17th and 18th Century Art

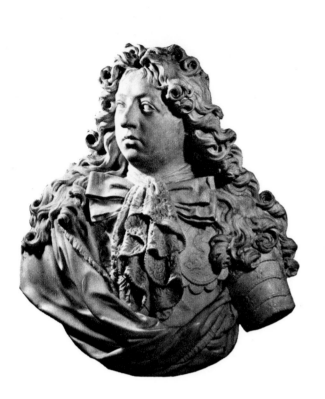

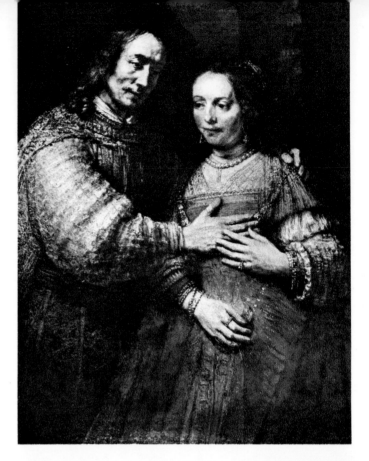

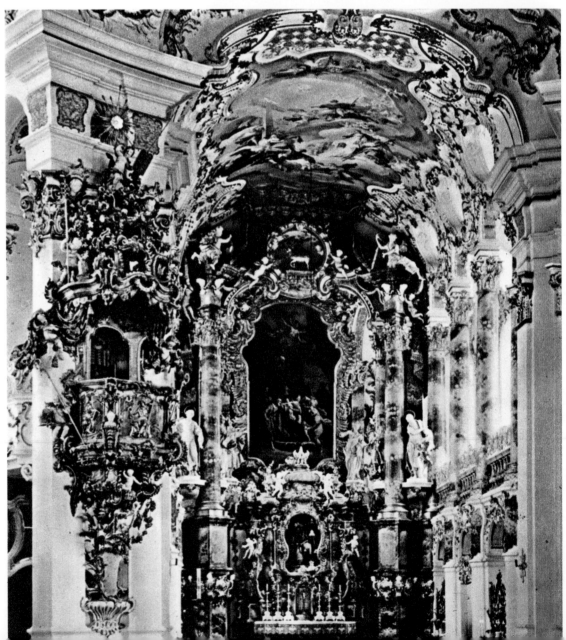

LIBRARY OF ART HISTORY

H. W. Janson,
General Editor

17th and 18th Century Art

BAROQUE PAINTING

SCULPTURE · ARCHITECTURE

JULIUS S. HELD

Professor Emeritus, Barnard College, Columbia University

DONALD POSNER

Professor, Institute of Fine Arts, New York University

PRENTICE-HALL, INC., *Englewood Cliffs, N.J.*
and HARRY N. ABRAMS, INC., *New York*

Sixth Printing

H.W. Janson GENERAL EDITOR

ISBN 0–13–807339–2
Library of Congress Catalogue Card Number: 79–127417

Printed and bound in Japan

EDITOR'S PREFACE

The present book is one of a series. *The Library of Art History* comprises a history of Western art in five volumes, devoted respectively to the Ancient World, the Middle Ages, the Renaissance, the Baroque and Rococo, and the Modern World. The set, it is hoped, will help to bridge a gap of long standing: that between one-volume histories of art and the large body of specialized literature written for professionals. One-volume histories of art, if they are to be books rather than collections of essays, must be—and usually are—the work of a single author. In view of the vast chronological and geographic span of the subject, no one, however conscientious and hard-working, can hope to write on every phase of it with equal assurance. The specialist, by contrast, as a rule deals only with his particular field of competence and addresses himself to other specialists. *The Library of Art History* fits in between these two extremes; written by leading scholars, it is designed for all those who are neither beginners nor professional art historians—educated laymen, upper-class undergraduates, and scholars in other fields who do not need to be introduced to the history of art but are looking for an authoritative guide to the present state of knowledge in the major areas of the discipline.

In recent years, such readers have become a large and significant group. Their numbers reflect the extraordinary growth of the history of art in our system of higher education, a growth that began in the 1930s, was arrested by the Second World War and its aftermath, and has been gathering ever greater momentum since the 1950s. Among humanistic disciplines, the history of art is still something of a newcomer, especially in the English-speaking world. Its early development, from Vasari (whose famous *Lives* were first published in 1550) to Winckelmann

and Wölfflin, took place on the Continent, and it became a formal subject of study at Continental universities long before it did in England and America. That this imbalance has now been righted—indeed, more than righted—is due in part to the "cultural migration" of scholars and research institutes from Germany, Austria, and Italy thirty years ago. The chief reason, however, is the special appeal of the history of art for modern minds. No other field invites us to roam so widely through historic time and space, none conveys as strong a sense of continuity between past and present, or of kinship within the family of man. Moreover, compared to literature or music, painting and sculpture strike us as far more responsive vessels of individuality; every stroke, every touch records the uniqueness of the maker, no matter how strict the conventions he may have to observe. Style in the visual arts thus becomes an instrument of differentiation that has unmatched subtlety and precision. There is, finally, the problem of meaning in the visual arts, which challenges our sense of the ambiguous. A visual work of art cannot tell its own story unaided. It yields up its message only to persistent inquiry that draws upon all the resources of cultural history, from religion to economics. And this is no less true of the remote past than of the twentieth century—if we are to understand the origins of nonobjective art, for instance, we must be aware of Kandinsky's and Mondrian's profound interest in theosophy. The work of the art historian thus becomes a synthesis illuminating every aspect of human experience. Its wide appeal is hardly surprising in an age characterized by the ever greater specialization and fragmentation of knowledge. *The Library of Art History* was conceived in response to this growing demand.

H.W. Janson

To
Anna and Michael
and to
Michael, Andrew, and Meredith

Contents

17th and 18th Century Art

Note on the Picture Captions

Unless otherwise noted, all paintings are oil on canvas, height preceding width. Measurements are not given for objects that are inherently large (architecture, architectural sculpture, wall paintings).

Introduction to Baroque Art

This book deals with the arts of architecture, sculpture, and painting from the late sixteenth to the late eighteenth centuries. Following a tradition by no means undisputed, we call this the period of the Baroque.

The origins of the word "baroque" are clouded.[1] It has been derived from *baroco,* a memory term coined by medieval logicians to designate a syllogism that antischolastic writers of the sixteenth century found particularly ridiculous; from *barocchio,* an Italian term used since the late Middle Ages for shady financial practices; or from the Portuguese *barocco,* a word used since the sixteenth century to describe pearls of irregular shape. Whatever its origin, "baroque" has been used since the eighteenth century in many contexts to denote things that are strange and bizarre.

When late eighteenth-century French and German writers spoke of baroque taste, they clearly took it to be an equivalent of bad taste. In the violent attacks made by Neoclassic critics on Italian art of the seventeenth and eighteenth centuries, "baroque" occasionally describes an extreme of aesthetic aberration. As a term for an entire style, however, the word is encountered only in the nineteenth century, and precisely when the wholesale denunciation of masters like Bernini and Borromini was about to give way to a more sympathetic view. This development first came to a climax in 1855, when the word *Barockstil* ("baroque style") was introduced by two influential publications: W. Lübke's *Geschichte der Architektur* and J. Burckhardt's *Cicerone.* Burckhardt actually became an apologist for the Baroque *malgré lui:* while still calling some of Borromini's works *Fratzengebilde* (caricatures), he could not help recognizing the beauty of many Baroque structures, and later spoke almost ruefully of his "baroque heresy." *Barock* (without the word "style") is used in 1873 by A. von Zahn, who states that "lately" artists and amateurs had begun to praise the so-called age of decadence.[2] It is very likely, indeed, that artistic currents of the 1860s—the architecture of Charles Garnier and the sculpture of J.-B. Carpeaux—had contributed to this reappraisal of Baroque art.

The first major investigation into the nature and the beginnings of the once-despised art was H. Wölfflin's *Renaissance und Barock* (1888).[3] Master of a concise literary style, Wölfflin described the formal qualities of Baroque architecture in terms that affected all later writings on the subject. The tendency to use the word "baroque" as a term to encompass all aspects of the seventeenth and much of the eighteenth centuries appeared first, however, in Italian writers: as early as 1895 Enrico Nencioni had spoken of *barocchismo* when he tried to characterize the civilization of the seventeenth century, and Corrado Ricci entitled a series of essays on seventeenth- and eighteenth-century personalities (including Mozart) *Vita Barocca*.[4] Alois Riegl, a Viennese scholar, tried to connect Baroque art more specifically with the cultural and intellectual history of the times; his lecture notes on the subject were posthumously published in 1908.[5] It did not take long for historians of other disciplines to adopt the convenient term: historians of music may have been the first to call one of the great ages in their art Baroque; historians of literature have followed (except in the Anglo-Saxon countries); and it is not uncommon to see references to Baroque philosophy, Baroque physics, Baroque medicine, and Baroque statecraft.

As both the term and the period to which it was applied became more familiar, it was inevitable that analogies were found between the Baroque and other periods. That the Hellenistic phase of Greek art had stylistic analogies with Baroque had been noticed since 1880; Wölfflin in 1888 spoke of the "ancient baroque." With his *Kunstgeschichtliche Grundbegriffe (Principles of Art History)* in 1915, Wölfflin furnished new underpinnings to this extension of the term, implying that the formal categories he used to distinguish Renaissance and Baroque corresponded to fundamental, if polar, modes in all artistic organization. (The possibility of recognizing the Baroque as a recurrent phenomenon had been envisaged by Friedrich Nietzsche[6] when he suggested that it was typical of late phases in cultural cycles.) Some German writers, such as Spengler, forgetting the importance of Italy for the genesis of the Baroque, took the extreme attitude that the Baroque, like the Gothic, expressed the deepest yearning of the "Germanic soul."

In the face of these speculative developments, many scholars felt the need to investigate more fully the nature of the historical Baroque. In his *Principles,* Wölfflin had tried to demonstrate that his "basic" formal categories were valid for all artistic media, and could be applied to all countries. In order to support a unified theory of the Baroque, some writers tried to credit it to some concrete historical forces, such as the Counter Reformation, political and economic absolutism, and the new science.[7] It was probably due to the desire to salvage a viable definition of the Baroque that much of the art of the sixteenth century following the High Renaissance was split from it and given a new name: Mannerism. In this view, rather than being antithetical to the Renaissance, Baroque was found to have a good many things in common with it.

In recent times scholars have been concerned rather more with the variety than with the unity of "Baroque" art. Some critics make chronological distinctions, such as early, high, and late Baroque; others distinguish a classicistic Baroque (a term first used in 1873) from what would have to be called a "baroque" Baroque, and recognize an early, high, and late "Baroque Classicism";[8] still others separate a "realist" Baroque from a "classicist" and a "decorative" one.[9] The potential confusion inherent in this terminological expansion is increased by the existence of "Rococo" as a style and period term.

The word "rococo" is based on the French *rocaille,* which refers to the shellwork and rockwork decoration of grottoes and fountains. By the middle of the eighteenth century *rocaille,* along with "grotesque," "arabesque," and "Chinese manner," became a synonym for "baroque"—another pejorative term for the free, irregular, and curvilinear decorative forms of the time.[10] At the end of the century the word "rococo," a witty combination of *rocaille* and *barocco,* was apparently coined by a student in David's studio.[11] In the nineteenth century "rococo" was sometimes used interchangeably with "baroque," but eventually it became attached exclusively to eighteenth-century phenomena.[12] Today, "Rococo" is often used to define an "age" of European art and culture extending from about 1700 to the French Revolution, and distinct from a seventeenth-century "Baroque age."[13] Many writers, however, consider the Rococo merely a French form of the late Baroque, and some tend to narrow its use even more, to a definition for the decorative and ornamental style of the Louis XV period. Yet others have elaborated on the term and created, for example, "Sonderrokoko" ("Special Rococo") for eighteenth-century ecclesiastical art in southern Germany.[14]

Understandably, some scholars, fearful that such terminological flexibility may lead to conceptual imprecision, have begun to reassess the validity and utility of many period and style rubrics. There is a growing tendency to restrict such terms to specific moments or trends in the history of art. Giuliano Briganti has proposed that the term "Baroque" be confined to the "generation of 1630" (in which he includes Rubens).[15] One of the authors of this book would prefer to call "baroque" only particular artistic modes that developed through the seventeenth and into the eighteenth century.[16]

It will be admitted, however, that there are general connections, often tenuous, to be sure, that link European art and artists during a period from, roughly, 1580 through the third quarter of the eighteenth century. In this book, as a matter of verbal and editorial convenience, this long and varied period is called "Baroque." With a lower-case "b," baroque is used to refer, in the fourth section of Chapter I, for instance, to a specific, distinct artistic trend during the time. "Rococo" appears in the chapters on the eighteenth century primarily to designate the final form of baroque styles.

If it is well-nigh hopeless to find a single formula for the art of the "Baroque period," one can nevertheless list a number of phenomena that seem peculiar to this age. Any student of Baroque art will be struck by its preoccupation with extreme physical size. Castles like Stockholm, Blenheim, and Caserta (figs. 295, 306, 375), monasteries like Einsiedeln and Melk (figs. 1, 398), astonish us with their sheer bulk; other buildings, like St. Peter's, Stupinigi, and Nymphenburg (figs. 2, 374, 417), reach out into space with the help of subordinate structures; some are integrated with open spaces, like the Zwinger in Dresden (fig. 400) and the Belvedere (fig. 395) in Vienna. Versailles

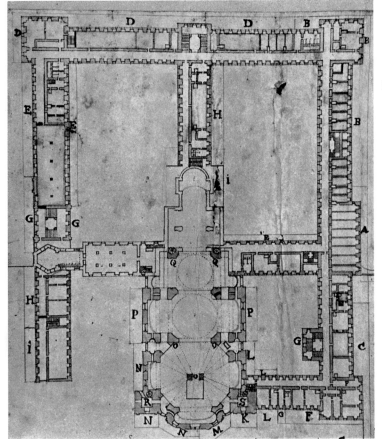

1. CASPAR MOOSBRUGGER. Plan, Benedictine Abbey at Einsiedeln. Begun 1719

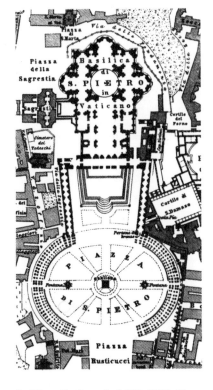

2. Plan, St. Peter's. 1506–1657. Rome

will always remain the prime example of Baroque expansion: it is not only the largest palace of all, but it, too, is part of an array of subsidiary structures. The huge buildings are themselves dwarfed by the vast gardens laid out in neat geometric patterns (fig. 141). Many grandiose plans ran afoul of harsh economic realities, but—as seen in contemporary engravings—they look like dreams of a megalomaniac. Cities were planned, or redesigned. Charleville, Montauban, Richelieu are early examples of whole communities planned in French provincial areas. In Germany the city of Karlsruhe still preserves its original plan (fig. 3), the castle of the prince forming the focal point for an interlocking system of radial, circular, and tangential streets.

To reach forth into space is a function natural to many styles of architecture: it becomes a meaningful symptom of the age if we realize that it is one of the basic gestures of Baroque art, from Caravaggio's *Martyrdom of St. Matthew* to Bernini's *St. Longinus* and Watteau's *L'Indifférent* (figs. 87, 57). About to be martyred, Ribera's *St. Bartholomew* (fig. 92) reaches out to the very limits of the large canvas. Andreas Schlüter's *Great Elector* (fig. 421) appears to trot swiftly through space, his glance scanning faraway distances.

Normal spatial limitations are disregarded. Bernini's figures burst from their niches (figs. 59, 70); in Pietro da Cortona's and Baciccio's (Giovanni Battista Gaulli) ceilings the action spills across the frames into adjoining fields (figs. 108, 122). On the ceiling in the Gallery of the Palazzo Farnese, Annibale Carracci had already painted figures who relate to one another across open spaces (fig. 95).

Space as interpreted by artists of the Baroque is both unified and unlimited. The medieval concept of distinct spatial spheres, suggestive of a permanent hierarchy of things, has completely vanished. Although seventeenth-century scholars might debate whether the totality of space was finite or infinite, they all agreed that it was continuous and indescribably vast. The far-flung distances traversed by Milton's Satan find their pictorial equivalent in the boundless spaces through which Rubens' Damned hurtle in their headlong fall (fig. 4). Equally unbounded, though more cheerful, are the heavens of Tiepolo's frescoes (fig. 354). In Claude Lorrain's landscapes (figs. 117, 118) or Watteau's *fêtes galantes* (fig. 313) the distant horizons are lost in a vaporous haze. Poussin's orderly world (fig. 161) as well as the chaotic one painted by Magnasco (fig. 359) have in common the suggestion of unlimited expanse.

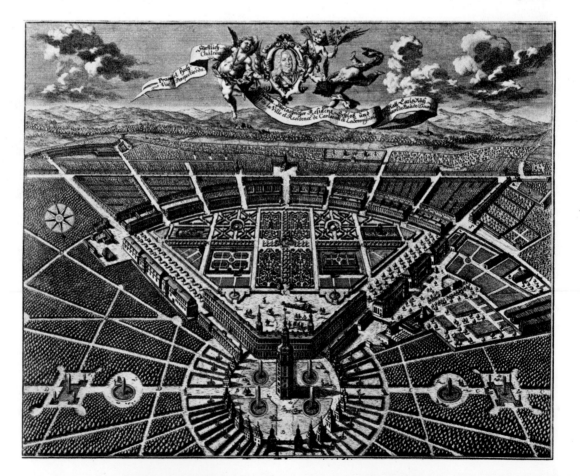

3. Plan, Town and Ducal Palace, Karlsruhe. 1715 (engraving of 1739)

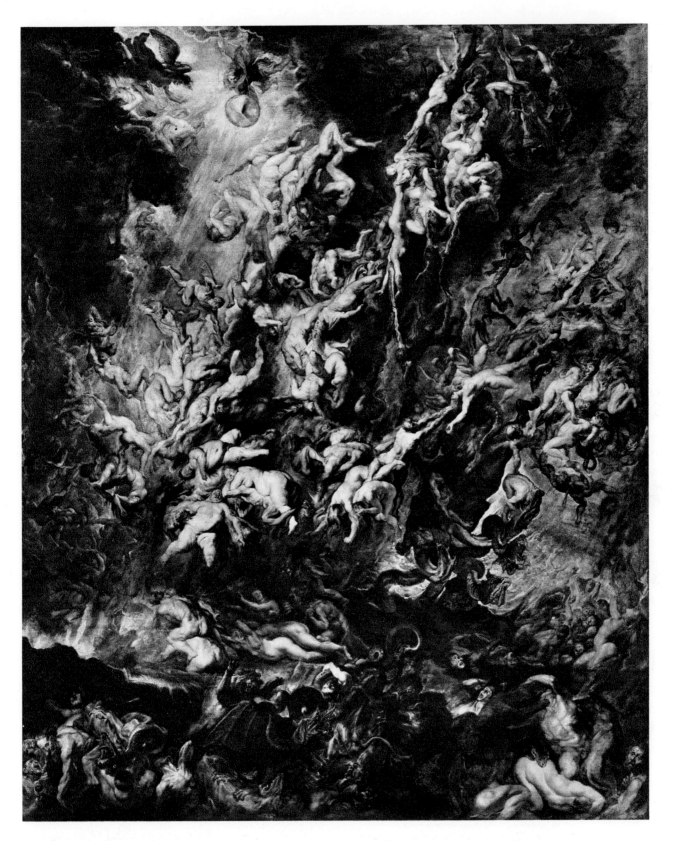

4. PETER PAUL RUBENS. *Fall of the Damned*. c. 1620. Panel, 9′4½″ × 7′4⅛″. Alte Pinakothek, Munich

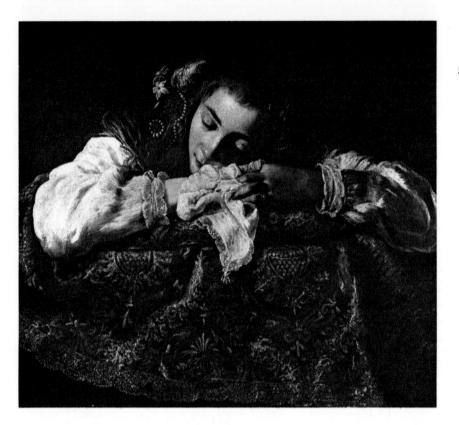

5. DOMENICO FETTI.
Girl Asleep. c. 1622.
26½ × 29⅛".
Museum of Fine Arts,
Budapest

With Rembrandt, space recedes into areas of shadow and mystery, while with Bellotto things far away remain as sharply defined as those near: but both artists share in the same concept of space.

The concept of a unified space involves the near as well as the remote. Caravaggio and his followers derived dramatic impact by placing the action close to the foreground (fig. 84). Fetti painted a startling close-up of a girl asleep over her needlework (fig. 5). Chardin's boys blowing soap bubbles from a window (fig. 325) are so close to us that we are tempted to touch them. Baroque space, with perfect logic, encompasses the world of the beholder. Bernini's *Beata Lodovica Albertoni* (fig. 65) and Asam's *St. George* (colorplate 59), not to mention innumerable illusionistic frescoes, involve the viewer by fusing their space with his.

Conventional boundaries inevitably were neglected. The principles of spatial illusionism, though first developed in the Renaissance, were systematically exploited only during the Baroque. In Versailles, the mirror's magic is used to trick the eye into seeing a much wider gallery than the one actually there. The curtains that Rembrandt and Vermeer painted into some of their pictures seem to have a reality distinct from that of the scenes they reveal. Liotard's enchanting *trompe l'oeil* of two plaster reliefs and bits of drawn paper painted against a simulated board is a model of optical illusionism (fig. 6). Borromini's little colonnaded corridor persuades the eye to see it as much bigger than it is (fig. 7); Bernini used the same device when he built the Scala Regia in the Vatican (fig. 35). The designers of stage sets, from Palladio to the Galli-Bibiena, were past masters of such effects.

Techniques that blurred the distinction between materials were helpful in denying actual lines of demarcation: painted wood, properly veined, could substitute for marble, and stucco for carved wood; graphic techniques were developed that made prints practically indistinguishable from drawings in chalk or pen.

Such substitutions illustrate the preoccupation of the age with technical virtuosity. Even minor artists handled their tools with astonishing dexterity. Never before or after were there so many supremely accomplished artisans, each one filled with pride and ambition—like that first met in

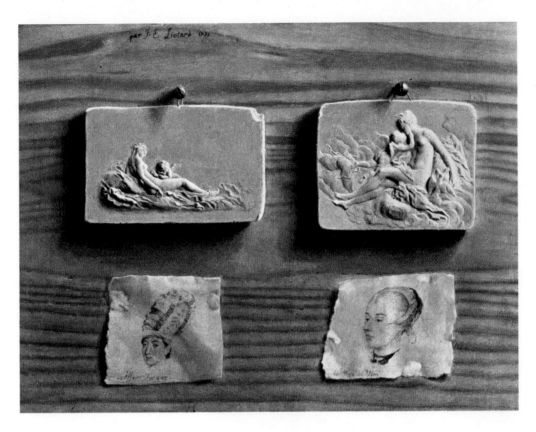

6. JEAN-ETIENNE LIOTARD.
Trompe l'oeil. 1771.
9½ × 12½".
Collection Dr. and Mrs.
Rudolf Heinemann,
New York

Cellini—to outdo all others. The technical expertness of Baroque gold- and silversmiths, blacksmiths making forged iron, glass blowers and cutters, makers of porcelain and terracotta, carvers in wood, stone, or ivory, weavers, and printers remains amazing to this day. Even in architecture much thought was expended on the creation of extraordinary effects: arches curving forward in space, walls undulating as if capable of motion, ground plans in unusual patterns, staircases providing optical surprises, supports carrying nothing, weights seemingly unsupported—such ideas are proof of a pervasive interest in technical fireworks.

Baroque art scored a breakthrough on yet another front. Compared with the figures in Baroque painting and sculpture, Renaissance figures are apt to look stolid, Mannerist ones inhibited. The Baroque artist took for granted that his characters were real people, caught in and reacting to specific situations. Observing man's behavior in moments of pleasure or trial, studying both empirically and theoretically expressions of passion and fear,[17] the Baroque artist explored a world as vast and exciting as that observed by his scientific contem-

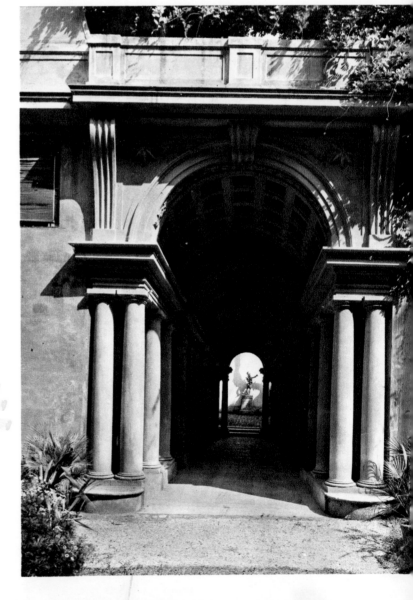

7. FRANCESCO BORROMINI.
Colonnade, Palazzo Spada.
c. 1635. Rome

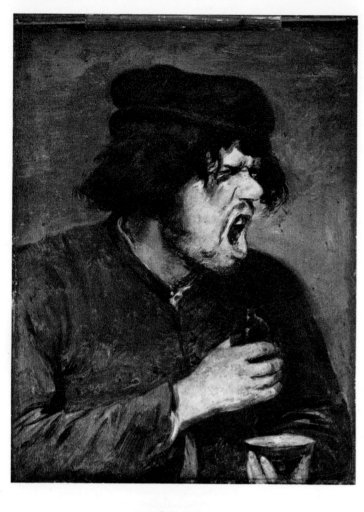

8. ADRIAEN BROUWER. *The Bitter Drink.* c. 1635.
Panel, 18¼ × 14″.
Städelsches Kunstinstitut, Frankfurt

poraries. Released from restraint, the emotional life asserts itself with freedom and spontaneity. Faces erupt in broad laughter (Honthorst, Hals, Steen) or are marked by a coy or sardonic smile (Vermeer, Velázquez, Hogarth). The voluptuous leer of a satyr (Rubens), the trembling ecstasy of a saint (Bernini), the agony of death (Schlüter), the half-touching, half-comic grief of a child (Jordaens), the shocked surprise of a man tasting a bitter drink (Brouwer; fig. 8), the willful facial distortions made by a deeply disturbed man in front of a mirror (Messerschmidt; fig. 9)—all these are studies of character and physiognomy that would have been impossible at an earlier age. Not surprisingly, Baroque artists were adept at making caricatures in the form of deft shorthand notations of actual personages (Carracci, Callot, Bernini, Tiepolo; fig. 356). Moreover, many artists of the period realized that the body is as eloquent a carrier of human emotion as the face. Poussin, whose sense of decorum restricted his use of facial expression, conveyed feelings of great subtlety and depth by gesture and bodily pose.

Equally revealing are scenes wherein action is suspended and the message expressively delivered in silence. The popular notion of Baroque art as melodramatic and rhetorical fails to include the many works marked by perfect stillness. We encounter figures in meditation (fig. 10) forming the visual counterpart to the "poetry of meditation":[18] peasants immobilized in simple poses (Le Nain; colorplate 18) and young women quietly absorbed in reading letters (Terborch, Vermeer). Though there are flamboyant still lifes, many more are indeed what the term implies. The element of time, as we shall see, plays an important role in works of this kind; rather than accentuating the fugitive quality of action, they convey the feeling of "timeless" continuity.

In the eyes of the Baroque artist man was not only capable of an unlimited range of emotions,

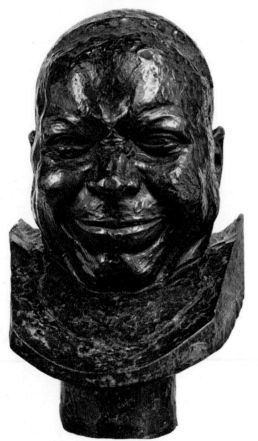

9. FRANZ XAVER MESSERSCHMIDT. *Grotesque Head.* c. 1770. Lead. Barockmuseum, Vienna

he was also of interest to the extent that he represented a specific social stratum. This appears most clearly in genre painting, whose subjects were perhaps the most interesting of the several new categories developed during this age. It is not surprising that at a time when much stress was laid upon distinctions of rank and class, genre actions were depicted on different social levels. Caravaggio painted gypsies (fig. 85) and cardsharps, and cast laborers and country folk in the roles of Biblical characters (fig. 86). Beggars, organ-grinders, street vendors, blacksmiths, and scullery maids appear with Ribera, Callot, Georges de La Tour, Rembrandt, and Velázquez. While the pictorial glorification of princes reached almost tasteless proportions, painters were also attracted by the ragged poor. Like the landscape painters who discovered the romantic charm of ruins (Seghers, Ruisdael), some artists were fascinated by the raw picturesqueness of human derelicts (fig. 11). There is no trace of callous ridicule in Velázquez's dwarfs and idiots (fig. 188). One can rather detect a degree of sympathy, a recognition of the bonds that tie the lowest to the highest—such as is expressed later in the prison scene of *The Vicar of Wakefield.* The extremes actually meet in such figures as the blind Belisarius (figs. 272, 332), the once great general now reduced to begging for alms.

In one further respect the artists of the Baroque struck out toward new goals: in regard to their own place in the social hierarchy. The process had begun in the Renaissance when a few artists were acclaimed, and nearly canonized, as creative geniuses. By the seventeenth century artists had developed a variety of means of blending into

10. **GEORGES DE LA TOUR.** *St. Mary Magdalen Meditating.* 1640–45. 50½×37″. The Louvre, Paris

11. Anonymous Italian artist. *Blind Beggar.* Second quarter 17th century. National Gallery, Rome

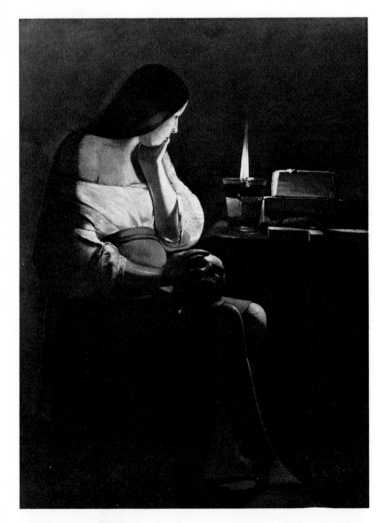

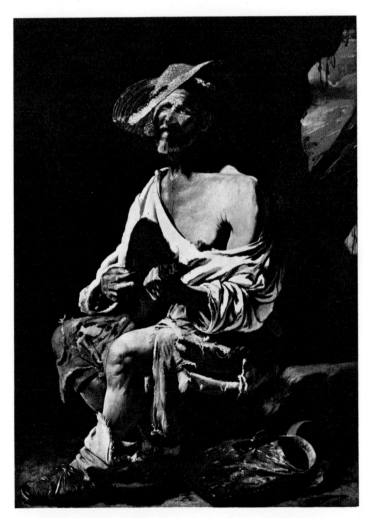

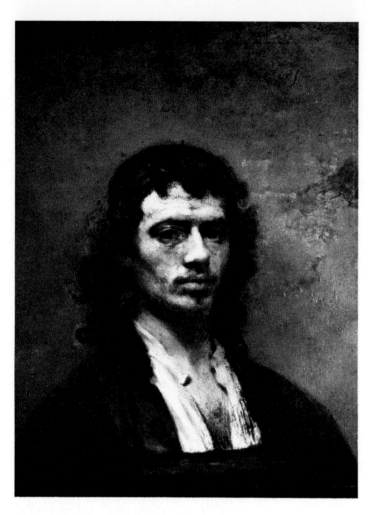

12. CAREL FABRITIUS. *Self-portrait*. c. 1650.
Panel, 25⅝ × 19¼".
Museum Boymans-Van Beuningen, Rotterdam

the social pattern. Some played the roles of *grands seigneurs,* surrounded by assistants and servants, and acquired eventually the very titles of nobility (Rubens, Van Dyck, Wren, Fischer von Erlach). Many, especially in the Netherlands, were regular businessmen, often combining art with commercial activities. In Italy, and later in Germany, artists were not infrequently attached to the household of a noble or a prince. In France and in some cases in England they found employment as pensioners of the state. The foundation of the French Academy in 1648 was the most important step in proclaiming the official function of the artist. Yet not all artists aimed at acquiring status and living a life of social respectability. There is evidence that some artists chose a bohemian existence in a more or less conscious protest against the conformist pressures to which they

were exposed. Antisocial behavior of artists is known from earlier centuries, but the social rebel seems to be a type appearing with the Baroque. A self-portrait like Fabritius'—with open shirt, revealing his hairy chest—would have been unthinkable before (fig. 12).

Baroque art was the art of a dynamic age, when the very foundations of the modern world were laid. Like the scientists with their new tools, such as the telescope and the microscope, the artists, too, discovered new worlds or found new ways of interpreting the old. They, too, "broke the circle" that tradition had forged,[19] but the paths they took differed from generation to generation and from country to country. For a survey of the development, it is the national schools with their marked identity that still furnish the most serviceable conceptual scaffolding.[20]

1

Italy in the Seventeenth Century

INTRODUCTION

The cradle of the Baroque was Italy, and the artistic capital of Italy was Rome. As time went on, other countries made their bid for leadership, but toward the end of the sixteenth century and in the first decades of the seventeenth, Rome attracted artists from all over Europe, as if by magic. To have made a mark in Rome was then for artists' reputations what favorable reviews in the leading cultural centers are to actors and musicians today. It must have been a source of justifiable pride for Rubens when in 1606 he obtained, over the heads of all Roman artists, the commission to decorate the high altar of the new church of the Oratorian brothers. Virtually every great artist of the Baroque in Rome had come from elsewhere. Carlo Maderno, Caravaggio, and later Francesco Borromini came from northern Italy, Annibale Carracci from Bologna, Pietro da Cortona from Tuscany, Gianlorenzo Bernini from Naples, Nicolas Poussin from France; yet Rome transformed them all, as they transformed her.

Many factors had contributed to this situation, but it was essentially connected with the Counter Reformation and the renewed vigor of the Roman papacy engendered by that movement. The Coun-

ter Reformation had been launched in the last sessions of the Council of Trent, when under the guidance of the Jesuits the Church began to assume a militant posture. Starting with Pope Pius V (1566–72), the chair of St. Peter's was occupied by men of great energy and vision. Pius himself adopted the Tridentine Profession of Faith (1566), formulated the Roman Breviary (1568), and reformed the Curia. He also condemned ancient statues as *idola antiquorum*. His successor, Pope Gregory XIII (1572–85), known for his calendar reform, was a strong supporter of the Jesuits. The church of Il Gesù, the first major work of art sponsored by the Company of Jesus, was built while he was pope. Sixtus V (1585–90) started a complete modernization of Rome by cutting long straight thoroughfares through its old quarters. Armenini, writing in 1586, noted the amazing increase in the construction of churches, chapels, and monasteries.[1]

Rome undoubtedly gained from the progress Catholicism made all over Europe. With the conversion and absolution of Henry IV (1595), France had again become a Catholic power. Flanders, Bavaria, and Austria were firmly in the

Catholic camp. The annexations of Ferrara (1598) and Urbino (1631) into the Papal State were signs of renewed territorial ambitions. At the same time the piety of such early leaders of the Counter Reformation as St. Charles Borromeo (d. 1584) and St. Philip Neri (d. 1595) yielded to a more relaxed attitude.[2] And whereas Popes Pius V and Sixtus V had come from the ranks of mendicant orders, the popes of the seventeenth century, like those of the Renaissance, came from prominent families: Aldobrandini (Clement VIII, 1592–1605), Borghese (Paul V, 1605–21), Ludovisi (Gregory XV, 1621–23), Barberini (Urban VIII, 1623–44), Pamphili (Innocent X, 1644–55), and Chigi (Alexander VII, 1655–67). They were elected by cardinals who were themselves members of the Roman nobility. Most of these popes were cultured gentlemen and generous patrons of the arts; they were surrounded by all sorts of *principi, marchesi,* and *cavalieri,* and aided by scholarly secretaries and expert advisers.[3] Of Urban VIII—known as a poet before he became a pope—it has been said that he would rather read a book on fortification than one on edification.

Yet by the middle of the century, papal power was again on the decline. Rome's voice carried little weight in the decisions of the Peace of Westphalia (1648). The great national states were capable of acting irrespective of what the Curia did or felt. While elsewhere in Europe a vigorous industrial and commercial life enriched most of the nations, the largely agrarian economy of Italy was unable to support indefinitely a profligate aristocracy rife with economic caprice and shameless nepotism. There was no sudden collapse but a marked slackening of the pace. Some fine monuments were added to the Roman landscape still in the eighteenth century, but it was also true that sheep, goats, and cattle had again taken over wide stretches of the town.

In the struggle that the rejuvenated church conducted against its foes, art had been given a special function. Painting and sculpture were recognized as excellent media of propaganda.[4] To be effective, works of art had to follow certain rules. All imagery had to be clear and truthful. Works that might arouse "carnal desire"[5] were inadmissible in churches. By contrast an unsparing realism in the rendering of Christ's suffering was proper and desirable.[6]

The Church made use of art the more willingly as her opponents had denied it a place in the houses of worship. The Calvinists, less tolerant than the Lutherans, had occasionally even destroyed art of the past because it might encourage idolatry. Thus Catholicism's emphasis on the adornment of churches was itself an answer to the reformers. Each new picture vindicated the place of imagery in worship and asserted the godly function of art.

Art was useful in other ways. Since the reformers attacked specific doctrines and beliefs, the Church used images to assert their truth. Faced with the reformers' denial that the Virgin played any significant part in God's plan for man's salvation, the Church intensified the cult of the Virgin, reflected in a wide increase of images depicting her life. Pleading with a mother's warmth and a woman's persuasiveness she is shown interceding for the sake of mankind. Countless images of the Immaculate Conception sustained the old belief that she had been conceived by God before all time, to be free from the stain of original sin.[7]

The Church reacted with similar force to the attacks made on the worship of saints. Scorning the skepticism of the Protestants, artists depicted saints in ecstasy, performing miracles, or suffering martyrdoms.[8] The authenticity of relics was upheld, and magnificent shrines were built to house them.

Of all the saints, Peter occupied a special place. The primacy of the popes was predicated on that of St. Peter, whom Christ had called the rock on which He would build His church. To mark the spot where St. Peter lay buried, Bernini erected his baldachin (see pages 63–64);[9] he also surrounded St. Peter's Chair *(Cathedra Petri)* in the apse of St. Peter's with a magnificent decorative

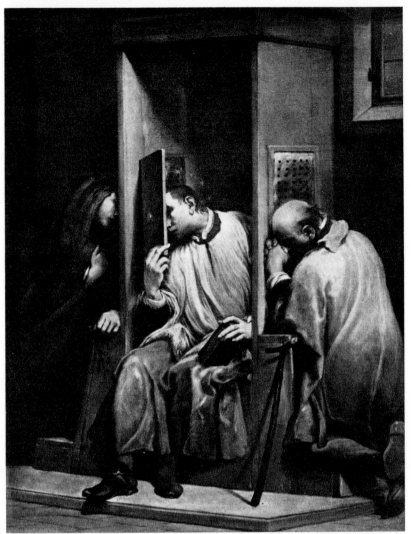

13. GIUSEPPE MARIA CRESPI.
*Confession of the Queen of Bohemia
to St. John Nepomuk.* 1743.
51⅛ ×47⅜".
Galleria Sabauda, Turin

composition. Both monuments give visible support to the papal claims to be the legitimate leaders of Christianity.

Art was enlisted, too, in the defense of the Sacraments. Calvinists had condemned Confession as useless since no amount of penance could change man's preordained fate. The Church, in response, encouraged the construction of large numbers of richly adorned and conspicuously located confessionals. In Crespi's painting (fig. 13) the act of Confession is depicted in all its humble intimacy. Christ himself is often rendered as comforter of the great penitents such as King David, the Prodigal Son, St. Mary Magdalen, the Good Thief, and St. Peter himself.

The polemical function of art was not its only one. Just as the new liturgy favored religious services that had the visual and acoustic appeal of a spectacle and the suspense of a drama, the new churches were made into edifices of unheard-of splendor. They welcomed the faithful with façades of majestic proportions and a full orchestration of columns, pilasters, niches, pediments, and figural and ornamental decor. The interiors, especially in the later phases of the development, were still more dazzling, culminating in the richly carved and painted decoration of the altars.[10] Through the symphonic accumulation of a variety of optical impressions, harmonized with an elaborate and stirring ritual, the worshiper is caught up in an emotional transport, carried away by an overwhelming appeal to all his senses (including smell, because of the incense burned). In its desire to glorify God and impress man, the Church during the Counter Reformation furthered immeasurably the forming of a new artistic ideal in which all arts contributed to the creation of a comprehensive work of art.

The principle laid down by the Church for the treatment of religious art remained valid—with local modifications—wherever Counter Reformation Catholicism held sway: Italy, Spain (and her colonies), France, Flanders, southern Germany, and Austria. Other types of subject matter, however, were developed during the Baroque period and flourished in the non-Catholic countries, especially the Netherlands. These developments in secular art will be treated in their appropriate context.

ARCHITECTURE

The first great church built for the Jesuit Order would have had a place in history for that reason alone. Il Gesù, started by Giacomo Barozzi, called Vignola (1507–1573) in 1568, offers even more: a milestone in the history of church architecture, "it has perhaps exerted a wider influence than any other church of the last four hundred years."[11]

Il Gesù owed this success largely to the satisfactory solution of an old problem: to integrate a central plan of building with a longitudinal one (fig. 14). The central plan had been a favorite idea of the High Renaissance, but the longitudinal one had the weight of tradition behind it—and tradition was important to the men of the Counter Reformation. Compared to a fifteenth-century structure that had had similar aims, Sant'Andrea in Mantua, designed by Alberti, Vignola's church is much more unified, with a clear subordination of all parts to a leading motif. The openings of the chapels hardly affect the impression of a compact space made by the nave beneath its huge barrel vault. The nave of Il Gesù is long enough to be felt as a longitudinal room, and short enough to make the visitor at once aware of the light area of the crossing under its soaring dome. A key role in the combination of the two systems, the longitudinal plan of the nave and the central plan of the dome, is played by the last bay, which, belonging to both, ties one to the other.

The design of the façade of Il Gesù (fig. 15) was not entirely new, but Vignola, and even more so his successor Giacomo della Porta, introduced a number of innovations that strongly affected the subsequent evolution of Baroque church façades. Like Alberti's façade of Santa Maria Novella in Florence more than a century earlier, that of Il Gesù consists of two stories, the upper being narrower than the lower. The difference is masked by two volutes bracing the upper story on either side. A wide pediment crowns this composition. A façade of this type had been built by Guido Guidetti for Santa Caterina dei Funari in Rome (fig. 16) only four years before Il Gesù was begun. Yet in Guidetti's façade an unbroken entablature kept the two stories completely apart; in Il Gesù all the major horizontal elements were broken in order to permit the vertical accents to continue unchecked from one level to the next. This verticalism—all the more important as the façade is as wide as it is high—marks the central bay particularly. In Santa Caterina dei Funari the pediment of the main portal remained below the horizontal division. At Il Gesù, a twin pediment above the central door overlaps the socle zone of the upper story, and a wall strip the width of the central bay continues it into the crowning pediment. In the earlier church, furthermore, all the lateral bays, on both levels, are treated in the

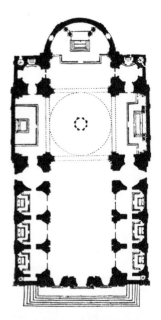

14. VIGNOLA. Plan, Il Gesù.
Begun 1568. Rome

15. VIGNOLA and GIACOMO DELLA PORTA.
Façade, Il Gesù. c. 1575–84. Rome

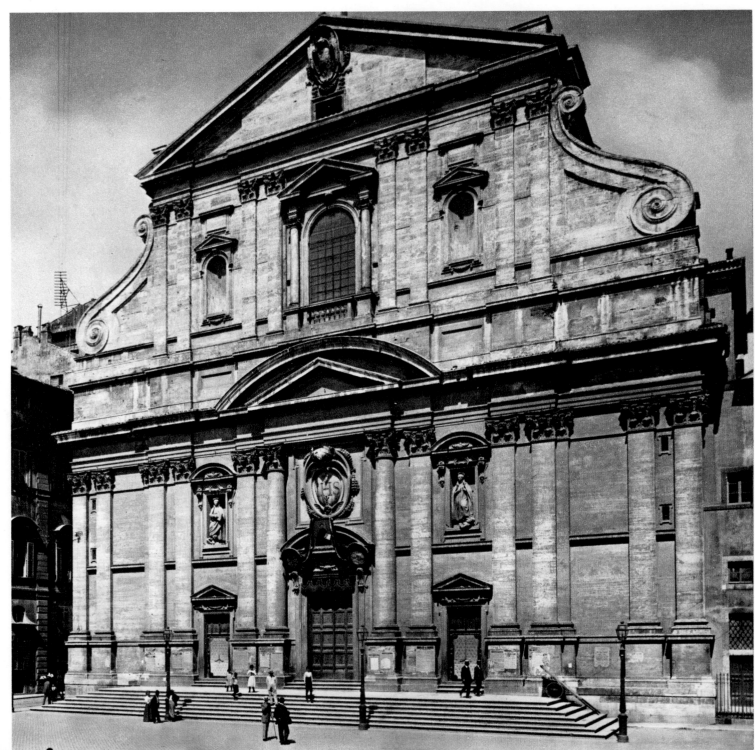

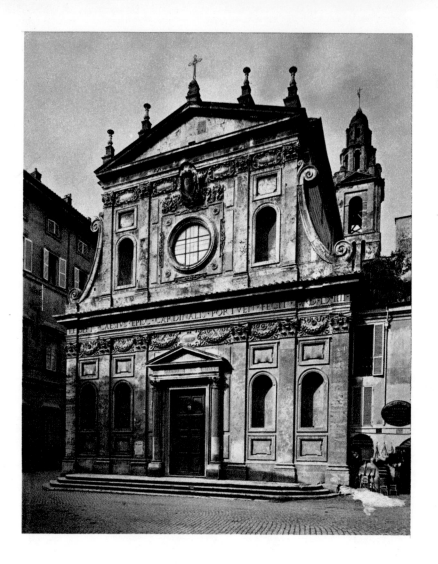

16. GUIDO GUIDETTI.
Façade, S. Caterina dei Funari.
Begun 1564. Rome

same way. In Il Gesù, those next to the central bay are marked by niches (and by doors on the ground floor), while the outermost bays below (and the areas that correspond to them above) are free of any embellishment. Thus a kind of hierarchy is established in which a powerful, dominant center is accompanied by subsidiary sections that differ among themselves in rank and value. This hierarchy has been further stressed by one crucial idea. The pilasters on the extreme bays are in a plane slightly behind that of the pilasters on the intermediate bays, while the latter, in turn, remain behind the columns framing the central portal. The central area, prominent already through its size and decor, thus literally stands out because of the slight forward motion of the whole façade from the sides to the center. The main gate welcomes the visitor by seemingly

moving out toward him, an idea that was elaborated imaginatively in later phases of the Baroque.

At Il Gesù, admittedly, this forward motion is somewhat hesitant and the relationship of the bays to each other not without ambiguities. In Carlo Maderno's (1556–1629) façade of Santa Susanna (fig. 17) there is no longer any ambiguity. The nearly equal balance between height and width at Il Gesù is replaced by a marked preponderance of the vertical, suggesting an upward surge of energies. Despite the relative narrowness of the façade, the bays are clearly distinguished from each other. The outer bays below, shrunk to near insignificance, are framed by shallow pilasters. The intermediate bays, stepped forward to be flush with these pilasters, are framed by columns below, pilasters above; on both levels these bays contain niches with figural sculpture.

26

The main bay is also framed by columns below and pilasters above, but they have again been moved forward by about half the depth of a column. Both the forward and the upward motion of Maderno's façade have more zest, as a result, than that at Il Gesù. While each bay is distinguishable from the next, Maderno managed to enhance the nobility of the central bay by making it appear that it alone is framed by *paired* columns or—on the upper level—pilasters.

The façade of Santa Susanna is remarkable for the clarity of its organization, which is all the more astonishing as it is richly covered with plastic decor making for a vivid interplay of light and shade. A work of surprisingly harmonious character, it seems to have revived some artistic principles of the High Renaissance. With its density of forms and its suggestion of motion in depth and height, it replaces the static equilibrium of the Renaissance with a new sense of dy-

17. CARLO MADERNO.
Façade, S. Susanna.
1597–1603. Rome

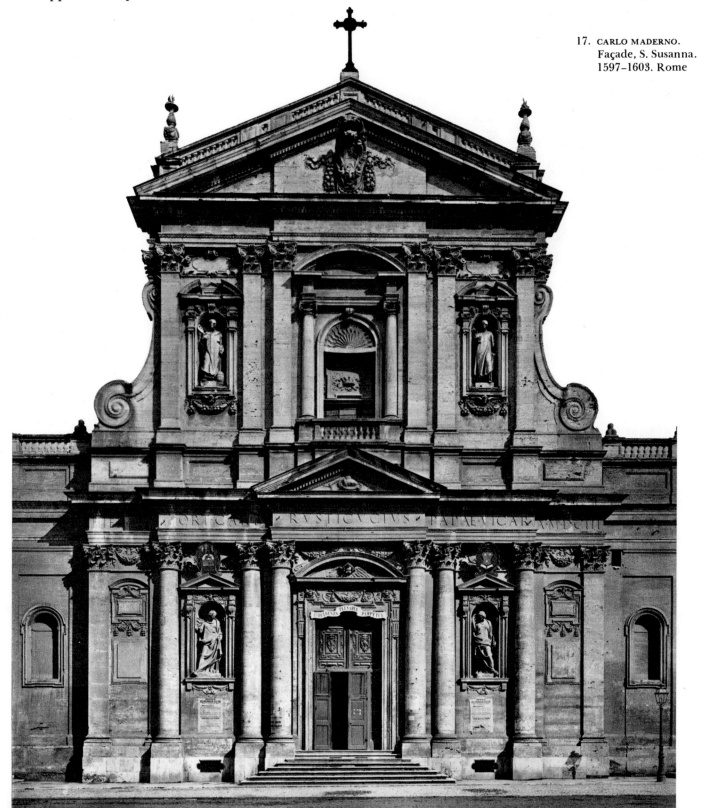

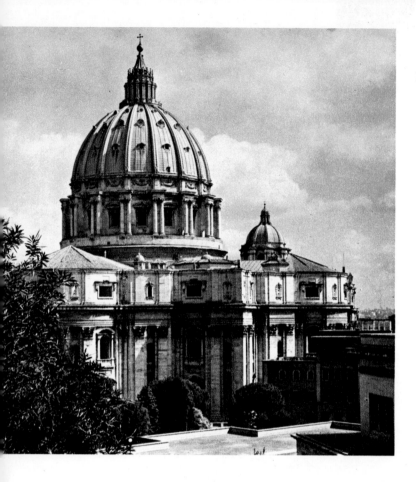

18. MICHELANGELO and GIACOMO DELLA PORTA.
Dome, St. Peter's. Finished 1593. Rome

ished in 1593 from the designs of Giacomo della Porta (fig. 18). Sixtus V also resolved the controversy about whether St. Peter's should be a central or longitudinal church by decreeing that the new building had to cover all the ground of Old St. Peter's, the venerable Early Christian basilica. He even determined much of the final phases of the history of St. Peter's (see pages 38–40) when, at his command and with some trepidation, Domenico Fontana engineered the transport of a great obelisk to the front of the church (1586), marking the spot that later served as the center of Bernini's colonnades.[12]

It was Maderno, however, who finally built the nave (fig. 19), patterning it on Il Gesù though unable, because of the great width of the building, to match the compact character of Il Gesù. His most important contribution to St. Peter's was the façade (fig. 20), which masks a large transversal entrance hall in the east of the building.[13] As planned, Maderno's façade was to be a restatement, in monumental terms, of the principles he had applied at Santa Susanna. His hand was forced to some extent: the colossal order and the attic story were legacies from Michelangelo's design. Maderno also had to make provisions for the benediction loggia above the main portal; from here the pope tendered his blessing *urbi et orbi*— to the city of Rome and the entire globe, a ceremony assuming special significance in a period of growing papal ambitions. Even the use of columns, ultimately derived from ancient temple façades, had been contemplated before. Rather than being hampered by these conditions, Maderno used them to his advantage.

The center of the composition is formed by a unit of three bays, of which the middle one is emphasized by width, proportion of its apertures, and decor. The next two bays on either side resemble, with modifications, the central bay but

namic urgency. Yet this partial return to principles of Renaissance design is found in other works of the first phase of the Baroque and represents an important aspect of the new movement.

The very year he finished the façade of Santa Susanna (1603), Maderno was appointed architect of St. Peter's. In the nearly one hundred years since it had been begun by Bramante in 1506, this vast structure had gone through periods of intense activity and long years of neglect. Bramante had planned it as a central building, but his successors (Raphael among them) had contemplated introducing the basilican plan, until Michelangelo (1546) emphatically reverted to the central type, albeit one of far greater concentration upon its main feature, the central dome, than envisioned by Bramante. The construction was pushed vigorously by Michelangelo, but the dome was unfinished when he died (1564). It was Sixtus V who decided to continue the construction, and the grandly soaring cupola was fin-

28

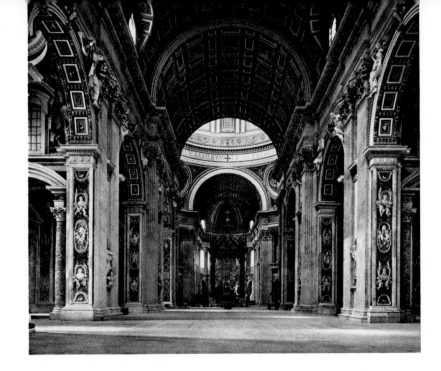

19, 20. CARLO MADERNO.
Interior of Nave and Façade,
St. Peter's. 1606–12. Rome

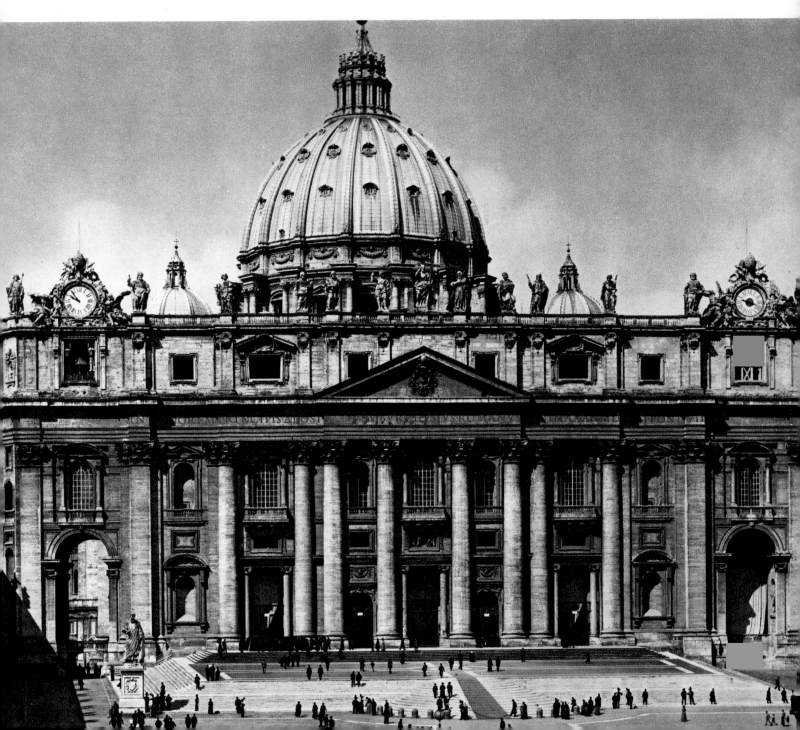

are stepped back so that the columns nearest the center stand in a corner rather than in front of the wall. These bays are followed by another pair, similar to the narrower ones of the center, but receding still farther; they are framed with pilasters instead of columns.

Maderno evidently organized the façade of St. Peter's like that of Santa Susanna in terms of five units, of which the four lateral ones are subordinated to the one in the center by a more modest treatment, and by their recession in depth. Yet by subdividing the central unit itself into three bays, with the lateral ones subservient to the one in the center, he created a rhythmically more intricate sequence, echoing on one level, as it were, and in telescoped fashion, the five-to-three relationship of the two stories at Santa Susanna.

At this point an old idea was revived. The younger Antonio da Sangallo, the architect who had preceded Michelangelo, had planned a façade flanked by two towers (1538). It was now felt that façade towers would give a strong vertical support to the huge dome, all the more so as the lengthening of the nave had made the lateral domes prac-

21. CARLO MADERNO and CARLO RAINALDI.
Façade, S. Andrea della Valle. 1624–29 and 1661–65. Rome

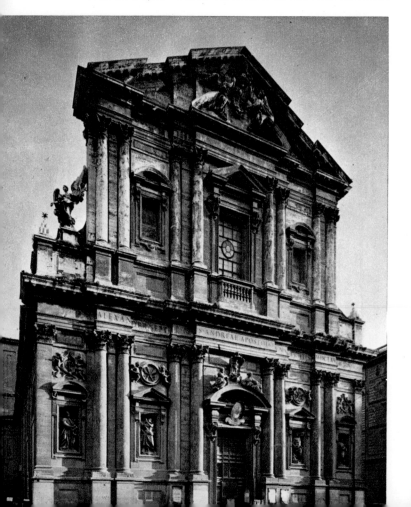

tically invisible. Two-tower façades were in the tradition of many medieval churches, and several had been projected or built on Italian soil in the sixteenth century (Santa Trinità dei Monti, Rome, 1495–1585; Santa Maria di Carignano, Genoa, begun 1577). Yet since the existing dome at St. Peter's was as wide as the five inner bays of the façade, Maderno had to extend the façade laterally if he wanted his towers to hold their own. This he did by adding another pair of wide bays containing arched passageways of huge proportions. These bays are flush with the last ones of the "original" façade and, like them, are flanked by pilasters. They are clearly an afterthought, and it does not help that they have on one side the strongly projecting terminal pilasters of the first plan while on the outside they are framed by shallower members.

When Paul V died in 1621, the tower idea was dropped; it was revived once more in the late 1630s, and Bernini actually built one tower. It had to be taken down when it appeared to be cracking (1646). Bernini made new plans that would have disengaged the towers from the façade, but the idea got nowhere. Consequently, the façade of St. Peter's remained without towers after all. The massive substructures built for the towers terminate now in an unworthy clock arrangement. The very idea, however, that the foremost church of Christendom was to have façade towers gave new luster to the old scheme: two-tower façades were built many times during the era of the Baroque.

Maderno's façade designs were widely imitated, both in Italy and abroad. The artist himself began one of the most splendid examples of Roman Baroque façades at Sant'Andrea della Valle (fig. 21), but it received its final form only in the 1660s. The vertical continuity of all orders and surfaces was here carried to such logical extremes that the crowning pediment was practically shredded to pieces in an effort to make it reflect all the ins and outs of the façade below. This, as well as the general effect of rhetoric caused by a multitude of columns and sculptured detail, is attributable to the later architects (Carlo Rainaldi—see pages 49–51—and Carlo Fontana), but Maderno's sense of rhythmic organization and his stepping forward of the façade toward the center still remain recognizable.

Maderno's contribution to the architecture of his time was less the result of a nimble imagination than of an ability to mold traditional concepts into a style that had logic, vigor and nobility. Some of his successors showed more freedom of invention and more gracefulness in detail. Maderno, however, remained unsurpassed for the articulateness and sensitivity of his architectural statements. In architecture his was the first authentic voice of the Baroque; its echoes were still heard in the eighteenth century.

The pattern of Il Gesù, modified with ideas derived from Maderno, may be seen in many Roman churches of the early seventeenth century. The most prominent were Santa Maria in Vallicella, the Chiesa Nuova (New Church) of the Oratorians (1575–1606); Sant'Andrea della Valle, built for the Theatines (1591–1623, except the façade); and two churches for the Jesuits, San Carlo al Corso (1612–72) and Sant'Ignazio (begun 1626). If nothing else, they provided artists with vast areas to decorate, especially as the taste for sumptuous ensembles grew with time. The character of the earlier churches was often greatly altered by these later additions. Il Gesù itself received most of its spectacular decor about a century after it had been built. The stuccos by Antonio Raggi in the nave and transept (after designs by G.B. Gaulli, called Baciccio; fig.122) were added 1669–83; an altar designed by Pietro da Cortona was placed there only after his death (1674–78); Baciccio's large paintings on the ceiling of the nave and the crossing were executed 1676–79; and the most celebrated piece, the altar of Sant'Ignazio in the left transept, was done in 1695–99 from Andrea Pozzo's design by a team of sculptors, most of them French.

Stylistically, these works reflect a concept of the function of decoration that had been developed by the great masters of the High Baroque: Pietro da Cortona (1596–1669), Gianlorenzo Bernini (1598–1680), and Francesco Borromini (1599–1667). Of these Cortona was primarily a painter, Bernini a sculptor, and, while Borromini was an architect first and last, he nevertheless was thoroughly familiar with the art of the stuccoworkers and throughout his career took a passionate interest in the smallest decorative details of his buildings. Hence all these artists conceived of decoration as an integral part of architecture; of Bernini, indeed, it has been said that he conceived architecture itself in sculptural terms. If the earlier buildings tended to be severe and majestic, the later ones were ingratiating and cheerful, a delight to the eyes and the analytical mind. Many of the key monuments of this period are small and intimate, and there is something of the beauty of finely assembled jewelry about them. They seem to reflect a religious attitude less concerned with the ardor of the missionary than with the aesthetic pleasure of a cultivated few.

With the reduction in scale and the growth of a more mundane outlook, the central type of planning came back into favor. The first contributions to this development were made by non-Roman artists, Francesco Maria Ricchino (1583–1658) and Baldassare Longhena (1598–1682). Ricchino, characterized by Wittkower as "perhaps the most imaginative and most richly endowed Italian architect of the early seventeenth century," was active in Milan. In San Giuseppe, a work of his youth, he made a significant experiment in creating a longitudinal progression in terms of two central units arranged one behind the other. Both follow the Greek-cross design, but the first one to be entered is dominant since it alone has a cupola. This unit determines the appearance of the outside, which shows two stories, the lower one rectangular and the upper in the shape of an octagon. The façade (fig. 22) is completely integrated with the body of the church; on the upper level it forms one side of the octagon. Ingenious though this solution may

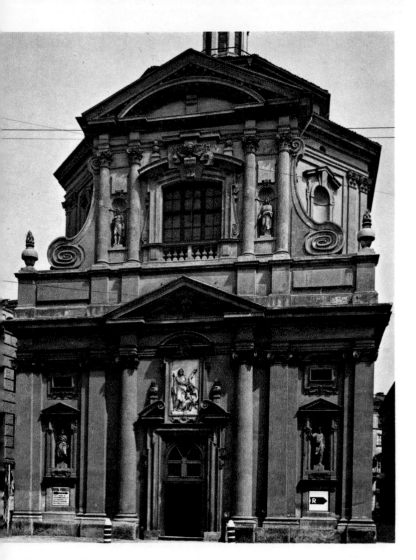

22. FRANCESCO MARIA RICCHINO.
Façade, S. Giuseppe. 1607–30. Milan

be, it is not entirely successful. The conflict between the function of the façade as a separate entity (stressed by the scrolls on either side of the upper story) and as a containing wall is not resolved. Nor is the façade completely unified in structure and decor. On the lower level the relief increases toward the central bay; on the upper the idea of a projecting center has been discarded, and the semblance of another three-bay arrangement, different from that below, has been created by the device of inserting niches with sculpture into narrow wall-strips that had been without accent below. The insertion of a segmental pedi-

ment into a triangular one is an early example of this theme.

Ricchino, no doubt, was full of ideas. The fact is, however, that not he but Maderno was the great leader of Baroque architecture in its first phase. This was due not only to the disadvantage Ricchino had in launching his ideas from "provincial" Milan. What he lacked was Maderno's sense of order and the gift of lending monumentality to projects of even limited scale.

Longhena's masterpiece, the Church of Santa Maria della Salute in Venice, was designed in 1630–31 in gratitude for the end of the plague.[14] It was finished only in 1687, though substantially according to plan. Here, too, we find a combination of two central units—each one, however, with its own dome (fig. 23). The first and dominant unit is an octagon surrounded by an ambulatory. Rectangular chapels mark the end of each axis except at the entrance and the opposite side, where an arch opens into the sanctuary. While a longitudinal axis is suggested by the view through this opening, the main octagon is treated with such regularity and the vistas in all directions are so similar in character that they tend to neutralize each other (fig. 24). Tall Corinthian columns in the angles of the octagon, and figures of prophets standing above them in the drum of the dome, are like guardians preventing escape. In a manner comparable to the ideals of the Renaissance, the bright, neatly ordered room rests within itself; motion is largely suspended. Nor is there much upward urgency. Judged only by its interior, the largest Baroque edifice in Venice is singularly devoid of excitement and drama.

Drama of a sort, however, is provided by its exterior (fig. 25). The location on the tip of the peninsula between the Grand Canal and the Canale delle Zattere was made for a grand effect, and Longhena used these possibilities with the skill of a stage designer. A series of twenty-odd steps leads from the water directly to the main entrance, designed as a tripartite triumphal arch with a pediment over the center. The chapels

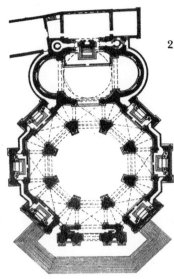

23. **BALDASSARE LONGHENA.**
Plan, S. Maria della Salute.
Begun 1631. Venice

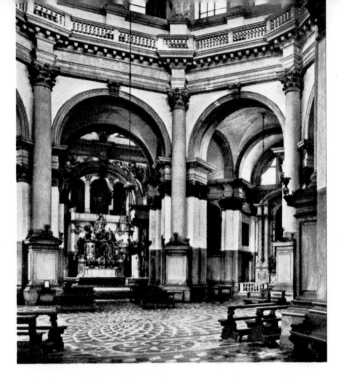

24. **BALDASSARE LONGHENA.**
Interior, S. Maria della Salute

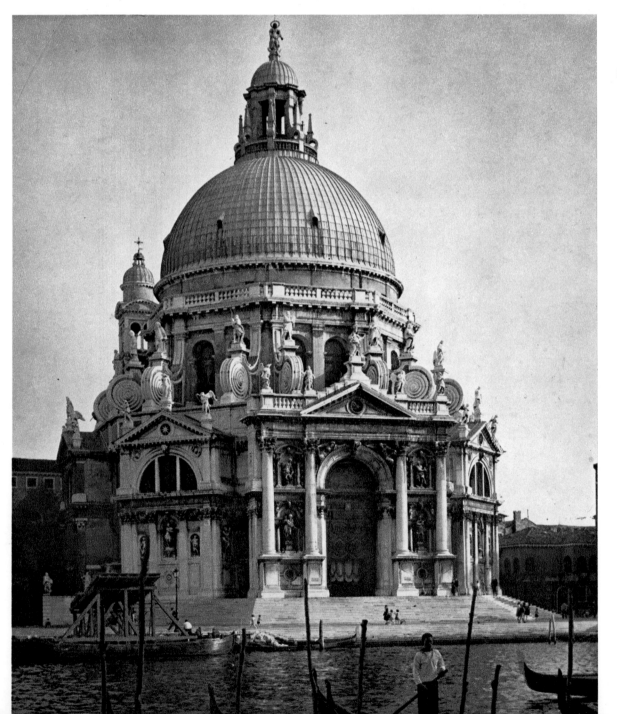

25. **BALDASSARE LONGHENA.**
Exterior,
S. Maria della Salute.
Begun 1631. Venice

33

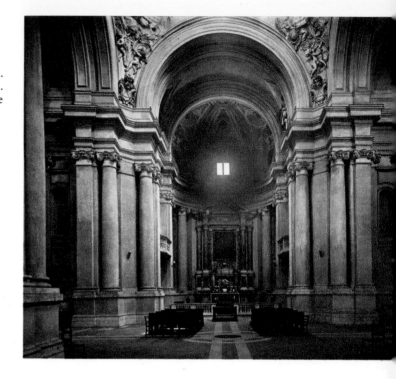

have façades of their own, designed in two stories: sculptures in niches below, and above, a semi-circular window, vertically subdivided in three. Sixteen richly curled volutes, rising above the ambulatories, abut the octagonal tambour, each of them enriched by a small platform supporting a freestanding carved figure. The octagon itself, with two arched windows to each side, ends in a balustrade. Up to this level the building is made up of many sculptural elements, designed to create a flamboyant effect. It was a stroke of genius to top off all this excitement with a singularly smooth, calm dome and no more than a gentle echo of the sculptural exuberance below in the lantern at the top. The quiet majesty of the cupola was realized by the device of a double shell with only the higher one visible on the outside. The dome, indeed, insures the impression of unity that the separate units of the lower part of the building would never have achieved. Only on close examination does one become aware of the clever device of a short circular drum that seems to rise without visible support from within the octagonal tambour, so freeing the artist from any obligation to create a formal transition between tambour and dome.

Santa Maria della Salute added to the skyline of Venice an unforgettably spectacular silhouette, and the eighteenth-century painters of Venetian *vedute* were understandably fond of it for this very reason (see colorplate 53). Yet the success of the building remains somewhat of a fluke. It is hardly accidental that despite its prominent place and its unquestionable, and deserved, fame, it remained an isolated piece. In the development of Baroque architecture Santa Maria della Salute is a revealing symptom, but of limited influence.

None of the churches built in Rome in the middle of the seventeenth century is as spectacular as Longhena's Santa Maria della Salute, but

in regard to structural originality, many of them surpass the proud edifice above the Grand Canal. Chronologically, Pietro da Cortona's Santi Martina e Luca came first; it was begun in 1635, in the form of a modified Greek cross (fig. 26), of which the main axis is slightly longer than the transversal one. Each arm of the cross ends in a rounded apse, and the corners of the crossing have been

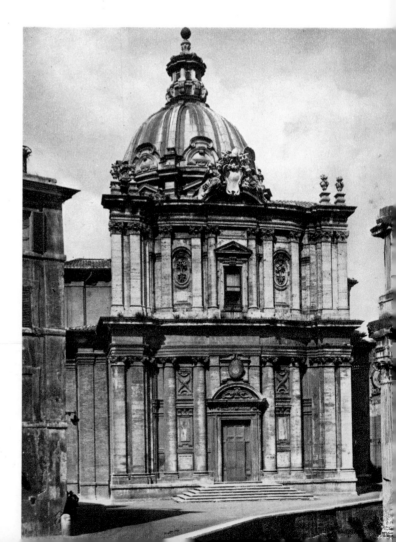

beveled off so that seen from the inside the shell of the building continues smoothly from one part of the building to the next. Pairs of freestanding columns placed all around the walls further unify the appearance. When he came to the façade (fig. 27), Cortona took the decisive step of introducing, if ever so slightly, a convex curvature between strong lateral piers marked by paired pilasters. The shape of the façade—two stories of equal width—is not unusual, but this curvature gives to it the impression of being shaped by pressures from within, the bottled-up forces of space. A glance at the plan of the church shows that it is the bulge of the western arm of the Greek cross that accounts for the curve of the façade; in other words, the façade is no longer a separate show-piece, as it was still with Maderno, but a flexible organism that may respond in many different ways to forces acting upon it.

The gentle forward motion of the façade of Santi Martina e Luca was realized at the expense of a strong central motif. Whatever hesitancy there was in this early work is completely gone in Cortona's brilliant façade of Santa Maria della Pace (fig. 28), added to a church of the fifteenth century (fig. 29). It is the first example of an arrangement in which the façade proper is only a part of a larger composition involving both width and depth, realized by partly ignoring, partly transforming existing conditions. The visitor is greeted by a semielliptical portico of six columns, forming three wide openings between them. Hidden in its shadow are the straight wall and plain portal of the fifteenth-century church. The part of the façade visible above the portico is richly organized in terms of pilasters, columns, and duplicated pediments. Its central section is conspicuously convex, echoing in a more restricted way the bold forward sweep of the portico. These two units owe much of their effect to the addition of two sets of lateral wings: low extensions on the ground level (one of which masks the mouth of a street) lend height to the façade proper by contrast, while above them concavely shaped wings make more dramatic the forward motion of the center. In order to allow for a proper appreciation

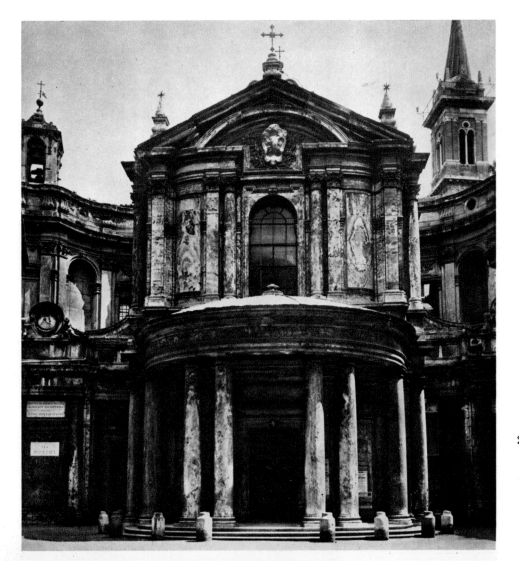

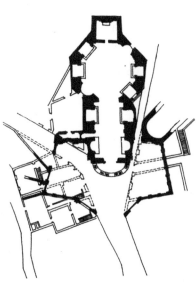

28, 29. PIETRO DA CORTONA.
Façade and Plan,
S. Maria della Pace.
1656–57. Rome

of this interplay of convex and concave elements, Cortona created a small piazza by razing buildings in front of the church.[15]

The beauty of Cortona's façade of Santa Maria della Pace, however, is not due to its striking spatial fantasy alone. All proportions have been chosen felicitously; the decoration is sparing and applied where it counts most. None is on the portico, whose severe Doric columns carry an unbroken entablature. In the upper story, Cortona stressed the continuity between wings and center by using the same order for both, and by providing an additional common element in the form of a stringcourse behind the orders. The motif of a segmental pediment inscribed into a gabled one, found in Ricchino's work, was given an interesting functional interpretation by connecting the triangular one with the firm corner pilasters, the curved one with the pilasters marking the extent of the forward curve of the walls. In the center, the segmental pediment is extended downward through the zone of the main entablature, a bold idea that provided space for an escutcheon surrounded by foliage.

Rich in subtle ideas, the design has the quiet assurance that comes with perfection. It has a theatrical flair but is not stagy; it is eloquent without being rhetorical; and despite its variety of motifs the beholder perceives its consummate harmony.

Pietro da Cortona is the author also of what is perhaps the most nearly ideal solution of the Baroque for the external organization of a dome. His own earlier one for Santi Martina e Luca had suffered from a lack of emphasis. By contrast his dome for San Carlo al Corso (fig. 30) is a masterpiece of lucidity and functional usefulness. As in domes of the Renaissance, cupola and drum are clearly separated. The eight very large window openings of the drum are separated by piers of compound pilasters flanked by Corinthian columns. These orders support a wide circular entablature decisively marking the top of the drum. Yet unlike Renaissance domes, the vertical flow of the piers is not stopped at this point but continues through the projecting imposts into spe-

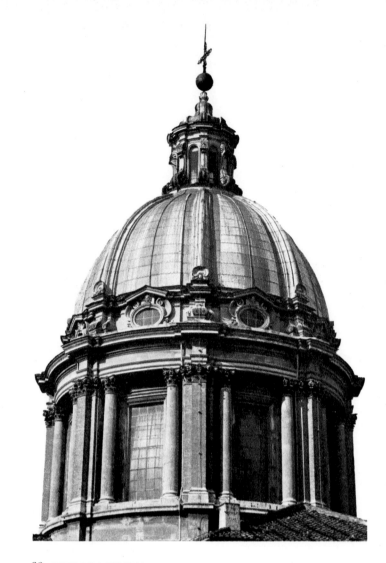

30. PIETRO DA CORTONA.
Dome, S. Carlo al Corso. Begun 1668. Rome

cially designed members of the attic zone, and from them into the ribs of the cupola itself. It was a particularly happy idea to insert oval windows under gabled moldings into each bay of the attic, providing not only an elegant topping for the plain windows below but an additional source of light for the interior as well. The lantern, finally, echoes on a smaller scale the major divisions below, substituting graceful scrolls for the clustered pilasters and columns. Again it is the feeling of proportional harmony that lends to Cortona's dome of San Carlo its special beauty.

Some of Cortona's buildings have been destroyed; many more remained projects never executed.

36

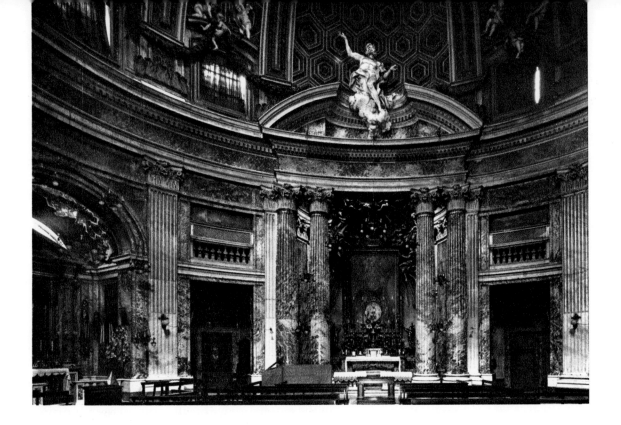

Yet the little that has survived assures him a place among the great Baroque architects equal to that which he unquestionably holds among Baroque painters (see pages 103–109).

Except for one earlier building, Bernini occupied himself with church architecture only late in life, and then only in small projects. He designed three central churches—one a Greek cross, one circular, and one an oval—accompanied by chapels. In all three the exteriors are relatively austere in contrast to the sumptuous interiors, in which not unexpectedly, sculpture plays an important role. The last two of these buildings, Santa Maria dell'Assunzione in Ariccia (1662–64) and Sant'Andrea al Quirinale (1658–70), are both at the center of larger spatial compositions demonstrating how the Baroque trend toward planning in multiple units can be realized even on a relatively small scale. In Sant'Andrea, a Jesuit sanctuary (fig. 32), Bernini provided the portal with a gracefully curving portico of two freestanding columns, different from but perhaps inspired by the portico of Santa Maria della Pace, standing on semicircular steps (of which there are today more than he planned). Their forward flow is con-

31, 32. GIANLORENZO BERNINI.
Interior and Façade,
S. Andrea al Quirinale.
1658–70. Rome

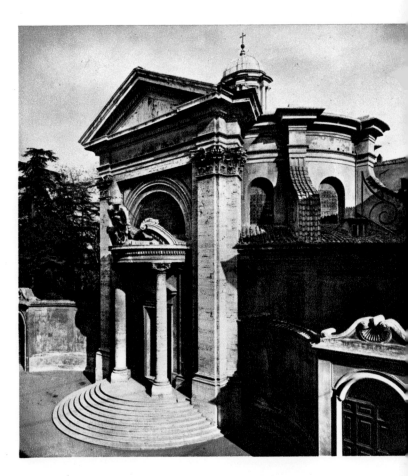

trasted to the concave movement of two low walls extending sideways like two welcoming arms. Above them appears the opposite curvature of the church itself, adding another element of curvilinear spatial motion. All these contrapuntally advancing and receding curves are anchored to one firm and determinedly frontal form, a simple, solid aedicula that marks the façade proper.

The interior (fig. 31; colorplate 1) offers the surprise of a ribbed and coffered dome that, being mantled in, is invisible from the outside. Moreover, instead of a variety of spatial motions, everything here is subordinated to the smooth continuity of the main oval. The long axis is placed transversally to the east-west axis of the church. The accompanying niches are hardly noticed. Only where an aedicula on fluted columns marks the opening to the main area do we become aware of an additional room. An inner sanctum has been created by a bulge in the outside wall, almost as if it had yielded to some spiritual fervor exuding from the region of the altar.

The impression of the interior is not dependent on spatial effects alone. Using marbles of many colors, with occasional touches of gold, Bernini gave to it a rich if mellow tonality. A glory of angels gambol above the main altar amidst some brilliant rays, and saints and angels, along with flowered garlands, are placed above the windows cut into the dome. All these details are in turn subordinated to the focal point of the composition: the figure of the titular saint, rising on clouds from the pediment of the aedicula framing the altar niche. Obediently curving inward, the pediment permits the saint to soar heavenward without any hindrance.

Of Bernini's secular buildings, none has come down without alterations. The most influential was his palace for Cardinal Flavio Chigi, designed as a block of seven bays accompanied by slightly recessed wings of three bays each (fig. 33). This beautifully balanced group was extended in the eighteenth century to more than twice its length, depriving Bernini's plan of its original proportions; nor did the building receive the sculptural decor Bernini had planned to rise above the cornice. The chief interest of Bernini's façade was in the emphatic rhythm of giant pilasters, uniting the two upper stories of a traditional three-story palace and following each in close succession. Giant orders had been used before by Michelangelo and Palladio and by northern "Palladians" (fig. 293), but in Bernini's Palazzo Chigi the system was given a "classical" formulation, beautifully expressing power and princely majesty; its role for later Baroque palace designs can be compared to that of Alberti's and Michelozzo's Florentine palaces for the Renaissance.

Bernini's most spectacular contribution to architecture was undoubtedly his wings and colon-

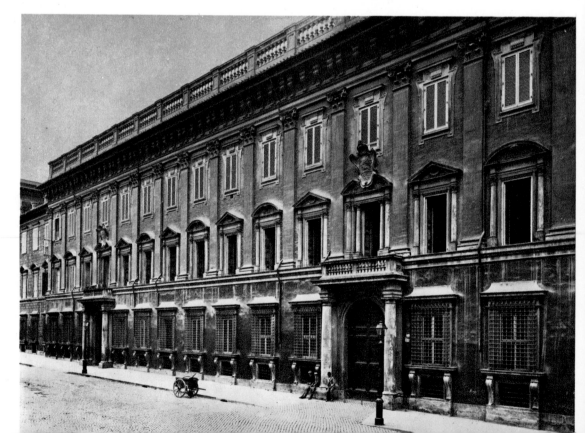

33. GIANLORENZO BERNINI.
Façade, Palazzo Chigi-Odescalchi.
Begun 1664. Rome

38

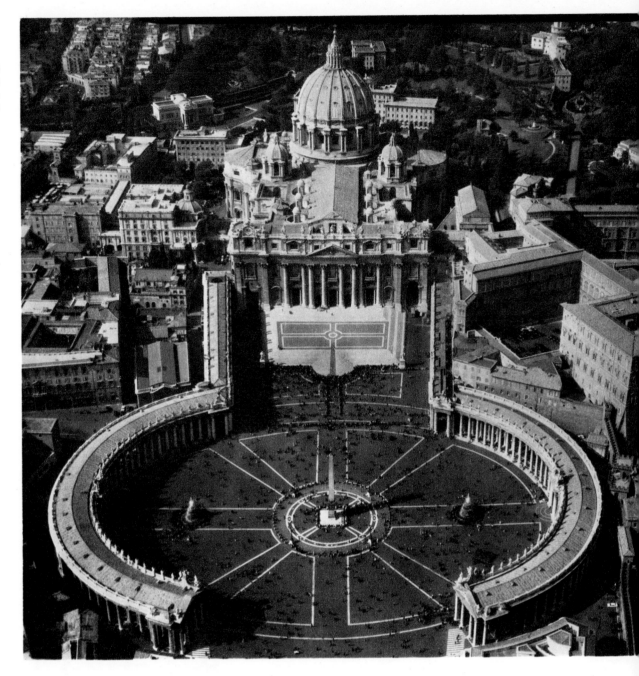

34. Air View of St. Peter's
including Colonnade
by Bernini, begun 1656.
Rome

nades for St. Peter's (fig. 34). Stretching forward
from Maderno's façade, the straight wings (or corridors) follow the downward slope of the ground
as they converge slightly toward each other. This
convergence, like so much at St. Peter's, was the
result of extant conditions, in this case buildings forming part of the Vatican palace. Yet Bernini made a virtue out of necessity: the converging wings, being of modest height, help to play
down the excessive width of the main façade
while emphasizing its height. Before this func-

tion is perceived, however, the visitor has been
scooped up, as it were, by the vast embracing
gesture of the colonnades.

The focal points of the huge oval formed by
the colonnades—the obelisk and the fountains—
had been emplaced long before. Whatever earlier plans had been envisaged for the area, they
surely had none of the incomparable majesty of
Bernini's solution with its more than 250 huge
Doric columns forming a triple corridor (the
central one barrel-vaulted) around the piazza (fig.

Italy in the Seventeenth Century / 39

2). Raised by a few steps above the square, the columns carry a wide entablature with a strongly protruding cornice. A balustrade hides the roof and incorporates above each column a huge, splendidly draped marble figure. Additional columns decorate the terminal points of the colonnades and the passages for vehicles at either end of the oval. Originally, Bernini had also planned a separate section closing off, except for two lateral openings, the piazza toward the east. Thus the full force of the wide sweep of the colonnades and of the vista of the church itself would have been felt only by one who had already entered the square. This section was never built, but until recent times a group of houses screened the approach to the colonnades, thus preserving the element of surprise. These houses were razed during Mussolini's era to make way for a wide, pompous boulevard, largely destroying the effect Bernini had planned.

In addition to their practical function and aesthetic appeal the colonnades are obviously of symbolic significance. Bernini himself compared them to "the motherly arms of the Church," ready to embrace believers and repentant heretics alike. Yet they are also undoubtedly symbols of physical power. Arranged four rows deep, the columns inevitably conjure up the image of a military force standing at attention, a visual equivalent of the *ecclesia militans* under the leadership of the Roman popes, even if by the time the monument was finished the centers of power had shifted elsewhere.

To achieve the effect of grandeur was Bernini's aim in another project connected with St. Peter's. His task in building the Scala Regia (fig. 35), the main stairs of the Vatican Palace, was made difficult because of the fearful limitations of space. How he solved this problem is characteristic of much of Baroque planning. With the help of perspective devices developed in stage design, he created the impression of a grand flight of stairs subdivided by columns into a barrel-vaulted center aisle and narrower side aisles. The eye imparts to the whole flight of stairs the proportions of the

opening, which is enriched by a grand escutcheon with the papal arms. Yet the magnificence of these stairs is only optical (fig. 36). Actually, the columns rapidly decrease in size so that at the end of the first straight run the distance from wall to wall is barely more than half of the width at the beginning. The lateral aisles, cramped enough to start with, are entirely eliminated in the second flight, which doubles back and thus is out of sight. An amazing tour de force, the Scala Regia typifies the tendency of the Baroque to welcome any means as long as they yield a desired effect—to be content, for instance, with the *illusion* of grandeur where conditions prevent its full demonstration.

Rejecting the constraint of rectilinear design and relying by preference on regular curvatures, Cortona and Bernini allowed their buildings to reach out into and to encompass space, not unlike the figures they rendered in painting and sculpture. Moving freely in space, their architectures were restricted only by the artists' deep respect for clear organization and harmonious proportion. The art of Francesco Borromini, the

35. GIANLORENZO BERNINI. Scala Regia. 1663–66. Vatican Palace, Rome

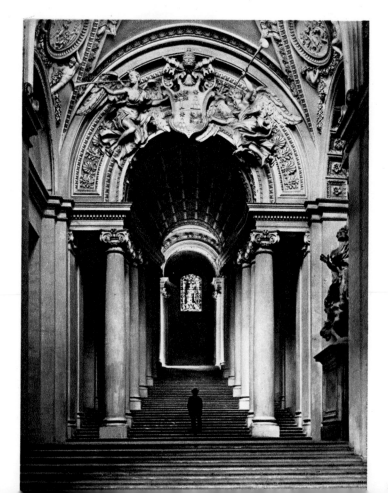

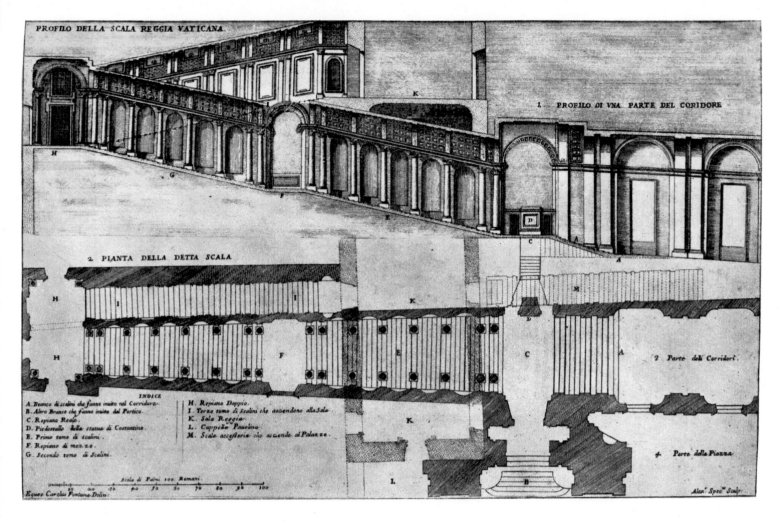

PROFILO DELLA SCALA REGGIA VATICANA.

1. PROFILO DI VNA PARTE DEL CORIDORE

2. PIANTA DELLA DETTA SCALA

INDICE
A. Branco di scalini che fanno inuito nel Corridore.
B. Altro Branco che fanno inuito dal Portico.
C. Repiano Reale.
D. Piedestallo della statua di Costantino.
E. Primo tomo di scalini.
F. Repiano di mezzo.
G. Secondo tomo di Scalini.
H. Repiano Doppio.
I. Terzo tomo di Scalini che ascendono alla Sala.
K. Sala Reggia.
L. Cappella Paulina.
M. Scala accessoria che ascende al Palazzo.

Scala di Palmi 100. Romani.
Eques Carolus Fontana Delin.
Alex. Spec. Sculp.

36. GIANLORENZO BERNINI. Plan and Elevation, Scala Regia (engraving by Carlo Fontana). 1663–66. Vatican Palace, Rome

third of the great architects of the High Baroque, was different. Where the first two aimed at order and regularity, he took pleasure in plans apt to mystify. Where they, especially in their most mature works, made use of the traditional vocabulary of architecture, Borromini developed his own personal idiom, in which conventional elements are associated with and occasionally supplanted by forms of picturesque originality.

His beginnings are largely hidden in the anonymity of the studios in which he worked. He assisted Bernini on the bronze baldachin in St. Peter's (see pages 63–64) and was employed in the construction of the Palazzo Barberini, but it is still uncertain how much of these works is due to his ideas. The first building entirely his own is the little church of San Carlo alle Quattro Fontane, affectionately known as San Carlino. Its

revolutionary character is best appreciated if one keeps in mind that it was built in the same decade that saw the construction of Longhena's Santa Maria della Salute and Cortona's Santi Martina e Luca. Starting with the tiny cloisters in 1634, Borromini built the church proper in 1638–41, except for the façade, which was added only in 1665–67. He began with plans for a longitudinally placed oval, accompanied by chapels of alternating shapes (fig. 37). As he progressed, he veered away from the concept of finite units; instead he favored merging the chapels with the main room. This was possible because he conceived of enclosing walls not as rigid boundaries but as delicate membranes capable of yielding to pressure. The oval from which he started is still visible in the marble pattern of the floor and the shape of the dome rising above the pendentives. The room

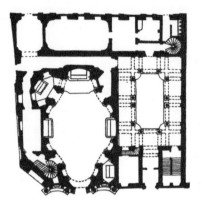

37. FRANCESCO BORROMINI.
Plan, S. Carlo alle Quattro Fontane.
Begun 1638. Rome

itself (fig. 38), however, vaguely recalling a Greek cross, bulges into relatively deep and narrow niches at either end of the longitudinal axis and wide but shallow ones in the transversal. All niches appear bigger than they are because of an illusionistic design of their vaults. Despite the fascinating flexibility of the spatial shell, the room is perfectly unified. Its walls are articulated by identical columns carrying a wide, continuous entablature that makes it easy to follow the "respiration" of the structure. A peculiar honeycomb pattern inside the dome, made up of hexagons, octagons, and Greek crosses, seems to give to the enclosing shell the ability to absorb, like some kind of soundproofing, the expanding spatial (and acoustic) energies. It has been pointed out that all of the curved surfaces, if completed, would form sections of five regular elliptical units.[16]

Thus what seems to be rather whimsical is actually based on careful geometric calculations, some of them possibly derived from age-old masons' practice.[17]

Consisting of two similarly proportioned stories, the façade (fig. 39) is very narrow and high— much higher, indeed, than warranted by the church behind it. On the ground floor the central bay curves forward while the lateral ones recede concavely. The oblique position of the four columns framing the bays, and the undulating entablature above them, clearly tie both concave and convex motions into one continuous rhythm. In the upper story all three bays are concave, but a little "sentry box" inserted in the central bay adds a convex countermotion. Above it two angels, apparently flying in front of the walls, hold a large oval medallion, tilting it forward to pro-

38. FRANCESCO BORROMINI.
Interior, S. Carlo alle Quattro Fontane.
Begun 1638. Rome

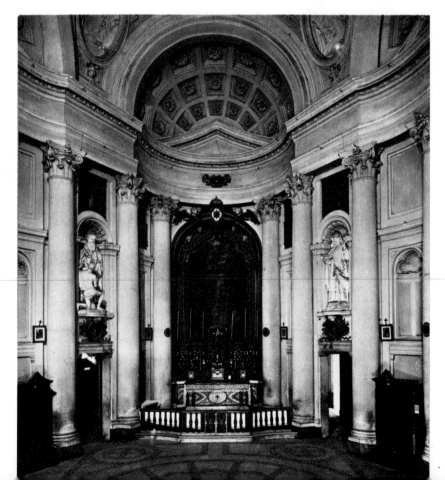

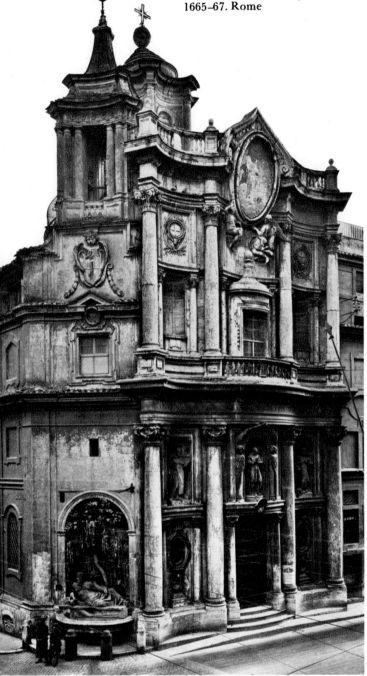

39. FRANCESCO BORROMINI.
Façade, S. Carlo alle Quattro Fontane.
1665–67. Rome

More than any other, the church dedicated to Sant'Ivo, patron saint of lawyers, reveals Borromini's ability to derive astonishing effects from seemingly simple premises. It was placed at the end of a long courtyard built by Giacomo della Porta for a school of higher learning that later became the University. The ground plan (fig. 40) is based on the form of a hexagonal star, or rather on the two equilateral triangles that by their interpenetration create such a star. By the surprisingly simple device of differentiating the shapes of the terminal points of these triangles Borromini created a most extraordinary interior. Instead of ending in three acute angles, one of the triangles terminates in semicircles or, spatially speaking, in semicircular niches.

The second triangle proceeds in the expected manner for about half the distance beyond the intersection, only to have its tip blunted by a convex curve, making the wall that corresponds to it look as if pushed in from the outside. Once inside the room (fig. 41), the visitor finds himself unable to establish anywhere the comfort of a clear axial reference. Wherever he stands, he sees before him a spatial unit differing from the one behind him; nor is there any formal correspondence along any transversal axis. Yet, just as in San Carlino, there is a strong awareness of unity; identical, elegantly fluted pilasters follow each other in close succession all around the walls. Above them a wide and perfectly "clean" entablature not only pulls all forms together but also permits us to see the basic pattern of the plan. Beyond this entablature, the view proceeds into the steeply rising dome (fig. 42), the height of which gives evidence of Borromini's preference for vertical motion. Furthermore, while the complex ground plan is carried up into the organization of the dome, Borromini used this higher sphere to reduce gradually the inherent elements of conflict by stressing the similarity of the six vertical piers, and by topping off their converging motion with a succession of perfectly circular forms that might suggest the watchful eye of God.

The outside of Sant'Ivo (fig. 43) is as unusual as

vide a better view from below. Moreover, the façade is not only conceived as a pliant spatial form but is also hollowed out by windows and niches and enlivened by sculpture, both figural and ornamental. Altogether it is an airy, rather playful design distinguished by a most imaginative conception and a superb execution of detail.

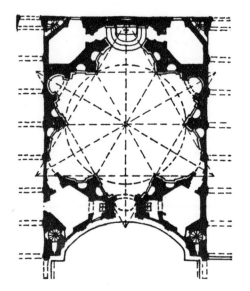

FRANCESCO BORROMINI.
S. Ivo della Sapienza.
1642–50. Rome

LEFT: 40. Plan

BELOW: 41. Interior

RIGHT: 42. Interior of Dome

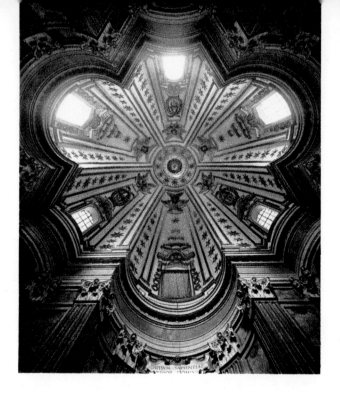

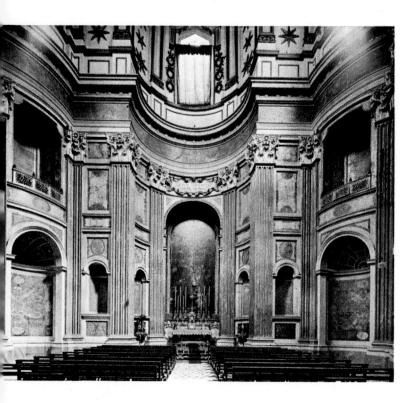

its interior. The shallowly concave façade adopts, with variations, the system of Della Porta's arcades in the courtyard. Borromini added an attic and placed on either side the Chigi emblem of six massed hills, resting on circular bases decorated with Chigi stars. (Stars are used as decoration in many other parts of the building.) The true Borromini touch appears above the façade, in the dome. The inner dome is largely hidden inside a drum, the six sectors of which bulge convexly like petals of a stylized rosette. The points of vertical stress are located in the recessed corners where the bulges meet behind compound pilasters. The upward motion of these members continues above the cornice of the drum in gracefully curved buttresses and is taken up by the paired colonnettes of the lantern. In calculated contrast to the convex curves of the drum, the horizontal members of the lantern recede concavely. The verticalism of the plan (supported at various levels by finial-like decorations) comes to a spirited, if somewhat exotic, climax in a spiraling pyramid enriched by many small flickering shapes; at this level, architecture seems to lose its material firmness and to dissolve into the surrounding air.

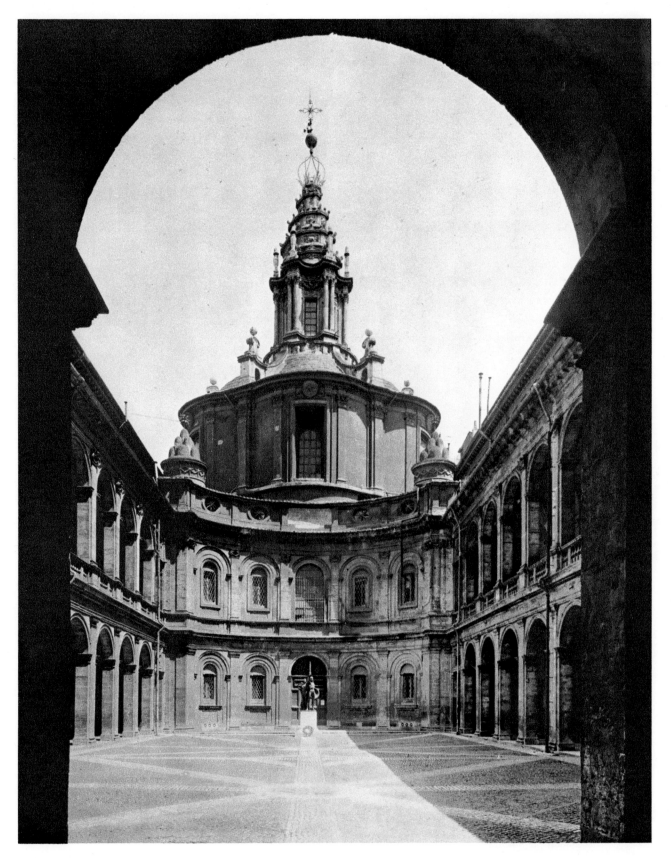

43. FRANCESCO BORROMINI. Exterior, S. Ivo della Sapienza. 1642–50. Rome

The principles of Borromini's architecture are well represented by San Carlino and Sant'Ivo. Yet almost every other of his buildings reveals unexpected and fascinating aspects. At Sant'Agnese in Piazza Navona, begun by Carlo Rainaldi (see page 50), Borromini achieved, by virtue of a concave center, a perfect combination of a two-tower façade with a high and commanding dome (fig. 44). There are the unfinished dome and slender, minaretlike tower of Sant'Andrea delle Fratte; the curiously wind-blown façade of the Oratory of San Filippo Neri, looking almost unsubstantial next to Rughesi's sturdy Gesù-type façade of the Chiesa Nuova; the façade of the College for the Propagation of the Faith with its seemingly irrational shift from bay to bay and the unorthodox handling of most details; and the interior of the church of the same College—one of Borromini's last works before his suicide in 1667—with its elimination of corners and the introduction of transversal vaulting devices to connect, Gothic fashion, the carrying members of one side of the room with those of the other.

Not one of these structures has the self-assured monumentality that marks even the smallest of Bernini's buildings. Yet by shunning, occasionally perhaps too demonstratively, anything that was conventional or "correct" (and thereby gaining the undisguised hostility of Bernini and his circle), Borromini encouraged all kinds of experimentation; the history of his influence has still to be written, but it is certain that the freedom of late Baroque architecture in southern Germany and Austria (see page 378) would have been impossible without the new conception of architecture Borromini had visualized in his work.

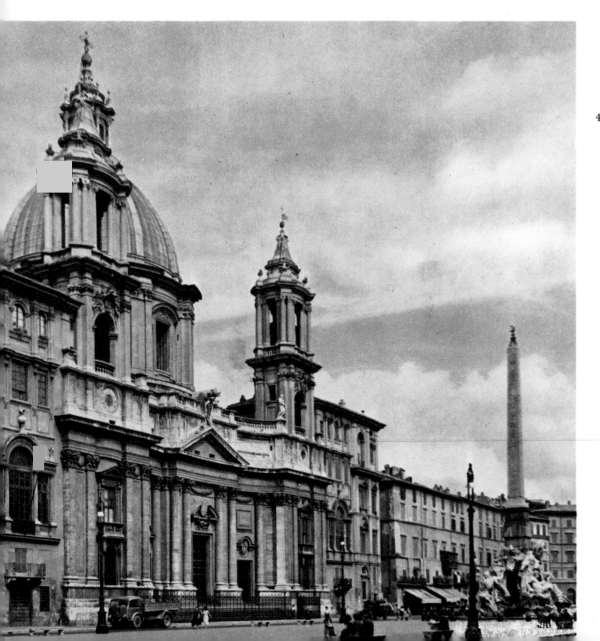

44. FRANCESCO BORROMINI.
Façade,
S. Agnese in Piazza Navona.
1653–66. Rome

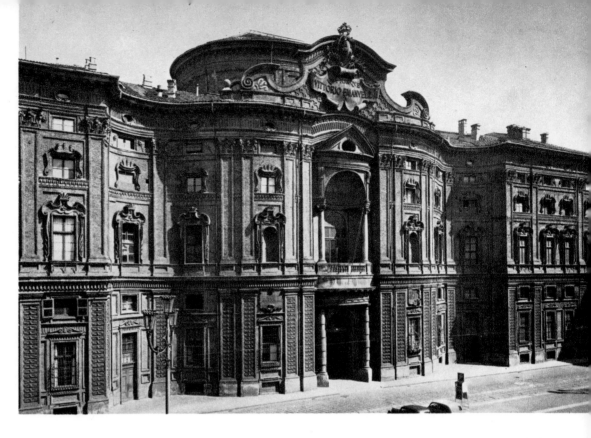

Borromini, however, was not the only southern influence active on these northern schools. They owed much to another Italian architect of the seventeenth century who was no less bold or unconventional. Yet Guarino Guarini (1624–1683), though indebted to Borromini, had an approach to architecture very different from Borromini's. While the latter retained throughout his life a mason's fascination with detail and gave to even his most bizarre creations a provocative elegance and grace, the former could not have cared less for such artisans' concerns. Guarini was an intellectual. A member of the Theatine Order, for which he built some churches, he was a teacher of philosophy and mathematics. He was fascinated with intricate geometric patterns, which he projected into three-dimensional reality, staggering the beholder with the ingenuity of the result more than captivating him with its beauty. With Borromini one always gets the impression that he loved improvisation and experiment; Guarini's art is decidedly cerebral and coolly calculated.

In his youth Guarini had been in Rome, but his entire career as architect took place away from that city. The first of the great traveling architects of the Baroque, he worked in places as widely separated as Messina, Paris, and Lisbon (and he made plans for churches in Munich and Prague). He finally settled in Turin. By a strange fate all the works done before he went to Savoy have been destroyed, but his plans have been preserved in engravings.[18] To his church in Lisbon he gave an undulating façade comparable to the façade of San Carlino; he was the first architect to apply the principle of undulation to a palace façade, in the Palazzo Carignano, Turin (fig. 45). He even inserted into the concave center of the façade a special convex unit that, despite its much larger size, clearly echoes the little "sentry box" of San Carlino.

Guarini apparently took special delight in devising new solutions for the construction of domes. His dome of the Chapel of the Holy Shroud in Turin rests on a circular drum whose six high arched openings are formed by highly decorated and unusually wide and stout piers. The implied hexagon is made explicit in the cupola by a sequence of six hexagonal stories formed by segmental ribs. As one looks up into this structure (fig. 46) one notices that each hexagon is inscribed into the one below it but shifted laterally by thirty degrees, so that the ribs of each

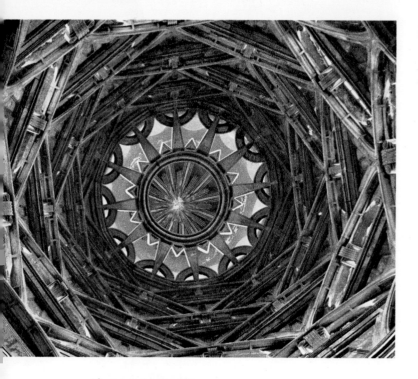

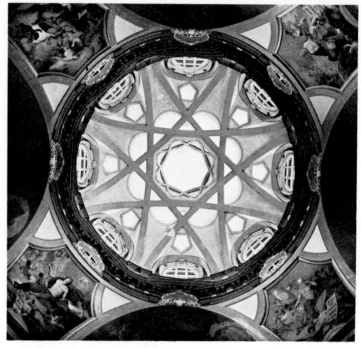

46. GUARINO GUARINI.
    Interior of Dome, Chapel of the Holy Shroud.
    1667–94. Turin

47. GUARINO GUARINI.
    Interior of Dome, S. Lorenzo.
    1666–87. Turin

of the upper polygons spring from the vertex of the one immediately below, just as the ribs of the first one spring from the vertex of the arches of the drum. Thus the first, third, and fifth hexagons parallel each other, as do the second, fourth, and sixth, though on a progressively reduced scale. A relatively simple geometric figure of inscribed hexagons has been projected into space in a daring feat of architectural engineering.

The same quality is seen in Guarini's Church of San Lorenzo in Turin, where an octagonal dome is supported by eight transversal ribs (fig. 47). At the point where these ribs first intersect, a second dome rises in the shape of a scalloped octagon. Since the ribs continue below this dome, each one intersecting with four others, they form a freestanding network that in its open center repeats once more the octagonal leitmotiv. The fantastic quality of this structure is enhanced by the contrast between the darker lower dome and the lighter upper one.

The bodies of these churches, too, can be described in terms of regular if complex geometric figures. In their three-dimensional development,

however, they come close to defying description. The Chapel of the Holy Shroud, for instance, is a cylindrical space, its walls divided by pilasters into seven bays of equal width plus one that is slightly wider. The drum, as we have seen, is circular, too. But the intermediary zone of the pendentives, contrary to all expectation, is organized by three large arches, one of which rises above the wide bay while each of the two others spans two bays by skipping one pilaster. The remaining three bays, located below the pendentives, are given convex curves reflecting the protrusion into the main room of three circular vestibules. The effect of all this is thoroughly bewildering, all the more so as Guarini, unlike Borromini, shunned the impression of unity. Rather he delighted in hinting at a multiplicity of spaces interpenetrating and at times even conflicting with each other.

This effect is still more pronounced in San Lorenzo (fig. 48). Its main spatial unit is inscribed into a square shell, but no single phrase can describe its interior dimensions. On seven sides of the main room are chapels alternating in depth but all opening in what may be described as a convex version of the so-called Palladian motif. Yet these chapels are not simply additions to the main room but are carved out of its mass, as it were, being created by walls that jut forward in shallow convex motions alternating with faintly polygonal ones. The entablature, again quite different from Borromini's treatment of that element, is broken up into short pieces, some straight, some curved, some jutting forward while others disappear into the depth of the chapels. On the eighth side, leading to the altar, there is a similar arcaded opening, but behind it lies a large oval room, placed transversally; instead of being carved out of the main room, it interpenetrates with it. The altar is outside this unit in a kind of ambulatory that hugs the curvature of the oval. Wherever one stands one sees fragmentary spaces whose connection with the other units is baffling.

If Borromini, as it has been said, eliminated the corner from architecture, Guarini can be said to have eliminated the quality of finiteness: the limits of the spatial units that make up his buildings cannot be grasped by those who stand in them. This was perhaps the architect's means

of conveying the concept of infinity. In a lighter vein, this concept was pursued still further by architects of the eighteenth century, like Vittone in Italy and Neumann in Germany (see pages 364, 392).

Different though they are in many respects, Borromini and Guarini have this in common: they prefer the seemingly unstable to the stable, the involved to the plain, the restless to the calm, the novel to the traditional. The extremeness of their position in seventeenth-century architecture has always been recognized. Neoclassic critics reserved their most scathing remarks for them. As architects, Cortona and Bernini were more moderate. Yet it is also true that in other media both artists took a more radical stance. In their formal turbulence Cortona's paintings and Bernini's sculptures seem to have more in common with the architecture of Borromini and Guarini than with the artists' own buildings.

If Borromini and Guarini were the leaders of the radical party of Italian seventeenth-century architecture, Carlo Rainaldi (1611–1691) may be said to have represented its right wing. His father Girolamo was a successful second-rater whose

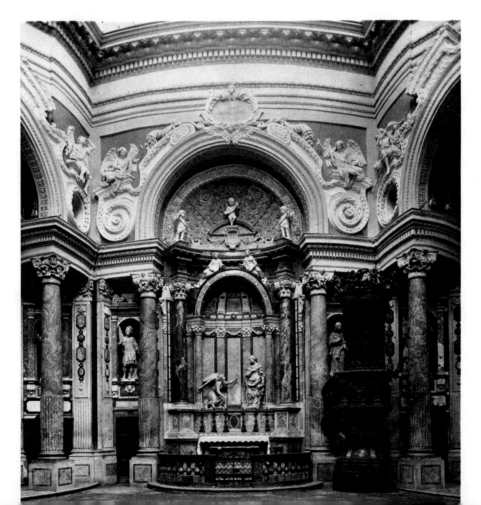

48. GUARINO GUARINI. Interior, S. Lorenzo. 1666–87. Turin

49

chief claim to historical notice is based on the fact that he finished the buildings on the Capitoline Hill, more or less in keeping with Michelangelo's plans. Carlo's own conservatism paid off handsomely; he was certainly one of the busiest Roman architects in the second half of the century.

Ironically, one Roman church is the work of both Borromini and Rainaldi, but not the result of collaboration. Sant'Agnese in Piazza Navona was begun and finished by Carlo Rainaldi, but his original plan for a traditional Greek-cross church was greatly altered when, soon after work began, he was dismissed and Borromini took over for an active span of two years (figs. 44, 49). The result, neither pure Borromini nor pure Rainaldi,

is not unpleasant but there is a hybrid quality to the church nevertheless (see page 46). In another of Rainaldi's major enterprises, the architectural organization of the Piazza del Popolo—the main entry into Rome—it was Bernini who crossed his path and modified the character of one of the two churches marking the angles of the three radiating streets. Entirely his own, however, is the large church of Santa Maria in Campitelli (fig. 50). Finished in the year of Borromini's death, it looks as if Borromini had never lived. Though Rainaldi had first planned a curved interior, he constructed in the end a building in which all major changes of direction are rectangular. (Only in the space below the dome are there obliquely

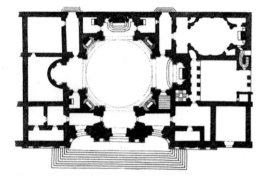

49. CARLO RAINALDI and FRANCESCO BORROMINI. Plan, S. Agnese in Piazza Navona. Begun 1652. Rome

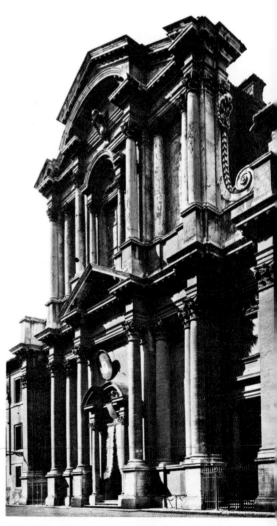

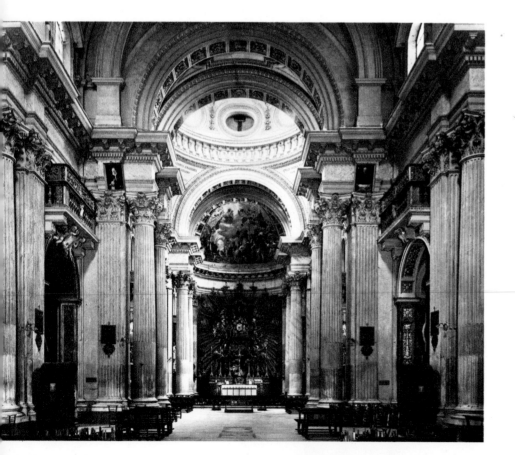

50, 51. CARLO RAINALDI. Interior and Façade, S. Maria in Campitelli. 1663–67. Rome

placed corner pilasters, and the apse is conventionally semicircular.)

Rainaldi's interior is fascinating because it exemplifies a concept of architecture basically opposed to that of the major Italian seventeenth-century architects. Uppermost with them had been the desire to create a continuous space, and to contain and shape imaginatively its dynamic properties. Rainaldi was primarily concerned with the plastic quality of the shell—a heritage from Michelangelo—enriching it lavishly with freestanding columns and deep niches. The same impression is obtained in the two-tiered and somewhat top-heavy façade (fig. 51). Rainaldi was sparing in sculptural decor, but employed a profusion of large and small columns to stress an unusually intense modulation in depth. His insistence on rectangularity (without Maderno's logical concentration toward the middle), combined with the exaggerated degree of recession within the façade, lends a harsh quality to the work; it is especially noticeable in the top pediment, where pieces of the cornice jut forward as if they had been cut out with scissors. (For Sant' Andrea della Valle, see page 30.) Yet it was Rainaldi rather than his greater contemporaries who most influenced later Roman architects, such as Carlo Fontana, Galilei, or Fuga (see pages 360–61).

SCULPTURE

The break with Mannerism came most slowly in sculpture.[19] Artists active around 1600 avoided posing their figures in torsions as extreme as those favored by Giovanni Bologna, but they had no positive aims of their own. The most one can say for the majority of sculptors contemporary with the painters Caravaggio and the Carracci is that occasionally they produced attractive pieces, as Stefano Maderno (1576–1636) did with his celebrated *St. Cecilia* (fig. 52). The gruesome theme of the dead martyr lying on the ground, her hands bound and her head partly severed from the body, has been made bearable by the beauty and grace of her figure and the lyrical flow of the lines of her hair and gown. In his youth, Francesco Mocchi (1580–1654) came perhaps closest to the innovations found in the painters of the period. His *Annunciation* in Orvieto (1603–8) is memorable for its energetic design and the penetrating characterization of the figures. His bronze equestrian statue of Alessandro Farnese (fig. 53) is filled with a driving motion that brings to mind Schlüter's statue of the Great Elector (see page 403). Mocchi's later works, however, did not fulfill the promise of his earlier ones.

The decisive change came only thanks to the genius of Gianlorenzo Bernini, born in Naples in 1598.[20] His father, Pietro, a sculptor of some competence, was his teacher, and Gianlorenzo assisted him after they had settled in Rome around 1605. By 1620 the son had left the father far behind. From that date until his death in 1680 Bernini's contemporaries acknowledged him as the greatest sculptor alive, and modern art history has concurred in this opinion, though perhaps for different reasons. The earlier fame of the master was largely due to his incredible virtuosity in handling marble, as in his early *Apollo and Daphne* (fig. 54), where he made believable—as if by magic—the metamorphosis of the skin of a maiden into the bark and leaves of a laurel tree. Today scholars are apt to stress the emotional depth of

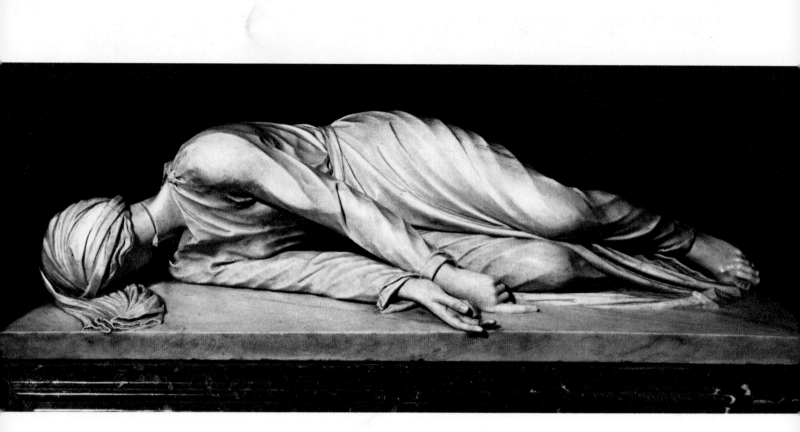

52. STEFANO MADERNO. *St. Cecilia*. 1600.
Marble, length 40″. S. Cecilia in Trastevere, Rome

Bernini's art and his intimate association with the spiritual forces of the Catholic revival. Their favorites are his later works, such as the two penitent saints in the Chigi Chapel of Siena Cathedral (fig. 59) or the angels with the instruments of the Passion in Sant'Andrea delle Fratte in Rome (fig. 64). This new approach has helped a reappraisal of works formerly judged too secular or too sensual. *St. Theresa in Ecstasy,* censured by the Victorians for its voluptuousness, is now recognized as the record of an intensely spiritual experience described by the saint herself in terms of sexual transport.

There is perhaps, a danger in stressing too much the spiritual element of Bernini's art. His work certainly is never gross, or lewd, or ignoble, but at all times it is magnificently carnal. Bernini never tired of glorifying the beauty of the nude human body, smooth but firm in adolescent angels and nubile women, swelling in muscular ripples in heroes and gods, sagging but still pulsating with life in ascetic saints. His basic artistic credo is so much like Rubens' that one is tempted to assume a connection. More than any sculptor before

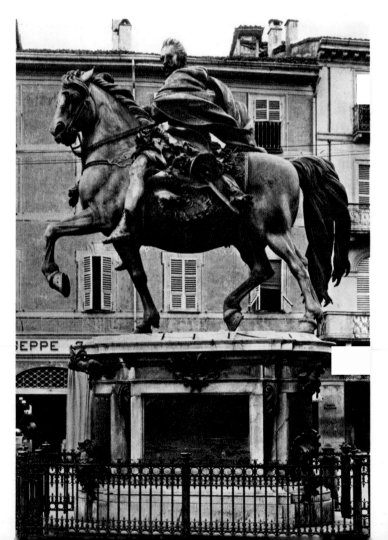

53. FRANCESCO MOCCHI.
Equestrian Statue of Alessandro Farnese. 1620–25.
Bronze, height c. 6′6½″. Piazza Cavalli, Piacenza

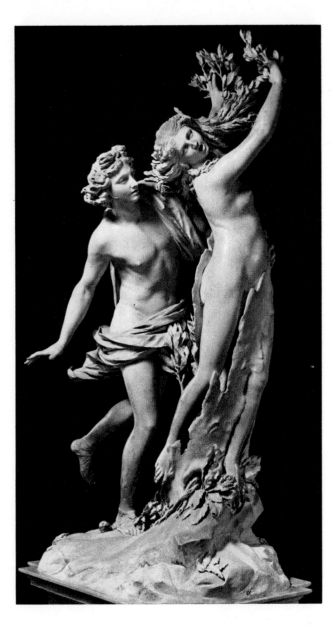

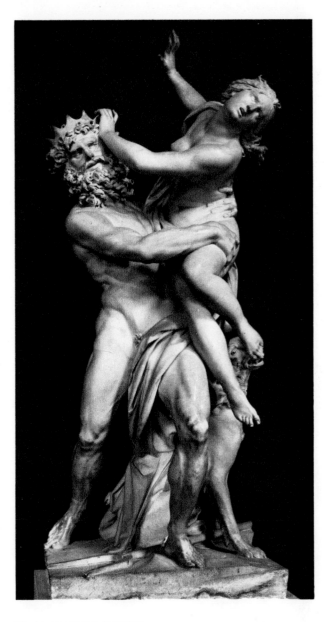

54. GIANLORENZO BERNINI.
Apollo and Daphne. 1622–25.
Marble, height 8′. Borghese Gallery, Rome

55. GIANLORENZO BERNINI.
Abduction of Proserpina. 1621–22.
Marble, height 7′4½″. Borghese Gallery, Rome

him, Michelangelo included, he makes us forget that his figures are made of marble and bronze. We expect stuffs to be pliant, flesh warm to the touch. We do not know what Pygmalion's sculpture looked like, but looking at those made by Bernini we can believe the legend.

As it always has for sensuous artists, human hair held a particular fascination for Bernini, and a technical challenge. He loved to show it in disarray, wind-blown, curling, and deeply hollowed out. In the *Abduction of Proserpina* (fig. 55)

strands of hair and beard flutter around Pluto's face like so many flames. Neptune's hair suggests waves lashed by tempestuous winds (fig. 370). The hair of women and angels is more gently animated. Wanting to be stroked with affection, it looks as if literally caressed out of the stone.

All this is indicative of the master's aim to use every part of his figures to express emotion. No matter what this emotion may be, it does not exist for Bernini unless it can be expressed by formal turbulence. Nothing is more characteristic than his treatment of drapery. Like Correggio, Barocci, and Rubens, he knew thoroughly that emotional excitement can be suggested vividly by agitated drapery folds. The first figure so treated is *St. Bibiana* (fig. 56). Vibrating delicately, her gown contributes greatly to the impression of the martyr's fervid devotion.

If St. Bibiana's gown seems stirred by a tender breeze, the mantle of St. Longinus (fig. 57) looks as if it were tossed and twisted by a violent wind. This accords well with the action of each figure: although transported by her vision, St. Bibiana modestly keeps her arms close to her body; St. Longinus, by contrast, stretches his arms out widely, abandoning himself wholly to the heavenly sights.

Most eloquent are the draperies in the St. Theresa group (fig. 58). The veil-like ones of the angel undulate around his body in a seductive manner, while the heavy masses of St. Theresa's

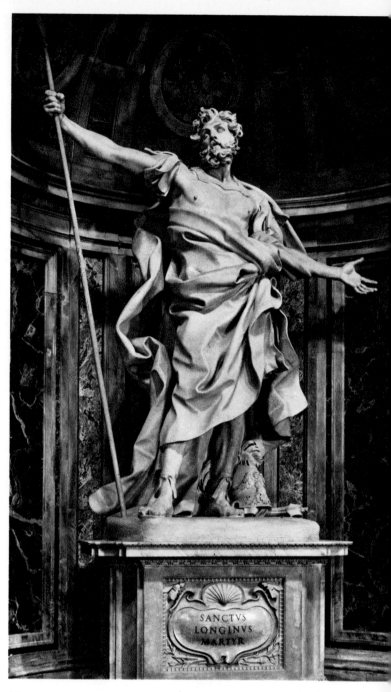

57. GIANLORENZO BERNINI. *St. Longinus*. 1629–38. Marble, height 14′6″. St. Peter's, Rome

Carmelite gown bury her body completely; only her face, hands, and—appropriately—discalced feet emerge from it.[21] Yet this voluminous robe contributes greatly to the expression of complete surrender and utter exhaustion. It hangs limply, as if all the vitality had been drained from it; many of its folds are deeply hollowed out, indicating a passive yielding to assaults from the outside.

56. GIANLORENZO BERNINI. *St. Bibiana*. 1624–26. Marble, height 7′10½″. S. Bibiana, Rome

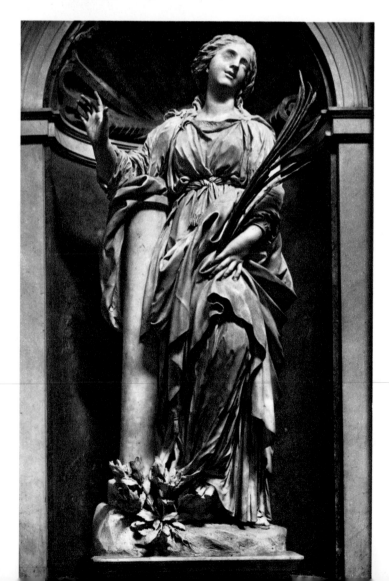

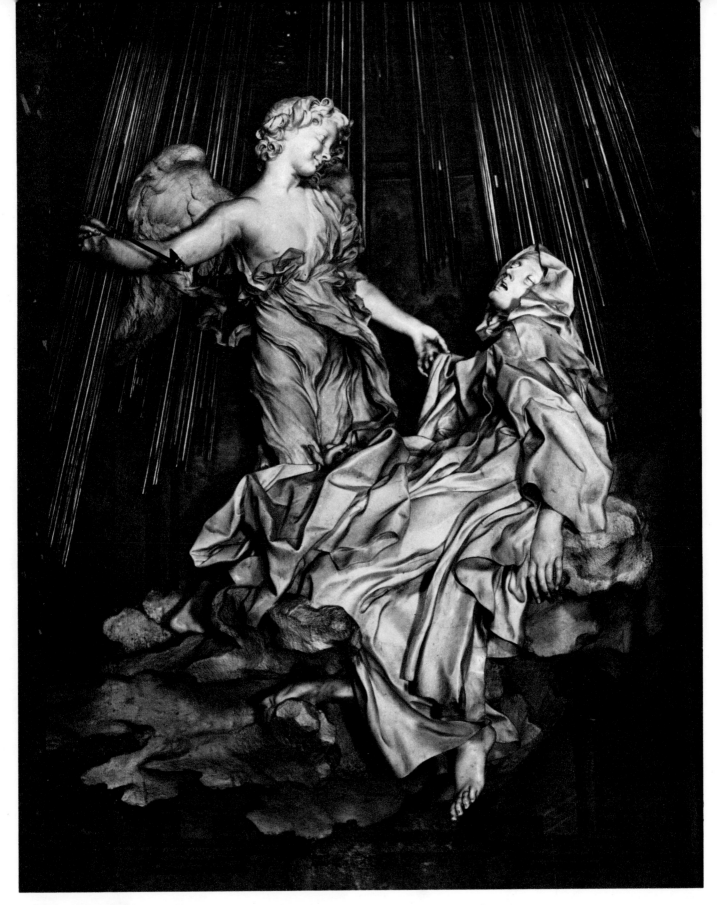

58. GIANLORENZO BERNINI. *St. Theresa in Ecstasy*. 1645–52.
Marble, height of group c. 11'6". Cornaro Chapel, S. Maria della Vittoria, Rome

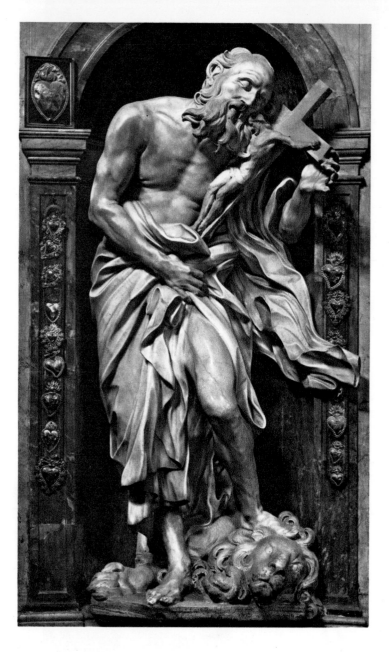

own fountains, a veritable cascade of the alb's thinly pleated folds rushes forth from under the protection of a smooth, large, and grandly sweeping cope.

Fully conscious of the expressive potential of hair and drapery, Bernini never neglected to study the primary carriers of emotional communication—faces and hands. The most violently distorted physiognomies belong to his early period, as they do in Caravaggio's and Rembrandt's art: Anchises' horror-stricken eyes as he is carried to safety from burning Troy by his pious son, David's furious concentration as he confronts his fearsome adversary (fig. 60); or the openmouthed shriek of a damned soul terrified by the fires of

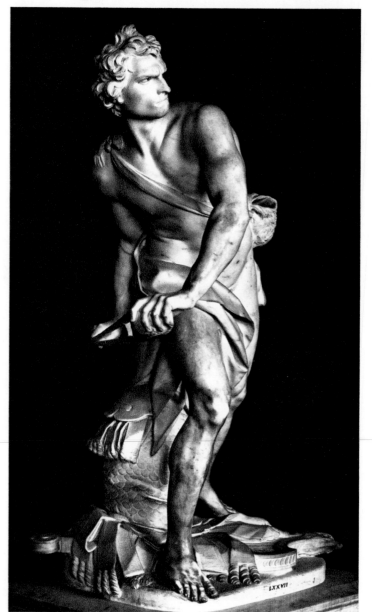

The draperies on the *St. Mary Magdalen* and *St. Jerome* (fig. 59) in the Chigi Chapel in Siena Cathedral are no longer comprehensible as complete raiments. They look like rags and tatters as they twist and flutter around the mortified bodies of the saints. (The rendering of *actual* rags would have offended decorum.) Thus they express the self-abasement and spiritual need of the saints.

Garments can also express power and majesty. The grandeur of Urban VIII enthroned above his own sarcophagus (fig. 61) is largely the result of Bernini's skillful manipulation of liturgical vestments. Like the streams of water in Bernini's

60. GIANLORENZO BERNINI. *David*. 1623. Marble, height 5'7". Borghese Gallery, Rome

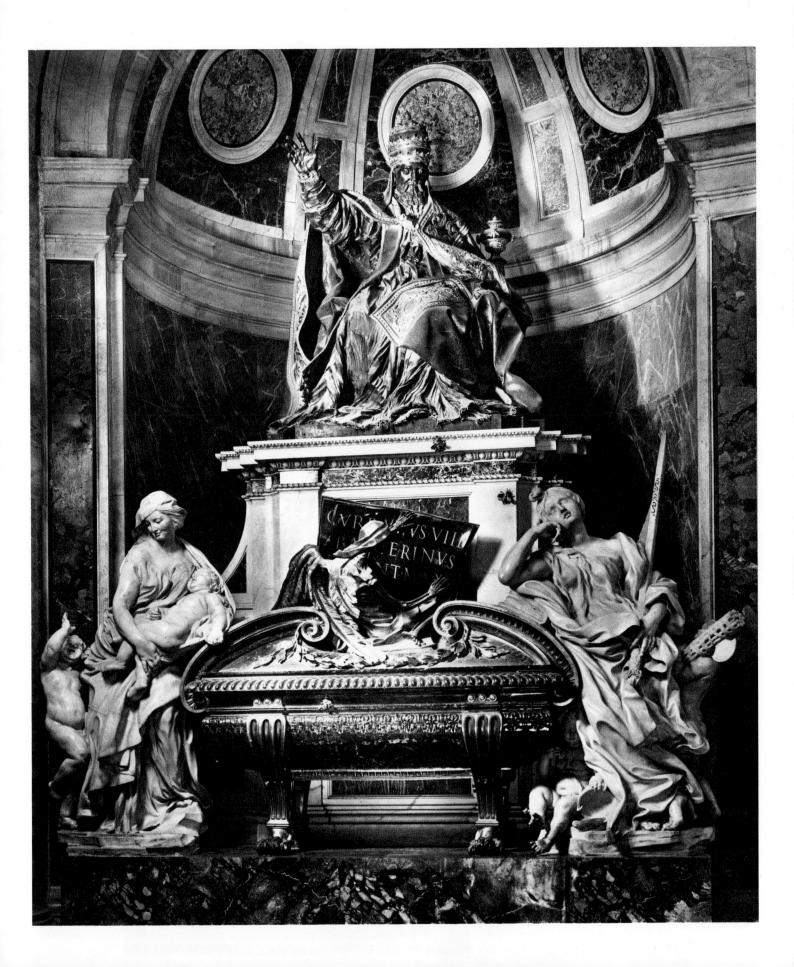

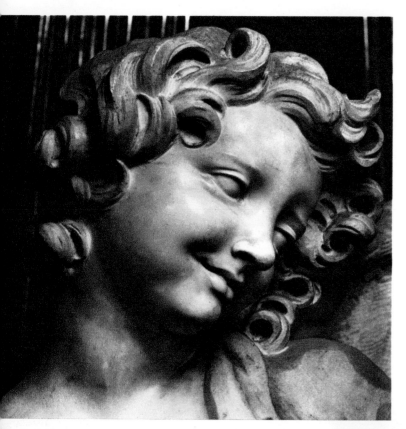
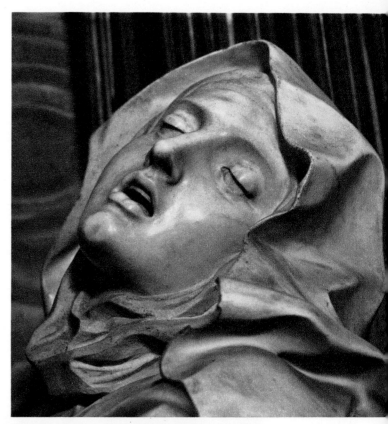

62, 63. GIANLORENZO BERNINI.
St. Theresa in Ecstasy,
details (see fig. 58)

64. GIANLORENZO BERNINI.
Angel with the Crown of Thorns. 1668–71.
Marble, height c. 9′.
S. Andrea delle Fratte, Rome

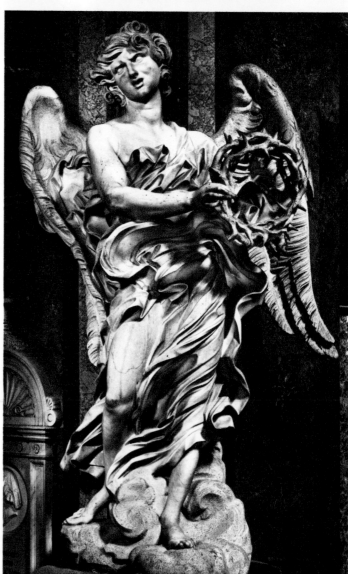

Hell. Bernini is less successful where more subtle emotions are needed. To express fear or pain in young women (figs. 54, 55), he relies on fairly standardized formulas, apparently afraid of marring the perfect symmetry or smoothness of their features.

The subtlety and differentiation of human physiognomy increased in the later decades of his activity. Among the best examples of this psychological refinement are the head of St. Theresa (figs. 62, 63), fainting with an almost audible moan, and of the angel who charms her with a roguish expression of heavenly joy. Equally acute as studies of character and emotion are the faces of the Fathers of the Church supporting the *Cathedra Petri* (colorplate 3), of the grieving angels (fig. 64) in Sant'Andrea delle Fratte, of blissfully smiling *Truth* (1646–52), and above all of the beatified Lodovica Albertoni, seen in the supreme agony

of death (fig. 65). With these works Bernini left far behind the Hellenistic examples of emotional sculpture (the *Laocoön* or the *Niobides*), though they had surely pointed the way.

This development was heralded in the 1630s by striking changes in his treatment of the portrait bust. His early portraits possessed what his mythologies or religious figures lacked—a high degree of individualization. It is quite possible that his early busts of a cool and efficient Pope Paul V, a witty and slightly cynical Monsignor Montoya (fig. 66), a haggard and weary Pope Gregory XV —all done between 1618 and 1622—are better likenesses than any of his later portraits.[22] Yet they lack the dramatic pose, the emphatic animation, and the characterization of each model as representative of a social group or psychological type that distinguish his later works. Scipione Borghese (fig. 67) is not only a clever and worldly

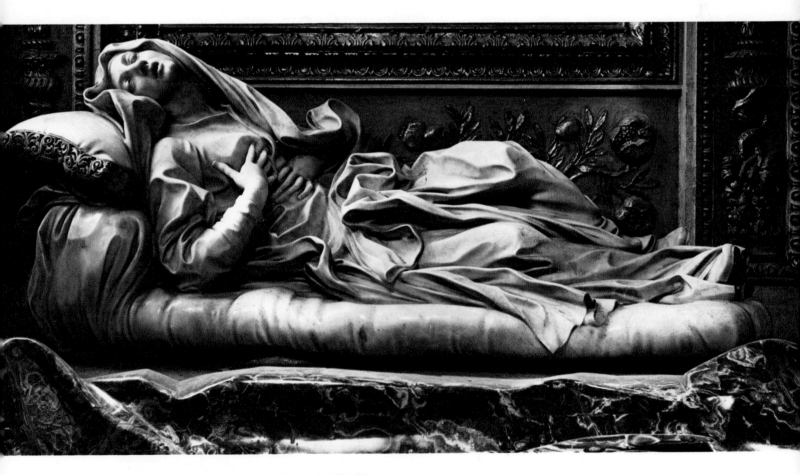

65. GIANLORENZO BERNINI. *Beata Lodovica Albertoni.* 1671–74.
Marble, length 6′2″. Altieri Chapel, S. Francesco a Ripa, Rome

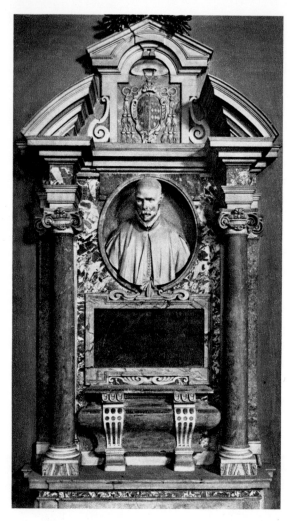

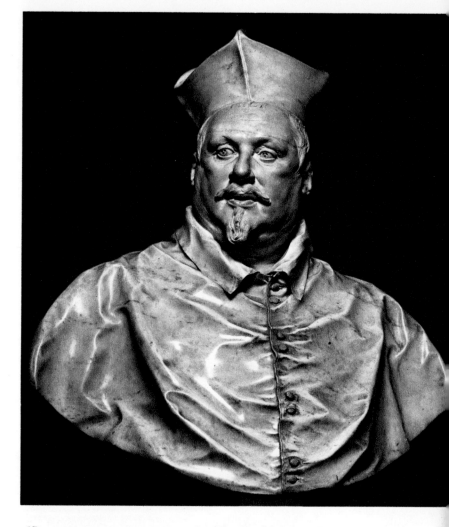

66. GIANLORENZO BERNINI.
Portrait of Monsignor Pedro de Foix Montoya.
1618–22. Marble, lifesize.
S. Maria de Monserrato, Rome

67. GIANLORENZO BERNINI. *Portrait of Cardinal Scipione Borghese.*
1632. Marble, height 30¾". Borghese Gallery, Rome

68. GIANLORENZO BERNINI.
Portrait of Costanza Buonarelli.
c. 1635. Marble, lifesize.
Bargello, Florence

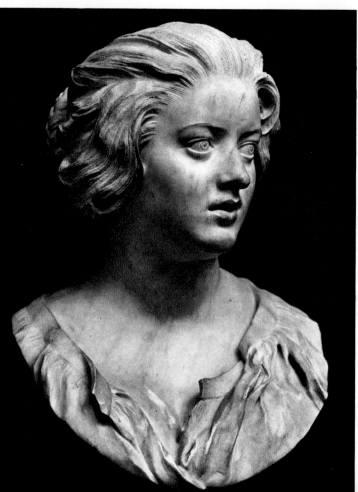

bon vivant; he also personifies a class accustomed to command, and expecting to be obeyed. The portrait of Costanza Buonarelli (fig. 68) belongs to the same period—a work forever stamped with the mark of Bernini's infatuation with the buxom young wife of one of his assistants. With her open blouse, her carelessly combed hair gathered in a knot, her wide-open eyes and parted lips, Costanza is the very image of a passionate female; indeed, she is the prototype of all aggressively erotic women, encountered henceforth in various disguises—most impressively in Goya's rapacious *Doña Isabel Cobos de Porcel* (National Gallery, London)—yet never rendered in art before Bernini.

The delicate balance between the typical and the individual that marks Bernini's portraits of the 1630s later gives way to a greater stress on the official aspect of portraiture. *Francesco I d'Este* (fig. 69) is primarily the image of a ruler. Working from painted portraits Bernini was clearly less interested in producing a likeness than a symbol of exalted majesty. The boldly convoluted drapery forms a base that skillfully avoids the effect of truncation common to all earlier busts. Aided by a broad lace collar and a grandly flaring wig, the silhouette rises with a minimum of interruption from the lower lateral ends of the drapery to the top. Two long curls frame the face pointedly averted from the beholder as from a person of no consequence.

Already his earliest sculptures had given notice that they needed wide spaces for their explosive energies. While Michelangelo had been content to show David quietly, if tensely, eyeing his adversary, Bernini caught him in the very moment of action, lunging violently forward (fig. 60). Bernini's Pluto strides mightily through space as he carries off his reluctant burden (fig. 55). In later years Bernini found ever new ways of extending

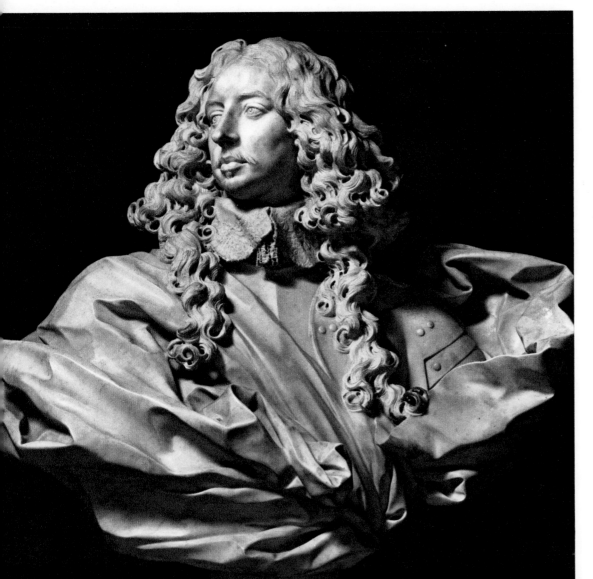

69. GIANLORENZO BERNINI.
*Portrait of
Francesco I d'Este.*
1650–51.
Marble, height 40″.
Museo Estense, Modena

61

the physical stage of his actors. Niches that formerly confined their occupants have no power over Bernini's figures. Early sculptures, like *St. Bibiana* and *St. Longinus* (figs. 56, 57), remain within their niches, but in action and expression point clearly beyond the allotted spaces. In the Chigi Chapel of Santa Maria del Popolo the action either bursts out of the niche, as with the prophet Habakkuk, whom an angel lifts up by a lock of hair (fig. 70), or the very reality of the niche as a part of the existing architecture is denied, as with the prophet Daniel, where the lion and the rock of the cave recede into undefined spaces.

Similar observations can be made on larger monuments such as the papal tombs in St. Peter's. Urban VIII (see fig. 61), his right hand raised in a gesture of blessing that strongly resembles a Roman imperial greeting, is enthroned above and slightly behind his sarcophagus flanked by the personifications of Justice and Charity. Although protruding from the niche, the tomb of the pope, like most earlier works (it was begun in 1628), was clear-

ly designed to fit into it. Its composition, assembling a number of separate units into one grand design, leaves the framing architecture inviolate.

Not so the late tomb of Alexander VII (colorplate 2). The niche makes its appearance only in the upper half of the composition, where the pope is shown kneeling in prayer. Underneath the pope's pedestal spreads a vast drapery of black marble. The skeleton of Death lifts this drapery in front, revealing a door supposedly leading to a tomb chamber. Most amazing are four allegorical figures surrounding the drapery. Two of them are placed so far in the background that they can be justified logically only if one assumes that there is no confining wall near them. Thus in this late work Bernini again completely disregarded the given architectural boundaries in favor of an impression of unlimited space.[23]

The altar of St. Theresa in Santa Maria della Vittoria is one of the finest demonstrations of what Bernini could do with sculpture if unhampered by existing conditions (fig. 71). The architecture of the altar has the shape of a convex aedicula, its coupled columns framing a vista into what seem to be distant spaces. The group of the rapturous saint and the smiling angel appear out there, placed on clouds and obviously meant to be no more than a vision that may vanish any moment in the heavenly light, the rays of which already surround it. Not content with the materialization of a mystic vision, Bernini also provided an audience. Above the passageways on either side of the chapel he installed illusionistic boxes which he filled with the busts of members of the Cornaro family. From these vantage points they watch, and in hushed voices discuss the miracle before them. Through these subsidiary figures the beholder himself is drawn into the composition, as if by proxy. The boundaries between illusion and reality, between art and nature, have become blurred as they did in spectacles on the Baroque stage. Yet they have not been wiped out: the saint's ecstasy takes place in a realm accessible only to the beholder's eyes.

Bernini used this idea again in the Altieri Chap-

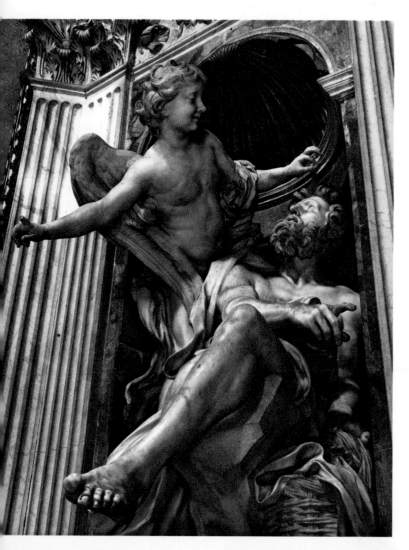

70. GIANLORENZO BERNINI. *Habakkuk and the Angel.* 1655–61. Marble, over lifesize. Chigi Chapel, S. Maria del Popolo, Rom

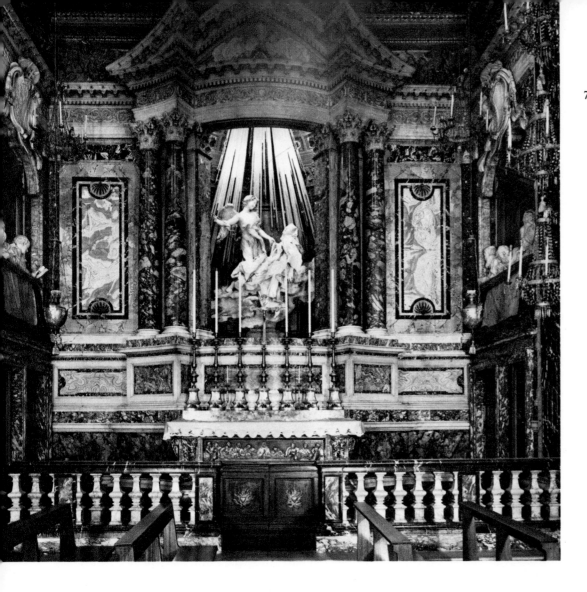

71. GIANLORENZO BERNINI. *St. Theresa in Ecstasy.* View of entire chapel. Cornaro Chapel, S. Maria della Vittoria, Rome

el in San Francesco a Ripa, dedicated to the Beata Lodovica Albertoni (fig. 65). The work is a masterpiece of descriptive realism. No detail seems to be missing from the embroideries of the pillow, the ruffled linen on the mattress, and the heavy drape covering the bed. Done in colored marble, this drape billows and flows out toward the beholder, who may well wonder if it is not real. And yet the artist made quite sure that no profane curiosity could deprive the work of its spiritual essence. Everything looks most tangible, but we cannot touch it. The space that holds the dying woman is both near and remote. We see her rather high above the altar and behind a large arch that appears even deeper than it is because of an illusionistic trick of foreshortening. An element of unreality is added by the light falling on her from con-

cealed windows. Thus on the one hand the Beata Lodovica Albertoni seems to belong to our normal sphere of sensory experience, while on the other she is obviously a mere apparition.

Tombs, altars, portraits, and freestanding figures were traditional themes of sculpture. Into each of these categories Bernini introduced strikingly novel ideas. Some of his most signal contributions to Baroque sculpture were made, however, in projects that practically had no precedents. Indeed, some are even difficult to classify. Is his baldachin under the dome of St. Peter's (fig. 72) a piece of sculpture, or is it architecture? The four huge twisted columns of bronze resemble richly carved statuary. Above each column stands a bronze angel, and behind these (and a few smaller cherubs) rise scrolls balancing—like so many trained seals—the narrow base on which huge bees, the Barberini's emblem, uphold in turn an orb and a cross.

Thirty years later Bernini covered the back wall of the apse of St. Peter's with a complex composition glorifying the *Cathedra Petri,* the Chair of St. Peter (colorplate 3), as that all-important object upon which was based the papacy's claim of an unbroken apostolic succession. In size alone the work by far exceeds any earlier decorative project. It consists of a variety of materials, among them stone, bronze, stucco, and glass. The center is occupied by a magnificent version of the papal throne (enclosing the modest "original" chair); it is surrounded by clouds rising like smoke all around, by fragments of columns, and by rays bursting forth from a brilliant circle of light in the midst of which hovers the dove of the Holy Ghost. Figural motifs appear in all sizes and on all levels, from the gigantic Fathers of the Church upholding symbolically rather than actually the Chair of St. Peter to the reliefs on the throne itself and the frolicking angels encircling the divine radiance above. It is a measure of Bernini's genius as a decorator that this fantastic conglomeration neither clashes with nor is overwhelmed by the quiet majesty of Michelangelo's architecture all around it. As a matter of fact, just as Bernini's colonnades added the last and crowning touch to the architectural history of St. Peter's, so his baldachin and *Cathedra Petri* formed the fitting climax of its interior decoration.

Finally, Bernini was responsible for a fundamental transformation of the design of fountains, traditionally entrusted to sculptors. Mannerist artists from Niccolò Tribolo to Giovanni Bologna had devised many fascinating solutions, adopting preferably the shape that called for a central "column" with one or more basins attached to it. The top of the column was formed by a piece of sculpture, generally a classical deity associated with water, like Venus or Neptune, and other figures were arranged more or less symmetrically around the central stem. The water was dispensed in carefully controlled jets, often creating ornamental patterns of great rhythmic elegance and charm.

No greater contrast to this Mannerist type of fountain can be imagined than Bernini's Fountain of the Four Rivers in the Piazza Navona (fig. 73). Located close to Borromini's façade of Sant' Agnese (and containing, according to Roman gossips, an ironic reference to it),[24] it looks as if a raw piece of nature had been left standing in the midst of a great city square. Water is no longer dispensed in graceful patterns and limited quantity; it gushes in unchecked profusion from amidst a tumble of rocks that also sustains a good deal of partly exotic vegetation. This startling piece of illusionism was not the product of a romantic "nature worship." Everything adds up to a well-planned allegorical conceit. On the wet and rocky ledges sit the four rivers, representing the then known continents; the rushing waters symbolize earth's bountiful supply of this life-giving element. But nature's raw forces, simulated below, are topped by a slender obelisk, symbol of order and wisdom. Thus it is man's control over nature, rather than untamed nature itself, that is proclaimed in this stunning composition.[25]

Other fountains designed by Bernini, such as the early *Barcaccia* in the Piazza di Spagna and the dynamically condensed Triton fountain in the Piazza Barberini, combine allegorical ideas with highly novel formal concepts. None, however, can compare with the Fountain of the Four Rivers in regard to the influence exerted on later fountain designs. Its most famous descendant is the Trevi Fountain (fig. 370), a work of the mid-eighteenth century that not only testifies to the long popularity of Bernini's ideas but also to the distance that separated his work from that of his epigones. Designed by Nicola Salvi, modified by Giuseppe Pannini, and decorated with sculptures by Pietro Bracci and Filippo della Valle, the Trevi Fountain is larger than any of Bernini's fountains. Here, too, "natural" rock forms a base above which rises a grand façade featuring in its center

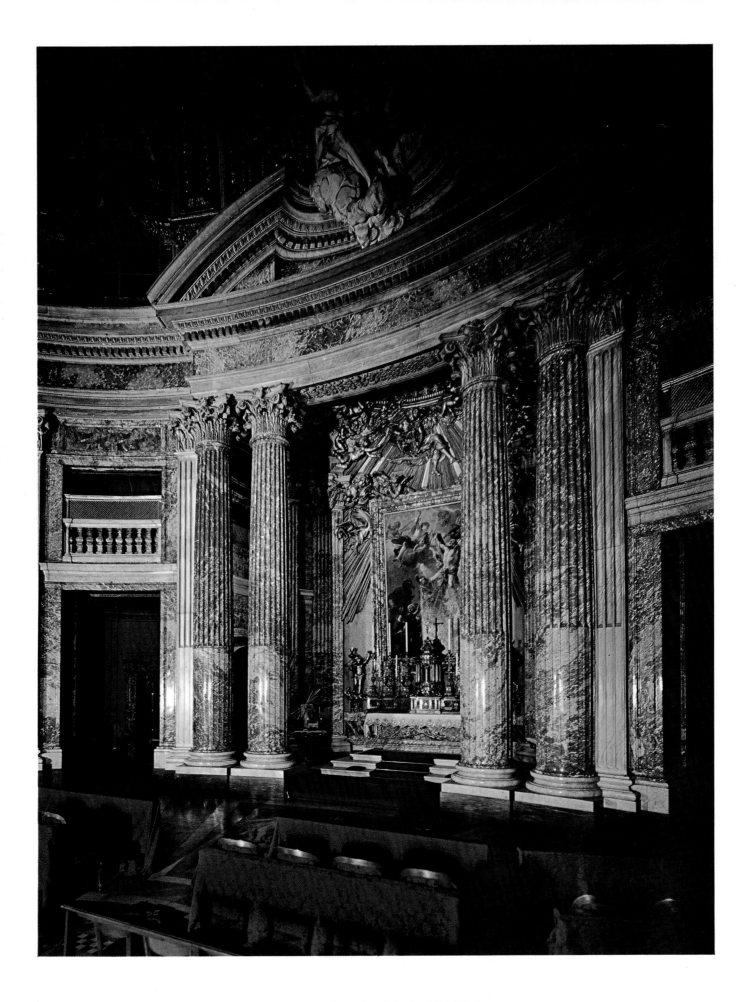

Colorplate 1. GIANLORENZO BERNINI. Interior, S. Andrea al Quirinale. 1658–70. Rome

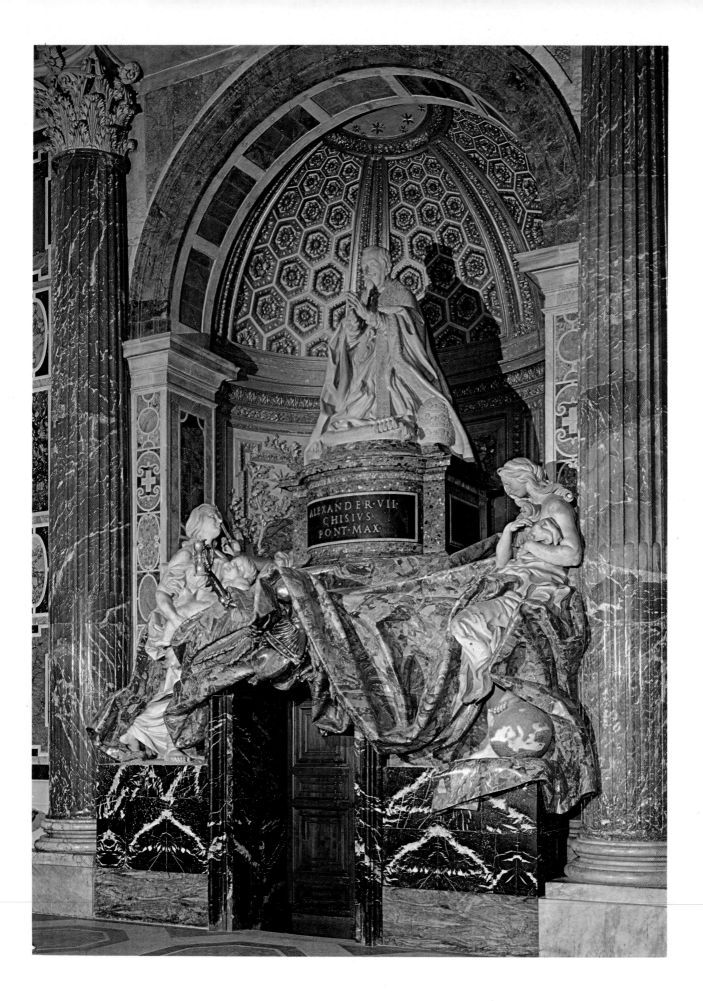

Colorplate 2. GIANLORENZO BERNINI. Tomb of Alexander VII. 1671–78.
White and colored marbles. St. Peter's, Rome

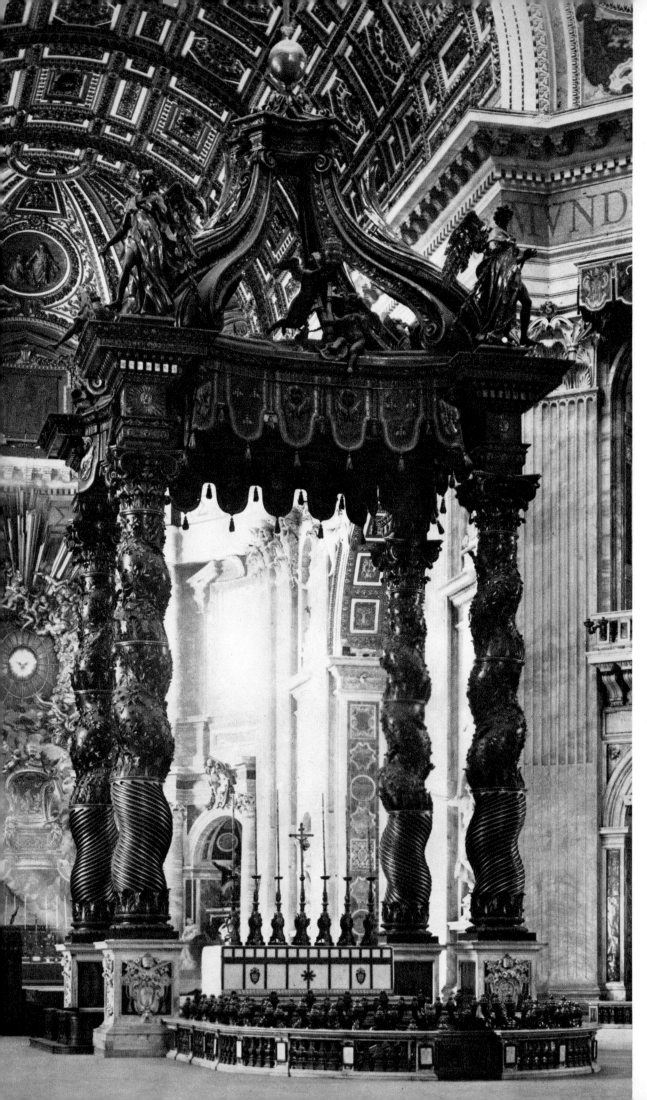

72.
GIANLORENZO BERNINI.
Baldachin. 1624–33.
Bronze, with gilding.
St. Peter's, Rome

a kind of triumphal arch. From it emerges the figure of Neptune, standing on a shell drawn by sea horses under the guidance of Tritons. (Behind him the arch turns incongruously into a niche.) As the commander of innumerable ribbons and sheets of water springing from the ledges below him, he postures prettily but without real force. The Trevi Fountain, indeed, is picturesque, like a spectacle, tailor-made for special effects of illumination catering to the tourist trade. Still, even though it may not be more than a pretentious bit of flummery, it is also a tribute to Bernini's concept of sculpture as an art capable of producing things that seem to grow, move, even breathe as freely as Nature herself.

This concept influenced the large majority of later sculptors, but few of them adopted it without reservations. Even among Bernini's contemporaries were artists who were either more moderate than he or were actually opposed to him. The strongest opposition came from François Duquesnoy (1594–1643), a Fleming who had arrived in Rome in 1618. No Flemish artist of his generation—even if hailing from Brussels—could avoid being familiar with and impressed by the art of Rubens. The chubby, agile *putti* of Duquesnoy's later years have always, and correctly, been accept-

ed as proof of Rubens' influence on his younger compatriot. Seen as a whole, however, Duquesnoy's art is much more restrained and "classical" than Rubens', and his most famous sculpture, *St. Susanna* (fig. 74), has more in common with Poussin and Sacchi than with Rubens; indeed, Duquesnoy knew the Frenchman well.

Given this background, Duquesnoy's style loses some of its mystery. Moreover, the classicism of a work like *St. Susanna* is clearly tinged with typical seventeenth-century attitudes. No earlier age could have produced the melodious fluency of her pose—already admired by Bellori—and her mood of tender enthusiasm. Though wearing the dress of a Roman matron, she lacks the ponderousness that so often goes with it. Other nonclassical details are the casual folds of her clinging dress and the soft waves of her lovely hair. Duquesnoy's classicism is obviously suffused with Baroque sensuousness.

Less subtle as an artist, but equally determined to reject the pictorial extremes of Bernini's art, Alessandro Algardi (1596–1654) was probably more influential than Duquesnoy. In technical skill he was Bernini's equal, and his marble portraits are unsurpassed in their imitation of textures such as silk, fur, hair, or skin. What he re-

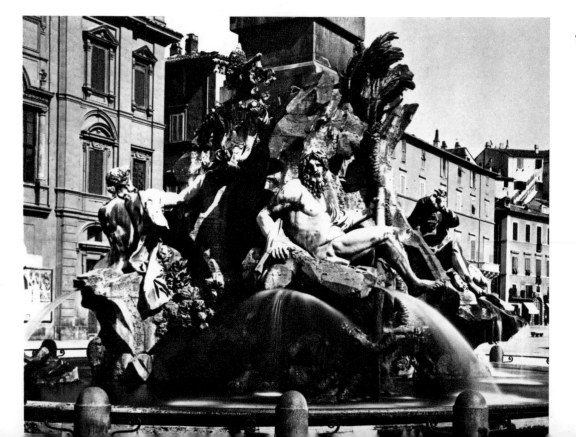

73. GIANLORENZO BERNINI.
Fountain of the Four Rivers.
1648–51. Travertine and marble.
Piazza Navona, Rome
(see also fig. 44)

jected was rhetoric, of form as well as of expression. Contrasted with the theatrical *mise-en-scène* of much of Baroque portraiture, the sobriety of Algardi's busts comes often as a welcome surprise. His tendency to avoid emotionalism is less of an asset in his narrative groups, tombs, and altars, because it is apt to make them appear competent but without fire, correct but without personal character.

These were hardly faults in the eyes of those critics who were disturbed by Bernini's subjectivism. What Algardi had to offer was something that could be learned, a language with rules like the one the Carracci had developed for painting a generation before. Although ever since the days of Ghiberti and Donatello Italian sculpture had been familiar with the technique of the pictorial

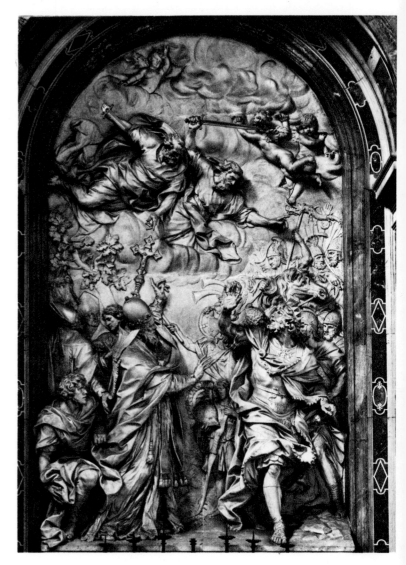

75. ALESSANDRO ALGARDI. *Meeting of Pope Leo I and Attila.* 1646–53. Marble, height c. 25'. St. Peter's, Rome

74. FRANÇOIS DUQUESNOY. *St. Susanna.* 1629–33. Marble, lifesize. S. Maria di Loreto, Rome

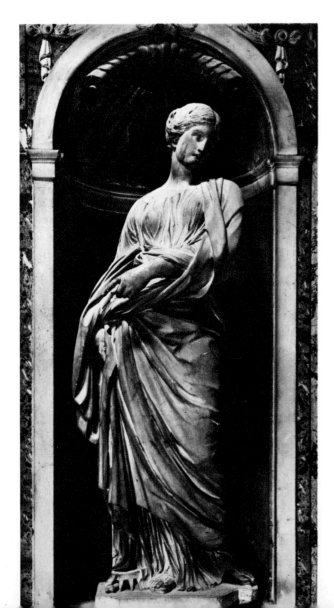

relief, Algardi applied it to larger fields than ever before, and enriched it by the inclusion of nearly full-round figures in the foreground. In this way he, too, came close to eliminating the invisible boundary that previously had excluded the beholder. In his relief of the *Meeting of Leo I and Attila* in St. Peter's (fig. 75), the king of the Goths seems just about to step from the relief. Just about —but not really. The equilibrium of the composition is too explicit, the frame too firm. And so it remains with most sculptors of the next generation, such as Ercole Ferrata (1610–1686), Antonio Raggi (1624–1686), and Domenico Guidi

Italy in the Seventeenth Century / 69

(1625–1701). They all tempered their Berninesque heritage with a good deal of Algardian academicism. Only Melchiorre Caffa (1635–1667/68) tried to follow Bernini's lead, but he died too young to change the trend. The presence in Rome of French sculptors in the wake of the foundation of the French Academy (1666) tended to reinforce a frigid formalism, or—with the approach of the eighteenth century—an elegant prettiness. An excellent example of how Bernini's ideas were purged of their power, to re-emerge in refined and inoffensive form, is Pierre Legros' (1666–1719)

strikingly lifelike figure of St. Stanislao Kostka on his deathbed.[26] It clearly is derived from Bernini's *Beata Lodovica Albertoni*, but instead of sharing the emotional depth of that work it comes rather close to the petty illusionism of a wax figure.

Just as Borromini's and Guarini's architectural ideas found their ultimate development in German and Austrian architecture of the eighteenth century, so Bernini's daring sculptural style had its strongest echo in the works of Schlüter, Permoser, the Asam brothers, and Ignaz Günther (see Chapter 10).

PAINTING

By the end of the 1560s there was, with the great exception of Venice, no really vigorous and creative school of painting in Italy. In Venice, Titian, Veronese, Tintoretto, and Jacopo Bassano were active, but the rest of Italy had succumbed to a rather mediocre, late Mannerist style. This style, despite some attractive products, had for the most part fallen to empty repetitions of decorative, highly artificial figural and compositional formulas (fig. 76), and it was really unable to express the new religious and spiritual ideals of the time. In 1563 the Council of Trent, as part of its work of

religious reform, had decreed that people should be "instructed" by art and "excited [by it] to adore and love God and to cultivate piety." The next year a prelate, Gilio da Fabriano, defined the contemporary problem when he denounced the kind of painting "that puts art before decency, . . . that considers it a great thing to twist a head, the arms, the legs, . . . that seems to prefer figures who do exotic dances and strike poses . . . rather than figures in contemplation."[27]

In the last decades of the century, in various Italian centers a number of artists independent-

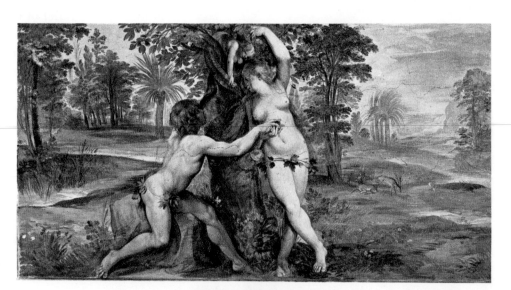

76. CAVALIERE CESARE D'ARPINO.
Temptation of Adam and Eve. 1602–3.
Fresco. Villa Aldobrandini, Frascati

ly began a spiritual and formal reformation of painting. To name only the most successful, there were: in Urbino, Federico Barocci; in Bologna, the Carracci; in Florence, Ludovico Cigoli; in Milan, Cerano; in Rome, Caravaggio and Annibale Carracci.[28] This reformation of painting produced not a unified style but several quite different stylistic solutions, each of which proved more or less fruitful for the art of the future. The main elements these new styles developed were naturalistic and emotionally forceful forms and clarity and directness of presentation. The Mannerist style had been generated from the art of central Italy, and understandably the "reform" artists, who tended to turn away from Mannerism, mostly sought inspiration in the naturalistic traditions of northern Italy, above all in the art of the Venetians and Correggio.

The earliest significant statement of the new artistic spirit is found in the work of Federico Barocci (1535–1612). By birth and training he belongs to the late Mannerist generation, but his art makes him a precursor and even a leader of the "reform" movement. Barocci spent almost the whole of his life in his native Urbino, but his works were much in demand, and he had commissions from all over Italy. In his twenties he worked in Rome for a short time with the Zuccari brothers, Mannerist artists who seem to have been distantly related to him, and his early work was much influenced by them. However, it was Barocci's discovery of Correggio that led him to a new artistic vision. Already in the 1560s he showed a feeling for space and atmosphere, for color and light, for naturalistic form, and for religious sentiment that contrasts markedly with the flat and dry formalistic conceptions of his Mannerist contemporaries. By 1569 Barocci had created his first great masterpiece, the *Deposition* (fig. 77). In this highly dramatic, colorful picture, unified by a warm atmosphere and fluid light, the figures appear solid and real. Figural activity has nothing of Mannerist ornamental artifice, and the powerful emotional content of the painting is convincing and touching. It was at least twenty years be-

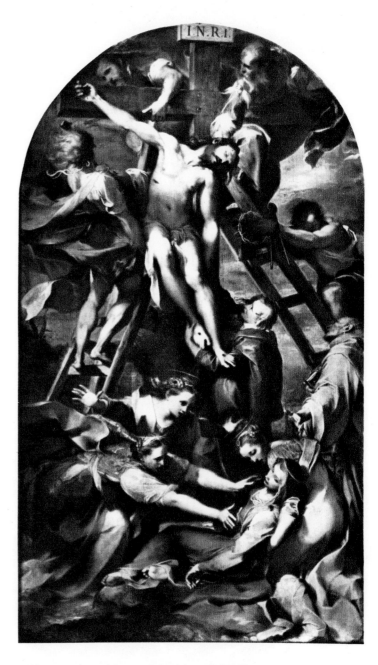

77. FEDERICO BAROCCI. *Deposition*. 1566–69. Cappella di S. Bernardino, Cathedral, Perugia

fore anyone but Barocci himself, except for artists in Venice, equaled this work in quality or in the warm, passionate naturalism of its style.

As Barocci's style developed, the space in his pictures became deeper, the atmosphere denser, the contrasts of color and of light and shade stronger, and the figural movement more flowing, rapid, and unified. In his later years he became a truly profound religious artist. Sacramental and ecstatic themes dominated his late work

Italy in the Seventeenth Century / 71

(the *Last Supper,* the *Circumcision,* the *Stigmatization of St. Francis,* the *Ecstasy of the Beata Michelina*). In the *Vision of St. Dominic* (fig. 78) of about 1593, the saint kneels in wondering devotion on a hilltop as the Virgin descends to give him the rosary. Here there is no scaffolding, none of the struts and beams that seem to support and organize the figures in the Perugia *Deposition.* Now it is the emotional content of the scene alone that binds the figures, who revolve and spin, with their broadly billowing draperies, in the ecstatic tempest. The spiritual excitement of the figures seems to create the space, to charge the atmosphere and make it glow with a dark luminosity.

Had Barocci worked in one of the leading artistic centers in Italy, his influence would surely have been much wider. As it was, his art was of great importance for Cigoli as well as for the Carracci. And he was clearly the forerunner of such great Baroque artists as Giovanni Lanfranco (fig. 103), Pietro da Cortona (fig. 110), and Bernini (fig. 58).

The artists who were most deliberate about the reformation of style were the Carracci. While the other reformers arrived at their solutions intuitively, the brothers Annibale (1560–1609) and Agostino (1557–1602), with their older cousin Ludovico (1555–1619), seem rather early in their careers to have recognized the poverty of the contemporary Mannerist style, and they soon began what might almost be described as a program of research and experimentation aimed at artistic revitalization. They traveled, studied the works of the masters, and were especially attentive to the art of Correggio and the Venetians, which they saw as the specific remedy for the decline of painting. According to their biographer Malvasia they were, from the first, outspoken in their opposition to the practitioners of central-

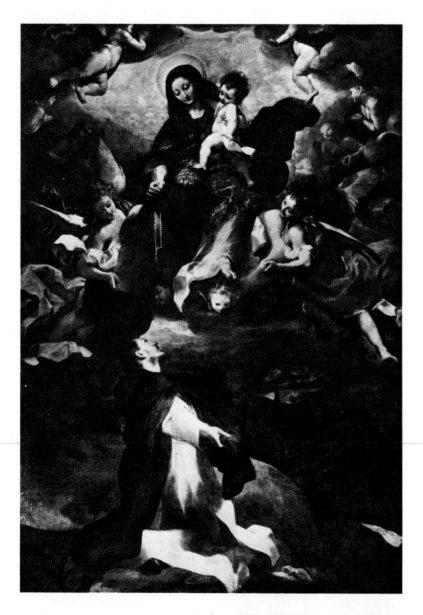

78. FEDERICO BAROCCI.
Vision of St. Dominic. c. 1592–93.
12′9⅝″ × 9′4¼″.
Bishop's Palace, Sinigaglia

Italian Mannerism. While young and struggling for success, Ludovico is supposed to have assured his cousins that "the Lombard style would prevail." They decided "to put aside timidity, to challenge the established masters and make themselves known";[29] thus it is not surprising that they incurred the animosity of older Bolognese artists.

Underlying the reform that the Carracci introduced was their new attention—one might even say dedication—to nature. This is most striking in a group of genre paintings by Annibale that date from the early 1580s; an example is the *Bean Eater* (fig. 79). This kind of coarse subject matter, presented with bold naturalism, and deriving in part from northern European painting, was popular around Bologna at the time. In Annibale's hands, however, the subject is treated with a new and remarkable visual objectivity. In the *Bean Eater* the play of light on the broadly blocked-out surfaces has been keenly observed; but even more important for the powerful, almost startling sense of reality is the uncompromising directness and immediacy of the presentation. The painter has interrupted the action, fixed the gesture, the open mouth, the glance, the unkempt hair. The setting, the peasant himself, and the objects on the table are represented with "artless" truth.

Annibale painted genre subjects only in his youth, but he and the other Carracci, in landscape and portrait painting and especially in their great number of drawings of all kinds, maintained throughout their lives a close contact with nature. Their approach to the problem of naturalistic representation became highly sophisticated: Agostino is known for his analytical studies of parts of the human body, and Annibale seems to have invented caricature in its modern sense, and even to have coined the word.[30]

In their religious work the Carracci showed that they understood and sympathized with the demands of Counter Reformation critics. In their own city of Bologna the archbishop, Gabriele Paleotti, in a book on art published in 1582, com-

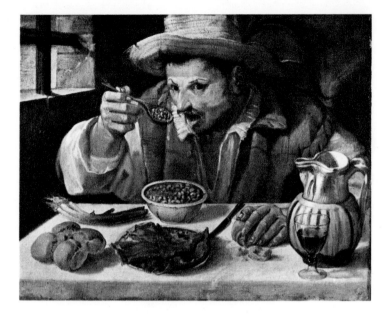

79. ANNIBALE CARRACCI. *Bean Eater*. c. 1583/84. 30¼×37¾". Colonna Gallery, Rome

plained about the kind of Mannerist pictures which "are seen every day in churches, and which are so obscure and ambiguous that instead of illuminating . . . they confound and distract the mind . . . to the detriment of devotion." Paleotti praised the artist who "knows how to explain his ideas clearly . . . and to render them intelligible and plain to all."[31] A few years later the Carracci began to provide distinguished examples of paintings that avoid obscurity and make a virtue of simple, plain speech. Ludovico's *Bargellini Madonna,* so called after the family that commissioned it (1588; fig. 80), is one of the finest of these early "reformed" works. The composition is derived from Titian's great *Pesaro Madonna,* but it has none of the inspiring monumental grandeur of its model. Instead, it charms us by its feeling of intimacy and pious devotion. Looking out at the spectator, the enthroned Madonna, with the Christ Child nestling in her lap, is an image of maternal sweetness. Surrounding her, three saints kneel in quiet adoration. St. Martha and St. Mary Magdalen in the foreground, lower than the other figures, seem almost to be in the beholder's space, and they make an easy transition between the worshiper and the Madonna.

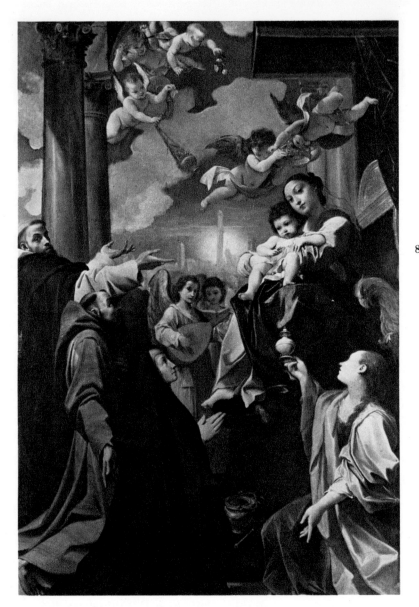

80. LUDOVICO CARRACCI.
*Madonna and Child with
Angels and Saints
(Bargellini Madonna).* 1588.
9'3" × 6'2".
Pinacoteca, Bologna

St. Dominic, standing at the left, turns toward us and directs our attention to the Virgin and Child. Farther back adolescent angels provide a musical accompaniment, while above, flying *putti* celebrate and prepare to crown the Madonna. In the distance, silhouetted against the rising sun, one sees the towers of Bologna. Here is the very spirit of Counter Reformation religion. For the faithful there is no barrier between the natural and supernatural spheres. The divine is in our midst. It is understood in human, warmly sentimental terms, and it speaks directly and simply to the worshiper.

The Carracci collaborated closely, especially on a number of fine fresco cycles that they painted in the Fava, Magnani, and Sampieri palaces in Bologna. In these paintings it is sometimes difficult to distinguish their individual contributions, and understandably critics came to speak of a "Carracci style." The artists themselves encouraged this idea, and when asked to explain who was responsible for the different parts of the frescoed decoration of the Palazzo Magnani, they answered only, "It is by the Carracci; we have all made it."[32] Nevertheless, the Carracci were temperamentally very different and their styles are for the most part quite distinct.

Ludovico, the oldest of the group, was closest

to the Mannerist generation, and Mannerist devices appear occasionally in his work throughout his life. However, his art is remarkable for its exploration and development of the pictorial possibilities of naturalistic light and figural movement. His later paintings, sometimes brilliantly forceful in their dramatic effects, may be sometimes lyrical and charming in their fantasy. Unlike his cousins, who tended to be conservative in their interpretations of traditional themes, Ludovico was astonishingly inventive in his treatment of religious subject matter. The Assumption of the Virgin, for instance, is almost invariably shown with the apostles around the already opened, empty tomb of Mary, some of them looking into it with surprise and some looking up at the Virgin (who usually fills at least half of the picture) as she ascends in a glory of clouds and angels. Ludovico painted this scene several times and always found new ways to convey its excitement and mystery. In a version that dates from 1608 or 1609 (fig. 81), it is not the vision of the divine that moves the beholder but the sense of physical reality, of human effort and strain, and of the awesome power of the miracle. The artist focuses on the drama of the actual opening of the tomb. The apostles press closely around, and three of them, huge and muscular, struggle to support and lift the heavy lid. The emptiness of the tomb explodes in their midst. They reverberate with the shock and gesticulate violently. In the foreground two apostles talk excitedly as they hold the shroud and flowers found in the grave. Only one apostle, in the background, has seen the heavenly vision. He spreads out his arms in adoration and looks up to where the slender cypresses point—to the small, light-filled opening in the clouds. The activity of the scene is intensified by the strong light that illuminates the figures in bold patches. And the two groups of gigantic apostles, compressed within the tall vertical frame, seem to burst diagonally upward with sudden swiftness as the tomb is opened.

In contrast to the dynamic compositions and animated pictorial effects that characterize

Ludovico's art, the work of both Annibale and Agostino tends to be controlled and restrained. Apparently they feared that a free, painterly style, if allowed to develop to an extreme, would result in a kind of visual confusion and complexity akin to the Mannerist style that they had struggled to overcome. In the 1590s they became seriously interested in the structured, carefully balanced art of the Roman High Renaissance, especially that of Raphael. The work of both brothers was relatively similar in intention, but Agostino, who made his main contribution as an engraver, was hardly the equal of Annibale as a

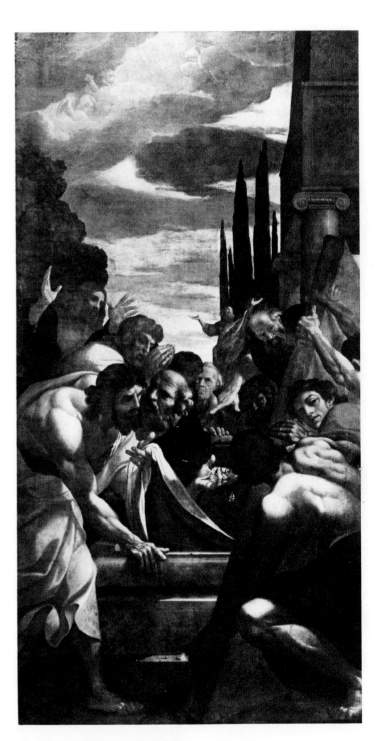

81. LUDOVICO CARRACCI. *Assumption of the Virgin.*
c. 1609. 21'10" × 11'4". National Gallery, Parma

painter. However, Agostino's most famous work, the *Last Communion of St. Jerome* of about 1592 (fig. 82), may serve to illustrate their general orientation in this period. In its color and light the picture clearly shows the influence of Veronese and Venetian naturalism. Indeed, there are some passages of extremely sensitive painting—for instance, the kneeling young monk, holding the crucifix, whose face is veiled by a liquid, transparent shadow. However, the light, diffused almost equally through the picture, and the color, unemphatic and toned down, create a quiet, harmonious scene that can be easily and uninterruptedly surveyed. There is—it takes a moment to realize it—a great deal of activity in the painting: a variety of attitudes, gestures, and expressions. But the composition has been so rigorously

systematized that the general impression is of utmost order and regularity. Vertically the painting is divided into two almost equal parts, and horizontally the architecture establishes a controlling symmetry. The arrangement of the figures echoes the masonry stage set. The groups at the sides mirror the architectural projections, and the movements of the foreground figures follow the same broad curve as the great central arch. The weighty, tectonic style evolved here was to be developed further and to have a great influence on the future of Italian painting; but this came about almost entirely through the subsequent work of Annibale, who soon left Bologna to work for Cardinal Odoardo Farnese in Rome (see pages 88–89).

In 1595, when Annibale arrived in Rome, Michelangelo Merisi da Caravaggio (1573–1610) had already been there perhaps for two or three years. Caravaggio was one of the youngest of the reform artists, and he was certainly the most original. Despite more or less adequate early training in his native Lombardy and a general familiarity with north-Italian pictorial traditions, he was anything but a "cultivated" artist when he came to Rome. His pre-Roman experience had not prepared him to sympathize with or to understand easily either the formalistic and frequently esoteric art of contemporary Roman Mannerists or the earlier ideal and learned art of Raphael and Michelangelo. Temperamentally contumacious, his reaction to the artistic milieu of Rome was stubbornly and even violently egocentric. He scandalized his contemporaries by insisting that the antique and the great masters were worthless as examples and that nature was a sufficient teacher. His works show that in reality he did study the art of the past, but his arrogant, aggressive attitude toward traditional artistic values, however much pretense, was the passionate expression of a sick, tormented spirit.

Caravaggio's life is a history of increasingly violent antisocial behavior. There is evidence, notably in his early works, of strong homosexual tendencies; toward the end of his life he was

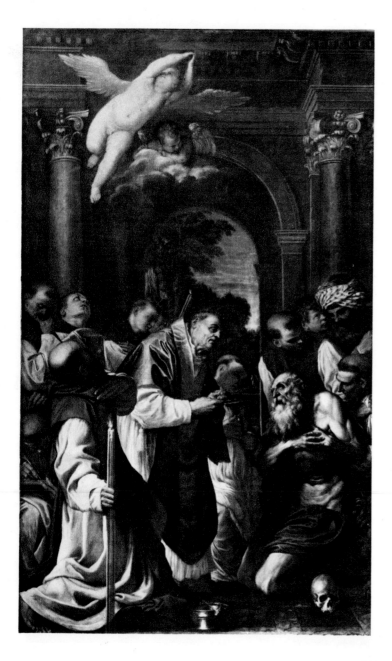

82. AGOSTINO CARRACCI. *Last Communion of St. Jerome*. c. 1592. 12'4" × 7'4". Pinacoteca, Bologna

forced to leave Messina after assaulting a teacher who suspected the artist of molesting his schoolboys. In Rome, Caravaggio was one of a gang of tough, sword-carrying, swaggering ruffians who appear frequently in his pictures (colorplate 4). From 1600 on, despite his professional success, his name began to appear in the police records. He was accused of attacking a man with his sword. Then there was a libel suit. Then arrest for showing disrespect to a police officer; for carrying arms without a permit; for assaulting a waiter; for breaking windows; for wounding a man after an argument over a prostitute. Finally, in 1606, he was forced to flee Rome after killing a man in an argument over a tennis game. In the remaining four years of his life he wandered from place to place—the Sabine Mountains, Naples, Sicily, Malta—becoming, within a period of five months in 1608, a Knight of the Order of Malta, its prisoner, and finally a fugitive from it. In 1609 he was caught by his enemies, knifed, and horribly disfigured. Finally, in the summer of 1610, he died of malaria after a mistaken arrest and a feverish walk across the burning sands of the beach at Port'Ercole. What is astonishing and wonderful is that a man so undisciplined and perverse could create beautiful, controlled masterpieces of the utmost refinement; that a man so brutal and violent could create some of the most profound religious paintings in the history of art; that somehow, through the terrible loneliness and tragedy of his life, he perceived a vision of incomparable poignancy and compassion.

As a young man, soon after he came to Rome, Caravaggio worked for a short time in the shop of Cavaliere Cesare d'Arpino (1568–1640), who was enormously successful and the favorite painter of the not very discriminating Pope Clement VIII (1592–1605). The artificiality of Arpino's work and its tasteful elegance (fig. 76) were for the most part antipathetic to Caravaggio, whose earliest works already show a feeling for solid, naturalistic forms. The young Caravaggio is said to have painted flowers and fruits in Arpino's shop—which suggests that he began his career as

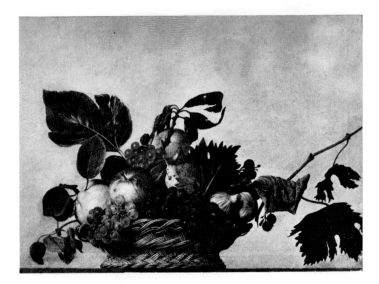

83. CARAVAGGIO. *Still Life*. Late 1590s. 17¾ × 23¼". Ambrosiana, Milan

a still-life painter—but his only certain still life known today seems not to date from his earliest period (fig. 83). Among the works produced during Caravaggio's first years in Rome are a number of paintings of young boys ornamented, as it were, by fruits and flowers or musical instruments, which allude to the sensual delights promised by or potential in the sitters. The *Bacchus* (fig. 84) is a splendid example. The subject and the half-length presentation have prototypes in earlier north-Italian art (*e.g.*, in Dosso Dossi) and even in antique sculpture. (In fact, the original buyers of such works, who undoubtedly had turned to antiquity for the justification of their sexual proclivities, may have related some of them to ancient representations of Antinoüs, the Emperor Hadrian's favorite.[33]) But Caravaggio's *Bacchus* is a unique and remarkably salacious treatment of the theme. The fleshy youth, with large lips and long eyebrows, his smooth white arm and chest bare and his vine-bedecked hair curled and pomaded like a geisha's, looks invitingly at the spectator. He proffers a glass of wine, held daintily with crooked little finger, while with his other hand he plucks at the black sash that holds his robe. Everything is suggestive: the undulating contour of shoulder and arm, the finely drawn folds of white drapery, the startlingly real bowl of overripe fruit.

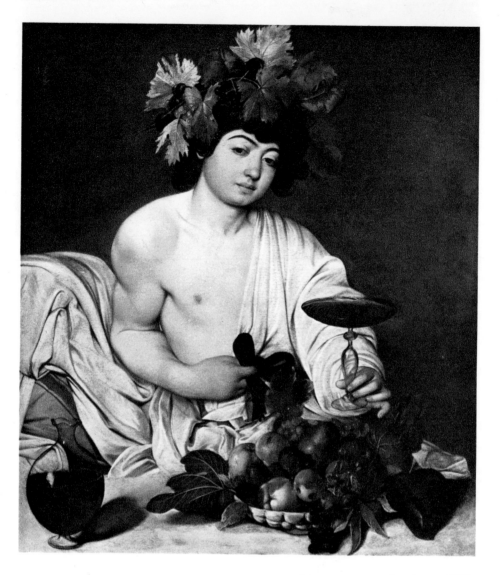

84. CARAVAGGIO. *Bacchus.* c. 1597.
37⅜ × 33½". Uffizi Gallery, Florence

If the *Bacchus* seems shocking to us, it is not
merely by its intentional impropriety but also because the artist has succeeded in narrowing, almost eliminating, the aesthetic distance between
the painted image and the spectator. Caravaggio's
solid forms, brought up close to the picture plane
and represented with mirror-like accuracy, cannot be relegated to any imagined, "other" en-
vironment. The plain background, the absence
of any painted "place," do not allow us to locate
them elsewhere but in our world. The spectator
is forced to respond immediately as if to real,
tangible presences, and it is the spectator to whom
Bacchus makes his overtures.

85. CARAVAGGIO. *Fortune Teller.* Late 1590s.
39 × 51½". The Louvre, Paris

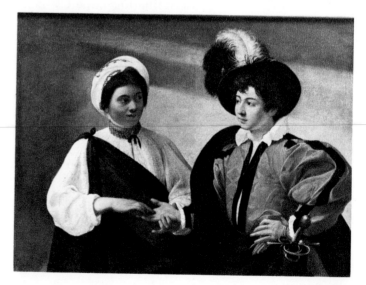

In the 1590s Caravaggio also made narrative genre pictures like the painting of an amorous young man having his fortune told (and his ring stolen) by a lovely gypsy girl (fig. 85). These themes have north-Italian precedents, although they derive ultimately from Netherlandish painting. The example of these works had enormous importance for the future of European seventeenth-century painting (see figs. 91, 225), but Caravaggio himself painted such subjects only in his early period before 1600.

About 1600 Caravaggio turned his powers of naturalistic representation almost exclusively to the depiction of religious subjects. There is a close connection between Caravaggio's religious conceptions and some of the ideas of the Counter Reformation: in particular the artist seems to have been influenced by the teachings of the great Roman reformer, St. Philip Neri (1515–1595).[34] St. Philip established a kind of "low church" in Rome, which emphasized humility and social equality in the religious sphere and, by appealing directly to the instincts and understanding of the common man, "popularized" religion. In a parallel way Caravaggio's art is deeply sympathetic to the common man, to the poor and the rejected, and makes its appeal in the most forthright, popular terms. The actors in the *Doubting Thomas* (fig. 86) are men of the people, proletarian types with large, heavy hands and features. Yet, despite their coarseness and poverty, despite the unkempt hair and torn, ragged clothes, these figures are invested with great spiritual dignity. The story is told with single-minded dramatic concentration. Again the background is empty. There are only the great solid figures, who watch with fierce intentness as the shocked Thomas, who had doubted the reappearance of Christ after the Resurrection, thrusts his finger into the open wound in his Lord's side. The brutal, even horrific sense of physical reality strikes directly at the emotions of the spectator; by it, and by the brilliant light that, like a spotlight from above, suddenly illuminates the figures, Caravaggio conveys the deep spiritual content of Christ's commanding words to Thomas: "Reach hither thy hand and thrust it into my side; and be not faithless but believing" (John 20:27).

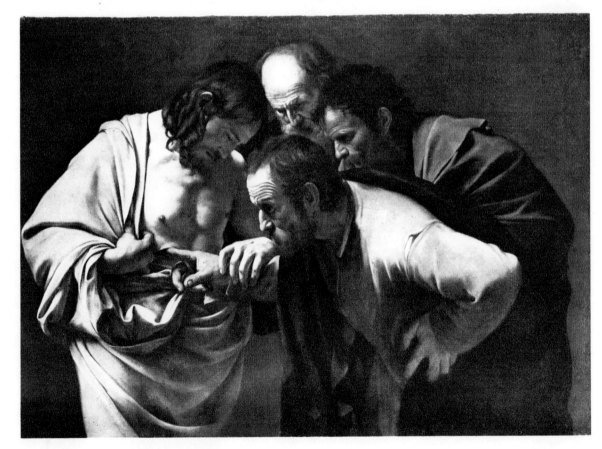

86. CARAVAGGIO.
Doubting Thomas.
c. 1601.
42⅛ × 57½".
Neues Palais, Potsdam

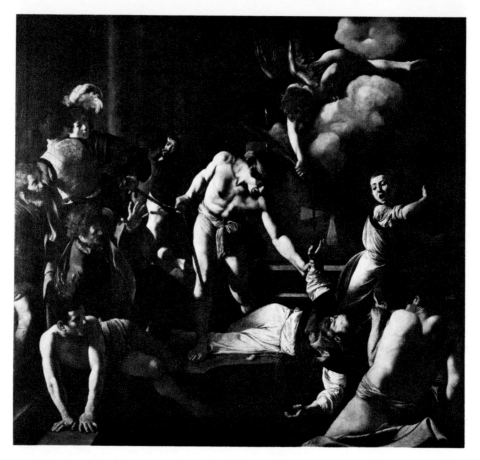

87. **CARAVAGGIO.**
Martyrdom of St. Matthew.
1599–1600.
c. 10'9" × 11'5".
Contarelli Chapel,
S. Luigi dei Francesi, Rome

The effectiveness of Caravaggio's so-called cellar light (a single strong light that seems to fall from a high, unseen window) is nowhere better seen than in the *Calling of St. Matthew* in San Luigi dei Francesi in Rome, painted in 1599–1600 (colorplate 4).[35] Here Christ and a companion silently approach the tax collector Matthew who sits with his agents. Christ's gesture, taken from Michelangelo's Adam on the Sistine Ceiling, seems to call forth and direct the beam of light that rakes diagonally down from above His head to strike and to convert the future apostle. Light for Caravaggio thus becomes the intangible but visible vehicle of divine grace and power.

In the *Calling of St. Matthew* the relatively soft atmosphere, the warm tonality, and the rich colors of the brightly dressed figures at the table clearly indicate the north-Italian origin of Caravaggio's style. The painter's contemporaries did, in fact, see the influence of Giorgione in this picture. Caravaggio's debt to the Venetian tradition is equally evident in the *Martyrdom of St. Mat-*

thew (fig. 87), the pendant to the *Calling* in the Contarelli Chapel in San Luigi. Here, for the first time, Caravaggio was confronted with a complicated, multifigure compositional problem. The problem was especially difficult for him because he habitually worked directly on the canvas, making few if any preparatory drawings (no drawing by him is known today). X-rays of the

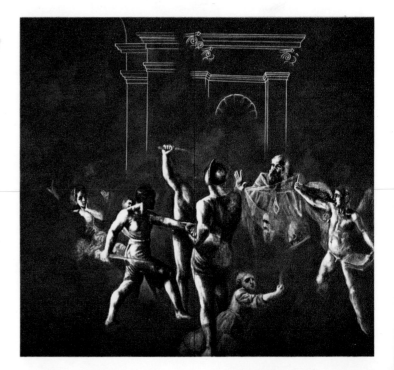

88. **CARAVAGGIO.** *Martyrdom of St. Matthew,*
reconstruction of first state
on the basis of X-rays

Martyrdom (fig. 88) reveal his uncertainties. Initially he conceived a very different composition which, in its use of a stabilizing architectural background and in its symmetrical disposition of the figures, is clearly based on a study of Roman High Renaissance compositions, especially of the paintings of the Raphael *Stanze*. However, Caravaggio was unable to invest this scheme with real dramatic clarity and power, and finally he abandoned his attempt to imitate the balanced monumentality of Raphael and turned instead to the freer, more dynamic compositional patterns of the Venetians. The final painting uses a rapidly revolving axial scheme that can be paralleled in the work of Tintoretto. The network of diagonal thrusts, and the figures of the saint, executioner, and fleeing acolyte, derive mainly from Titian's now destroyed *Death of St. Peter Martyr,* formerly in Santi Giovanni e Paolo in Venice.

The genesis of the *Martyrdom of St. Matthew* makes it especially clear that despite Caravaggio's "naturalism," and despite his own wish to be free of the weight of authority, his art was rooted in the grand traditions of the Italian Renaissance. Indeed, the monumental and dignified figure of the Virgin holding the large, heavy Christ Child in the *Madonna of Loreto* of about 1604–5 (fig. 89) recalls the ponderous gravity of forms designed by artists like Andrea del Sarto (*e.g.,* the *Madonna of the Harpies* in the Uffizi Gallery, Florence).[36] One need not wonder that the great traditionalist Poussin was particularly interested in this painting by Caravaggio (fig. 158).

In the *Madonna of Loreto* Caravaggio's representation of the two humble pilgrims—simple people who seem spiritually illumined by the profound earnestness of their faith—was considered objectionable by many of his contemporaries. To official, conservative taste it seemed disrespectful to show in an altarpiece the muddy feet and poor, dirty clothes of the pilgrims. This was only one of several instances when Caravaggio's "social realism" met with disapproval. His first altarpiece of *St. Matthew* for the Contarelli Chapel (now destroyed; formerly in the Kaiser-Fried-

rich-Museum, Berlin), and the *Death of the Virgin* (the Louvre, Paris), were actually rejected by their commissioners because of their improprieties. One should not, however, assume that Caravaggio was a misunderstood artist. His paintings were appreciated and avidly collected; he was patronized by distinguished members of the nobility and the high clergy; and after 1600 he never lacked commissions for important, well-paid church pictures. He could have had a prosperous, official success, but his violent behavior, as if spurred on by an unconscious desire for self-destruction, became more frequent and intense as his success grew. It put him beyond the pale of social acceptability and finally forced him to leave Rome.

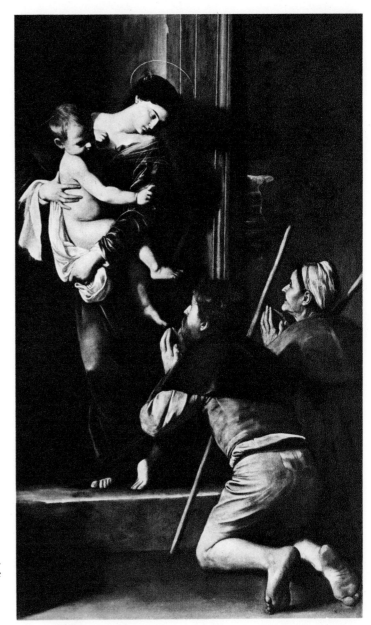

89. CARAVAGGIO. *Madonna of Loreto.* c. 1604–5.
8'6⅜" × 4'11". S. Agostino, Rome

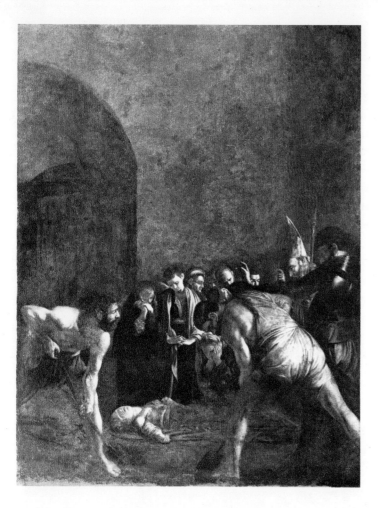

90. CARAVAGGIO. *Burial of St. Lucy.* 1608.
13′4⅝″ × 9′10½″. S. Lucia, Syracuse

In his post-Roman period there was a change in Caravaggio's style that was only partly anticipated in his late works in the capital. Compositions like the *Burial of St. Lucy* of 1608 (fig. 90) are astonishingly simplified, and almost planimetric in design. There is a minimum of activity; the figures are stiff and grouped closely to form a long wedge across the bottom of the canvas. Above them is a vast emptiness. Light and atmosphere seem to decompose the forms. A sense of great quiet, overwhelming in its dignity and sadness, pervades these pictures and seems to suggest that somehow, in his sufferings as a fugitive, as an outcast, Caravaggio had found a kind of spiritual repose.

Caravaggio's style attracted a great many imitators and followers in Italy. It was easy to adopt his genre types, some of his more striking pre-

sentational devices, and his strong chiaroscuro. But few painters really understood the profound religious significance of his works. Artists like Saraceni and Gentileschi managed to produce more acceptable, *bourgeois* versions of Caravaggesque naturalism. Others, like Manfredi, Valentin de Boulogne, and Honthorst, were attracted by the low-life aspects of Caravaggio's work and tended to exaggerate and vulgarize them. Furthermore, they revived the pure genre subjects that Caravaggio himself had given up by the end of the 1590s (fig. 85). The Frenchman Valentin de Boulogne (1594–1632), who spent his entire working career in Rome, where he arrived about 1612, was one of the most gifted of the latter group. His tavern scene or *Concert* (fig. 91) is obviously related to the left side of Caravaggio's *Calling of St. Matthew* (colorplate 4). But—to say nothing of the evident difference in subject—Valentin's figures have nothing of the smart refinement of Caravaggio's. His men are sinister, swarthy types, and the woman and young boy are plain and lethargic. There is, in short, a grossness here that Caravaggio would not have tolerated. Nevertheless, in Valentin's hands, such subjects are endowed with fine, romantic overtones. The atmosphere is dense, gray, and fuming, and the figures, who seem barely conscious of each other, almost glow with a passionate melancholy.

Caravaggio's influence spread rapidly throughout Italy, but nowhere did it have greater success than in Naples, where the master had been twice, in 1607–8 and in 1609–10. There Caracciolo, called Battistello (c. 1570–1637) was one of his earliest and best followers, and on the basis of Caravaggio's style he founded the modern Neapolitan school of painting. However, the greatest artist working in Naples in the early seventeenth century was a Spanish follower of Caravaggio, Jusepe de Ribera (1591–1652), known in Italy as Lo Spagnoletto.

Almost nothing is known of Ribera's early career. Before he went to Italy (by 1615, when he is documented as being in Rome), he may have studied with Francisco Ribalta (see pages 175–77)

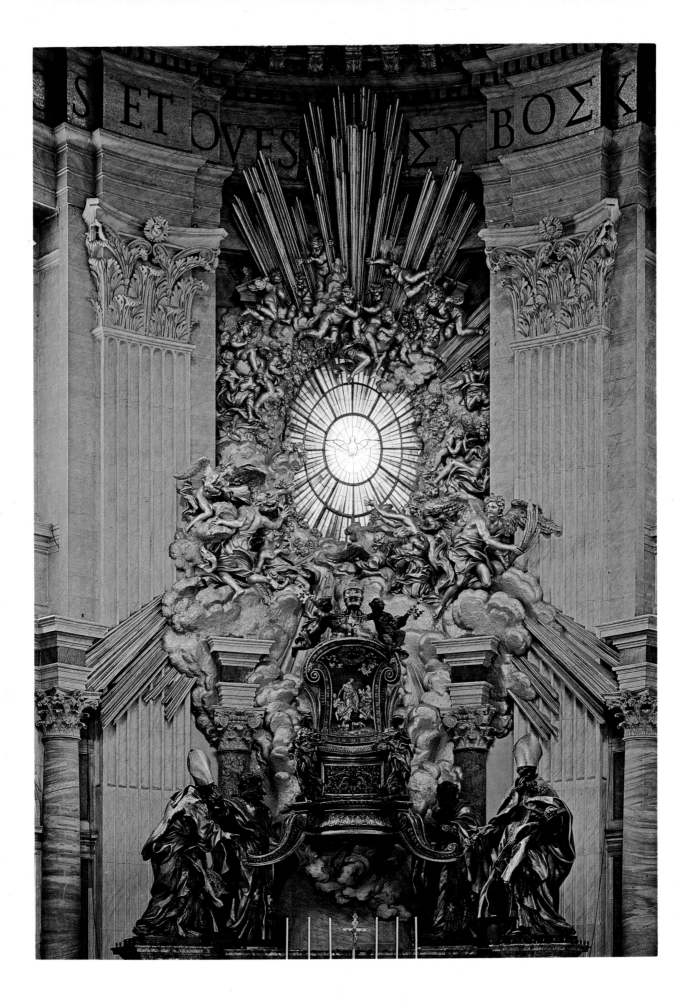

Colorplate 3. GIANLORENZO BERNINI. *Cathedra Petri*. 1656–66.
Gilt bronze, marble, and stucco. St. Peter's, Rome

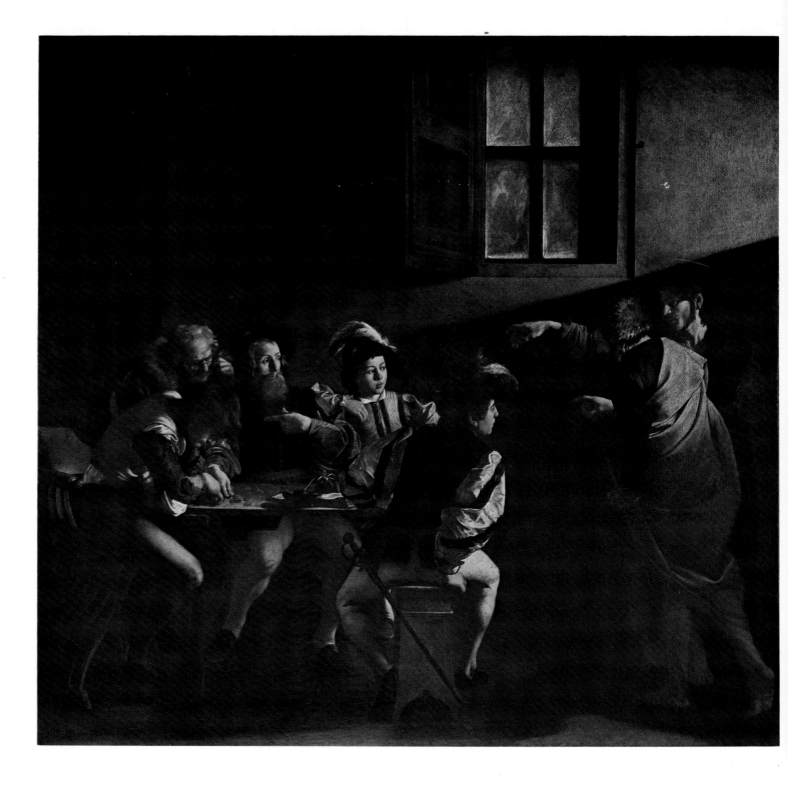

Colorplate 4. CARAVAGGIO. *Calling of St. Matthew*. 1599–1600.
11′1″ × 11′5″. Contarelli Chapel, S. Luigi dei Francesi, Rome

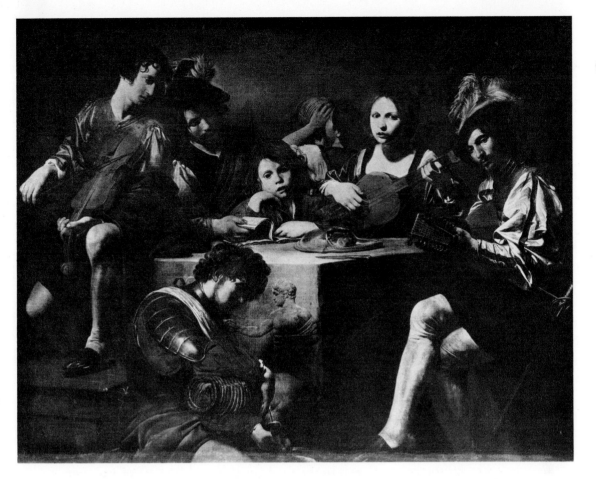

91. VALENTIN DE BOULOGNE.
Concert. c. 1620.
68 × 88"
The Louvre, Paris

in Valencia, but this is still uncertain.[37] Apparently he settled in Naples before 1620, having already been to Parma, and he had stayed long enough in Rome to gain a good reputation as a follower of Caravaggio. In Naples, which had been under Spanish rule since the fifteenth century, he made an almost immediate success. A great many of his works were sent to Spain, and Ribera belongs, of course, as much to the history of Spanish art as to the history of Italian art. His paintings were, in fact, one of the principal means by which Caravaggism was carried to Spain, and his influence on Spanish painters—late Ribalta, Zurbarán, Velázquez, Murillo—was considerable. However, for Italy, which Ribera found more sympathetic than his native country, he provided one of the crucial links between the generations of Caravaggio and Luca Giordano (see pages 121–22).

There is a group of etchings by Ribera from the early 1620s, but his first signed and dated paintings (the *Drunken Silenus* in the Naples

Picture Gallery and the *St. Jerome* in the Hermitage Museum, Leningrad) are from 1626. By this time he had developed a powerful, independent version of Caravaggesque naturalism. Ribera is famous for his depictions of old, withered skin, of swollen joints and toothless mouths. He developed a technique in which the marks and lines traced by his coarse brushes in the wet paint create an exciting surface texture and intensify the naturalistic illusion. But his was not an empty, virtuoso naturalism. The topography of the human flesh was for Ribera the mirror of the human spirit, and by baring the nerves at the very surface of the skin he makes us acutely sensitive to the inner life of his heroes. In the great *Martyrdom of St. Bartholomew* of 1630 (fig. 92) the saint, pathetically unprotected in his nakedness, is stretched and twisted beyond the limits of human endurance. One feels the pain in the knotted muscles of his legs, in the aching ribs beneath the rough, taut skin of his chest. The saint, about to be flayed, looks to Heaven and, as he is slowly lifted by dreadful machinery, his martyrdom takes on the aspect of Christ raised on the Cross.

In contrast to the rather hermetic compositional style of Caravaggio, Ribera's broad V-shaped composition is open and spacious, and it seems to reflect the style of early baroque masters like Lanfranco and Guercino (see pages 98–102). The strong, dramatic contrasts of light and shade were of course learned from Caravaggio, but Ribera abandoned the spotlight effect of the older master's illumination. Furthermore, Ribera's insistent individualization of types, forms, and textures goes far beyond the intention of Caravaggio's more generalized naturalism.

It was through his unrelenting concentration on the physical presence of the individual that Ribera created such searching portrayals of human character as the *Boy with a Clubfoot* of 1642 (fig. 93). Here, in the ugly, terribly deformed child, who is silhouetted against the sky as he shoulders his cane like a musket and strikes a proud, military pose, there is a strong note of mock heroics—which gives way suddenly, beneath the boy's penetrating gaze and broad, open smile, to a poignant image of indomitable courage and human dignity. The picture also conveys a specifically Christian message. The clubfooted boy is an object of pity, but he is in the service of God: he wears his deformity like a uniform and carries his exhortation to charity like a divine commission.

In Naples, Caravaggism, although it had been much transformed, survived longer than elsewhere in Italy. Only in the mid-1630s, mainly through the influence of Roman painting, did Neapolitan artists begin to turn away from a dark, strongly naturalistic style. In Ribera's late work his palette became lighter and brighter, the paint surfaces thinner and more transparent, and the forms and compositions quieter and more idealized. In Rome this "ideal" style, which had its origins in the art of Annibale Carracci, began to dominate by the second decade of the new century, and by 1620 Caravaggism no longer had real vitality there. However, in the late 1620s in Rome a new type of low-life genre was developed that subsumed and gave a kind of second life to Caravaggio's innovations. This was the style of the Bamboccianti.

The style takes its name from Pieter van Laer (1592/95–1642) who, because he was deformed and ridiculously disproportioned, was nicknamed "Il Bamboccio" (which may be translated roughly as "Big Baby") by the society of Netherlandish artists living in Rome.[38] Bamboccio was born in Haarlem, but nothing is known of his work or education before 1625, when he arrived in Rome, where he stayed until 1639. Apparently, he was responsible for the development of the small genre picture that seems rather like "a window open on the street." The *Farrier* (fig. 94) is typical of his everyday city scenes. Earlier Netherlandish genre painting (*e.g.,* Brueghel) was, of course, one source of this style. But these objective yet sympathetic portraits of the life of the proletariat, seen in the shadows and half-shadows of an urban setting, are something new, and owe very much to Caravaggio's tenebrist style and to his revolutionary conception of the dignity of the common man. Some of the Bamboccianti were Italians (for instance, Michelangelo Cerquozzi), but the style appealed especially to Northerners, and had considerable influence outside Italy, for instance in France, in the work of the Le Nain brothers (see pages 147–49).

It is interesting and important that in Italy the best interpreters of Caravaggio's style were generally non-Italian artists. Indeed, it was outside Italy, in the work of artists like Georges de La Tour, Zurbarán, and Rembrandt, that Caravaggio's popular realism proved most fruitful. In Italy, Caravaggism could not really compete with a grand, ideal manner that was rooted in the nation's past and that took its authority from the remains of ancient sculpture and from the monumental styles of Raphael and Michelangelo.

Annibale Carracci was responsible for reviving

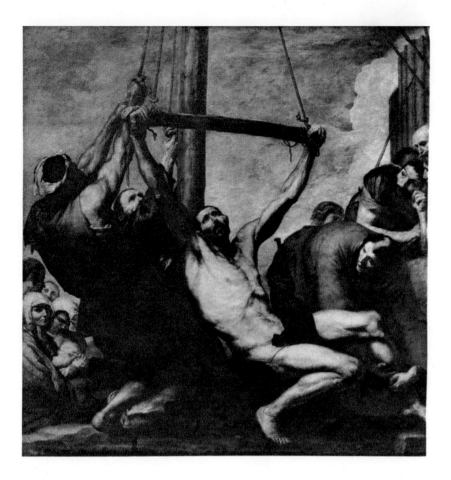

92. **JUSEPE DE RIBERA.**
Martyrdom of St. Bartholomew.
1630. 6′×6′6″.
The Prado, Madrid

94. **PIETER VAN LAER**
(IL BAMBOCCIO).
Farrier. c. 1635.
18½×14½″.
Collection Corrado Zingone, Rome

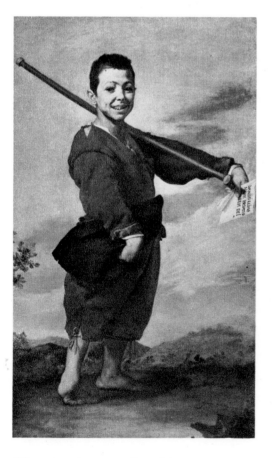

93. **JUSEPE DE RIBERA.** *Boy with a Clubfoot.* 1642.
64½×36¼″. The Louvre, Paris

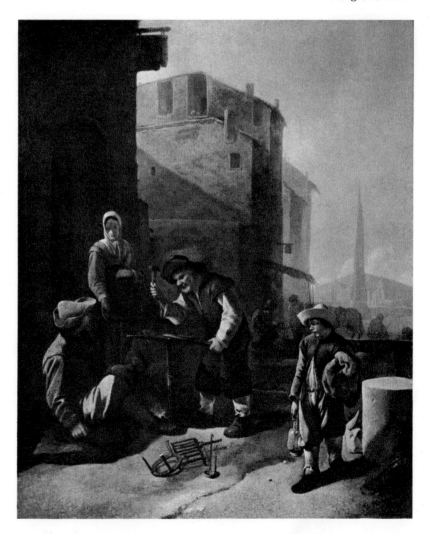

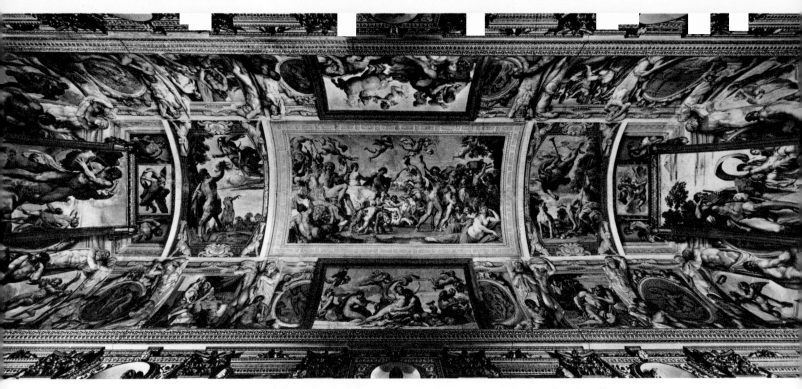

95. ANNIBALE CARRACCI. Ceiling Fresco. 1597–1600. Gallery, Palazzo Farnese, Rome (see colorplate 5)

the classical and Renaissance heritage of Italian painting. Although his work in Bologna had been distinguished, it was really during the last four-teen years of his life (1595–1609), spent in Rome, that he became an artist of international impor-tance and great historical significance. Unlike Caravaggio he was a learned artist with a deep, passionate respect for tradition. In late Bolo-gnese paintings by Annibale and by his brother Agostino there is already evidence of a predis-position for the art of the Roman High Renais-sance (see page 75), and once in Rome Annibale began to reconstruct his style on the basis of his direct experience of the works of Raphael, Mi-chelangelo, and antique sculpture. His Roman compositions acquired a new grandeur, became images of an ideally beautiful world, sometimes almost remote in their aesthetic abstraction. His weighty figures, rhythmically balanced, move and turn with stately ease, and in type and propor-tions closely resemble the statues of the ancients. In Rome his forms came to be defined with great clarity and precision as his line became sharper,

his light more general, and his color more local-ized

Annibale's greatest achievement is the fresco decoration of the Gallery of the Palazzo Farnese in Rome (fig. 95; colorplate 5). The frescoes of the vault celebrate the indomitable power of sen-sual love,[39] and the fact that they were made to decorate a palace inhabited by Cardinal Odoardo

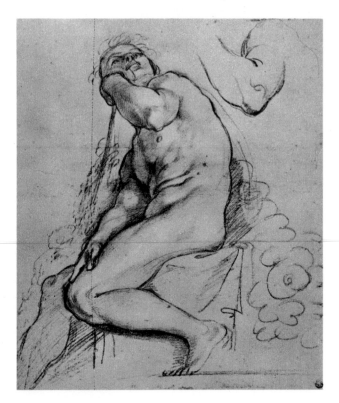

96. ANNIBALE CARRACCI. *Nude Youth.*
Study for a figure in the Ceiling Fresco
of the Farnese Gallery. c. 1598.
Blue chalk heightened with white, 19½ × 15⅛".
The Louvre, Paris

Farnese, great-great-grandson of Pope Paul III, is a sure sign that the severe, ascetic phase of the Counter Reformation was fast coming to an end. The vault of the gallery was painted about 1597–1600, and was apparently designed for the occasion of Ranuccio Farnese's wedding (Ranuccio was Odoardo's elder brother). The side walls, illustrating the more sober subject of love controlled by virtue, and especially by the virtue of the Farnese family, were not painted until 1603–4. Annibale alone was responsible for the pictorial conception of the whole and for most of the actual execution, although Agostino, who was in Rome from 1597 to 1599, painted the two long scenes on either side of the central painting of the vault, and Annibale's students assisted him on the wall frescoes.

The design of the vault, with its painted architecture and seated nude youths (fig. 96), brings Michelangelo's Sistine Ceiling instantly to mind. And the amorous divinities could not have been realized without the example of the figures in Raphael's frescoed Sala di Psiche in the Farnesina. However, Annibale's scheme has a unity and an effusive richness of movement that cannot be paralleled in Renaissance art. Beginning from the cornice the various elements are locked together into a complicated structure that seems self-supporting and that culminates in the central painting of the *Triumph of Bacchus and Ariadne*. The spectator is immediately caught up by the luxuriance of pictorial forms—and moved from one dazzling level of pictorial illusion to another: from the painted architecture of the vault itself, seemingly hung with framed easel pictures, to the simulated sculptural decoration, marble herms, and bronze medallions that sometimes disappear behind the "easel" pictures; to the "real" flesh-colored nude youths who sit on pedestals at the edge of the cornice; and finally to the blue sky "outside," seen through the openings at the corners, where pairs of *amorini* wrestle on the exterior balcony. The brilliance of a unifying, painted sunlight floods the vault, illuminating the "pictures," making the "marble" shine, and giving a radiant glow to the "living" figures. Everything is convincing; everything is painted.

In contrast to the spirit of joyful abandon in the Farnese Gallery, Annibale's Roman religious paintings are imbued with a sense of noble gravity. In the *Three Marys at the Tomb* of about 1600 (fig. 97), the figures might be actors in a Greek

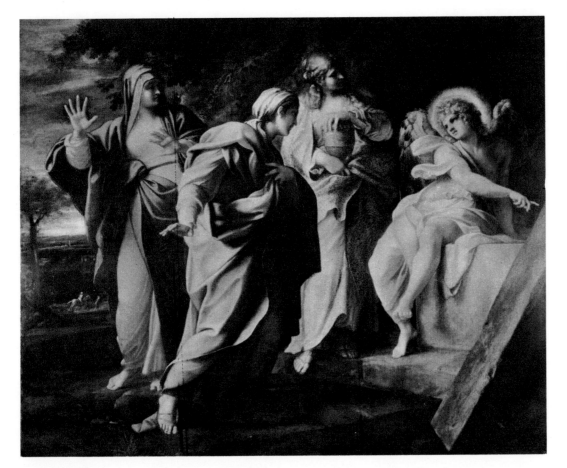

97. ANNIBALE CARRACCI. *Three Marys at the Tomb.* c. 1600. 47⅝ × 57¼". Hermitage Museum, Leningrad

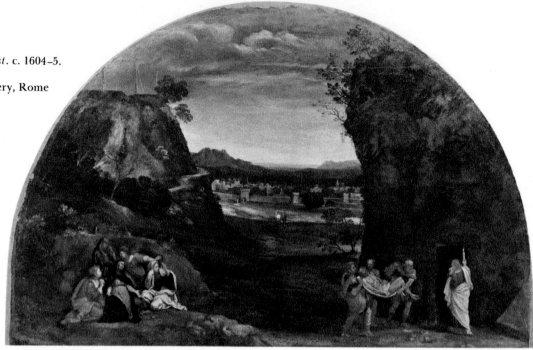

98. ANNIBALE CARRACCI.
Entombment of Christ. c. 1604–5.
47¾ × 74⅜".
Doria Pamphili Gallery, Rome

tragedy. Confronted by the angel, who points grandly to the empty tomb of Christ, the Marys express their surprise with dignified, rhetorical gestures. This is the sphere of the ideal, where perfect, impersonal beings act out the great dramatic moments of human history. Annibale's high diction stands in direct opposition to the common speech of Caravaggio. Yet, when one compares the *Three Marys* with the *Calling of Matthew* (colorplate 4), there are evident similarities. Both artists create heavy, solid forms and set them in a convincing, ample space. And although Annibale's later work was more austere, around 1600 his debt to his north-Italian sources is still very clear in the sensuous light and atmosphere of his pictures. Also, the ideality of Annibale's forms should not obscure his great reliance on nature. His paintings were carefully prepared by numerous drawings made from life. For him the ideal was not an arbitrary, imagined conception, as it was for the Mannerists, but something actually existing in nature, and requiring the learning and genius of the artist to be perfected and made manifest.

Indeed, in landscape too Annibale was able to discover the rigorous laws of a grand and noble design. In Rome, partly inspired by the great experiments in this genre that Polidoro da Caravaggio had made in San Silvestro al Quirinale a century before, Annibale altered his earlier, essentially Venetian landscape style and created what has come to be known as the "ideal landscape." A powerful example is the austere *Entombment of Christ* (fig. 98), one of a series of six landscape lunettes with Biblical subjects. The landscape has a kind of natural, architectural order, and is conceived as a stage for human action. One can trace the path from Golgotha on the left down to the harsh terrain where the women lament, and then across the arid ground to the cliff where the men carry Christ to his tomb. The small figures are grouped in front of the masses of rock on either side of the picture, and Christ's separation from the living seems symbolized by the vacant plain in the center, which stretches back to the city and the mountains in the distance. Bathed in a melancholy, autumnal light the scene takes on a tragic grandeur. Pictures like these had an enormous influence on the later development of landscape painting, and they inspired such artists as Domenichino, Poussin, and Claude Lorrain (fig. 118), while more immedi-

90

ately, around 1600, they were important for the German painter Adam Elsheimer (colorplate 6; see page 208).

Landscape painting in the seventeenth century was considered a special field (along with portrait, genre, and still life, a *"petite manière"*) and its history tends to reflect developments in the dominant field of history painting—that is, the illustration of historical, religious, mythological, or allegorical figure subjects. In Rome, Annibale Carracci and Caravaggio had together "reformed" history painting. For the next generation Mannerism no longer had any appeal, and it was the styles of these two masters that provided the points of departure for later painting in Rome and, indeed, in most of Italy. Annibale's special contribution was to show the way back to the heritage of Raphael and Michelangelo, and to show that it was not entirely incompatible with the painterly styles of northern Italy. Ultimately, it was Annibale's pupils and associates who marked out the main directions for the future. They were equipped, as were none of Caravaggio's followers, with a deep understanding of past traditions, and also with the technical training necessary for the great decorative enterprises that were to play such a large role in the history of seventeenth-century Italian painting.

The oldest of the Carracci followers was Guido Reni (1575–1642), who had studied in their shop in Bologna before coming to Rome in 1601 or 1602. In Rome, he did not work with Annibale (who disliked him personally), although he remained on intimate terms with the latter's pupils. For a short time, about 1604–7, he was infatuated with Caravaggio's art,[40] but by the end of the first decade he had created a personal and very pure "ideal" style. The finest of his early masterpieces is the *Aurora* fresco, painted in 1613–14 on the ceiling of the Casino Rospigliosi in Rome (fig. 99). In the lovely, flowing linear rhythms traced across the surface by the figures and their wind-blown draperies, it is obvious that the picture is indebted to ancient relief sculpture. Aurora, scattering flowers over the earth, leads the way. Phoebus-Apollo, his chariot drawn by handsome piebald horses through the rarefied, luminous atmosphere, is surrounded by the dancing Horae. In its perfect, measured ideality this painting might be understood as the seventeenth-century counterpart to Raphael's *Galatea* fresco in the Farnesina.

In 1614 Reni moved permanently to Bologna, where he soon came to dominate the Bolognese school. His genius overshadowed all others, and none could escape his influence. In his art he

99. GUIDO RENI. *Aurora*. 1613–14. Ceiling Fresco, Casino Rospigliosi, Rome

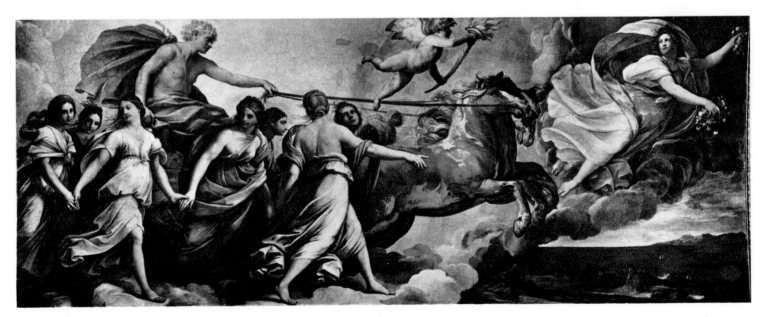

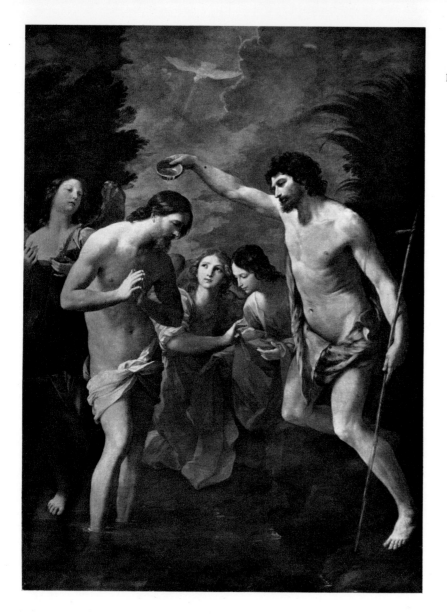

100. GUIDO RENI.
Baptism of Christ. 1622–23.
8′7¾″ × 6′1¼″.
Kunsthistorisches Museum, Vienna

created a repertoire of "perfectly" proportioned figures, exact poses, gestures, and expressions. Guido's "divine grace," in pictures like the *Baptism of Christ* (fig. 100), results from wonderfully confluent patterns of dance-like movements exquisitely executed by an ideal company. His expressions—for instance, the upturned eyes and open mouths—can be worn by rapturous angels, ecstatic Magdalens, and suicidal Cleopatras (colorplate 7). These are not the mawkish masks that nineteenth-century imitations would suggest, for they are not intended as naturalistic representations but as part of an elevated poetic vocabulary. Just as one conceives a set of ideal proportions for the human body, so Reni conceived a set of

ideal configurations of physiognomy and posture for emotional expressions.

Reni was one of the truly great colorists of the century. His *Cleopatra* of about 1638–39 belongs to the period that began in the late 1620s, when he abandoned his earlier dark, "golden" manner and adopted a bright, "silver" palette. Here the broadly painted color surfaces dazzle the spectator with their sharp brilliance. The exalted operatics of the scene are given a gloriously luminous expression by the pearl-gray flesh of the queen, set off by the sharp violets, the biting blues, and the hot orange-golds of the draperies.

Reni had little feeling for the truly tragic, and equally little for the epic. His is a world of melo-

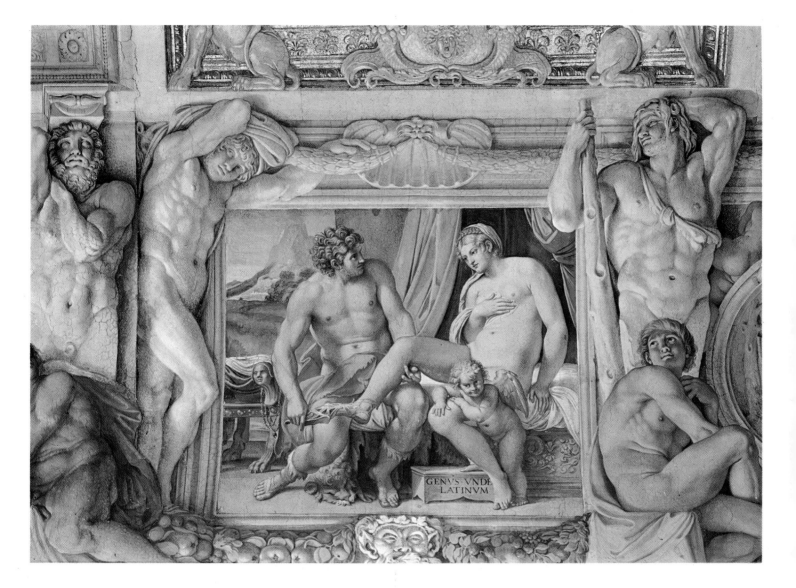

Colorplate 5. ANNIBALE CARRACCI. *Venus and Anchises*. Ceiling Fresco, detail. 1597–1600. Gallery, Palazzo Farnese, Rome

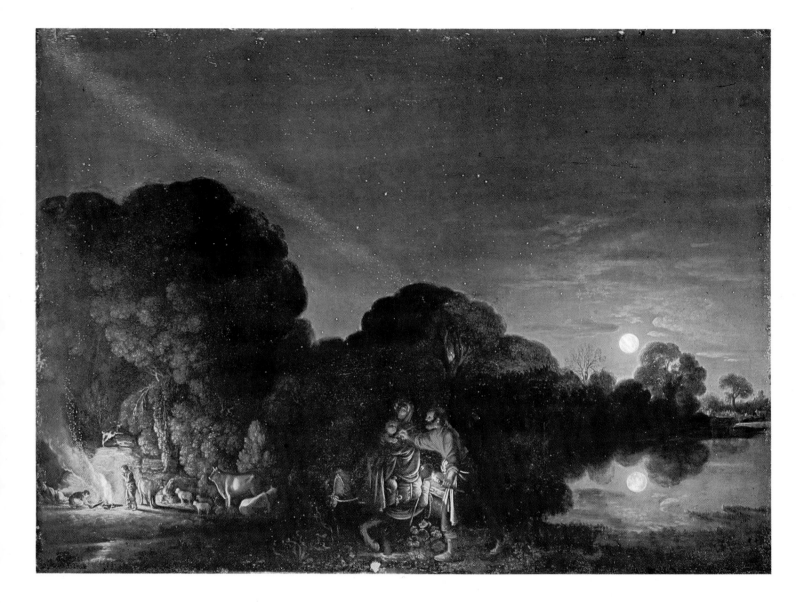

Colorplate 6. ADAM ELSHEIMER. *Moonlit Landscape with the Flight into Egypt*. 1609.
Copper, 12¼ × 16⅝″. Alte Pinakothek, Munich

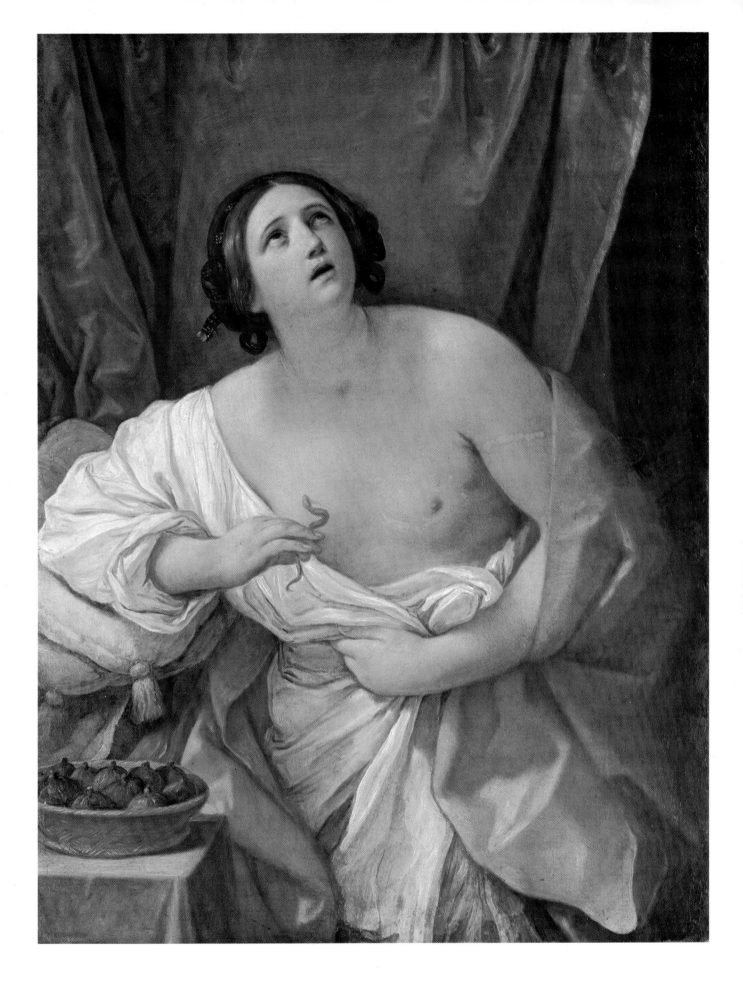

Colorplate 7. GUIDO RENI. *Cleopatra*. c. 1638–39. 37¾ × 47½″. Pitti Gallery, Florence

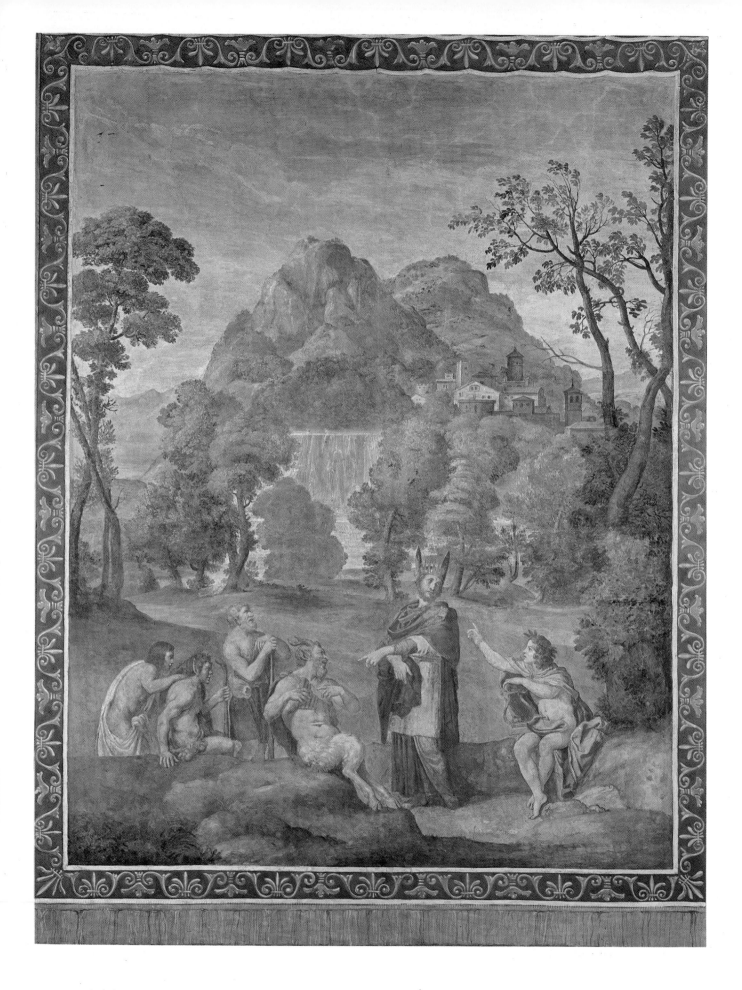

Colorplate 8. DOMENICHINO. *Punishment of Midas*. 1616–18.
Fresco, 8′9¼″ × 6′9¾″. National Gallery, London

drama, but refined—perhaps even made sublime —by an exquisitely graceful line, by singing color, and by sensuous paint surfaces. He had a host of followers and imitators, but no equal. The only artists working in Bologna who could be considered rivals, Albani and Guercino (see pages 101–102), were both influenced by him.

Francesco Albani (1578–1660), after his early training with the Carracci in Bologna, went to Rome about 1602 and became one of Annibale's chief assistants. Like Reni, he was very successful in Rome, but decided to return to Bologna toward the end of the second decade. In his early work he was quite close to Annibale, but usually—and sometimes distressingly—sweeter. He was most original in small landscape paintings, where his lyricism and feeling for light anticipate Claude Lorrain. In his altarpieces he was only occasionally capable of a strong, personal statement, as in the *Annunciation,* known as the *Annunciation of the Beautiful Angel,* of 1633 (fig.

101). There is a remarkable sense of grave decorum in this severely constructed composition. The matronly Virgin stands with great dignity as the Angel Gabriel, in a rush of wind and light, glides into a pose of adoration. Stylistically, the picture seems to fall precisely between the heroic rhetoric of Annibale (fig. 97) and the refined lyricism of Reni (fig. 100).

Annibale Carracci's favorite pupil and his most faithful follower was Domenico Zampieri (1581–1641), known as Domenichino. He too had studied with the Carracci in Bologna, but essentially his art was formed under the close supervision of Annibale after he came to Rome in 1602 or 1603. In a series of mythological landscape frescoes (1616–18) for the Villa Aldobrandini in Frascati, he excels in dramatic narration and even rivals his master in the creation of ideal landscapes. For one of these scenes, the *Punishment of Midas* (colorplate 8), Domenichino was partly dependent on a drawing by Annibale[41]

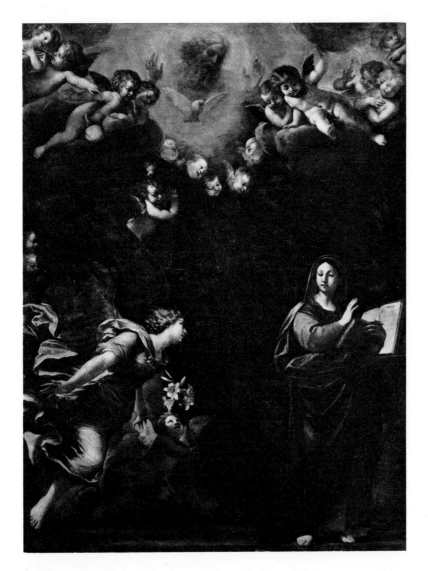

101. FRANCESCO ALBANI.
Annunciation of the Beautiful Angel.
1633. 11'11⅝"×8'6".
S. Bartolommeo, Bologna

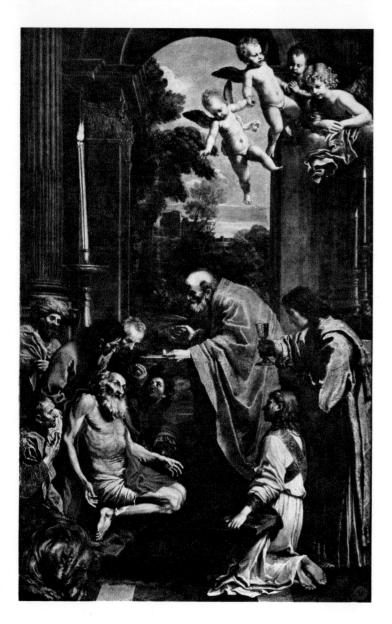

102. DOMENICHINO. *Last Communion of St. Jerome.* 1614. 13′9″ × 8′4½″. Vatican Gallery, Rome

Domenichino's landscapes have always been appreciated, and their importance for the history of landscape painting was very considerable. However, the artist's reputation, which in the nineteenth century reached astonishing proportions—some considered him second only to Raphael—was based on his narrative incisiveness in studied, balanced figure compositions like the *Last Communion of St. Jerome* of 1614 (fig. 102). This picture is derived from Agostino Carracci's version of the same subject in the Bologna Pinacoteca (fig. 82). Like most artists of his generation, Domenichino no longer felt it necessary to insist, as did the reform artists in reaction to Mannerism, on the density and weight of forms. His composition is consequently much more open and spacious than Agostino's. But Domenichino was also a greater artist than Agostino. The dramatic variety and descriptive precision of his picture make Agostino's forms and figures seem characterless; and compared with the subtleties of placement and movement of Domenichino's composition, Agostino's design appears dull and heavy-handed.

Beginning around 1617, Domenichino's works show his attempt to enliven his style by a new animation and excitement. To a large extent the results are disappointing, and his only major work of this later period that is an undisputed masterpiece is the fresco decoration of the apse and pendentives of Sant'Andrea della Valle in Rome (1622–27). Essentially, the change in Domenichino's paintings reflects the competition and growing popularity of the new baroque style. The early champion of this style in Rome was another of Annibale Carracci's pupils, Giovanni Lanfranco (1582–1647), whose work overshadowed Domenichino's before the end of the second decade.

After some early training with Agostino Car-

—but only partly; the splendid integration of the figural composition and the monumental landscape seems to be entirely his own. The amusing story is told with a dispassionate innocence that makes it the more charming. King Midas was present at a musical contest between Pan and Apollo. An inveterate blunderer, Midas decided for Pan. As Midas points to the satyr the indignant Apollo, with an answering gesture, seems to cry "Ass!" and, indeed, makes ass's ears sprout from the hapless king's head. Behind Midas the trees and the great mountain peaks solemnly echo the ridiculous transformation.

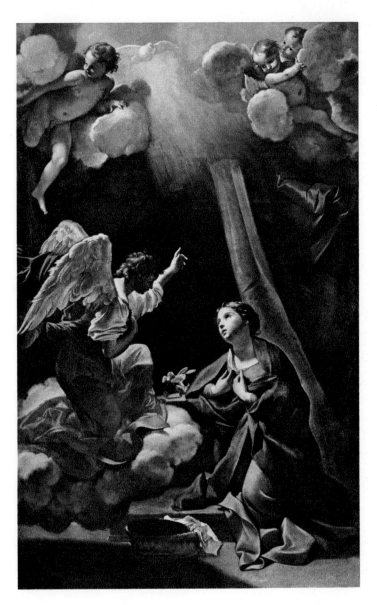

103. GIOVANNI LANFRANCO. *Annunciation.*
c. 1616. 9′8½″ × 6′. S. Carlo ai Catinari, Rome

racci in Parma, Lanfranco came to Rome in 1602 to study with Annibale. He produced some interesting works in the first decade of the century, some of which show his knowledge and appreciation of Correggio. However, it was during his stay in the Emilia from 1610 to 1612 that he really matured and, on the basis of his renewed experience of the illusionism of Correggio and of the animated, coloristic art of Ludovico Carracci and Schedoni, developed a highly original and influential style. His *Annunciation* (fig. 103) is in complete contrast to the meditative, tectonic style that Domenichino was then practicing (fig. 102). Lanfranco believed in ideal beauty, decorum, and other principles of the grand manner, but he rejected the relatively static, balanced groupings, the carefully constructed stages, and the generalized light that Domenichino had taken over from Annibale's late style. The *Annunciation* is a highly dynamic conception. The forms turn in space, and the whole seems to spiral diagonally upward. The structure of the room disappears as it is miraculously invaded by the angel who flies on a cloud and by the divine light that flows like a rushing stream down the curtain from the Holy Ghost to the Virgin. Light, color, and movement all contribute to the unity and to the explosive emotionalism of the scene. Parallels for this style can be found in the work of Ludovico Carracci (fig. 81), who was surely one of its sources, but one is reminded most of all of Correggio and Barocci (fig. 78). Indeed, Lanfranco's contribution was to bring to and to develop in Rome an aspect of the north-Italian pictorial tradition that had not really been known there previously. His paintings precede Bernini's comparable stylistic experiments in sculpture (see pages 51–63) by several years, and were undoubtedly one of Bernini's sources.

In contrast to Domenichino, whose style de-

manded slow, painstaking preparation and execution, Lanfranco aimed at immediacy, painting with a lively, quick brush stroke. He worked rapidly, and his paintings were much in demand. He was an especially gifted decorator, and his grandest work in Rome is his fresco of the *Assumption of the Virgin,* of 1625–27, which decorates the dome of Sant'Andrea della Valle (fig. 104). The fresco is based on Correggio's dome painting in the Cathedral of Parma, but its powerful activity and luministic unity are new. Photographs must inevitably do the painting an injustice. The enormous surface, high above the

104. GIOVANNI LANFRANCO.
Assumption of the Virgin.
1625–27. Fresco.
Dome of S. Andrea della Valle,
Rome

spectator, is transformed into a light-filled empyrean. The heavenly host, bathed in a blue-green atmosphere, surrounds the dazzlingly bright figure of Christ in the lantern, while the Virgin, almost lost in the turbulence of clouds and angels, ascends with arms outstretched toward her Son. What captivates the spectator is not so much the illusionistic effects as the overwhelming density and accord of the visual impressions. In the seventeenth century the dome was compared to a musical orchestration "when all the sounds together form the harmony."[42]

After the Sant'Andrea dome Lanfranco painted a number of impressive frescoes in Rome and in Naples, where he worked from 1634 to 1646. However, it was his activity in Rome from 1613 to 1630 that is of greatest historical interest, for then he was instrumental in directing Italian painting toward the baroque style. This painterly style represents only one trend in what we have come to call, somewhat ambiguously, "Baroque art" (see pages 12–13). In a sense, this style can be understood as an extreme statement of a pictorial idea that was characteristic of all the art of the age: that aesthetic space and real space can be convincingly related and imaginatively unified. The "reform" generation introduced this idea, which was to a certain extent the reintroduction, after the interlude of Mannerism, of a Renaissance concept. Characteristically, in pictures around 1600 painted forms are forced forward as if into the spectator space. In general, the next generation developed the idea in a new way through the creation of a painted space that becomes an extension of the real space and allows the spectator to move imaginatively into the picture. (The difference between the two generations can be seen by comparisons of Domenichino and Agostino Carracci: figs. 82, 102; of Lanfranco and Caravaggio: figs. 89, 103; of Guercino and Annibale Carracci: figs. 95, colorplate 9). This idea was most completely realized in the illusionistic masterpieces of the baroque style (figs. 108, 122), but the extremity of such statements met strong, and frequently successful, opposition. In the 1620s in Rome the baroque style dominated the more "rational" linear and constructed style that was represented early in the century by Annibale Carracci, Reni, Albani, and Domenichino; but, as we shall see, the latter trend had a distinguished future in the art of Sacchi and Poussin.

Outside Rome, toward 1620, painters were also experimenting with a baroque style. Giovanni Francesco Barbieri (1591–1666), who was called Guercino because he was squint-eyed, grew up in Cento, a small town near Bologna. Almost self-trained, he created a personal style on the basis of his study of the Ferrarese painter Scarsellino and of Ludovico Carracci. In a letter of 1617 Ludovico announced the arrival in Bologna of this young man: "a great draughtsman and a most felicitous colorist; he is a prodigy of nature, a miracle . . . who astonishes the leading painters."[43] Indeed, his drawings still excite our ad-

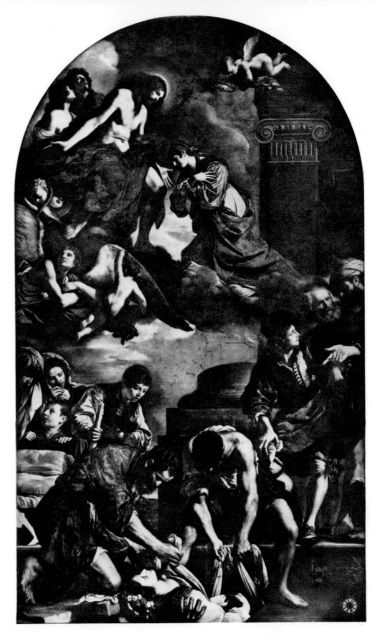

105. GUERCINO. *Burial of St. Petronilla.* 1621–23. 23′7″ × 13′10″. Capitoline Gallery, Rome

miration, and one is still astonished by the boisterous freedom of pictures like the *Burial of St. Petronilla* (fig. 105), which was painted during Guercino's stay in Rome from 1621 to 1623. The picture seems to be constructed of active fragments of form and light that arrange themselves in discontinuous, diagonal patterns. There is no rest for the spectator; caught up, for instance, by the swift movement that runs down from the right edge of the canvas to the grave at the bottom, his glance is violently turned about in mid-course by the youth who twists his body and head sharply around.

The conception of the scene is also novel and exciting. Above, St. Petronilla, who chose death rather than marriage to a pagan, is received by Christ in Heaven; below, she is seen again, being buried. And here Guercino has used the lower frame as the near edge of the grave, so that when the painting was in its original location in St. Peter's, the saint seemed to be lowered out of the picture and into the altar-tomb that actually enshrines her remains. Thus, for the communicant at the altar, the divine vision was united with the mystery of the Mass through the sacrifice of the saint, and belonged at once to the world of painted illusion and miraculous reality.

The power and originality of Guercino's style can be easily appreciated in another of his Roman works, the *Aurora* fresco in the Casino Ludovisi (colorplate 9). The ceiling demands comparison with Reni's fresco of almost a decade earlier in the Casino Rospigliosi (fig. 99). Reni's painting, like those of Annibale in the Farnese Gallery (fig. 95), is a *quadro riportato;* that is, it simulates an easel picture that has been affixed to the ceiling. Guercino has conceived instead an illusionistic view from below *(di sotto in sù)* that, in combination with the painted architecture by Agostino Tassi (a landscape painter and a specialist in illusionistic perspectives), suggests that the ceiling is open to a view of the heavens where Aurora in her chariot comes speeding by. Correspondingly, instead of Reni's graceful rhythms and relief-like composition, Guercino creates an open, dynamic, three-dimensional design.

Soon after Guercino left Rome to work again in Cento and Bologna, he surrendered to the quiet, ideal style of Reni. His later work tends toward sentimentality, and, although individual paintings can be quite impressive (fig. 106), in general his work ceases to be of great historical interest.

The young Guercino, and also Lanfranco, were once thought to have derived their styles from Caravaggio, but it is now clear that although they knew something of Caravaggio's work (Lanfranco of course knew it well), they took very little from him directly. Neither was really interested in Caravaggio's popular realism, and in contrast to Caravaggio, who used light to emphasize the three-dimensional solidity of form within a limited space, they were both concerned with expanding space and creating atmosphere, and they used light independently of form to animate the surface and depth of their pictures. In this, of course, their art is related to Ludovico Carracci and is ultimately dependent on Correggio, Tintoretto, and some aspects of Titian.

It is curious that the painterly tradition of sixteenth-century Venice did not generate its own baroque style. As if oppressed by the city's past grandeur, native Venetian painters in the first years of the seventeenth century could produce little more than pale imitations of Veronese, Tintoretto, and Titian. It took foreigners to rediscover the Venetian tradition and to give it new life. The Roman Domenico Fetti (1589–1623) came to Venice via Mantua in the early 1620s; Bernardo Strozzi (1581–1644) came from Genoa in 1630. Both had been exposed to the

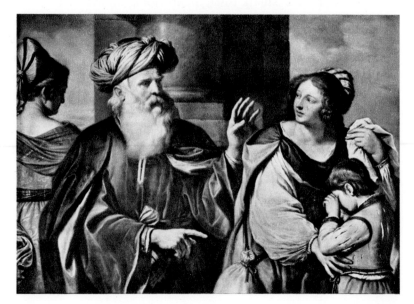

106. GUERCINO. *Expulsion of Hagar.* 1657–58. 45¼ × 60". Brera Gallery, Milan

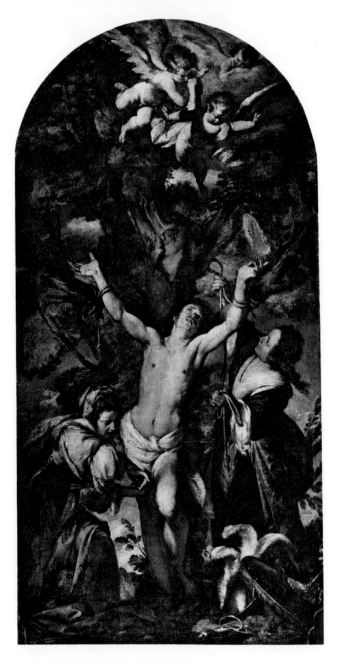

107. BERNARDO STROZZI. *St. Sebastian*. c. 1635.
14′1″ × 6′5″. S. Benedetto, Venice

works of Rubens, and in Venice the paintings
of Veronese and other Sixteenth-century Venetian masters helped them enrich their vigorous
baroque styles (figs. 5, 107). Jan Liss (1595/97–
1629/30), another foreign artist who had came to
Venice (in the early 1620s), was a German who
had studied in Holland. His mature paintings,
like the *Toilet of Venus* of about 1626 (colorplate
10), are treated with a coloristic sensuousness

that is wholly Venetian. Here, set off against the
blue-gray of the curtain and the bright, cool
blue of the sky, the nude goddess and her hand-
maidens reflect the warmth of the red and red-
violet draperies. The motifs are largely drawn
from works by Titian, and the bright, high-keyed
color shows Liss's great dependence on Veronese.
However, in the exuberance of the figures and
in the cool, rippling light that flows over the
forms there is an emotional and pictorial unity
that is entirely new. Later Venetian artists, like
Francesco Maffei (c. 1600–1660) and Sebastiano
Mazzoni (c. 1611–1678; a Florentine by birth
and training), produced excellent and original
versions of a baroque style; but only in the eighteenth century did Venetian post-Renaissance
painting gain international significance.

It was in Rome, around 1630, in the art of
Pietro Berrettini da Cortona (1596–1669), that
the Italian baroque style in painting found its
richest seventeenth-century expression. Cortona
went to Rome about 1612 after his early training in Florence. His earliest known works date
around 1620 and show him to be still closely associated with the rather provincial group of Florentine artists then active in Rome. At this time,
however, he was also studying the remains of antiquity, the "antiquicizing" paintings of the Renaissance artist Polidoro da Caravaggio, and, in
general, educating himself. He was soon patronized and encouraged by the learned antiquarian
circle of Marcello Sacchetti, Cardinal Francesco
Barberini, and Cassiano dal Pozzo, and by the
end of the 1620s he was producing important
works in painting and beginning his career as an
architect (see pages 34–37).

His paintings of the third decade show Cortona
making use of the lessons of Annibale Carracci,
Reni, Domenichino, Lanfranco, and also of Titian. The influence of Titian's famous "Bacchanales," which had come from Ferrara into the
Ludovisi collection in Rome,[44] is especially evident in his *Triumph of Bacchus* (c. 1624; Capitoline Gallery, Rome) and *Rape of the Sabine
Women* (c. 1629; colorplate 11). In the latter the

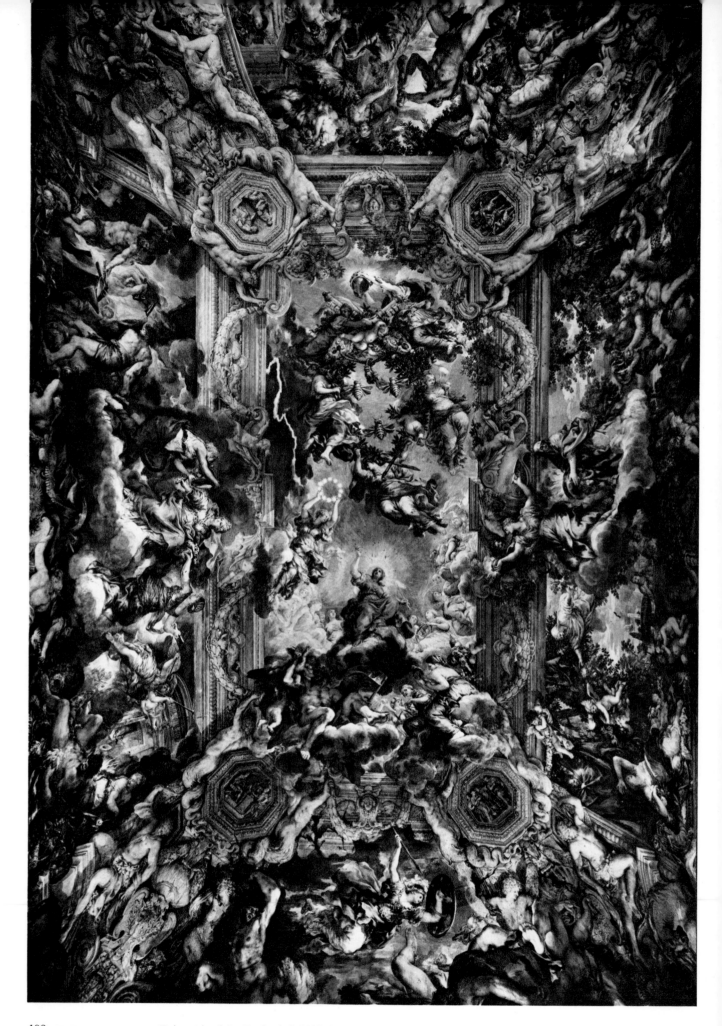

108. PIETRO DA CORTONA. *Triumph of the Barberini*. 1633–39.
Ceiling Fresco, Gran Salone, Palazzo Barberini, Rome

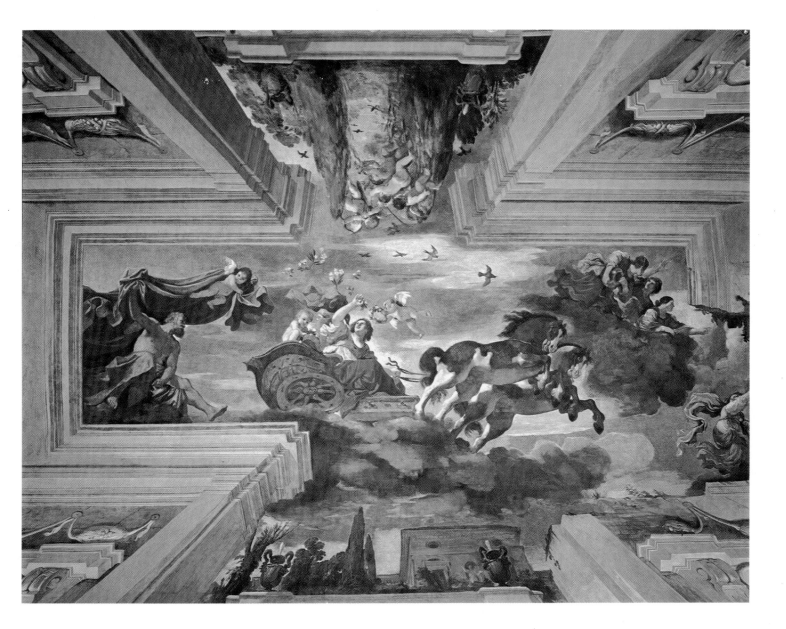

Colorplate 9. GUERCINO. *Aurora*. 1621. Ceiling Fresco. Casino Ludovisi, Rome

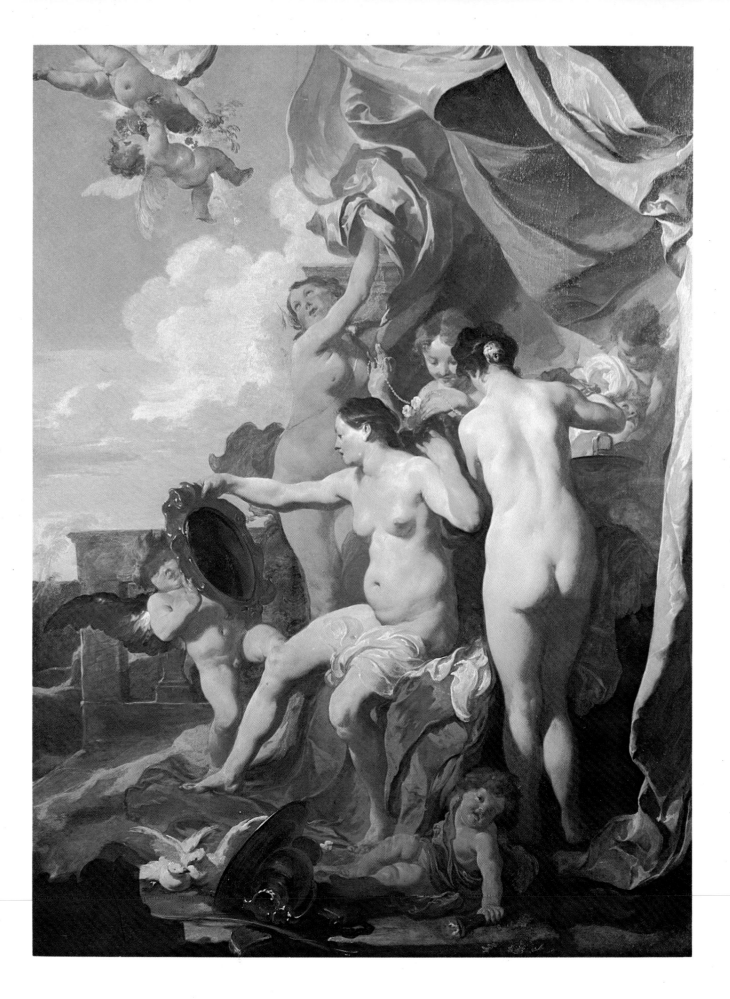

Colorplate 10. JAN LISS. *Toilet of Venus*. c. 1626. 31½ × 23½".
Collection Schoenborn, Pommersfelden

bright light and color create effects of richness and sensuosity that add a new dimension to the baroque style in Rome. Here archaeological detail provides an erudite background for the action; the rapid brushwork and the figures placed on contrasted diagonal axes give the impression of violent activity. The scene does lack convincing emotion or narrative incisiveness, and the figures seem posed—the group at right is, in fact, derived from Bernini's *Abduction of Proserpina* statue (fig. 55)—but the picture is intended as a gorgeous spectacle, and as such it succeeds brilliantly.

Between 1633 and 1639 Cortona painted the vault of the *gran salone* of the Palazzo Barberini (fig. 108). This was the most important decorative commission of the 1630s, and Cortona produced a fresco that is for Roman baroque painting what Michelangelo's Sistine Ceiling is for Roman High Renaissance painting—the grandest and most complete statement of its aesthetic ideals. Painted in the palace of a great Roman family whose glory and virtues it celebrates, the ceiling underlines the secularizing trends of the seventeenth century. The iconographic program was devised by the poet Francesco Bracciolini. On the coving of the vault mythological scenes portray, through allegory, the virtuous accomplishments of the then reigning Barberini pope, Urban VIII. In the principal field the substance and the embellishments of the Barberini name are revealed. Just below the center of this field, Divine Providence, one of whose emblems is the bee, points to the three bees of the Barberini insignia surrounded by the laurel of immortality, which is held by the virtues, Faith, Hope, and Charity. Immortality herself flies to set a stellar crown upon the family coat of arms, while above, two more crowns are added: the papal tiara and the poet's laurel (Urban VIII was a gifted poet). The allegorical conceit actually completes Sacchi's ceiling of *Divine Wisdom* in another room of the palace (see pages 109–111).[45]

All these elements have been fused in a breathtakingly dense pictorial orchestration. Cortona's debt to Annibale Carracci, and to Lanfranco and Guercino, is evident, but his design is, nonetheless, one of astonishing originality. Actually, it appears that he began with a scheme that was fairly close to the Farnese Gallery decoration; this

109. PIETRO DA CORTONA. Ceiling Fresco, Sala di Giove. 1643–46. Palazzo Pitti, Florence

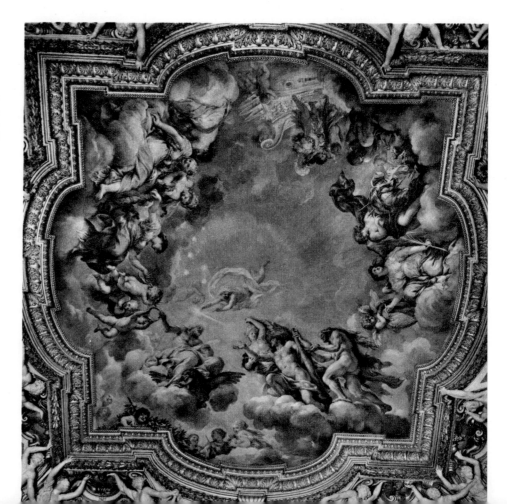

can still be seen in the painted architectural framework and in the decorative "sculptured" caryatids. Cortona has opened the vault, however, and the architecture merely defines the different spatial levels. The figures are not confined by frames; they exist within and beyond the room and flow in great waves from compartment to compartment. The vault is filled with a unifying light and atmosphere that, together with the continuity of movement, merges the spectator space with the imagined space of mythology and allegory.

On the Barberini ceiling all is painted. In his ceiling designs for a suite of rooms in the Palazzo Pitti in Florence (1641–47), Cortona combined paintings with real architectural and sculptural decoration (fig. 109). These ceilings, commissioned by Grand Duke Ferdinando II, follow a rather elaborate allegorical program apotheosizing the Medici and illustrating their princely virtues. The virtues are associated with the planets, for which the individual rooms are named.[46] The type of ceiling decoration that Cortona used in the Palazzo Pitti can be related to some of his earlier works in Rome, but it is probable that he developed it in the 1640s as a result of his impressions during a short stay in Venice in 1637. The typical Venetian ceiling decoration (*e.g.*, Veronese's in San Sebastiano, Venice) also encloses painted fields, seen *di sotto in sù*, in richly carved enframements. Indeed, the most striking difference between the Pitti ceilings and the Barberini vault is the rigorous separation of elements in the former compared with the interpenetration of forms in the latter. This change, however, is the corollary of a change in stylistic conception that had great importance for later painting. The Barberini ceiling depends for its effect essentially on the density and movement of plastic masses: even the atmosphere is thick and heavy. The Pitti ceilings are conceived instead largely in terms of the animation of space and of luminous volumes of atmosphere. Now the painted figures gravitate toward the periphery of the ceiling, leaving the centers open and thus increasing the sense of space. The delimiting frames really provide a kind of skeletal structure that controls and gives shape to the movement of space, and the white and gilt stucco ornamentation reflects light and brightens the room. The airiness, the rapidity of movement, and the gaiety of color in these ceilings represent a first step toward Rococo style, and ultimately they lead to the great ceiling decorations of Tiepolo (see pages 340–41).

After Cortona returned to Rome in 1647, he frescoed the vault of the gallery of the Palazzo Doria-Pamphili (1651–54) and the nave, dome, and apse of Santa Maria in Vallicella (1647–65). It was perhaps natural that as a painter-architect Cortona should have made his most important contributions in monumental ceiling decorations. His easel paintings count many masterpieces, however, and in his late work he proved a power-

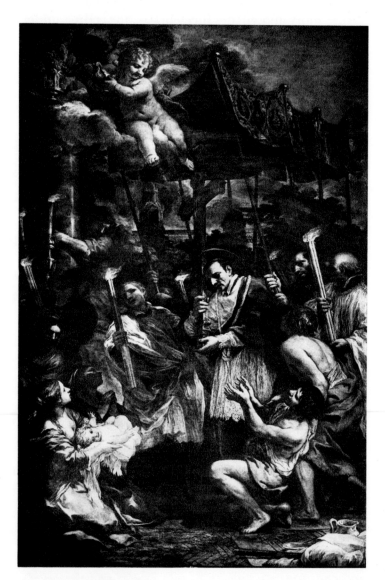

110. PIETRO DA CORTONA.
Procession of St. Carlo Borromeo. 1667.
S. Carlo ai Catinari, Rome

108

ful religious painter. One of his finest altarpieces is the *Procession of St. Carlo Borromeo* of 1667 (fig. 110). The picture represents the saint carrying the reliquary of the Holy Nail among the plague-stricken. The handling is very broad and free, merging the figures with the surrounding atmosphere. Dramatic illumination and repeated diagonals give the painting an intense energy. The night air seems charged, and the marching figures, ablaze with light, appear to surge out of the picture toward the spectator.

Cortona's works are the most spectacular achievements of mid-seventeenth-century Italian painting. His baroque style, however, represents only one of the directions that painters were pursuing in those years. Indeed, Cortona's two most distinguished contemporaries, Sacchi and Poussin, appear quite clearly as his stylistic opponents. Andrea Sacchi (1599–1661) returned to Rome in the early 1620s from Bologna, where he had gone with his teacher Albani. His first important work in Rome, the altarpiece in Sant' Isidoro, is, as one might expect, indebted to Albani and Ludovico Carracci. Sacchi quickly grasped the nature of modern trends in Rome, and his *Miracle of St. Gregory* of 1625–27 (in the Vatican Gallery) is as masterful an example of the baroque style as any of the contemporary works of Pietro da Cortona. However, Sacchi's strong ties, through Albani, to the tradition of Annibale Carracci and Raphael acted as a restraint on his formulation of an early baroque manner and made Cortona's work around 1630 appear to him not a logical consequence of modern style but an unreasoned and extravagant pictorial experiment.

Partly in reaction to Cortona, Sacchi began to place heavy emphasis on draftsmanship and on compositional order and clarity. His ceiling fresco in the Palazzo Barberini, painted between 1629 and 1631 (fig. 111), may be understood as his manifesto. Iconographically, this ceiling and Cortona's ceiling in the *gran salone* of the palace (fig. 108) are interrelated. Sacchi's enthroned Divine Wisdom, whose attribute is the sun, sup-

plements the images of Divine Providence and Immortality in the later fresco. Together, their symbols—the sun, bees, and laurel—compose the Barberini insignia. Sacchi's design was wholly modern: the ceiling is open to the heavens and filled with clouds and light. However, the centralized composition is stable and finely balanced. The figures are relatively few and clearly defined, and the result is a grand, dignified allegorical vision (Divine Wisdom and the personifications of her qualities ruling the world through the Barberini family) that is immediately legible. Cortona's answer to this was the ceiling of Divine Providence.

The two ceilings are paradigms of the possibilities of mid-century style, and artists and critics debated their merits.[47] Sacchi and his supporters insisted that a painting must be composed according to the Aristotelian rules for tragedy: above all, it must have a minimum of actors and be characterized by grandeur and clarity. They accused Cortona of being unconcerned with the poetic substance of his work and losing it in the confusion of superficial magnificence. No one in the seventeenth century would have challenged Horace's dictum *"ut pictura poesis,"* which identifies painting with poetry (see page 370). What the Cortona camp argued was that painting could be like epic poetry, which brings together and binds a multitude of persons and events. The dispute had no real issue. The two concepts of painting developed side by side, and although for short periods one dominated the other (for instance, in the 1640s, when Cortona was in Florence, Sacchi's style was pre-eminent in Rome), both survived and proved fruitful for the future.

It is difficult today to assess Sacchi's merits as an artist. He worked little and slowly and depended much on fine, careful drawing and on subtle adjustments of color and tone. Unfortunately, many of his paintings cannot be easily studied, either because of their location (the important series of the *Life of St. John the Baptist*, painted between 1639 and 1649, has always been almost

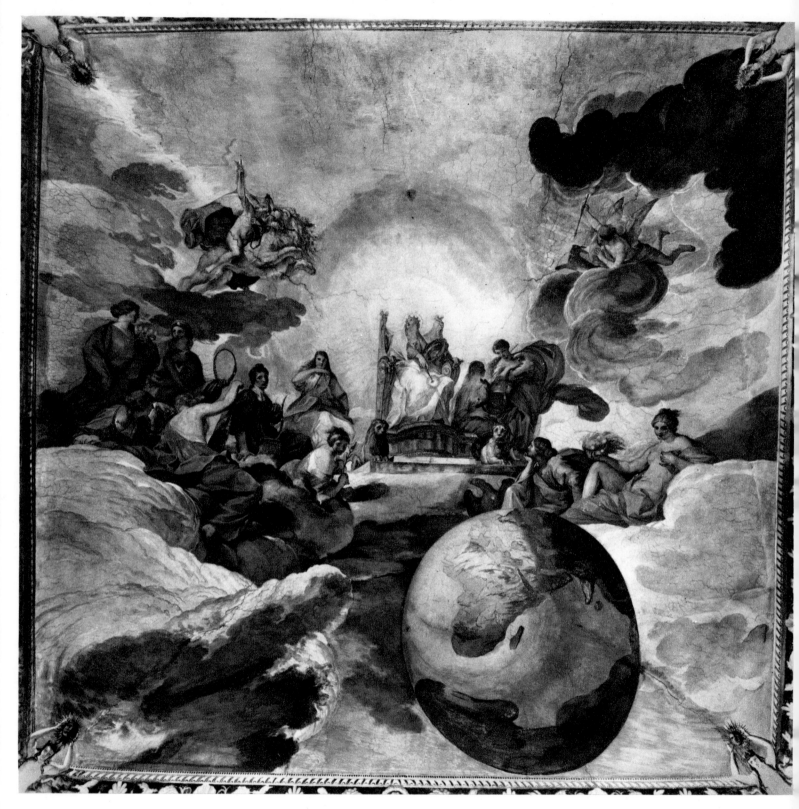

111. ANDREA SACCHI. *Divine Wisdom*. 1629–31. Ceiling Fresco, Palazzo Barberini, Rome

invisible since it is placed high in the lantern of the Lateran Baptistery in Rome), or because of their poor condition. However, his *Vision of St. Romuald,* which dates from 1631 (colorplate 12), is a superb example of the application of his pictorial principles to the problem of the altarpiece. The saint describes his vision, seen in the background, of the souls of dead monks of his order ascending a ladder to heaven. His companions listen quietly, with deep seriousness. There is almost no activity, and certainly no excitement or rapturous emotionalism. It is in the slow rhythms of precise gestures and expressions and in the quiet, closely knit harmony of whites and grays that the artist expresses the grave, inner drama of the scene.

Sacchi's style was paralleled in the paintings of the French artist Nicolas Poussin (1594–1665). Almost nothing is known of Poussin's work before he came to Rome in 1624. He was apparently discovered in Paris by the Italian poet Cavaliere Marino, for whom he made some drawings, which are now mainly preserved in Windsor Castle. Poussin followed Marino to Rome and soon joined Cortona and Sacchi as a member of the circle of Cardinal Barberini and Cassiano dal Pozzo. In the 1620s he too learned and practiced the modern, baroque style. He was especially appreciated in those years for his poetic mythological paintings, which were strongly influenced by Venetian art. In fact, Poussin had gone to Venice on his way to Rome, and he undoubtedly knew works by contemporaries like Liss (colorplate 10) as well as the famous masterpieces of the previous century. And in Rome, he, like Cortona, studied Titian's "Bacchanales." A typical picture of his early Roman period is his *Death of Adonis* (c. 1628; fig. 112). It is freely composed and broadly handled. The rich color and the raking light of the setting sun provide a marvelous romantic ambience for this illustration of Ovid's tale of how Venus poured nectar on the blood of her dead lover Adonis and thus created the anemone.

From his early biographers we know that even in France Poussin had developed a profound respect for Raphael and for the art of the ancients. It is not too surprising, therefore, that in 1630/31 Poussin decided to ally himself with Andrea Sacchi against the extreme baroque style that Cortona was developing; his paintings in the first years of the thirties are, in fact, es-

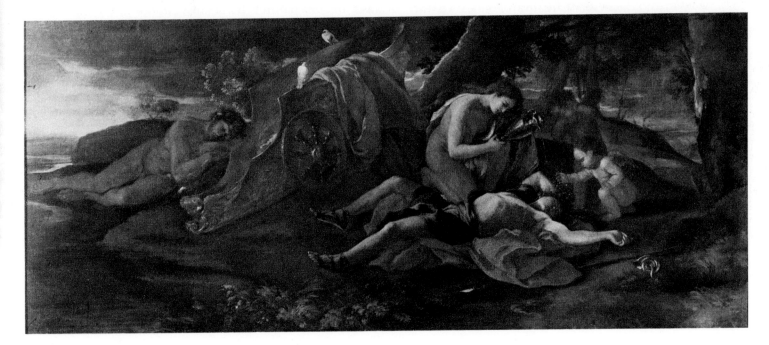

112. NICOLAS POUSSIN. *Death of Adonis.* c. 1628. 22½ × 50⅜″. Musée des Beaux-Arts, Caen

111

pecially close to Sacchi's. Poussin's sensuous and painterly *Death of Adonis* has much in common with Cortona's *Rape of the Sabine Women* (colorplate 11). But his own version of the *Rape of the Sabines* (c. 1636; colorplate 13) is something quite different. In the cool, clear air the forms are defined with hard, sculptural precision. The façade of a Roman Basilica appears like a backdrop for the action "on stage," which begins with a start as Romulus gives the signal for his men to seize the Sabine women. In Cortona's painting, tumultuous confusion is suggested by dense knots of active figures, by the freedom of handling, and by the light and color that merge and bind the forms. In Poussin's painting, violence and turmoil appear almost as the mathematical result of a graph of patterns of energy and movement. Romulus' gesture is answered by a series of movements across the picture at right angles to his staff. The main figure groups are tightly knit and suggest interlocking pyramidal structures. Bright areas of primary colors intensify the dramatic effect of the painting, but, by their placement, they also help tie the complex scheme together.

As a narrator Poussin was much superior to Cortona. Nothing in Cortona's *Sabines* can compare for dramatic power with the horrified old woman and the desolate infant in Poussin's painting—or with the old man on the right who struggles desperately with the Roman to save his daughter. At the same time Poussin goes beyond Andrea Sacchi in the rigorous intellectualism of his style. For Poussin the antique was not merely an ideal but an inspiring and incontrovertible authority (incidentally, several of the figures in his *Rape of the Sabines* are derived from ancient statues). For him pictorial discipline came to mean more than aesthetic propriety; it was the expression of a moral conviction. "I flee confusion," he wrote; "it is as inimical to me as shadows are to the sunlight."[48] His pictures are illumined by his passion for clarity, for precision of expression, for the dignity and beauty of the ideal.

Poussin remained apart from the "official" art world of Rome, where he painted hardly any altarpieces and no frescoes. He preferred to paint relatively small-size cabinet pictures for private patrons, which gave him greater freedom in his choice of subject and mode of expression. He played a significant role in the development of Italian painting until 1640, and the influence of his early work can be seen in the romantic art of such men as the Genoese Giovanni Benedetto Castiglione (c. 1600/10–1665; fig. 113). But after 1640, though he lived in Italy, Poussin worked primarily for French patrons and was not a great influence on Italian art. His later career belongs to the history of French painting, and it must be treated in another chapter (see pages 151–52).

Mid-century landscape painting in Italy shows a stylistic dichotomy that is analogous to what has been seen in figure painting. In the work of Salvator Rosa (1615–1673), we find romantic, picturesque landscapes whose ultimate origins are in a Netherlandish tradition that was brought to Italy in the sixteenth century by such artists as Matthew and Paul Bril, and then continued in the new century by Agostino Tassi and others. Rosa was born near Naples, but he lived most of his life in Florence and Rome. Although active as a history painter, he is most famous as a landscapist. Typical of his landscapes is the *Bandits on a Rocky Coast* (fig. 114). The romantic, slightly sinister overtones of the subject are supported by the dark tonality of the painting and by the inhospitable, even menacing character of the landscape elements: jagged rocks, turbulent water, and swift-moving clouds. The sharp diagonals of the composition and the rapid brushwork seem to reveal the nervous inner life of nature.

Closely related to Rosa, and surely influenced by him, was Gaspard Dughet (1615–1675), Poussin's brother-in-law and often called Gaspard Poussin. Dughet, who was a Roman by birth, owes much to Poussin's landscape style (see pages 158–59), but his feeling for the wildness and

112

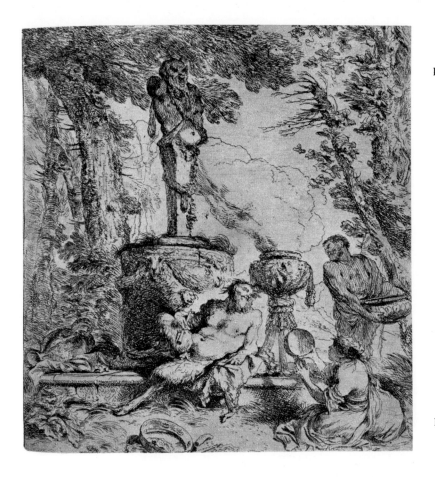

113. **GIOVANNI BENEDETTO CASTIGLIONE.**
Festival of Pan. 1648. Etching.
The Metropolitan Museum of Art, New York
(Pulitzer Bequest, 1917)

114. **SALVATOR ROSA.**
Bandits on a Rocky Coast. c. 1656.
29½ × 39⅜".
The Metropolitan Museum of Art, New York
(Charles B. Curtis Fund, 1934)

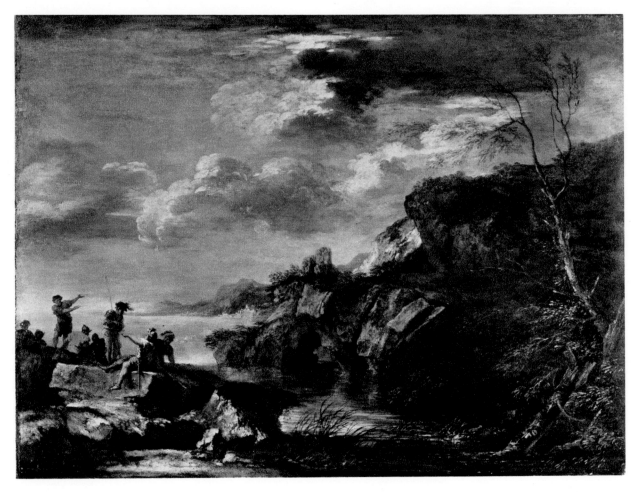

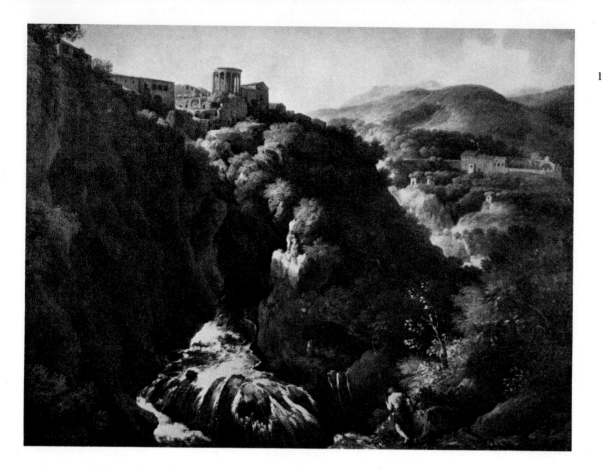

115. GASPARD DUGHET.
View of Tivoli.
c. 1645–50.
28¾ × 38⅜″.
Hatton Gallery,
University of
Newcastle-upon-Tyne

fertility of nature was quite personal. In such a painting as the *View of Tivoli* (fig. 115), man and his creations yield to the sublime grandeur of cliffs, cascades, and impenetrable vegetation.

In contrast to these picturesque and, we may say, baroque conceptions of nature, Claude Gellée, called Claude Lorrain (1600–1682), perhaps the greatest landscapist of the century, produced an idyllic version of the "ideal landscape." Claude is usually considered a French painter, but except for one short trip to his native Lorraine (1625–27), he spent his entire working career in Italy, where his art formed and matured. In Rome about 1620 Claude became a student of Agostino Tassi, a talented but minor painter. His wonderful seaport scenes (colorplate 14), one of his favorite early subjects, have immediate precedents in the work of Tassi, and the small figures and the architectural backgrounds that complete these pictures reveal his close contact with the Bamboccianti. His luminism certainly derives in part from Elsheimer (see page 208), and around 1640 the structured landscapes of Domenichino and, through the latter, of Annibale Carracci influenced him greatly.

Claude's intuition of the transforming power of light and atmosphere is, however, something without precedent. No one before him had turned to face and paint the sun as its light filters through the morning or evening air. In the *Seaport Scene* of 1639, water and architecture and figures are animated by the light of the setting sun. Delicate weblike patterns are created by the riggings of the great ships silhouetted against the sky, and the serenity and vastness of the world seem revealed in this moment of time caught on canvas.

Behind Claude's paintings lie not only preparatory sketches but also remarkably sensitive drawings made from nature, mostly on expeditions in the Roman Campagna. These drawings are unrivaled in their startling immediacy, capturing

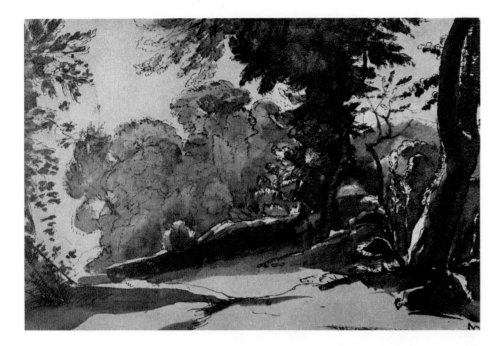

116. CLAUDE LORRAIN.
Woods in Sunlight.
c. 1640–45. Pen and ink wash.
Teyler Museum, Haarlem

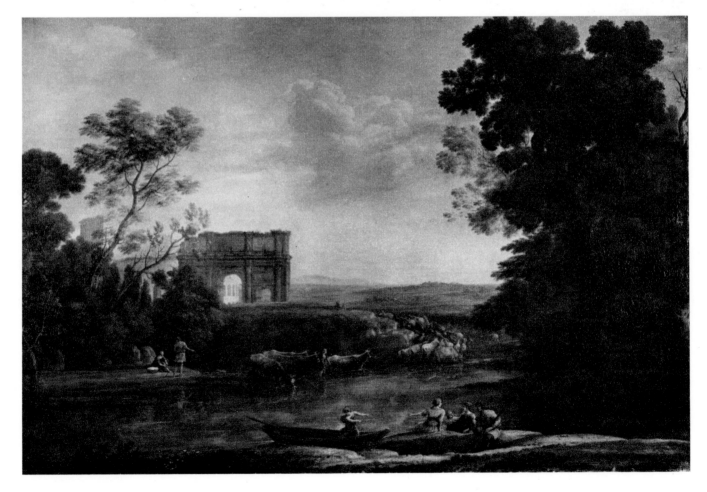

117. CLAUDE LORRAIN.
Landscape with the Arch of Titus
(Decline of the Roman Empire).
1661. 26 × 39″.
Collection Duke of Westminster

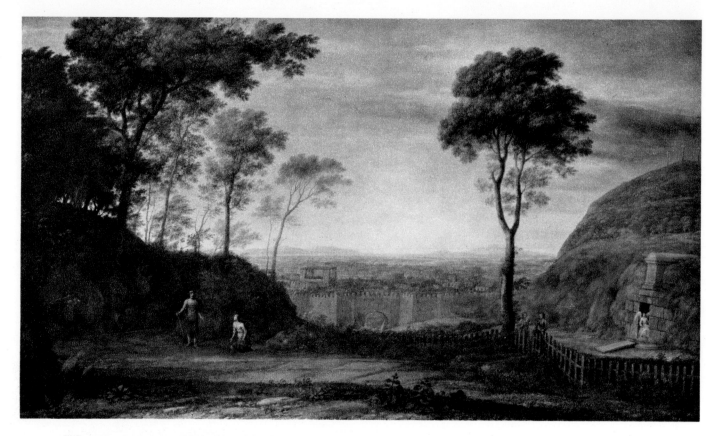

118. CLAUDE LORRAIN. *Landscape with Christ Appearing to the Magdalen.* 1681.
32¾ × 54¾". Städelsches Kunstinstitut, Frankfurt

the limpidity of the air and the play of light over a plain, on rocky cliffs, or in a corner of a wood (fig. 116). And these direct impressions of nature, intensified, expanded, and controlled, became the poetic substance of Claude's idyllic landscape paintings.

As Claude's art developed, as his vision of nature became grander, space and distances increased, and his compositions became simpler, broader, and more majestic. Narrative elements, which had played a relatively minor role in his early landscapes, gained considerably in importance, and the mood of his stories and the mood of nature—now serene and nostalgic (fig. 117), now solemn and melancholy—are perfectly attuned. In the very late (1681) *Christ Appearing to the Magdalen* (fig. 118), Claude went back to a painting that stands at the very beginning of the seventeenth-century tradition of the ideal landscape: Annibale Carracci's *Entombment of*

Christ (fig. 98). He took over the composition with its grave, dramatic dignity, but the sentimental content is entirely his own. Broader and deeper, seen in subdued light, the landscape is suffused in a vibrant, moist atmosphere that is at once somber and magically tender.

After Claude there was no landscape painter of the first rank in Italy until the eighteenth century. The history painters continued to do important work, although quality in this field too was declining toward the end of the seventeenth century. The generation of history painters that followed Cortona and Sacchi was led, in Rome, by two painters who continued the stylistic dichotomy that their elders had initiated. Carlo Maratta (1625–1713) was a student of Sacchi's and, although his early work shows a certain degree of stylistic experimentation, essentially he followed faithfully in the direction that his master had marked out. His ceiling of the *Tri-*

116

umph of Clemency in the Palazzo Altieri in Rome (fig. 119), painted in the 1670s, appears to be a busier and more effusive version of Sacchi's ceiling in the Palazzo Barberini (fig. 111). However, except for the concession to a general taste of the late seventeenth century, it is basically in keeping with the decorative principles expounded by Sacchi. One has very much the feeling that Maratta was an epigone, for his style seems to have come too easily to him, and his paintings lack a spark of creative passion. However, one

119. CARLO MARATTA. *Triumph of Clemency.* 1670s. Ceiling Fresco, Palazzo Altieri, Rome

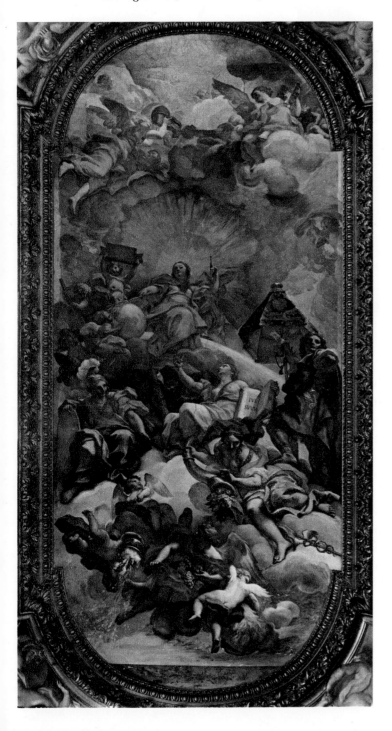

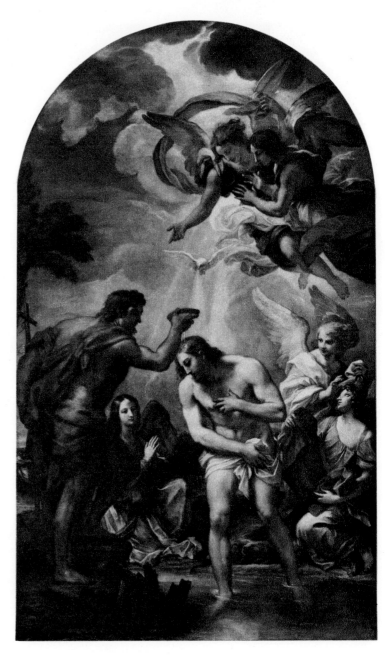

120. CARLO MARATTA. *Baptism of Christ.* c. 1697. S. Maria degli Angeli, Rome

must admire his extraordinary competence and the natural nobility of his inventions. Paintings like the *Baptism of Christ* (c. 1697; fig. 120), with their large, ideally proportioned figures and highly formalized compositions, have something of the grandeur of sculptural monuments. The fact that the *Baptism* is related to a version of the subject by Albani, in the Bologna Pinacoteca,

Italy in the Seventeenth Century / 117

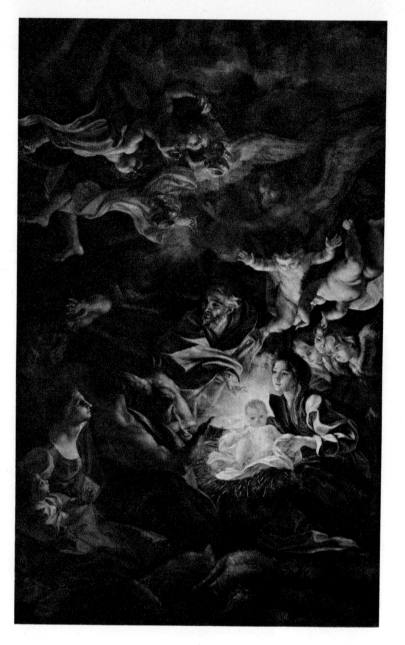

121. BACICCIO.
Adoration of the Shepherds. c. 1672.
13′9⅜″ × 6′8¾″.
S. Maria del Carmine, Fermo

underlines Maratta's role in passing on the tradition of Annibale Carracci, Albani, Sacchi, and others to the eighteenth century, when Benedetto Luti, Pompeo Batoni, and finally Anton Raphael Mengs, among others, were indebted to him.

Maratta's antipode in Rome was Giovanni Battista Gaulli (1639–1709), called Baciccio. He came from Genoa, where he had known works by Rubens and Van Dyck as well as by Strozzi, and on a trip to Parma he studied Correggio. The influence of these artists appears clearly in his easel pictures, which are vigorously baroque in design, warm and luminous in color, and free and broad in handling (fig. 121). In Rome, where he arrived about 1657, he was closely associated with Bernini. Baciccio's greatest work, the ceiling of the nave of the Church of Il Gesù in Rome (fig. 122), painted between 1676 and 1679, may have benefited from Bernini's advice as well as from his example.[49] The ceiling depends on illusionistic methods that Bernini had developed on a small scale in his chapel designs, the ceiling

OPPOSITE: 122. BACICCIO.
Triumph of the Name of Jesus. 1676–79.
Ceiling Fresco, Il Gesù, Rome

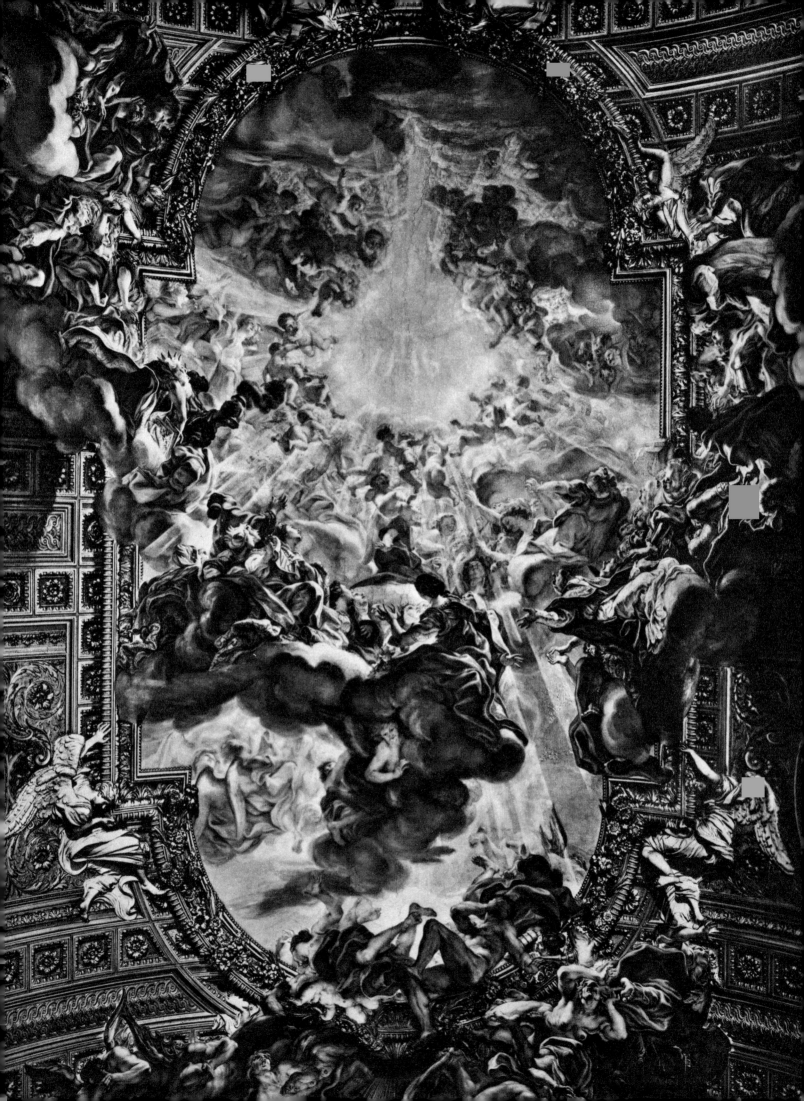

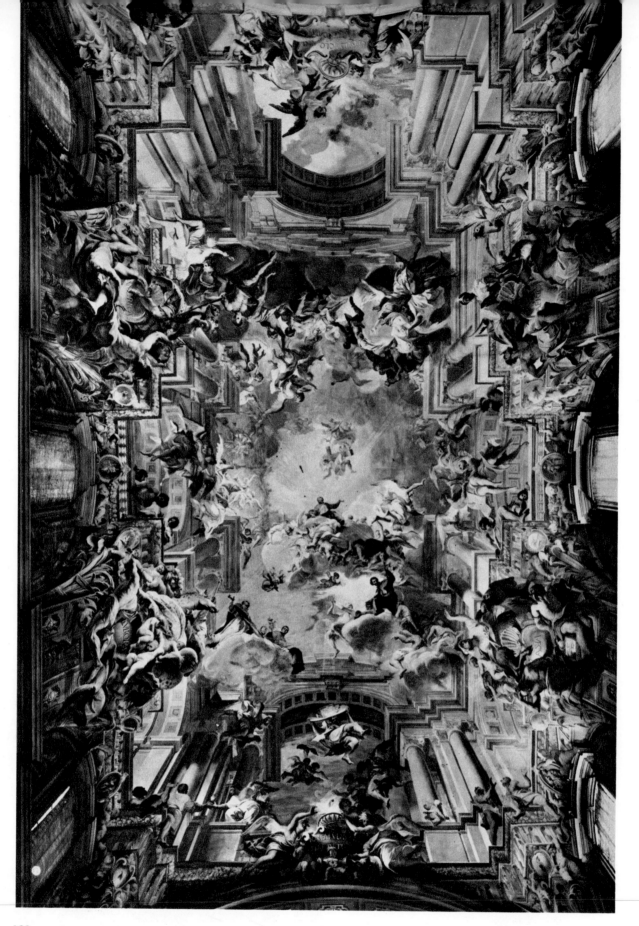

123. ANDREA POZZO. *Entrance of St. Ignatius into Paradise.* 1691–94. Ceiling Fresco, S. Ignazio, Rome

of the Cornaro Chapel in Santa Maria della Vittoria (1645–52) being the most advanced. In this system, painting is merged with real architecture and sculpture in a single illusionistic vision; Cortona's Barberini ceiling of 1633–39 (fig. 108) must be considered the principal inspiration for this mode of ceiling decoration, as only a small step was needed to convert Cortona's simulated unification of painting, architecture and sculpture into three-dimensional reality. Not surprisingly, it was a sculptor-architect, Bernini, who took that step; Cortona, in his ceiling frescoes in the Palazzo Pitti (fig. 109), had meanwhile developed another type of decorative system, where painting and real sculpture and architecture are separable, if interrelated, units in the design. Baciccio, following Bernini's lead, completely integrated the three media on his Gesù ceiling. There colored, three-dimensional stuccowork is combined with painted forms and superimposed on the architecture. Through the sculpture and the real and painted light and shadow the illusion gains relief and becomes tangible. In Il Gesù the earthbound spectator is offered, like a promise, a view of Heaven, where the faithful adore the name of Christ. And he sees the damned spilling out over the frame as they are thrust from Heaven by the splendor of Christ's name.

The fullest expressions of the baroque style in painting are found in the field of monumental ceiling decoration. Here, partly by drawing on the other visual arts, painters created extremes of illusionism and powerful rhythms of color, light, and form that cross vast surfaces to grip and overwhelm the imagination and emotions of the spectator. Aesthetically, the vault of Il Gesù is probably the most successful Roman ceiling decoration of the last third of the century. It does have distinguished rivals though, especially the ceiling in Santi Domenico e Sisto, Rome (1674–75), by Domenico Maria Canuti and Enrico Haffner, and Andrea Pozzo's ceiling of the nave of Sant'Ignazio, Rome (1691–94; fig. 123). The latter is hardly a profound artistic statement, but it is the most dazzling tour de force of *quadratura* painting (*e.g.*, illusionistic painting of architectural perspectives) of the century.

One ceiling decoration outside Rome must be mentioned: the vault of the Gallery of the Palazzo Medici-Riccardi in Florence (figs. 124,

124. LUCA GIORDANO. *Apotheosis of the Medici Dynasty.* 1682–83. Ceiling Fresco, Palazzo Medici-Riccardi, Florence

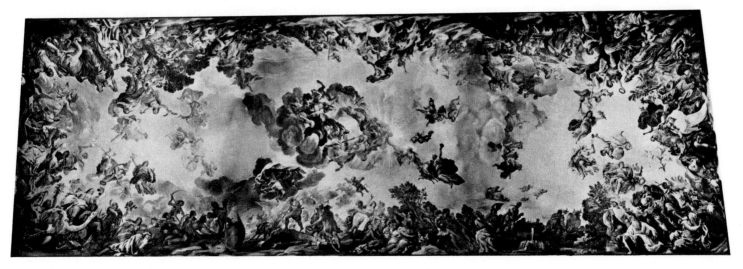

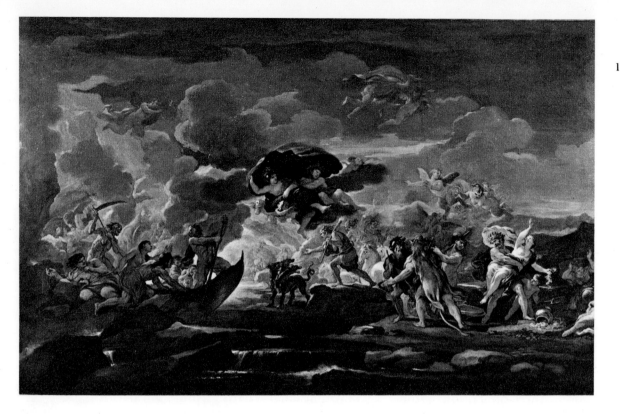

125. LUCA GIORDANO.
Pluto and Proserpina.
1682. Oil sketch.
Collection Mahon,
London

125), painted by Luca Giordano (1634–1705) in 1682–83. Giordano was born and trained in Naples, where he first studied—and, indeed, imitated—the work of Ribera. He was influenced by Lanfranco's baroque style in Naples, and, later, he studied Cortona's art in Rome and Florence. Constantly on the move, he traveled throughout Italy and went finally, in 1692, to work for a decade in Spain. Giordano was extraordinarily prolific, and his speed in painting earned him the nickname "Luca fa presto." Only in recent years has the true importance and quality of Giordano's work begun to be recognized again. Giordano carried the baroque style to new heights of facility and creative spontaneity. In his frescoes he perfected a coloristic style, first adumbrated by Cortona, in which flat areas of high-keyed color, often juxtaposed without tonal transitions, produce a vision of unprecedented brilliance and limpidity. The Florentine ceiling, which owes very much to Cortona's late decorations, is remarkable for its spaciousness, its very bright color, and flickering rapidity of movement. The forms are small in relation to the total space and have little of the heavy plasticity characteristic of seventeenth-century art. Indeed, the lightness, the coloristic brilliance, and sparkling animation of the fresco unmistakably announce the coming of the Rococo.

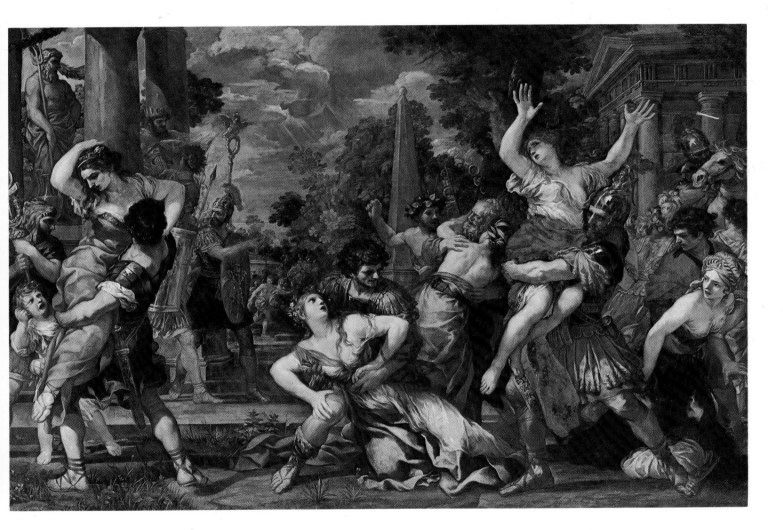

Colorplate 11. PIETRO DA CORTONA. *Rape of the Sabine Women*. C. 1629.
9′ × 13′10″. Capitoline Gallery, Rome

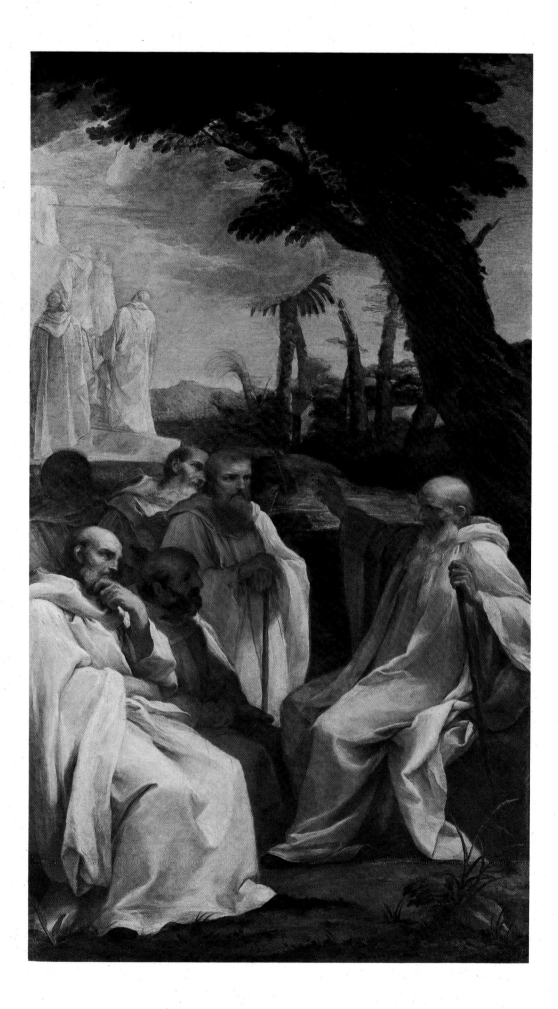

Colorplate 12.
ANDREA SACCHI.
Vision of St. Romuald. 1631.
9'10⅛" × 9'2¼".
Vatican Gallery, Rome

Colorplate 13. NICOLAS POUSSIN. *Rape of the Sabine Women*. c. 1636. 61×82½″.
The Metropolitan Museum of Art, New York (Dick Fund, 1946)

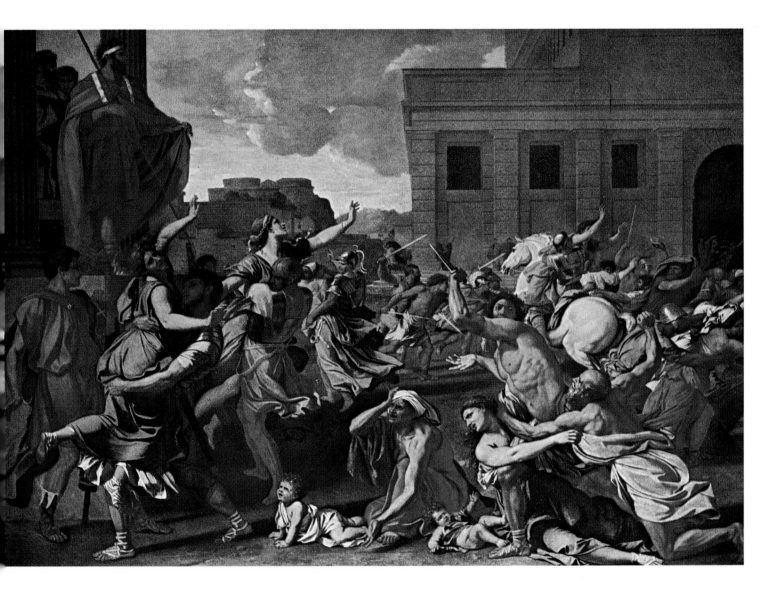

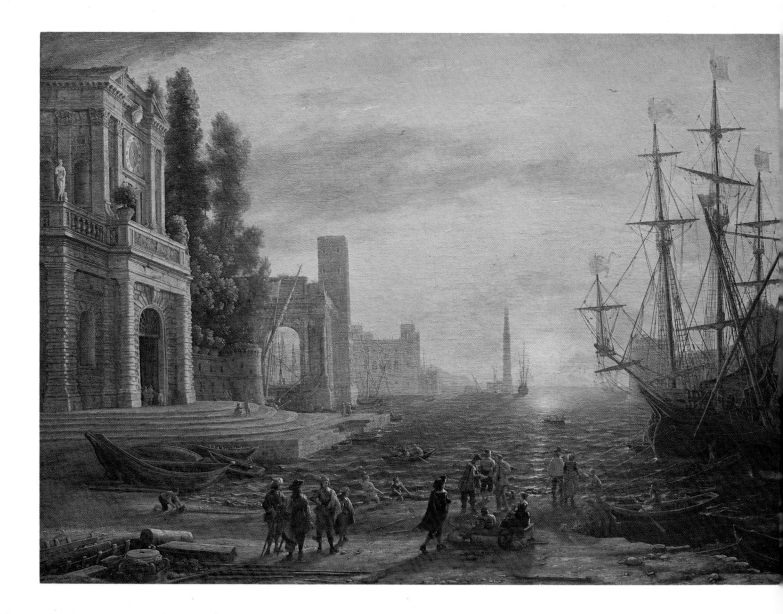

Colorplate 14. CLAUDE LORRAIN. *Seaport Scene*. 1639. 58½×76¼".
National Gallery, London

2

France in the Seventeenth Century

ARCHITECTURE

Henry IV's conversion to Catholicism in 1593, and the consequent acceptance of his authority throughout France, may be considered the first major step in the transformation of that country into a modern nation-state. The beginning made by Henry IV and his minister Sully toward national unification and centralization of power was continued (after the weak and nearly catastrophic rule of Maria de' Medici [1610–1624]) by Louis XIII and Richelieu, and later by Mazarin. When Louis XIV, assisted by Colbert, took over the reins of government in 1661, the authority of the crown was unchallenged and France was the dominant power in Europe.

The arts in France kept pace with the progressive consolidation and strengthening of the nation. In general, in the first quarter of the seventeenth century there was a continuation of the artistic patterns of the previous century; during the next fifteen years or so French artists imported and absorbed the lessons of modern Italian art; in the period from about 1640 to about 1660, in the art of François Mansart and Nicolas Poussin, the most original and undoubtedly the finest French achievements of the century were made. After

1660 there was a final consolidation and expansion of earlier accomplishments under the aegis of official academies of art.

The character of French architecture at the beginning of the seventeenth century was largely determined by Henry IV, who was especially concerned to make practical and aesthetic improvements in the city of Paris. During his reign streets were widened and paved, new quarters were built and old ones renovated. Following the king's directions, architects like Claude Chastillon and Louis Métezeau executed schemes many of which, characteristically, had been envisaged in the sixteenth century. One of these, the Place des Vosges (fig. 126), formerly known as the Place Royale, goes back to an idea of Catherine de' Medici's in the 1560s. Under Henry IV, beginning in 1603, the square was planned, and plots were sold to buyers who agreed to build according to the pre-established architectural design. For himself the king had the central, higher pavilions built on either side of the square. The houses are of brick and stucco, and the continuous line of arcades, windows, dormers, and roofs enclosing the Place des Vosges creates a restrained, graceful pattern

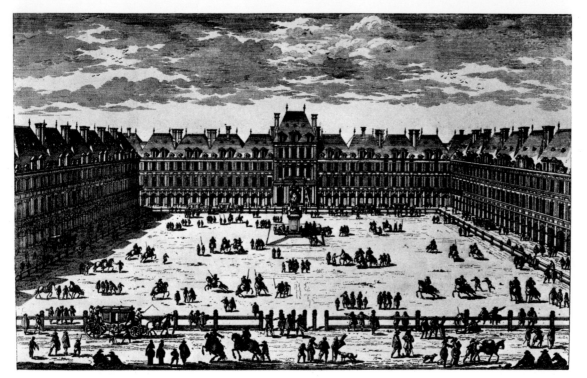

126. Place des Vosges
(formerly Place Royale).
Begun 1603. Paris
(17th-century engraving)

that still suggests residential quiet and dignity.

Architectural achievements at the beginning of the century consisted less in new ideas or inventions than in the assurance and competence with which projects were realized. The most notable architect of this period was Salomon de Brosse (1571–1626), whose best-known works today are the Palais de Justice at Rennes and the Luxembourg Palace in Paris. The latter, begun in 1615 for Maria de' Medici, is not significantly new in plan (fig. 127). The scheme, with its main block flanked by two wings, and the court thus formed

enclosed by a screen in front, goes back to sixteenth-century château plans. The specific source here seems to be the château of Verneuil of about 1565, designed by Jacques du Cerceau, who was, in fact, De Brosse's maternal grandfather. The architect's personality asserts itself most forcibly in his feeling for mass and weighty articulation. The domed entrance pavilion of the Luxembourg (fig. 128), for instance, is given bulk and density by the projecting columns, the broken line of the entablatures, and the aggressive rustication of the entire surface.[1]

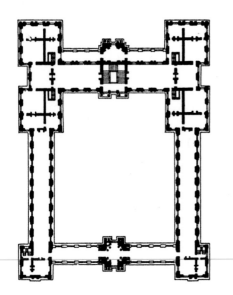

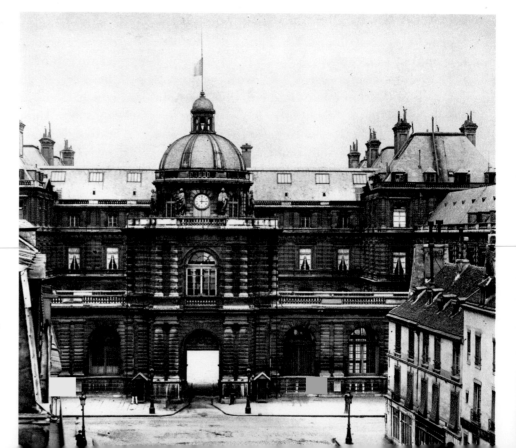

127, 128. SALOMON DE BROSSE.
Plan and Entrance Pavilion,
Luxembourg Palace.
Begun 1615. Paris

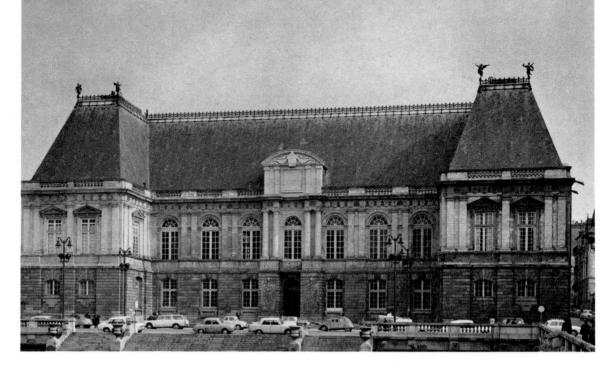

129. SALOMON DE BROSSE.
Exterior, Palais de Justice.
Begun 1618. Rennes

The Luxembourg has an air of ponderousness; in his later works at Rennes (fig. 129) and at the château of Blérancourt, which seem especially important for François Mansart, De Brosse shows the same seriousness, but he tends to be more economical in his means and more insistently correct in his use of the classical vocabulary, while at the same time highly inventive. In general, his style seems to have been inspired largely by works of the "classical" phase of sixteenth-century architecture (c. 1540–c. 1565). In 1619, in fact, De Brosse was responsible for an edition of Jean Bullant's treatise, *Règle générale d'architecture* (1565).

The influence of contemporary Italian architecture appears in France most strikingly in the work of Jacques Lemercier (c. 1585–1654), who returned to Paris by 1615 after about seven years in Italy. He became the favorite architect of Cardinal Richelieu, for whom he designed the Palais Royal, the town of Richelieu, and other works. One of the buildings commissioned by Richelieu is the Church of the Sorbonne, begun in 1635. In plan and elevation the church is almost entirely Roman in design; it has been noticed, in fact, that in many respects the church is a direct imitation of San Carlo ai Catinari in Rome (1612–20).[2] The church has two façades, one on the street and one in the court of the Sorbonne. To make it possible to see the dome in conjunction with the street, or west, façade (fig. 130), Richelieu had the Place de la Sorbonne cleared of buildings. This façade, with its superimposed Corinthian and Composite orders, its rhythm of alternating bays marked by columns and pilasters, and its volutes uniting the high upper story and broad lower story, evidently belongs to the tradition of Roman design rep-

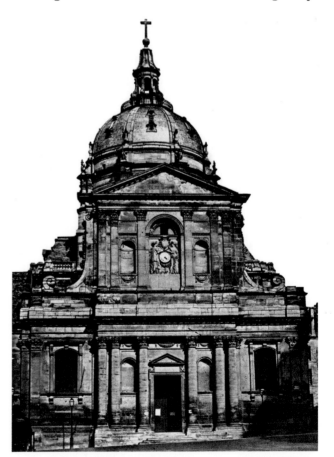

130. JACQUES LEMERCIER.
West Façade, Church of the Sorbonne.
Begun 1635. Paris

resented by Giacomo della Porta's Il Gesù façade (fig. 15).

It is significant that Lemercier's church was begun just three years before Borromini began San Carlo alle Quattro Fontane in Rome (fig. 39). The distinctive character of French seventeenth-century architecture is to a large extent explained by the fact that in the years when the baroque style was being formed in Italy, French artists were taking the conservative, "academic" tradition in Italian architecture as a point of departure for the development of their national style.

Lemercier was the kind of competent architect who offers his patrons dependability and accommodation rather than genius. Very different was François Mansart (1598–1666), who would seem to have carried inventive fertility to extravagance, and artistic integrity to obstinacy. In 1645 Mansart was commissioned by Anne of Austria to undertake a huge project for the Convent of the Val-de-Grâce in Paris. The plan (fig. 131) involved the building of a church and forecourt, additions to the convent, and the construction of a palace for the queen. Mansart had agreed to complete the church within a year and a half, but work soon fell behind schedule and expenses rose above estimates as the architect apparently changed and reworked his plans with grand indifference to the will of his patron. In 1646 he was replaced by Lemercier; all that is left of Mansart's independent work is the ground plan of the church (although partly altered), the elevation up to the first cornice, and the record of his ideas that survives in the commemorative medal and in preparatory drawings.[3]

Mansart seems to have been trained under De Brosse, and, although he never went to Italy, it is evident that his knowledge of Italian architecture, gained mostly through books, was exhaustive. The general plan for the Church of the Val-de-Grâce, with its aisleless, barrel-vaulted nave and side chapels, is dependent on Vignola's plan of Il Gesù (fig. 14), a scheme that had already been introduced to France, primarily by the Jesuit architect Etienne Martellange (1565–1641). Here,

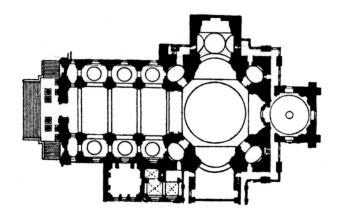

131. FRANÇOIS MANSART. Plan, Church of the Val-de-Grâce. 1645–62. Paris

however, the nave culminates in an expanded, undulating space created by the play of semicircular choir and transept apses around the domed crossing. This idea derives from Palladio's design of the Redentore in Venice.

Mansart's ability to find new forms and combinations, and to use ideas deriving from Italian and also French sixteenth-century traditions, appears in one of his earliest buildings, the Church of Ste. Marie de la Visitation in Paris, begun in 1632. The church is planned as a central domed space with radiating chapels (fig. 132). Its sources are to be found in Michelangelo's plan for San Giovanni dei Fiorentini, and in chapel designs by Philibert de l'Orme and Jacques du Cerceau.[4] However, the Church of the Visitation has an unmistakable seventeenth-century character. Unlike his models, Mansart avoided an absolute regularity of plan and created instead a pattern of related spaces that vary in size and shape.[5] Furthermore, by sinking the central floor below the level of the chapels, a dramatic heightening of the interior effect is produced. Nevertheless, for all its modernity in seventeenth-century terms, there is, in the Church of the Visitation, a sense of harmony and fine balance that differs greatly from the emotionalism and activity of such Roman baroque designs as Borromini's San Carlo (fig. 37). Mansart insists on the "classical" circle rather than the "baroque" oval for his main form; he establishes a regular rhythm of small and large bays; and he uses relatively severe and classically correct decorative detail.

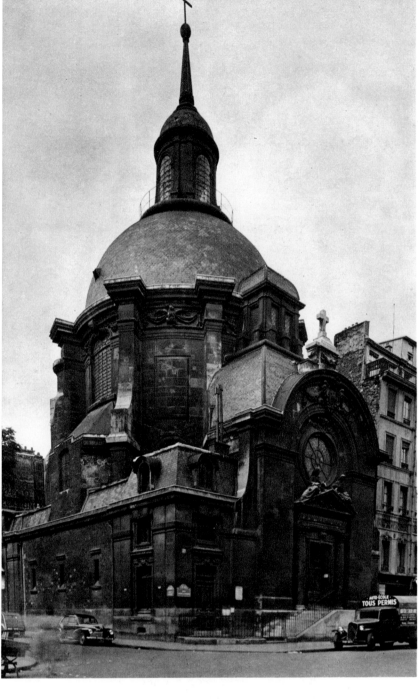

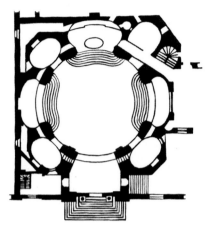

132, 133. FRANÇOIS MANSART.
Plan and Façade,
Ste.-Marie de la Visitation.
Begun 1632. Paris

The Church of the Visitation belongs to the early phase of Mansart's career, when he had still not freed himself from De Brosse's influence and was first developing the inventive classical style of the Val-de-Grâce. This is revealed especially on the exterior of the building (fig. 133), where the majestic portico is played off against the great cylinder of the church proper (the attached building to the left of the portico is a nineteenth-century addition). Instead of following classical precedent and crowning the portico with a triangular pediment (as at the Pantheon in Rome, where the same elements, rotunda and portico, are involved), Mansart used a monumental arch after the example of such sixteenth-century French architects as Du Cerceau.

The most impressive of Mansart's surviving buildings are at Blois and the château of Maisons.

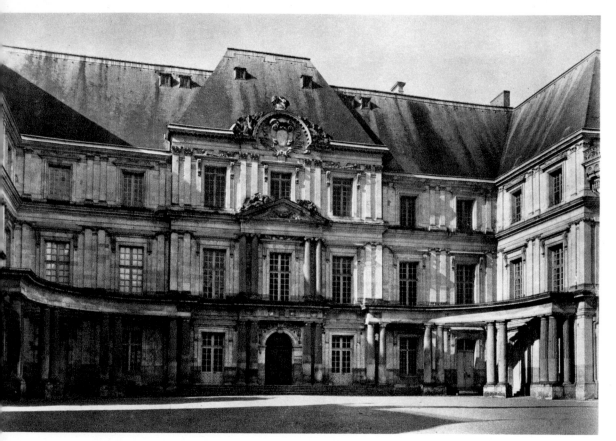

134. FRANÇOIS MANSART.
Exterior of the Orleans Wing
Château of Blois.
Begun 1635

135. FRANÇOIS MANSART.
Section, Grand Staircase, Château of Blois

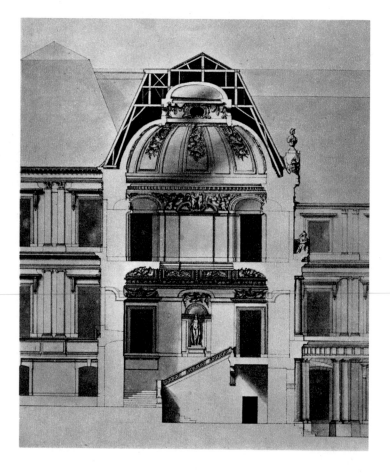

Beginning in 1635 Mansart worked for three years at Blois for Gaston d'Orléans, Louis XIII's brother. Gaston's original plan was to demolish the sixteenth-century buildings at Blois and to construct a new, huge palace. Apparently the project proved too expensive. As it is, the severely monumental block that was actually executed is one of the finest works of the century (fig. 134). Of particular interest is the grand staircase (fig. 135). The stairs themselves carry only to the first floor; on the second floor is a continuous gallery, and above that a dome and lantern. Mansart devised the idea of opening the first-floor ceiling to a view of the gallery and to the dome above, thus creating an unexpected sensation of spaciousness and luminosity. This device of the cut-off ceiling or dome with a view into the space beyond was anticipated in the small domes of the Church of the Visitation, and projected for the main dome of the Val-de-Grâce. Its final realization was in Jules Hardouin-Mansart's Church of the Invalides (fig. 148).

Between 1642 and 1646 François Mansart built

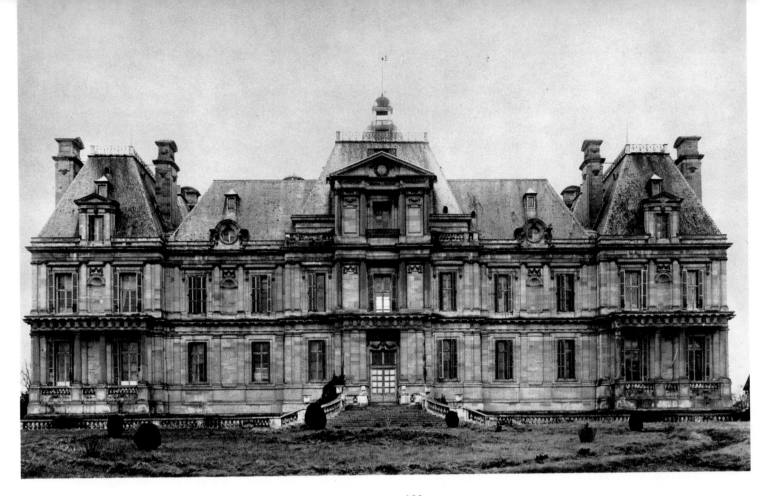

136. FRANÇOIS MANSART
     Garden Façade, Château of Maisons. 1642–46

137. FRANÇOIS MANSART and JACQUES SARRAZIN.
     Vestibule, Château of Maisons. 1642–46

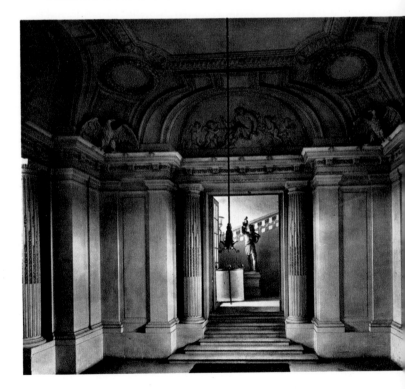

the château of Maisons, just outside Paris (figs. 136, 137). Elements of its design can be traced back to De Brosse, and in part it elaborates on ideas that Mansart had formulated at Blois. Nevertheless, it is a remarkable and completely original product of the architect's maturity. Unlike the traditional château, which is planned in units around a central court (fig. 127), Maisons is designed as an independent, freestanding building, like an Italian Renaissance palace and, significantly, like De Brosse's château of Blérancourt. It is composed of a main block flanked by two projecting pavilions. Each of these three massive units is separately roofed,[6] and the grouping and articulation of their parts is complex and varied. Yet all elements are brilliantly interrelated in an over-all design that makes every detail seem the logical consequence of a closely reasoned plan. On the garden façade the dominant theme of three related masses is reflected in the division of the main block into a central pavilion and two side sections. It is stated in the A-B-A rhythm of the frontispiece, which is repeated, with the relation of wall to opening reversed, by the windows and niches on the end wings and on either side of the central pavilion. By breaking the outline of the roof Mansart insists on the division of the main block into three units and, in addition, on the five-part rhythm that is created across the entire façade. The latter is echoed in the grouping of the five middle bays of the building. The theme of the pedimented frontispiece and rising roof behind it is sounded again in the pedimented dormers and high roofs of the end wings. The deep recesses and the columns of the upper two stories of the frontispiece reappear in the porticoes on the ground floor of the side pavilions.

The wall surfaces of Maisons, primarily articulated by pilasters, are treated with linear severity. The surface planes are always stressed, but at the same time the building is emphatic in its plastic, sculptural qualities. Flanked by the two end wings, the wall of the central block moves forward in a series of steps that culminate in the frontispiece with its recessed middle bay of door and windows. This movement in depth is, of course, heightened by the play of light and shade on the building. In his very real concern for space and movement, Mansart reveals his community with seventeenth-century architects everywhere in Europe. However, at Maisons and in other works, Mansart expresses a distinct and characteristically French approach to art. Essentially, in his insistence on clarity of relationships, in his inventive and sophisticated application of the classical

vocabulary, and in his predominant use of planar, rectilinear forms, Mansart created an architecture that makes its primary appeal to the intellect; as such, despite such details as the broken pediment, it is far removed from the subjective and frequently "licentious" architecture of the baroque style in Italy and elsewhere.

At Maisons one is also able to appreciate Mansart's brilliance and originality in planning and decorating interior spaces. In the vestibule, for instance, the smooth planes of paneling and pilasters are combined with full columns to create a space that is rich in movement and plasticity. The sharply cut stone, without color, provides dignified, elegant ornamentation. The over-all effect is one of classical perfection. Mansart was no pedant, however, and in the vestibule he felt he could relax the severity of his classicizing posture. Almost playfully, he designed a charmingly incorrect Doric frieze and unconventionally filled the flutings of the Doric columns with sprays of foliage.

In the 1660s Mansart was, of course, one of the architects considered for the project to complete the Louvre. His independent and arrogant temperament would seem to have made it a foregone conclusion that he was not to be chosen by the efficient administrator Colbert. However, a large group of drawings by Mansart for the Louvre survive today. Unlike Perrault and his circle (colorplate 16), Mansart approached the problem in terms of traditional French design; his own work at Blois and Maisons stands behind his project for

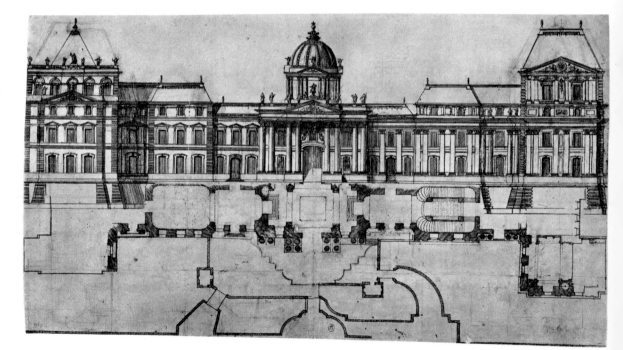

138. FRANÇOIS MANSART.
Project for ground plan
and elevation of
East Façade, Louvre.
c. 1664.
Pen and ink, and black chalk.
Bibliothèque Nationale,
Paris

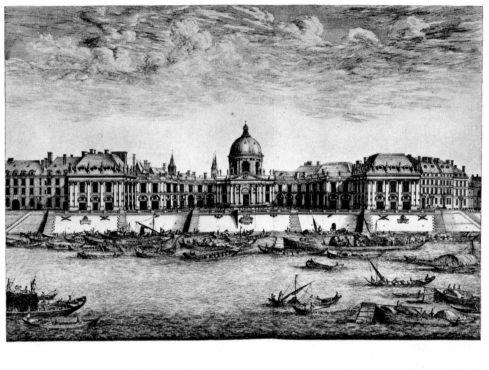

139. LOUIS LE VAU.
Exterior, Collège des
Quatre Nations
(Institut de France).
Begun 1662. Paris
(etching by
Israel Silvestre, 1670)

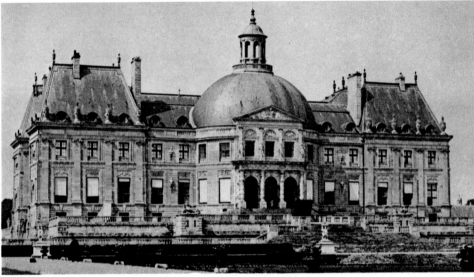

140. LOUIS LE VAU.
Garden Façade,
Château of
Vaux-le-Vicomte.
1657–61

the east façade of the Louvre (fig. 138). This is the work of an old man, who was no longer in touch with the needs and ideas of the time; but the inexhaustible fertility of his mind is astonishing. The architect presents alternatives, variations, and combinations on left and right sides of his plans and on flaps and overlays added to them.

A more businesslike architect than Mansart was Louis Le Vau (1612–1670). Beginning in the late 1630s he was a highly successful builder of private town houses and country châteaux, and before 1660 he had become one of the artists favored by the state. In 1654 he succeeded Lemercier as architect of the Louvre, and in 1662 he began the Collège des Quatre Nations (the present Institut de France; fig. 139). He used a classical vocabulary, but with a certain carelessness, as he strove for grand and picturesque effects. His most impressive building is the château of Vaux-le-Vicomte (fig. 140), built for the minister of finance, Fouquet, between 1657 and 1661. Like Mansart's Maisons, it is planned as a massive freestanding block, but it has none of Mansart's subtlety of design and detail. The great oval salon (an early and important example of such a room rising open through two stories) looks rather swollen and even out of place in its projection on the garden façade, and the frontispiece seems pasted on rather than being logically related to it. Yet the total effect is bold and imposing and, set in Le Nôtre's garden (colorplate 15), the château stands in weighty splendor.

André Le Nôtre (1613–1700), who has a good claim to being the greatest artist in the history of European landscape architecture, came from a family of royal gardeners. He learned the craft under his father, who was head gardener of the Tuileries. In addition, Le Nôtre studied in the shop of the painter Simon Vouet, and he received sound architectural training, perhaps with Lemercier or François Mansart. By 1635 he had been appointed First Gardener to Monsieur, the king's brother. The main forms of the classical French garden, where nature is ordered according to regular, symmetrical, and carefully delineated patterns, had been established in the sixteenth century. Le Nôtre's contribution consisted in perfecting a conception of the formal garden in which all parts are seen in terms of a vast, unified, three-dimensional composition, carefully related to and harmonized with the building. In his plans irregularities of terrain are considered and used to advantage. He insists on variety in forms and motifs, and he constantly offers surprises and new vistas to the spectator. There is always, however, controlling and linking all elements, a dominant scheme that seems worked out with mathematical exactitude. Le Nôtre played down the use of the relatively small, complexly patterned floral areas which proliferated in sixteenth-century gardens. Instead, he gave a major role in his designs to water—to the shimmering play of fountains and, above all, to the calm, luminous expanses of canals and pools, with their brilliant reflections.

At Vaux-le-Vicomte, Le Nôtre created his first great work. Behind the château the ground falls away gradually toward a small valley. Le Nôtre designed a progression of descending terraces that are marked by transverse axes and bisected by a broad central axis. The terrace nearest the house is dominated by the carpetlike, colorful *parterres de broderie* (such designs originated in embroidery patterns). Farther on, the beds are plain, vast stretches of green, surrounding circular fountain pools and accented by lines of topiary work. Continuing past the semirustic "grotto," the central axis begins to rise slowly as it climbs a hill, and the view culminates in the distance in a statue of Hercules, seen against the dark background of the woods.

The building, gardens, and decoration of Vaux were created by a team of artists: Le Vau, Le Nôtre, Le Brun (see pages 160–64). This team was taken over by Louis XIV, and, in the 1660s, it was put to work at Versailles. Louis XIII had built a small château there, and his son conceived the idea of constructing a palace, gardens, and town on the site. The land was swampy, water was scarce, anticipated expenses were astronomical; but at Versailles Louis XIV saw his chance to dazzle the world with the grandeur of his projects and with his power to realize them. The immensity of the scheme is best seen in old plans (fig. 141). Three avenues, the central one leading from Paris, cross the town and converge on the Place d'Armes, which opens onto the courtyard of the palace. From the other side of the palace the central axis cuts a path through the formal gardens, a great area subdivided into handsomely patterned squares and rectangles, and sweeps down to the Basin d'Apollon (Apollo, the sun-god, is a symbol of Louis XIV). Beyond begins the Grand Canal, stretching (incredibly, considering the original scarcity of water) more than a mile. Subsidiary axes crisscross the park, which, in some sections, is labyrinthine, but the main lines of the plan rule the whole. Le Nôtre's feeling for space and mass appear in the immense vistas that he created, in the great mirrors of water, and in the bulk and volume of the trees that define and model spaces. At Versailles, Le Nôtre had an almost unlimited field for "architecting" nature. The result was that the land was bent to an ideal of geometric

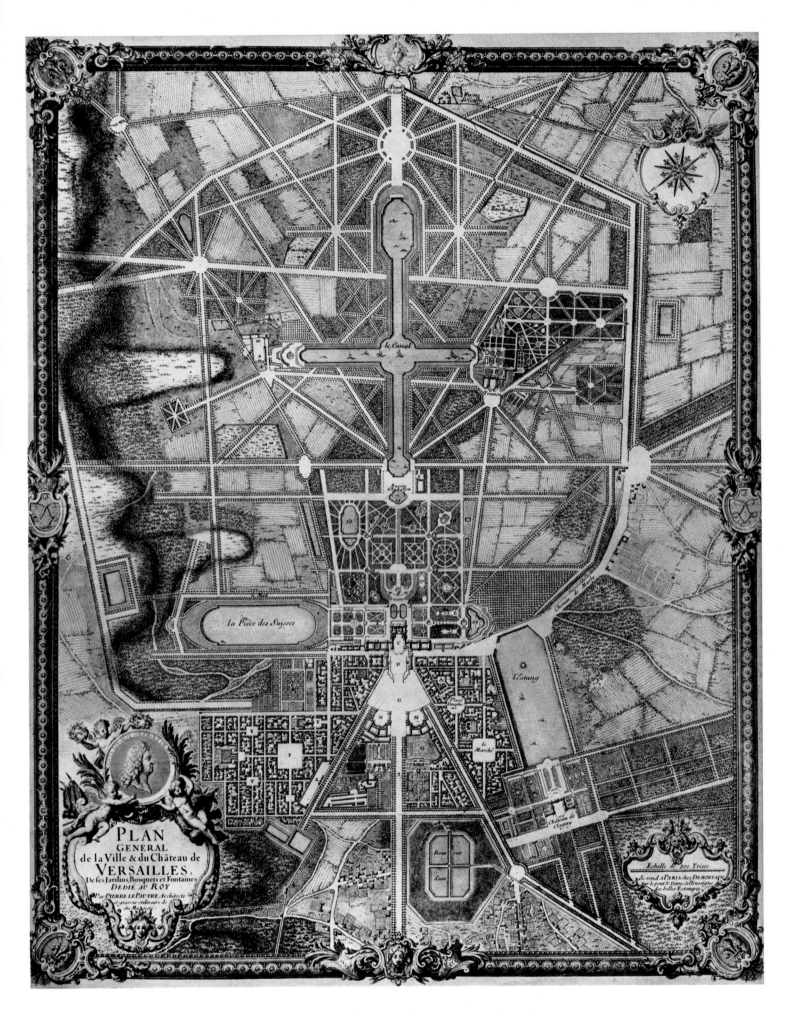

141. Plan, Versailles (town, palace, and gardens). 1660s (engraving by Pierre Le Pautre)

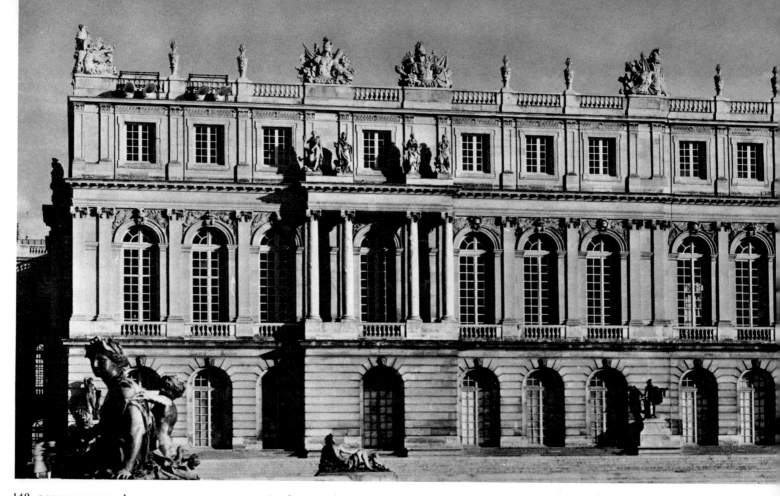

142. LOUIS LE VAU and JULES HARDOUIN-MANSART. Garden Façade (portion), Palace of Versailles. 1669-85

rationality and harmony, an ideal not far removed from Poussin's vision of the classical landscape (fig. 161).

Major construction at Versailles continued well into the eighteenth century. The over-all plan developed in stages, and from the beginning Versailles was a work of true collaboration. Le Nôtre's ideas were worked out with Le Vau and then with Jules Hardouin-Mansart, who succeeded Le Vau as architect in charge of Versailles. Le Vau was responsible for the first major enlargement of the château. In 1669 construction was begun according to a plan that preserved the old structures on the court side but encased them in a new building on the garden front. In its scale, its treatment of masses, and sense of proportion, this façade (known from engravings) was one of Le Vau's masterpieces. The haughty first story, articulated with Ionic pilasters and columns and crowned by the square bays of the attic, rests splendidly on the solid base provided by the ground floor. Today, the noble elevation can be only partly appreciated (fig. 142). In Le Vau's façade of twenty-five bays, solidity and depth were produced by setting back the middle eleven bays. Beginning in 1678, however, these bays were filled in by Jules Hardouin-Mansart to create the Galerie des Glaces (Hall of Mirrors; fig. 143); at the same time Mansart's addition of lateral wings, which tripled the width of the façade (fig. 144), completely destroyed the scale and proportion of Le Vau's design.

The Galerie des Glaces is one of the most dazzling interiors in a palace renowned for its splendor. The gallery is about two hundred and forty feet long and is flanked by two large square rooms, the Salon de la Guerre and the Salon de la Paix. Le Brun decorated the barrel vault of the gallery with paintings glorifying Louis XIV. The walls are richly ornamented with white and colored marbles and gilded bronze. The gallery can be

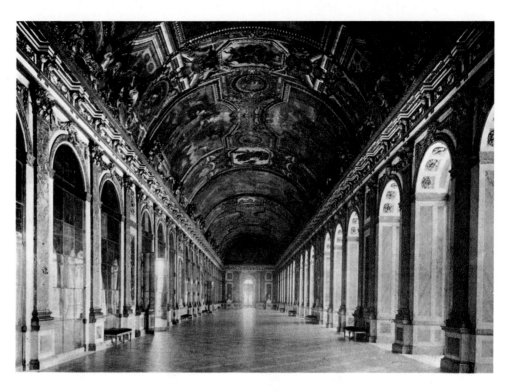

143. JULES HARDOUIN-MANSART
and CHARLES LE BRUN.
Galerie des Glaces.
Begun 1678. Palace of Versailles

properly appreciated only as one walks the long distance from one end to the other. The continuous row of arched windows opening on the garden and, on the opposite wall, the huge mirrors that reflect light and seem to extend space create a sensation of grand and stately formality.

Regrettably, the superb Staircase of the Ambassadors at Versailles was destroyed to make room for new constructions during the reign of Louis

144. Air View, Palace of Versailles

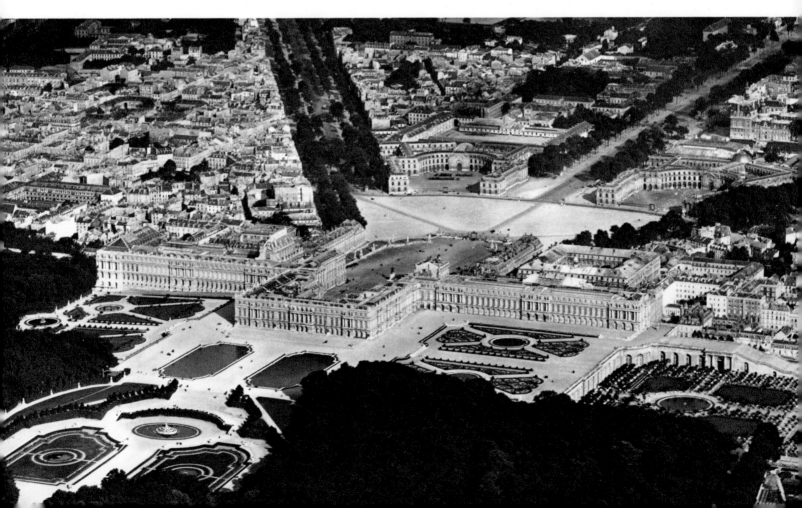

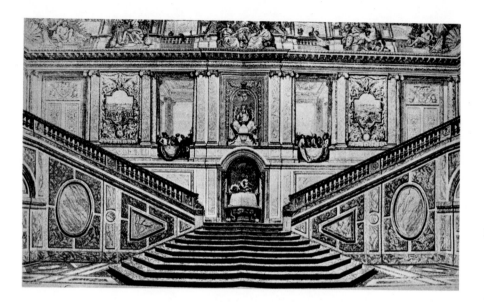

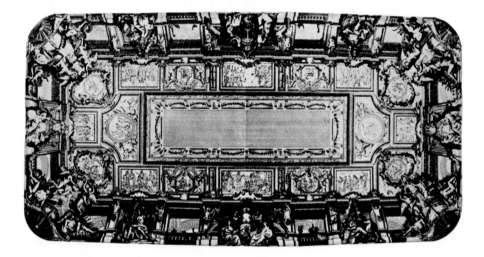

145, 146.
LOUIS LE VAU and FRANÇOIS D'ORBAY.
Staircase of the Ambassadors,
and Ceiling (by CHARLES LE BRUN).
1671–80. Palace of Versailles
(18th-century engravings)

XV. Some idea of its magnificence is conveyed by Chevotet's print (fig. 145). The staircase, begun in 1671 and finished in 1680, had probably been planned by Le Vau, but its final form must owe much to his assistant, François d'Orbay (1631–1697), who was in charge of the actual construction.[7] Le Brun was responsible for the decoration (fig. 146). The hall was narrow, but the design made maximum use of the available space. The broad first flight of stairs led to a landing dominated by a fountain and surmounted by a bust of Louis XIV (by Jean Warin). From here a long flight on either side led to a gallery above. The illusionistic paintings on the walls and vault expanded the space, and the sumptuous paneling of colored marbles was radiant in the light that fell from the skylight.

Versailles was the king's project. The Louvre was really the project of his minister Colbert, who considered the palace in Paris the main showplace of the state. The building of the modern Louvre was begun in the mid-sixteenth century and continued by the architects of Henry IV and then, under Louis XIII, by Lemercier. Le Vau completed work begun by Lemercier, and by the early 1660s the one outstanding task that remained was the construction of the great east façade. Designs proposed by Le Vau and François Mansart (see pages

134–36) did not satisfy Colbert, who then asked the leading architects of Italy—Bernini, Pietro da Cortona, and Rainaldi—to submit plans for the palace. Bernini's ideas (and his reputation) warranted an invitation to Paris.

The ultimate rejection of Bernini's plans for the Louvre symbolize a major shift in the geographic orientation of European art. For centuries Italy had dominated the art of Europe, and Colbert had imagined that only in Italy could he find artists capable of doing justice to the grandeur of the French monarchy. However, after the months that Bernini spent in Paris in 1665, it became evident that French temperament was not in sympathy with an Italian Baroque style and, furthermore, that national pride and ambition would not endure the arrogantly superior posturings of foreign artists.[8] The Louvre was to be finished by Frenchmen, and in the next few decades French art, following the political fortunes of the nation, was to achieve hegemony in Europe.

In 1667 Colbert created a Buildings Council to settle the problem of the Louvre design. The council consisted of Le Vau, the painter Le Brun, and Claude Perrault (1613–1688), who was a practicing physician, a scientist, scholar, and architectural theorist, and responsible for an edition of Vitruvius in 1673. Perrault's brother Charles served as secretary of the council. The plan submitted by the committee for the east façade of the Louvre was executed between 1667 and 1670 (colorplate 16). Since the seventeenth century there have been partisans of Le Vau and of Perrault in assigning primary responsibility for the scheme.[9] Important elements in the design clearly depend on Le Vau, but the final result has an archaeological cast that points to the erudite Perrault. The central block and the colonnade are adaptations from Roman temple designs, and, though the coupled columns, for instance, are decidedly "modern," the details are treated with exemplary correctness. Thus the façade may evoke an image of the French crown as the patron and protector of the Western classical tradition. The real brilliance of the scheme, however, is in the sense of majesty and noble repose that it conveys. The central pediment creates the only break in the long horizontal line of the entablature, which sweeps across some five hundred and sixty-five feet. The end pavilions provide quiet but solid terminations for the building. And rising from the simple, unornamented first story is the soaring colonnade with its rhythmic continuity of paired Corinthian columns, a fluted screen in front of the shadowed loggia.

Apparently, the Louvre experience convinced Colbert of the need for a permanent, professional body through which the government could create standards for the nation's architecture and supervise its development. In 1671 he ordered the establishment of the Royal Academy of Architecture. Significantly, the Academy's first director, François Blondel (1617–1686), while a capable designer, was primarily an architectural theorist. Blondel gave public lectures at the Academy,[10] and the academicians assembled regularly in an effort to codify the "rules" of architecture. The treatises of the "authorities" (such as Vitruvius and Palladio) were studied and compared, and the buildings of ancients and moderns were analyzed. While unanimity of opinion on such matters as the precise nature of *le bon goût* in architecture could not be expected, at least general principles could be established, and these helped to define and promote the national style. No one in France questioned the ideal of rational, clear, and harmonious architectural expression, and it could easily be agreed that the broken pediments and extravagant ornamental forms used by Borromini and his followers were contrary to good sense and to the best examples of antiquity. The principle of "decorum" was invoked to justify the use of the high French roof, which, one argued, was dictated by the northern climate. The Academy's influence, however, extended beyond aesthetic matters to the practical business of construction. The Academy offered advice on such technical details as the use of cramps for masonry; it helped to clarify laws and customs that concerned architects and builders; it located and assessed the quality of stone quarries. Largely as a result of the Academy's activities the development of French architecture was assured stylistic coherence and a very high level of competence in design and construction.

The leading French architect of the end of the seventeenth century was Jules Hardouin-Mansart (1646–1708). He had been a student of his great-uncle François Mansart, but he also learned much from the aggressive, grandiose style of Le Vau. He was well suited to continue work at Versailles, which, as has been mentioned, was put in his charge in 1678. The chapel at Versailles and the Church of the Invalides (fig. 147) in Paris are probably his most impressive works. The latter,

begun in 1676 but only finished in 1706, was added to Libéral Bruant's building for disabled soldiers (1670–77). Its centrally planned space and the interior elevation (fig. 148) are derived from one of François Mansart's designs for the Bourbon funerary chapel at St. Denis.[11] The most remarkable feature of the interior is the high dome, where Mansart used the device invented by his uncle (see page 132), the cut-off ceiling. The inner, first dome rises from a high drum pierced by tall, large windows. This dome is cut off at the top, and the spectator looks through it to the second dome, where a painted heavenly apparition (*St. Louis in Glory,* by La Fosse) suggests an infinite space

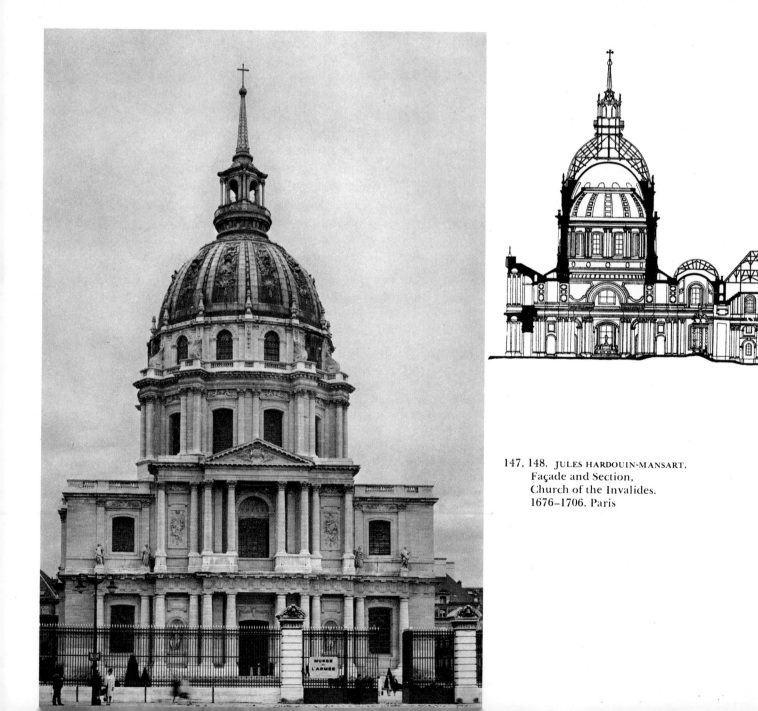

147, 148. JULES HARDOUIN-MANSART.
Façade and Section,
Church of the Invalides.
1676–1706. Paris

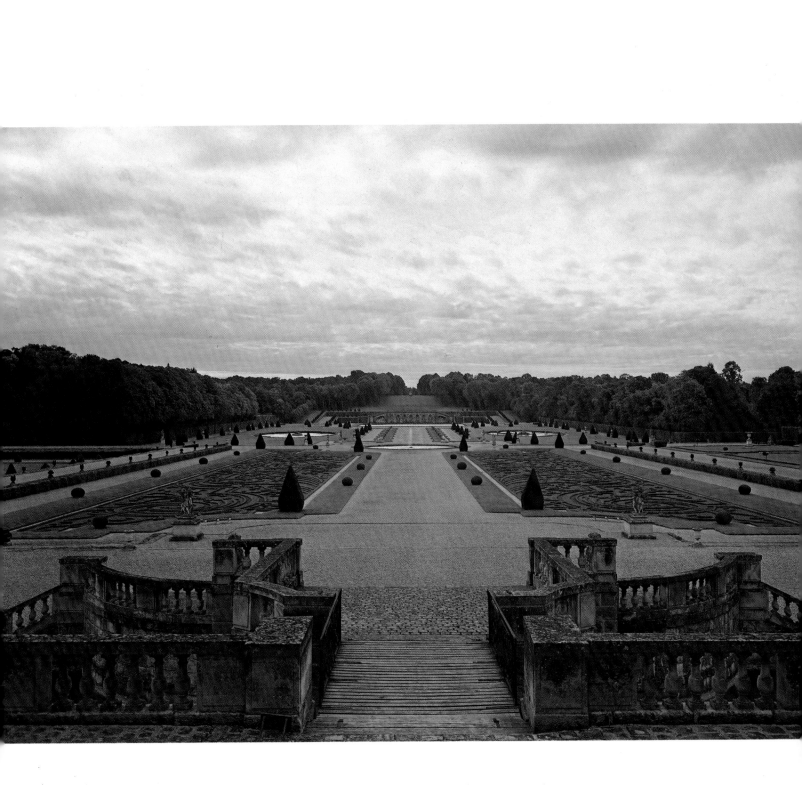

Colorplate 15. ANDRE LE NOTRE. View of Garden, Château of Vaux-le-Vicomte. Begun 1657

Colorplate 16. LOUIS LE VAU, CHARLES LE BRUN, and CLAUDE PERRAULT. East Façade, Louvre. 1667–70. Paris

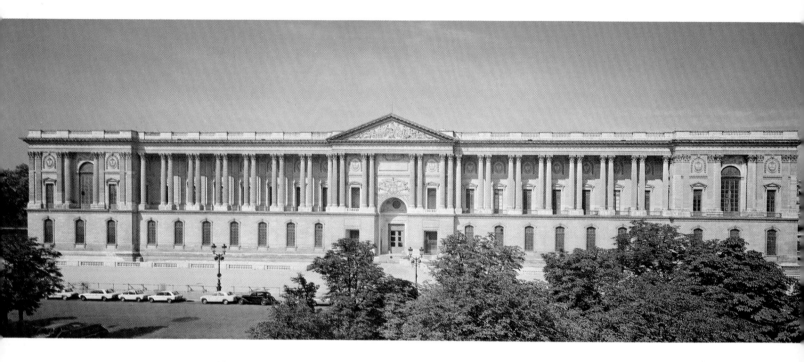

above. The sense of openness, and also of drama, is enhanced by the light filling the upper space, coming from hidden windows in the outer dome.

Mansart insists on sharply defined, precise, and correct articulation of details, and in the dome, for instance, he stresses the unbroken lines of the cornices. However, the grandiose, dramatic organization of space is quite unlike François Mansart's restrained and subtle compositions. On the façade, too, although the carefully planned disposition of rectangular shapes recalls the elder Mansart (see fig. 136), the massing of elements, with forceful projections and deep recesses, produces a complexity that seems aimed more at richness of effect than at intellectual excitement. The drum is de-signed with an alternating rhythm of one and two windows and buttresses between them. This is unconventional, but effective in creating movement. The dome itself, with its drum and attic, seems to telescope upward as it continues the vertical thrust of the columns below.

A comparison of Jules Hardouin-Mansart with his uncle suggests the change that occurred in French art after 1660. The taste of the age no longer encouraged a purposefully restrained style like that of François Mansart; Jules Hardouin-Mansart, by combining lucid, rigorous organization and aggressive monumentality, provided the perfect architectural expression for the reign of Louis XIV.

PAINTING

Seventeenth-century painting in France may be said to begin only around 1625. Early in the century, "official" court painting, represented by the second school of Fontainebleau (artists like Ambroise Dubois, Toussaint Dubreuil, and Martin Fréminet), was characterized by a conservative, mediocre Mannerist style. In Lorraine, then politically independent, Jacques Bellange was working between 1600 and at least 1617, but he practiced an extreme late Mannerist style that, rather like El Greco's in Spain, properly belongs to the history of sixteenth-century art.

Jacques Callot (1592/93–1635) seems to bridge the two centuries, although his work never quite took root in the new one. Callot returned to his native Lorraine in 1621 from Italy, where he had gone about 1610. He had worked for a decade in Florence as an engraver at the court of Cosimo II de' Medici, and it is the sophisticated hyper-elegance of the Tuscan court that provides the background for Callot's witty, incisive, and still Manneristic representations of festival scenes, *commedia dell'arte* characters, and similar subjects. However, in much of his work after his

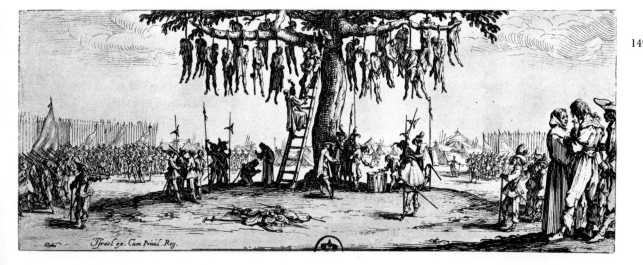

149. JACQUES CALLOT.
*Miseries of War:
Hangman's Tree.*
1633. Etching.
Bibliothèque Nationale,
Paris

return to Lorraine there is a new directness in pictorial approach and a new seriousness in content. He produced gripping war scenes that seem to anticipate Goya (fig. 149), religious prints of great poignancy, and sensitive landscape drawings and etchings. Still, although aspects of Callot's work may have been of some importance for Georges de La Tour,[12] in general he stands outside the main trends in the development of French art. Indeed, it was modern Italian art, especially the styles of the Carracci and Caravaggio schools, that was the primary source for painting in France in the seventeenth century.

Caravaggism was brought to France fairly early in the century. It had relatively little success in Paris,[13] but its importance was great in the provinces, where it provided a modern foundation for the new generation of painters and where, in some instances at least, its direct, naturalistic approach was probably felt to accord well with local religious attitudes.[14] As early as the second decade Louis Finson, a Flemish follower of Caravaggio, came from Italy and settled in Provence. Many others, like Nicolas Tournier in Toulouse and Jean Leclerc in Lorraine, imported and disseminated the style in France; but the most brilliant and original French artist who derived from Caravaggio was Georges de La Tour of Lorraine (1593–1652).

Little is known of La Tour's early career. It is not unlikely that he went to Italy before 1620, although there is no proof for such a trip. It seems certain, however, that he traveled in Holland in the early 1620s and came in contact with some of Caravaggio's Dutch followers. There is, in fact, in La Tour's early works an emphasis on naturalistic surface effects and a use of a relatively high-keyed palette that suggest, in particular, the influence of Terbrugghen (colorplate 35). However, even in his early paintings La Tour's own personality is strikingly evident in his tendency to create surface patterns and to generalize and stylize forms. The *Woman with a Flea* (fig. 150), probably dating from the mid-1630s, is a low-life theme which is also known from exam-

ples in Dutch art.[15] However, the coarseness of the subject has been transmuted by La Tour's feeling for the inherent geometry of form. Surfaces are to be read as broad planes of colored light and shade; a sharp line defines edges and contours; in front of the bare wall the severe verticals and horizontals of the chair play against the curves of the figure. The stylization and formal abstraction of La Tour's works seem extraordinarily modern (fig. 10), and it is no accident that after having been long forgotten, the artist was rediscovered in the twentieth century.

La Tour's paintings are predominantly night scenes, illuminated by candle or torchlight, a device that he probably learned from Honthorst's circle (colorplate 30). However, unlike Honthorst, and unlike Caravaggio, La Tour did not assign to light a primarily dramatic or naturalistic function. For him light was another element of pictorial pattern and stylization and it serves at once to animate and to unify the forms. In *St. Irene Curing St. Sebastian* (colorplate 17), the flames of the torch, curving like twisted ropes, throw an

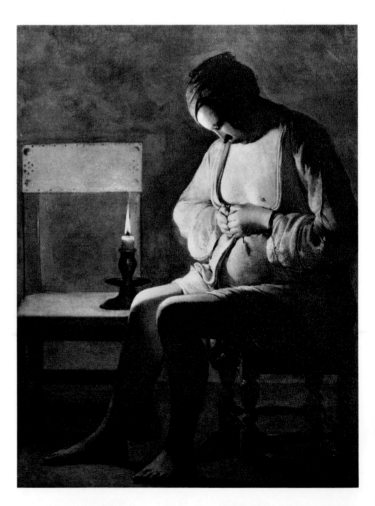

150. GEORGES DE LA TOUR. *Woman with a Flea.*
c. 1635. 47¼ × 34⅝".
Musée des Beaux-Arts, Nancy

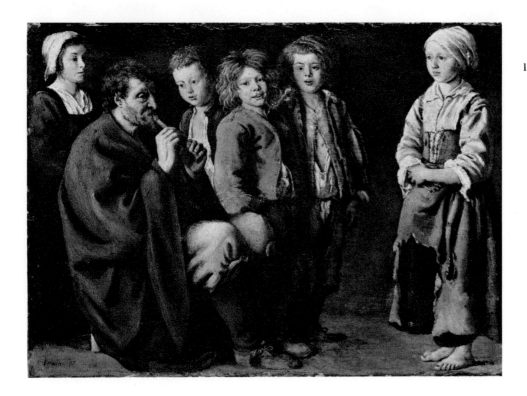

151. ANTOINE LE NAIN.
Village Piper. 1644.
Copper, $8\frac{1}{2} \times 11\frac{1}{2}''$.
Detroit Institute of Arts

even, coppery light on the figures and create a rhythmic sequence of illuminated planes. The effect is ostensibly naturalistic, but one soon realizes that the flickering activity of torchlight has been quieted, and that the smooth, generalized light surfaces are the result of invention and not observation. An air of compelling mystery is created by the treatment of light and form in La Tour's religious paintings like the *St. Sebastian* (which work, incidentally, is ultimately derived from Caravaggio's *Entombment of Christ* in the Vatican Gallery). Details disappear in the warm glow of his strange light, and the essentials of form and gesture, generalized and refined, and arranged with almost mathematical precision, appear as frozen abstractions in the stillness of night.

The painting of the Le Nain brothers may be considered dependent on Caravaggism if this movement is understood in the broadest sense. Major questions still remain to be solved regarding the work and careers of the three brothers: Antoine (1588–1648), Louis (1593–1648), and Mathieu (1607–1677). We know that they came from Laon, near the Flemish border, but there is

no record of their activity before they established themselves in Paris about 1630. They had a communal shop and apparently collaborated on some paintings, and it is frequently difficult to distinguish their hands. Although they produced some history pictures and altarpieces, they are known principally for genre painting, in which they did their best work. This field was, of course, considered a minor artistic activity in the seventeenth century, and, although the brothers were successful enough to attract imitators, their work could not exercise any real influence on the main trend in French painting.

The Le Nains' paintings offer no sure starting point for identifying their individual personalities; scholars have divided pictures by, and accepted as, Le Nains into three more or less coherent groups and, on the basis of the source literature, given a name to each. Antoine was known for miniatures and small portraits; a group of genre pictures, mostly small and many painted on copper, with suggestions of the influence of Netherlandish sixteenth-century art, are attributed to him (fig. 151). Far superior in quality is the group given to Louis, who was traditionally

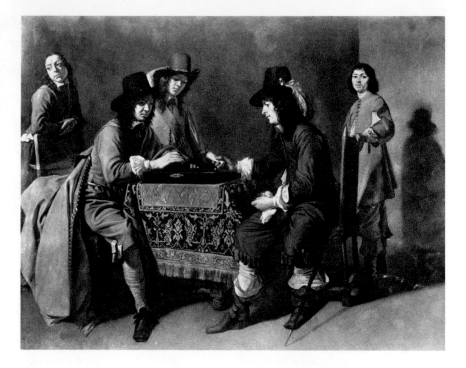

152. MATHIEU LE NAIN.
Trictrac Players. c. 1660.
$35\frac{3}{8} \times 47\frac{1}{4}''$.
The Louvre, Paris

called "le Bon" or "le Romain." The latter epithet suggests that he had been to Rome, and this is supported by the paintings given to him, which seem strongly influenced by Bamboccio and his followers. However, in paintings like *The Cart* (colorplate 18), rural scenes are substituted for Bamboccio's urban scenes (fig. 94).

Most often in Louis' work families of peasants sit or stand in or outside their homes and look gravely, even melancholically, at the spectator. Activity is kept to a minimum. Details are handled with strong realism, and everything is immersed in a cool, grayish light. There is something almost puritanical about these severely static compositions and monumentally stolid figures; and in the light of the artist's uncompromising naturalism, they convey a profound feeling for human dignity and worth.

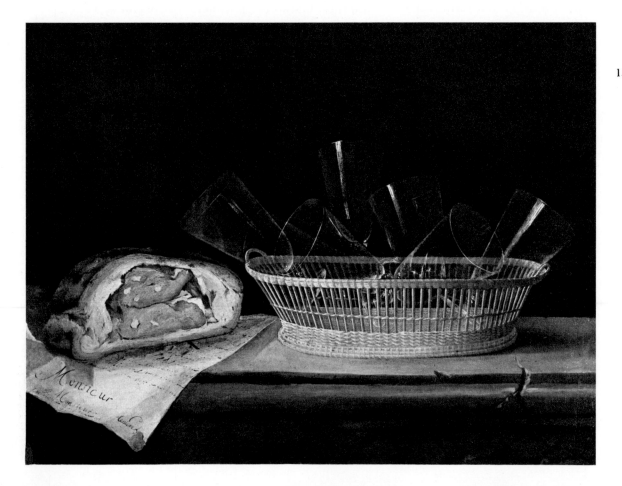

153. SEBASTIEN STOSKOPFF.
Pâté and Basket of Glasses.
$19\frac{1}{2} \times 25''$.
Musée des Beaux-Arts, Strasbourg

Mathieu was certainly influenced by his brother Louis, but he specialized in what may be called bourgeois genre scenes. He was a member of the Paris militia, and many of his pictures, like the *Trictrac Players* (fig. 152), represent officers gaming or drinking. Mathieu's paintings have nothing of the sober, studied organization or psychological penetration of Louis' works, but they are admirable for their liveliness and acuity. Interestingly, his pictorial solutions are often quite similar to those evolved by such Dutch painters as Thomas de Keyser, Van der Helst, and Terborch, and it seems certain that he was familiar with Netherlandish painting of the first half of the century.

In general, the art of the Netherlands had a rather limited influence in France. French still-life painters, men like Sébastien Stoskopff (1597–1657), whose work (fig. 153) has come to be appreciated again only in recent years,[16] of course stand as important exceptions. Otherwise, it is notable that even Rubens' *Maria de' Medici* cycle, painted for the Luxembourg Palace in the 1620s (see pages 204–205), aroused little enthusiasm among French painters. However, Philippe de Champaigne (1602–1674), who was born and trained in Brussels, shows, especially in his early

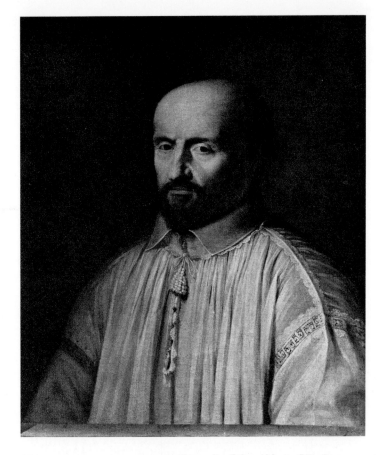

154. PHILIPPE DE CHAMPAIGNE. *Portrait of the Abbot of St. Cyran.* 1643. 29×22½". Museum, Grenoble

155. PHILIPPE DE CHAMPAIGNE. *Mother Agnes and Sister Catherine.* 1662. 65×90⅛". The Louvre, Paris

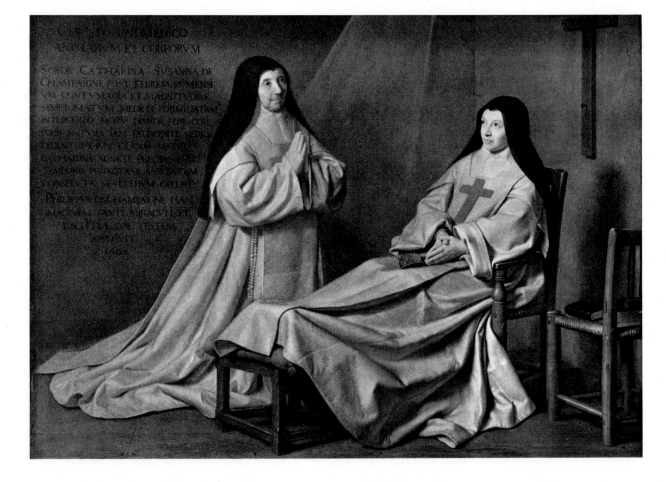

works, his indebtedness to Rubens. This is evident in his lighting, his smooth handling, and in some of his realistic types; but from the beginning he tended to avoid the baroque exuberance of Rubens' compositions. Champaigne moved to Paris in 1621 and soon became successful as a religious painter. However, his finest works are his portraits; in these he never flatters his sitters, yet he invests them with grave and imposing dignity (fig. 154). The seriousness and candor of his style were not attuned to the superficial and glamorous ideals of the aristocracy and the socially ambitious bourgeoisie, and he was patronized largely by intellectuals and serious men of finance and government. It seems wholly fitting that he was the favorite painter of the severe, self-disciplined Cardinal Richelieu.

In the 1640s Champaigne came in contact with the Jansenists, who practiced an extremely rigorous, austere, and unorthodox form of Catholicism. The painter's daughter was a nun in the Jansenist Convent of Port-Royal, and his own strong sympathies with the movement seem reflected in the increasing solemnity of his style. Champaigne's masterpiece is the *ex voto* of 1662 (fig. 155), which celebrates the miraculous cure of his daughter, Sister Catherine, who had been paralyzed for over a year. Sister Catherine and Mother Agnes, the prioress of the convent, are seen in prayer. The forms are arranged with a

kind of geometric precision against the bare background, and they are defined with the same sharp clarity as the explanatory inscription at the left. The colors are restrained, grays and blacks predominating. There is none of the display of emotion and excitement so typical of the Italian and Flemish Baroque; here the miracle proceeds from the passionate solemnity of prayerful meditation.

Although La Tour, Louis Le Nain, and Champaigne were rivaled by few other French painters, they were essentially the product of local or peripheral artistic trends. The main tradition of French seventeenth-century painting was developed in Paris, and had its roots in the style of the Carracci and their followers. This style was introduced to France by Simon Vouet (1590–1649), who, at the beginning of his career, had actually been a follower of Caravaggio. Vouet was trained in France as a portrait painter, and he traveled to London, Constantinople, and Venice before he went to Rome in 1614. In Rome he was immediately attracted by the Caravaggesque style, and his earliest known paintings, portraits and genre pictures dating from around 1615, are closely related to the work of Manfredi and Valentin de Boulogne (fig. 156; see fig. 91). In the 1620s, when the popularity of Caravaggism was declining in Rome, Vouet began to study the works of the Carracci and their followers, especially Guido Reni, and he learned also from con-

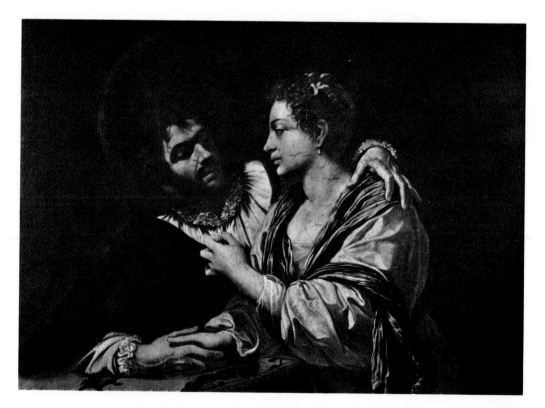

156. SIMON VOUET. *The Lovers*
c. 1617. 38½ × 53½"
Collection Pallavicini, Rome

temporary Genoese and Venetian artists. By the time he returned to France he was thoroughly familiar with modern Italian painting. His reputation had grown considerably in the twenties, and in 1627 Louis XIII called him to Paris and appointed him First Painter to the King.

Vouet was ambitious and willing to please. These qualities, supported by his marvelous facility as a painter and his experience in Italy, made him eminently suited for the role he was called on to play in Paris. He established a large shop to execute the great number of commissions that he received from the king, the queen mother, and especially from members of the newly rich and powerful middle class. His patrons generally wanted showy, decorative pictures, painted in the modern "Italian manner" and untroubled by intellectual complications or deep feeling. Vouet's French works draw extensively on Italian models, but his interpretations of them tend invariably toward the pretty and the ornamental. At their best Vouet's works are enchanting in their decorative exuberance. The *Toilet of Venus* (fig. 157), which dates from the late 1630s, is based primarily on one of Francesco Albani's versions of the theme, while the figure of Venus is taken from Annibale Carracci's *Venus and Anchises* (colorplate 5). It is characteristic that the anatomical solidity of the figures and the weighty composition of Annibale's fresco are replaced in Vouet's work by brightly colored polished forms bound together by an elaborate and elegant curvilinear network, which is rather like a sumptuous ribbon on a gift package.

Vouet trained the leading artists of the next generation—Le Sueur, Le Brun, Mignard—and through him the main ideas of modern Italian painting were first established in Paris. This is what his contemporaries meant when they credited Vouet with being the first to introduce *le bon goût* to France.[17] It was not Vouet, however, but the expatriate Nicolas Poussin who provided the basis for a distinct French style in the seventeenth century. Vouet's great contribution had been to prepare France to understand and assim-

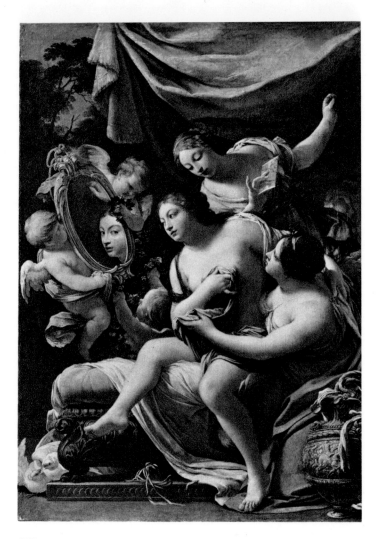

157. SIMON VOUET. *Toilet of Venus*. Late 1630s. 65⅜ × 45". Carnegie Institute, Pittsburgh

ilate Poussin's style, which was, of course, predicated on recent developments in Italian art (see pages 111–12).

In the late 1630s the king and Richelieu began to press the by then famous Poussin to return to France. Poussin went to Paris, although with misgivings, in 1640. The artist was well treated, but the commissions he was forced to accept were not to his liking. Poussin preferred to paint relatively small easel pictures, but in France, besides large altarpieces, he was charged with such work as the decoration of the Long Gallery in the Louvre.[18] Also, although his position was secure, he suffered from the jealousy of many French artists (especially Vouet), who quite understandably felt threatened by him. Finally, in 1642, Poussin returned to Rome, where he remained until his death in 1665.

Despite its short duration, Poussin's stay in Paris was crucial for his own development and for the development of French art. Poussin made new friends and patrons in Paris, and after his return to Italy the bulk of his production was destined for France. Many of Poussin's patrons, mainly minor civil servants, bankers, and merchants, participated in or were in sympathy with the revival of Stoic philosophy in seventeenth-century France. What these men wanted from the arts was not a glamorous display of the kind that Vouet offered his patrons, but lucid, didactic illustrations of human behavior in the context of serious ethical problems.[19] Although Poussin, before he went to France, had already created dramatic narratives such as the *Rape of the Sabine Women* (colorplate 13), in which he emphasized the expression of human passions, his preference then was for many-figured, romantic, picturesque subjects. After 1640, certainly inspired by his new friends, he concentrated on more profound religious and historical themes. Scenes from the Bible that illustrate individual moral decision (fig. 160), and paintings of ancient Stoic heroes (fig. 161), are characteristic of his mature works.

French artists were quick to recognize the power and vitality of Poussin's art. Moreover, the lucidity of his style, with its descriptive precision and reasoned organization, appealed to a passion for order and clarity that had by then become an important part of the nation's cultural character (and which has suggested the term "classical" to describe French culture of the seventeenth century). This French ideal of form and expression illumines the dramas of Corneille and the writings of Pascal and Descartes;[20] and it even seems to distinguish the works of La Tour and Louis Le Nain from those of Italian and Netherlandish Caravaggisti and Bamboccianti. But, in painting, this ideal received its finest and most complete realization in the art of Poussin.

Poussin's style represents an extreme statement of the so-called classical trend in seventeenth-century painting. It is based above all on devotion to the art of antiquity and that of Raphael, and to the more recent example of the Carracci and their followers. Because of his concern for clarity and conciseness and for ideal beauty, Poussin had little sympathy with the baroque exuberance of Pietro da Cortona or the naturalism of Caravaggio and his followers. It is therefore somewhat surprising to find Poussin going back to Caravaggio's *Madonna of Loreto* (fig. 89) for his representation of the *Holy Family with Saints Elizabeth and John* in the Musée Condé, Chantilly, of about 1640, for which there is a preparatory drawing in Windsor Castle (fig. 158). However, Poussin's picture must be understood as a critique of Caravaggio. What the Frenchman appreciated was essentially the grand monumentality of Caravaggio's *Madonna,* and even this group, which he studied carefully, he rearranged so that the Virgin is balanced and steadied. She stands straight and tall with the majesty of a queen. Caravaggio's coarse peasants, his deep mysterious shadows, and his diagonal composition were eliminated or revised. Poussin's figures are defined with sharp clarity in a light-filled space,

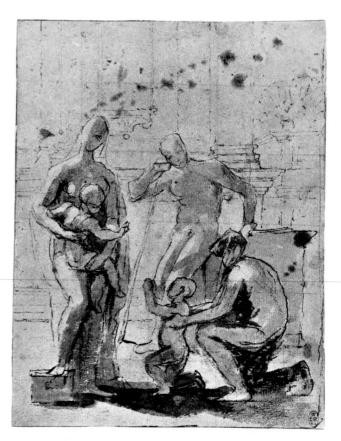

158. NICOLAS POUSSIN.
Holy Family with Sts. Elizabeth and John. c. 1640.
Ink wash and chalk, 8⅜ × 6⅜".
Windsor Castle

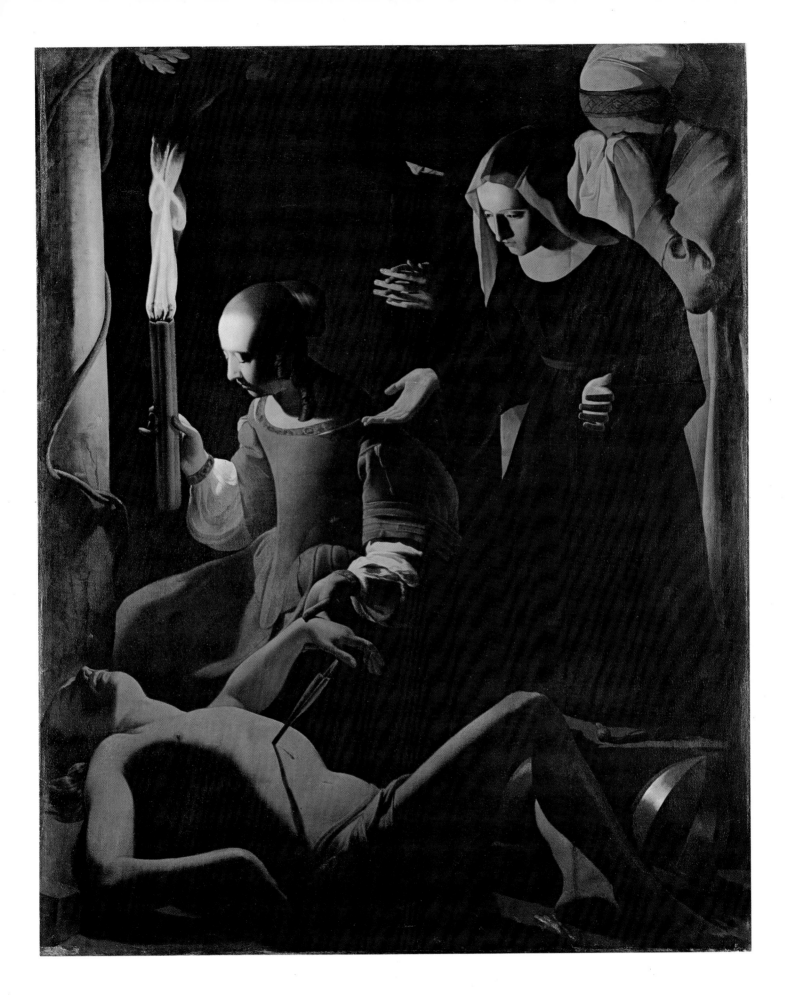

Colorplate 17. GEORGES DE LA TOUR. *St. Irene Curing St. Sebastian*. c. 1648. 63 × 50¾".
Dahlem Museum, Berlin

Colorplate 18. LOUIS LE NAIN. *The Cart*. 1641. 22 × 28¼". The Louvre, Paris

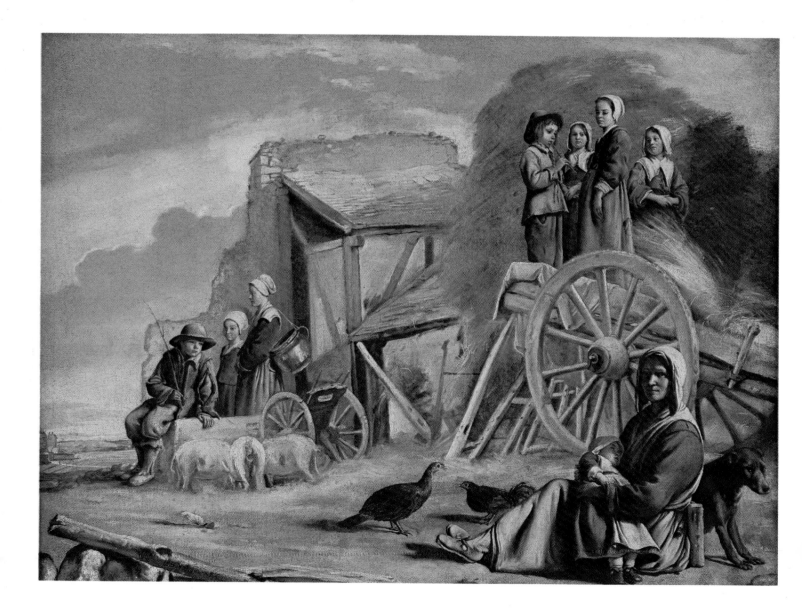

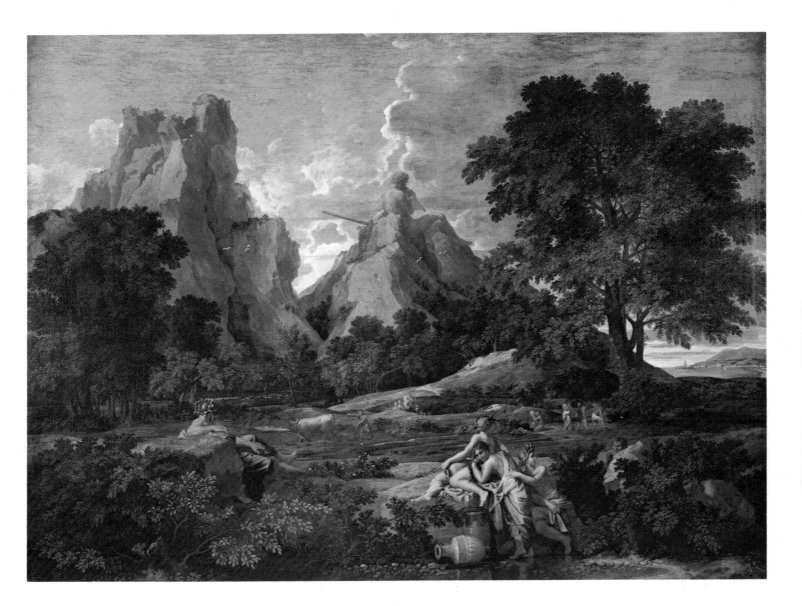

Colorplate 19. NICOLAS POUSSIN. *Landscape with Polyphemus.* Late 1650s. 58¼ × 77½″.
Hermitage Museum, Leningrad

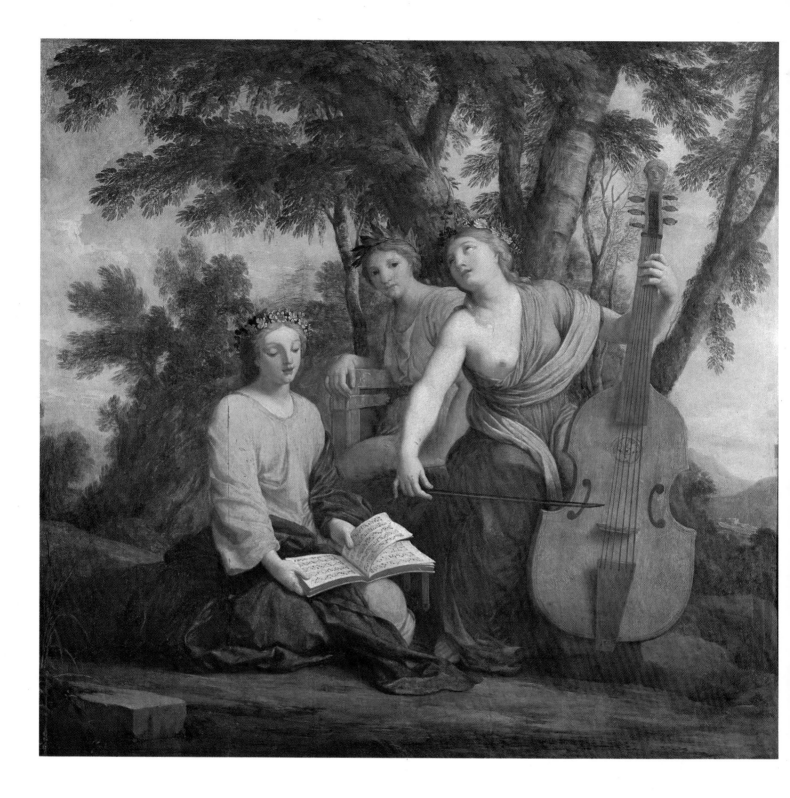

Colorplate 20. EUSTACHE LE SUEUR. *Muses Polyhymnia, Melpomene, and Erato.* c. 1645. 52 × 54⅜″.
The Louvre, Paris

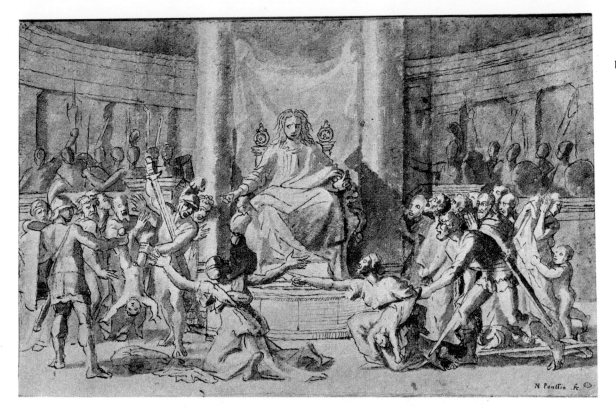

159. NICOLAS POUSSIN.
Judgment of Solomon.
1649.
Pen and bistre wash,
9⅝ × 15⅛".
Ecole des Beaux-Arts,
Paris

and their arrangement on the picture plane makes the whole resemble a sculptured low relief.

By the mid-1640s Poussin had developed a new grand style, his *maniera magnifica*. In this period his initial ideas, sometimes startlingly violent in their emotionalism (fig. 159), were carefully ordered and adjusted. His forms now have a new monumental solidity, and his compositions are sometimes rigid in their severity and laconic organization. Stylistically, the grandeur and concentrated dramatic power of this phase of his art reflect, above all, his intense devotion to the example of the late works of Raphael. Behind Poussin's *Judgment of Solomon* (fig. 160) there is Raphael's version of the subject in the Vatican Loggie, and also Raphael's *Blinding of Elymas* and *Death of Ananias* from the series of Vatican tapestries. Poussin's enthroned Solomon, enclosed

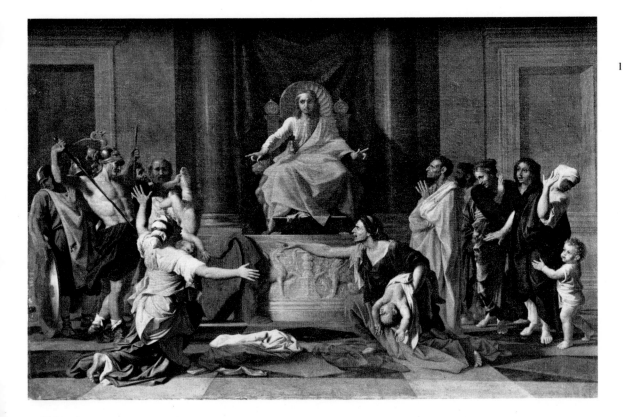

160. NICOLAS POUSSIN.
Judgment of Solomon.
1649.
39⅜ × 59".
The Louvre, Paris

157

by two great columns, is placed on the picture's central vertical axis. The upper edge of his footstool marks the horizontal axis. The other figures are grouped symmetrically beneath and on either side of the king, who has just ordered the disputed infant to be divided. The gesture of the soldier on the left, who is about to execute the command, is answered by gestures of horror from the chorus of onlookers at the right. In the foreground the wicked mother with her dead child shrieks her assent to Solomon's order; the good mother opens her arms in a plea for the life of the child. Thus the wise Solomon makes his judgment. On this theater-like stage the passions of man are revealed with stark and compelling directness.

Although Poussin painted landscapes early in his career, he began to take a serious interest in the subject only toward the late 1640s. Inspired by the ideal landscapes of Annibale Carracci and Domenichino (fig. 98; colorplate 8), Poussin's landscape pictures of this period show a similar but still more developed feeling for the structure and organization of nature. They almost seem composed of geometric solids, carefully placed and balanced in a deep, exactly measured space and sharply defined in the clear, bright sunlight. In *The Ashes of Phocion Collected by His Widow* (1648; fig. 161), stately trees with thick foliage stand like pylons at the entrance to the landscape.

A road curves gently back across a grassy field to the city of Athens. Behind, in the distance, are the rugged mountains of Attica. This is a "civilized" landscape, dominated and given shape by man. It is Poussin's vision of the natural world of his beloved ancients, where buildings and temples establish the pattern for the architecture of nature.

This painting is one of a pair; the other, the *Funeral of Phocion,* is now in the collection of the Earl of Plymouth. The Athenian general Phocion, whose story is told by Plutarch, was a Stoic hero. Because of his courageous dedication to truth Phocion was falsely condemned for treason, executed, and refused burial within the city walls. The *Funeral of Phocion* shows his body being carried out of the city. After Phocion was cremated his widow gathered his ashes, which, with the advent of a new and just regime, were given deserved honor.

Landscapes became increasingly important for Poussin, and they almost dominate the production of his late period. In what may be called his old-age style, beginning toward the mid-1650s, Poussin was more relaxed, no longer so severe, and his compositions were treated with greater freedom of organization, while his handling was broader and looser. This corresponds to a change in subject matter in the artist's final period. In his late works, often iconographically enigmatic,

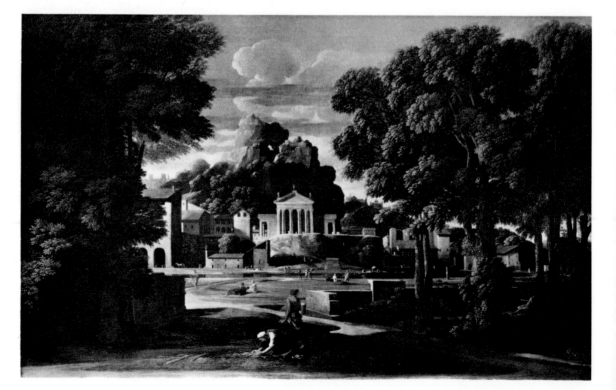

161. NICOLAS POUSSIN.
The Ashes of Phocion Collected by His Widow.
1648. 45⅝ × 69¼".
Collection Earl of Derby, Knowsley, England

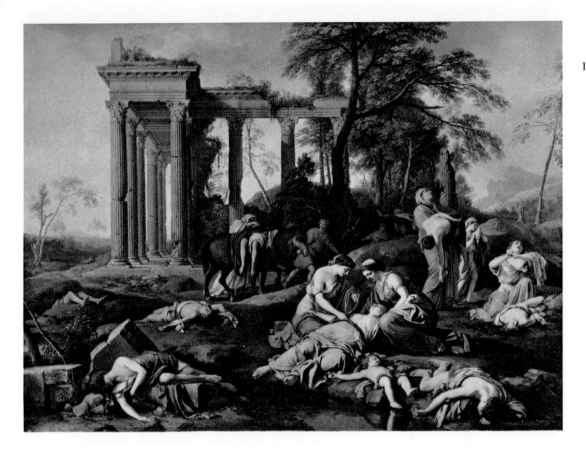

162. LAURENT DE LA HIRE.
*The Children of Bethel
Mourned by Their Mothers*
1653. 38¼ × 50¾".
Museum, Arras

an idyllic lyricism tends to replace the heroic didacticism of his earlier subjects. The old Poussin, perhaps influenced by the philosophic speculations of friends and acquaintances,[21] turned to themes of cosmic significance. The efforts of individual man are ignored or appear inconsequential in these pictures that stress the primacy of nature and its unalterable laws: the grand patterns of history; the rhythm of change of the seasons; the continual transmutation of the elements; the recurrent cycle of life and death.[22] In Poussin's *Landscape with Polyphemus* (colorplate 19), probably dating from the late 1650s,[23] man, diminutive in the middle distance, takes his first steps toward civilization as he begins to till the soil. Nature is still wild, luxuriant in its growth. The air is vibrant, tremulous. The giant Polyphemus, perhaps representing the earliest age of the earth, seems to grow out of the living rock. He pipes his love song to the green-haired nymph Galatea, who hides from him in the foreground. She and her companions may represent the secret forces of nature.

From the 1640s on, French painting was decisively affected by the art of Poussin. His influence is very clear in the works of such artists as Philippe de Champaigne,[24] Laurent de La Hire (1606–1656), and Eustache Le Sueur (1616–1655). Although he lacked Poussin's vigor, La Hire produced works that impress us by their fine feeling for linear precision, calculated arrangement, and tonal control (fig. 162). Le Sueur began his career as a student of Vouet's, and his works from about 1640 show him completely dependent on his master. However, in the second half of the 1640s he abandoned Vouet's elegant and ornamental style and turned to Poussin and Raphael (whose works he knew mainly through engravings) for inspiration. His *Muses* (colorplate 20), painted about 1645, is obviously modeled after figures in Raphael's *Parnassus,* while in the linearism and dominant planarity of the composition the artist was following the lead of Poussin's contemporary style. Le Sueur did not have Poussin's masculine force and intellectual profundity, but his work is distinguished by graceful, gentle forms as well

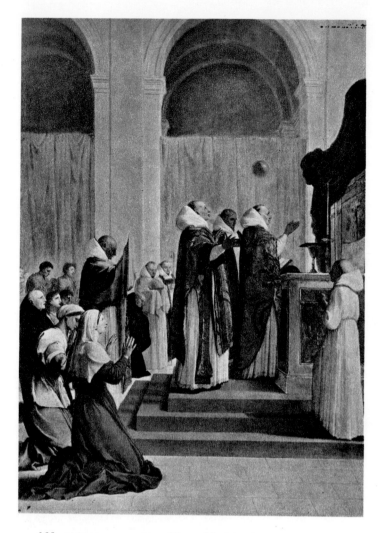

163. EUSTACHE LE SUEUR. *Mass of St. Martin of Tours*. 1655.
44⅞×33⅛". The Louvre, Paris

as by luminous, delicate color.

Le Sueur's late religious paintings are especially appealing for their sense of calm and dignified piety. The *Mass of St. Martin of Tours* (fig. 163) was painted in the last year of Le Sueur's life. It illustrates the story of the bishop, St. Martin, whose archdeacon was slow to obey his order to give clothing to a beggar. When the poor man complained, St. Martin, preparing to celebrate Mass, gave him his own tunic. During the Mass a ball of fire, signalizing St. Martin's virtue, miraculously appeared above his head. Like Philippe de Champaigne (fig. 155), Le Sueur shows an emotional reticence in depictions of miraculous events that seems characteristically French. Indeed, this attitude was fostered by the teachings

and activities of such leading French religious figures as St. François de Sales and St. Vincent de Paul, whose "devout humanism," with its emphasis on reasonableness and on social service, might be described as a French "classical" Catholicism. In the *Mass of St. Martin* the composition, closed behind by the great arches and the broad expanse of curtains and constructed of repeated verticals and horizontals, suggests the sober calm of pious devotion. The miracle causes no excitement; only a few figures are aware of it, and their gestures are restrained and quiet.

Le Sueur, who died young, was overshadowed by another member of his generation, Charles Le Brun (1619–1690). Le Brun studied with Vouet before going to Rome in 1642, where he was in contact with Poussin. Many of the paintings he made in Rome and in the years immediately following his return to Paris in 1646 are close imitations of Poussin's work. As Le Brun developed a personal style in the 1650s, however, he proved able to make use of contemporary Italian sources as unlike Poussin as Pietro da Cortona. In his decorations at Vaux-le-Vicomte in the late 1650s, and later in the Louvre and Versailles (fig. 143), he adapted elements of Cortona's baroque style in order to satisfy his patrons' taste for elaborate and luxurious display as well as for controlled expression.

It is probable that Le Brun was an artist spoiled by a too easy success. His early works indicate natural gifts that were never completely realized, and only occasionally did he produce a really first-rate work. One of them—indeed, one of the finest portraits of the century—is the equestrian portrait of his first patron, the chancellor Séguier (fig. 164). The picture, which has been called the "French classical answer" to the baroque equestrian portrait type created by Rubens and Van Dyck,[25] possibly shows Séguier at the entry of Louis XIV and Maria Theresa into Paris in 1660. It is at once highly naturalistic in treatment and extremely formalized in presentation. The chancellor sits on his handsome horse in the very center of the composition. His pages seem to revolve around him as the procession moves forward at a ceremonial pace.

Le Brun's artistic talents were complemented by his administrative and political abilities. In 1648 he was the leading spirit behind the foundation of the Royal Academy of Painting and Sculpture. The original purpose of the Academy was to free artists from the still medieval restrictions of the old painters' guild and to elevate their social and intellectual status. In the first decade of its existence the Academy was rather loosely organized and fairly tolerant in its aesthetic position. By the 1660s, however, Le Brun managed, with the official support of the king's minister Colbert, to gain control of the Academy, and he held it until Colbert's death in 1683. As chancellor of the Academy he dictated the art theory of the institution and directed its pedagogical program. Success for an artist in Paris was now possible only through the Academy, and success in the Academy depended on Le Brun's favor.

The doctrines of the French Academy were the most rigid in Europe. Based on earlier art

164. CHARLES LE BRUN. *Equestrian Portrait of the Chancellor Séguier.* Before 1661. 9'8⅛" × 11'6¼". The Louvre, Paris

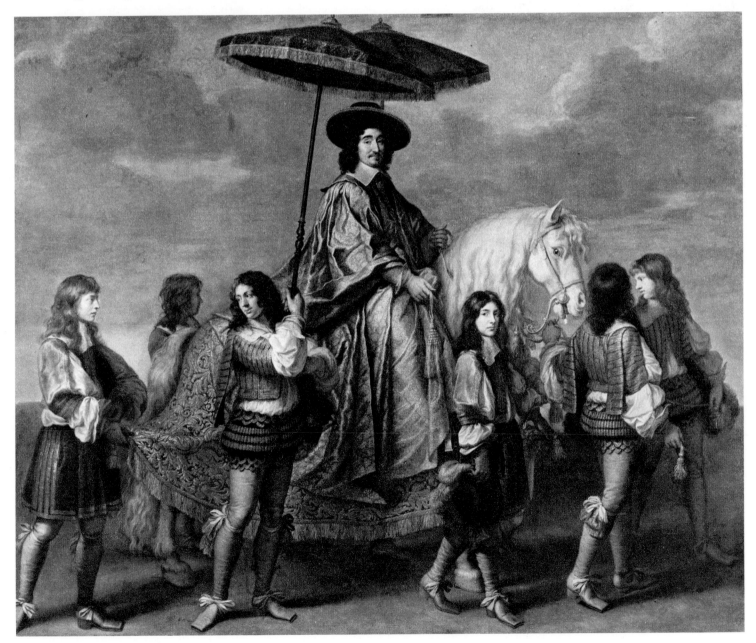

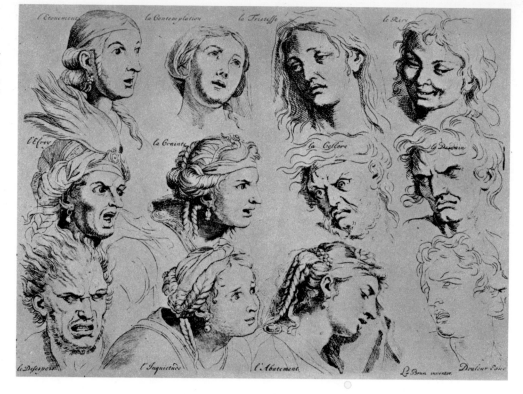

165. CHARLES LE BRUN.
The Expressions
(from *Traité des passions*,
Paris, 1698)

writers, from Leon Battista Alberti to Franciscus Junius, artistic theory in France was developed and codified during the 1660s and '70s in the course of lectures and discussions in the Academy and in writings of men like Fréart de Chambray who were connected with the Academy.[26] Convinced that art was a rational activity, the theorists analyzed the "parts" of painting—invention, expression, composition, drawing, and color—and strict rules for them were established. Le Brun himself lectured on expression, providing visual touchstones for the representation of specific passions (fig. 165). The rules undoubtedly hampered the development of genius, but they assured a relatively high level of artistic competence. The artist was to be learned and well versed in history and literature, for his pictures had to be morally enlightening in content and accurate in detail. For Le Brun and his circle the severe art of Poussin, and that of Poussin's ideals, antiquity and Raphael, provided the unimpeachable examples for the modern painter. In practice artists could not always be faithful to these examples, and, as we have seen, Le Brun himself, especially in his decorations, introduced elements derived from Cortona's work. However, such

compromises were subtly explained or, more often, conveniently ignored.

In France, academies owed their success in large part to their effectiveness as instruments of the state. Richelieu and Mazarin had succeeded in establishing the absolute authority of the monarchy and in bringing France to a position of unassailable dominance in Europe. Under Louis XIV, Colbert continued their work and expanded the bureaucratic machinery of government. Colbert recognized that the arts could serve the interests of the nation and played an active role in encouraging and directing their development. The academies trained and organized cadres of artists to execute the great projects of the reign of Louis XIV. The art of France contributed to the extension and deepening of the nation's influence beyond its borders; the cult of Poussin, who was known as the "French Raphael," added to the glory of France. In 1666 the French Academy in Rome was founded; by the end of the century French art had taken the pre-eminent position in Europe.

Le Brun was the ideal man to lead official French painting in these years. A highly competent artist, he was also extremely versatile: he

162

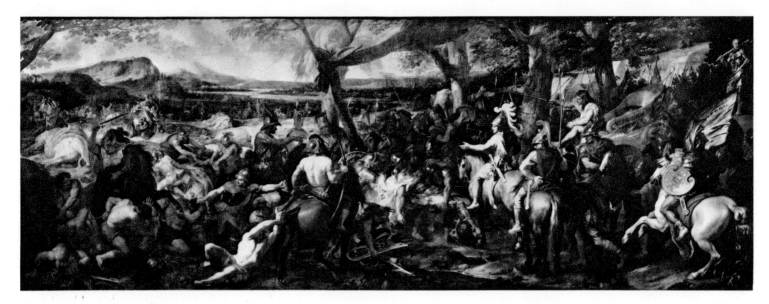

166, 167. CHARLES LE BRUN.
Defeat of Porus by Alexander.
1665–68. 15′5″ × 39′4½″.
The Louvre, Paris

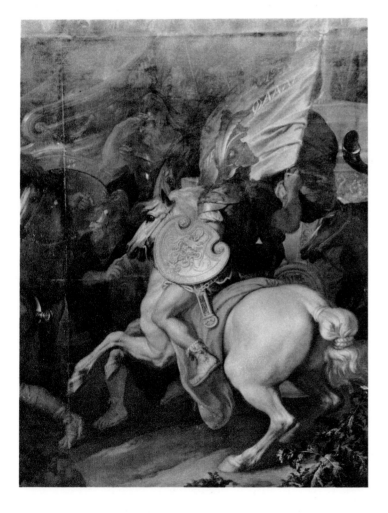

administered a huge shop; he painted easel pictures and monumental decorations; he designed tapestries, sculpture, and *objets d'art;* he participated—or interfered—in official architectural enterprises. The Sun King's palaces owe very much to Le Brun for their splendor. The artist himself considered the series of five paintings known as the *Battles* or *Triumphs of Alexander* his greatest artistic achievement. The series, executed between 1661 and 1668, alludes to Louis XIV in the guise of Alexander the Great. Louis-Alexander is the virtuous prince, deserving and destined to rule the world. The last picture in the series, the *Defeat of Porus by Alexander* (figs. 166, 167), illustrates royal magnanimity. The wounded Indian king Porus is brought before the triumphant Alexander, who, satisfied with his victory, impressed by the nobility of his opponent, and certain of Porus' faithful service in the future, grants him continued dominion over his land. The state recognized the propaganda value of the *Alexander* series, and tapestries and prints were made after it and sent to rulers throughout Europe.[27]

Artistically the *Alexander* paintings are disappointing. The *Defeat of Porus* and others in the series attempt, without success, to rival the great battle pictures of the Renaissance, like Leonardo's *Battle of Anghiari* and Raphael's *Repulse of Attila.* Le Brun's enormous canvases (the *De-*

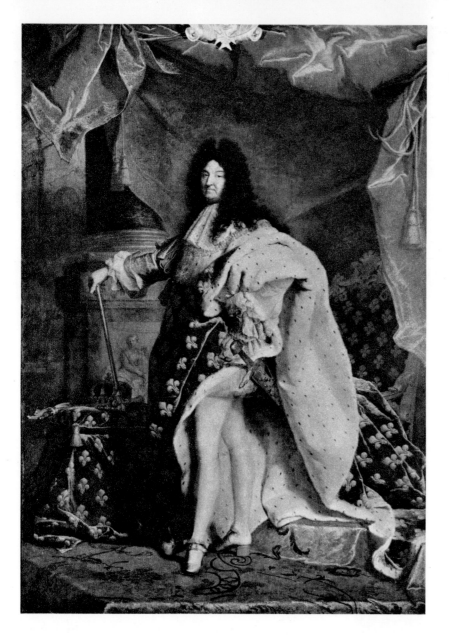

feat of Porus measures about fifteen by forty feet) may be accurate in historical detail, and they follow the "rules"; but they lack inventive felicity, and today seem overbearing and boring in their bombast and pomposity.

History painting continued as the dominant category in the last decades of the century, but notable achievements were also made by the portrait specialists Nicolas de Largillierre (1656–1746) and Hyacinthe Rigaud (1659–1743), who produced somewhat different versions of a grand style in portraiture. Rigaud's best-known work is the full-length *Portrait of Louis XIV* of 1701 (fig. 168). The king, wearing his heavy robes eas-

ily, stands with regal aloofness and looks almost condescendingly at the spectator. With the column and curtain behind, and the abundance of rich, colorful stuffs, this is an image of self-confident power and nonchalant luxury.

The brilliant color of Rigaud's portrait reveals the influence of Flemish painting, which grew in France in the last quarter of the century. Following the lead of Poussin, most French artists had thought of color as a servant and support of the essential structure created by drawing. In the early part of the century the coloristic style of Jacques Blanchard (1600–1638), who had returned to Paris from Venice in 1629, had little

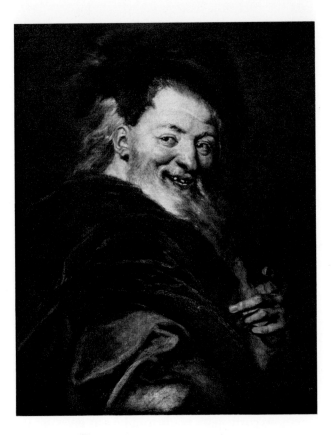

169. ANTOINE COYPEL. *Democritus*. 1692.
27⅛×22½". The Louvre, Paris

influence. However, around 1670, in reaction to the narrow and rigid position taken by Le Brun and his circle, a number of artists and critics began to champion the cause of color, which was to triumph in the eighteenth century. Roger de Piles, a great figure in the history of art criticism, published several books that focused attention on the coloristic art of the Venetians, of Correggio, and of Rubens, and thus challenged the supremacy of drawing. At the same time, artists like Charles de La Fosse (1636–1716) and Antoine Coypel (1661–1708), inspired by the great masters of color, pointed the way to a new direction for French painting.

Coypel's *Democritus* (fig. 169) is patently an imitation of Rubens. La Fosse's ceiling of the Salon d'Apollon of 1681 in the palace of Versailles, for which a sketch exists in the Rouen Museum (fig. 170), shows the results of his stay in northern Italy between 1660 and 1663. The design, the figure style, and the luminous atmos-

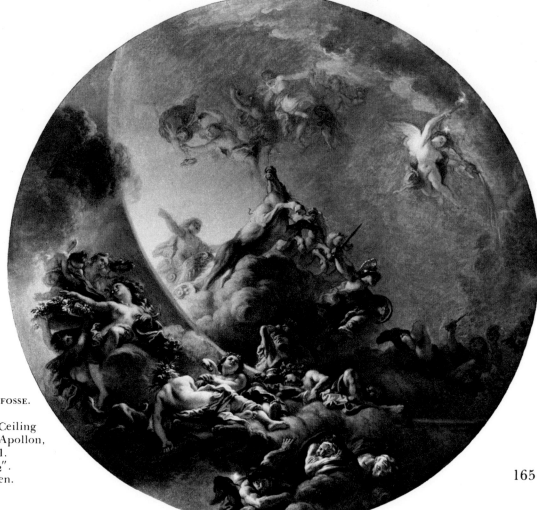

170. CHARLES DE LA FOSSE.
Sunrise.
Oil sketch for Ceiling
of the Salon d'Apollon,
Versailles. 1681.
Diameter, 38½".
Museum, Rouen.

phere are ultimately dependent on Correggio, and the bright color and spirited brushwork reveal the influence of Venice. The lightness and animation of such paintings as this anticipated and led to the Rococo style of the next century.

A group of related disputes—"Quarrels"—occupied the last decades of the seventeenth century. The Quarrel concerning Color *versus* Drawing was only one of them. The rules established by the Academy were attacked and opposed by the idea of the liberty of genius. In the Quarrel of Ancients *versus* Moderns the authority of the great masters of the past was challenged in the name of progress and relativity of judgment. Artists were searching for new expressive tools, and the Quarrels, above all, broke the restraints of Academic doctrine and cleared the path for new developments in French art.

SCULPTURE

It was not until the second half of the seventeenth century that French sculpture arrived at a level of quality comparable to that of the architecture and painting of the period. Sculptors like Jacques Sarrazin (1588–1660), Jean Warin (1604–1672), and the brothers François and Michel Anguier (c. 1604–1669 and c. 1613–1686 respectively) were excellent craftsmen and were not unaware of new developments in the arts, but they lacked sufficient genius to produce memorable works.

Sarrazin is probably the most interesting of the older French sculptors of the seventeenth century. He spent more than fifteen years in Rome, beginning in 1610, and he was largely responsible for familiarizing French sculptors with recent Italian ideas. He himself created a type of classical style that seems to parallel Poussin's manner and that perhaps appears to best advantage in the context of François Mansart's architecture. In the 1640s Sarrazin was responsible for the sculptural decoration of the château of Maisons; the linear finesse and cool reserve of his statues and reliefs there (fig. 137)[28] are in perfect harmony with Mansart's architectural style.

Although French seventeenth-century sculpture was slow to develop, it has the distinction of including, in Pierre Puget (1620–1694), the greatest sculptor of the century after Bernini. Puget was born in Marseilles. He belonged to a family of masons and stonecutters, and he was trained as a sculptor of ship ornament. Between about 1637 and 1643 he was in Florence and Rome. According to tradition, he was engaged to work under Pietro da Cortona on the decoration of the Palazzo Pitti in Florence (see fig. 109), but he seems to have spent only a short time in Florence and his activity there cannot now be traced. Puget studied painting in Italy, and when he returned to the south of France he began a short career, just before 1650, as a painter,[29] although he also worked as a designer of ship decoration.

The earliest known sculptural work by Puget, the portal of the Hôtel de Ville in Toulon (fig. 171), was commissioned in 1656. The design of the portal itself, with two atlantes used as brackets to support a balcony, is based on a motif common to contemporary ship decoration and goes back to sixteenth-century Italian prototypes, but Puget used the scheme with a remarkable and wholly original feeling for its expressive possibilities. The two figures, representing youth and old age lifting and supporting their burden, seem to suggest the unending toil that is man's lot on earth. Beneath the crushing weight of the balcony the plastic density and compactness of their supple bodies, buried below the waist in a mass of drapery, is marvelously effective. The young man (fig. 172), one hand on his back for balance, the

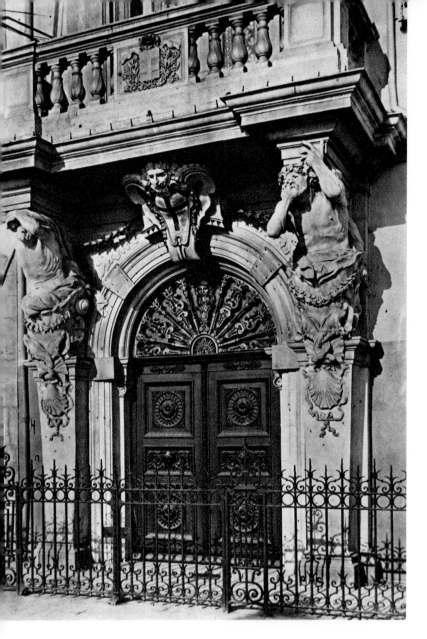

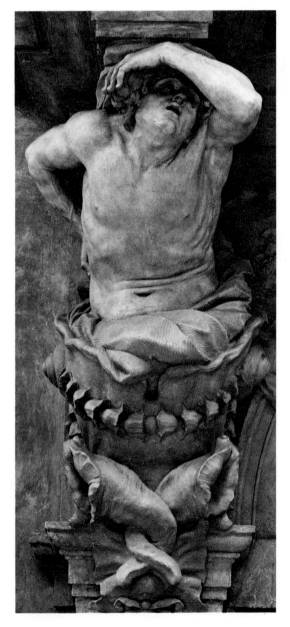

171, 172. PIERRE PUGET.
Portal, Hôtel de Ville.
1656. Toulon

other above his head to steady the load, arches his muscular body as he lifts the weight to his shoulders. His expression is strained; physical effort becomes a symbol of the anguish of the soul. Stylistically, Puget's figures may be related to the stucco sculptures designed by Cortona for the Palazzo Pitti and perhaps also to some of Bernini's works, but in spirit they are closest to Michelangelo's *Bound Slaves,* which Puget must have known and loved.

Soon after the Toulon portal was completed, Puget came to the attention of Parisian patrons, and it seems that on a commission from Fouquet he left France for Italy about 1660 probably to obtain marble for statues for the château of Vaux-

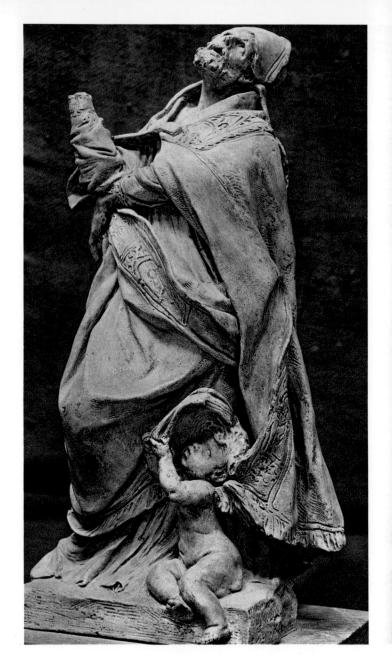

le-Vicomte. Fouquet was arrested for embezzlement late in 1661, and the sculptor, finding himself with no definite prospects for work in France, decided to settle in Genoa, where opportunities were plentiful. Puget's Genoese period, which lasted until 1668, was abundantly productive. However, his greatest project in Genoa was only partially realized. Around 1663 the Sauli family commissioned Puget to decorate their church, Santa Maria Assunta di Carignano. A great baldachin, to stand under the dome, was designed by Puget, and four statues by him were projected for the niches in the piers of the crossing. Regrettably, of this grand scheme only two statues were finished by Puget: the *St. Sebastian* and the *St. Alessandro Sauli* (a *St. Mary Magdalen* and a *St. Jerome* were planned for the other niches).[30]

The *St. Alessandro Sauli* is Puget's most extreme baroque work (fig. 173). The composition is based on an ascending spiral, and the figure seems to spin in space as he throws back his head in ecstasy. One arm crosses his body, the other is raised to Heaven; his bishop's robes billow out in broad, full folds. The statue owes a great deal to the example of Bernini, but Puget's personal sensibility lends it a new grace of form and a certain psychological elegance. The figure is dominated by the pattern that sweeps around him, that seems to pull him upwards into the light-filled dome above. Thus his ecstatic transport is refined to an exquisite ravishment.

Soon after he returned to France, Puget succeeded in obtaining royal commissions for sculpture. Of a number of works destined for Versailles, the *Milo of Crotona* (fig. 174) is the most famous. It was begun in 1671 and completed in 1682. Milo was a Greek athlete who caught his hand in a tree stump he was trying to uproot and, while trapped, was attacked and killed by wild animals. The baroque character of Puget's image is emphatic, perhaps most of all in his preparatory drawing at Rennes (fig. 175). The strong diagonal thrust of the composition, Milo's twisting pose, the forceful, naturalistic handling of anatomy, and the intense emotionalism of the figure all relate this work to the style of Bernini and his followers. There are crucial differences, however. Indeed, the *Milo* probably owes more to ancient statues like the *Laocoön* than to Bernini. Furthermore, unlike Bernini's works, Puget's statue is contained, limited by the steep triangular shape that the forms compose. Movement in the statue is organized along an unbroken line that rises from the tree stump, continues across Milo's arm, and returns to its starting point through the

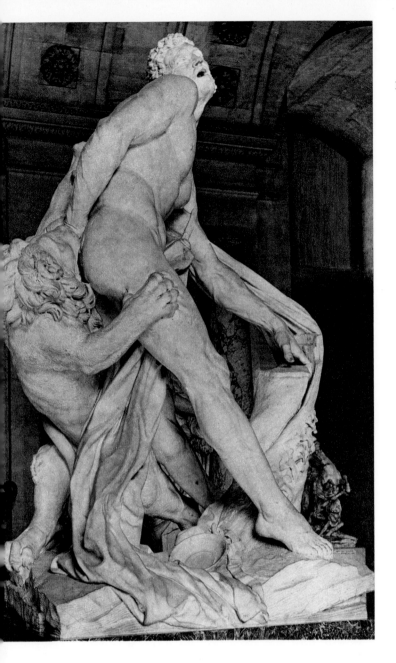

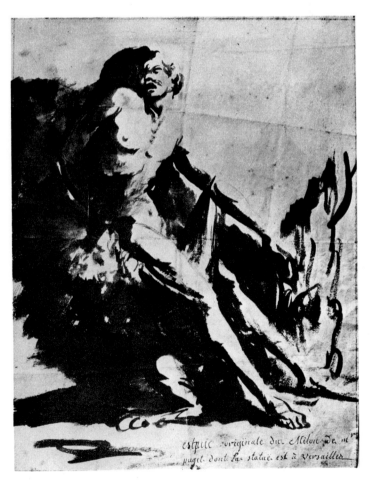

174. PIERRE PUGET. *Milo of Crotona*. 1671–82.
Marble, height 8′10½″
The Louvre, Paris

175. PIERRE PUGET.
Preparatory drawing for *Milo of Crotona*.
c. 1671. Brush and ink wash, 9½ × 7″.
Museum, Rennes

descending arc of the athlete's torso and legs. In addition, in its main view the statue has a minimum of spatial movement and is almost planar in appearance. The result, in Puget's group, is that movement and emotion are held in check, and a certain aesthetic distance is imposed between the statue and the spectator. These characteristics, which distinguish the French artist's work from Bernini's, are typical of Puget's post-Genoese period, and they reflect a basic change in his aesthetic approach. In the Toulon atlantes (fig. 171) figural movement and anatomy are the direct expression of psychological and physical

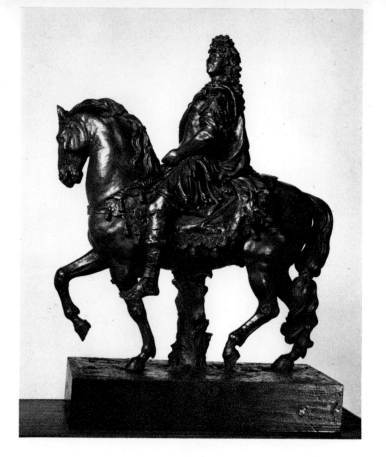

176. FRANÇOIS GIRARDON.
Model for Equestrian Statue of Louis XIV. 1683–92.
Red wax, height 30¼".
Art Gallery, Yale University, New Haven
(Gift of Mr. and Mrs. James W. Fosburgh)

states of being. In the artist's statues after about 1670 movement and anatomy become visual signs, part of an "operatic" vocabulary, and in the *Milo*, for instance, anguish and pain appear only as formalized, anecdotal details in a narrative context that is wittily expressed by the organization of the statue.

Many of the features of Puget's late work can be paralleled in other French art of the time, and although some of them were anticipated in his Genoese statues, they were not clearly formulated until he began working for Versailles. Yet if this suggests the intrinsically "French" character of Puget's mature sculpture, it is nevertheless true that the stylistic orientation of his work was always a little too "Italian" to appeal strongly to French taste in the seventeenth century. This fact, aggravated by court intrigues and by the artist's difficult temperament, prevented Puget from ever really achieving an official success. The tragedy of Puget's life was that his ambitions and abilities were largely wasted. *"Je me suis nourri aux grands ouvrages,"* he wrote, *"je nage quand j'y travaille; et le marbre tremble devant moi, pour grosse que soit la pièce."* ("I nourish myself on great works. I am in my element when I work on them; and the marble trembles before me, however large the piece.") He was given too few opportunities to nourish himself.

An artist whose work was better attuned to official French taste was François Girardon (1628–1715), who carried Sarrazin's manner into the second half of the seventeenth century. Girardon spent some years in Rome at the end of the 1640s, and after his return to France he was closely associated with Le Brun on the work at Vaux-le-Vicomte, the Louvre, and finally Versailles. Indeed, Girardon might be said to have produced a sculptural version of Le Brun's style of painting.

Girardon's monumental equestrian statue of Louis XIV (fig. 176), made for the Place Vendôme and destroyed during the French Revolution, parallels the style of Le Brun's *Portrait of Séguier* (fig. 164) in its rejection of dynamic, baroque forms. Characteristically, the sculptor's design is based on an antique model, the statue of Marcus Aurelius on the Capitoline Hill in Rome. Girardon's best-known work, the lifesize marble group of *Apollo and the Nymphs* (fig. 177), was commissioned in 1666 and finished in 1672. Originally it formed part of the Grotto of Thetis in the park of Versailles. This grotto was destroyed in 1684, and when Girardon's group was moved to its present location at Versailles in 1778 two of the figures were unfortunately rearranged. The group represents the sun-god Apollo at day's end, served and refreshed by six of Thetis' nymphs.[31] The composition was designed to contain a variety of poses harmoniously arranged on a symmetrical plan. The individual forms, beautifully idealized in type and proportion, are finely, precisely carved and smoothly polished. The sources of Girardon's inspiration are not difficult to find.

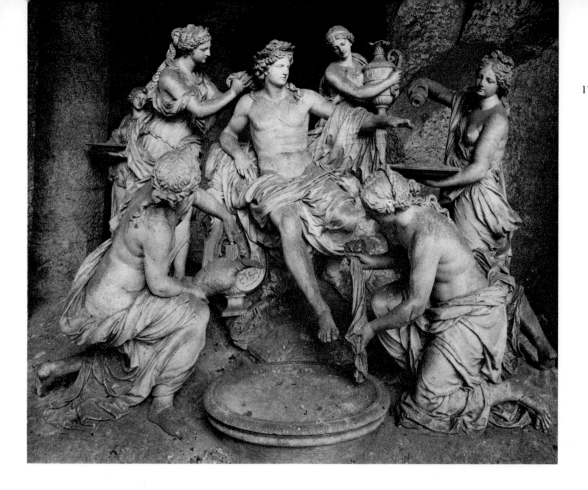

177. FRANÇOIS GIRARDON.
Apollo and the Nymphs.
1666–72.
Marble, lifesize.
Versailles

The Apollo is clearly based on the ancient statue in the Vatican, the *Apollo Belvedere;* the nymphs, and the composition of the group itself, show that the sculptor was a diligent student of Poussin's paintings. The total effect, however, has a charming, courtly propriety that belongs entirely to the age of Louis XIV.

Between 1675 and 1694 Girardon created his masterpiece, the tomb of Cardinal Richelieu (fig. 178) in the Church of the Sorbonne in Paris. In its original position in the choir (it is now in the transept), the tomb's main view showed the cardinal, supported by "Piety," looking up in devotion to the altar. The mourning figure of "Christian Doctrine," seen from behind, is de-

rived from a figure in Poussin's *Extreme Unction* (now in the Duke of Sutherland collection). The planarity of the triangular composition, hardly relieved by the gentle turning movements of the figures, the long, quiet descent from the figure of Piety to the mourner, and the vast stretch of plain drapery that covers the bier—together these produce a moving experience of deep, but controlled feeling. The sentiment is one that we have come to associate with French art, and it is wholly unlike the emotionalism of most Italian Baroque tombs (colorplate 2).

Girardon was also a portrait sculptor, but in that field he was surpassed by Antoine Coysevox (1640–1720). Coysevox was trained in the Acade-

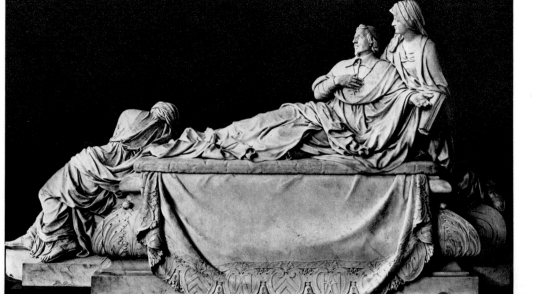

178. FRANÇOIS GIRARDON.
Tomb of Cardinal Richelieu.
1675–94. Marble.
Church of the Sorbonne,
Paris

171

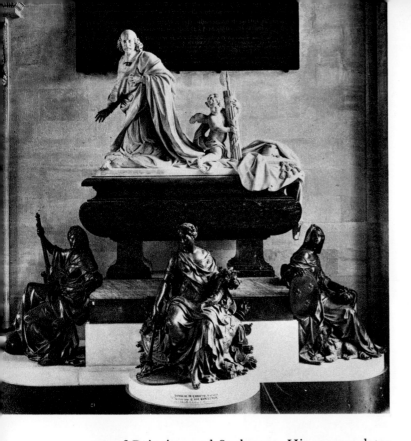

of course knew. The head rests solidly on the broad base of the richly clothed body. The surfaces are rendered with brilliant naturalism, and the bust is animated by the treatment of the hair and clothes and by the movement of the head, slightly turned and glancing upward. Compared to the aggressive, extroverted character of Bernini's state portraits (fig. 69), this bust seems restrained and almost placid. But it combines, like the architecture of Jules Hardouin-Mansart and the paintings of Le Brun, those essential traits of Louis XIV's France, a formal sense of order and control and a magnificent, self-confident pomp.

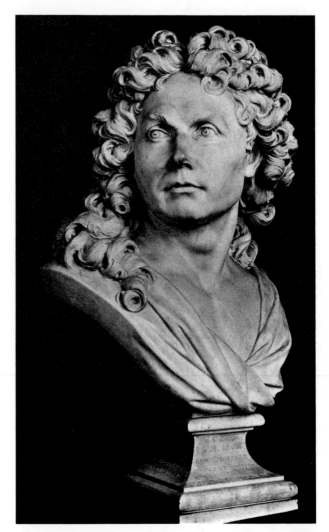

my of Painting and Sculpture. His success dates from the late 1670s, when he joined the team of artists who were creating Versailles. He was a prolific artist, and his garden sculpture, interior decorations, and tomb designs (fig. 179) are often of very high quality. But his great gift was for portraiture. In his portrait busts Coysevox developed both an official, grand style and an informal, highly naturalistic manner. In the latter, understandably reserved for portraits of his friends and colleagues (fig. 180), he shows a spontaneity and directness of characterization that was to lead directly to the main tradition of the eighteenth century.

Coysevox's feeling for individual character appears also in his state portraits, although it is naturally restrained by the requirements of official formality. The marble bust at Versailles of the eldest son of Louis XIV, the Grand Dauphin (colorplate 21), is a relatively early example (c. 1680) of the sculptor's grand style in portraiture. The somewhat sulky and overfed nature of the Dauphin comes through beautifully in this bust. The portrait formula that Coysevox uses is certainly related to the portrait style of Bernini, whose bust of Louis XIV at Versailles Coysevox

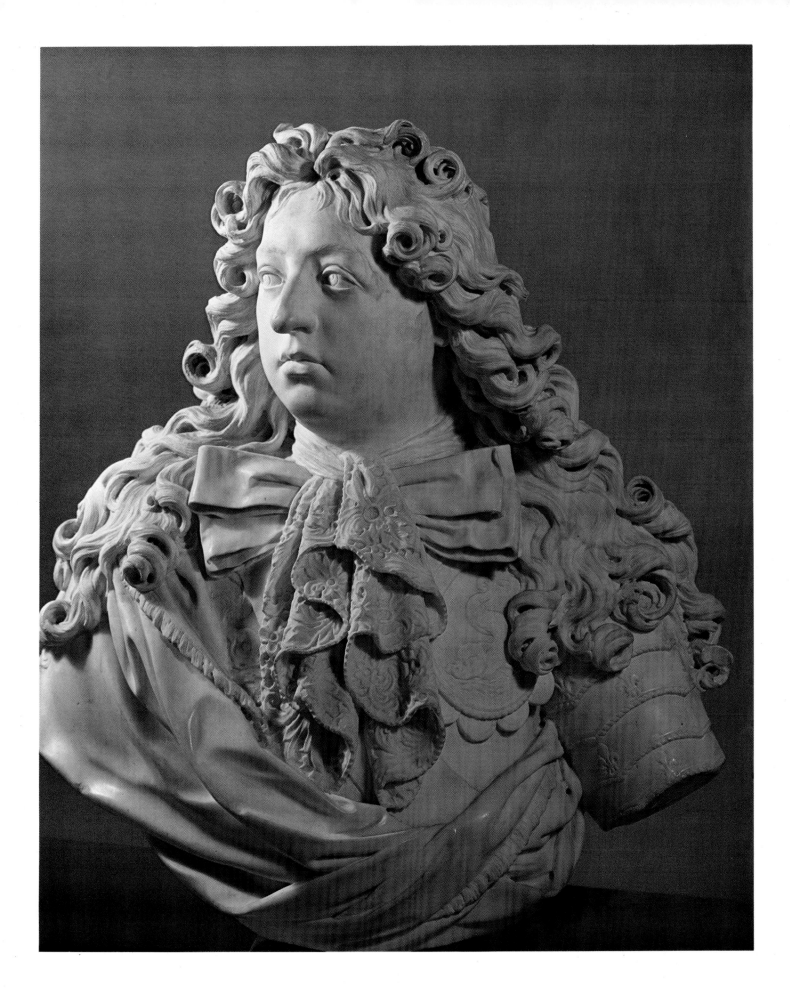

Colorplate 21. ANTOINE COYSEVOX. *Grand Dauphin*. c. 1680. Marble, height 24¾″. Versailles

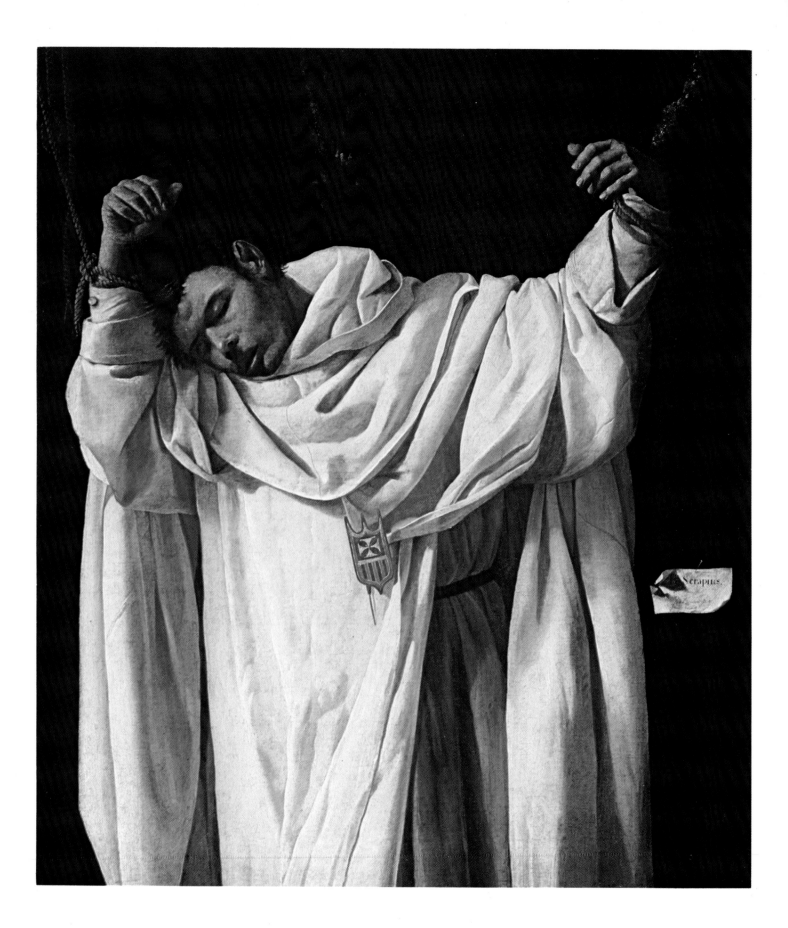

Colorplate 22. FRANCISCO DE ZURBARAN. *St. Serapion*. 1628. 47⅛ × 40¾″. Wadsworth Atheneum, Hartford

3

Spain in the Seventeenth Century

PAINTING

Spanish power and wealth were at their height in the sixteenth century when, after the unification of the country under Ferdinand and Isabella (1474–1504), Spain was enormously enriched by the exploitation of the newly discovered lands of America. However, the sixteenth century only prepared the "Golden Age" of Spanish art which began shortly after 1600, when the nation's political and economic powers were already beginning to decline.

There were notable achievements in all the visual arts of Spain during the seventeenth century, but painting was unquestionably dominant. In the sixteenth century, largely because of Spain's possessions and connections in Italy and in the Netherlands, Spanish painters were familiar with the main developments in contemporary European art. Venetian traditions, which were well known in Spain, were especially significant for the origin and development of seventeenth-century Spanish painting.

The influence of Venetian art is very clear in the work of Francisco Ribalta (1565–1628), who was the most distinguished Spanish painter of the first years of the century. The early sources of Ribalta's style were primarily the works of Juan Fernández Navarrete (El Mudo), who had studied in Venice under Titian, and the paintings of the Venetian artist Sebastiano del Piombo that were available in Spain. Until about 1612 Ribalta's work was strongly marked by late Mannerist formulas, but in his later period these gradually disappeared as the artist evolved a warm, naturalistic style that parallels, and was influenced by, new developments in Italian art. One of Ribalta's finest paintings is the *St. Francis Embracing Christ on the Cross* (c. 1620; fig. 181). The iconography is novel and is based on mystical, poetic images rather than on an event known from the St. Francis legends. The saint stands on a crowned leopard lying at the foot of the Cross, thus symbolizing his suppression of pride and worldly goals. With his eyes closed, his cheek pressed against the Saviour's side, he embraces the body of Christ. Dolorous angels surround the pair, and one comes to Christ with a crown of flowers to replace the crown of thorns that He bestows on St. Francis. The visionary quality of the picture obviously reflects the impassioned piety so characteristic of the Counter Reformation in Spain, and is reminiscent of the writ-

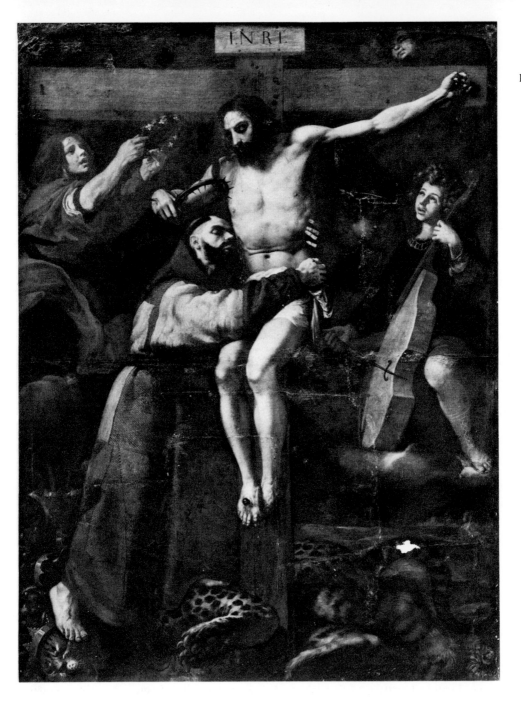

181. FRANCISCO RIBALTA.
*St. Francis Embracing
Christ on the Cross.*
c. 1620.
7′6½″ × 5′6⅞″.
Provincial Museum,
Valencia

ings of such sixteenth-century Spanish mystics as St. Theresa and St. John of the Cross. Indeed, similar subjects had been treated in the previous century in a Mannerist style by painters like El Greco, and Ribalta's real innovation is less in his iconography than in his mode of presentation. The vision is depicted with a new dramatic simplicity. The figures are normally proportioned and wholly natural in their movements and emotions. The picture's appeal is in its directness and in its convincing sense of tangible presence.

The monumentality and naturalism of Ribalta's picture, its broad handling of form, and its painterly treatment of light are ultimately Venetian in origin, and they especially bring to mind the art of Titian. However, another source for Ribalta, suggested by the dramatic lighting in his painting, was Caravaggio's style, which was known in Spain very early in the century.[1] Indeed, a signed copy by Ribalta of one of Caravaggio's paintings still exists,[2] and the work of the Italian artist was probably a main source of inspiration in the development of Ribalta's forceful and naturalistic late style.

Caravaggio's importance for the history of seventeenth-century painting in Spain cannot be exaggerated. His artistic innovations were crucial for the formation of the leading Spanish artists of the century: Ribera, Zurbarán, and Velázquez. Ribera was active in Italy, and has been discussed in another chapter (see pages 82–86). Zurbarán and Velázquez, who were both students in Seville around 1615, knew Caravaggio's style mainly through copies and through the works of the master's imitators. Both recognized, however, that in its expressive and representational possibilities Caravaggism was incomparably superior to any of the styles practiced by contemporary Spanish artists.[3] Both men, too, had the genius to go beyond Caravaggio's style and to create a personal and lasting art of their own.

Almost nothing is known of the earliest period of the career of Francisco de Zurbarán (1598–1664). Only one certain painting (a rather clumsy *Immaculate Conception,* dated 1616) exists from the years before about 1625. However, many of his works of the late 1620s appear strongly influenced by Caravaggio's style. The signed and dated *St. Serapion* (1628; colorplate 22) is obviously dependent on the descriptive techniques and presentational devices invented by Caravaggio (fig. 86). The dark background is empty; the figure of the saint, filling the canvas, is pushed forward toward the spectator, and the details are rendered with an emphatic realism. The bright light that falls on the figure from the upper left has a forceful dramatic impact, and it creates the bold chiaroscuro that gives weight and solidity to the forms. Furthermore, Zurbarán's very conception of St. Serapion is indebted to Caravaggio. The coarse Spanish features of the martyred monk (who actually was English) stamp him as a man of the people, and

the image was meant to evoke an immediate response of sympathetic identification in the painter's audience.

Caravaggio's influence cannot, however, entirely explain the impression made by the *St. Serapion.* In Zurbarán's feeling for linear pattern and for striking color harmonies—in this instance a marvelously subtle play of whites against the dark background—the artist expresses a personal sensibility; and in the emotional content of the picture he reveals a character that seems particularly Spanish. Serapion's pose in death and the abundance of exquisite drapery lend the image a haunting, dignified air, and the painting has a fierce, compelling intensity that derives from Zurbarán's combination of an insistent formal pattern and an almost brutal realism.

During his career Zurbarán was influenced by Velázquez, Ribera, and finally by Murillo. Zurbarán also seems to have appreciated the old, still medieval artistic traditions of Spain. It is because of this that his work frequently has an air of deliberate provincialism and suggests connections with folk art and with contemporary Spanish sculpture (see pages 189–93), where popular traditions remained strong. Such a painting as the *Temptation of St. Jerome* (1638–39; fig. 182) is wonderful in its sophisticated "primitivism." The story is told with utmost directness. St. Jerome makes an angular, patterned gesture of horror as he turns away from the music-making women conjured up by his own sensual desires. For the figure of St. Jerome Zurbarán imitated the painterly manner of Ribera (fig. 92), but the rather stylized linear treatment of the women, who go about their business of temptation with professional seriousness, suggests a comparison with the painted and clothed figures of the native tradition of Spanish sculpture (fig. 198). Zurbarán's sharp, linear handling of form, his patterning of surfaces, and his strong, bright colors, which are perhaps reminiscent of Gothic paintings, impart a sober, grave simplicity and an almost archaic quality to his work. Understandably, Zurbarán's art was espe-

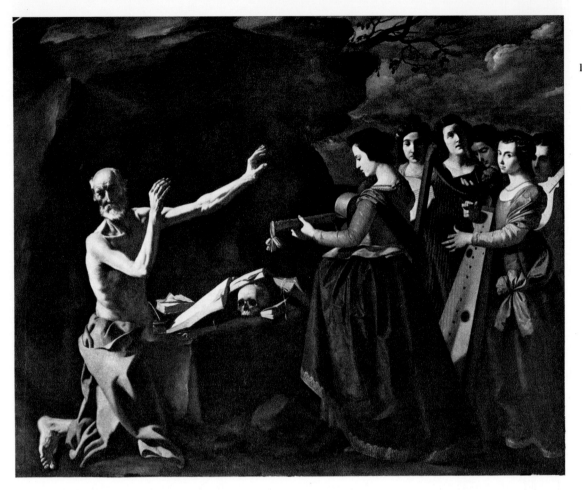

182. FRANCISCO DE ZURBARAN.
Temptation of St. Jerome.
1638–39. 41 × 73".
Hieronymite Monastery,
Guadalupe

cially appealing to the severe, ascetic taste of the monastic orders, and the artist created most of his work for them.[4]

Zurbarán is known primarily as a painter of religious subjects, but he also proves to have been a very fine still-life painter. He was not an innovator in this field; his still lifes belong to a tradition already established by such artists as Blas de Ledesma, Sánchez Cotán, and Juan van der Hamen. This Spanish tradition drew on both Nether-landish and Italian (specifically Caravaggesque) sources.[5] Zurbarán shows an extraordinary mastery of the type in his *Still Life with Oranges* of 1633 (fig. 183), the only signed example among the few surviving still lifes attributable to Zurbarán. Critics frequently speak of the mystical quality of this painting. Indeed, the austerity of the setting, the limitation to three groups of objects and the deliberateness with which they have been arranged in a row, the strong light focused

183. FRANCISCO DE ZURBARAN.
Still Life with Oranges. 1633.
23½ × 42".
The Norton Simon Foundation,
Pasadena

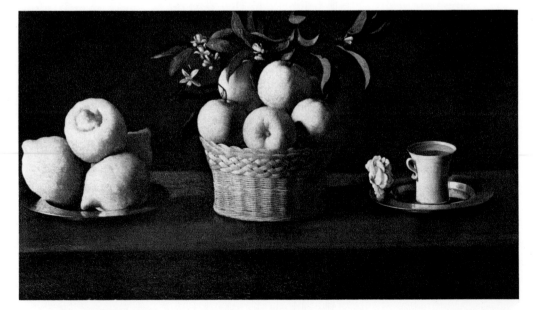

on them, and the intense realism of treatment—all contribute to the impression of secret meaning.

The products of the last fifteen or twenty years of Zurbarán's career tend to be disappointing. Murillo's great success led Zurbarán to emulate the younger man's style, which was not really suited to his talents or temperament.

Zurbarán's contemporary, Diego Rodriguez de Silva y Velázquez (1599–1660), to give his full name, was the greatest Spanish painter of the age. In 1616 Velázquez completed five years of apprenticeship with the Sevillian painter Francisco Pacheco. Pacheco was a mediocre but perceptive and cultivated artist, and in his studio, which was a center of intellectual life in Seville, Velázquez was introduced to poets and scholars as well as painters. The primary influence on the young Velázquez, however, was Caravaggio's style. Caravaggesque methods are dominant in Velázquez's early religious pictures, portraits, and, above all, in his *bodegones*. In the early seventeenth century, *bodegón* ("eating house") was the Spanish term for paintings of figures with food, drink, kitchen utensils, and the like. This type of picture had originated in Northern Europe around the middle of the sixteenth century, and toward 1600 it was well known in Italy (fig. 79) and Spain. The type was enriched in Italy by the pictorial techniques of Caravaggesque realism (fig. 91), and in this modern form it was taken up by Velázquez.[6]

Old Woman Cooking Eggs (fig. 184) is dated 1618. The half-length figures emerging from the dark background, the strong chiaroscuro, and the unmitigated realism of figural types and of still-life details are largely derived from Caravaggio's style. However, neither Caravaggio nor any of his followers ever approached everyday scenes with Velázquez's sovereign sense of detachment.

184. DIEGO VELAZQUEZ. *Old Woman Cooking Eggs.* 1618. 39×46″. National Gallery of Scotland, Edinburgh

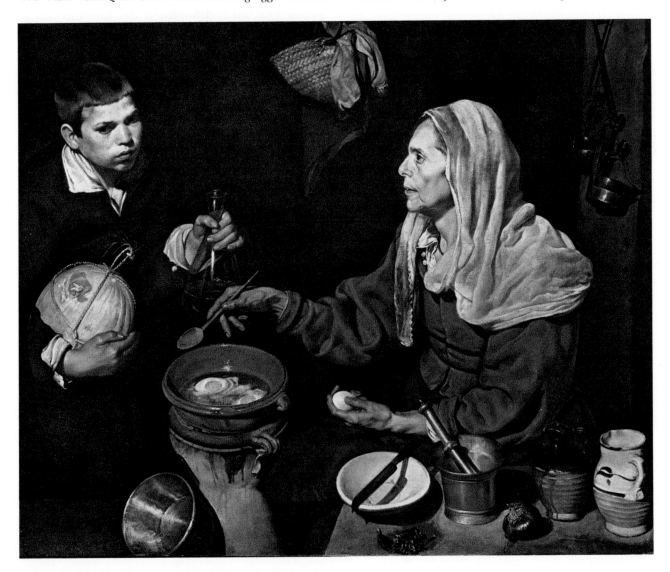

For Velázquez, the forms do not exist as parts of a meaningful event, and there is, indeed, a strange lack of dramatic or psychological connection between the figures. The objects, whether human figures or inanimate things, seem to be only optical data for an exercise in the poetry of naturalistic techniques of representation. Indeed, it is just Velázquez's dispassionate attitude toward low life, involving neither mockery nor sympathy, combined with his feeling for poise and balance in the arrangement of shapes, of illuminated surfaces, of colors, and of textures, that gives this *bodegón* its impressive, even noble character.

Old Woman Cooking Eggs was painted when Velázquez was only nineteen. Although there are still some awkward passages that reveal his inexperience, the painting has a technical virtuosity that completely overshadows the work of contemporary Spanish painters. It is not surprising, therefore, that within a few years after his admission to the Sevillian painters' guild in 1617 his reputation was known to art lovers at the court in Madrid. Velázquez visited Madrid in 1622, when he painted a portrait of the poet Gongora (fig. 185). The following year he was called to court by the king's minister, Count-Duke Olivares. His success was immediate. Velázquez's first portrait of Philip IV in 1623 greatly pleased the eighteen-year-old monarch, and the artist was admitted to the king's service, in which he remained until his death.

Velázquez's early full-length portraits, such as the *Infante Don Carlos* (c. 1627; fig. 186), belong to an international portrait tradition that was established in Spain in the sixteenth century by the Flemish painter Anthonis Mor and continued principally by Sanchez Coello and Juan Pantoja de la Cruz. The scheme used by these artists involved silhouetting the figure against a neutral background and isolating it by eliminating accessories or at least reducing them to a minimum. What Velázquez brought to the formula was a Caravaggesque feeling for three-dimensional form, and also the suggestion of a surrounding atmosphere.

Seen against the grayish-olive background, his elegant black clothes ornamented by a heavy gold chain and by the Golden Fleece that hangs on a black silk ribbon, the king's younger brother Don Carlos is portrayed with the same fine, objective realism as the forms in *Old Woman Cooking Eggs*. However, Velázquez does not only describe the external appearance of his subject; he also discovers personality. The restrained, rich color harmony, the splendidly nonchalant pose, the wonderfully negligent manner of holding a glove by one of its fingers, and the fixed, superior expression reveal the haughty, determined character of the prince. In this portrait, with the exception of the simple indication of the floor line and the figure's shadow, Velázquez does not use perspective devices to create depth. Instead, he depends on relatively fluid handling and the control of light and tonal rela-

185. DIEGO VELAZQUEZ.
Portrait of Gongora. 1622.
19¾ × 15¾".
Museum of Fine Arts, Boston
(Maria Antoinette Evans Fund)

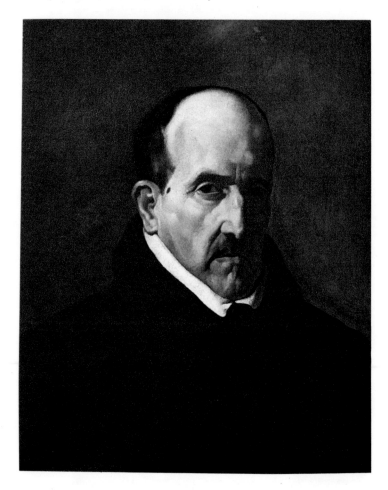

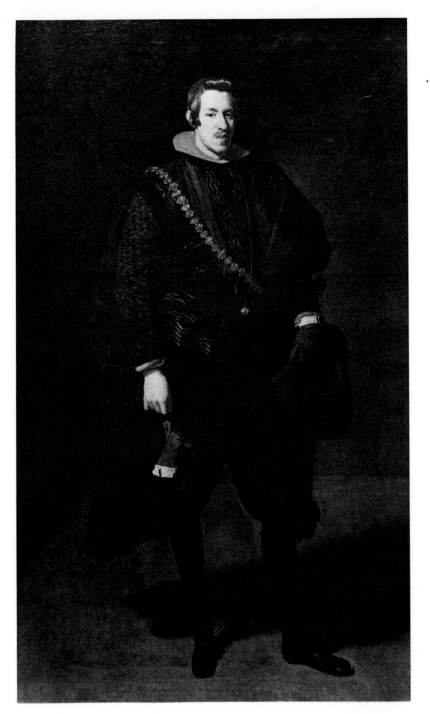

186. DIEGO VELAZQUEZ.
Portrait of the Infante Don Carlos.
c. 1627. 82¼ × 49¼".
The Prado, Madrid

tionships to immerse the figure in a convincing atmospheric space. This is a departure from the dry, linear manner of most earlier Spanish portraitists, and to some extent also a departure from Caravaggio's emphatic concern with the plastic solidity of form. The painterly elements in Velázquez's style point especially to an understanding of elements of the Venetian tradition.

Venetian painting was brilliantly represented in the royal collections, but its full impact on Velázquez came only with Rubens' visit to Madrid in 1628–29. Rubens' passion for Titian and his appreciation of the Venetian master's late manner, expressed in his own coloristic style as well as in his numerous copies after Titian (see pages 198–99), revealed to Velázquez the full power and

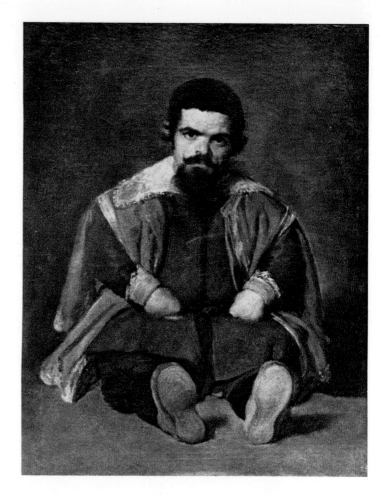

poetry of Titian's color, light, and handling. Despite two trips to Italy (1629–31 and 1649–51), where Velázquez studied Raphael, Michelangelo, and Correggio as well as the Venetians, and where he met Ribera and many of the most famous Italian artists of the time, no influence was so important for the artist's mature period as his experience of the art of Venice and, above all, of Titian.

The *Portrait of Philip IV* in the Frick Collection, New York (colorplate 23), is known as the "Fraga Philip" because it was painted in the city of Fraga in Aragon, where Velázquez had accompanied the king in 1644 on a military campaign. It shows Velázquez's developed manner and clearly reveals his debt to Venetian pictorial methods. In this painting the artist's style is literally daz-

zling. The red and silver campaign dress is brilliantly resonant against the umber background. The transparency of the surfaces and the looseness of the brush strokes seem to dissolve form; yet they also create space and atmosphere and, almost magically, coalesce to model form in light (fig. 187). This technical wizardry, which anticipates the spectator's perceptive responses and recognizes that eye and mind will grasp and organize visual suggestions,[7] is what made Velázquez so exciting for nineteenth-century painters such as Manet.

It seems that Velázquez's portraits of Philip IV are not absolutely faithful to appearance. At the very beginning of his career the king's painter evolved a refined formula for the royal physiognomy. It was not meant to beautify the unfortunate Hapsburg face but to "ennoble" it and to fix an image of a commanding, superior being.[8] In a sense, then, in his portraits of the king the artist created, rather than revealed, personality.

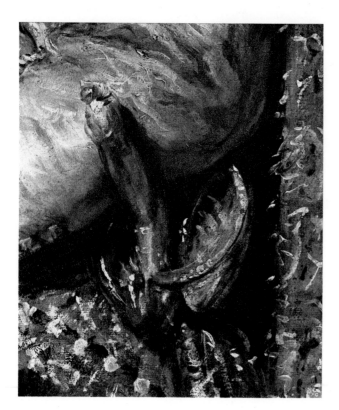

187. DIEGO VELAZQUEZ. *Portrait of Philip IV*
(detail of sword hilt). 1644.
Copyright The Frick Collection, New York
(see colorplate 23)

At the opposite pole from Velázquez's paintings of the quasi-divine monarch is another kind of court portrait, his pictures of the dwarfs, jesters, and idiots that Philip, like many seventeenth-century princes, collected for his amusement. These people were regarded as barely human, and their deformities seemed evidence that they had been denied God's grace. In portraits like the *Sebastián de Morra* of the mid-1640s (fig. 188), Velázquez is not gentle or sympathetic. The dwarf sits on the ground like a child, soles up, and his short arms terminate in little stumps of hands. But the picture's fascination is in the revelation of character, for the deformity of body is seen as a corollary of the state of the soul. Sebastián de Morra stares petulantly at the spectator, at once pathetic and bitterly mean.

After Velázquez entered the royal service he was primarily active as a portraitist. He seems to have stopped painting *bodegones* in the 1620s, and the majority of his religious pictures date from the years before 1630. Velázquez felt at ease with any subject matter, however, and in his later period a considerable number of works have religious, mythological, historical, genre, or landscape themes.

The *Surrender of Breda* (fig. 189) was painted in 1634–35 to commemorate the Spanish victory over the Dutch in 1625. Velázquez, who had never been to Breda nor seen the Dutch commander, composed his picture from prints and descriptions of the event, and there is evidence that he derived some of the main elements of the composition from sixteenth-century Bible illustrations.[9] Consider-

189. DIEGO VELAZQUEZ. *Surrender of Breda*. 1634–35. 10′1″ × 12′1½″. The Prado, Madrid

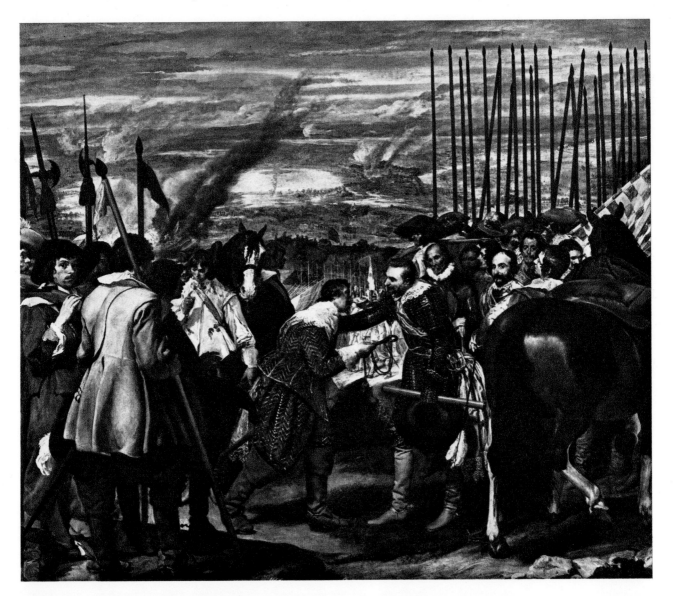

ing this, the painting has an astonishing quality of vivid reportage. The scene is made still more immediate and convincing by the liquid spontaneity of the brushwork, creating a cool, luminous atmosphere that envelops the figures and flows across the landscape into the far distance. However, the natural and unaffected presentation is the result of careful deliberation, and it is put at the service of a highly complex composition designed to reveal the character and the underlying significance of the episode. In Velázquez's painting the natural structure of appearances reflects a transcendent moral order. The two groups of soldiers have gathered above the field of battle. On the right the victorious Spaniards press close behind their general and his noble mount. Their lances, a bold rhythm of twenty-nine verticals (which have given the picture the name "Las Lanzas"), are raised high in a proud martial display. On the opposite side the defeated Dutch troops stand wearily and rest their halberds on their shoulders. In the center Justinus of Nassau bows as he hands the key to the city of Breda to his opponent, Ambrosio Spínola. The latter, who became famous for his clemency at Breda (the surrender terms were exceptionally lenient), puts his arm on Justinus' shoulder in a superb gesture of noble magnanimity. Virtue is the conqueror; the message reflects the gentlemanly, Christian code of seventeenth-century imperialism, and it appears again in Le Brun's *Defeat of Porus by Alexander,* made for Louis XIV (fig. 166). A comparison of the two pictures reveals a community of ideals, but it also reveals Velázquez's unique powers of realization.

In 1656 Velázquez painted the monumental *Portrait of the Royal Family* (fig. 190). A characteristically romantic shift of emphasis in the nineteenth century gave the picture its present title, *The Maids of Honor.* There is nothing quite like it in art before Velázquez's time, certainly not in Spain.[10] In its exceptionally broad handling and daring formal abbreviations (which cannot be adequately conveyed by a small illustration), it is the master's boldest experiment in naturalistic techniques. "Naturalism," for Velázquez, as for all seventeenth-century artists, was not essentially a device for describing the world as it is but, rather, for revealing a higher order of visual and intellectual relationships. In the last century, however, critics tended to interpret Velázquez's naturalistic art in terms of nineteenth-century stylistic intentions. Thus *The Maids of Honor* was believed to be a candid representation of an actual event. The action is not entirely clear, however, and alternative stories have been invented to explain the picture (Velázquez was painting the royal couple when the princess and her companions interrupted, and vice versa). There has thus been much inconclusive speculation about the subject of the huge canvas that the artist is shown painting, and it has been proposed that the uncertainty of meaning was deliberate. However, the supposed ambiguities in *The Maids of Honor* exist only when one assumes that its organization is primarily narrative in structure. Actually, the picture is based on an almost unprecedented artistic intuition of the formal and psychological interrelationships immanent in an instant of time. The specific action is incidental. The central theme of the painting is the awareness of the royal presence, in which the main participants, socially and psychologically disparate, are momentarily united: Velázquez at his easel, brush in hand; the princess, who was about to take the glass of water offered her; the princess' dwarf at the right; and the marshal in the passageway beyond the room—all turn silently toward the king and queen, who stand at the invisible border line between real and painted space, and are reflected in the mirror on the far wall. The painting is virtually inexhaustible in its visual and intellectual subtleties. The mirror image is set between two poles of visual reality, with the "painted" scenes above it and the "picture" of the marshal framed in the doorway next to it. The paintings, of Apollo and Pan and of

OPPOSITE: 190. DIEGO VELAZQUEZ. *The Maids of Honor.* 1656. 10′5″ × 9′. The Prado, Madrid

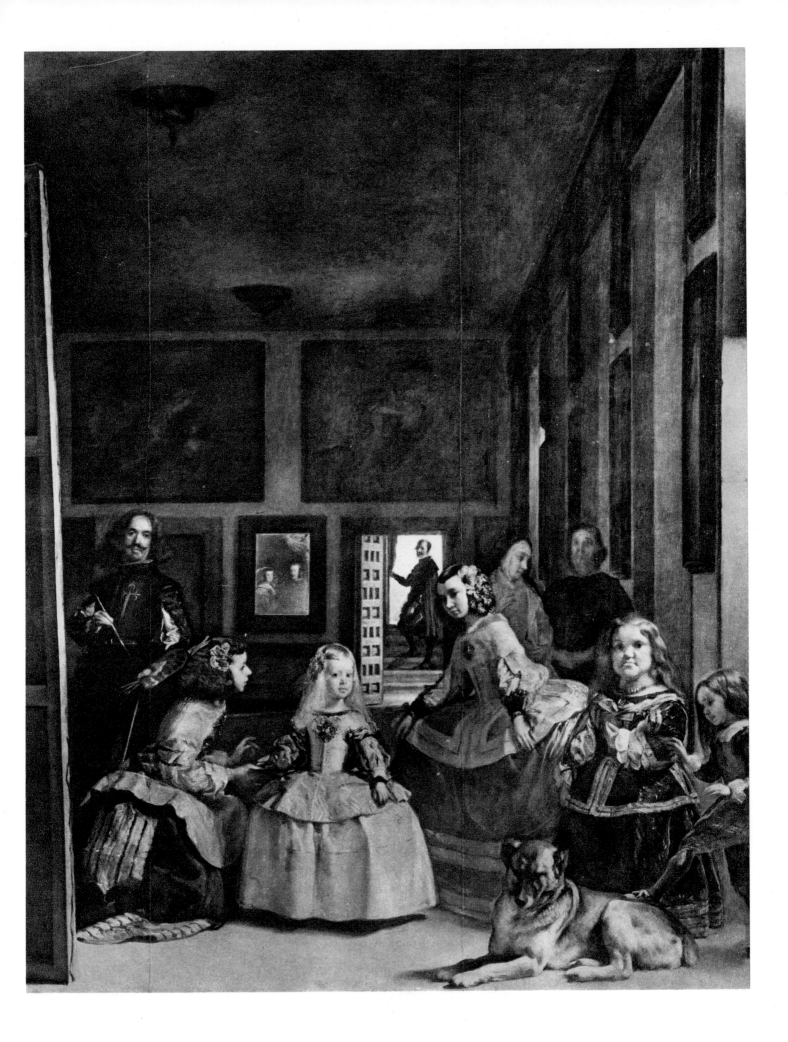

Pallas and Arachne, allude to the divine nature of true art. What is most extraordinary, however, is the complete identification of the imagined position of the king and queen with the real position of the spectator. The lifesize canvas of the artist's studio—its light and atmosphere, and the figures in it—becomes an extension of real space. And the total involvement of the spectator in this silent drama of mutual awareness makes *The Maids of Honor* the most sophisticated and perhaps the most profound illusionistic painting of the seventeenth century.

A younger member of Velázquez's generation, Alonso Cano (1601–1667), must at least be mentioned. He was a talented and versatile artist who was a sculptor and architect (fig. 200) as well as a painter. Cano had been a student with Velázquez in Pacheco's shop in Seville, and in 1638 he went to Madrid, where he was influenced by Velázquez and by the Venetian pictures in the royal collection. Cano seems to have been a quarrelsome man, and his difficulties with the civil authorities were in some part responsible for his many changes of residence (Madrid, 1638–44 and 1657–60; Valencia, 1644–45; Granada, 1652–56; Malaga, 1665–66). Cano's paintings show a strong, often original, but not brilliant personality. One of his best pictures, the signed *Descent into Limbo* (c. 1650; fig. 191), is especially impressive for the raking diagonals of the composition, the bold silhouetting of the figures, and the sensuous coloring. It is also noteworthy as one of the rare Spanish paint-

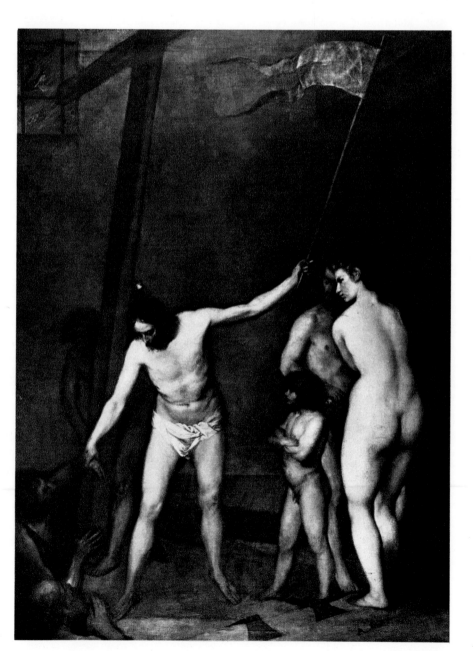

191. ALONSO CANO. *Descent into Limbo.* c. 1650. 66×47½″. Los Angeles County Museum of Art

186

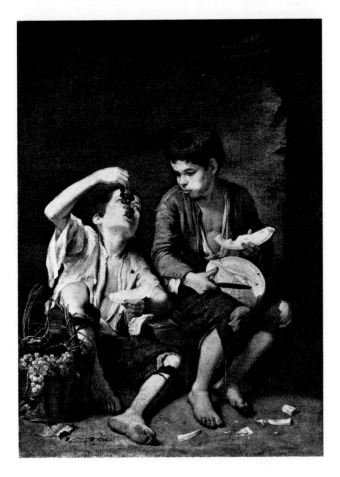

192. BARTOLOME ESTEBAN MURILLO.
Boys Eating Grapes and Melon. c. 1650.
57 × 41½". Alte Pinakothek, Munich

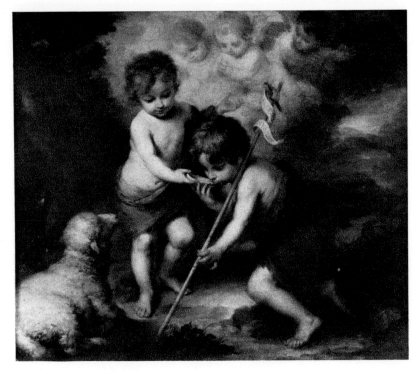

193. BARTOLOME ESTEBAN MURILLO.
Infant Christ and St. John the Baptist. c. 1670.
41 × 48¾". The Prado, Madrid

ings of the seventeenth century to concentrate on the representation of the nude figure.

The last great painter of Spain's Golden Age was Bartolomé Esteban Murillo (1617–1682), who was born in Seville, where he was active all his life. The works of Zurbarán and, to some extent, of Ribera influenced Murillo's early style, but beginning in the 1650s, presumably after a trip to Madrid, he developed a warm, coloristic manner that depends on the examples of Rubens and Van Dyck, of the mature Velázquez, and of Venetian painting. Murillo's European reputation was once greater than Velázquez's. This is probably because his buoyant and facile art makes a pictorial and emotional display that is more closely related to Flemish and Italian Baroque styles and also more widely accessible than is Velázquez's subtly restrained art.

Murillo's well-known paintings of street urchins, flower girls, and the like reveal especially well the anecdotal and deliberately engaging character of his art. Genre pictures, like *Boys Eating Grapes and Melon* of about 1650 (fig. 192), are based on the *bodegones* of the earlier decades of the century (fig. 184), but Murillo's naturalism is clouded by an atmosphere of pathos and charm, and the subjects of his works have been transformed into generalized, touching "folk types."[11] The ragged children in the Munich painting stuff themselves with an avidity that is at once gross and cute; in other pictures they play dice or search themselves for fleas. They are meant as poetic and sentimental images of spoiled innocence—the earthly version of a divine but equally sentimental image that Murillo has given us (fig. 193).

Murillo's range of subject matter was wide, and the charm and immediacy of his style, and his narrative skill, have given his works in all categories a great popular appeal. As a religious painter Murillo is particularly famous for his representa-

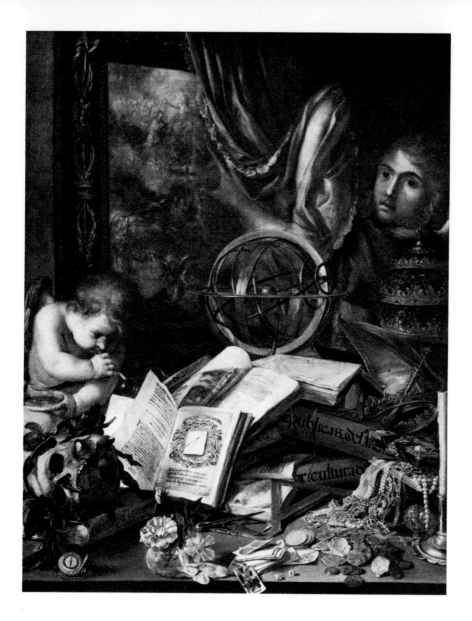

194. JUAN DE VALDES LEAL.
Vanitas. 1660.
51½ × 39″.
Wadsworth Atheneum,
Hartford

tions of the *Immaculate Conception* (colorplate
24). The city of Seville was especially devoted to
the cult of the Immaculate Conception, and Murillo painted the subject about fifteen times. The
structure and sentiment of his versions of the
theme are partly influenced by Guido Reni;[12]
their sensuous handling, the warmth and depth
of the atmosphere, the exalted prettiness of the
model, and the melodious flight of Rubensian
putti give them a sweetness and grace of such
positive force that pious sentiment is elevated to
poetry.

An artist who contrasts sharply with Murillo
is Juan de Valdés Leal (1622–1690), whose works
are especially interesting for their passionate

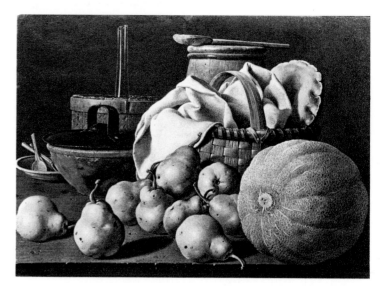

195. LUIS MELENDEZ. *Pears and Melon*. Mid-18th century. 25 × 33½″.
Museum of Fine Arts, Boston (Margaret Curry Wyman Fund)

188

religious intensity. Apparently trained in Cordova by a relatively minor artist, Antonio del Castillo, Valdés Leal settled in Seville in 1656. In his works religious devotion is expressed by active, overcrowded compositions complemented by dramatic, brilliant color and rapid brushwork. His choice of subjects frequently shows a quasi-medieval obsession with themes of death. The *Vanitas* (fig. 194) belongs to a Spanish tradition of allegorical representations of Vanity that go back ultimately to Netherlandish late medieval art. Heaped on the table are the symbols of worldly wealth, power, wisdom, culture. But there is also a death's-head, and a *putto* blowing bubbles, a symbol of transience, to point to the futility of earthly ambitions and accomplishments. A curtain is pulled aside to reveal a transcendent truth in the image of the Last Judgment.[13]

The quality of Spanish painting began to decline in the last decades of the seventeenth century. During the next hundred years, although there were native artists such as the excellent still-life painter Luis Meléndez (1716–1780; fig. 195), Spanish painting was dominated by foreigners: Luca Giordano, Corrado Giaquinto, Giambattista Tiepolo, and Anton Raphael Mengs. Only in the second half of the eighteenth century did Spain again produce a truly great artist, Francisco Goya (1746–1828)—but he belongs to the history of the modern world.

SCULPTURE

In the history of Spanish sculpture of the seventeenth and eighteenth centuries, three facts are of central importance: sculpture was almost exclusively religious in subject matter; it was primarily popular in orientation; its main medium was polychromed wood. In the sixteenth century, Spanish sculptors knew and adapted many of the accomplishments of Italian sculpture, but native medieval practices persisted. Around 1600, in the works of Juan Martínez Montañés (1568–1649) in Seville and Gregorio Fernández (1576–1636) in Castile, a sculptural tradition was created that makes use of Renaissance forms in pose and gesture and also continues the popular realism of late medieval art. To a great extent the early development of Spanish seventeenth-century sculpture parallels the development of contemporary painting. Mannerist formulas, gradually abandoned, were replaced by more naturalistic conceptions of figural structure and movement and by a new directness in dramatic approach. In a statue of *St. Bruno* by Fernández (1634; fig. 196), the long, straight folds of the habit emphasize the solidity of the stance and the bulk of the simple, broadly blocked-out forms. The monumentality and the intense realism of detail in works like this (fig. 197) suggest comparison with some of the paintings of the time. Actually, close contacts between painters and sculptors in the period facilitated an exchange of influence. Alonso Cano was both a painter and sculptor as well as architect; Velázquez was a friend of Montañés; and it is possible that Zurbarán worked as a painter of statues.

Fernández's *St. Bruno* was carved for a retable. Similar works were made for the *pasos*—that is, lifesize groups of sculptured figures representing Passion scenes to be carried in procession during Holy Week. In either case the statues were almost always painted, and frequently they were designed

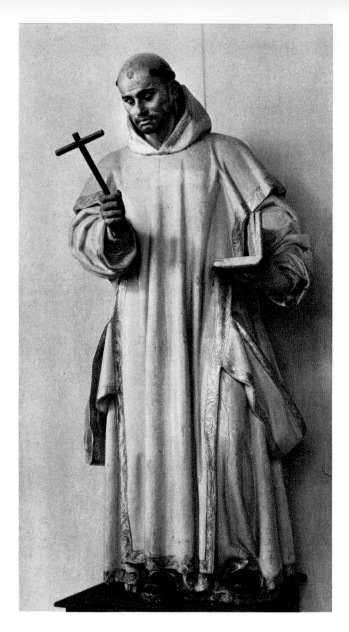

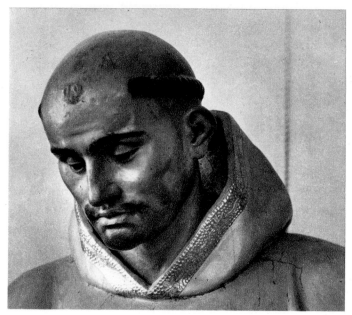

196, 197. GREGORIO FERNANDEZ.
St. Bruno. 1634.
Wood, polychromed.
Museum, Valladolid

198. PEDRO DE MENA.
Sorrowing Madonna (detail).
c. 1650. Wood, polychromed.
Chapel of N. S. de los Dolores,
Cathedral, Seville

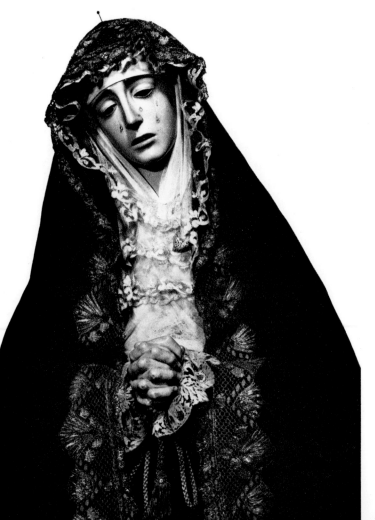

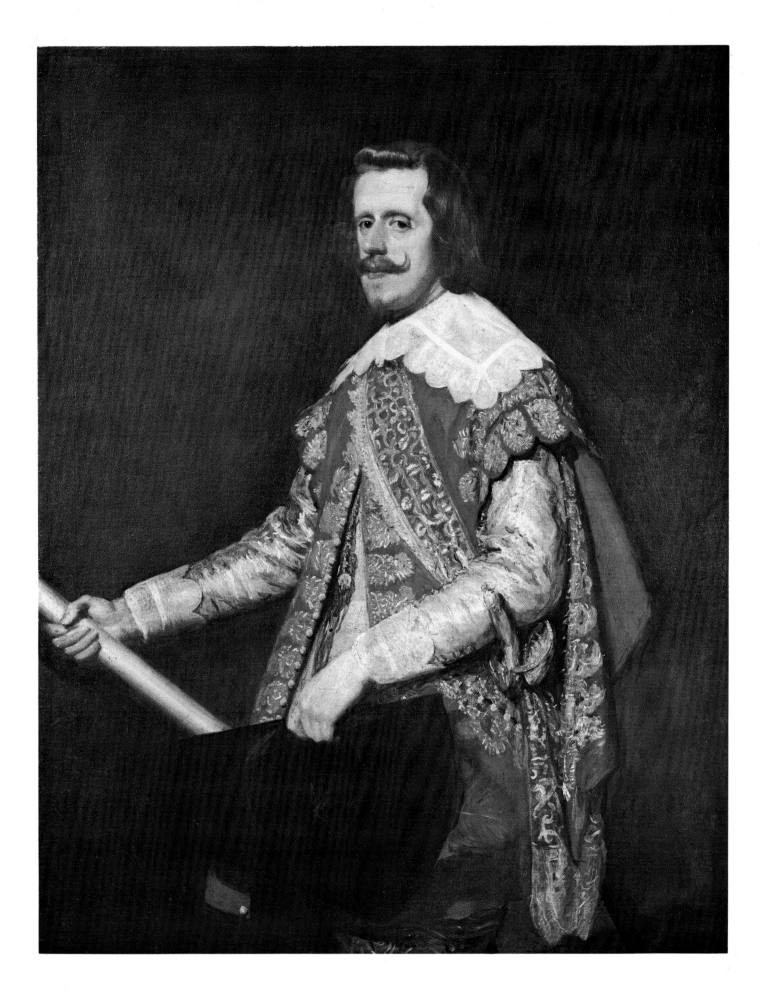

Colorplate 23. DIEGO VELAZQUEZ. *Portrait of Philip IV (Fraga Philip)*. 1644. 51⅛ × 39⅛″.
Copyright The Frick Collection, New York

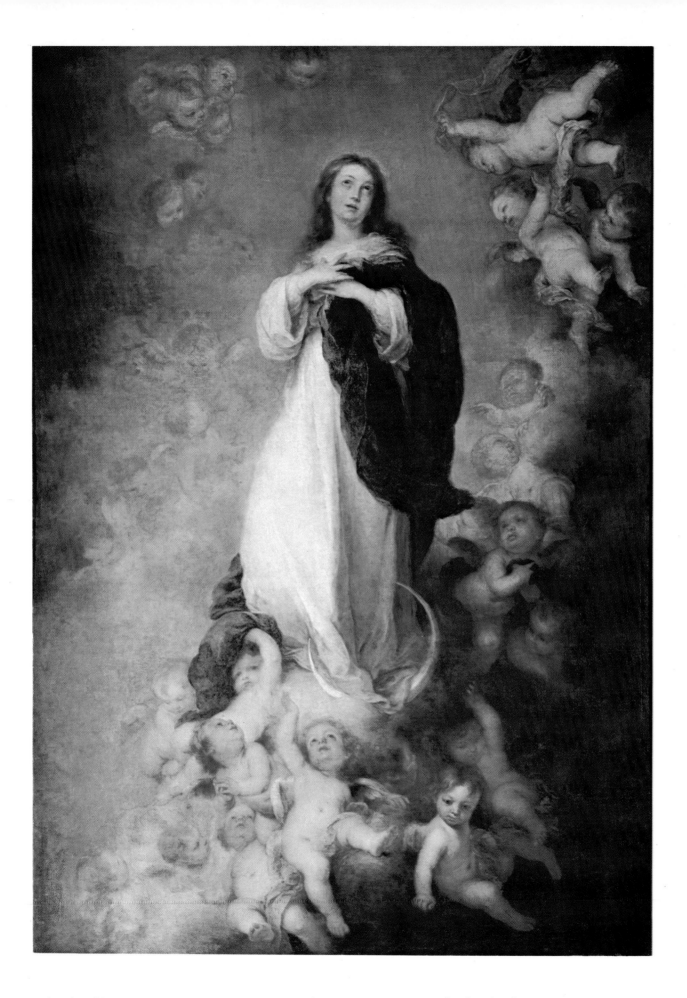

Colorplate 24. BARTOLOME ESTEBAN MURILLO. *Immaculate Conception*. c. 1660. 8′9⅞″ × 6′8¾″. The Prado, Madrid

to be dressed, like enormous dolls, in real clothing. Pedro de Mena's *Sorrowing Madonna* in the Cathedral of Seville (fig. 198) is an excellent example of a statue *de vestir*. In such works the illusion of real existence is heightened by the fact that redressing or rearrangement of clothing can change the appearance and character of the image.[14] The Spanish passion for realism even led to the use of glass eyes, glass tears, and real hair for statues. These works were designed to convey religious sentiment in the most direct and widely comprehensible terms. The artistic devices used are those that appeal strongly to an unsophisticated, popular audience, and, actually, it is not always easy to draw a precise line between high art and folk art in Spanish sculpture.

The sculptural tradition that began around 1600 remained vital well into the eighteenth century. It was always a local tradition, however, having virtually no influence on the history of sculpture outside Spain. Nevertheless, many distinguished, and sometimes great, works were created by Montañés, Fernández, and, later, by such artists as Alonso Cano, Pedro de Mena (1628–1688), and Francisco Salzillo (1707–1783).

ARCHITECTURE

All the arts in seventeenth-century Spain are strongly marked by regional and personal differences of style. Unlike painting and sculpture, however, architecture was not dominated by great inventive personalities or unified by a coherent, national aesthetic. Sixteenth-century architecture in Spain had culminated in the majestic, if coldly Italianate, Escorial, which was completed in 1582 by Juan de Herrera. The severe Herreran style began to be replaced in the first decades of the seventeenth century with a new freedom and animation in the design of ground plans and elevations. The oval plan became popular in the early years of the century, as in Sebastián de la Plaza's Bernardas Church (1617–29) in Alcalá de Henares (fig. 199), where alternating oval and rectangular chapels surround the oval nave. These new developments in Spanish architecture depended largely, of course, on the importation of ideas from Italy, and they were augmented by a revival of the Spanish penchant for decorative forms and surfaces. But these elements were not

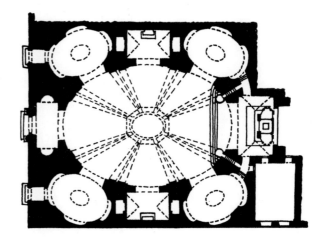

199. SEBASTIAN DE LA PLAZA.
Plan, Bernardas Church. 1617–29.
Alcalá de Henares

molded into a distinct Spanish architectural tradition until the turn of the next century.

Among the few notable achievements of seventeenth-century architecture in Spain, Alonso Cano's façade for Granada Cathedral (fig. 200) may be mentioned. Cano designed the façade just before he died in 1667, and it was built on the foundations of Diego Siloe's early sixteenth-century church. The deep recesses are, therefore, Siloe's responsibility. Cano created a design of patterned linearity. The round windows and round-headed arches play against the sharp, straight lines of the layered planes that give relief and movement to the surfaces.

Cano's detail can hardly be considered correct or classical, but he was sparing in his use of ornament, which is in sharp contrast to the free and abundant application of ornament that primarily characterizes the architectural manner formed about 1700. This manner, closely related to the international Rococo style, is usually called "churrigueresque," after the Churriguera family of ar-

chitects. The rubric is not entirely apt, for the work of most members of the family is actually rather restrained in comparison to the typical productions of the style to which they gave their name. They did, however, help to revive and modernize some aspects of plateresque design (so called because of the apparent connection with silverwork decoration) that had been characteristic of Spanish architecture in the fifteenth and early sixteenth centuries. In the eighteenth century, in the brilliant work of men like Pedro de Ribera (c. 1683–1742) and Narciso Tomé (d. 1742), the new style achieved real distinction. Tomé's *Trasparente* (an immense altar scenery where the Holy Sacrament is housed in a glass— *i.e.,* "transparent"—receptacle) in Toledo Cathe-

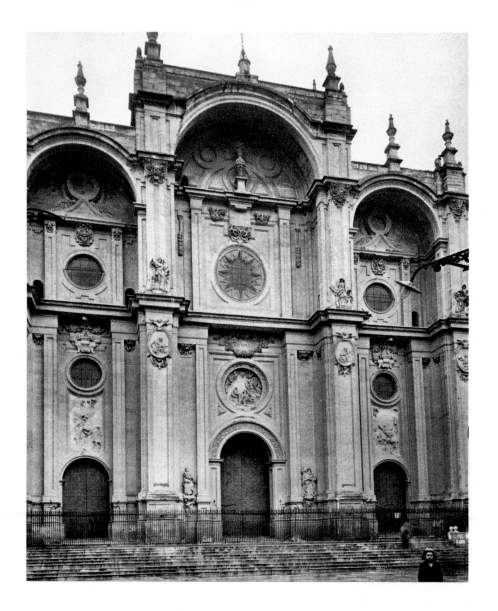

200. ALONSO CANO.
Façade, Cathedral.
Begun 1667. Granada

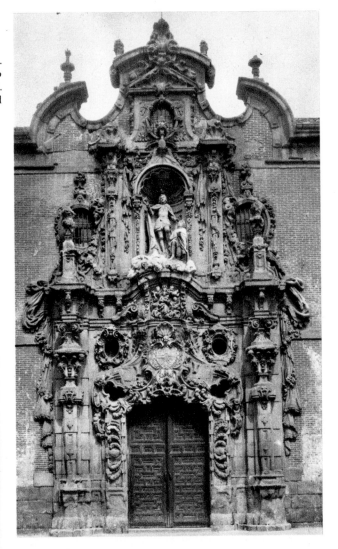

202. PEDRO DE RIBERA.
Portal, Hospicio de San Fernando
(now Museo Municipal).
1722. Madrid

201. NARCISO TOME. *Trasparente*. 1732.
Marbles, bronze. Cathedral, Toledo

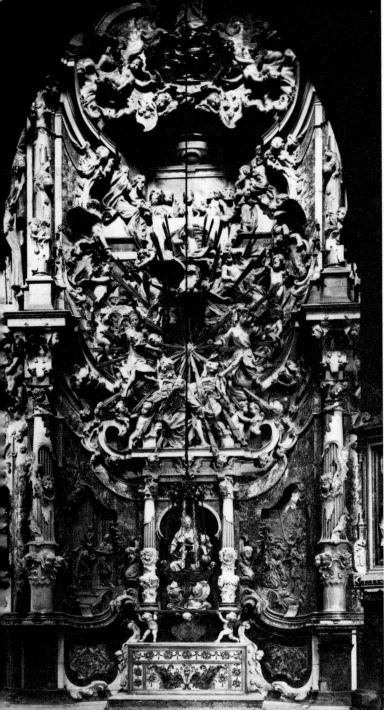

dral fuses architecture, sculpture, and light into a dizzying spectacle (fig. 201) that is unfortunately almost impossible to appreciate through photographs. Pedro de Ribera's portal of the Hospicio de San Fernando in Madrid (fig. 202), as much sculpture as architecture, is surely related to French Rococo design. However, the thick, almost choking growth of ornament that covers the surface, and the bizarre treatment of standard architectural forms, have a sumptuous earthiness that recalls the plateresque and is specifically Spanish. It is interesting that this architectural style was nowhere more at home than in the Spanish colonies of America, where it easily absorbed elements of the traditions of Indian art, and reached extremes of decorative exuberance undreamed of in Spain.

Spain in the Seventeenth Century / 195

4

Flemish Painting in the Seventeenth Century

Forming part of the declining Spanish empire, but physically separated from it by the vigorous and largely hostile kingdom of France, the southern Netherlands (somewhat incorrectly called Flanders) played an unhappy role in the seventeenth century. While sharing a common history, culture, and language with the Dutch, the Flemish were parted from their northern neighbors by religion, social structure, and economic interest. Well-meaning though the Spanish governors were (especially Albert of Austria and his wife and successor Isabella, daughter of Philip II of Spain), they were unable to stem the tide that inexorably reduced the country to political impotence and economic ruin. There were times when things seemed to look up. A truce in the war with the Dutch (1609–21) provided a breathing spell. Even when war was resumed, no major battle was fought on Belgian soil. The arrival as governor of no less a person than the brother of the king of Spain (1634) was greeted with high hopes. Moreover, while commerce was ruined, other activities flourished. The Church made the country into a powerful bastion of the Catholic faith. Churches whose works of art had been de-

pleted by Calvinist iconoclasts were newly decorated. The Antwerp publishing house of Plantin, founded by a French Huguenot, became the leading center for theological and humanist publications. Whatever hopes people may have had, they were dashed in 1648: by closing the harbor of Antwerp "in permanence," the Peace of Westphalia deprived the country of its lifeblood for close to two hundred years.

Despite these adverse conditions, Flanders had a rather active artistic life. It was the doing of only one man, however, that transformed an activity having purely provincial significance into one echoing throughout Europe. That man was Peter Paul Rubens (1577–1640).[1]

Born in Germany to Flemish parents, Rubens had his training in Antwerp. From his teachers he inherited an unreserved admiration for the masters of the Italian Renaissance. Contact with humanist scholars alerted him to the beauty of ancient art and civilization. Between 1600 and 1608 he traveled in Italy and briefly in Spain, copying ancient sculptures (fig. 203) but paying attention also to the artistic movements of his own time. In the end he fused the many divergent influences into a style of unquestioned unity and originality.

Recognition of his genius came quickly. In Italy he worked for the Gonzaga at Mantua, for the wealthy families at Genoa, and for the Oratorians at Rome. When he had returned to and settled in Antwerp, commissions and honors came in ever-growing numbers. He built a palatial house[2] where he installed a valuable collection of classical sculptures. To be received by Rubens was considered a distinction. It was not that he had assumed the manners of the aristocracy (although he had); nor that he was rich (although he was). From all accounts it becomes clear that Rubens' great attraction—outside the recognized authority of his art—was his intellectual eminence. Adept in many languages, keenly interested in all aspects of the contemporary scene and well informed through an extended correspondence, he was ideally suited for services far exceeding those normally entrusted to an artist. For many years he was confidential adviser to his sovereign, the archduchess Isabella. As her special envoy he made trips to Spain, England, and Holland, carrying out delicate diplomatic missions. When he finally relinquished these arduous tasks to divide his time between his house in Antwerp and his country place near Brussels, he was known as Sir Peter Paul Rubens, having been knighted by Charles I of England in addition to having been ennobled by the king of Spain (fig. 204).

203. PETER PAUL RUBENS. *Younger Son of Laocoön.* 1600–1608. Drawing after the Laocoön. Black chalk, 17⅜ × 10⅜". Ambrosiana, Milan

204. PETER PAUL RUBENS. *Self-portrait.* c. 1633–35. Black and white chalks, 18¼ × 11¼". The Louvre, Paris

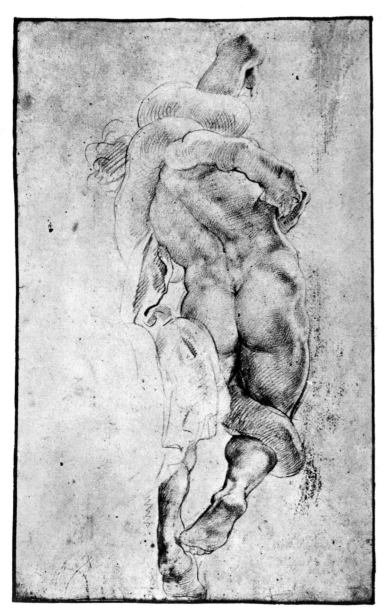

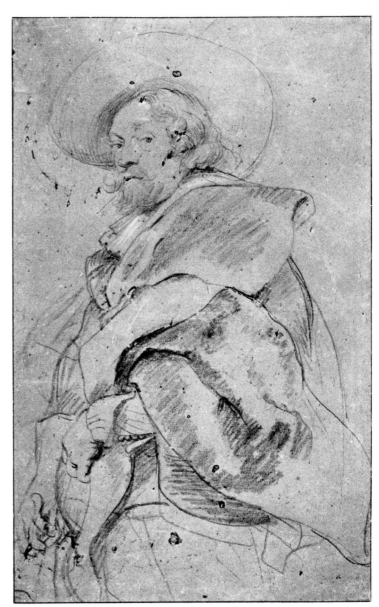

His wide range of activities and interests never interfered seriously with his work as an artist. Unlike the unrestrained and passionate figures in many of his canvases, Rubens conducted his own life austerely and with utter discipline. He organized his workshop efficiently to cope with his many commissions. In large paintings he did employ assistants, but he was able to apply the finishing touches with such skill that he could truthfully claim even these products as his own work. He trained a whole school of engravers to reproduce his paintings, since he shared the view, first encountered with Italian artists of the sixteenth century, that the invention of a picture was of a higher order than its execution. In addition to painting he furnished drawings for altars, tombs, title pages and book illustrations, for the sculptural decoration of architecture, and for the ephemeral structures of popular pageantry. He planned books on ancient cameos and on the rendering of human emotions, but the only literary pieces known today are a short passage on the imitation of ancient statues and the foreword to a book of engraved architectural drawings of Genoese palaces. It is safe to say that no artist of the seventeenth century, not even the amazingly productive Bernini, equaled Rubens in the variety of projects in which he was engaged and the number of works actually finished.

Although slightly younger than Annibale Carracci and Caravaggio, Rubens was still a man of their generation. Like them, he turned his back on the outworn formulas of Mannerism, feeling a need for a fresh approach to nature and a more liberal use of the artistic tradition. But whereas Caravaggio's figures had moved slowly and hesitantly, Rubens' are buoyant and possessed of an elastic energy. Rubens' figures command a wider range of emotions than Annibale's, and they know passions that those of the Bolognese master either suppressed or never felt. If Annibale made humans into gods, Rubens made gods human, in flesh and in spirit. True to his Flemish heritage, Rubens retained in his pictures the specific appearance and texture of things—one might even say their feel and their smell—but nothing is ever vulgar or foul. Close to nature, like Caravaggio, he idealized it, like Annibale. The greatness of his art, to put it in the form of a paradox, is that it is naturalistic and idealized at the same time.

Rubens differed from his contemporaries in Italy most emphatically in his use of color. For the Bolognese, color, though treated occasionally with Correggesque delicacy, was essentially a pleasant embellishment of a design. Caravaggio's colors were plain and solid, like the people he depicted. For Rubens, color was an all-important element of expression. Before the observer of his works can decipher the subtle intricacies of the actions or appreciate the wealth of meaningful detail, he is strongly affected by Rubens' color. Its common denominator is brightness, and its basic message is one of beauty and cheer.

Rubens' choice and treatment of color was not the same at all times. In the beginning of his career he was committed to a juxtaposition of bright local colors not unlike the uncomplicated color patterns found in contemporary Flemish flower pieces. During the 1620s, Rubens' handling of color changed, as did his style in general. Newly sensitive to the special beauties of Titian's paintings, he profited from the opportunity of a prolonged visit to Madrid to copy the Venetian master's paintings in the royal collections. Flesh, especially of women and children, is now painted in floating tones of mother-of-pearl. Rather than juxtaposing large color areas as he had done before, he broke them up and blended them more subtly, achieving a coloristic oscillation of great variety and charm. Contrary to Titian's late work, however, the character of Rubens' color scale remained bright; he never stopped using his characteristic pinkish lake, light ocher, or cerulean blue, all mixed and generously highlighted with white. Where the subject demanded darker tones —as in night scenes, or grim narratives such as the *Slaughter of the Innocents* (fig. 205)—he still gave them a luminous transparency; and no matter how frightful the subject, Rubens never per-

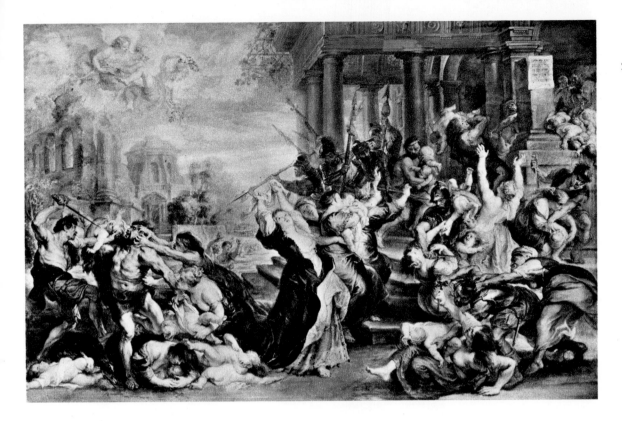

205. PETER PAUL RUBENS.
Slaughter of the Innocents.
c. 1635. 6'6⅜" × 9'11".
Alte Pinakothek, Munich

mitted it to disturb the coloristic harmony of the whole.

If Titian's influence was supreme in Rubens' later work, Michelangelo dominated his early career. In his *Rape of the Daughters of Leucippus* (fig. 206) he not only conceived the whole group in sculptural terms but even borrowed the central nude from Michelangelo's Medici tombs. The *Judgment of Paris* (colorplate 25), on the other hand, is a typical late work imbued with the spirit of Titian. Instead of being isolated from the landscape, the figures are embedded in it; instead of forming a sculptural unit, they move about freely in space. Light and shade are not used to stress roundness of form but to suggest a mellow atmospheric ambience. Rubens was always con-

206. PETER PAUL RUBENS.
Rape of the Daughters of Leucippus.
c. 1616–17. 7'3½" × 6'10¼".
Alte Pinakothek, Munich

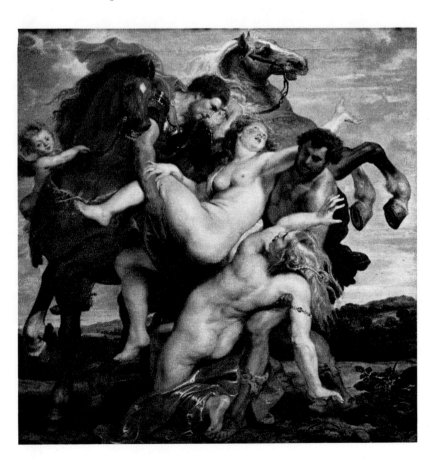

cerned with human action, but whereas in his earlier work he stressed the physical aspects of action, in later ones he was more concerned with mood and psychological experience.

Two categories of work stand in the center of Rubens' activity: the altarpiece and the pictorial cycle, often consisting of independent though thematically connected tableaux. The altarpieces were either in the traditional, if slightly archaic, form of the triptych or consisted of large single paintings to serve as the focal area of the modern type of Baroque altar.

The Cathedral of Antwerp still has three major works of this kind, two of them fairly early triptychs. Now balancing each other against the piers of the crossing, the triptychs, one with the *Raising of the Cross* (fig. 207), the other with the *Descent from the Cross*, are impressive examples of the sculptural style of the years 1610–15. One of the latest and loveliest of all his altars is in the St. Jacobskerk (Church of St. James) in the very chapel where the master was subsequently buried. Here, the Virgin is adored by saints (fig. 208) in an intimate gathering, painted with such personal warmth that one can understand the old legend attached to it that says the saints are disguised

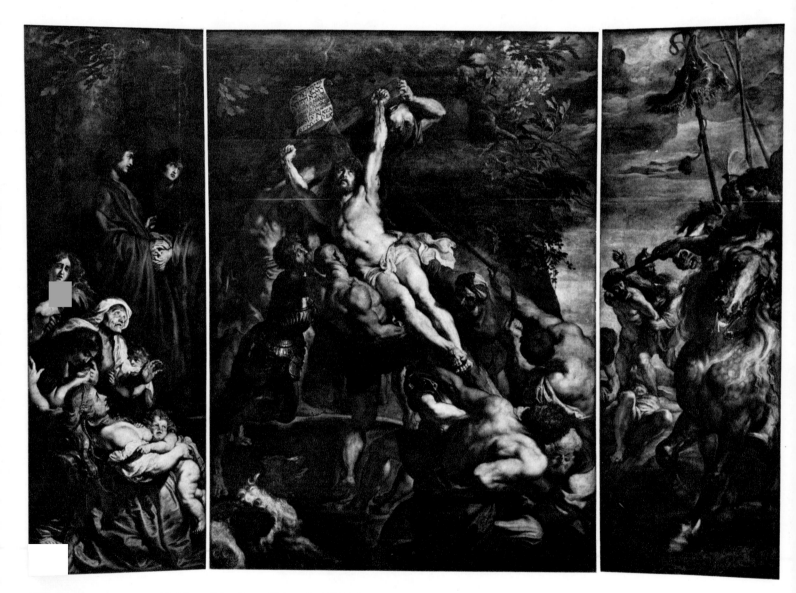

207. PETER PAUL RUBENS. *Raising of the Cross*. Triptych. 1610–11.
Panel; center 15′2″ × 11′2″, each wing 15′2″ × 4′11″. Cathedral, Antwerp

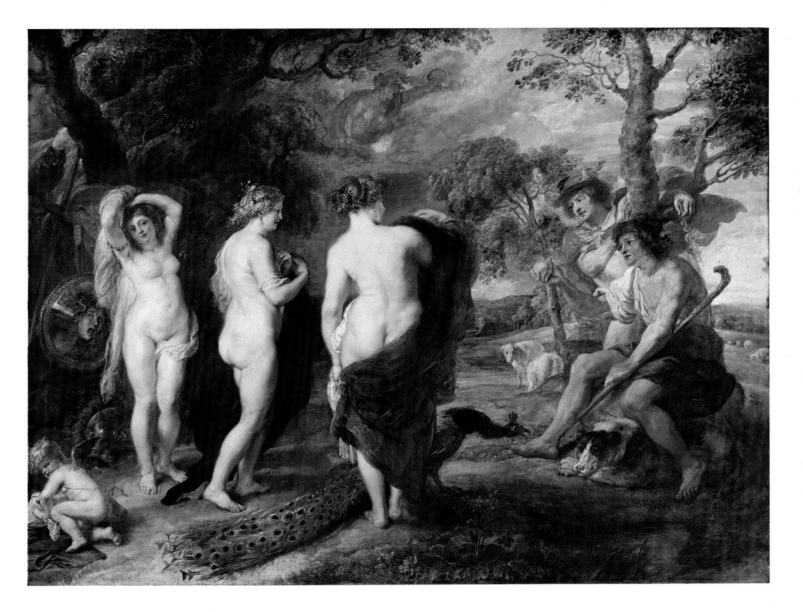

Colorplate 25. PETER PAUL RUBENS. *Judgment of Paris*. c. 1638. Panel, 57⅛×76⅜". National Gallery, London

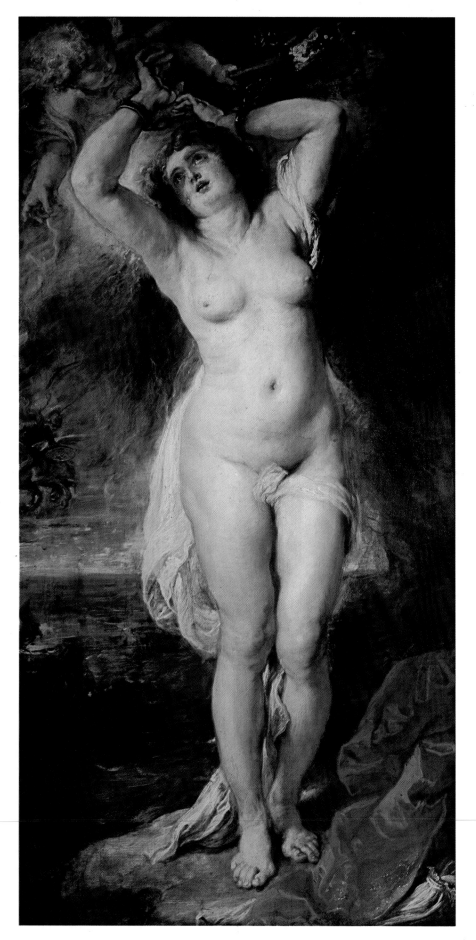

Colorplate 26.
PETER PAUL RUBENS.
Andromeda. c. 1635.
Panel, 75 × 37".
Dahlem Museum, Berlin

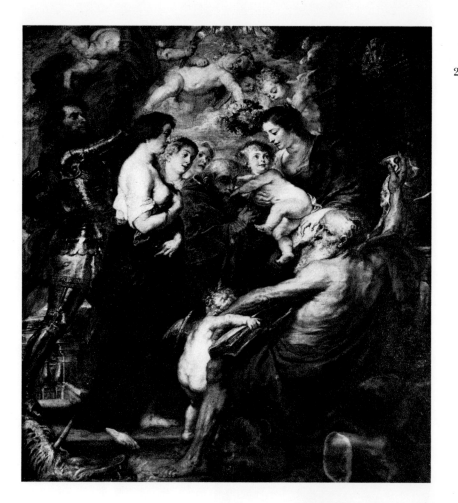

208. PETER PAUL RUBENS.
Madonna with Saints. 1639.
Panel, 6'11⅛" ×6'4¾".
St. Jacobskerk, Antwerp

portraits of Rubens himself and of his family. Of the paintings now dispersed, two particularly grand ones are in Vienna, together with the oil sketches Rubens had made for them. Painted before 1620 for the high altar of the Antwerp Church of the Jesuits, they have particular interest for showing how art was engaged in pleading special causes: St. Ignatius of Loyola and St. Francis Xavier (fig. 209), the two Jesuits whose miracles were so vividly displayed in these majestic canvases, had not yet been canonized when Rubens painted them. We may assume that the Antwerp Jesuits enlisted the aid of the great painter, to promote with the visual reality of his art the pending claim for their sainthood.

Vienna owns another triptych in which Rubens had the opportunity to do homage to both

209. PETER PAUL RUBENS.
Miracle of St. Francis Xavier. c. 1616–17.
Oil sketch, 41¼×28½".
Kunsthistorisches Museum, Vienna

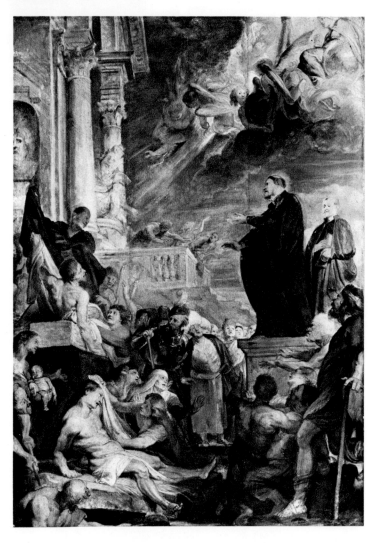

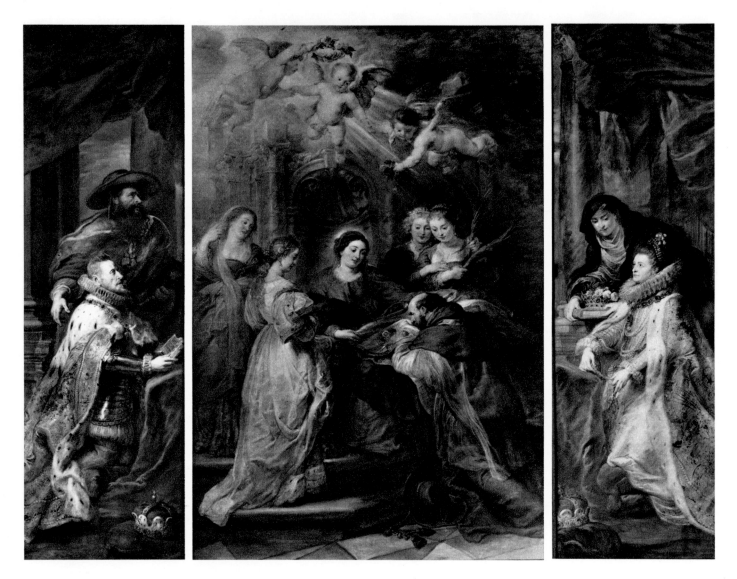

210. PETER PAUL RUBENS. The Ildefonso Altar. Triptych. 1630–32.
    Panel; center 11′6″ × 7′8½″, each wing 11′6″ × 3′6″. Kunsthistorisches Museum, Vienna

religion and secular patronage (fig. 210). While
in the central panel St. Ildefonso receives a chas-
uble from the very hands of the Virgin, Archduke
Albert and Archduchess Isabella, dressed magnificently, watch from the wings. (When Rubens
painted the piece, Albert was dead and Isabella
wore only the habit of the Poor Clares.) The
glorification of the deity in terms of secular rulers, an old theme of Christian art, had been given
new impetus in the Renaissance. It was left to
Rubens to project into the religious sphere the

full pomp of pageantry surrounding the mon-
archs of the Baroque period.

No wonder he was the perfect artist to give
form and substance to what has been aptly termed
the theme of the secular apotheosis. Several of his
large cycles glorify great princes of his time in
transparent historical or mythological disguise:
a series of tapestries describing the life of Emperor Constantine may contain allusions to Louis
XIII of France.[3] Of two projected cycles dedicated to the lives of Maria de' Medici and her

husband, Henry IV, only the first was finished, though the second was well advanced when the project was abandoned. Painted for a large room in the Luxembourg Palace (now in the Louvre), the twenty-one canvases of the story of Maria de' Medici form the perfect example of the courtly allegory of the Baroque.[4] In dignified grandeur, subtlety of thought, and sheer pictorial magnificence, the cycle remained unexcelled.

The cycle of Maria de' Medici can be understood properly only if it is realized that a fundamental tenet of the age of absolutism places the lives of princes entirely outside the realm of common mortals. Thus from her very birth Maria leads a charmed existence. Heaven and earth combine to smooth her path. Classical gods and allegorical personifications surround her admiringly, if necessary acting as obedient servants.

In the scene where Henry IV, not unlike Tamino in *The Magic Flute,* falls in love with a painted image (fig. 211), it is Hymen, the god of marriage, accompanied by Cupid, who presents the portrait of Maria to his view. Jupiter and Juno look down from clouds, the very model of nuptial bliss. Eager *putti* remove the instruments of combat, to indicate that the event interrupted one of Henry's campaigns. France herself, a helmeted figure behind the king, shares his admiration for the foreign princess who will be the future queen.

The true glory of such a picture, however, is not conveyed by the mere identification of its cast and their doings. It lies in the incomparable ease with which Rubens combined beings from different spheres in a common action, in the smooth flow of motion from one figure to the next, in the spaciousness of the whole composition, with its perfect balance between solid bodies and airy intervals, and in the controlled exuberance of its colors.

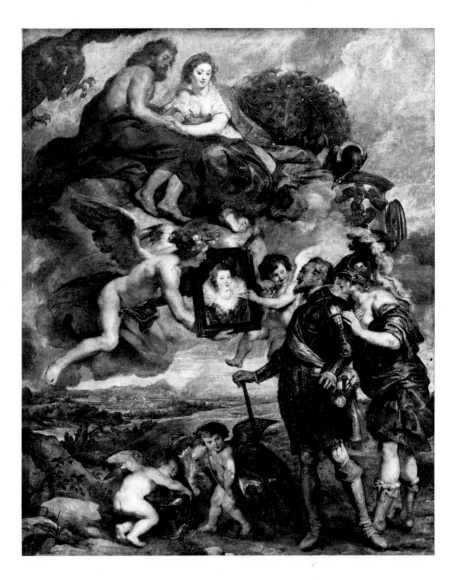

211. PETER PAUL RUBENS.
*Henry IV Receiving the
Portrait of Maria de' Medici.* 1622–25.
12′11⅛″ × 9′8⅛″.
The Louvre, Paris

205

212. **RETER PAUL RUBENS.** *Apotheosis of James I.* Sketch for ceiling of Banqueting House, Whitehall.
c. 1629. Panel, 35½ × 22″. Mrs. Humphrey Brand, Glynde Place, Glynde, England

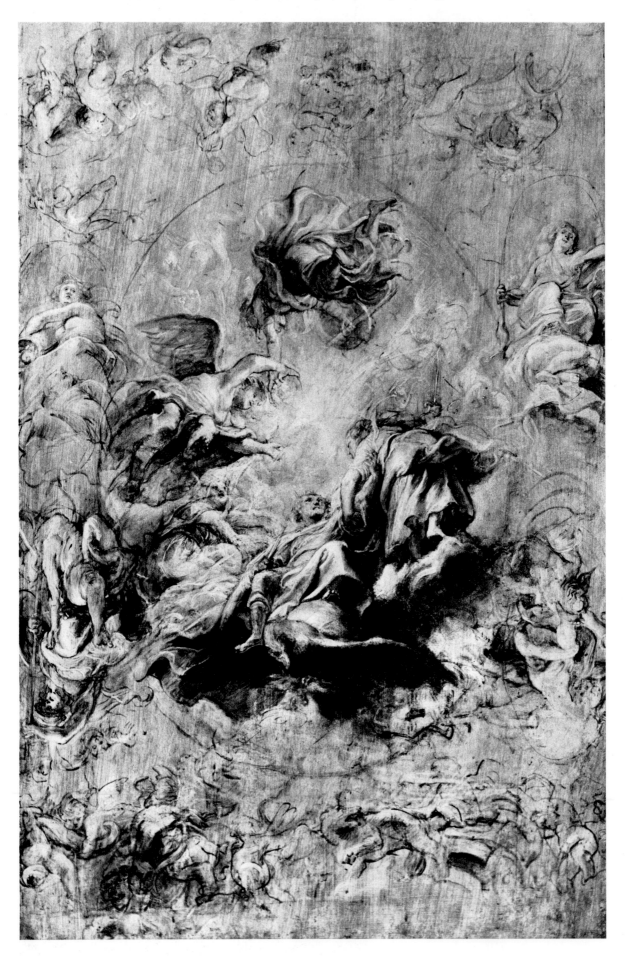

The only cycle by Rubens still in its original place is the ceiling of Inigo Jones's Banqueting House at Whitehall in London (see pages 284–85). Here, too, the program was political. By glorifying James I, Rubens was proclaiming the happy union between England and Scotland and extolling, incidentally, the reigning king. In one of the three central canvases two women, personifying the two countries, hold each a crown over the head of the infant Charles I; a third, Britannia, ties them together, "perfecting the Union."

How clearly Rubens visualized the final arrangement of the nine panels making up the entire decoration may be seen in a little-known but fascinating sketch which probably represents Rubens' first approach to the problem (fig. 212).[5] The central oval depicts James I carried to Heaven on the wings of an eagle; he is aided and joyously welcomed by personifications of Religion and Justice, Wisdom and Victory. Four Virtues in smaller ovals (two of them painted "upside down" to indicate the direction and angle from which the finished canvases were to be seen) and processions of playful cupids controlling wild animals fill the remaining spaces. Not since Correggio's dome fresco in the Cathedral of Parma had the open spaces of the sky been populated with figures so much at home in the ethereal element. As realized in its final installation, including the two large rectangular scenes added to the seven units sketched on the Glynde Place panel, the plan for the Whitehall ceiling is obviously indebted to Venetian ceilings of the Renaissance, particularly to Veronese's paintings on the ceiling of the Church of San Sebastiano in Venice.[6]

In 1634 Rubens had an opportunity to devise for his home town a pageant that subtly combined erudition, courtly politesse, and special pleading. For the arrival of the new governor, Cardinal-Infante Ferdinand of Spain, the city of Antwerp planned a truly princely welcome. After some delays, the triumphal entry finally took place on April 17, 1635. The prince passed beside stages and rode through arches erected from

Rubens' designs.[7] Each structure had its own story to tell, but one theme was stressed more or less overtly in them all: Antwerp's dire need of help and hope for succor. The city longed for peace and a resumption of trade; contemporary writers compared her to Andromeda, chained to a rock, and the Spanish prince was hopefully greeted as a new Perseus come to rescue her; indeed, this may be the hidden meaning of one of Rubens' most beautiful mythological paintings of this period, the moving *Andromeda* (colorplate 26), in which Antwerp-Andromeda is shown at the very moment when a torchbearing cupid points out to her the approach of her gallant liberator. On one of the stages of the triumphal entry the archduke saw the Temple of Janus, from whose depth the blindfolded Fury of War bursts forth, brandishing a sword and a torch (fig. 213). On one side Ferdinand's aunt, the archduchess Isabella, assisted by Peace, Piety, and the genii of Love and Friendship, desperately tries to close the doors of the temple, while on the other Discord and the Fury Tisiphone pull them open. The themes of the blessings of peace and the ravages of war are still further developed

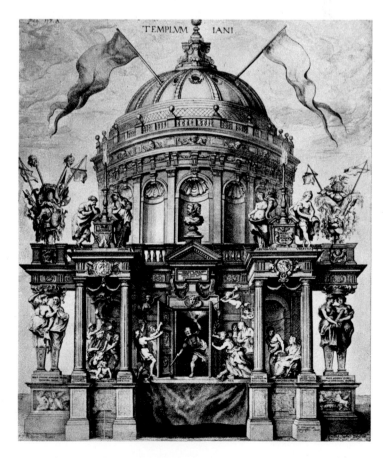

213. THEODOR VAN THULDEN. *Temple of Janus,* from *Pompa Introitus Ferdinandi.* 1641–42 (etching after Rubens, 1635)

in appropriate personifications and complex arrangements of trophies.

Commissions like the Medici cycle, the Whitehall ceiling, and the *Triumphal Entry of Ferdinand* were only a few of the vast enterprises the Rubens studio was called upon to complete. An unending stream of battle scenes, hunting scenes, classical and legendary subjects suitable for the decoration of princely dwellings, in addition to religious pictures for public and private devotion, issued from the artist's studio.

Burdened with many duties and commissions, Rubens yet found time to paint for his own pleasure. The most delightful products of his leisure are his landscapes and peasant scenes.

At the end of the sixteenth century, two distinct trends in landscape painting had crystallized. One, represented by such artists as Lucas van Valckenburgh and Joos de Momper (fig. 214), continued the rendering of mountainous views and open rural settings in the realistic, if picturesque, manner of Pieter Bruegel the Elder (1520?–1569). The other trend, derived from Italian prototypes (Titian) and developed chiefly by Gillis van Coninxloo (1544–1607), Paul Bril (1554–1626), and Jan Brueghel (1568–1625), transformed the parklike glades of Venetian art into romantic forest sceneries as a fitting setting for stories taken from the Bible and from ancient lore (fig. 215). Although one of Rubens' teachers, Tobias Verhaecht (1561–1631), belonged to the first of these schools, Rubens himself was more deeply indebted to the second.

Yet just as Rubens' human beings strike us with the forthrightness of their actions and the truth of their feelings, so Rubens' landscapes, with their individualized trees, plants, and rock formations, are clearly based on direct study of nature, whereas those of Van Coninxloo and his school follow stereotyped formulas. It is very likely that this naturalism of Rubens' landscapes owed something to the friendship he had struck up in Rome with the German painter Adam Elsheimer (1578–1610).[8] In the beginning of his career Elsheimer himself had painted in the Van Coninxloo tradition, brought to Germany by Flemish refugees. Under the influence of Caravaggio, his style changed in Italy, where his forms gained realism as well as solidity; he observed light effects and introduced into landscape painting the lovely motif of the full moon reflected on a still sheet of water. Moreover, he was the first artist to paint the nocturnal sky not with an arbitrary, purely decorative distribution of stars, but with the exact constellations familiar to people of the Northern Hemisphere—a feat probably not unconnected with the fact that he was a contemporary of Kepler and Galileo (colorplate 6).

Despite their poetry and realism of detail, Elsheimer's landscapes lack what those of Rubens possess in abundance: a feeling of motion (fig. 216). With Rubens, wind and weather buffet and leave their mark on trees, clouds drift overhead, waters rush down mountains, and the rainbow swings its luminous and graceful arc across the skies. His most personal landscapes belong to his

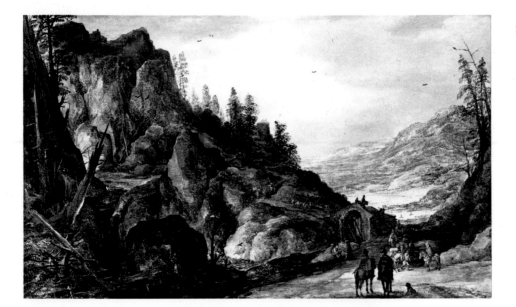

214. JOOS DE MOMPER. *Mountain Landscape.* c. 1600. Panel, 18⅛ × 29⅛". Rijksmuseum, Amsterdam

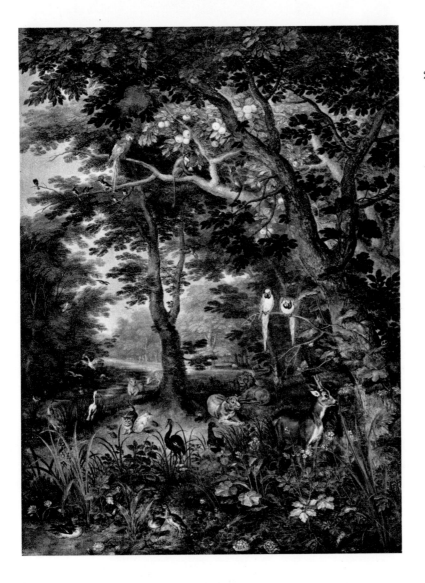

215. JAN BRUEGHEL.
Paradise. c. 1610–20.
Panel, 23¼ × 16½".
Dahlem Museum, Berlin

216. PETER PAUL RUBENS.
*Landscape with Storm,
and Philemon and Baucis.*
c. 1624. Panel, 4′ 9⅞″ × 6′ 10¼″.
Kunsthistorisches Museum,
Vienna

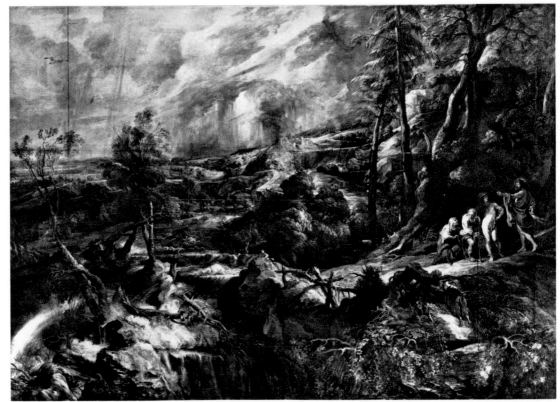

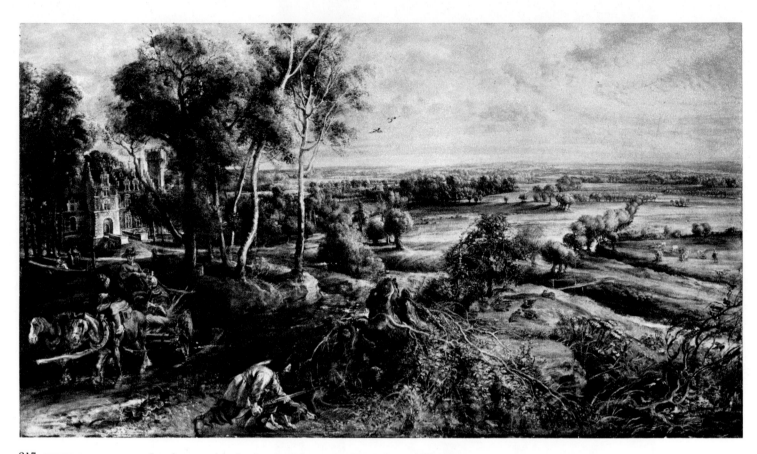

217. PETER PAUL RUBENS. *Landscape with the Castle of Steen*. c. 1636. Panel, 4'5" X 7'9". National Gallery, London

last years, when, as the owner of a great estate, he had ample opportunity to observe the countryside (fig. 217). And although the origins of his landscape style lie elsewhere, he saw nature increasingly with the eyes of his great Flemish forerunner, Pieter Bruegel.

Bruegel may also have stimulated him to paint the activities of the Flemish peasantry. In one memorable picture Rubens rendered a rustic festival in which the earth fairly shakes under the rollicking forms of peasants drinking, dancing, and making love (fig. 218). In another panel peasants dance under a big tree in a humorously mixed-up pattern, their sturdy bodies moving gracefully to the rhythm of the music (fig. 219).

"Graceful" is a word that could never have been used to describe Bruegel's peasants. What links

Rubens' figures with those of his great Flemish predecessor is their vitality and the recognition of the force of man's animal drives. But no matter how passionate Rubens' peasants are, they are never uncouth or lumpish like Bruegel's. The secret, perhaps, lies not only in Rubens' personal inclination toward a world that is perfect rather than defective: his landscapes and peasant scenes may be another form of tribute to the culture of the ancients. Rubens knew the bucolic poems of Vergil and Horace. When he transformed a Bruegelian harvest festival into a peasant bacchanal, he was probably aided by the recollection of Horace's *"nunc est bibendum, nunc pede libero | pulsanda tellus"* (*Odes*, I, 37: "Now is the time for drinking, for stomping the ground with an unrestrained foot."). If anything, it was

210

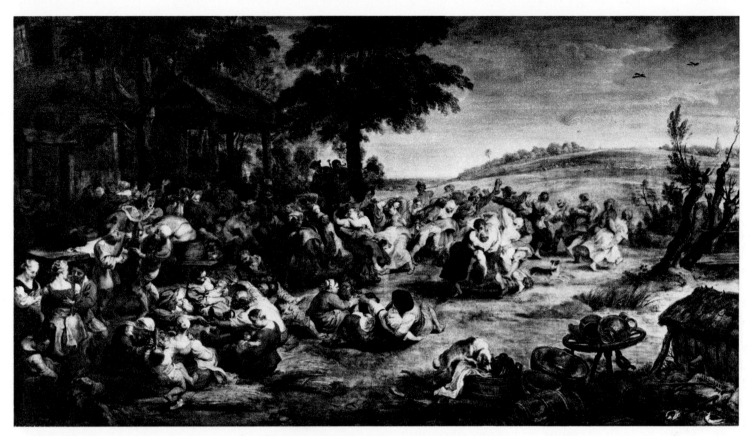

218. PETER PAUL RUBENS. *Kermesse*. c. 1630–32. Panel, 4′10⅝″ × 8′6¾″. The Louvre, Paris

219. PETER PAUL RUBENS. *Peasants Dancing*. c. 1636. Panel, 28¾ × 39¾″. The Prado, Madrid

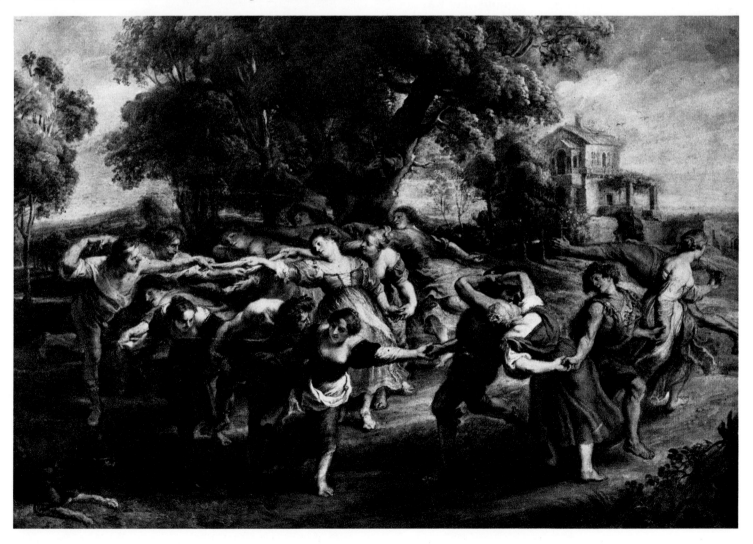

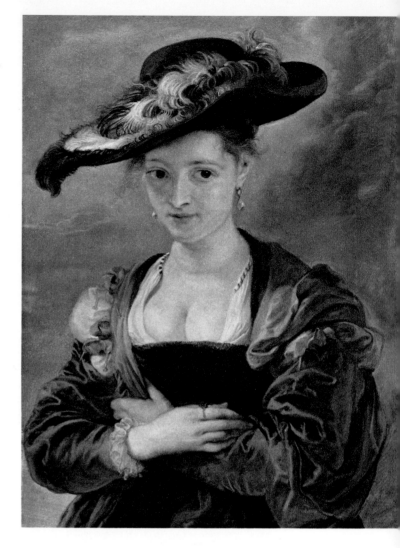

220. PETER PAUL RUBENS.
"Chapeau de Paille." c. 1620–25. Panel, 31×21½".
National Gallery, London

the civilizing influence of the classical tradition that made graceful athletes out of boors.

Indeed, at the very core of Rubens' art lay his passionate interest in the world of classical antiquity. It is reported that while he painted he listened to a reader reciting the works of ancient authors. He exchanged learned letters on archaeological problems with an equally dedicated French scholar. The largest category of his drawings may well have been the detailed copies he made after ancient monuments.[9] His work abounds in figures more or less freely derived from ancient sculptures. What matters, however, is the complete dedication of his life as well as his art to an ethos he had derived from the ancients. When he built his house he had inscribed on it mottoes from Juvenal praising moderation and equanimity. Even in his most dramatic subjects he aimed at measure and harmony. He was not a classicist; he did not try, as did Poussin, to follow specific classical precepts and to formulate an art closely resembling that of the ancients. What he tried to do was to create a world distinctly his own, but worthy of and permeated by the ideals of beauty and nobility that he recognized as the essence of classical culture. In this, by the verdict of posterity, he was successful.

Rubens had many pupils and imitators, but only one worthy of his genius. The life span of Anthony van Dyck was brief (1599–1641).[10] Twenty-two years younger than Rubens, he died a year and a half after his master. Almost as if he had felt that his time was limited, Van Dyck was feverishly active from the beginning. At the age of nineteen he was received as master in the artists' guild. His whole career appears to have been a race to catch up with Rubens, but when the mantle of the master finally was ready to descend on his shoulders, Van Dyck's health was no longer capable of sustaining the burden. Though he may have failed in his life's ambition, he had accomplished a great deal, particularly in the field in which Rubens had engaged only reluctantly: official portraiture.

The major types of portraiture had been established in the sixteenth century by masters such as Holbein, Titian, and Anthonis Mor. Baroque portraiture was largely concerned with the problem of how to suggest, and do justice to, the social position of the model without losing spontaneity of pose and expression. Rubens was at his best when he chose the model himself, in portraits of his own family and friends. The so-called *"Chapeau de Paille"* (fig. 220) will surely forever remain the most enchanting example of a portrait painted, perhaps literally, *con amore*.[11] To gauge fully Rubens' range as a painter of portraits it is useful also to examine his *Thomas*

Howard, Earl of Arundel (colorplate 27). Arch and curtain indicate a palatial setting; the sparkling armor and the helmet are symbols of courage and high rank. Self-assurance, if not pride, determines the attitude, with the head turned outward, allowing the earl to throw a perfunctory glance at the beholder. As the true climax of the composition, the face mirrors the dignity, high intelligence, and sensitivity of the man whom Rubens himself called an evangelist of the arts.[12]

While Rubens painted portraits only reluctantly, Van Dyck delighted in and was swamped with portrait commissions wherever he went, in Flanders, Italy, and England. It is easy to see why. No one before him had given his models a similar mixture of aristocratic refinement and casual elegance. Van Dyck's sitters wear their splendid costumes with perfect ease. Most of them look tall and slim; no one could ever imagine their long hands and tapering fingers holding anything but a fan, a book, a walking stick, or a piece of jewelry. They lack the physical strength and

the intellectual eminence that Rubens stressed in his portraits; instead, they are apt to be delicate, somewhat effeminate, moody, perhaps even blasé. The haughty grandeur of *Elena Grimaldi* (colorplate 28), one of a brilliant group of portraits done in Genoa around 1625, is underscored by the introduction of an obsequious young Negro slave holding a red parasol over her head. Of his English portraits none is finer than the portrait of Charles I, known as *Le Roi à la chasse* (fig. 221). Standing on a knoll like a commander overlooking a battlefield, and shaded by a tree extending over him like a canopy, the king is imbedded in compositional devices proclaiming his royal eminence. Yet all the concrete physical symbols of his rank are omitted. In his casual riding clothes, his hat at a rakish angle, the monarch represents above all the very model of a gentleman. The social ideal, first formulated by Baldassare Castiglione in his book *The Courtier* and revived under the Stuarts by such writers as Henry Peacham, is here depicted to perfection

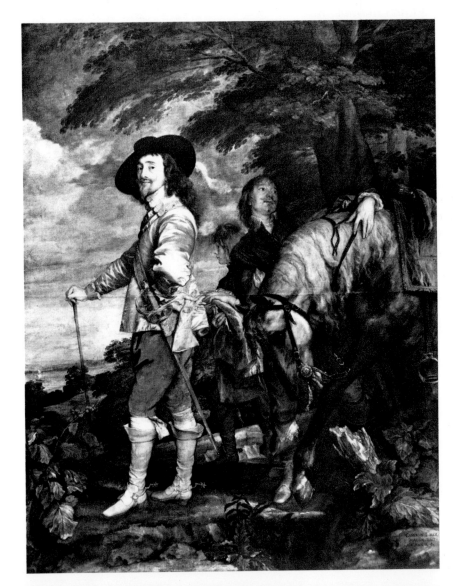

221. ANTHONY VAN DYCK.
Charles I at the Hunt. 1635.
8'11" × 6'11½".
The Louvre, Paris

213

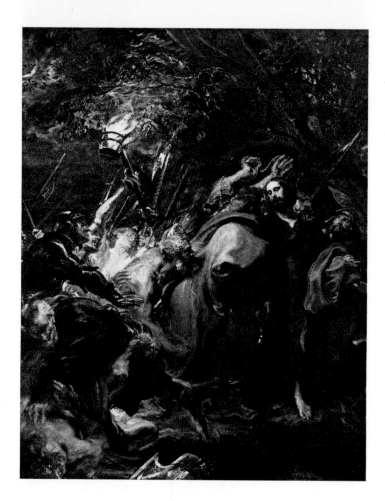

222. ANTHONY VAN DYCK. *Betrayal of Christ.*
c. 1620. 55 × 44½".
Minneapolis Institute of Arts

in the figure of the "Cavalier King." Like many other portrait formulas by Van Dyck, the pattern of this picture was repeated and paraphrased many times over; amusingly enough, a last echo of Van Dyck's portrait of the staunch spokesman for the divine right of kings is found in Charles Willson Peale's portrait of General Washington.

While Van Dyck is remembered most for his portraits, his contributions to narrative painting were by no means negligible. In early works such as the *Betrayal of Christ* (fig. 222) he creates a scene of fierce action and emotional intensity, all the more exciting because it is seen in the flickering light of torches and portable braziers. Such efforts, painted under the eyes of Rubens and surely in competition with him, give way in later years to subjects more congenial to Van Dyck's gifts and temperament. In his religious scenes he painted comely Madonnas adored by

223. ANTHONY VAN DYCK.
Rinaldo and Armida. c. 1629. 7'9" × 7'6".
Baltimore Museum of Art
(Jacob Epstein Collection)

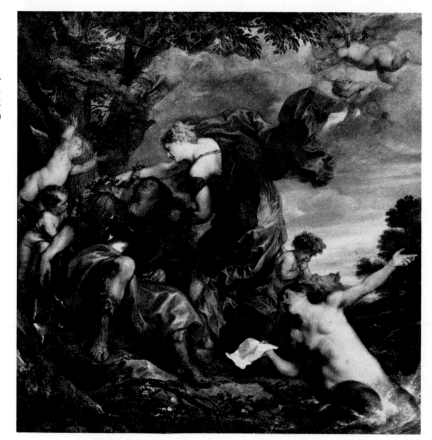

214

suave and gentle saints, or Lamentations permeated by an elegiac pathos. He also painted several versions of the incident taken from Tasso's *Gerusalemme Liberata,* in which Rinaldo happily succumbs to the wiles of Armida (fig. 223). He was evidently fascinated by a hero who, unlike the manly, active types of Rubens, voluptuously yields, if only temporarily, to the enticements of a pretty enchantress.

After the death of both Rubens and Van Dyck (1641), the "prime painter" of Flanders (in the opinion of Sir Balthasar Gerbier) was Jacob Jordaens (1593–1678).[13] Unfortunately, he maintained this standard of quality for only a few more years. From the middle of the century onward his art went into decline, paralleling the lethargy that came over Flanders as a whole. In contrast to Rubens and Van Dyck, who were often abroad and worked for an international clientele, Jordaens hardly ever traveled. His is an unsophisticated art, full of native strength and

given to a boisterous sense of humor. His figures resemble those of Rubens in size and glowing health, but they lack grace and elasticity; like those of Caravaggio—who influenced Jordaens strongly—they stay close to the earth, of which they seem a part. Unlike Caravaggio's, however, which are apt to be somber in color, Jordaens' pictures are colorful and gay. They are also rambling. Thus the "Finding of the Tribute Money," the actual subject of the picture, occupies only a marginal area of the large canvas in Copenhagen (fig. 224). More important to Jordaens seems to have been the opportunity, suggested by the subject, of painting a ferry boat ready to push off, filled with a picturesque crowd including, besides the muscular sailors, old men, Negroes, a young woman holding on to a straw hat, a crying baby, a horse, and a cow, all seen in the glaring light of a hot summer day.

More than those of any other Flemish artist, works like these express visually that primitive

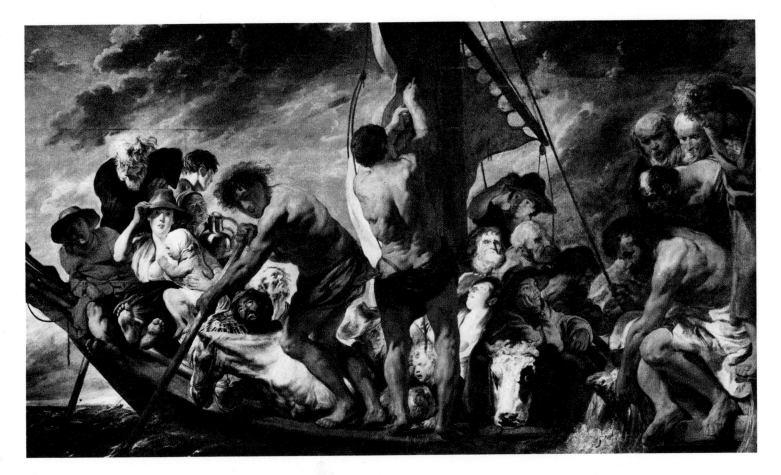

224. JACOB JORDAENS. *"The Ferry Boat of Antwerp" (St. Peter Finding the Stater).* c. 1630. 9'2⅛" × 15'3¾"
Statens Museum for Kunst, Copenhagen

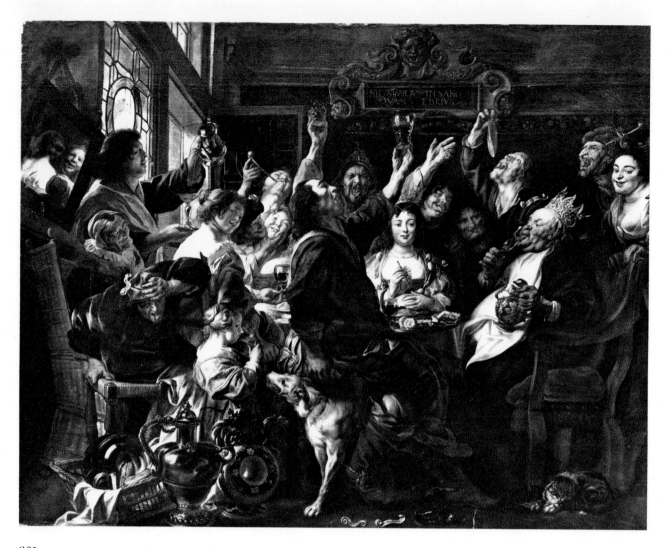

225. JACOB JORDAENS. *The King Drinks*. 1656. 7'11¼" × 9'10⅛". Kunsthistorisches Museum, Vienna

joie de vivre the sixteenth-century Flemish poet Cornelius Crul had put into words:

> *Oh Lord who maketh apples, pears, and nuts,*
> *Be praised for thy good cheer,*
> *For meat and fish that taste so good,*
> *For butter, bread, for wine and beer.*

Indeed, food plays a prominent role in Jordaens' pictures. He loves to show people sitting around the dinner table (fig. 225), either acting out Aesop's fable of the peasant who invited a satyr to dine with him, or celebrating the feast of Epiphany with the customary mummery and gargantuan meals. On many of these noisy and occasionally indelicate banquets Jordaens in- scribed moralizing proverbs, castigating the folly of inebriation and gluttony. While he may have used this subterfuge to assuage some pedestrian moralists, Jordaens had no intention of seriously censuring the exuberance of his characters and their fondness for food, drink, and companion- ship. He included himself, after all, and many members of his family in some of the wildest revels.

Jordaens' use of proverbs is of special interest. In giving pictorial form to the metaphorical content of proverbs he continued an old tradi- tion that had reached a high point with Pieter Bruegel. For Bruegel the proverb was a means of exposing human folly. The characters usually do what the proverb, explicitly or by implication, warns them to avoid. With the help of the proverb collection published by the Dutch poet Jacob Cats (see page 227), Jordaens selected proverbs, preferably those with a positive message. In contrast to Bruegel's pessimism, Jordaens represents the optimism of the Baroque. *The Eye of the Master Makes the Horse Fat* (colorplate 29) is the title of one of these scenes, and a flourishing horse, indeed, occupies the center of the stage, symbolizing the results of good management. Since the horse is dappled, Jordaens included the figure of Mercury, who, according to the theories of equine astrology, has a salutary planetary influence on horses of this type.

Rubens, Van Dyck, and Jordaens undoubtedly were the leading Flemish masters of the first half of the seventeenth century, but they were not alone. The efficient organization of the Rubens studio gave new impetus to the process of specialization that had started already in the sixteenth century. Thus the landscapes in some of Rubens' pictures are painted by Jan Wildens, the animals and fruit by Frans Snyders, and the flowers by Jan Brueghel. These men were not assistants in the literal sense: they were themselves heads of large studios. Rubens called on their services as the need arose. In addition, there were independent painters like Theodor van Loon and Caspar de Crayer in Brussels, Theodor van Thulden in Antwerp, Jan Janssens in Ghent, and Jacob van Oost in Bruges, who helped fill the growing demand for large-scale religious paintings. The ability of Flemish painters to work on a monumental scale was widely recognized. In the middle of the century Amalia of Solms, the widow of Frederik Hendrik of Orange, called a team of Flemish painters, among them Jordaens and Van Thulden, to The Hague to assist in the decoration of a residence she had built near the town, known as *Huis ten Bosch* (House in the Woods).[14]

Despite the wars that had separated Flanders from Holland during most of the first half of the seventeenth century, cultural contacts were maintained in many fields. The movement of artists from one country to the other, while not completely free, at least did not present insuperable difficulties. Of the several examples of such travels known, the most interesting is the case of Adriaen Brouwer (1606–1638). Studying with Frans Hals in Haarlem, he concentrated on depicting the squalid life in rural taverns that he plainly knew well, and not only as a remote observer. Taking pleasure in shocking the sensibilities of well-mannered society, he animated his scenes far beyond the placid examples of his Dutch contemporaries. His peasants, a very different breed from the handsome outdoor types of Rubens, are exaggerated physiognomically to the point of caricature; completely uninhibited, they smoke (then a disreputable activity), drink, play cards, fight, vomit, and relieve themselves. So spontaneous are their actions, so close to life their appearance, that we are apt to forget that these pictures are essentially variations on the traditional theme of Gluttony. In other scenes he showed village surgeons treating their doubly unfortunate patients (fig. 226); and he occasionally painted some gloomy landscapes. What gives to all these works their undeniable distinction

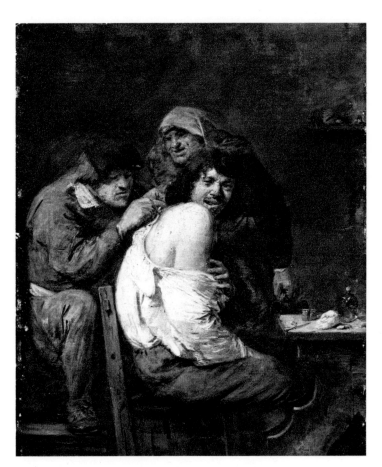

226. ADRIAEN BROUWER. *The Village Quack.* c. 1636–37. Panel, 13⅜ × 10⅝". Städelsches Kunstinstitut, Frankfurt

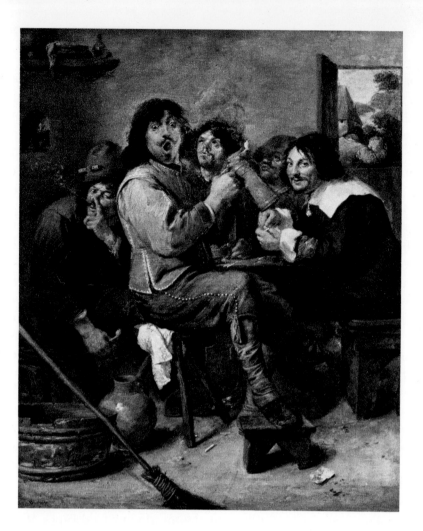

227. ADRIAEN BROUWER.
The Smokers. c. 1636.
Panel, 18 × 14⅜".
The Metropolitan Museum of Art,
New York
(Michael Friedsam Collection, 1931)

is his uncanny ability to bring his unsavory characters to life, and to combine them in dramatic actions. He also suggests vividly the smoky, reeking atmosphere of his disorderly farmhouses and inns. Above all, he painted with great freedom and with such boldness that his panels seem much larger than their actually quite diminutive size. Beginning with a relatively crude palette, Brouwer developed a highly sophisticated sense of color, closer, it seems, to the early works of Van Dyck than to those of Rubens. In his late works, like the *Bitter Drink* (fig. 8) and the *Smokers* (fig. 227), a masterful study of character is supplemented by a scintillating, if softly toned, use of color.

Brouwer's paintings occupy an important place in the rapidly growing peasant genre. A whole school, active in both Flanders and Holland, can be traced to Brouwer's direct influence. His ideas were prettified, bowdlerized, and anecdotally enriched by David Teniers (1610–1690). The Dutch painters Isaac (1621–1649) and Adriaen (1610–1685) van Ostade depicted rickety peasants' homes and their smoke-filled inns with an engaging gentleness of color but with little interest in human drama or intensity of facial expression. One young Dutch painter alone seems to have been attracted precisely by these aspects of Brouwer's art: from a larger historical point of view, Brouwer's chief merit may well have been the strong influence he exercised on the early works of Rembrandt.

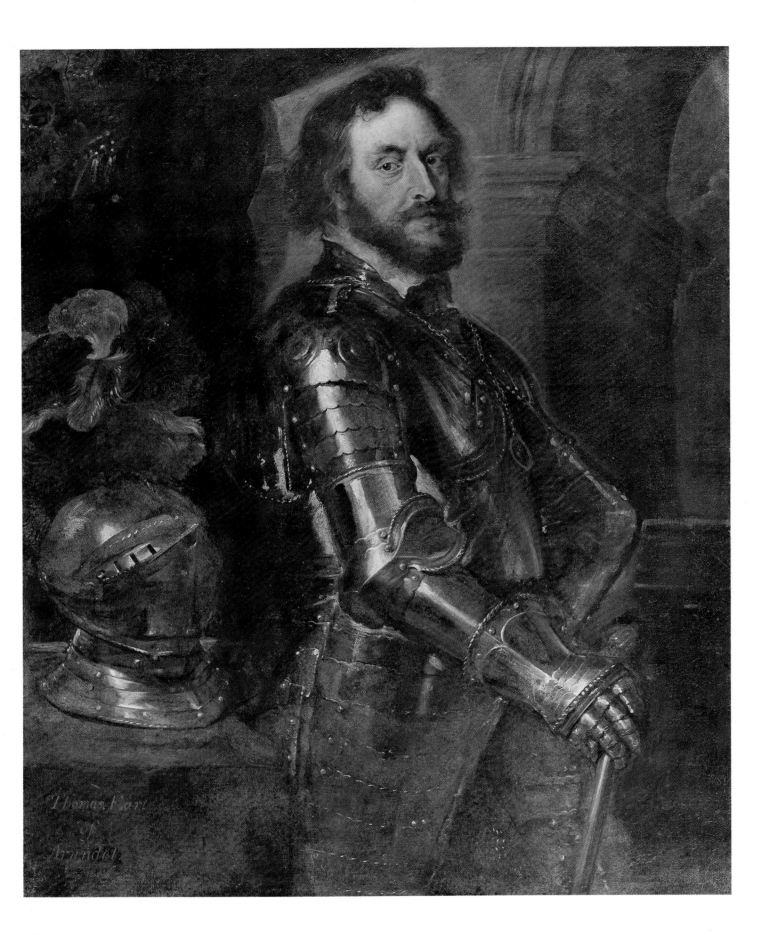

Colorplate 27. PETER PAUL RUBENS. *Portrait of Thomas Howard, Earl of Arundel.* c. 1630. 54 × 44⅞".
Isabella Stewart Gardner Museum, Boston

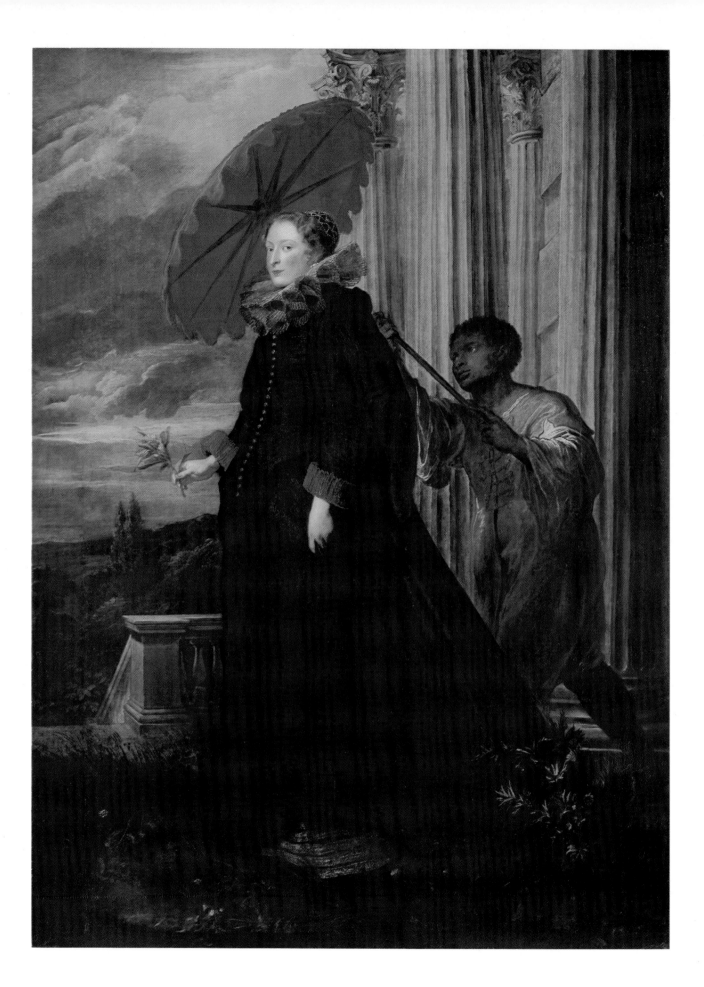

Colorplate 28. ANTHONY VAN DYCK. *Portrait of the Marchesa Elena Grimaldi.* c. 1625. 97 × 68".
National Gallery of Art, Washington, D.C. (Widener Collection)

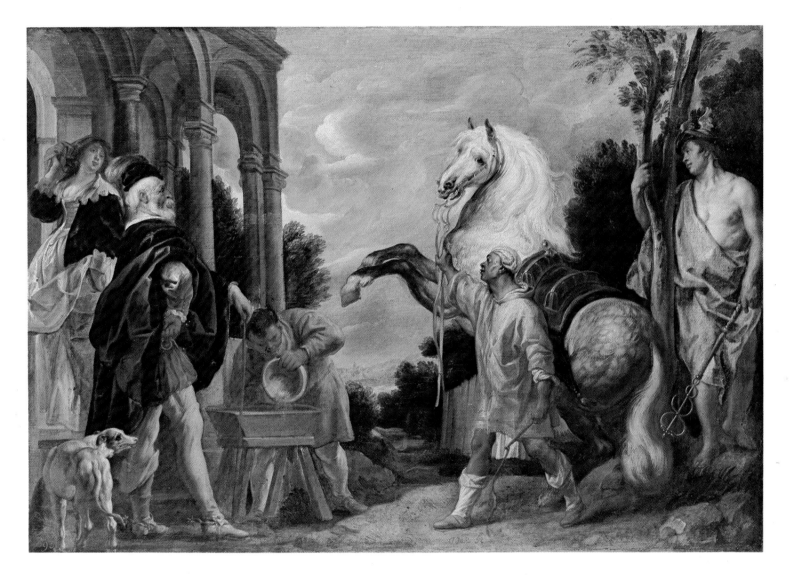

Colorplate 29. JACOB JORDAENS. *The Eye of the Master Makes the Horse Fat.* c. 1645. 32×44⅛″.
Gemäldegalerie, Cassel

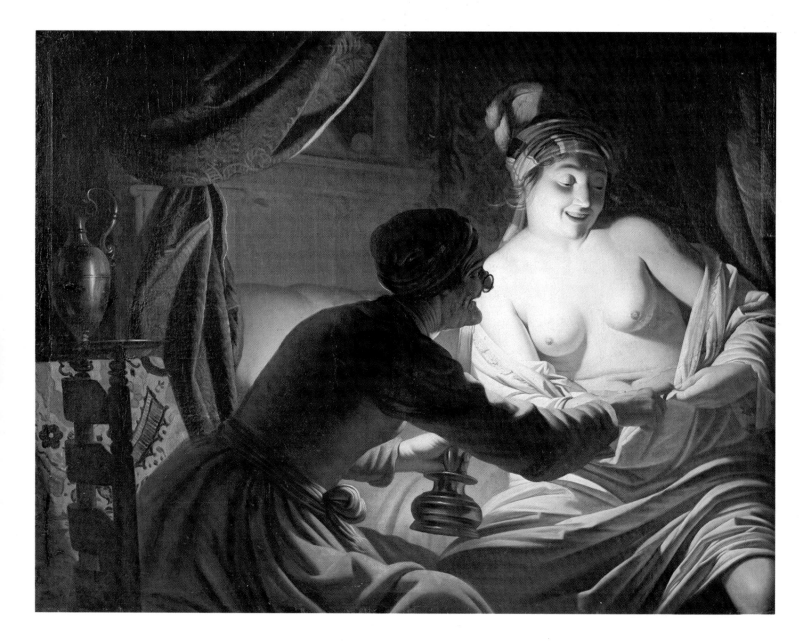

Colorplate 30. GERARD HONTHORST. *Merry Flea Hunt*. c. 1625–30. 41⅜×53½".
Öffentliche Kunstsammlung, Basel

5

Dutch Painting in the Seventeenth Century

The rebellion in the Netherlands against Spanish domination succeeded in freeing only the seven northern provinces, frequently called Holland after the name of the largest and wealthiest province. By the truce of 1609, Spain virtually recognized the independence of these United Provinces. The war continued after the expiration of the truce in 1621, and it was for the Dutch a mere holding action; never seriously threatened, their republic grew into a power of the first rank.

When peace finally came in 1648, Holland's prosperity was unequaled in Europe. Banking, commerce, industry, and agriculture flourished alike. In rivalry with the English, Dutch ships plied all the oceans, linking the motherland with newly founded colonies in the Americas and the East Indies. Calvinism was the official religion, but dissident groups such as the Mennonites and even Catholics were tolerated; Jews as well as English Separatists found it a haven from persecution.

In a Calvinist country no demands were made on art for the sake of worship: Dutch churches were whitewashed and bare of painting (see fig. 245). Most commissions came from private individuals or professional organizations. For some of the greatest Dutch artists, including Frans Hals, Rembrandt, and Gerard Terborch, portraits were the chief source of income. Yet it is certain that commissions were insufficient to sustain the ever growing number of artists. Thus for the first time in history, artists produced largely for the open market.[1] In other words, painters, like manufacturers, were faced with the need of producing negotiable merchandise.

This they managed to do. We know that pictures were used in payment of debts, as collateral on loans, and as objects of investment if not speculation. The Dutch (and to a lesser extent the Flemish) both encouraged and regulated the activities of professional art dealers. Many painters, among them Rembrandt, found dealing in art and antiques a tempting (if risky) mode of increasing their earnings.[2] We know of lawsuits about the genuineness of paintings and regulations concerning art auctions. With art firmly established as a recognized facet of Dutch capitalism, it is little wonder that many young men chose it as a profession. The result, however, was an oversupply of paintings and a lowering of prices; and although it was bound to set up a vicious circle, the depression of prices forced artists to step up production. Hence many of these pictures were produced at great speed. Albrecht Dürer once boasted that a picture he did in Venice was completed in five days: many Dutch landscapes may have taken less than a day to paint.

Pictures painted primarily for a middle-class population had to be relatively small to fit modest dwellings. It was equally desirable that the subject matter be easily comprehended and of general interest. Once an artist found he had a special skill in any one subject he was likely to repeat it. The system discouraged experimentation and favored specialization. Collaboration of several specialists on one picture was not uncommon.

The choice of themes may have been influenced by the growth of a national consciousness and the pride of the Dutch in the country they had wrested from two powerful foes, the sea and the Spaniards. Their fishing boats and their warships, the windmills and the churches, the cattle and the markets, the very food on their tables—these were the visible tokens of their national identity and of a way of life they had fought for and were ready to defend again.

There is, then, some truth in the popular notion that Dutch seventeenth-century painting is an expression of Dutch patriotism. But this is not the whole story.

To begin with, the "realism" of Dutch painters was selective. Cheerful subjects were preferred to disturbing ones. Unpleasant incidents were given a humorous or moralizing slant. The ministrations of a village quack or the visits of traveling dentists were shown as popular attractions made more rewarding by the suffering of the hapless patients. The ailments of languishing young ladies (fig. 228) were recognized by sly old physicians as *minne pijn* ("lovesickness"). Save for an occasional tailor, baker, weaver, or blacksmith, men are rarely shown at work. To judge by Dutch painting, life was an almost continuous enjoyment of leisure.

Pictures of catastrophes, such as the Delft pow-

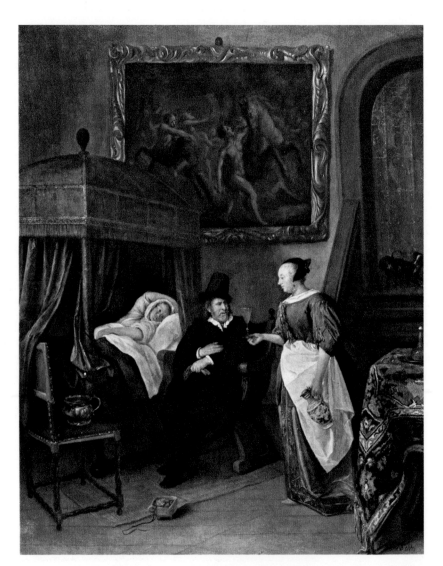

228. JAN STEEN. *The Lovesick Maiden.* Third quarter 17th century. Panel, 23¾×19¼". Mauritshuis, The Hague

224

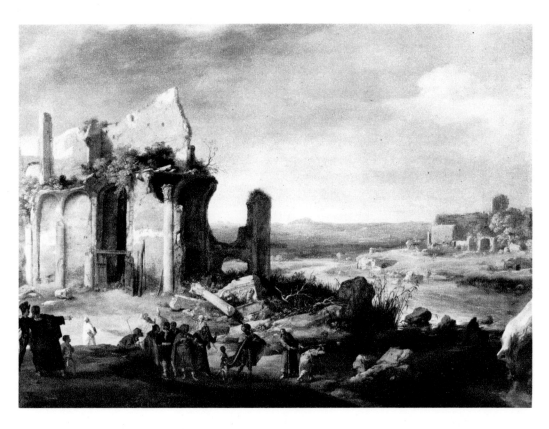

229. BARTHOLOMEUS BREENBERGH.
Moses and Aaron
Changing Waters of Egypt
into Blood. 1631.
Panel, 23⅝ × 32⅞".
J. Paul Getty Museum,
Malibu, California

der explosion of 1654 and the ruins of the Amsterdam town hall after the fire of 1652, are exceptional. If storms at sea are shown, they primarily demonstrate the stout Dutch defenses that protect the land, or the seaworthiness of the boats and the courage of their sailors.

Moreover, the Dutch did not paint only their own country. A large group of painters, such as

Bartholomeus Breenbergh (c. 1599–1655/59; fig. 229), Jan Both (1618–1652), and Nicolaas Berchem (1620–1683), specialized in Italian scenes. Allaert van Everdingen (1621–1675) visited Sweden and Norway and henceforth specialized in waterfalls and craggy cliffs enhanced by the peaked silhouettes of the northern spruce (fig. 230). After having spent seven years in Brazil, Frans Post

230. ALLAERT VAN EVERDINGEN.
Swedish Landscape.
Mid-17th century. 53¾ × 71¼".
Museum Boymans-Van Beuningen,
Rotterdam

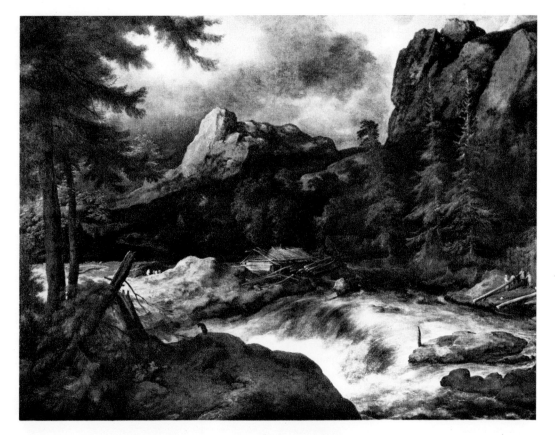

(c. 1612–1680) continued painting Brazilian scenery to the end of his long life.[3] Other artists depicted the colorful life of foreign nations. Pieter van Laer (1592/95–1642; see page 86) and his followers did Roman street scenes with peasants, beggars, or masked revelers. More exotic still are large canvases by Aelbert Eeckhout, who portrayed the weird appearance of South American Indians (fig. 231) and painted still lifes of their handicraft and tropical fruits.

Dutch painting, however, was not based on observation alone: some of the best of it brought to life narratives from sacred or secular literature or rendered allegories and emblems.

Though there was no official place for religious painting (save for occasional works done for Catholic churches), Biblical subjects abound in Dutch art; they were meant for contemplation rather than worship. Under the influence of Adam Elsheimer (see pages 208 – 210) and Paul Bril, several Amsterdam artists (such as Pieter Lastman, 1583–1633) early in the century painted stories from the Bible; their pictures are generally small and characterized by romantic settings and fanciful costumes.

The anachronisms in these works extended also into the representations of medieval or classical subjects. Dutch women modeled for the goddess Diana in paintings by Van Loo and Vermeer without changing their clothes: no Dutch painter was ever a classicist in the manner of Poussin. But it escaped the Dutch no more than people elsewhere that stories from the distant past contained valuable analogies to contemporary situations. Thus the story of Claudius Civilis, a Batavian who had fought against the Romans, acquired a topical significance since the Dutch, claiming the old Germanic hero as their ancestor, saw in his exploits a parallel to their own revolt against Spain.[4] The new town hall of Amsterdam was decorated with paintings of the struggle of the Batavians (see page 247), as well as with reliefs of mythological subjects appropriate to their location: the *Fall of Icarus*, for instance, was placed above the door of the Chamber where business failures had

to be declared. A print of *Flora's Chariot of Fools* (fig. 232) is a satirical allegory on the mad tulip speculations of the 1630s.

For all its supposed realism, Dutch art frequently made use of allegory. Emblem books—a creation of the sixteenth century—had their greatest vogue in Holland. They furnish evidence to suggest that deeper meanings may lie hidden in simple genre scenes.[5] Half-length figures in genre actions may illustrate the five senses (fig. 233), the seasons, or vices like gluttony or greed. For from being the harmless record of a normal bedtime ritual, Gerard Honthorst's *Merry Flea Hunt* (colorplate 30) hints at the fate meted out to another kind of nocturnal "visitor" by the two laughing women, most certainly a procuress and prostitute. Pictures within pictures (in paintings by Metsu, Steen, Vermeer, and others) often suggest meanings not immediately obvious from the action in the foreground.[6]

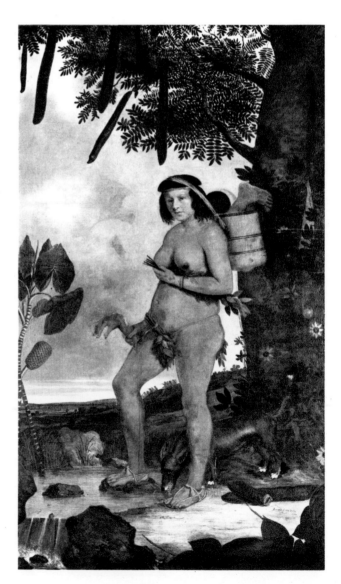

231. AELBERT EECKHOUT. *Tapuya Woman.*
1641. 8'8" × 5'2½".
Nationalmuseet, Copenhagen

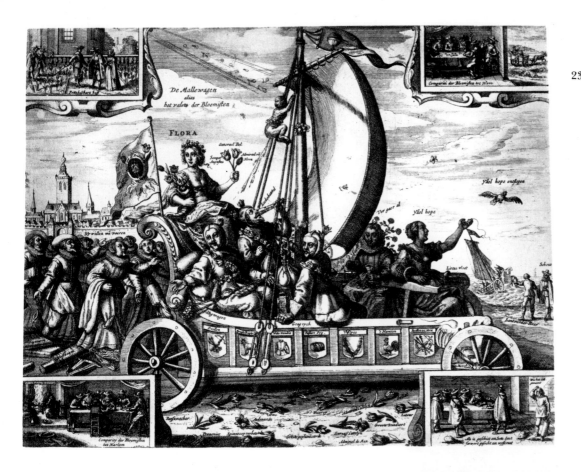

232. CRISPIJN DE PASSE.
*Flora's Chariot of Fools
(Flora's Mallewagen).* 1637
(engraving, after
Hendrick Gerritsz. Pot).
Rijksmuseum, Amsterdam

Still lifes of old books, candles, clay pipes, and musical instruments were easily understood as allegories of vanity, even without the human skull added by some masters.[7] A good many associations, quickly grasped by their contemporaries, may be lost to us. In a poem "On the Image of a Fisher Girl from Scheveningen Carrying a Basket with Fish on Her Head," Jacob Cats contrasts servitude in the city to liberty at the seashore, even if bought at the price of a hard and meager existence. Frans Hals had painted such a picture (fig. 234), and we may wonder whether he had had in mind something akin to Cats's thought. Even a prosaic artist like Hals was not above using emblematic elements, carrying special messages for the initiated.

All the achievements that have given Dutch seventeenth-century painting its eminent place in the history of art were accomplished within the chronological limits of two generations. In the beginning of the century Mannerist traditions

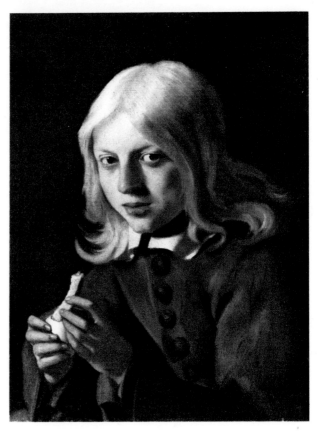

233. MICHIEL SWEERTS. *Allegory of Taste.*
Mid-17th century. 21¼ × 16⅛".
Staatsgalerie, Stuttgart

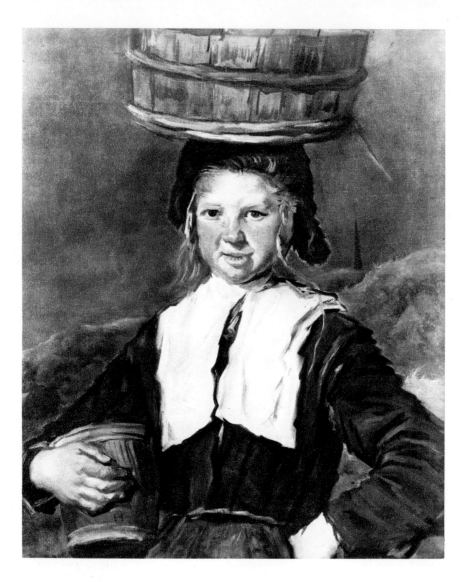

234. FRANS HALS.
Fisher Girl. c. 1635.
Panel, 25 × 19⅝".
Art Museum, Cincinnati
(Mary Hanna Collection)

were still quite strong, especially with artists in Haarlem and Utrecht. Younger masters, like soldiers trying to establish a beachhead, struck out in different directions but shared one common desire: to replace the stilted pictorial language of the Mannerists with forthright and simple statements.[8] By 1625, the new generation of painters was firmly established: among them were Hercules Seghers (1589/90–after 1632), Gerard Honthorst (1590–1656), Dirk Hals (1591–1656), Jan van Goyen (1596–1656), Pieter Jansz. Saenredam (1597–1665), Salomon van Ruysdael (c. 1600–1670), Simon de Vlieger (c. 1600/5–1653), Aert van der Neer (1603–1677), and Rembrandt van

235. THOMAS DE KEYSER. *Portrait of a Woman.*
1628. Panel. 31½ × 25".
Museum of Fine Arts, Budapest

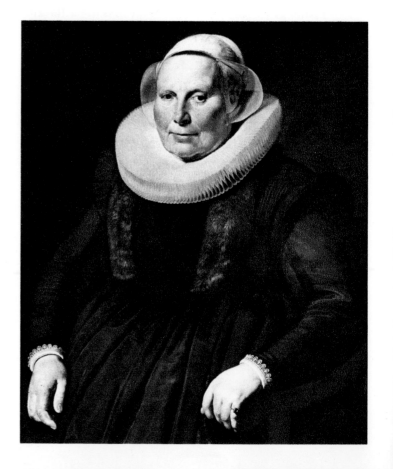

Rijn (1606–1669). Frans Hals (c. 1580–1666) is a tangible figure only after his thirtieth year.

Looking at the last decades of the century, we find them devoid of any major artistic accomplishment. Many of the best painters were dead (Rembrandt; Frans Hals; Jan Vermeer, 1632–1675) or approaching the end (Jan van de Capelle, c. 1624–1679; Jan Steen, 1625/26–1679; Jacob van Ruisdael, 1628/29–1682). Others continued along established paths without introducing new ideas. Moreover, French influences gained in popularity. With Adriaen van der Werff (1659–1722) an ideal of elegant virtuosity supplanted the solid merits of earlier Dutch art.

In the period encompassing virtually all major achievements of Dutch art (1610/20–1670/80), a crucial development took place around the middle of the century. It coincides with the emergence, in the Peace of Westphalia (1648), of Holland as one of the great political and commercial powers of Europe. Up to the middle of the century Hollanders are depicted as men of simple tastes and frugal habits. After 1650 we notice a trend toward luxury, possibly connected with the fact that more people were able to live on income from investments. It is instructive to compare portraits painted in the 1620s and '30s by Frans Hals (fig. 234) and Thomas de Keyser (fig. 235) with those done after the middle of the century by Gerard Terborch (c. 1617–1681; fig. 236) and Bartholomeus van der Helst (1613–1670). On the one hand we are confronted with hardy, reliable, uncomplicated types dressed in fabrics of sturdy quality and dull color; on the other we are admitted into the company of figures dressed in delicate silk and other fine materials: even the chairs are velvet-covered. With the refinement of fashion goes an aura of social exclusiveness and polite manners.

Similar distinctions can be traced through all categories of subjects. Still lifes painted before 1650 (fig. 237) are apt to assemble objects made of glass, pewter, and earthenware; the food is plain fare—bread, cheese, smoked ham, herring, and beer. Still lifes painted after 1650 (fig. 238; color-plate 31) are more likely to include objects made

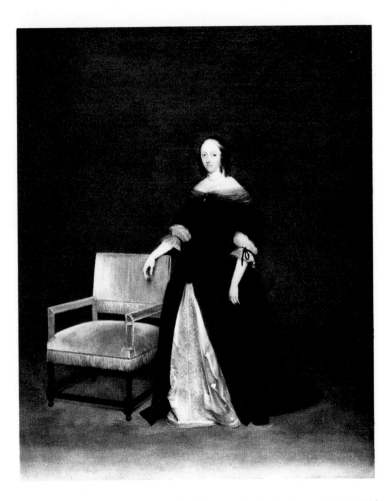

236. GERARD TERBORCH. *Portrait of Geertruid Marienburg (1645–1722)* c. 1670. 32 × 25½". National Museum, Prague

of silver, gold, crystal, and porcelain; the food might include lobsters, peaches, and wine.

Interiors painted before the middle of the century, in works by Pieter Codde (1599–1678), Jakob Duck (c. 1600–after 1660), and Anthonie Palamedes (1600/1–1673), are generally plain, with wooden floors and meager decoration. Those done later, in paintings by Jan Steen, Pieter de Hoogh (1629–after 1684), Gabriel Metsu (1629–1667), and Jan Vermeer, more often than not have marble flooring, magnificent curtains, and pictures in gilt frames. Like the stately mansions that began to rise along the fashionable canals of Amsterdam, they mirror clearly the tastes of a rich society.

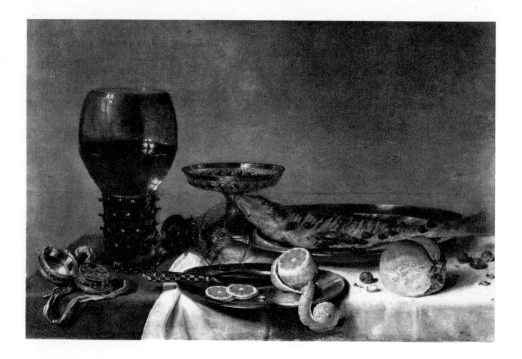

237. **PIETER CLAESZ.**
Still Life. 1629.
Panel, 18⅛ × 27⅛″.
Mauritshuis, The Hague

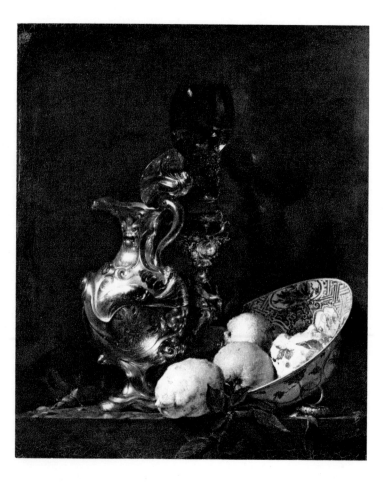

More was involved, however, than the exchange of one set of motifs or one fashion for another. If we examine subjects where the visual data could not have changed much from the first part of the century to the second, we see that the very style of painting changed. Most instructive is the development of landscape. In the works of Hercules Seghers (fig. 239; see also page 236), Jan Porcellis (1584–1632), Jan van Goyen, and Salomon van Ruysdael, Holland is a different country from that depicted by Philips Koninck (1619–1688; fig. 240), Aelbert Cuyp (c. 1620–1691), Jacob van Ruisdael, and Meindert Hobbema (1638–1709). Earlier artists saw a nearly monochromatic world in which all forms were in tones of brown and gray. No such generalization is possible about later landscapists, who agree only in the conviction that color be assigned a more dynamic role. Whereas

238. **WILLEM KALF.** *Still Life with Nautilus.*
After 1650. 28⅛ × 24½″.
Rijksmuseum, Amsterdam

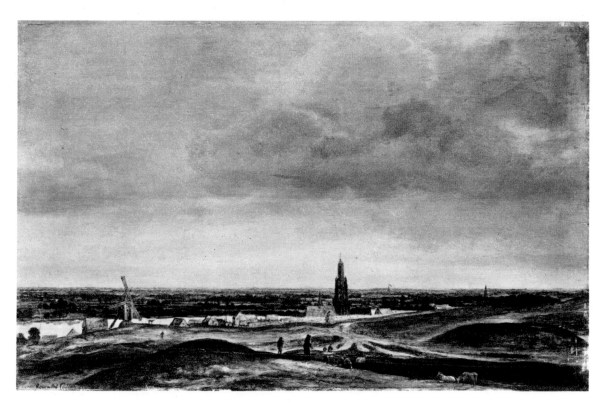

239. HERCULES SEGHERS. *View of Rhenen*. c. 1630. Panel, 16½ × 26¼″
(upper portion added later; original dimensions 8½ × 26¼″). Dahlem Museum, Berlin

240. PHILIPS KONINCK. *Extensive Landscape with a Hawking Party*. c. 1670. 52¼ × 63½″. National Gallery, London

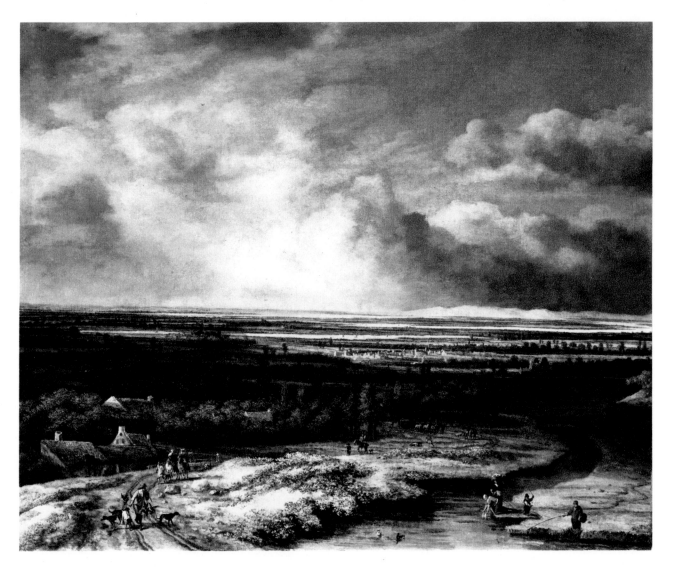

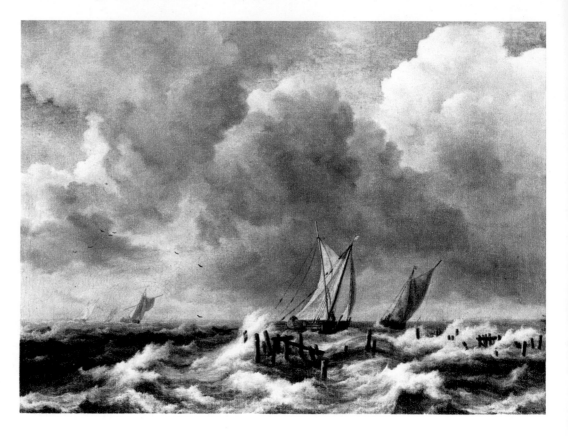

241. JACOB VAN RUISDAEL.
The Haarlem Sea.
Third quarter 17th century.
21¾ × 25¾".
Musées Royaux des Beaux-Arts,
Brussels

earlier landscapes appear to have been painted under skies permanently overcast, the late ones acknowledge the wide potentialities of outdoor light. Cuyp (colorplate 32) studied the effects of moist sunsets and painted gold-rimmed clouds floating below a cerulean sky. Light and shadow are contrasted dramatically in landscapes by Jacob van Ruisdael and Koninck and seascapes by Willem van de Velde (1633–1707).

The very texture of objects seen in nature seems to change when we come to the younger generation: forms gain density and weight (fig. 241). Foaming waves battering the pilings in a sea storm by Jacob van Ruisdael leave no doubt about the formidable power of masses of water; by contrast the lacelike undulations of waves in Van Goyen's panels (fig. 242) never threaten even the lightest fishing vessels. And compared to the structural

242. JAN VAN GOYEN.
*Landscape with Rippled Sea
(View of Dordrecht).*
1644–53. 38¼ × 58¼".
Musées Royaux des Beaux-Arts,
Brussels

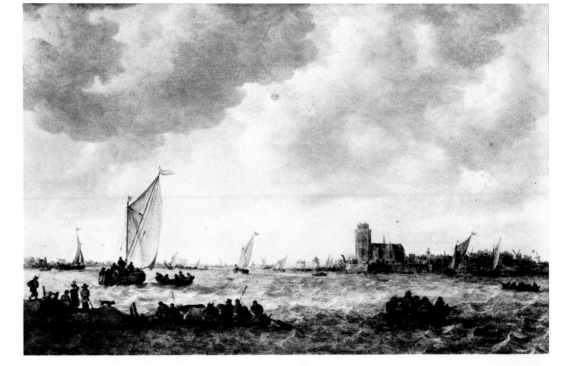

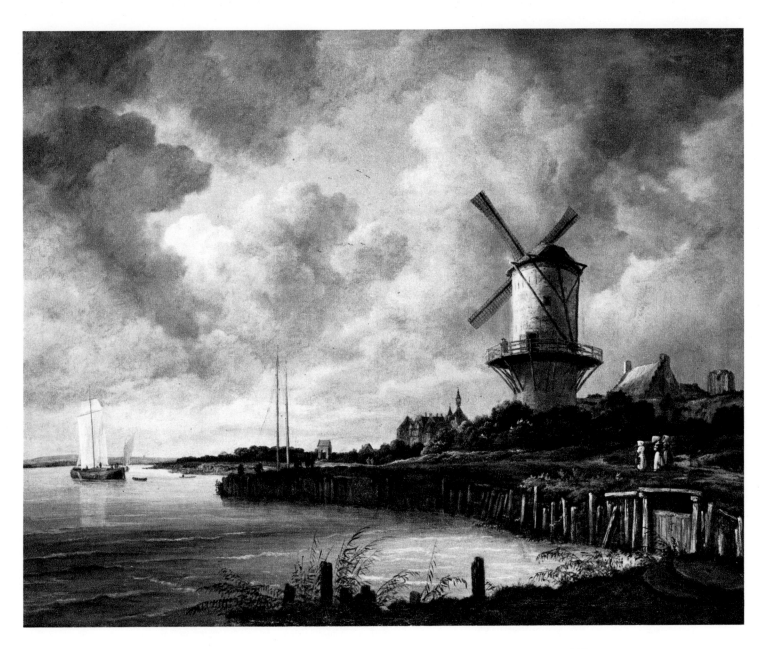

243. JACOB VAN RUISDAEL.
Windmill near
Wijk-bij-Duurstede.
c. 1665. 32⅝ × 39¾".
Rijksmuseum, Amsterdam

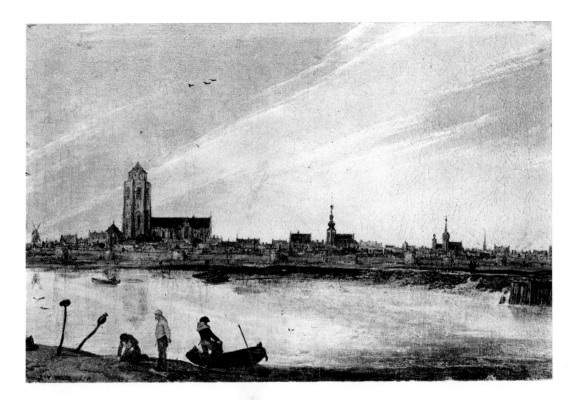

244. ESAIAS VAN DE VELDE.
View of Zierikzee.
c. 1615. 10½ × 15¾".
Dahlem Museum, Berlin

firmness of the Delft skyline painted by Vermeer (colorplate 44) or the rugged masonry of the windmill near Wijk as seen by Jacob van Ruisdael (fig. 243), the buildings in landscapes by Esaias van de Velde (c. 1591–1630; fig. 244), Van Goyen, or even Van der Neer look flimsy and insubstantial. In the paintings of the first half of the century trees are apt to be scrubby and stunted; of the second half, majestic and luxuriant. In paintings by Molijn, Van Goyen, and Seghers, the countryside looks arid and uninviting; in those of Koninck, Ruisdael, and Cuyp, it appears fecund and widely cultivated.

It is likely that as recorders of the actual scenery men like Van Goyen and Salomon van Ruysdael deserve our confidence more than Jacob van Ruisdael or Aelbert Cuyp. The Jewish cemetery near Amsterdam (colorplate 33), which Jacob van Ruisdael painted in two powerful canvases, still exists near a quiet little brook. In Ruisdael's paintings this modest flow is changed into a rushing mountain stream and the background is enlivened by ruins of a Gothic building that never stood there at all. Stimulation of a poetic mood or philosophic reflection through calculated manipulation of landscape elements is more charac-teristic of the period after 1650 than before. Earlier, only Seghers in his haunting etchings (fig. 247), Rembrandt in a few paintings, and Aert van der Neer in his moonlight studies had used landscape for emotional effects, but Ruisdael went far beyond them in his romantic approach. In the *Jewish Cemetery* the silent tombs, the crumbling ruin, and a blanched tree trunk combine in an eloquent *memento mori,* while growing bushes and trees, foaming waters, and drifting clouds speak of the renewal of life.

Analogous observations could be made about other categories, but it suffices to look briefly at the painting of church interiors. Those painted by later artists, such as Emanuel de Witte, are exciting with their profusion of flags, tombs, epitaphs; elegant people walking in the majestic halls provide additional spots of color (colorplate 34). By contrast an artist like Saenredam, who formed his style before the middle of the century, stressed the bareness of whitewashed walls (fig. 245); what figures he introduced were rendered in dark accents.

Of all the stylistic elements contributing to the unique qualities of Dutch painting in the third quarter of the seventeenth century, light had a

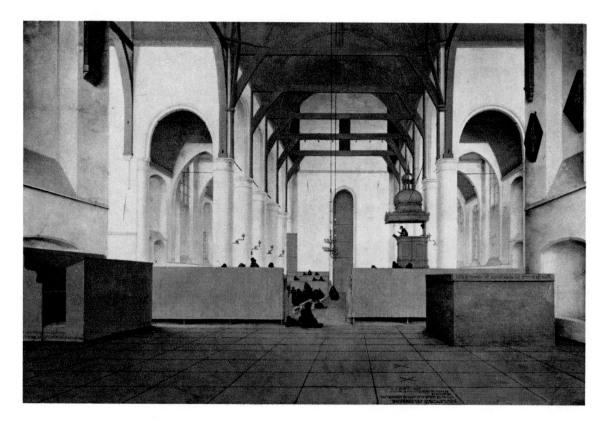

245. PIETER JANSZ. SAENREDAM. *Interior of the Church of St. Odulphus, Assendelft.* 1649. Panel, 19½ × 30″. Rijksmuseum, Amsterdam

234

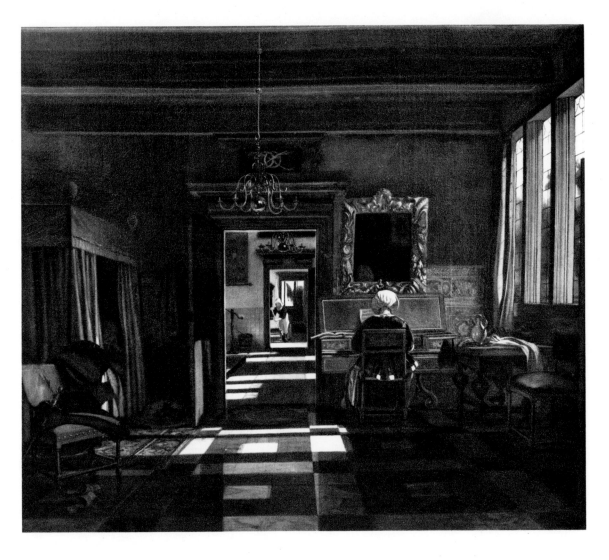

particularly important function. Brutal Caravaggesque contrasts had been common during the earlier period. In the second half of the century, artists delighted in painting the seemingly capricious gliding of the sun's rays over floors and walls, flashing back from glass or metal, giving sudden radiance to tiled roofs, or bleaching linen spread on the meadows. In pictures where all physical action has come to a standstill, the wandering of the light alone provides the beholder with a sense of motion (fig. 246).

This motion involves the category of time. As we become aware of the impermanence of the light-and-dark patterns in the picture and realize that they must inevitably, if imperceptibly, change, we are also forced to see the scene in time as much as in space. Using the silent movement of

light for suggesting the passing of time was not altogether new. The slow but constant flow of the minutes and the hours had been implied before in works such as Dürer's engraving of *St. Jerome,* Piero della Francesca's *Sinigaglia Madonna,* and even Jan van Eyck's *Arnolfini Wedding.* In these works the effect was still closely allied to a subject of absorbing interest. In the paintings of the later Dutch masters, nameless and sometimes faceless people are caught in trivial activities and inhabit fragments of space without import. It does not matter who they are or what they do. With a delicious sense of recognition we share in a pervasive mood of peace and harmony, all the more beguiling as there seems to be neither a beginning nor an end to it. Only a superficial formulation would claim for these pictures that in them we can see "time stand still." Actually, the unbroken continuity of time is the essence and deepest mystery of these works.

Against this general background of Dutch painting a few artists stand out with contributions sufficiently personal to warrant separate discussion. Rembrandt, of course, is in a class by himself. If Frans Hals and Vermeer are sometimes bracketed with him, it is for reasons not always germane to genius—admiration for the bravura technique of Hals and consciousness of the extreme rarity of Vermeer's works. Virtually forgotten for about two hundred years, both masters owe their modern fame to critics of the late nineteenth century; other figures deserve recognition for talents not substantially less than theirs. Hercules Seghers is one—an artist fearfully poor while he lived but now increasingly admired for his few paintings and extremely rare etchings. Many of his landscapes portray a world caught in an inexorable process of corrosion and decay. He etched ruins, old books with wrinkled leaves, a skull, a sinister storm at sea, dead trees, and parched plains. One of his finest prints, touched up faintly with watercolor, is of a tree almost floating in space, its trunk no more than an insubstantial accumulation of dots, its branches drooping like the lines of a dirge (fig. 247). Seghers, however, was also among the first to catch the beauty of a perfectly flat country where only a church spire or the arm of a windmill breaks through the low, straight line of the horizon (see fig. 239).

More than the other Dutch schools, that of Utrecht was in particularly close touch with the developments in Italy. It was a group of Utrecht masters, each of whom had worked for a considerable time in Rome, that spearheaded Caravaggio's influence in the European North, and among these Utrecht "caravaggisti" Hendrick Terbrugghen (1588–1629) was by far the most interesting.[9] Despite the brevity of his life Terbrugghen's art has considerable range and individuality. Unlike

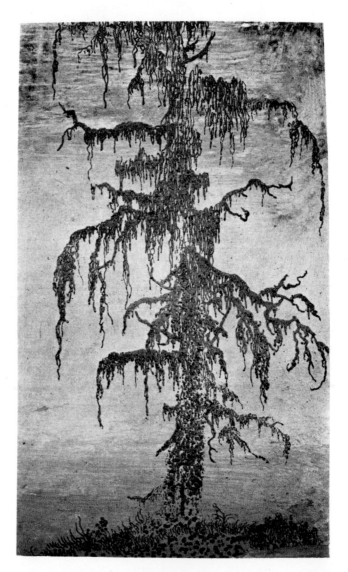

247. HERCULES SEGHERS. *Pine Tree*.
c. 1630. Etching, 6⅝ × 4".
Rijksmuseum, Amsterdam

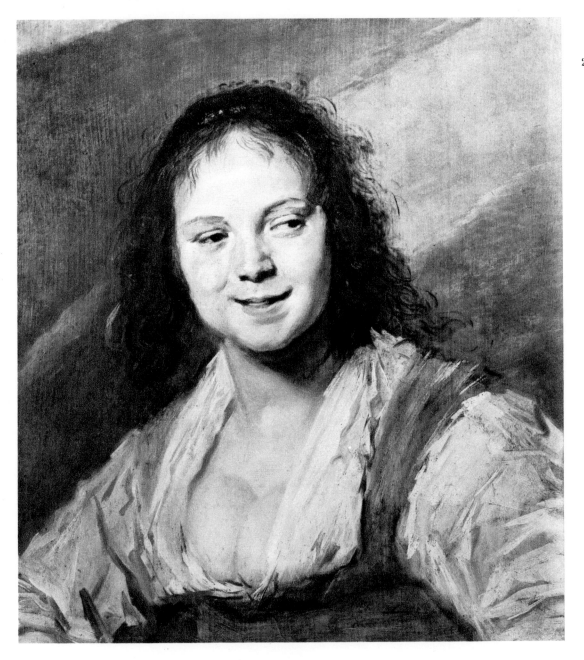

248. FRANS HALS.
Gypsy Girl. c. 1635.
22⅞ × 20½".
The Louvre, Paris

most of the Dutch painters of his generation, he was an accomplished colorist, notable for piquant harmonies of lilac, rose pink, and lemon yellow, frequently relieved by a soft gray. While the surface modulation of other Utrecht painters of this group—such as Honthorst and Baburen—is generally harsh, that of Terbrugghen shows an almost imperceptible transition between light and dark. Pictures like the softly illuminated *Boy with Wineglass* (colorplate 35) make it easy to understand why certain of Terbrugghen's paintings have been attributed to Jan Vermeer van Delft.

Despite obvious technical differences, the many half-length figures by Frans Hals of laughing musicians, topers, gypsy girls (fig. 248), and children plainly prove the artist's acquaintance with the Utrecht followers of Caravaggio. Born in Flanders, Hals came to Haarlem as a child and seems to have stayed there all his life. A sociable man and careless manager, Hals was often in financial trouble, but probably knew that he could always redeem himself by painting another portrait. He never seems to have lacked commissions, and the reason is easy to see: he imparted to his models a certain *élan vital*, all the more convincing as he evidently had an unfailing ability to catch a "spitting" image. Each of his models appears as an unmistakable individual, brought to life with deft, sure strokes of the brush.[10]

Hals is best known for his outgoing, optimistic portraits of the 1620s and '30s. His coloristically most subtle portraits were painted in the 1640s, and his psychologically most penetrating ones in the 1640s and '50s, when the ebullience of his earlier portraits gave way to a harsh, severe, sometimes almost sullen expression.

For all the liveliness of his conception and technical virtuosity (which was already a legend in the master's own time), Hals showed little imagination when it came to posing his models. Like a routine photographer he had a set of standard attitudes that he repeated with only token varia-

tions. Among them is a pose, not even invented by him, in which the seated model leans one arm on the back of a chair and looks at the beholder over it (fig. 249).

The assets as well as the limitations of Hals's art are evidenced by his group portraits. Groups of men (and eventually of women, too) bound together by mutual interests and common activities were more often portrayed in Holland than anywhere else in Europe.[11] The tradition goes back to the beginning of the sixteenth century; the first groups so portrayed were men who together had made a pilgrimage to Jerusalem or who had joined a company of the civil guard. While later in the century pious sight-seeing trips to the Holy Land became less fashionable (and more difficult), the joining of military guilds remained popular: companies of riflemen, named for such saints as George, Sebastian, and Hadrian, continued to be active patrons. Indeed, their airs grew more martial and their outfits more colorful as their mili-

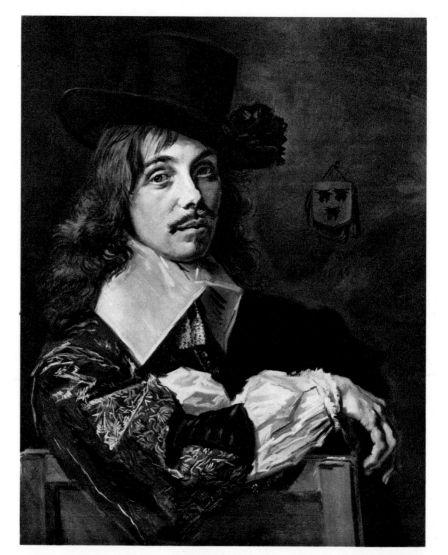

249. FRANS HALS.
*Young Man in a Large Hat
(Balthasar Coymans).*
1645. 11½ × 9⅛".
National Gallery of Art,
Washington, D.C.
(Andrew Mellon Collection)

238

Colorplate 31. WILLEM KALF. *Still Life*. c. 1665. 25⅝ × 21¼″.
National Gallery of Art, Washington, D.C. (Chester Dale Collection)

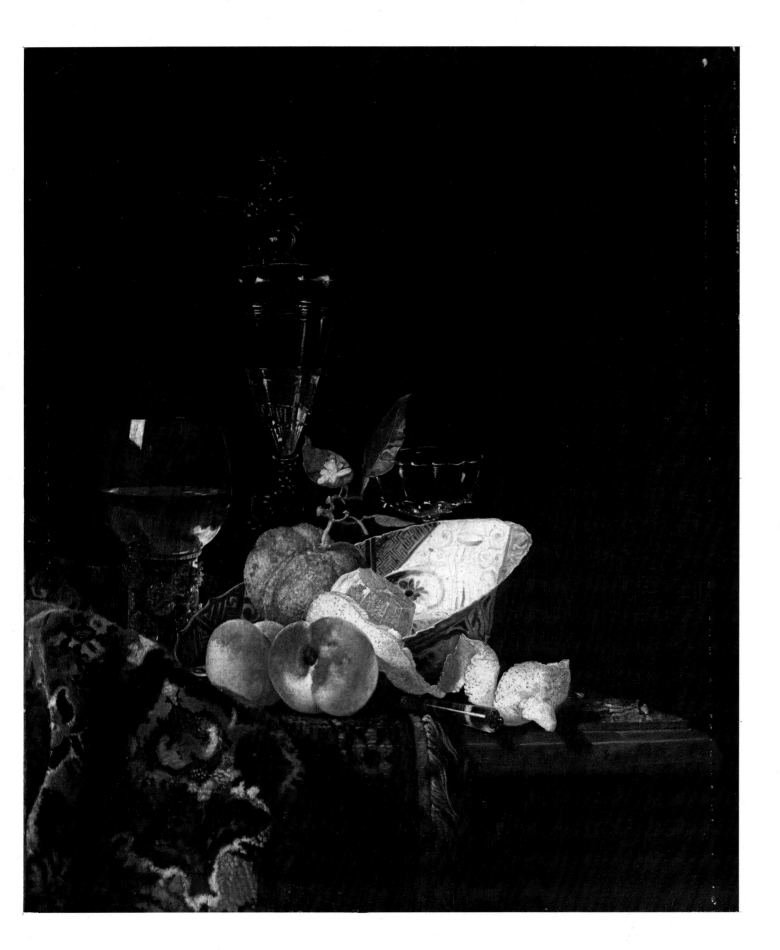

Colorplate 32. AELBERT CUYP. *A Herdsman with Five Cows by a River*. c. 1655. Panel, 17⅞ × 29⅛″.
National Gallery, London

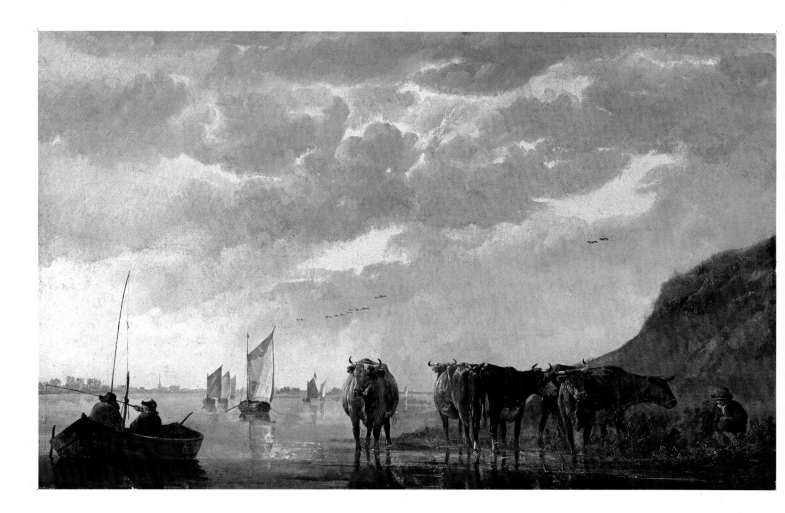

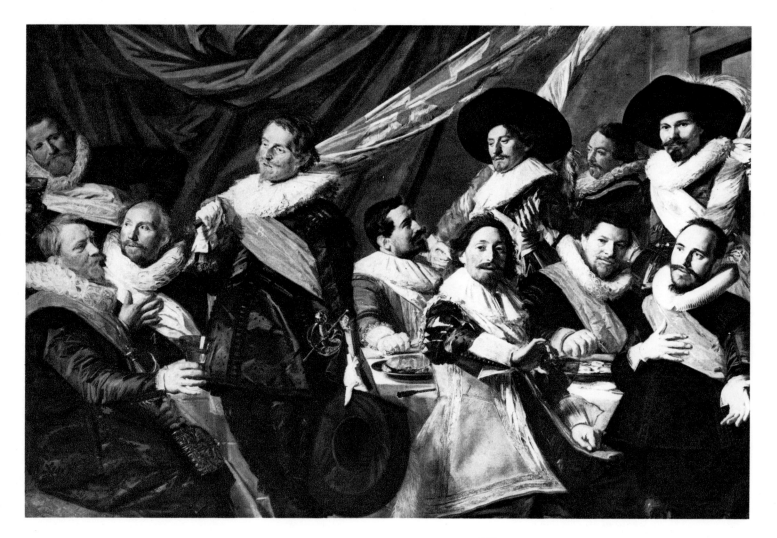

250. FRANS HALS.
*Banquet of Officers of the Civic Guard
of St. George at Haarlem.*
1627. 5′10½″ × 8′5⅜″.
Frans Hals Museum, Haarlem

tary value and readiness for combat declined.

When Frans Hals was first charged with painting such a military guild (1616),[12] he adopted an established compositional pattern, arranging his models informally around a banquet table and giving prominence to the officers—captain, lieutenant, and flag-bearer. In two group portraits of the 1620s, he made an effort to avoid the looseness of this arrangement (fig. 250): he distributed the figures fairly regularly over the canvas, giving each one about the same amount of space. While some of the men look out of the picture, most of them try to establish, through gesture, glance, or turn of the body, some measure of contact with their fellows. In this effort, however, they fail. Ultimately, Hals's concern was with isolated indi-

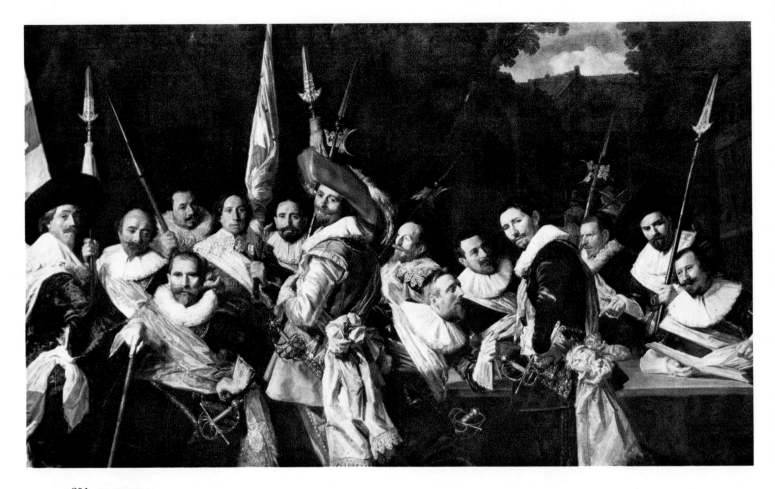

251. FRANS HALS.
*Assembly of Officers and Subalterns
of the Guard of St. Hadrian at Haarlem.*
1633. 6'9½" × 11'6⅝".
Frans Hals Museum, Haarlem

viduals, and their eloquent gestures, their smiles, and their invitations to drink remain unanswered. Watching them, one is reminded of a party where everyone talks and no one listens. The sense of unity, so clearly aimed at by compositional devices, is lost because Hals was unable to unite his models in a common action.

He never again tried a "dramatic" configuration. In his group portraits of 1633 (fig. 251) and 1639, most figures turn outward again; in the former, Hals achieved an air of easy informality that makes this perhaps his most successful portrait of militia men. In the later one he reverts to the primitive device of lining up his men in rows. As usual, each man is a distinct and striking personality, Hals himself appearing among them. Yet the whole is an almost pathetic admission of insufficiency, all the more dismal as it was done in the same year in which the most dramatic of all military group

242

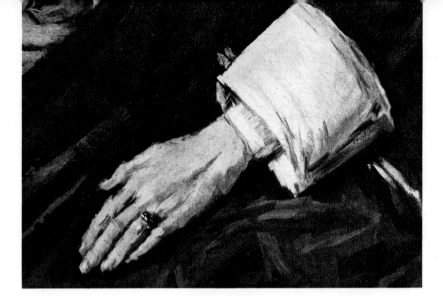

252. **FRANS HALS.**
*Women Regents of the
Old Men's Home at Haarlem*
(detail of brushwork; see colorplate 36)

portraits was begun: Rembrandt's *Night Watch* (fig. 257).

The last of Hals's group portraits are of so-called regents—trustees of commercial, professional, or charitable organizations. Traditionally they were shown sitting around a table, which presented no problem, since there were rarely more than six figures to accommodate, including the servant standing in the background. Shortly before his death, Hals painted the men and women regents of the Haarlem old men's home (colorplate 36). Nothing could be more artless than the compositional arrangement of these canvases; yet these paintings by an artist well past his eightieth year are remarkable performances. The women sit rigidly in fearsome propriety. One is tempted to scan their faces, as one might those of a jury, to discover what their attitude might have been toward those in their charge. It may be our own softness that fails to see compassion in these dour faces, or generosity in these bony hands. Even compared with Rembrandt's *Syndics of the Drapers' Guild* (fig. 258), finished only a few years before, Hals's latest canvases stand their ground. What they lack in the suggestion of action and unspoken drama they make up for by the somber dignity of the group as a whole and a near-magical economy and freedom of execution (fig. 252).

A widespread notion holds that Rembrandt van Rijn[13] was an outsider in Dutch seventeenth-century painting. Nothing is further from the truth. As a painter of Biblical and mythological subjects he continued the tradition of his master Pieter Lastman and other Dutch followers of Adam Elsheimer. Like dozens of others he painted the portraits of Dutch middle-class citizens, undoubtedly to their complete satisfaction. If he occupied a special place it is because, in plain fact, he was the one great genius in a country teeming with men of talent. Rembrandt towers over them by virtue of his great range, his productivity, his wealth of imagination, and his depth of feeling.

Tracing the development of Rembrandt's art during the forty-four years of his active life (his first works date from 1625), one notices a basic change of direction taking place during the 1640s. In works of the first twenty years of his activity, Rembrandt's characters are possessed of powerful physical energies that are released by violent action in space. They gesticulate freely, their faces yield readily to emotional impulses, and their silhouettes undulate picturesquely. Later in his career the figures are likely to be heavy and blocklike, and they move slowly and deliberately, if at all. Their physical existence is subordinated to their intense psychological life; what they do is less important than what they feel. Indeed, the weight of their thoughts is apt to impede their capacity for action.

What is true of individual figures applies to his compositions as a whole. Agitated and full of contrasts in Rembrandt's earlier work, the compositions conform more to classical patterns in his

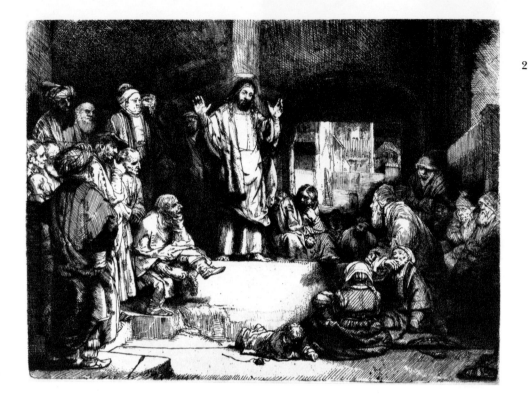

later. Only during the earlier part of his career (chiefly the 1630s) do they reflect an influence from Rubens. Recollections of the Italian Renaissance are manifest in works of the 1650s, such as the severely rectilinear etchings of the *Petite Tombe* (fig. 253) or the *Ecce Homo* (fig. 254).[14]

As one would expect, Rembrandt handled color very differently in his early work and in his late. His earliest paintings still have traces of the garish colorism found in much Dutch art of the beginning of the century. In the 1630s his colors are blended more harmoniously, occasionally approaching the monochrome, though where it suited the subject they still could speak in loud

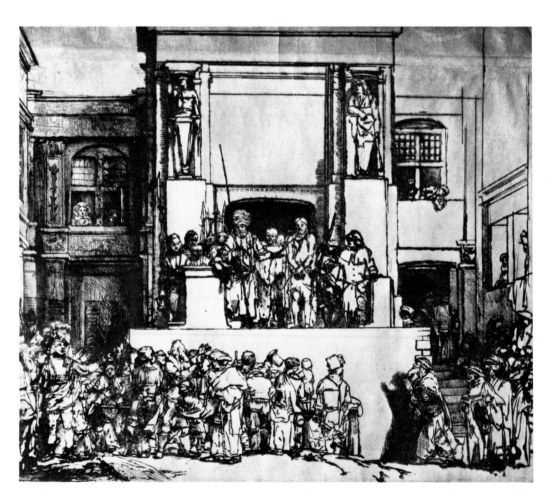

244

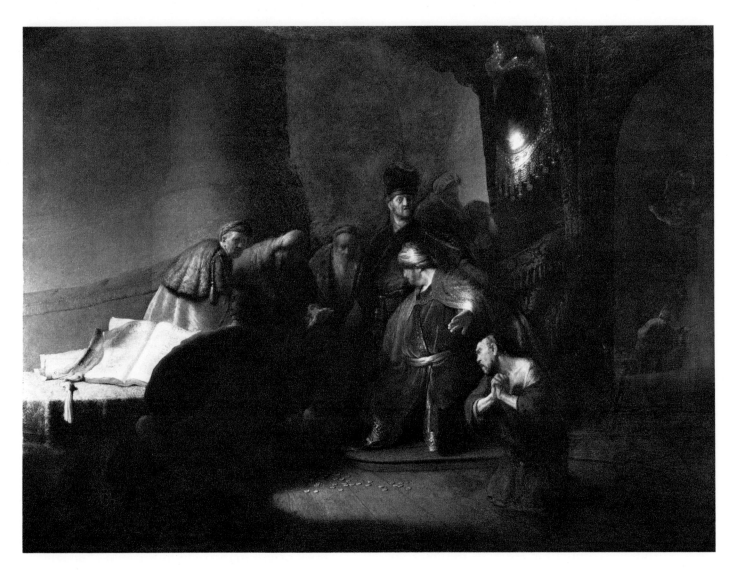

255. REMBRANDT. *Judas Returning the Thirty Pieces of Silver.* 1629. Panel, 31 × 40½".
Collection Marchioness of Normanby, London

contrasts. Scumbled and glazed, Rembrandt's late colors gleam with a new luster. The pigments, often applied in heavy impasto, have a radiance as if they themselves were charged with light.

It is easy to see that in its main outlines Rembrandt's development parallels that of Dutch painting in general. No matter how personal their message, Rembrandt's later works are in essential agreement with works of other Dutch masters of that period. The precious glow of his colors brings to mind still lifes by Kalf or Van Beyeren; the subtlety of his light effects recalls seascapes by Van de Capelle and church interiors by De Witte. Rectilinear stage patterns are combined with quiet figures in Terborch and Pieter de Hoogh; the

trend toward majestic forms and somberness of mood is in many of Jacob van Ruisdael's landscapes. By contrast, the interest in detail and in linear agitation combined with relatively flat color schemes found in his earlier work is related to Dutch landscape and genre painting of the 1630s and early '40s.

That for a considerable part of his career Rembrandt was in tune with the artistic currents of his time can be shown also by the acclaim given to his works from the very beginning. His painting of *Judas Returning the Thirty Pieces of Silver* (fig. 255), each piece lying on the floor before the astonished and disgusted priests of the temple, was greatly admired by Constantijn Huygens

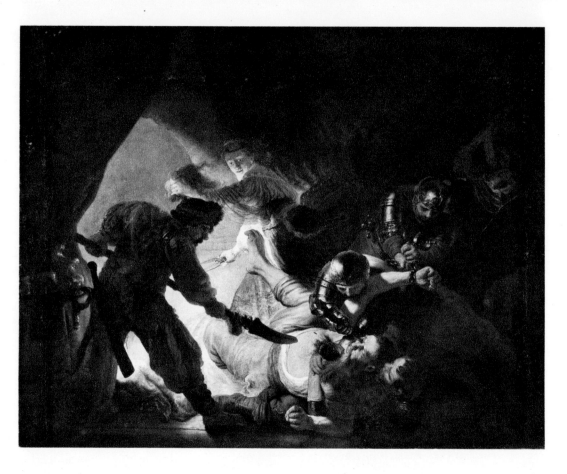

256. REMBRANDT.
Blinding of Samson.
1636. 7'9" × 9'11".
Städelsches Kunstinstitut,
Frankfurt

(see page 285).[15] Through Huygens' intercession Rembrandt received the commission to paint Passion scenes for the prince of Orange. In gratitude he painted for Huygens the most sanguinary of his early paintings, the large *Blinding of Samson* (fig. 256).

Even before this Rembrandt had been asked to portray Dr. Nicolaas Tulp, a famous physician, giving an anatomical demonstration (colorplate 37); it was this commission that encouraged Rembrandt to move from his native Leyden to Amsterdam. Pictures portraying teachers of anatomy dissecting corpses before a watchful throng (not always of doctors) had been painted earlier. The demonstration traditionally used the bodies of executed criminals, the only ones available for that purpose. Rembrandt was the first to see the dramatic possibilities of the theme, with its implied reference to crime and punishment and its overt contrast between speaker and watchful listeners.[16] Sitting on one side of the bloated and brightly lit corpse (of an imbecile who had been

hanged for murder), Tulp holds the exposed tendons of the arm with a forceps, inviting his hearers to compare the findings with illustrations in a book placed in the right foreground. Though every figure in the picture is a portrait, Rembrandt concentrated on action rather than likeness, introducing a new phase in the development of the group portrait.

In 1642, ten years after this work, Rembrandt finished a military group portrait that differed from traditional patterns of such themes as much as the *Anatomy* had from its prototypes. Known—erroneously—as the *Night Watch* (fig. 257), the picture shows a company of militia commanded by Captain Frans Banning Cocq preparing to march into the early morning sun. They are assembling in front of a high arched gate, and the painter delighted in showing the bustle, the confusion, even the noise (drums beating, dogs barking, a shot being fired) of such a scene while lending suitable prominence to the tall figure of the captain as he gives marching orders to the short lieutenant walking at his side. Contrary to a popular legend, the picture was well received. Its colorful costumes, some with medieval associations, and its bold foreshortenings and striking contrasts of light and dark pleased a taste for romantic self-glorification that was especially strong in Amsterdam toward the middle of the century.

Later commissions include a second *Anatomy*, today known only from a fragment that survived a fire and from a sketchy drawing made to test two alternative frames. The largest canvas Rembrandt ever painted was another commission, intended for the new town hall of Amsterdam (see pages 226, 286). It depicted the Oath of the Batavians under Claudius Civilis and was to form part of a cycle extolling this legendary Batavian hero.[17] For reasons that can at best be surmised, Rembrandt's huge canvas was excluded from the final hanging; in the end, Rembrandt himself cut it down to its central group, and only this fragment (still one of

257. REMBRANDT. *Night Watch*. 1642. 11'5¾" × 14'4½". Rijksmuseum, Amsterdam

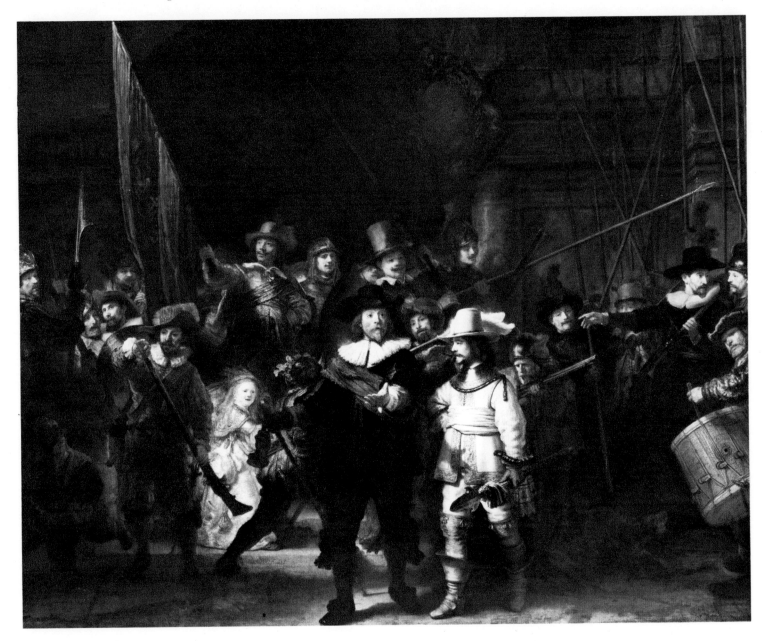

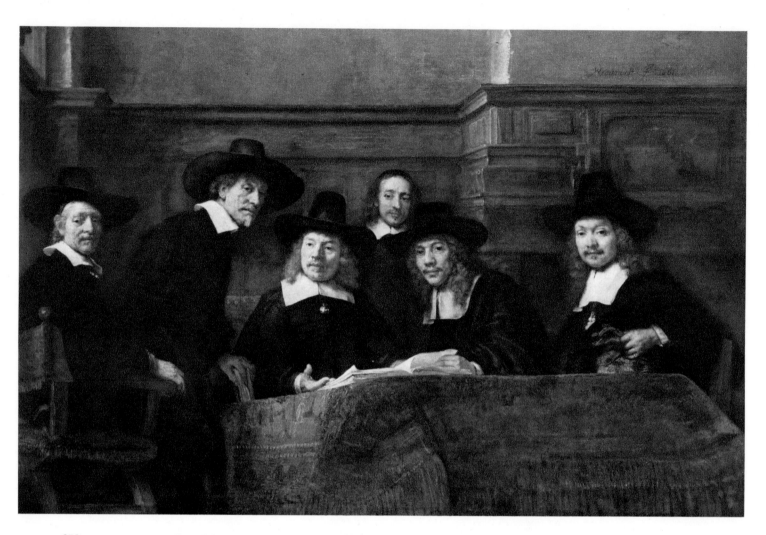

258. REMBRANDT. *Syndics of the Drapers' Guild*. 1662. 6'3⅞" × 9'2". Rijksmuseum, Amsterdam

the master's largest pictures) is preserved (color-plate 38). Assembled around a table like the disciples at the Last Supper, and illuminated by a bright but hidden light, a small band of solemn men vow their fealty to their tall, one-eyed leader. The unusually light colors are applied in broad strokes, as Rembrandt recognized that the picture was to be seen from a great distance.

Even after this fiasco Rembrandt received another major commission, to paint the syndics of the drapers' guild, attended by their servant (fig. 258). The poses of these men are so active and their expressions so keen that many interpreters have been tempted to read the picture as the re-

cord of a definite situation in which the syndics confront, and react to, an unseen audience.[18]

Private commissions received by Rembrandt include three canvases for Don Antonio Ruffo, a collector in faraway Messina, among them the picture of Aristotle negligently touching the golden chain, symbol of princely favor (fig. 259), and of Homer dictating his poetry (fig. 260).[19] Rembrandt also contributed a few etchings for book illustrations, none more interesting than a set of four designs for a treatise by Rabbi Manasseh ben Israel.

But commissions account only for a small percentage of Rembrandt's work. An event from the

248

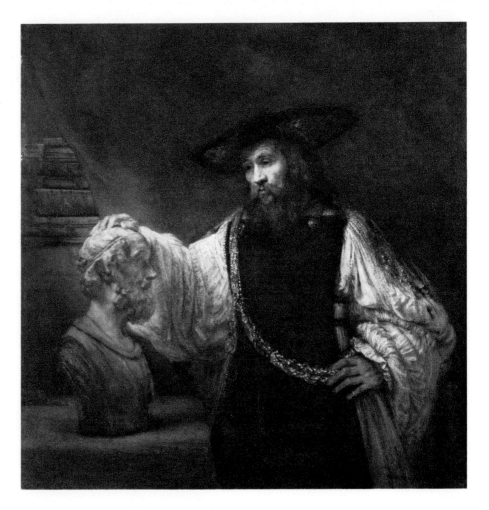

259. REMBRANDT.
Aristotle with the Bust of Homer.
1653. 56½ × 53¾".
The Metropolitan Museum of Art,
New York (purchased with
special funds and gifts of friends
of the Museum, 1961)

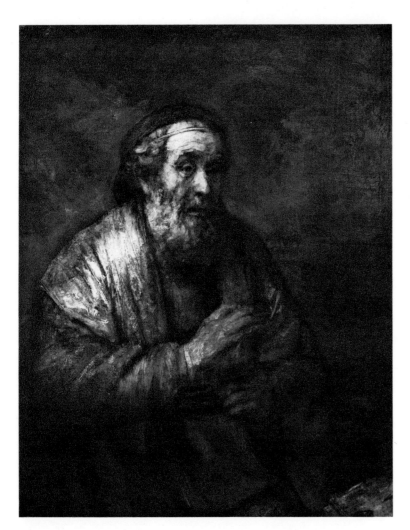

260. REMBRANDT.
Homer Dictating His Poetry.
1663. 42½ × 32½".
Mauritshuis, The Hague

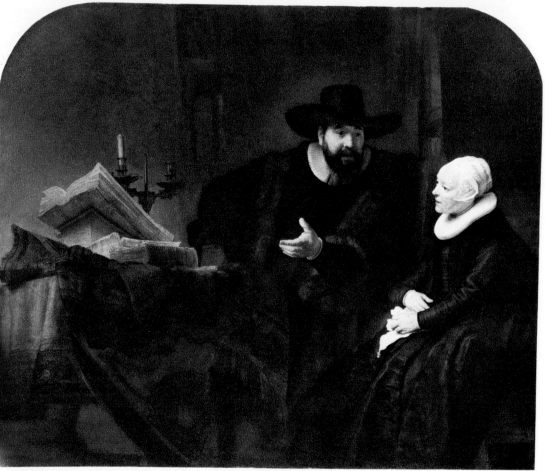

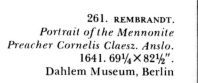

261. REMBRANDT.
Portrait of the Mennonite Preacher Cornelis Claesz. Anslo.
1641. 69¼ × 82½".
Dahlem Museum, Berlin

middle of the master's career throws some light on his private aims as an artist. Paraphrasing a slightly shopworn conceit, Joost van den Vondel, the foremost Dutch poet of the seventeenth century, had hinted at the limits of the painter's craft when he commented on a portrait etching of Rembrandt's of 1641 (rendering Anslo, a popular Mennonite preacher): "He who wants to 'see' Anslo must hear him [speak]."[20] Rembrandt's answer to Vondel came in a painting done a year later (fig. 261). This time Anslo, no longer alone, turns from his books to a woman (perhaps his wife) whom he appears to be comforting, accompanying his words with an eloquent gesture of his hand. Skillfully foreshortened and illuminated, this hand serves as the focal point of the composition.

The painting may not have altered Vondel's view of painters, but it shows clearly that Rembrandt appreciated the role of the spoken word and tried to find a visual equivalent for it. Again

and again he chose themes showing the confrontation of a speaking individual with an audience ranging from a state of near apathy to rapt attention. The works include St. John trying to arouse an obtuse multitude, Joseph recounting his dreams, Christ as a boy arguing with the elders or as an adult seriously addressing the sick and the halt (fig. 262), Homer keeping spellbound a group of admirers (fig. 263). Speakers and audiences are involved also in his approach to many of his commissions, such as the two Anatomies and the *Syndics*. The "speaking" hand of the captain is the hub around which revolve the varied and picturesque activities of the *Night Watch*.

In all these subjects Rembrandt reveals an intense concern with the various aspects of human interaction. It is hardly surprising that he had an abiding interest in the basic forms of this interaction—those manifest among members of one family. He clearly took great interest in the lives

250

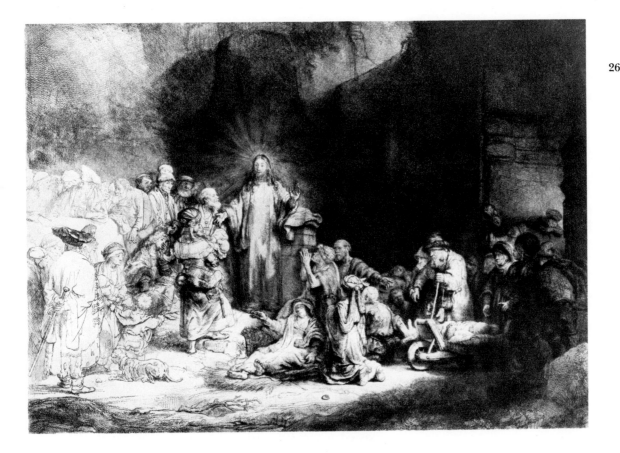

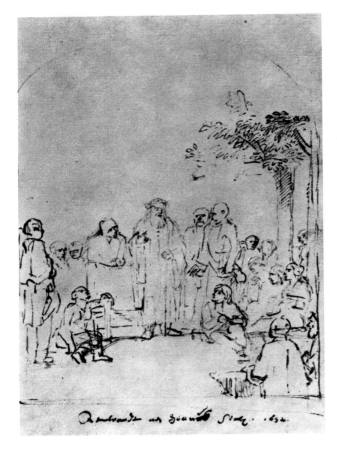

263. REMBRANDT. *Homer Dictating His Poetry.* 1652.
Pen and ink, 10×7¼". Six Collection, Amsterdam

of those nearest to him. Until her death in 1639, his mother was one of his favorite models. So was his wife Saskia from the time of their engagement in 1633 until her untimely death in 1642. When Hendrickje Stoffels succeeded her—albeit without the blessing of the church—she took Saskia's place in his art as well. Of his four children with Saskia, three died in infancy, but the last, Titus, lived to the age of twenty-seven and figures more frequently in Rembrandt's later works than any other person.

Family scenes, of parents alone or with children, are frequent in Rembrandt's work. We can watch the Holy Family secure in their home, presenting the Child in the temple, taking Him on the flight into Egypt, or returning from there, the boy walking between them. Rembrandt painted Jacob blessing his grandsons Ephraim and Manasseh (colorplate 39), a silent family gathering made particularly meaningful by the presence of Ashnath, Joseph's Egyptian wife.

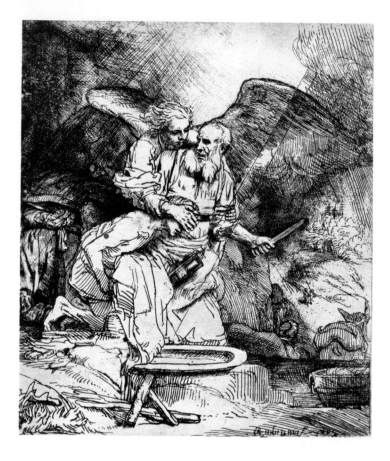

264. REMBRANDT.
Sacrifice of Isaac. 1655. Etching.
British Museum, London

The bond between father and son assumed a particular significance for Rembrandt in the last decades of his life. The Bible offered this theme in several familiar stories. One of these is the Sacrifice of Isaac. Rembrandt had dealt with it in an early painting, stressing the savage efficiency with which Abraham prepared the grisly task and his surprise at being suddenly interrupted (the idea of showing the knife dropping from his hand Rembrandt derived from a play by the French poet Beza, of 1549–50). Another is an etching in which the father seems to answer the son's embarrassing question with a trustful gesture to Heaven. The most moving interpretation of the theme is given in an etching of 1655 (fig. 264). Without taking recourse, as he had done before, to depicting tears on the old man's cheeks, Rembrandt succeeded in expressing in Abraham's face the unspeakable agony through which the patriarch passed when God asked him to be the agent of his only son's death.

Father and son are the central characters of the Book of Tobit, which may be one reason why Rembrandt illustrated it more often than any other Biblical text of similar length. The repentant return of the prodigal son to his father, finally, was dealt with by Rembrandt in all media. In the earlier formulations, in drawing and etching (fig. 265), father and son rush toward each other with gestures of contrition on the son's part, signs of eager welcome and succor on the father's. In his late painting (fig. 266) all physical motion has ceased, even among the observers watching in silence. The son is entirely encompassed by the father, who gathers the returned son to him by laying both hands on his back. In contrast to the earlier works, where each figure played an equal

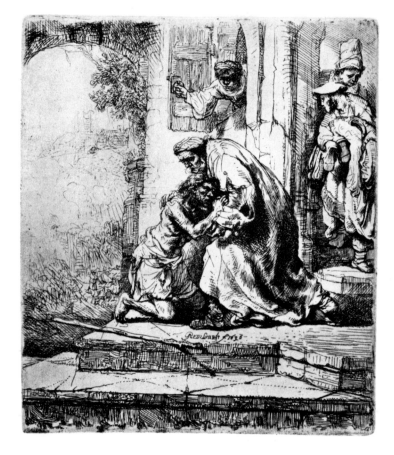

265. REMBRANDT.
Return of the Prodigal Son. 1636. Etching.
Fitzwilliam Museum, Cambridge, England

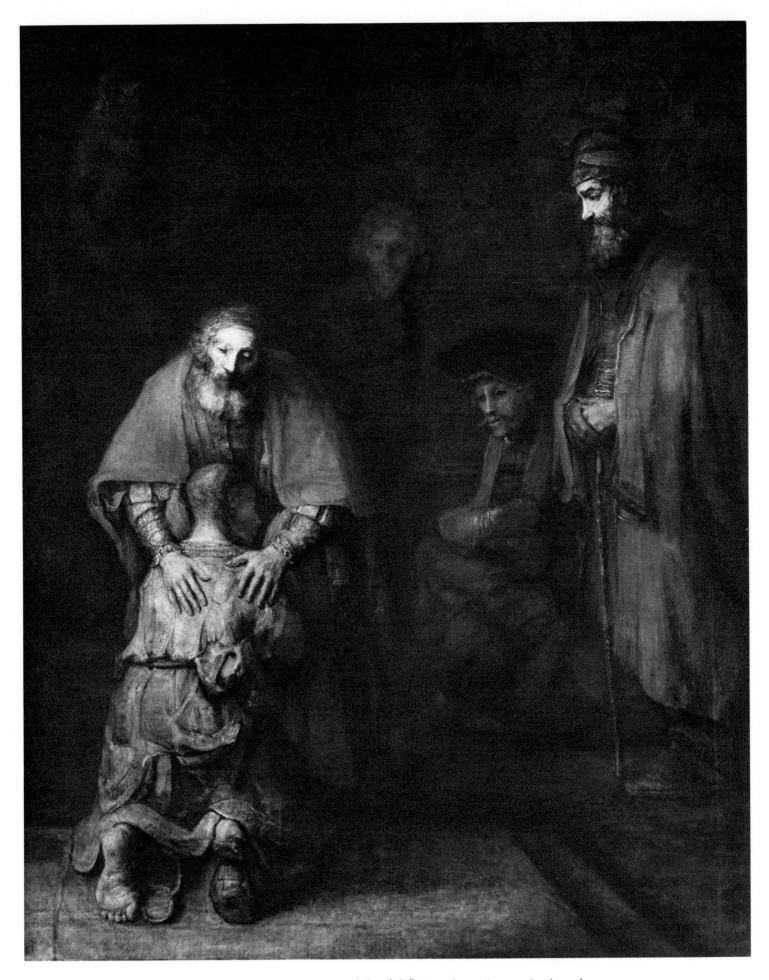

266. REMBRANDT. *Return of the Prodigal Son.* c. 1665. 8′8″ × 6′8¾″. Hermitage Museum, Leningrad

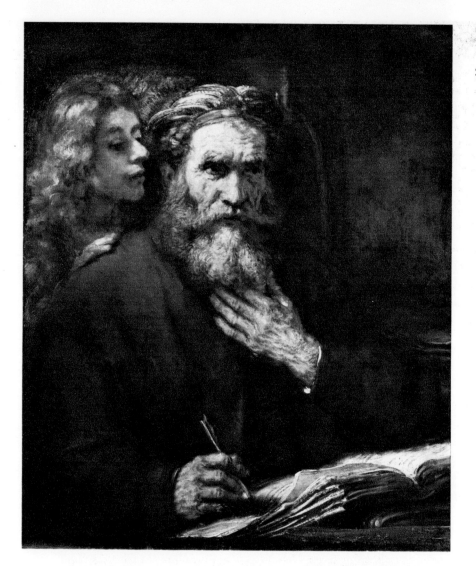

267. REMBRANDT. *St. Matthew.*
1661. 37½ × 32".
The Louvre, Paris

part in the drama, the emphasis is now entirely on the old man who finds fulfillment in the exercise of charity.

The increasing depth of Rembrandt's interpretations of the theme of father and son probably reflects the artist's own affection for his son Titus. In a painting of St. Matthew (fig. 267) Rembrandt gave Titus' features to the angel, the source and symbol of divine guidance. It may be more than coincidence that Rembrandt, who had survived other crises, including bankruptcy, professional disappointments, and Hendrickje's death (1663), died one year after the loss of Titus.

Recognizing these powerful bonds of kinship, Rembrandt also saw man surrounded by supernatural forces. Unlike Rubens and most Italian masters of the Baroque, who permitted men, an-

gels, gods, and allegorical personifications to mingle in perfect equality, Rembrandt stressed the unexpected and miraculous when mortals meet the divine. Influenced by Elsheimer, he depicted the moment when Philemon and Baucis recognize with awe the two gods whom they had sheltered in their modest dwelling. He showed Abraham waiting humbly on his visitors, sensing the emanation of a higher power. The doubting Thomas draws back in sudden shock as he recognizes Christ, and the disciples at Emmaus realize with fear (in the earlier versions; fig. 268) or in deep emotion (fig. 269) that their companion is the Saviour risen from the grave.

Rembrandt was fascinated by stories in which God's will is communicated to man through the intercession of angels. As a painter of angels he

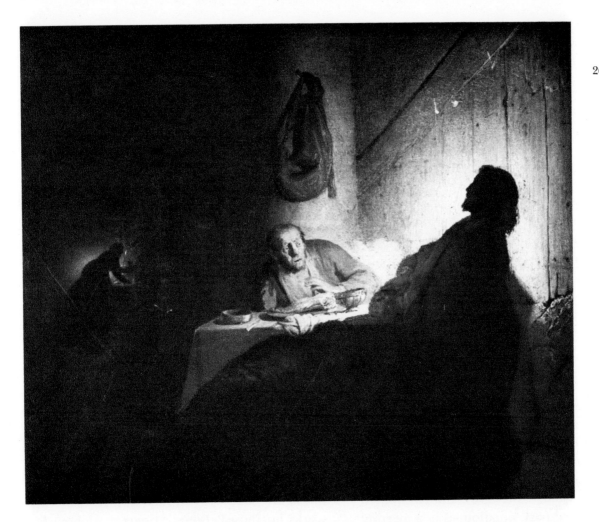

268. REMBRANDT.
Supper at Emmaus.
1628–30.
Oil on paper
pasted on panel,
14½ × 16⅛".
Jacquemart-André
Museum, Paris

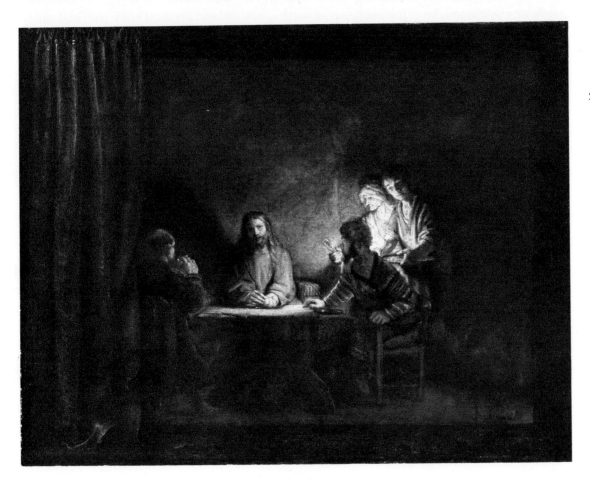

269. REMBRANDT.
Supper at Emmaus.
1648. 34⅞ × 43¾".
Statens Museum
for Kunst,
Copenhagen

255

had no equal in the seventeenth century. They come to protect and to save, as in Abraham's sacrifice, in the rescue of Ishmael, or in Tobias' travels and the healing of Tobit's blindness. Angels are found in Lot's flight from Sodom, Jacob's dream, Elijah's rest on Mount Horeb; it is an angel who brings cheer to Manoah, explains Daniel's vision, and chastises Balaam (colorplate 40). These subjects and many others appear in Rembrandt's work, in addition to those of the New Testament involving angels, such as the Annunciation to the Shepherds, the Rest on the Flight into Egypt, Christ's Agony in the Garden, and His Resurrection.

Rembrandt's angels are full-grown youths with large wings; the classical *putto* occurs only rarely. These heavenly messengers, whether coming or going, are invariably accompanied by bursts of light. Darkness, on the other hand, is characteristic of man's normal existence. Far from holding terror, it spells a degree of security. In an etching erroneously called *Reclining Negress*, shadows seem to protect as with a blanket the nude body of a sleeping woman (fig. 270). But confronted with an extraordinary situation, as in a meeting with God or angels, or challenged, be it for good or for evil, man must leave the safe shadows of his ordinary life and face the searching light, as do the Batavians when they swear their oath (colorplate 38), the Magi as they come into the presence of a higher King, or St. Peter in the Denial (fig. 275).

Only in his later years did Rembrandt realize the full symbolic force of light and darkness. At first, darkness was mere absence of light. The 1640s, as in many other things, were the decisive years for his mature conception of the meaning of shadow; in these years he began to back away from success, to live unobtrusively for his own work. From then on the shadows in his paintings became less impenetrable and more filled with their own life. Shadow held out the promise of comfort and peace; light coincided with exaltation, excitement—and danger.

Human interaction, and man's confrontation with the supernatural world, were urgent problems for Rembrandt because he was tragically aware of man's essential isolation. The loneliness of life is the most pervasive theme of the master's later works, even where they involve more than one figure. Solitary figures abound also in his early works, but those Bellonas, Minervas, Sophonisbas, apostles, and rabbis act as if they counted on an

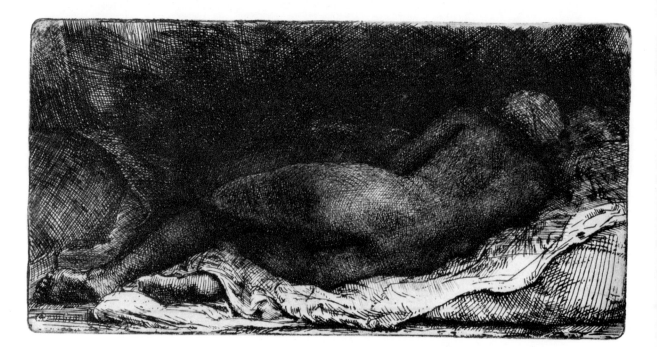

270. REMBRANDT. *Reclining Nude*. 1658. Etching. The Metropolitan Museum of Art, New York (Bequest of Mrs. H. O. Havemeyer, 1929)

256

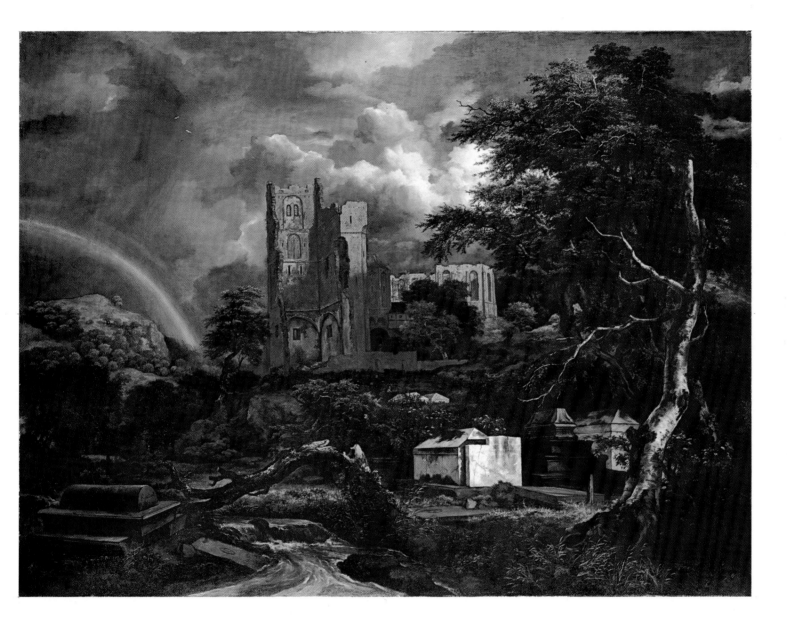

Colorplate 33. JACOB VAN RUISDAEL. *Jewish Cemetery*. c. 1655. 56 × 74½". Detroit Institute of Arts

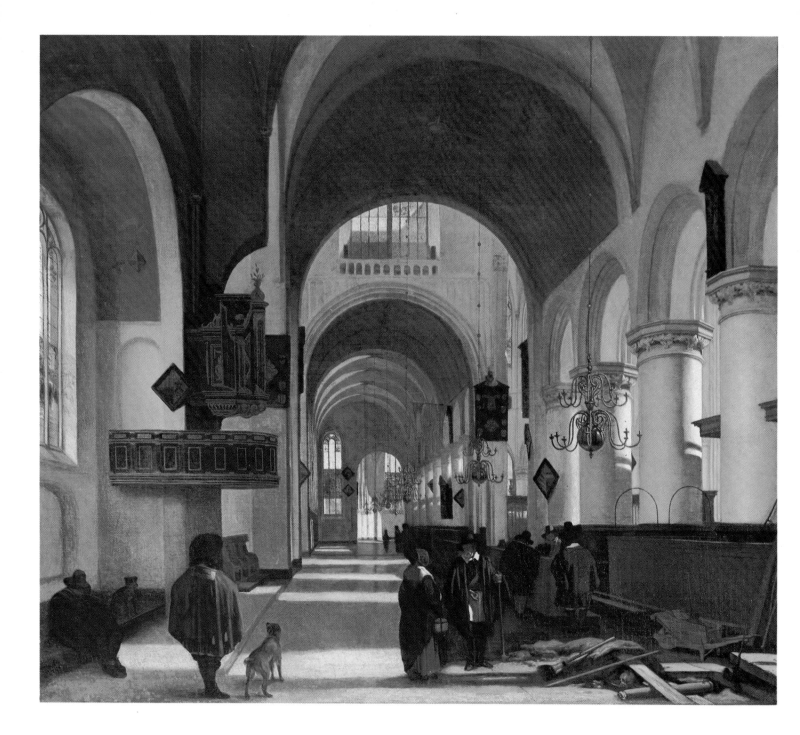

Colorplate 34. EMANUEL DE WITTE. *Interior of a Church*. 1668. 38¾ × 44″.
Museum Boymans-Van Beuningen, Rotterdam

Colorplate 35. HENDRICK TERBRUGGHEN.
Boy with Wineglass. 1623.
26½×22¼".
North Carolina Museum of Art, Raleigh

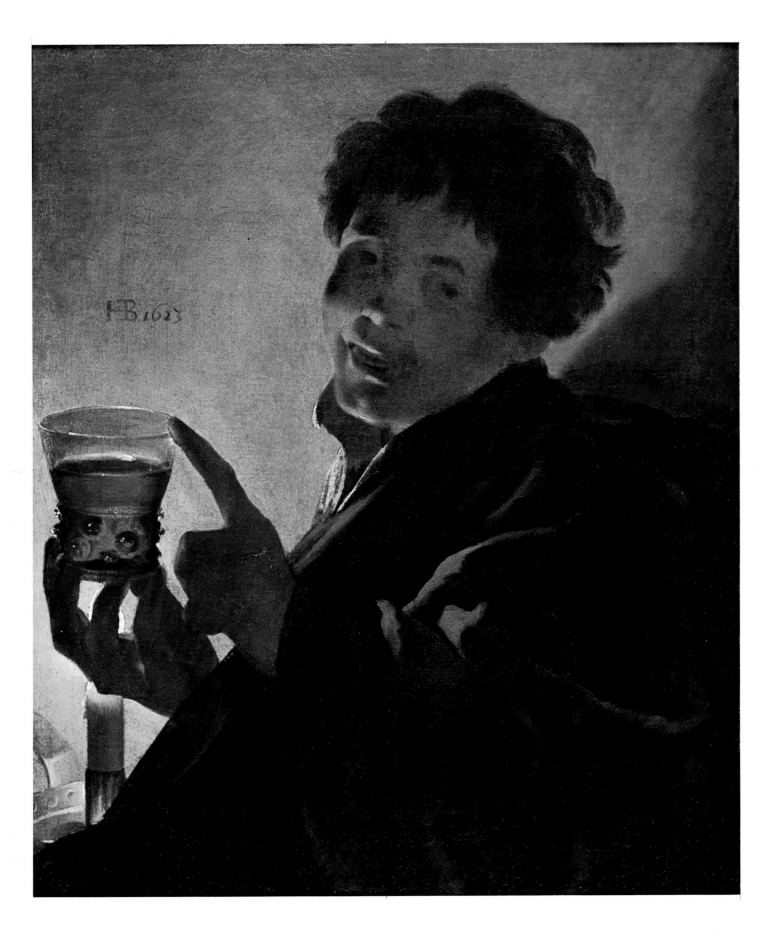

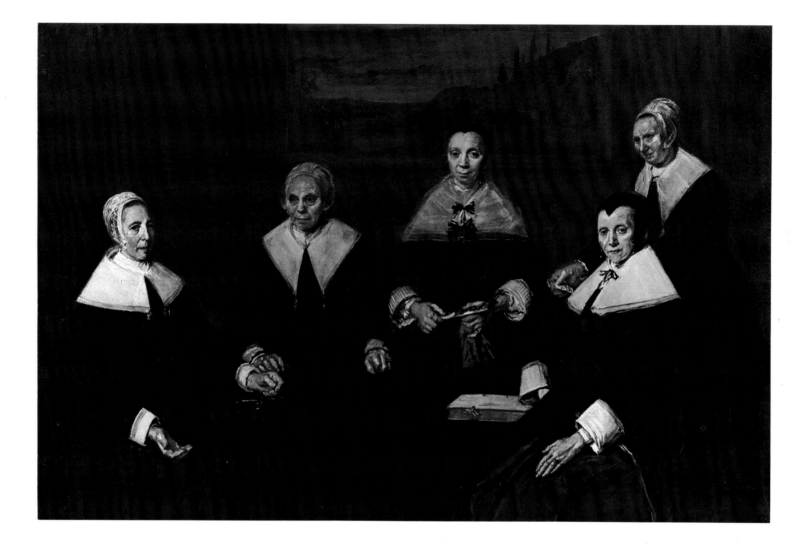

Colorplate 36. FRANS HALS. *Women Regents of the Old Men's Home at Haarlem*. 1664. 67×98″.
Frans Hals Museum, Haarlem

Colorplate 37. REMBRANDT. *Anatomy Lesson of Dr. Tulp*. 1632. 63¾ × 85¼″. Mauritshuis, The Hague

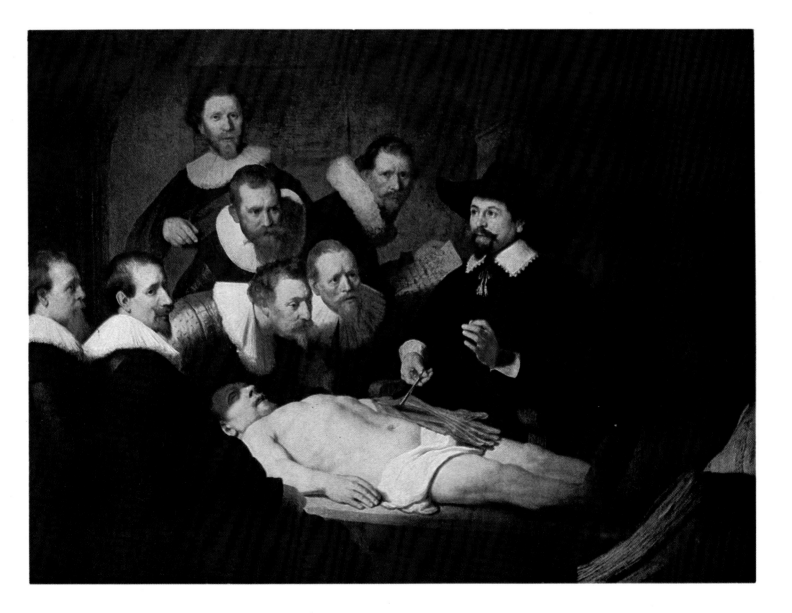

Colorplate 38. REMBRANDT. *Oath of Claudius Civilis*. 1661/62. 6′4⅛″ × 10′1″. Nationalmuseum, Stockholm

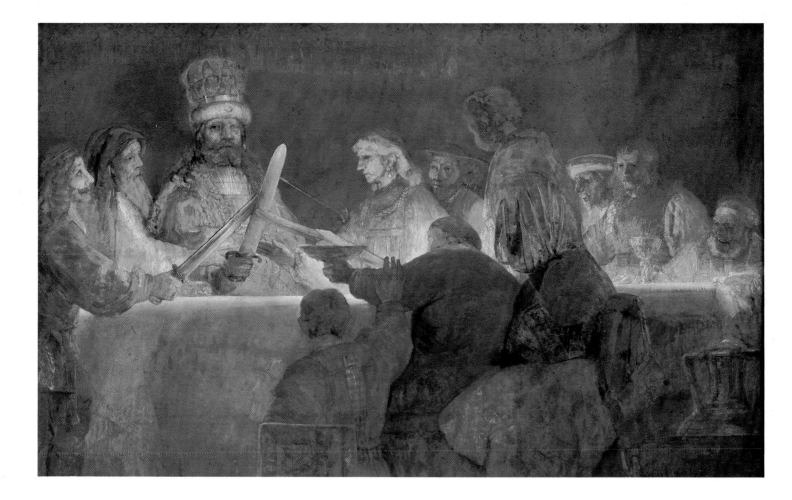

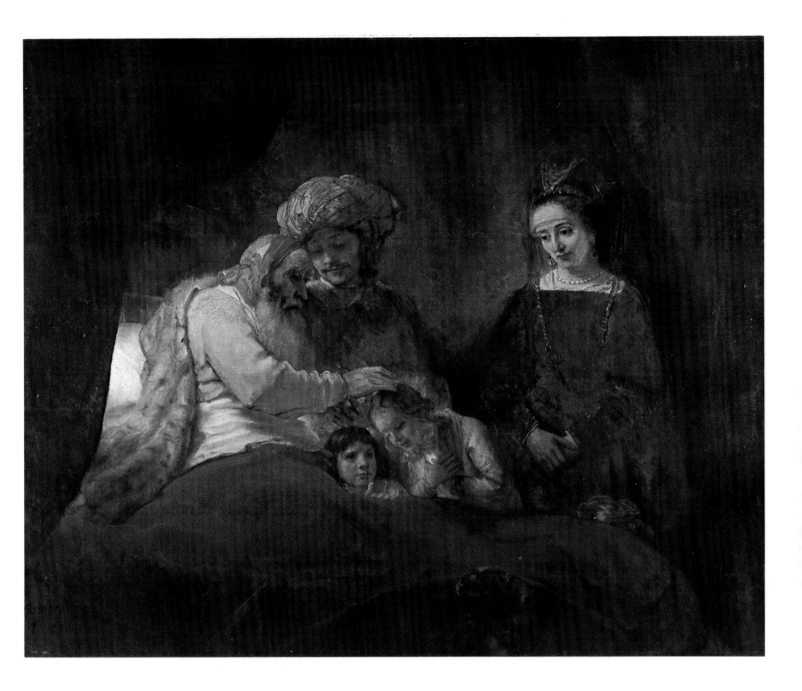

Colorplate 39. REMBRANDT. *Jacob Blessing the Children of Joseph*. 1656.
68½ × 83½". Gemäldegalerie, Cassel

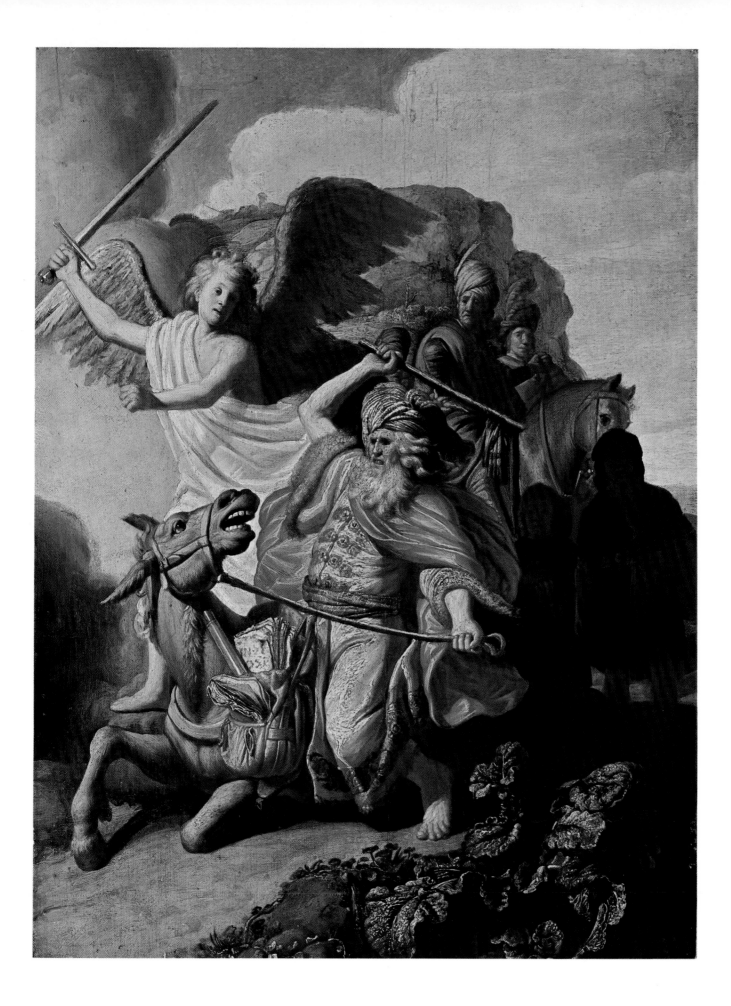

Colorplate 40. REMBRANDT. *Balaam and the Ass*. 1626. Panel, 25½ × 18½″. Cognacq-Jay Museum, Paris

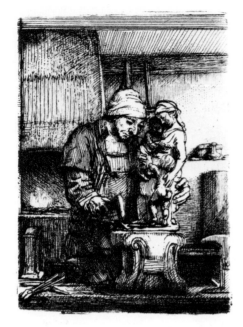

271. REMBRANDT. *The Goldsmith.*
1655. Etching (facsimile size).
The Metropolitan Museum of Art,
New York (Dick Fund, 1927)

272. REMBRANDT. *Blind Belisarius.* c. 1660.
Pen and ink, 6½ × 4⅞". Dahlem Museum, Berlin

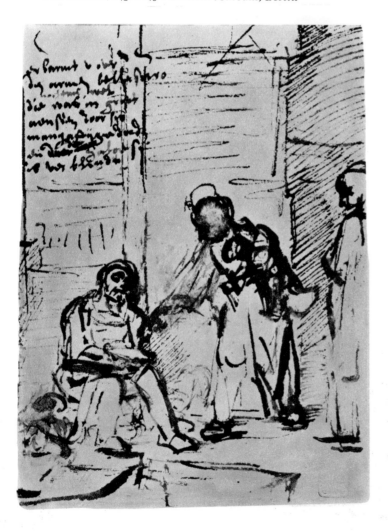

audience. And for the scholars buried in cavernous rooms, the outside world is as close as the next window.

In the decades after the *Night Watch,* Rembrandt painted such figures as monks and hermits who are bound to lead a secluded life. His portraits became increasingly introspective, the sitters occasionally supporting their heads as if deep in thought. In a tiny etching of 1655 Rembrandt depicted a goldsmith totally absorbed in his work (fig. 271) as he presses a small sculpture (personifying Charity) close to his body. By being at one with his work, the artist is effectively separated from the world without.

Blindness, a frequent theme in Rembrandt's art, is a pictorial metaphor for loneliness. *Blind Belisarius* (fig. 272) is doubly outcast, being also reduced to begging. For Homer, blindness is a source of strength: as Rembrandt painted him in a late work (fig. 260) he seems to be illuminated from within. His physical blindness is a symbol of the alienation of genius—the loneliness that is the price of creativity.[21]

For the poet and the artist, loneliness may have its rewards. But Rembrandt knew also of situations where the hopelessly final isolation of man is revealed in all its stark pathos. Holding David's fateful letter, Bathsheba (the Louvre, Paris) seems

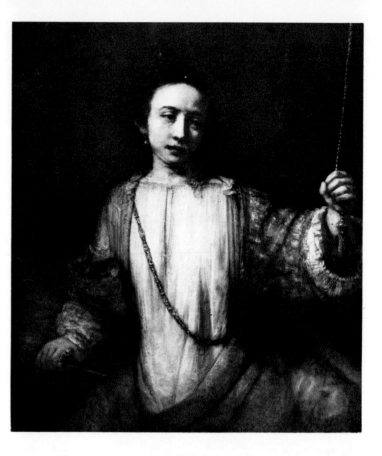

273. REMBRANDT.
Lucretia. c. 1666.
43½ × 37⅜".
Minneapolis Institute of Arts
(The William Hood Dunwoody Fund)

to ponder sadly a decision she alone must make. Twice in his last years Rembrandt painted the suicide of Lucretia, once as she seems to address the dagger (National Gallery of Art, Washington, D.C.) and again after she has driven home the weapon (fig. 273); in each case, contrary to the classical text telling her story, she is alone. As he appears in the painting *David Before Saul* (fig. 274), King Saul is an old man, aware of his physi-cal decline and spiritual isolation, made all the more poignant by the Oriental splendor of his outfit. St. Peter (fig. 275), his craggy face in the full light of a candle, faces the questioning sol-diers alone; though a true rock of a man, he is revealed to us as a troubled, faltering human be-ing. In *Haman's Dismissal* (fig. 276) Rembrandt juxtaposed three men, each shaken by thoughts that are his alone.[22]

274. REMBRANDT.
David Before Saul.
c. 1657–58. 51⅜ × 64½".
Mauritshuis, The Hague

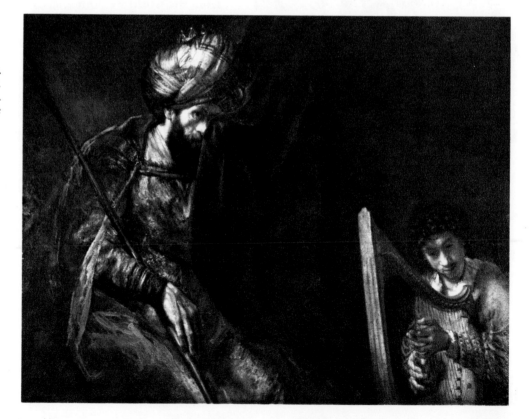

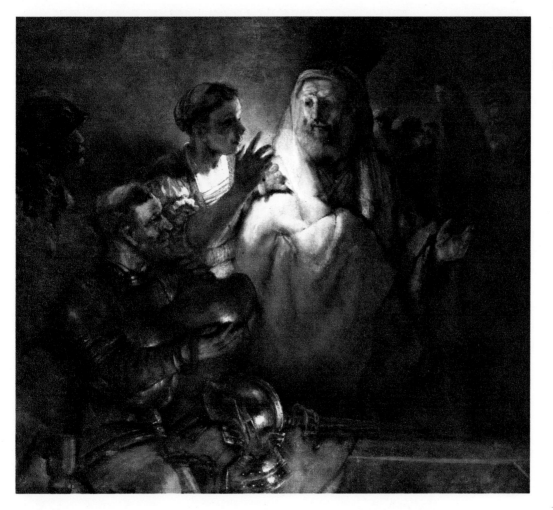

275. REMBRANDT.
Denial of Peter. 1660.
60⅝ × 66½".
Rijksmuseum, Amsterdam

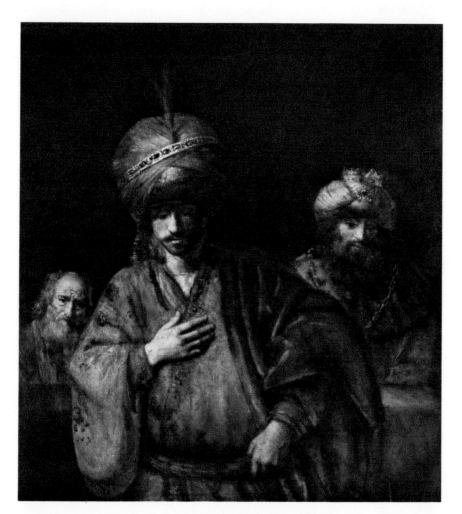

276. REMBRANDT.
Haman's Dismissal. c. 1665.
50 × 45⅝".
Hermitage Museum, Leningrad

267

The knowledge that every man (*pace* John Donne) *is*, after all, an island unto himself lends a tragic character even to the theme of love. The so-called *Jewish Bride* (colorplate 41) is probably the portrait of an actual couple, not necessarily Jewish, in the guise of Biblical lovers like Isaac and Rebecca, or Jacob and Rachel. As a token of his affection the man drapes a chain over the "bride's" shoulders while she, in a gesture of abiding beauty, touches and gently presses his right hand to her heart. Yet close as the two young people are, they are also separated, first by the striking red-yellow contrast of their costumes, but more profoundly by their expressions. In a preliminary drawing the man had looked smilingly in the young woman's face. Now they look past one another, each occupied with feelings and thoughts that can never be completely shared. Even in the closest of human relationships, Rembrandt seems to say, there remains an unbridgeable gap, a condition—unavoidable as the curse of original sin in theology—that compels us to live alone.

Here, perhaps, lie the roots of Rembrandt's persistent concern with his own image. Only one artist before Rembrandt had had a similar disposition toward self-portraiture—Albrecht Dürer. In Dürer's case a forgivable vanity had been joined to a keen awareness of a great historical mission. Rembrandt's self-portraits are more numerous than Dürer's, and they were done for various reasons. At first he tried to catch fleeting expressions. During the 1630s and early '40s he traced the transformation of a plain and homely youth into an affluent gentleman, occasionally choosing fanciful dress or poses derived from Raphael or Titian. The late self-portraits (colorplate 42) are different; they probe below the surface as if he thought a constant scrutiny of himself might yield answers otherwise not attainable. What he finally sees in the mirror is the face of a man who has gained the strength to bear the fate of loneliness without yielding to bitterness or despair.

No account of Rembrandt's art, no matter how cursory, can avoid paying special tribute to his drawings. About twelve hundred are still extant, surely only a fraction of all he did. If Rembrandt's etchings were the chief reason for his fame in the eighteenth century and his paintings foremost in people's minds when his star rose steeply in the second half of the nineteenth, the "modern" image of Rembrandt is strongly molded by a universal admiration for his drawings.

In drawings we see how quickly Rembrandt's hand reacted to what he saw with his physical eye, or with his mind's. Moreover, the drawings permit us to see the wide range of Rembrandt's interests—his studies of classical busts, Renaissance drawings and prints, and, most remarkable, contemporary Mughal miniatures (fig. 277). He studied rare animals (lions, elephants, and camels) from life, and a skeleton rider and horse from an anatomical theater. There are delightful studies of mummers on parade, exotic bowmen, mothers struggling with unruly children, or dentists triumphantly exhibiting a pulled tooth. Although he painted and etched many beautiful landscapes,

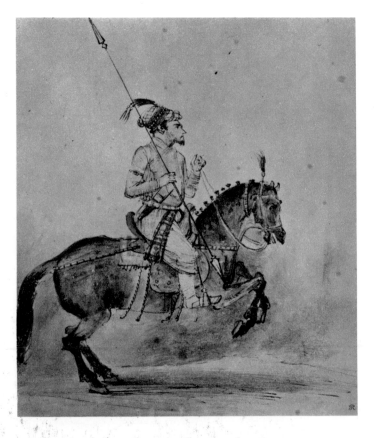

277. REMBRANDT. *Man on Horseback* (copy of Mughal miniature). c. 1654/56. Pen and wash with chalk, 8⅛ × 7". British Museum, London

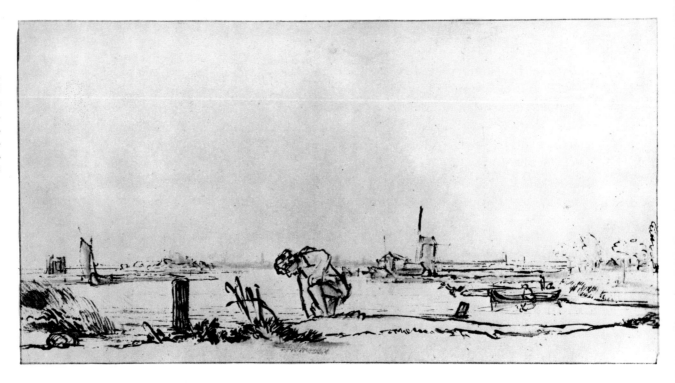

278. REMBRANDT.
*View of the Amstel
with a Man
Bathing.* c. 1654–55.
Pen and ink,
and wash, 5¾ × 10¾".
Dahlem Museum,
Berlin

Rembrandt's landscape drawings are perhaps the most admirable of all for their perfect suggestion of depth and aerial perspective, realized with a minimum of detail (fig. 278).

Done with the utmost freedom, many of Rembrandt's drawings allow us to watch the creative process itself. In narrative scenes he often began by indicating the stage with a few lines; the more distant figures are generally drawn first, in strokes that barely touch the surface of the paper, followed by those closer to the foreground, done in bolder lines. There is something uncanny about

the master's performance in drawings such as the *Mocking of Christ* (fig. 279). Drawn in pen, without preparatory lines in pencil or chalk, each figure is given a telling pose, from the unconcerned though watchful guards to the kneeling mockers and the pitifully huddled figure of Christ. More astonishing still is the balance of the whole, the infallible justness of the intervals between the figures. Technically no more than a rapid sketch, the drawing has the finality of a great work of art.

In the history of drawing this is a novelty. Most draftsmen before Rembrandt distinguished clear-

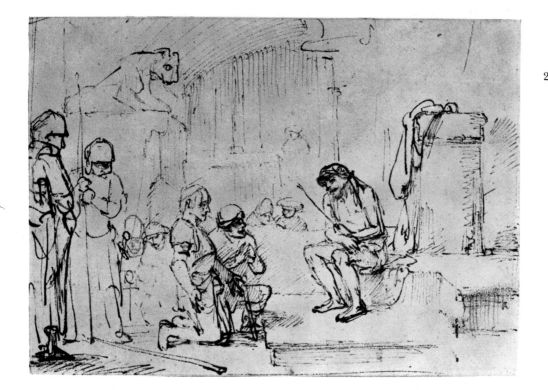

279. REMBRANDT.
Mocking of Christ.
c. 1652–53.
Pen and ink,
6¼ × 8½".
Pierpont Morgan Library,
New York

ly between preparatory sketches, marked by traces of trial and error, and finished drawings, done neatly and in detail. Rembrandt was the first great master to make drawings worthy of being appreciated as end products while preserving the freshness of a first draft.

By the standards of the seventeenth century Rembrandt was an old man when he died at sixty-three. Many of the finest Dutch painters died much younger.[23]

Yet there is probably no Dutch painter whose early death is more deplorable than that of Carel Fabritius (1622–1654), a pupil of Rembrandt's who at the age of thirty-two was killed in a powder explosion at Delft (fig. 12). Compared to that of most of the other masters who died young, his extant oeuvre is small (though it may have been larger than we know). What it lacks in numbers it makes up in originality, and his most personal achievements belong to the very end of his life. His career as an artist was cut short precisely at the point when he had completely freed himself from the influence of his master.

Two of his last works are like manifestoes of a new trend in art. The setting of his *Guardsman* (fig. 280) of 1654, seen from nearby, is an assembly of fragmentary units, sections of a stair and a house entrance, parts of the shallow arches of a town gate surmounted by the lower half of an old relief of St. Anthony, a column partly fused with a low wall and decorated with little posters, branches of vine supported by a few pieces of red fencing—all the most ordinary things, deliberately presented as unworthy of special interest. In front of the wall a shabby guard lounges on a low

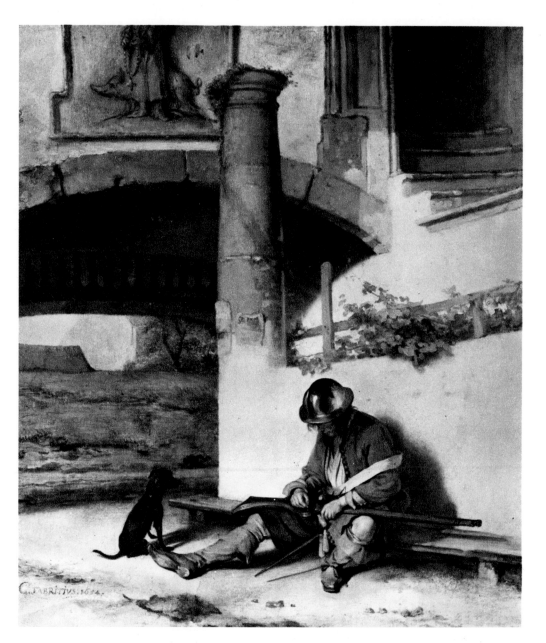

280. CAREL FABRITIUS.
Guardsman. 1654.
$26\frac{3}{4} \times 22\frac{7}{8}''$.
Staatliches Museum, Schwerin

270

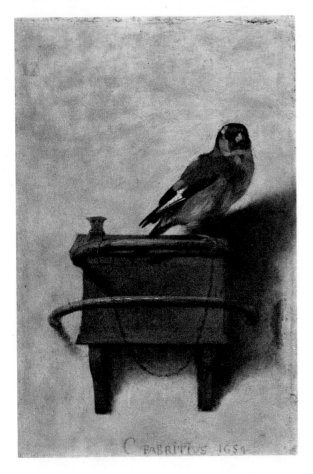

281. CAREL FABRITIUS. *Linnet.* 1654.
Panel, 13⅞×9″. Mauritshuis, The Hague

bench examining a rifle in his lap; his face is largely obscured by a plain helmet. A black mongrel, as motionless as his master, sits beside the soldier. Nothing could be further from Rembrandt's concern for human feeling and interaction than this scene; Fabritius tells no "story." His "theme" is the subtle harmony of light colors, dominated by bright areas of roughly plastered walls, and the mood of drowsy inertia of a small town on a warm summer day when the silence is the greater for the faint hum of insects. And in stressing the peculiar magic of this sunlit stillness, Fabritius created the first masterpiece of Dutch painting that conveys irresistibly the even pulse beat of time.

The *Linnet* (fig. 281), also of 1654, is deservedly one of the most popular Dutch pictures. Fabritius signed it in large letters, conscious, perhaps, of its bold novelty. Even if painted, as has been suggested, as a *trompe l'oeil,* it remains remark-

able as an almost revolutionary artistic statement. We see a little bird sitting on one of the curved rungs of its perch, its foot chained to a sliding ring; behind the asymmetrically placed bird is a white wall on which fall the shadows cast by bird and perch. The picture is broadly painted, and the bird is done in a few summary areas of color. Uncluttered, airy, both informal and monumental, the picture devaluates the significance of subject matter and glorifies the autonomy of art, anticipating the "art for art's sake" of the nineteenth century. Its enduring appeal is surely due to its very simplicity. Like the *Guardsman* it signified a fundamental break with Rembrandt's concept of art.

In a poem on Fabritius' death, Arnold Bon, a bookdealer in Delft, consoled himself with a reference to Jan Vermeer, who "masterfully followed Fabritius' path." Vermeer obviously adopted some of Fabritius' ideas, but he was influenced by other artists as well, among them Terbrugghen. Even for his two splendid landscapes he relied on formulas found before by other, if minor, artists. If historical greatness were measured solely by an artist's degree of originality, it is doubtful that Vermeer would occupy the place he does.

What distinguishes Vermeer's best works from those of his forerunners and models is his uncompromising insistence on nothing less than perfection. A slow worker, he probably painted not many more than the forty-odd pictures that are still preserved. Not until Ingres was there another artist who worked as deliberately as Vermeer, and the results were in each case pictures distinguished by immaculate craftsmanship, perfect balance, and cool, tastefully combined colors. They also deal with pleasing, winsome subjects. With sure instinct, Vermeer applied the lesson he had learned from Fabritius to the themes ideally suited for it, the middle-class domestic genre already cultivated by Dou, Terborch, Metsu, and Steen. Yet the fashionable young women of his pictures, in the same way as Fabritius' guardsman, are simply one still-life element among the rest. In the early *Girl Reading a Letter* (fig. 282) the motionless figure

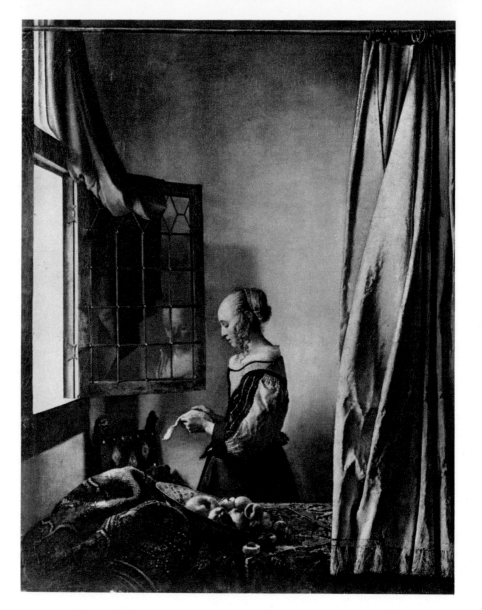

282. JAN VERMEER.
Girl Reading a Letter. c. 1655–60.
32⅝ × 25½″
Staatliche Kunstsammlungen, Dresden

takes its part in a planimetric pattern formed not only by things (window, curtain, table, and still life) but by the very intervals between them. In a later picture (fig. 283) the young woman is wedged between furniture and irregular areas of wall space like a bouquet in a tight vase.

The density of pattern increases in works done toward the end of Vermeer's career. Pictures like the *Girl Pouring Milk* (fig. 284) still show the uncrowded simplicity as well as the textural firmness derived from Fabritius. The *Woman with Maid* (Rijksmuseum, Amsterdam) and the *Artist in His Studio* (colorplate 43) are complex in design and silkily smooth in execution. The artist's

accomplishment becomes something of a tour de force, the laborious if amazingly successful solution of an intricate problem of compositional organization. Gone now is the delectable suggestion, typical of his earlier works, of pictures conceived in a happy moment of poetic inspiration. His last paintings, indeed, show a rapid artistic decline.

Vermeer's approach to his subject matter also underwent a gradual change. Leaving aside a few early experiments with mythology and Caravagesque genre, we find his characteristic subjects first in pictures of the second half of the 1650s. Modeled in striking plasticity, and completely

272

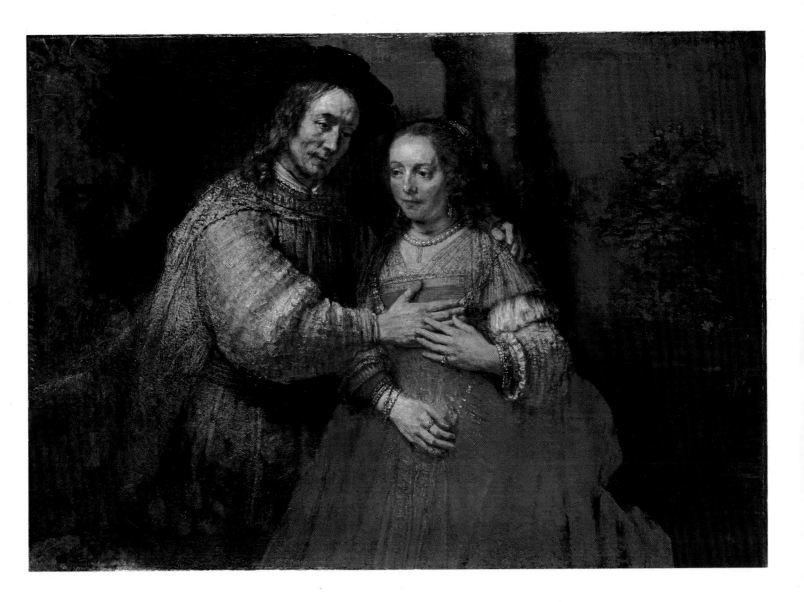

Colorplate 41. REMBRANDT. *"Jewish Bride."* c. 1665. 47¾ × 65⅜". Rijksmuseum, Amsterdam

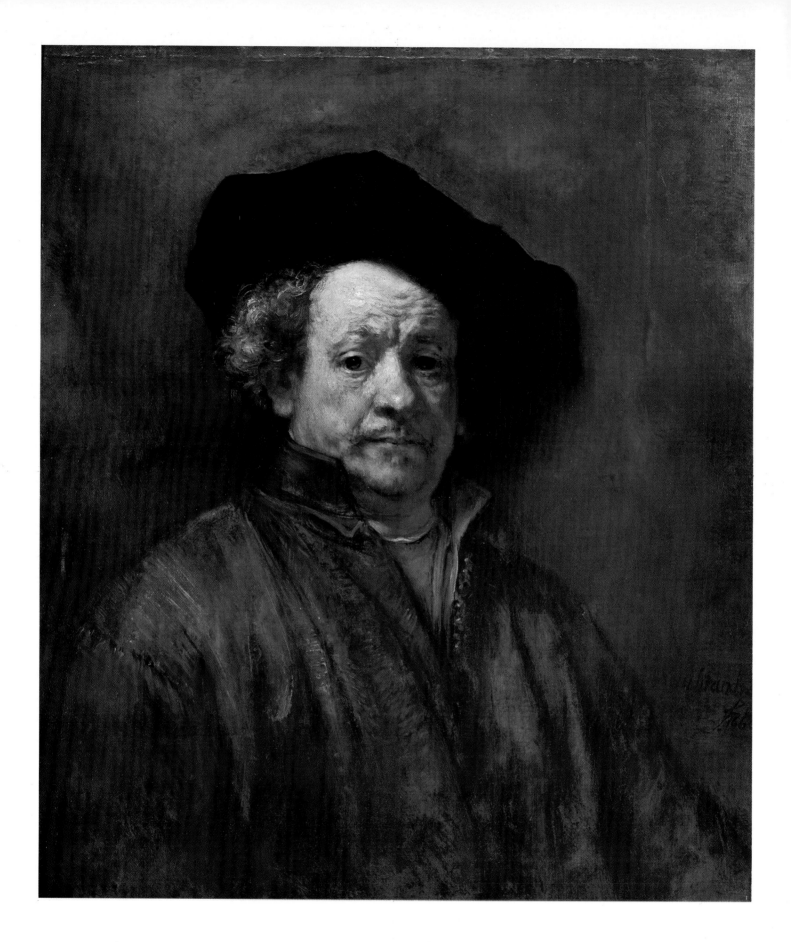

Colorplate 42. REMBRANDT. *Self-portrait*. 1660. 31⅝ × 26½″.
The Metropolitan Museum of Art, New York (Bequest of Benjamin Altman)

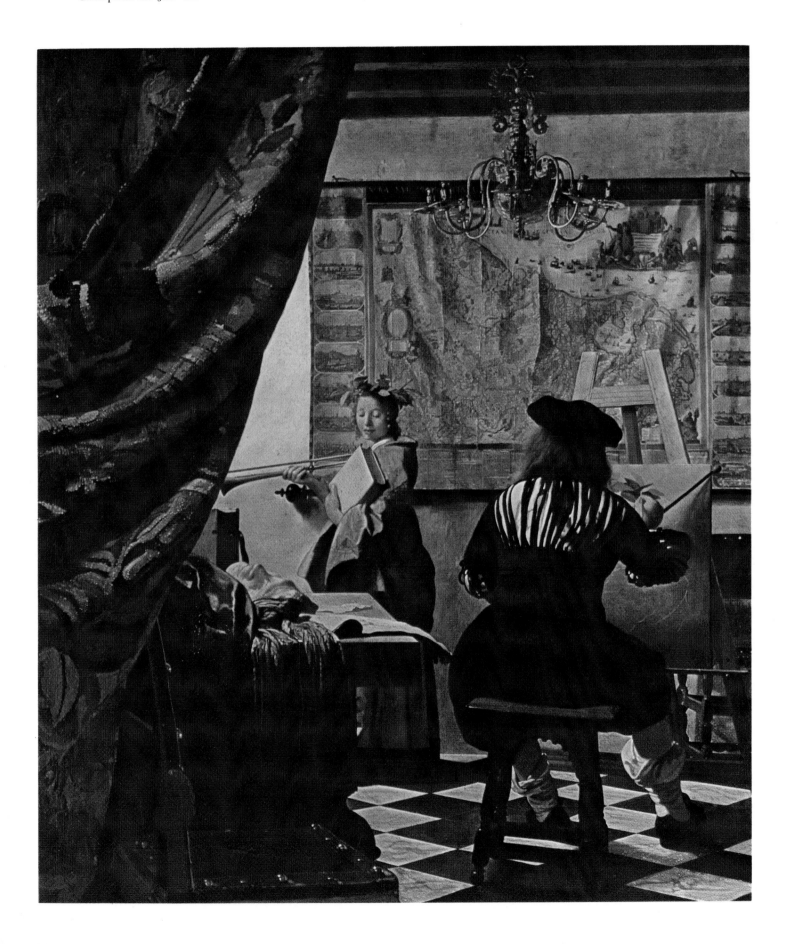

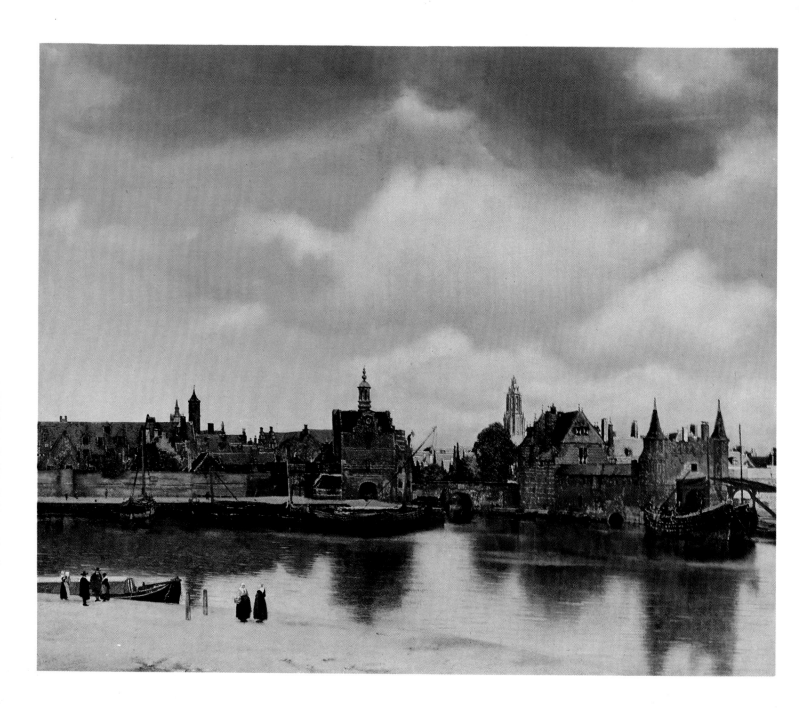

Colorplate 44. JAN VERMEER. *View of Delft*. c. 1658. 38½ × 46¼″. Mauritshuis, The Hague

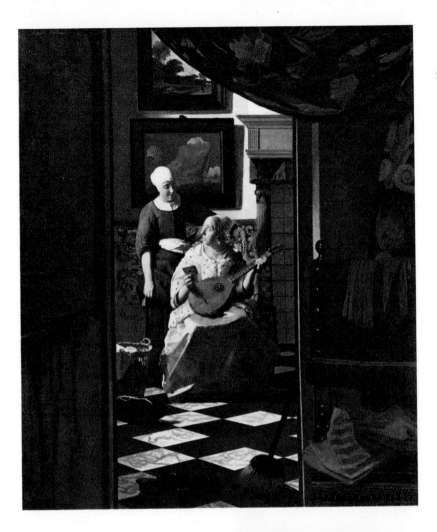

283. JAN VERMEER.
The Letter. c. 1666. 17¼ × 15¼".
Rijksmuseum, Amsterdam

284. JAN VERMEER. *Girl Pouring Milk.*
1655–60. 18 × 16⅛".
Rijksmuseum, Amsterdam

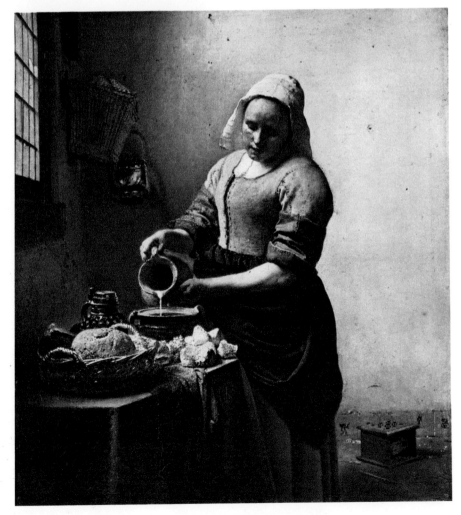

absorbed in their doings, these figures, often shown in profile, are immobilized like Egyptian reliefs. In the 1660s one notices a shift from unbending figures to more flexible ones. Some begin to smile, and when there is more than one figure they are apt to be involved in some trivial genre action, occasionally drawing the beholder into the act. Vermeer was never very explicit about these actions: some of the fascination comes from the vague feeling that there is more to them than meets the eye. He sometimes gives hints of submerged meanings by using pictures, mirror reflections, or objects such as musical instruments as clues. Behind the staid façade seems to lurk occasionally a less than respectable social behavior.[24]

In other pictures Vermeer revealed an interest in intellectual activities; twice he painted geographers (or astronomers) in their shaded studios (fig. 285), possibly inspired by Rembrandt's etching known as *Dr. Faustus*. His most ambitious allegorical work (and one of his largest) is the *Artist in His Studio* (colorplate 43), probably no less than a glorification of the art of painting itself.[25] The demure model poses as Clio, the muse of history and of fame, and the objects on the table (book, paper, and a plaster cast) reinforce the basic theme. Mysterious and allusive and forever tantalizing because we see only the back of the artist, this picture forms a fascinating Northern counterpart to another seventeenth-century exaltation of the painter's craft, Velázquez's *Maids of Honor* (see pages 184–86).

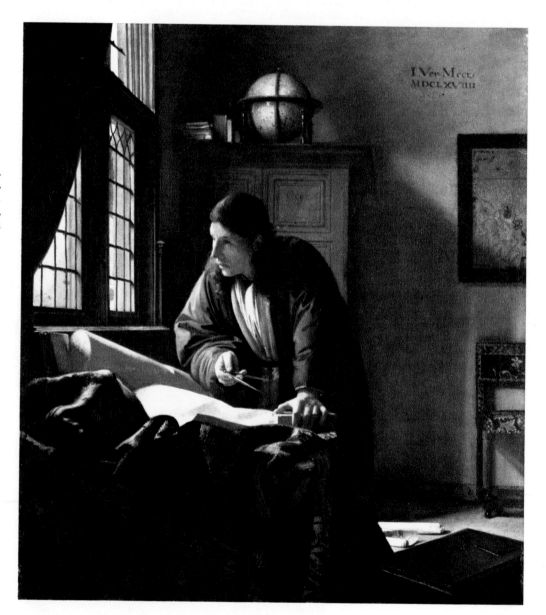

285. JAN VERMEER.
The Geographer. 1669.
20⅞ × 18⅜".
Städelsches Kunstinstitut,
Frankfurt

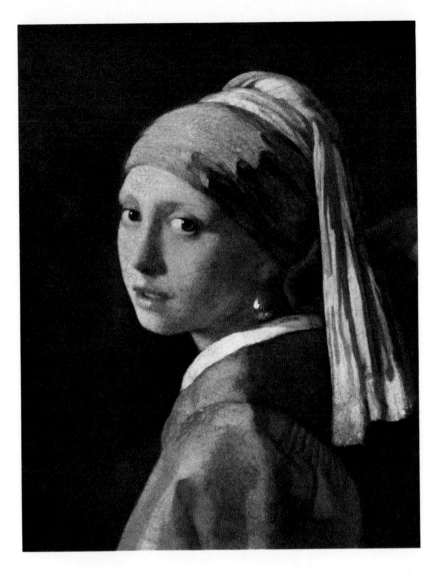

286. JAN VERMEER.
Girl with Yellow Turban.
1660–65. 18¼ × 15¾".
Mauritshuis, The Hague

Vermeer's fame ultimately rests on a handful of pictures outstanding for their sustained purity of mood, their compositional cohesion, and their almost miraculous subtlety of execution. The *Girl with Yellow Turban* (fig. 286) is such a work. In contrast to Terbrugghen's gregarious and buxom beauties, from which she probably derives, Vermeer's girl is the embodiment of gentleness and delicacy, her face of almost evanescent shades touched up by a few highlights of floating lightness. Symbolically condensed into a tiny area at the center of the picture, all the marvels of color and light seem to be repeated in the pearl hanging from the girl's ear. The whole picture, indeed, is like a painted jewel.

There is an element of coyness in the girl's turn of head, a faint hint of sensuousness in her parted lips. Yet whereas in comparable works by other masters (Rubens' *"Chapeau de Paille,"* fig. 220; or Bernini's *Costanza Buonarelli,* fig. 68) one senses the emotional involvement of the artist himself, Vermeer's eroticism is intellectual rather than sensual. Whatever passion there was in Vermeer, it was directed toward purely artistic goals. He loved his labor, and his works are a labor of love.

There are two pictures in Vermeer's oeuvre in which the subject may have aroused in him a modicum of affection. They are the only landscapes preserved by the artist and perhaps the only ones he ever painted.

As landscapes they belong to the special category of city views, practiced particularly in the second half of the seventeenth century by a group of highly skilled specialists, among them the brothers Berckheyde (fig. 291) and Jan van der Heyden. Vermeer's pictures have little in common with the products of these masters. He avoids what they aimed at—the picturesque view, the oblique angle, the stress on prominent edifices, in short what may be called the sightseer's approach, revived again by the Venetian painters of *vedute* in the eighteenth century (see pages 349–52). Both of Vermeer's landscapes create a sense of distance between the beholder and the scenery. Rather than being welcomed into the

scene, he is, in the most literal sense, confronted by it. Even the *Street in Delft* (fig. 287) is in a way a panorama. We see the small group of buildings from the other side of the street, but the artist does not invite us to cross it. Despite the few motionless people and the piece of land in the foreground of the *View of Delft* (colorplate 44), the canal fulfills a similar function, separating the town from the viewer. Of the two, the *Street in Delft* seems to be the simpler work, but its simplicity is deceptive. It actually is a masterpiece of calculated contrasts and correspondences. Al-

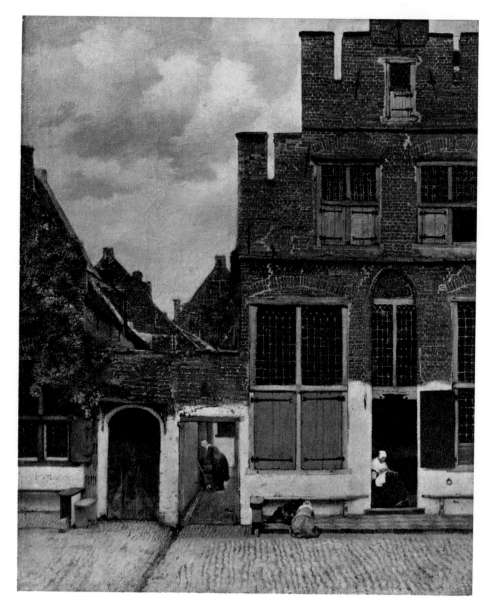

287. JAN VERMEER. *Street in Delft*. c. 1658. 21⅜ × 17⅞". Rijksmuseum, Amsterdam

though of moderate dimensions, the house at the right seems large because of the lower structures at the left. Since the left side contains also a variety of recessional motifs, the proud frontality of the dominant building is even more conspicuous. Yet there are no conflicts. The ups and downs of the roof lines are subtly coordinated, and the mellow color scheme (despite the fact that the green of a vine has turned blue) is still beautifully adjusted to the russet of the brick walls.

The model for the *Street in Delft* was surely a real street. As far as we know, Vermeer never left his native city. His *View of Delft* suggests that he was deeply attached to the charms of the old town. Whatever his reasons for painting the skyline of Delft, he created what is by all odds the finest Dutch landscape of the seventeenth century.

This is indeed more than the picture of a particular town. For Vermeer's contemporaries each building was an identifiable structure in a unique topographical context. For us the secret of the picture's greatness lies elsewhere. Though it represents but a section of one Dutch town, Vermeer's canvas has become a symbol of the whole country. This, in fact, *is* Holland. Here are its horizontal expanses under a wide sky, lively with leisurely clouds; its quiet waters, mirroring buildings and trees, carrying the boats essential to its way of life. The few figures are solid, slow, and primly keeping their distance. These are their houses, built of brick and mortar and roofed with bluish slate or red tiles. And this is the ever changing light that at this moment leaves the foreground in the shade of clouds while in the distance some orange roofs and a slender steeple beam in the sun.

The radiance of the church tower is as meaningful as its relative smallness within the plan of the whole picture. Religion had its place in the Dutch scheme of things, but that place was clearly defined and circumscribed. Vermeer's *View of Delft* is not only sheer optical poetry: it also is a witness to an eminently rational social system in which the Church fulfilled its appropriate functions. The fostering of enthusiasm or ecstasy was not among them.

6

Northern European Architecture in the Seventeenth and Eighteenth Centuries

During the period of the Baroque, the Protestant countries of the European North produced only one religious edifice of a monumental scale—St. Paul's in London. There was, however, a lively activity on the parish level, especially in London after the fire of 1666, which destroyed eighty-seven churches, and again when the new Tory and High Church government in 1711 passed an act for "Building . . . fifty new churches of stone and other proper Materials . . . "[1] Some churches were built in Holland, but the old Gothic churches provided ample space for most needs. Around 1700 Nicodemus Tessin planned a majestic church in Stockholm to serve as the burial site of Swedish kings, but the money for it was spent on the foreign wars of Charles XII; and a grandly domed church planned in Copenhagen in the middle of the eighteenth century was actually built only in the nineteenth.

The chief tasks confronting architects in these areas were secular, such as the erection of stately mansions for a prosperous urban society. A lively building activity went on in university towns such as Oxford and Cambridge. Hospitals, almshouses, customhouses, exchanges, and other types of government buildings were erected or at least planned. In Holland municipal initiative was responsible for some exquisitely designed weighing houses[2] as well as new town halls. Not all the ambitious projects for castles and country residences were realized, but some of the finest works of the period were created for patrons in high places.

The architects responsible for these undertakings were well acquainted with achievements elsewhere in Europe, primarily in Italy but increasingly in France. The spread of architectural ideas did not, however, depend on firsthand acquaintance. The first Palladian vogue in northern Europe, for instance, was sustained by Palladio's own publication of his designs (1570); the growing popularity of French plans was abetted by Jean Marot's *L'Architecture française* ("Le Grand Marot") of the late seventeenth century, a book remarkable also for its inclusion of seventeen engravings of the newly discovered ruins of Baalbek in Syria.

In England the man of destiny was Inigo Jones (1573–1652). Talented in many fields, he was famous for the ingenious staging of Stuart masques, especially those of Ben Jonson, his exact contemporary. Although unacquainted with practical architecture, he was slated in 1613 to be Surveyor of the King's Works, a position of vast authority subsequently occupied by Wren and Vanbrugh. To prepare himself for his job, he spent nineteen months in Italy, traveling together with Thomas Howard, the earl of Arundel, the most sensitive art patron and collector in England (colorplate 27). Another "steady companion" was Palladio's *Quattro libri dell' architettura*.[3]

It is hard to imagine a more radical break with tradition than that presented by Jones's Queen's House in Greenwich, designed in 1616 for Anne of Denmark, wife of King James I, and finished, after an interruption of about twelve years, in 1635 for Henrietta Maria, wife of King Charles I. Traditional English architecture had indulged in picturesque silhouettes and a multitude of decorative devices. All these fanciful elements were swept away by Jones in favor of the utmost clarity and restraint.

The structure was, as a contemporary called it, "some curious devise" enabling the Queen to go from the palace gardens to the park without contaminating herself with the traffic (and dirt) of the public road that separated them. Jones solved the problem by erecting two rectangular buildings of identical size on either side of the road and connecting them with a bridge.[4] In Palladian fashion, each of these buildings was planned symmetrically and the size of the rooms graded in simple proportionate relationships. The northern block, facing the river, contains the largest room, a central hall measuring forty feet in all directions. Despite some later changes the outside of the building still impresses us with its quiet dignity and unobtrusive elegance. Most fascinating are the differences between the two façades. The center portion projects slightly in both but whereas the façade toward the park has five windows below, in harmony with the intercolumniations of an open loggia above, the north façade (fig. 288) is pierced by only three windows on each level. This simplicity, however, is made up for by a double stairway, flanked by balustrades that continue laterally along a platform and form a parallel to a similar balustrade at the top of the structure. As a result, the north front, marking the main approach, is more majestic and aloof, the one toward the south more gracious and informal.

If Queen's House was essentially a modest structure (unsuited for the role it was eventually to play as the focal point of a grandiose sequence of

288. INIGO JONES. North Façade, Queen's House. 1616–35. Greenwich, England

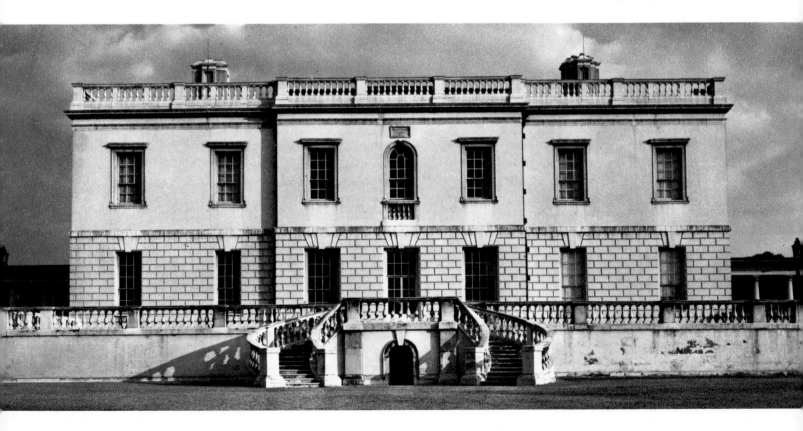

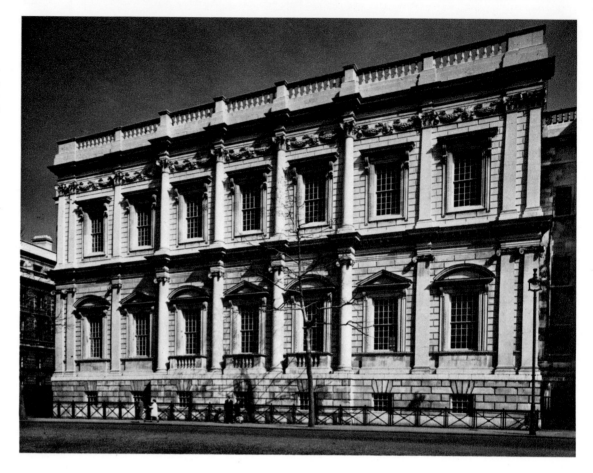

289. INIGO JONES.
West Front, Banqueting House,
Whitehall Palace.
1619–22. London

buildings), Jones's so-called Banqueting House for Whitehall was the very opposite. Replacing an older hall consumed by fire in 1619, it was intended as the setting "for the display of royal might and glory,"[5] serving for the reception of foreign princes, the ratification of treaties, and for all official ceremonies including royal masques. (With ironical appropriateness, the beheading of Charles I was staged on a platform in front of Jones's hall.)

The testimony of the structure, unfortunately, is blurred by later changes. Once subtly differentiated by three kinds of stone of different colors, its exterior is now uniformly whitish gray. The interior, happily cleansed of the clutter of an army museum, is rather bare and probably too light. Originally the hall was richly decorated with paintings, tapestries, and flags, and received its light chiefly from the windows above the balconies. The crowning splendor of the hall is fortunately intact: Rubens' ceiling glorifying James I in nine large canvases (see page 207).

The Banqueting House is unusual in several respects. Its "façade" (fig. 289) is actually the side elevation and has no entrance: access to the structure is from the end. Another peculiarity is the contrast between the exterior and the room behind it. Seen from the outside, the Banqueting House resembles a palazzo with two stories of equal height above a high podium.[6] The inside consists of only one large hall having the proportion of a double cube. A modicum of correspondence between interior and exterior is established by the organization of the hall in terms of two superimposed orders divided by a cantilevered balcony.

Although unconventional, Jones's Banqueting House is a most handsome and harmonious building. It looks appropriately festive with its subtle interplay of rusticated surfaces and finely proportioned orders, the sculptured masks and swags of fruit that link the capitals in the upper tier, and the determined spatial motion of the two entablatures that break forward above the orders, insuring a strong vertical integration of the whole design. The crowning balustrade, built here long before it appeared at Queen's House, set a fashion repeated almost endlessly in later British architecture.

Jones's Palladian Baroque found an echo in a development of urban architecture of more than local significance. In response to the rapid growth of London's population, some enterprising individuals began to obtain licenses for the development of entire streets. They sold plots, or finished houses built in conformity with a standard plan. Thus in the late 1630s a certain William Newton obtained a license to construct fourteen houses in Great Queen Street and thirty-two houses on the west side of Lincoln's Inn Fields. The only house surviving, though not entirely intact, is the so-called Lindsey House, built for Sir David Conyngham. Although certainly not designed by Jones,[7] it has much of the moderation and masculinity Jones himself had recommended for the exterior of buildings. One can hardly think of a more successful adaptation of a classical vocabulary to a domestic dwelling, or one of more harmonious proportions.

Jones's influence soon spread to the Continent, especially the Netherlands. The major representatives of this new architecture were to be found in two centers—at The Hague, the residence of the princes of Orange, and at Amsterdam, with its proud and wealthy patrician society.

A central figure at The Hague, besides Prince Frederick Hendrik himself, was Constantijn Huygens (1596–1687; see page 246), a learned amateur who kept abreast of new ideas. Poet, diplomat, scholar, and art lover, he officially occupied the position of secretary to the prince of Orange. The prince had strong ties with France, and French was the language of his court. Huygens, however, had been in Italy, too, and knew Palladio's buildings; he also had twice visited England, and it is certain that he saw both the Banqueting House and the still unfinished Queen's House. He probably had some concrete opinions on architecture when he joined forces with a gifted young architect, Jacob van Campen (1598–1657). One of the fruits of their collaboration, Huygens' own house, has disappeared. Its neighbor, a residence built in 1633–35 for Prince Maurice of Nassau, the governor of Brazil, still survives and—known as the Mauritshuis—

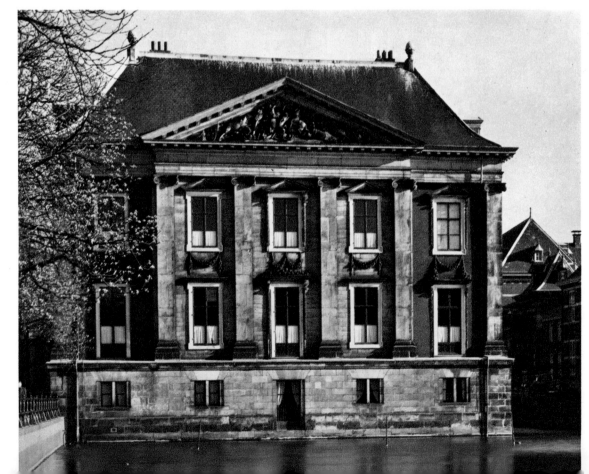

290. JACOB VAN CAMPEN and CONSTANTIJN HUYGENS. Canal Façade, Mauritshuis. 1633–34. The Hague

today houses one of the finest Dutch museums (fig. 290).

A freestanding block consisting of two equal stories above an inconspicuous ground floor, and topped by a high hipped roof (of French derivation), the Mauritshuis is as radical a departure from earlier Dutch practices as Jones's buildings are from English. Instead of the dazzle of multi-tiered gables enriched with scrolls, herms, urns, and a proliferating rustication, Van Campen's building features a continuous sequence of colossal Ionic pilasters, carried all around the block. At the front and back they are incorporated into formal façades, though one differs greatly from the other. In the back, where the building rises directly from the edge of the town's central pond, the height of the ground floor is added to the whole composition and carries five bays; the three central bays are somewhat narrower and project slightly, and are crowned by a wide, sculpture-filled pediment.

The main façade is richer, but less harmoniously organized. Since the ground floor was all but invisible, the architect increased the vertical axes to seven bays, to counteract the impression of excessive width. Again the three central bays project and are provided with a pediment, but since they are rather narrow the pediment is much shorter and less dominant than in the back.

The rooms of the interior are symmetrically grouped around a spacious central staircase that widens to a hall-like space on the upper level. Even though the house of a prince, the Mauritshuis manages to remain above all a house. Few of the later buildings of the Dutch Palladian trend can compare with its simple dignity. The house built by Justus Vingboons in 1662 for the Trip brothers in Amsterdam may be more grandiose with its tall fluted pilasters and sumptuous carvings, yet the very rhetoric of such later buildings increases one's appreciation of the sturdy plainness of the Mauritshuis.

Van Campen was the architect in charge when the city of Amsterdam decided to build a new town hall to replace the medieval one (which providentially burned down during the early stages of the work). The new hall turned into Holland's greatest architectural enterprise of the seventeenth century.

Stately town halls had for a long time been the visible manifestations of urban power and pride. This is as true of towns such as Florence and Siena as it is of Bruges and Tournai. Later the cities of Nuremberg and Augsburg had erected magnificent town halls, before the Thirty Years' War abruptly halted such projects. The last major town hall built in the Netherlands was that of Antwerp, designed by Cornelius Floris in 1561–65. By the middle of the seventeenth century the northern Netherlands was the only remaining country where the citizens of large towns could still shape their own destinies, and, of all Dutch towns, Amsterdam was by far the largest and most prosperous. The burgomasters of Amsterdam did not care only for adequate space for a greatly expanded administration; they also desired the new town hall to be a symbol of the greatness of a city that had recently emerged with new glory from the negotiations of the Peace of Westphalia (1648; see also page 196).

Van Campen's building—finished from his designs after he had unaccountably been dismissed—is worthy of these efforts. Covering a block 280 feet wide and 235 feet deep, it is particularly imposing because of its height—110 feet, not counting the tower (fig. 291). To reach this height, Van Campen superimposed, on a high ground floor, two nearly identical stories, each with two rows of windows—oblong below, square above—united by giant orders of pilasters.

The central space of the interior is occupied by the Burgerzaal (fig. 292), a huge room extending to the full height of the two principal stories (reminiscent of Jones's Banqueting House) and obtaining its light from two large courtyards on either side. Even by the standards of Baroque art, this is a room of incomparable grandeur and by far one of the largest spatial units within a secular structure built anywhere in the seventeenth century.

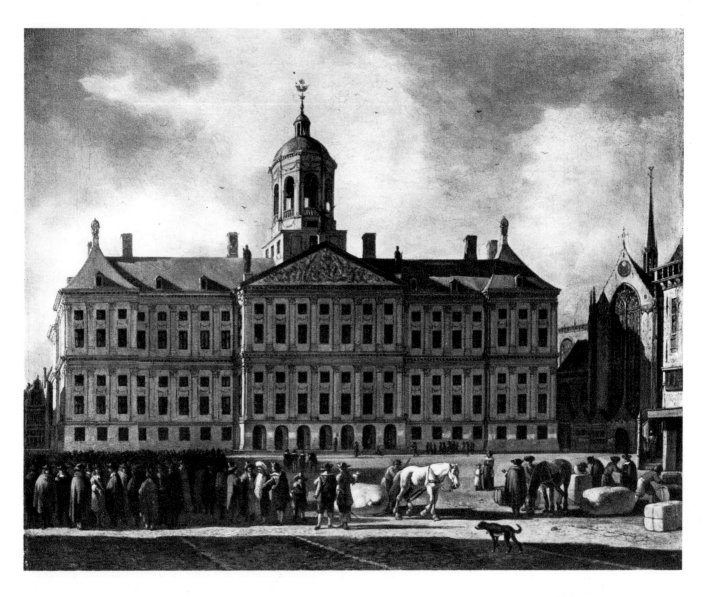

291. GERRIT BERCKHEYDE.
View of the Amsterdam Town Hall.
c. 1675. 13¼ × 16⅜″.
Rijksmuseum, Amsterdam

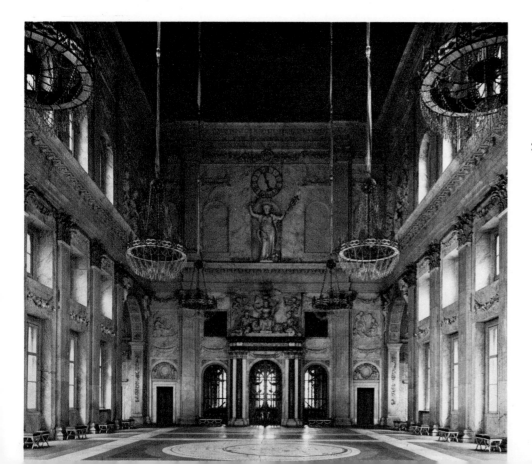

292. JACOB VAN CAMPEN.
Interior of the Great
Central Hall, Town Hall.
Begun 1648. Amsterdam

287

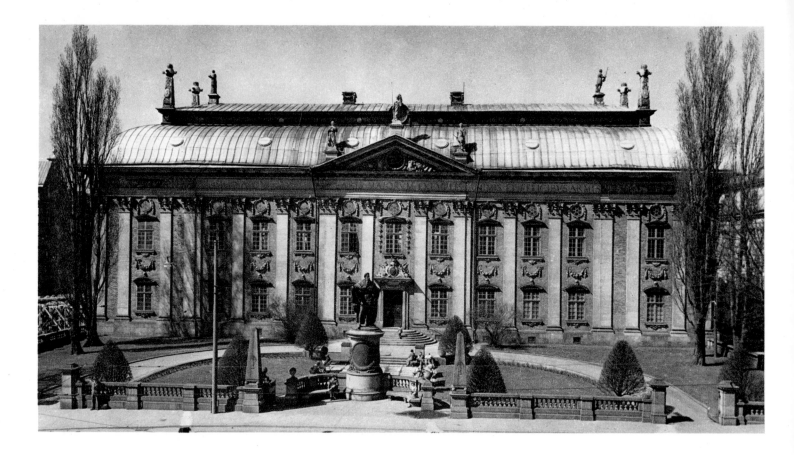

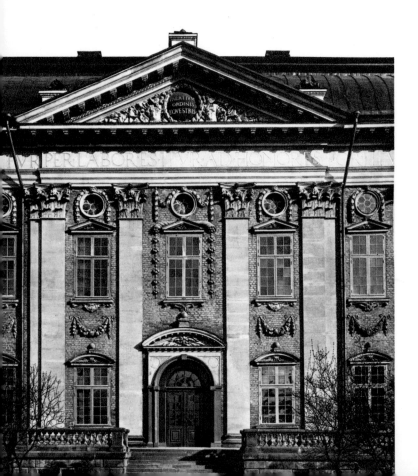

293, 294. JUSTUS VINGBOONS.
Street (above) and Garden Façades,
Riddarhuset. 1653. Stockholm

Impressive for its sheer size, the Amsterdam town hall is also an instructive example of the fundamental relevancy of the decorative program in Baroque buildings.[8] In sculptures and paintings, most of them mythologically or allegorically embroidered, the themes of triumph and civic virtue are conjoined. The man chiefly responsible for the sculptured decoration was Artus Quellinus I (1606–1668), a Fleming whose style was derived from Rubens; it is an irony of history that Rubens' artistic ideals were used to glorify a city that more than any other had insisted on the complete humiliation of Rubens' own town, Antwerp.

The Dutch version of Palladian classicism spread rapidly beyond the borders of the country, particularly to some courts in northern Germany (where the princes of Orange had close dynastic ties) and to commercial centers like Hamburg and Bremen. In many places this influence was spearheaded by Dutch architects. In Sweden the most important project in the middle of the century, the so-called Riddarhuset in Stockholm (fig. 293), an assembly-house for the nobility, was redesigned by the Dutch architect Justus Vingboons (1653), though its final appearance owes much to Vingboons' successor, Jean de la Vallée (1620–1696). A shallow building, only three axes in depth, it has façades on street and garden, both employing in a characteristically Dutch manner giant Corinthian pilasters set against a brick wall decorated with garlands of fruit between the windows. Both façades put stress on their main entrances by crowning the three central bays with a pediment (fig. 294), but whereas the lateral extension of the garden façade continues on either side the quiet rhythm of five identical bays, the more dynamic street façade accentuates each of the end-bays, resulting in a more pronounced movement in depth and a reduction in the total number of bays from thirteen to eleven. A row of circular windows in an attic zone (a curious anticipation of Wren's long row of oculus windows on the park façade of Hampton Court) and a peculiar roof with a double curvature (a hallmark of later Swedish Baroque architecture) appear here for the first time. Nor was the Riddarhuset

the first example of Dutch Palladianism in Stockholm: as early as 1646 Louis de Geer, a wealthy industrialist from Holland, had used the Mauritshuis as a model for his own residence.[9]

The relatively plain language of Dutch Palladianism was insufficient, however, to do justice to the architectural aspirations of an ambitious royal court. When the foremost Swedish architect of the Baroque, Nicodemus Tessin the Younger (1654–1728), built the royal palace of Stockholm (fig. 295) around the turn of the century, he relied heavily on the vocabulary of Roman Baroque (though it may not be wholly accidental that the width of the edifice consists of twenty-five window axes—precisely the number in Van Campen's Amsterdam town hall). Entirely personal and most ingenious is Tessin's use of the terrain. Placing a huge block, made up of four wings enclosing a square courtyard, on the brow of a low hill, he enriched it with ramps, terraces, and lower projecting wings (two of which flank an elevated garden). Partly surrounded by water, this majestic ensemble still dominates Stockholm, even though nothing came of the plan to tie it into a still vaster urban development.

One of the most harmonious projects of city

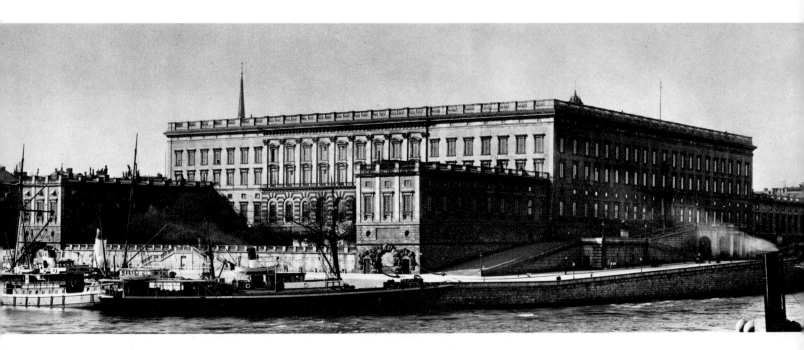

295. NICODEMUS TESSIN THE YOUNGER. Exterior, North Façade, Royal Palace. c. 1700. Stockholm

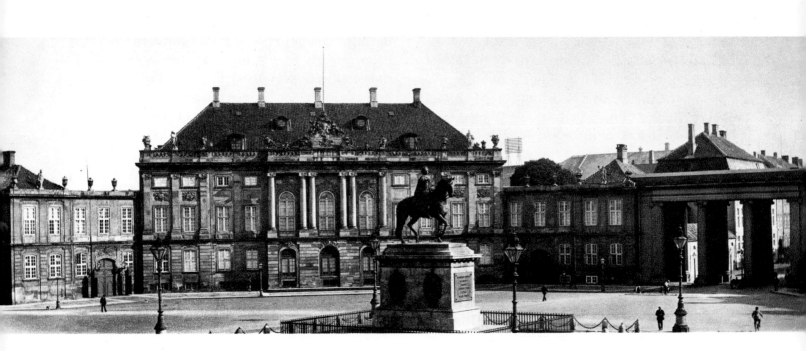

296. MARCUS TUSCHER and NICOLAI EIGTVED.
Exterior of Palace, Amalienborg.
Begun 1749. Copenhagen

planning was realized in Copenhagen at the very
end of the Baroque era. The royal patron, King
Frederick V, seems to have taken an active part
in working out the details of this plan with his
two architects, Marcus Tuscher (1705–1751) and
Nicolai Eigtved (1701–1754). Though one of the
buildings has since become the royal residence
(fig. 296), the project, known as Amalienborg
(begun 1749), was designed for occupancy by
members of the court. In the center, an octagonal
plaza was formed by diagonally cutting back the
four corners of a street crossing (fig. 297). The
frontages thus won were built up with four cen-

297. *View of Amalienborg*
(engraving by Le Clerc, 1766).
Copenhagen

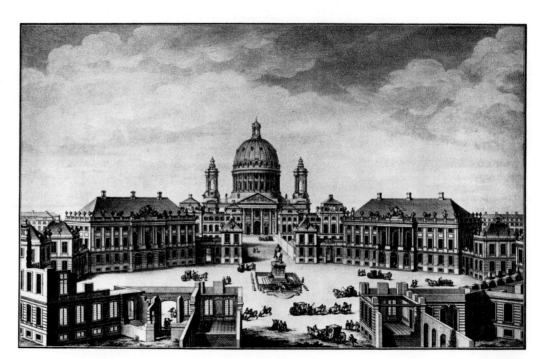

tral palaces, each having short lower wings. The schema is continued along the streets with more modest structures. Enough of the original plan has been preserved to make Amalienborg a major architectural delight in Scandinavia.

However aesthetically rewarding much of Scandinavian Baroque architecture may be (not to mention Leningrad's grandiose palaces built in the eighteenth century), it was literally and figuratively marginal. We must return to England for another major contribution to the mainstream of Baroque architecture.

The new period of English architecture—and probably its greatest—was ushered in by a disaster of unparalleled magnitude: the blaze that leveled over thirteen thousand houses in London in the first days of September, 1666. Not unlike the blitz of 1940, this provided unexpected opportunities for architectural renovation. The most important project was the rebuilding of St. Paul's, where the fire had put an end to all halfhearted attempts at restoration. Whoever was to build it had to begin from scratch.

Ground for what was to become the almost mythical beacon of London was broken in 1675, the year before J. Hardouin-Mansart began the Church of the Invalides, the proudest Parisian church of the Baroque (fig. 147). The architect was Christopher Wren (1632–1723), who since 1669 had been Surveyor-General—a position from which he directed the destinies of English architecture for several decades. A student of science and mathematics, Dr. Wren had been professor of astronomy at Oxford, but in the early 1660s he became interested in architecture and designed some university buildings at Oxford and Cambridge. On his trip to the Continent in 1665–66 he appears to have had contact with some of the leading French and Italian architects, but he never actually went to Italy. Paris had begun to supplant Rome as the world capital of art.

Wren's first plan for St. Paul's was in the form of a Greek cross, its arms connected by segmental curves. The idea of a central building was given up in favor of a longitudinal plan (fig. 298), precisely as it had been done at St. Peter's in Rome and, as there, largely for the sake of tradition. St. Paul's has much in common, indeed, with English Gothic cathedrals (fig. 299). Its total length of five hundred feet comes close to that of such hallowed examples as Canterbury, Lincoln, and York. Like many of its Gothic predecessors, the nave is as long as the choir; and Wren used the typically Gothic device of flying buttresses in its construction, though he concealed them behind a wall that seems to add a second story above the side aisles. The extension of the dome to include the full width of the side aisles was surely due to Wren's thorough acquaintance with Ely Cathedral.

It must be admitted, however, that St. Paul's does not achieve the complete artistic unity that a less eclectic master might have been able to give it. The persistent use of two sharply separated stories of equal height for a building of this size (possibly a carry-over from Jones's Banqueting House) deprives it of monumentality (fig. 300). The design works best in the transept façades, which Wren enriched with gracefully curved porticoes probably derived from Santa Maria della Pace or Sant'Andrea al Quirinale. On the main facade Wren combined with an almost perverse innocence the most contradictory elements, from a loggia formed by coupled columns obviously based on Perrault's façade of the Louvre (colorplate 16) to towers which in their freestanding parts are full of Roman reminiscences, including some very Borrominesque curvatures and perforations.

The dome, undoubtedly the most striking and most successful part of St. Paul's, was done last. Wren made the final plans around 1704–5, and the structure was completed by October, 1708. Its great height was achieved by adopting the principle—no longer new—of freeing the exterior appearance from the interior construction.[10] Wren used this opportunity to design a work of classic simplicity that is still echoed in the domes

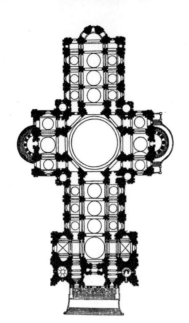

298. CHRISTOPHER WREN.
Plan, St. Paul's Cathedral.
1675–1710. London

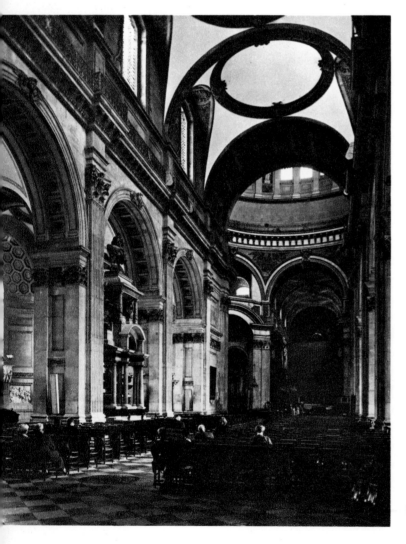

of the Paris Panthéon (originally Ste.-Geneviève) and the Capitol in Washington. The peristyle of the tambour (despite the walling up of every fourth intercolumniation) is strongly reminiscent of Bramante's Tempietto of 1504; as in that building, the cupola rises on a drum emerging from behind the balustrade that crowns the peristyle. Only in the lantern does the severity of this arrangement give way to a more complex play of forms, though even here Wren remains more classical then Hardouin-Mansart at the Church of the Invalides.

Despite its shortcomings, St. Paul's remains one of the major churches of the Western world, and the inscription on Wren's tomb inside the church could justifiably call it the true monument to the artist: *si monumentum requiris, circumspice* ("if you seek a monument, look around you"). For a fair appraisal of Wren's work posterity—fortunately—is not confined to St. Paul's alone. He is credited with no less than fifty-one churches rebuilt after the great fire, and he showed a remarkable versatility in planning these modestly sized buildings.

299. CHRISTOPHER WREN.
View toward transept, St. Paul's Cathedral

300. CHRISTOPHER WREN. West Façade, St. Paul's Cathedral. 1675–1710. London

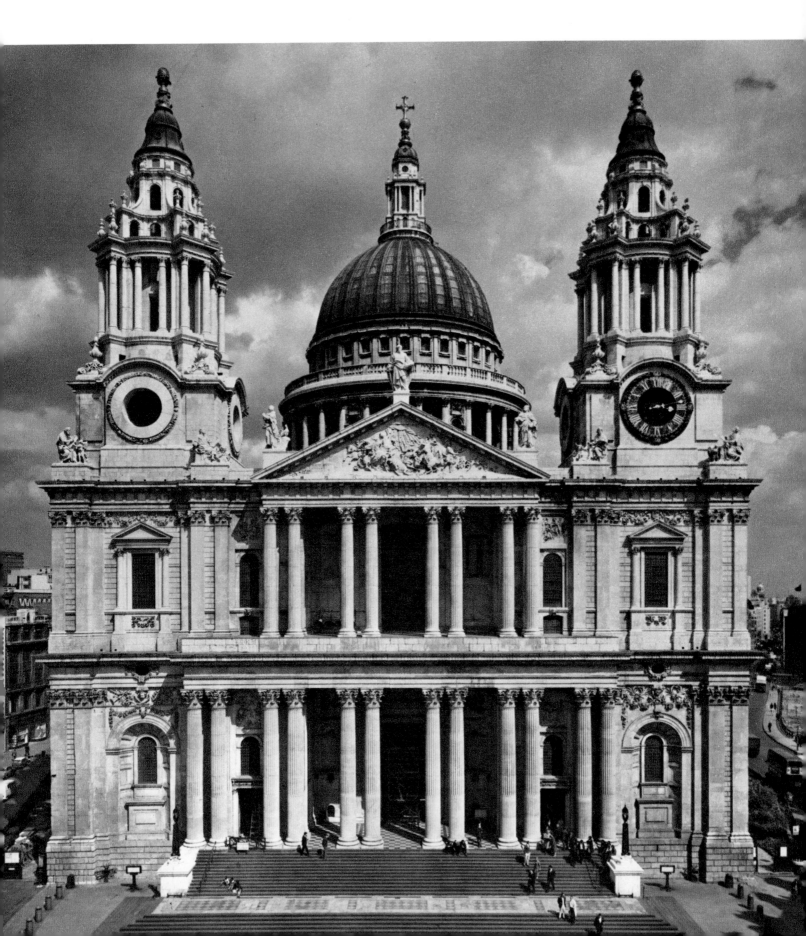

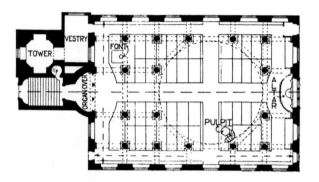

301. CHRISTOPHER WREN.
Plan, St. Stephen's, Walbrook.
1672–87. London

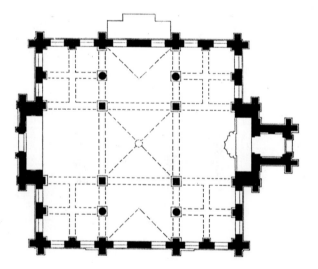

302. JACOB VAN CAMPEN.
Plan, New Church. Begun 1645. Haarlem

The most ingenious is St. Stephen's, Walbrook (figs. 301, 303), and it is fortunate that this masterpiece of mathematical calculation escaped the fury of the second great London fire, which doomed so many other churches by Wren. To appreciate the originality of St. Stephen's one ought to compare it with the New Church at Haarlem, built by Van Campen (begun 1645; fig. 302). Van Campen's was a remarkably clear and logical structure in which a Greek cross was inscribed into a square ground plan. St. Stephen's, too, is a central church, though the ground plan is a short rectangle rather than a square. But whereas in Van Campen's church the central feature is a traditional crossing with cross-rib vaults, Wren's church has a central dome floating above an octagon of arches, which issues in turn from a square formed by twelve freestanding columns. (Toward the entrance another row of four columns aids in establishing a short vaulted nave and lower side aisles.) In order to have the eight arches of the octagon of equal height, the distance between the columns in the longitudinal and the transverse axes had to be larger than elsewhere in the church—with the result that the plan, especially as seen beneath the dome, approximates a Greek cross. Despite the structural complexity, the solution looks surprisingly light and effortless. There are few churches to which the shopworn expression calling architecture "frozen music" may be applied with more justification. Its component "tunes"—the main rectangle, the inner square, the Greek cross, the octagon, and the circle of the dome—are interwoven with utmost rationality and precision. This was clearly not a house for enthusiastic worshipers;[11] it was a temple for people who put faith in reason in order to arrive at a reasonable faith. Spinoza might have felt at home in Wren's church.

Most of the parish churches built from Wren's plans represent that ideal of "plainness and duration" that he considered the principal requirement of their exterior.[12] Only the design of the steeples—one to each church—prompted him to

294

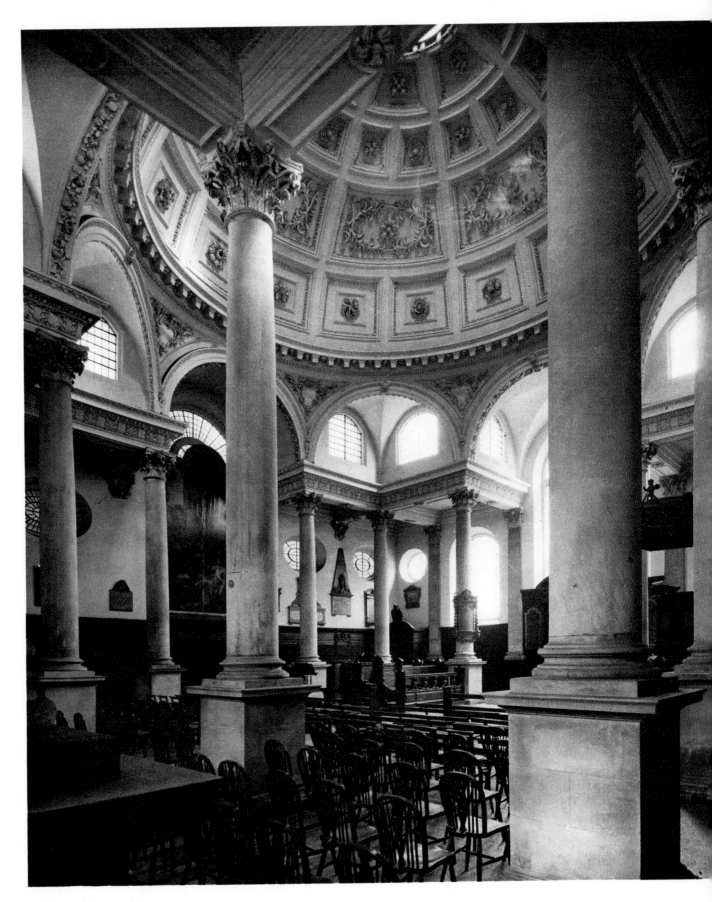

303. CHRISTOPHER WREN. Interior, St. Stephen's, Walbrook. 1672–87. London

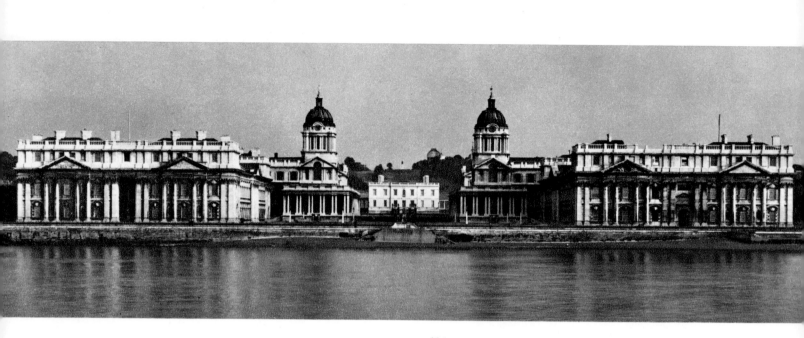

304. CHRISTOPHER WREN. Exterior, Greenwich Hospital. Completed 1705

rather elaborate efforts, since he thought that "handsome spires or lanterns" are adornments of the whole town.

Of the many large-scale architectural compositions for which Wren made plans, Greenwich Hospital (fig. 304) is the only one that reflects to a considerable extent his intentions, but even these plans were the result of a compromise. He had hoped to close the vista formed by four long blocks with a great domed structure, but was forced to abandon the idea to avoid impeding the view of Queen's House lying farther up the hill. His solution—to narrow the second courtyard by providing the block on either side with colonnades and to mark their narrow "fronts," facing the river, with domed towers—resulted in a spatial composition of undeniable grandeur despite the absence of a dominant center. The only inside room equal to the majestic exterior is the "Painted Hall" decorated by James Thornhill (fig. 305), which one enters under the tower at the right.

As an architect Wren seems to have worked with great facility of imagination, and he had moments of truly inspired brilliance. Yet his in-

305. CHRISTOPHER WREN. Painted Hall, Greenwich Hospital. Ceiling Painting by James Thornhill, 1708–27

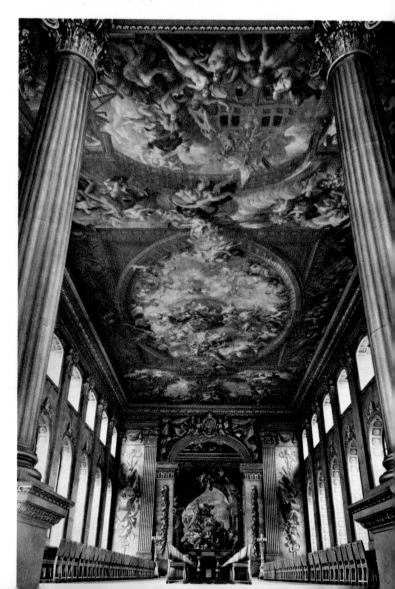

296

tellect was clearly more powerful than his commitment to a particular formal idiom. He designed with his brain rather than his heart, relying on knowledge more than passion. Essentially, he believed in the value of compromise; in this he suited well the temper of his country and the society that made up his patrons. Although he did not escape a final disappointment—being dismissed in 1718 as Surveyor-General of the Royal Works—he retained the gratitude of a nation whose desire for greatness he was the first to express in the language of stone.

What Wren lacked John Vanbrugh (1664–1726) possessed to the highest degree: a robust personal vision and a firm will to see it realized. He, too, had come late to architecture and like Wren often left the elaboration of details to Nicholas Hawksmoor (1661–1736), a true professional. Where Wren was committed to civilized urbanity and common sense, Vanbrugh aimed at a display of "masculinity" and raw grandeur. It is hardly accidental that all Vanbrugh's major works are secular, where an expression of sturdy power was not inappropriate. With Castle Howard, built for the Earl of Carlisle, England received its first example of a sprawling princely residence, dominated by a high central block enclosing a domed hall and distinguished by a façade that has a more than fortuitous kinship with that of St. Peter's.

Vanbrugh is best known for Blenheim Palace (1705–22), the most conspicuous symbol of the might of England's ruling class (figs. 306, 307). This enormous pile was built, largely from public

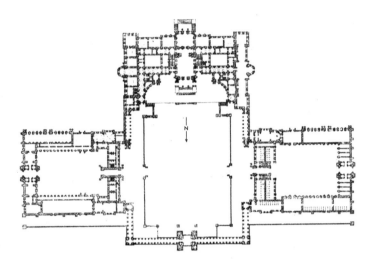

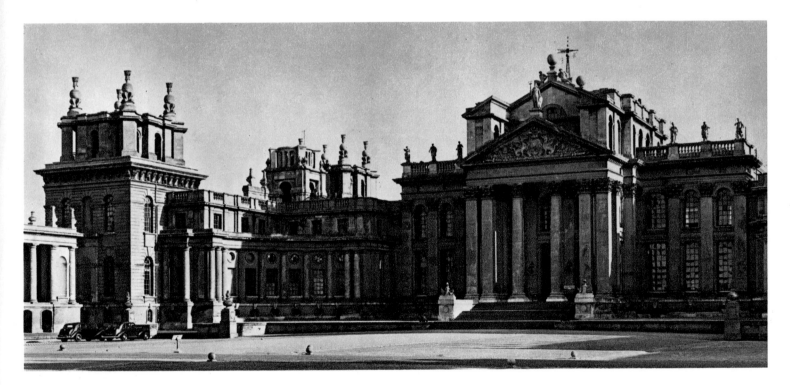

306, 307. JOHN VANBRUGH.
Plan and Entrance Façade, Blenheim Palace.
1705–22. Woodstock

funds, for John Churchill, duke of Marlborough, the colorful statesman and popular military hero. His role in English history can be compared to that of Prince Eugene of Savoy in Austria—his ally in the campaign of Blenheim for which the palace was named. But Blenheim is a far cry from the Vienna Belvedere, built for Prince Eugene (fig. 395). There is no Austrian lightness and grace in Vanbrugh's structure; nothing but colossal columns and pilasters would do for the *corps de logis,* while fat thirty-foot finials add their weight to the squattish corner towers. Contemporary skeptics were not slow to jest about the excessive weightiness of the structure, and its disregard for convenience and comfort. Yet Blenheim was not meant to be a mere private residence but a national monument embodying, as Vanbrugh put it, "Beauty, Magnificence, and Duration." Vanbrugh avoided any impression of formal fluency; Italian architects would have shuddered at his brutality in running the wings up against the corner towers at right angles.

The purest display of Vanbrugh's intentions as architect is found in a relatively small building (fig. 308) that, moreover, has come down only as a shell: Seaton Delaval, Northumberland (1717–28). The over-all impression is grandly gloomy, evoking unmistakably the massed and muscular power of medieval fortresses. A severe rustication, extending even to two pairs of flanking columns, gives the center of the building a defiant air, and the undecorated octagonal towers reinforce this impression. Even the stairs to the main portal evoke memories of drawbridges let down. What is left of the interior proclaims clearly that the chief element of architecture is the walls, not the orders. It may well be that of the three qualities of architecture stressed by Vanbrugh, the last—duration—was the one uppermost in his mind. Although ravaged by fire, Seaton Delaval has justified this trust.

As the eighteenth century progressed, a strong classical trend reappeared, though it was by no means unopposed. The leaders of this movement

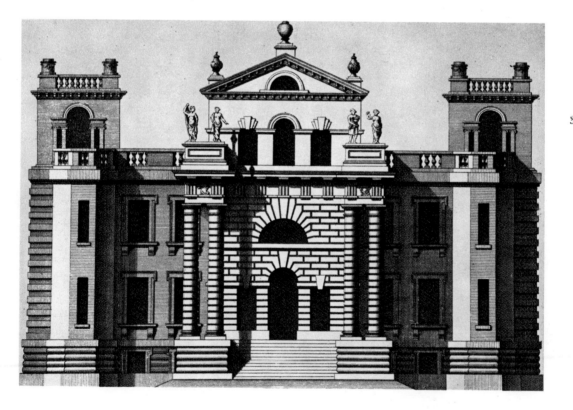

308. JOHN VANBRUGH. Engraving of Façade, Seaton Delaval. 1717–28. Northumberland

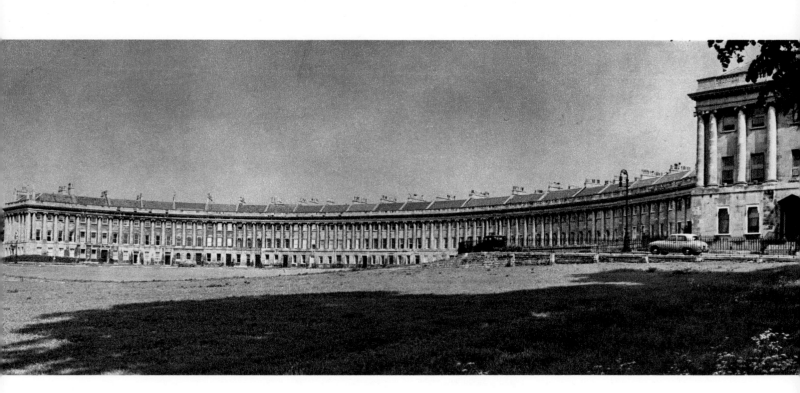

309. JOHN WOOD THE YOUNGER. Royal Crescent. 1767–75. Bath

were by origin or sympathy associated with the Whig party, the political instrument of the big landowners and merchants. Just as in politics they disliked Catholicism and royal privilege, so in architecture they objected to any formal quality that evoked the memory of Roman Baroque. The men who articulated the new credo were learned amateurs rather than artists. Anthony Ashley Cooper, third earl of Shaftesbury (1671–1713), had been the first to plead the case of classicism, and of an Academy as an institution to foster its goals. The key figure of this development, however, was Richard Boyle, third earl of Burlington (1694–1753), who with the help of the architects Colen Campbell and William Kent made Palladian villas fashionable, supporting the vogue with his own publication of Palladio's designs (1730). Inevitably, this trend stimulated a Jonesian revival, which was aided by Kent's publication in 1727 of Jones's designs. Buildings like Chiswick House (1725), near London, or Holkham Hall, Norfolk (1734), represent well the neat regularity

and almost aseptic purity of the style propagated by the earl of Burlington. The frigidity of this architecture was offset by a relaxed and informal treatment of the gardens; following Shaftesbury's criticism of the rigid geometry of the French gardens, associated as they were with princely arrogation, Kent, among others, designed gardens emulating nature's own order as an expression of personal freedom and independence. Known as the "English garden" and gradually enriched with picturesque motifs such as medieval ruins or Chinese pavilions, the deliberately irregular garden design quickly spread to the Continent (where the backgrounds in Watteau's paintings had prepared a favorable climate of taste).

The Palladian fashion was not limited to the houses of the landed gentry. It also affected the tradition of serial town architecture. The men who introduced Palladian principles into multiple dwelling units were John Wood the Elder and his son John the Younger (1728–1781). Both were active in Bath, the fashionable spa; the most

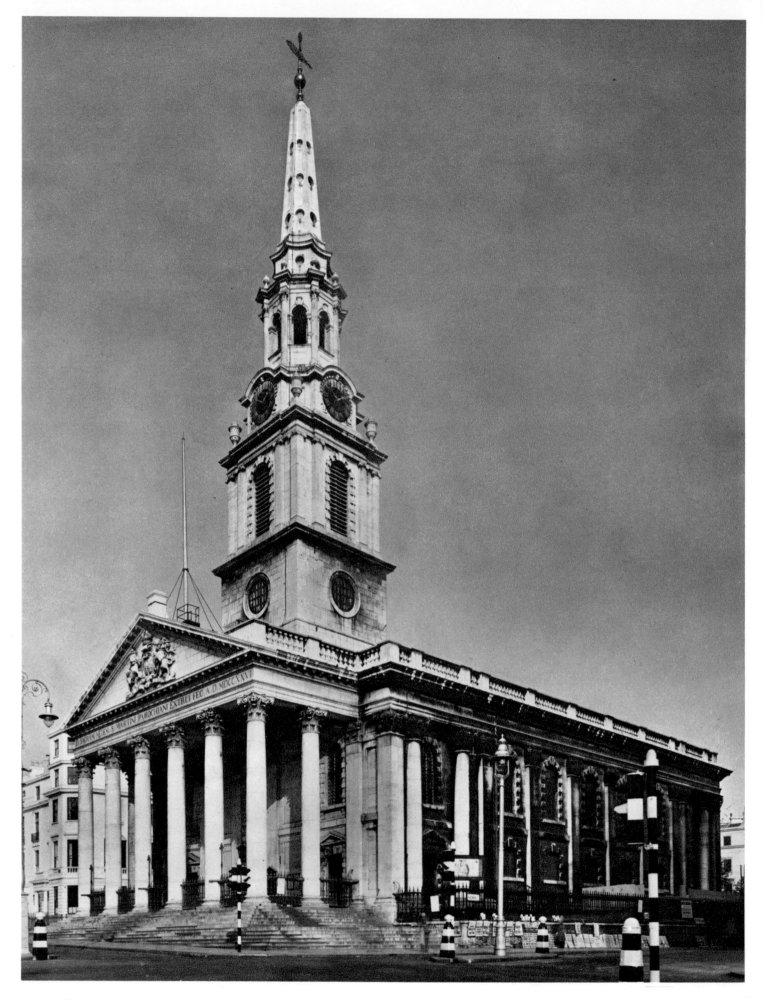

310. JAMES GIBBS. St. Martin's-in-the-Fields. 1721–26. London

spectacular of these blocks made up of "one-family houses" is the Royal Crescent, the work of the younger Wood (fig. 309). Thirty houses are combined into a vast concave body of palatial appearance. With its majestic phalanx of attached Ionic columns and its unbroken entablature and balustrade Wood's Royal Crescent strikingly visualizes both the remarkable cohesion of English high society and its proud exclusiveness.

If the architects associating with the earl of Burlington are representative of what may be called Whig aesthetics, James Gibbs (1682–1754) was the exponent of Tory taste. Issuing from Wren's circle, but trained by Carlo Fontana in Rome, he introduced principles of Roman Baroque architecture into England. In his churches of St. Mary-le-Strand (1714) and St. Martin's-in-the-Fields (fig. 310) he strongly articulated the exterior with pilasters, columns, and large pedimented windows (reminiscent of Roman palaces more than of churches) and in both buildings

created an organic unity between the muscular body of the church and the soaring energies of the steeple. In the curved portico of St. Mary-le-Strand he emulated Pietro da Cortona's portico of Santa Maria della Pace more wholeheartedly than Wren had done in the transepts of St. Paul's. Gibbs's chief homage to Roman Baroque, however, is the Rotunda, known as the Radcliffe Camera Library (fig. 311), at Oxford (1739–49). Its rusticated, polygonal ground floor lends it a fortresslike ruggedness and forms an effective contrast to the proud opulence of the main part of the cylindrical structure. Even though the dome, rising from a much reduced perimeter, fails to match the monumental shapes below, Gibbs's "camera" proclaims loudly the merits of the sculptural concept of architecture so dear to the Italian tradition. Yet it is significant for the scientific and rational climate of eighteenth-century England that he stated this in a building dedicated to the advancement of knowledge, not to the service of God.

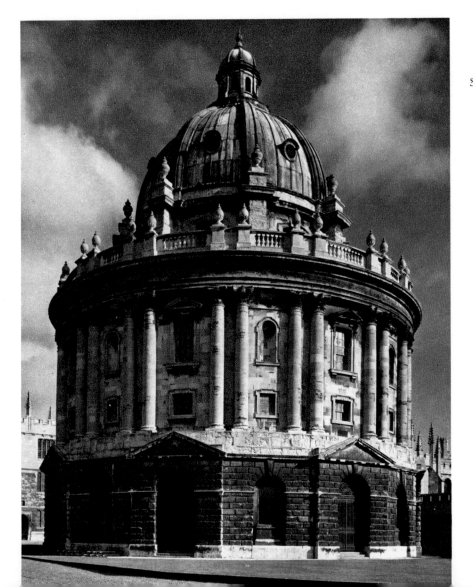

311. JAMES GIBBS.
Exterior, Radcliffe Camera
(now Radcliffe Library).
1739–49. Oxford

301

7

France in the Eighteenth Century

PAINTING

The artistic trends that appeared in France in the last decades of the seventeenth century were partly inspired, and certainly encouraged, by the newly assertive tastes of Parisian society. The intellectual independence, the wide range of interests, and the elegant intimacy of social life in Paris were increasingly cultivated in reaction to the heavy, authoritarian formality of the court at Versailles. The grand scale of the royal style of life and art could not be emulated by the merely rich, and new ideals, closer to normal human dimensions, were needed to satisfy the cultural aspirations of those who chose, or who were forced, to remain independent of the court. In Paris the leading "tastemaker" was Philippe, duke of Orléans. His art collection in the Palais Royale included great works by the Venetians, Correggio, Rubens, Van Dyck, and Rembrandt, and he had admiration for the younger generation of French colorists. Art responded to the new demands; depictions of the amusements, the pleasures, the variety of life, and the sensuous charms of color began to replace the didactic or propagandistic subjects and the essentially linear style of the seventeenth century. By the beginning of

the eighteenth century Parisian tastes were affecting art at Versailles and, when Philippe d'Orléans became regent after the death of Louis XIV in 1715, their ascendancy in France was unchallenged.

Although the gradual transformation of French painting can be traced back to the 1670s,[1] the specific character that it took during the eighteenth century was in large part determined by Antoine Watteau (1684–1721). Watteau was born in Valenciennes, a city on the Flemish border that had only been secured as French territory by the Treaty of Nijmegen in 1679. Indeed, when Watteau came to Paris about 1702 he associated himself with the colony of Flemish artists there, and his early work included genre pieces in the manner of the Netherlandish little masters. During his years in Paris though, Watteau studied the paintings of the Venetians and of Rubens, and he was impressed by the spirited lightness of Charles de La Fosse. He worked for a time with the decorator Claude Audran, and he contributed to the ornamental vocabulary of the eighteenth century by helping to develop, for instance, the *chinoiseries* and *singeries* (decoration based on

Oriental subjects and monkey motifs) that soon became very popular.

A crucial early influence on Watteau's development was the art of Claude Gillot (1673–1722), with whom he worked from about 1704 to about 1707. Gillot's manner contributed to the creation of Watteau's elegant figure style, and it was Gillot's example that led Watteau to one of his most important themes: the theater, especially the Italian *commedia*. In art around 1700 the comedians (represented a century earlier in the prints of Jacques Callot) were the subject of a popular but minor genre that was treated in an amusing, anecdotal fashion by Gillot and others (fig. 312). Watteau transformed the genre. He recognized the essential verisimilitude and the psychological range of the stock types of the *commedia,* and in his art the fantasy of the stage and the reality of everyday life are merged. Actually, this was not only based on poetic intuition. In the eighteenth century the conventions

of social ritual—the playful dalliance of mistresses and lovers in shady *allées,* the gallant conversation, the ballets, and the pastoral masques—stylized an important part of upper-class life and made it a kind of theatrical endeavor. One of the traditions on which Watteau drew was the illustration of contemporary manners and fashions; it was one of the primary sources for his creation of an entirely new genre in painting: the representation of the *fête galante,* the amusement and entertainment of elegant society. Thus, in his works, theater and life become one in a comedy of love and desire, of frustrations, of missteps, and of chance discoveries. The *Mezzetin* (c. 1718; colorplate 45) is one of Watteau's friends dressed in the brilliantly striped costume of the *commedia dell'arte* character. He plays his mandolin in the perfumed intimacy of a verdant garden. The statue in the background, a woman with her back turned to Mezzetin, clarifies the theme of longing and still unrequited love.

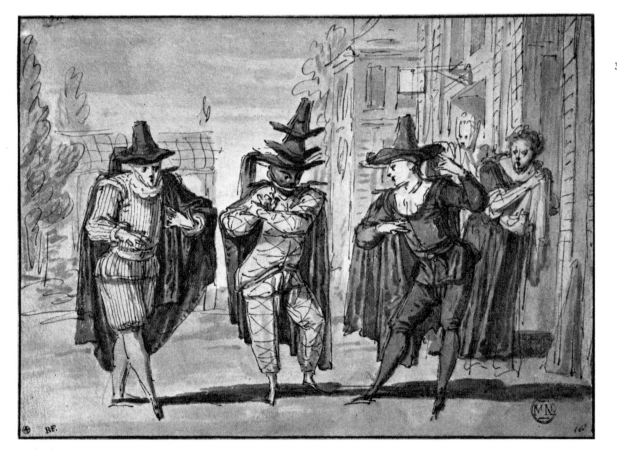

312. CLAUDE GILLOT.
*Scene from
"Death of Maître André."*
c. 1700.
Pen and wash drawing,
6¼ × 8½".
The Louvre, Paris

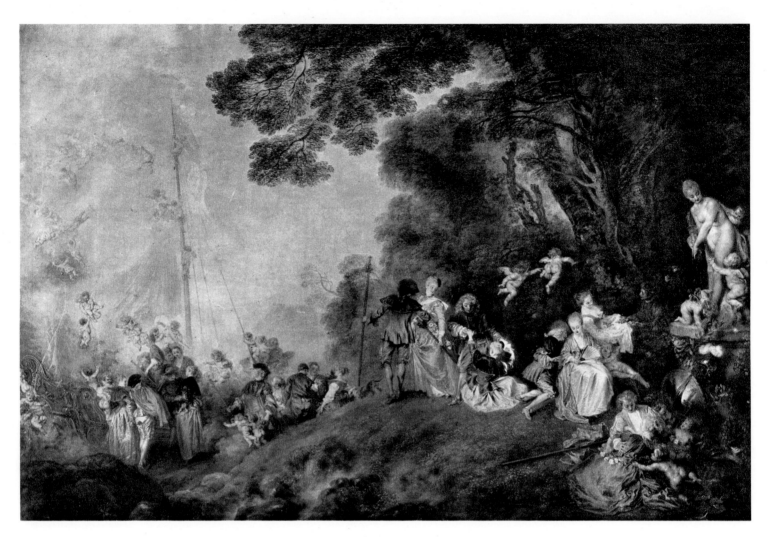

313. ANTOINE WATTEAU. *Pilgrimage to Cythera*. c. 1718. 50¾×76¼". Dahlem Museum, Berlin

The famous *Pilgrimage to Cythera* exists in two versions: the first in the Louvre (1717) and the later one (c. 1718) in the Berlin Museum (fig. 313). The painting recalls Rubens' *Garden of Love* (Prado, Madrid), and Watteau's debt to Rubens is especially clear in the picture's sensuous color and atmosphere. However, the vaporous glazes, the graceful arabesque of the composition that sweeps from the statue of Venus down the hill to the boat, and the light, almost weightless figures, dressed in shimmering satins, who move across the landscape give the painting a lyrical delicacy and elegance that belongs entirely to the eighteenth century. The picture illustrates the end of a voyage to Cythera, the island of love,

where Venus rose from the sea. The participants have come and made their offerings to the goddess and now, at sunset, they prepare to leave for the mainland. They rise slowly from their amours; some look back sadly and turn away reluctantly from the scene of their idyl. The pilgrimage has been an escape into the world of sweet fantasy, yet the return to reality cannot be unaffected by it. Watteau's subject was drawn from a play by Dancourt (*Les Trois cousines*, 1700), where the theme is explained in the verse *"Venez à l'île de Cythère / En pèlerinage avec nous. / Jeune fille n'en revient guère / Ou sans amant ou sans épous."* ("Come to the island of Cythera on a pilgrimage with us. A maiden hard-

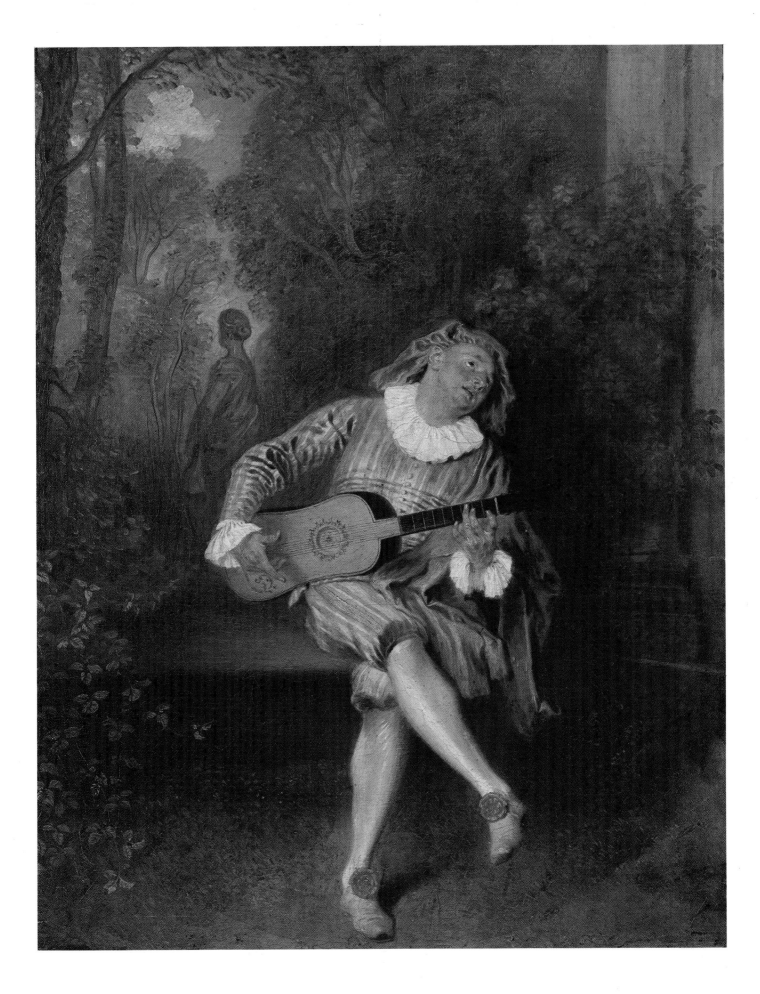

Colorplate 45. ANTOINE WATTEAU. *Mezzetin*. c. 1718. 21¾ × 17″. The Metropolitan Museum of Art, New York

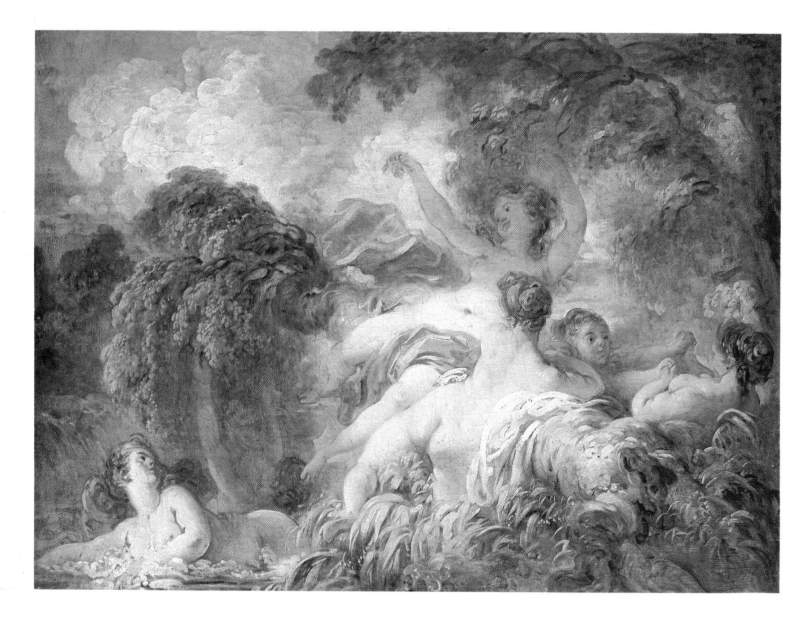

Colorplate 46. JEAN-HONORE FRAGONARD. *Bathers.* c. 1765. 25¼ × 31½″. The Louvre, Paris

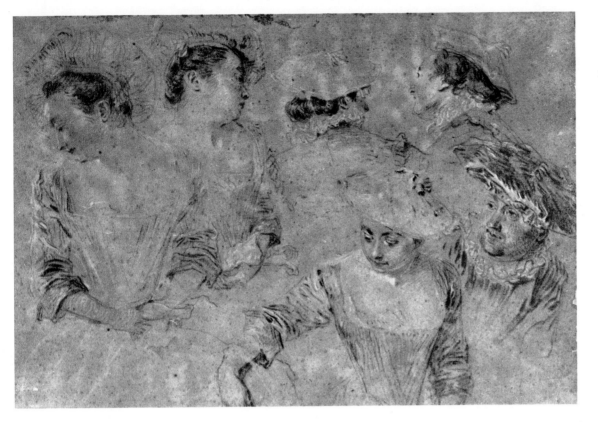

314. ANTOINE WATTEAU.
Six Figures.
Chalk, three colors,
6×12"
The Louvre, Paris

ly ever returns from it without a lover or a husband.")²

Watteau was one of the world's great draftsmen. He drew incessantly from life, capturing the inflections of a gesture, or the nuances of a pose or attitude (fig. 314). His favorite medium was sanguine, to which he often added black and white chalks. His line has a rapid, nervous vitality, and is supremely confident in grasping form and movement. Whether he worked with one chalk or three, his drawings have a coloristic luminosity that makes them seem almost painted. Apparently, most of Watteau's drawings were not made with specific paintings in mind. When composing his pictures, however, he would make a rather free selection of figures and attitudes from his pages of life studies and group them melodiously into a *fête galante* or a scene of comedians. Thus his pictures almost never have clearly defined narratives, but his actors are always endowed with a wonderful, lifelike spontaneity.

One of the most remarkable products of the eighteenth century is the painting *Gersaint's*

Signboard (fig. 315). Watteau, who became ill from tuberculosis, had been in England from 1719 to 1720, where the climate had aggravated his illness. On his return, for amusement and, he said, "to get the stiffness out of my fingers," he asked a friend, the art dealer Gersaint, if he could paint a signboard for his shop. It was one of his last works, and it is reported to have been painted in eight days. It is at once a perfect advertisement and a brilliant representation of a "page from Parisian life." Gersaint's shop is shown hung thick with a choice selection of paintings; the management appears cultivated and solicitous; and one can apparently depend on the staff's care in packing and shipping. Clearly, Gersaint caters to people of refinement and taste. The shop is presented as completely open on the street. On the pavement at the right a dog searches itself for fleas. At the left a lackey looks dully at the portrait of Louis XIV being packed (the name of the shop was "Au Grand Monarque"). With more lively interest, and with a light, elegant step emphasized by the fine creases of her long,

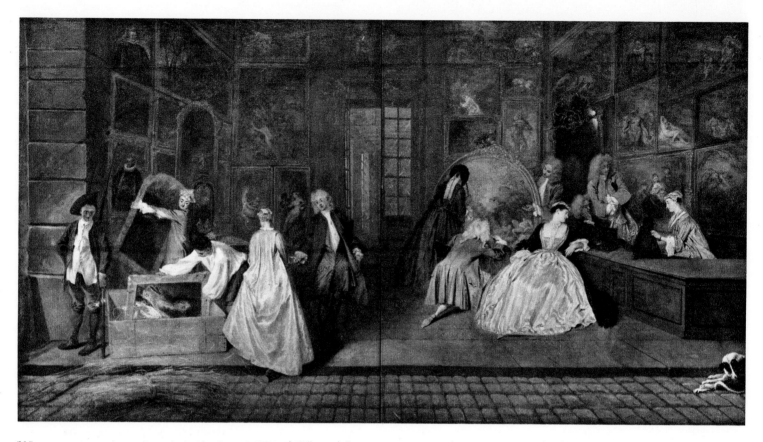

315. ANTOINE WATTEAU. *Gersaint's Signboard*. 1721. 5'3¾" × 10'1". Palais Charlottenburg, Berlin

sweeping gown, a lady turns to glance at the portrait as she enters the shop after her gallant. On the other side the amateurs study Gersaint's works of art. Every pose and gesture is incisive and true. Watteau has created a cast of real characters, who act out a little comedy on an urban stage.

Watteau invented or perfected new genres, in which painting could sparkle with a charm, a freedom, and a fantasy hardly known before. Yet it was through a still deeper poetry that Watteau lifted his scenes of the escapades and games of a frivolous society to the level of great art. His works convey his feeling for the preciousness and elusiveness of the moment; they strike with gentle ironies; and sometimes, as in the *Gilles* (fig. 316), they touch us with a deep, melancholy pathos.

The influence of Watteau's style was far reaching. The graceful, decorative patterns of his com-

positions; the tall, slender, and rather adolescent figures with their agile, elongated hands; the splendid elegance of his costuming; the delicacy of his color; the crisp activity of his brushwork—all were perfectly attuned to the taste of the century. In the works of François Boucher (1703–1770) these elements were carried to a charming, although sometimes banal, extreme of seductive prettiness. Boucher, a favorite of Madame de Pompadour, for whom he began working in 1746, was the leading exponent in painting of the *style Louis XV*, which can be considered the full flower of the Rococo. Boucher was a prolific artist, and his production ranges from monumental mythologies to portraiture, modish genre, pastoral and Oriental subjects (fig. 317), and ornamental design. His taste was essentially formed by his teacher, the fashionable François Lemoyne, and he was influenced by aspects of contemporary Venetian

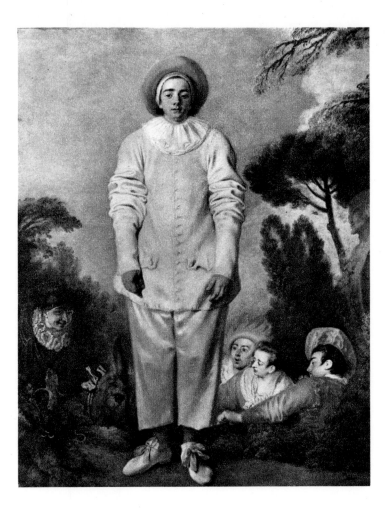

316. ANTOINE WATTEAU. *Gilles.* c. 1717–19.
72⅜ × 58⅛". The Louvre, Paris

painting. Boucher's most intimate experience of
Watteau's art came in the 1720s, when he was
commissioned to make etchings after works by
Watteau. However, he had none of Watteau's intellectual or spiritual resources, and he developed
a highly ornamental style that depends heavily
on a glamorous display of pastel colors and brilliant brushwork, and frequently on the outspoken eroticism of figures and compositions. Yet
Boucher cannot be dismissed as merely pretty
or superficial. His was a truly poetic vision—
expressed by consummate draftsmanship and
breathtakingly facile brushwork—of an eternally
happy never-never land where the sun always
shines, and where gods and men, and Nature

317. FRANÇOIS BOUCHER.
Chinese Fishing Scene. 1742.
15⅝ × 25".
Musée des Beaux-Arts, Besançon

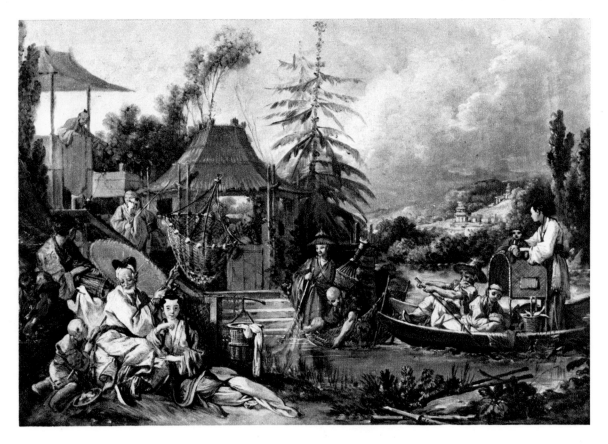

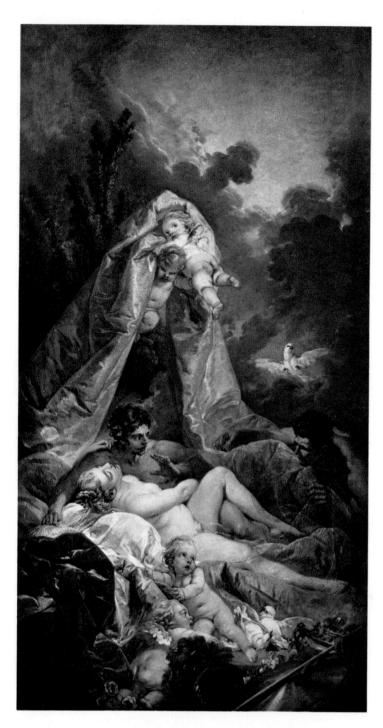

318. FRANÇOIS BOUCHER. *Mars and Venus Caught by Vulcan.*
c. 1754. 64½ × 32¾". Wallace Collection, London

herself, are irrepressibly playful. In such a work
as *Mars and Venus Caught by Vulcan* (fig. 318),
figures, draperies, trees, and clouds are unified in
a voluptuous play of irregular, complex Rococo
rhythms and dominated by a typical eighteenth-
century zigzag pattern that rises with swift, spirited animation; the scene is radiant with light
and tantalizing in its suggestiveness.

It was Diderot who remarked that Boucher's
pupils "hardly know how to handle a brush . . .
before they take to weaving garlands of children
[and to] painting chubby pink bottoms."[3] He
may have been thinking of Jean-Honoré Fragonard (1732–1806), who, after an early apprenticeship with Chardin (see pages 314–18), studied
with Boucher for about four years. Fragonard
continued the subjects and the style of the Rococo
until they had become outmoded, and he died
impoverished and forgotten. However, it was
Fragonard's role to be, as the Goncourt brothers
put it, "the master of a dream world," a world "lit
by the vast wood blaze of the festivities of the
Trianon—the final bonfire of the eighteenth
century!"[4] Learning from Boucher, but surpass-
ing him, Fragonard transformed Watteau's wist-
ful serenity into a joyful abandonment to the
pleasures of the senses and the urgings of passion.

In works like the *Happy Accidents of the
Swing* (fig. 319) "Frago," as he was known, delights the eye with a natural gaiety and exquisite
finesse that were only rarely approached by
Boucher's self-consciously chic style. The *Swing*
was commissioned by the Baron de Saint-Julien
in 1767. The character of the society in which
Fragonard's art flourished is nicely revealed by
the fact that the baron dictated the subject,
specifying that his mistress be depicted on a swing
pushed by a bishop (an irreverent pun: Saint-
Julien was the *Receveur général des biens du
Clergé*), and that the baron himself be shown
"in a position to observe the legs of this charming
girl."[5] The lady rides high; her shoe flies off, her
lovely pink dress billows out like a flower un-
folding to uncover slightly more than a well-
turned leg. The gentleman hiding in the bushes,

310

his arm outstretched, thrills to the hoped-for sight, while a statue of a smiling cupid (cleverly copied from Falconet; fig. 334) commands a discreet silence. The scene is embroidered by patterns of branches, leaves, and flowers that are as frivolous and gay as the subject itself.

The *Swing* is painted in Fragonard's "finished," decorative style. Pictures like his *Bathers* (colorplate 46) are still freer and bolder in handling. The *Bathers* is almost a sketch, brushed in rapidly with broad strokes. The sunlit warmth of the vision is captivating, and the voluptuous richness of the paint surface is positively delicious. Here the mischievous eroticism of the *Swing* is replaced

by the unashamed sensuality of a frolic in the sun, and the delightful freedom and roseate glow of nudity become the expressions of a buoyant and abundant nature.

Among the most enchanting aspects of Fragonard's art are his landscapes. He took up landscape during his first stay in Italy, where, having won the Prix de Rome, he was a student at the French Academy in Rome from 1756 to 1761.[6] A deservedly famous group of paintings and drawings by Fragonard were made of the Villa d'Este at Tivoli. In a beautiful sanguine drawing he shows the *grande allée* of the garden and captures the sensation of airy heights and

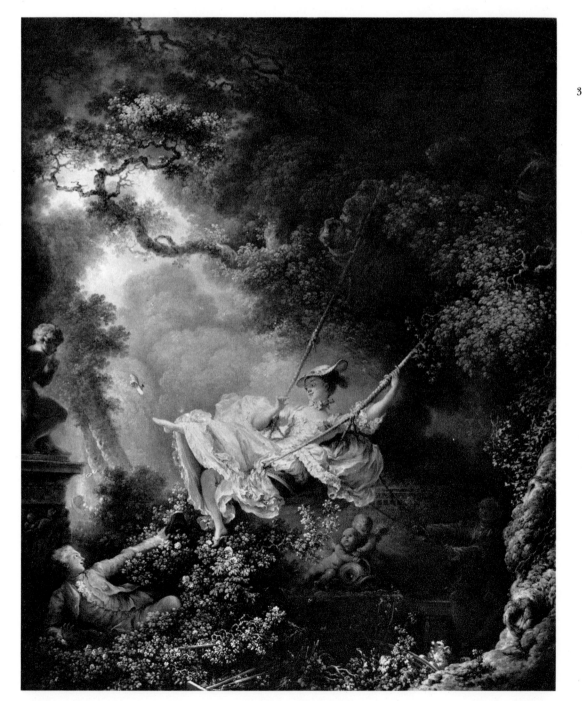

319. JEAN-HONORÉ FRAGONARD.
Happy Accidents of the Swing.
1767. 31⅞ × 25⅜".
Wallace Collection, London

311

luminous distance (fig. 320). The sun plays brightly in the foliage and spreads itself warmly across the path. The majestic cypresses rise effortlessly, and they gently, almost caressingly, lean toward each other; in the distance through the tall, narrow opening between the trees, the villa with its stepped terraces is dimly visible. Fragonard made nature as light and graceful, as Rococo, as the eighteenth-century ladies and gentlemen who enjoyed it.

In Rome, Fragonard had been a close friend of Hubert Robert (1733–1808), who had become a student at the French Academy in 1754. However, Robert remained until 1765 in Italy, where he studied the works of Pannini and Piranesi (see page 352) and developed an attractive landscape style that depends heavily on the picturesque effects of architectural elements and especially of architectural ruins. The artist came to be called "Robert des ruines" for his romantic pictures of real or fancied, ancient or modern ruins. In a painting made between 1786 and 1788 he depicted an actual scene of the demolition of the houses on the Pont au Change in Paris (fig. 321). The painting is ostensibly documentary, but its primary concern is the suggestion of the changing face of the world, and the engaging picturesqueness of a scene created by the work of demolition, which has piled up huge masses of earth and stone in front of the buildings on the far side of the bridge. It is interesting that in its

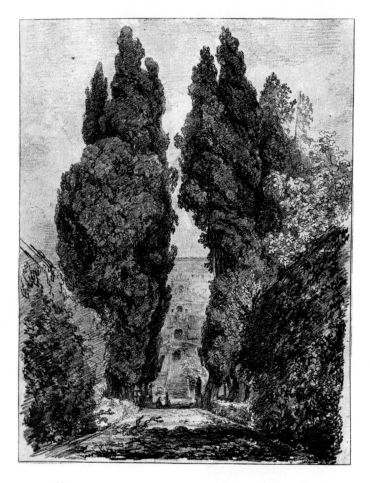

320. JEAN-HONORÉ FRAGONARD.
The Great Cypresses at the Villa d'Este, Tivoli.
1756–61. Sanguine, 19 × 13¾".
Musée des Beaux-Arts, Besançon

321. HUBERT ROBERT.
Demolition of the Houses on the Pont au Change.
1786–88. 34 × 62½". Musée Carnavalet, Paris

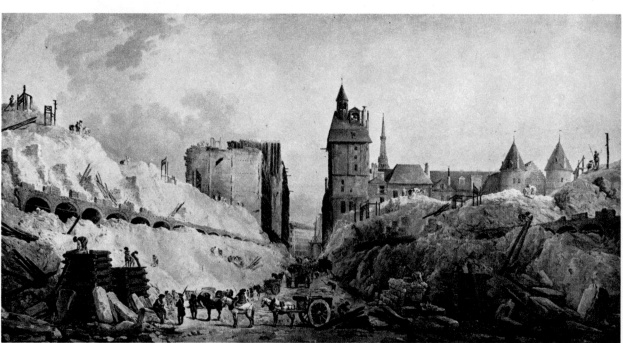

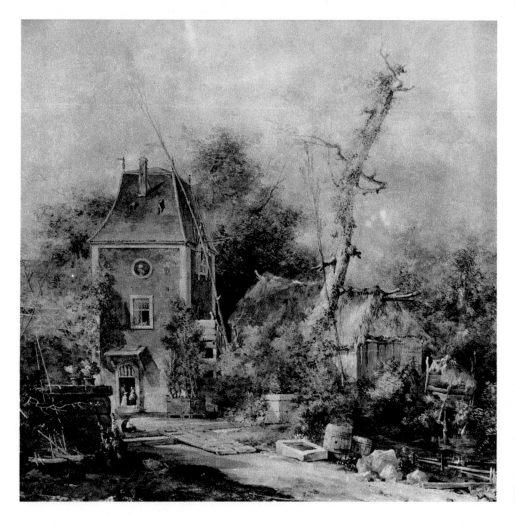

322. LOUIS-GABRIEL MOREAU THE ELDER.
La Maison du Jardinière. 1786.
Gouache, $17\frac{1}{2} \times 17\frac{3}{4}''$.
Weil-Picard Collection, Paris

general treatment the picture is very like Frago-nard's drawing of the *Villa d'Este* in Besançon. Both artists make use of similar devices of atmosphere, scale, and perspective to create spaciousness and a long, accented vista. In both works, too, as in many eighteenth-century landscapes, man appears diminutive in relation to the vastness of his surroundings, which, unlike the seventeenth century, the new age did not feel could be rigorously dominated and patterned by man.

In France, Hubert Robert designed some gardens "in the English manner." It is characteristic of the eighteenth century that the classical French garden, which had been perfected by André Le Nôtre (see page 136), lost favor and was superseded by the contrived "natural" irregularity and variety of English garden design[7] (see page 299). Indeed, it was the happy accidents and the wonderful surprises of untended nature that provided the main themes for the century's land-

scape artists. In a lovely gouache sketch by Louis-Gabriel Moreau the Elder (1740–1806), dated 1786 (fig. 322), the picturesque charms of nature are revealed in the sunny disorder of a rustic house. The sketch is contemporary with the "hamlet" built by Richard Mique (and perhaps suggested by Robert) for Marie-Antoinette on the grounds of the Petit Trianon at Versailles (fig. 323). There, in her private village—complete

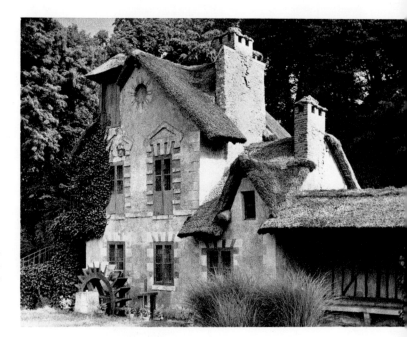

323. RICHARD MIQUE.
Hameau de la Reine, Petit Trianon, 1783.
Versailles

with a parsonage, a mill, and a dairy—the queen and her friends played at the simple rustic life.

Because the eighteenth century delighted in the vision of nature and man unspoiled by the vices of advanced civilization, it encouraged the development of the "minor" categories: landscape, still life, popular everyday scenes. In these fields, it was supposed, the unadulterated beauties of nature and the spontaneous (therefore good) aspects of human life were revealed. It is not surprising, then, that Dutch seventeenth-century art was now popular and influential in France. Fragonard, for example, painted a number of landscapes in the manner of Ruisdael, and in the art of Jean-Baptiste Siméon Chardin (1699–1779) Dutch still-life and genre painting were naturalized in France.

Chardin could not have learned very much from the third-rate artists who were, in the most superficial way, his teachers—Pierre-Jacques Cazes and Noël Coypel. But Coypel seems to have used him to paint still-life details in his paintings, and this may have helped to direct the young artist's talents. Nevertheless, Chardin ap-

pears to have been largely self-taught. Evidently he studied Flemish and Dutch still lifes while he was painting the same subjects from nature. By the end of the 1720s he was producing masterpieces. In 1728 he was admitted to the Academy of Painting and Sculpture, and within a decade he was famous. Chardin's still lifes exhibit considerable variety. There are freshly killed rabbits or pheasants lying limply on a table; a basket of opulent fruits; colorful flowers in a pretty porcelain vase; elaborate compositions of musical instruments or of the paraphernalia of the painter (fig. 324). However, Chardin is best known for his simple arrangements of a few, familiar objects: a copper pot, an earthenware jug, apples or oranges, with perhaps a single scallion. Dutch still-life painting was the main source for pictures like the *Silver Goblet* (colorplate 47). However, in contrast to the shining clarity and precision that characterizes the rendition of surfaces in the work of Claesz. or Kalf (figs. 237, 238), Chardin's manner is soft and atmospheric. Actually, it seems that Chardin's handling was largely inspired by Rembrandt, and, like the Dutch master's, his

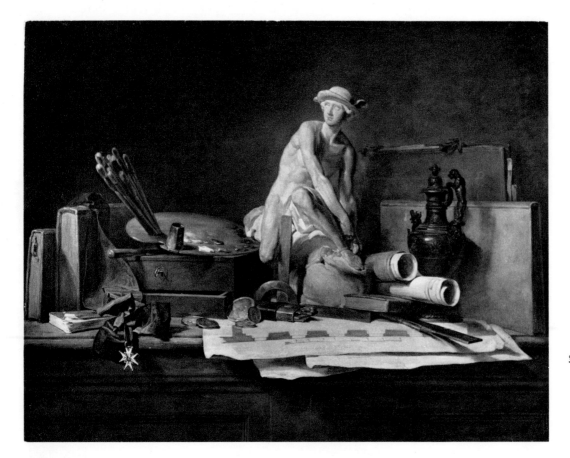

324. JEAN-BAPTISTE SIMEON CHARDIN. *Attributes of the Arts*. 1766. 44⅛ × 55½". Minneapolis Institute of Arts

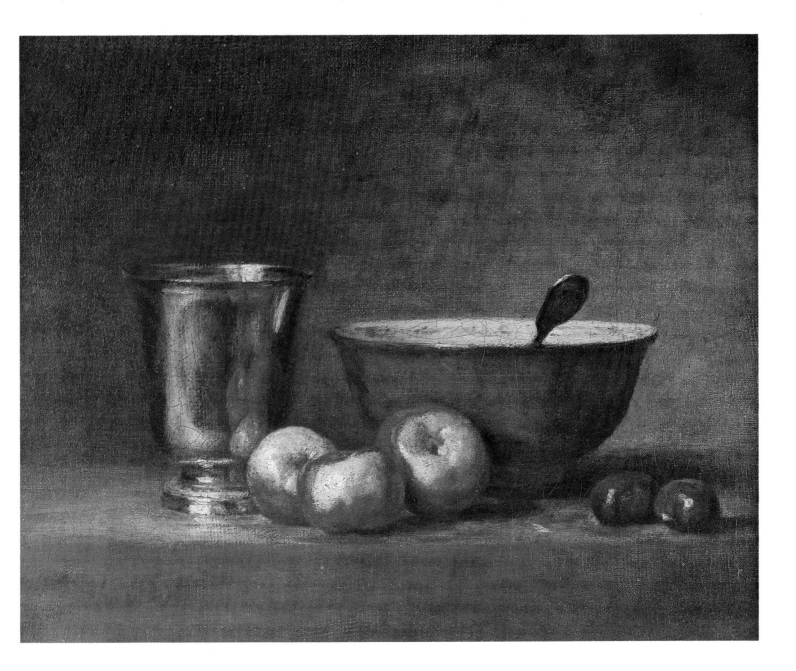

Colorplate 47. JEAN-BAPTISTE SIMEON CHARDIN. *Silver Goblet.* c. 1760. 13 × 16⅛″. The Louvre, Paris

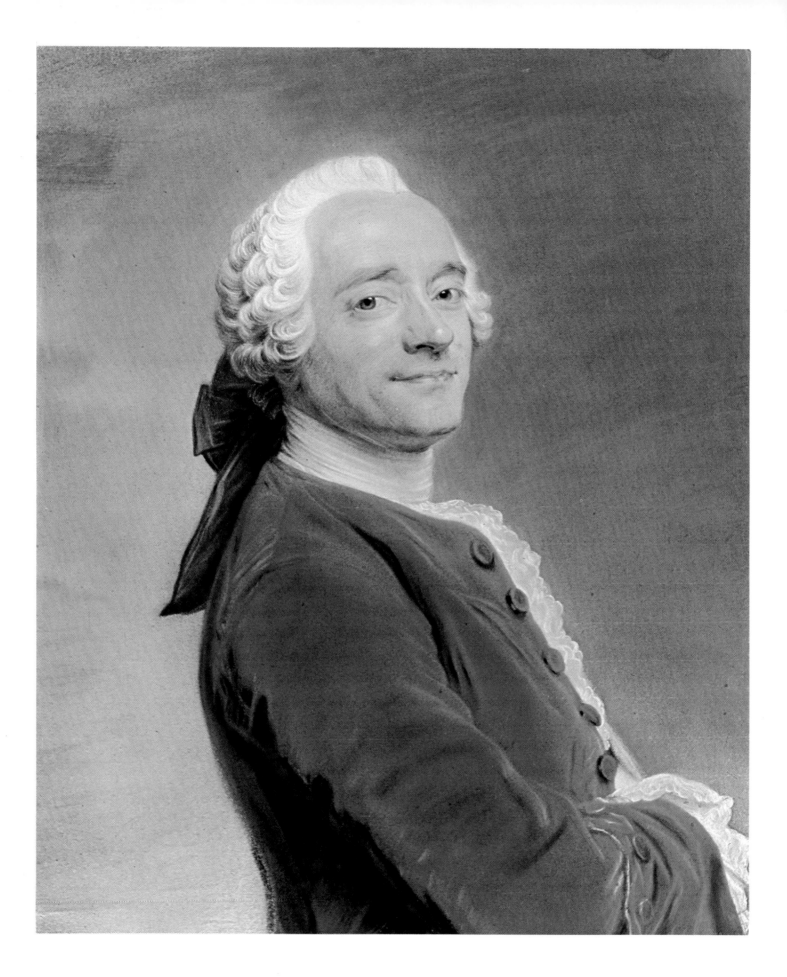

Colorplate 48. MAURICE QUENTIN DE LA TOUR. *Self-portrait*. 1751. 25¼ × 21⅝″. Musée de Picardie, Amiens

touch is free, creating objects with patches of color, blurring edges and merging forms; sometimes his surfaces are thick and impasted, sometimes they are covered by the merest glaze of color. And the magical result, in the Goncourts' phrase, is a "sensation of the actual presence of things." In the *Silver Goblet* a few objects that seem to be enhanced by the patina of familiarity and domestic use, are grouped closely on a plain table in the half-light of the corner of a room. They are transformed by the artist's revelation of harmonies and correspondences of color, shape, and texture, and by his discovery of the almost musical notes produced by the redness of the apples and the redness of their reflections—bright and sharp on the goblet, duller on the warm brown of the bowl.

Chardin began painting genre subjects in the early 1730s. In this field, too, he revealed the beauty inherent in the commonplace scene. His subjects range from a boy blowing bubbles (fig. 325) or constructing a house of cards, to a scullery maid bending over her pots, to a mother listening to her young daughter say grace (fig. 326). Like his still-life paintings, Chardin's genre pictures were mainly dependent on Netherlandish prototypes[8] (fig. 284), but his figure style and his serene approach to everyday reality were not uninfluenced by Watteau (fig. 315). Works like the *Benediction* (fig. 326), however, draw, as do most of Chardin's still lifes, on a special aspect of eighteenth-century taste. Here, ordinary, everyday things and events are revealed as the bearers of wholesome, honest pleasure. The good *maman,* firm but gentle, pauses as she sets the table to hear the younger child finish reciting grace. The older girl, playing the serious grownup, watches her sister attentively. This is a sentimental depiction of the virtues of bourgeois domesticity, but it is sincere and unaffected, and it continues to

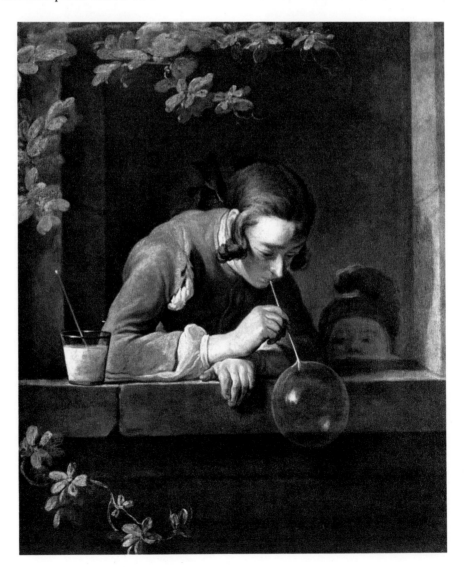

325.
JEAN-BAPTISTE SIMEON CHARDIN.
Soap Bubbles. c. 1732.
36⅝ × 29⅜".
National Gallery of Art,
Washington, D. C.
(Gift of Mrs. John W. Simpson)

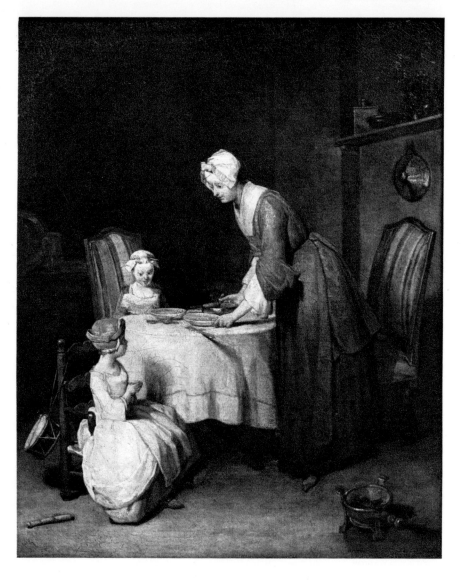

326.
JEAN-BAPTISTE SIMEON CHARDIN.
Benediction. 1740.
19¼ × 15⅜".
The Louvre, Paris

charm us by its natural tenderness and intimacy.

Ideals of naturalness and intimacy also affected portraiture in the eighteenth century. Instead of formal attitudes or the display of rank and position, which generally characterize seventeenth-century portraits in France (fig. 168), most artists now concentrated on physiognomy, on the nuances of expression, and on the spontaneous gesture, and they sought to capture the essence of the individual personality. The leading French artists of the century—Watteau, Boucher, Fragonard, Chardin—were all fine portraitists. They, and the portrait specialists of the age—Jean-Marc Nattier (1688–1766), Louis Tocqué (1696–1772), Maurice Quentin de La Tour (1704–1788), Jean-Baptiste Perronneau (1715–1783), and others—

brought portraiture to a remarkable level of excellence. Nattier's specialty, a seductive version of a portrait formula that had been developed in the previous century, was to portray his sitters in the guise of classical divinities (fig. 327). In general, though, the French eighteenth-century portrait is distinguished by its attention to the head, by its reticent use of accessory details, by its informality of pose, and, above all, by its intimacy.

Maurice Quentin de La Tour was the outstanding French portrait specialist of the century. He worked almost exclusively in pastel, a medium that was admirably suited to the contemporary taste for immediacy and delicacy.[9] The artist has left us a vivid record of the great personalities of the age—princes, *grandes dames, philosophes,* artists, dancers. La Tour himself is seen in his *Self-portrait* of 1751 (colorplate 48). His strong head is beautifully modeled, and the whole form is surrounded by a delicate atmosphere created by the powdered chalks. The artist leans back at a rakish angle, and he fixes the spectator with a sharp, rather sly glance and an ironic smile. Many of La Tour's portraits are only sketches, instantaneous notes of the structure of the head and of the characteristic movement of the mouth or the eyes (fig. 328). But he always grasps those essential traits that particularize and animate the individual. Indeed, it is precisely the instinctive gestures, the turn of the head, the glance, the fleeting expression—frequently caught by the artist, it seems, while his subject is engaged in the play of lively conversation— that reveal the mind and temper of the sitter.

Eighteenth-century society took pleasure in the sparkle of sophisticated individuality, in intellectual freedom, and in social license, but also

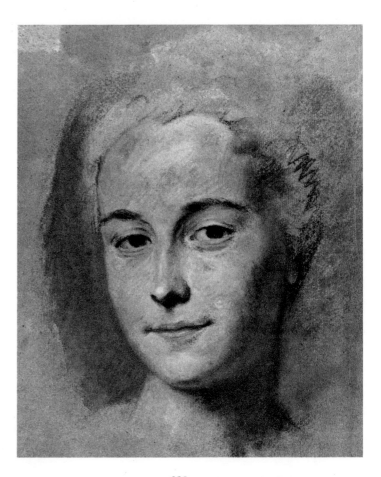

328. MAURICE QUENTIN DE LA TOUR.
Portrait of the Dancer Camargo.
Mid-18th century. Pastel.
Museum, St. Quentin

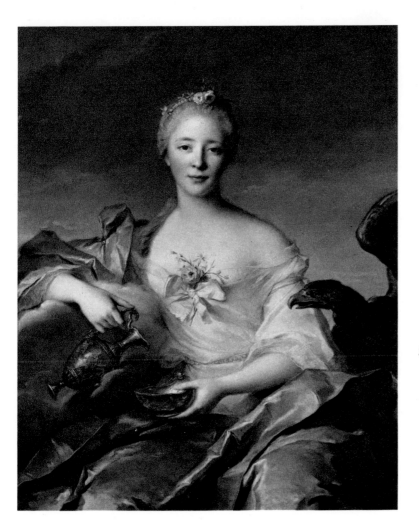

327. JEAN-MARC NATTIER.
Madame de Caumartin as Hebe.
1753. 40¼ × 31⅞".
National Gallery of Art, Washington, D.C.
(Samuel H. Kress Collection)

319

believed in the virtues of the "simple" people, and it thrilled to visions of ingenuous morality. An early generation had enjoyed both Boucher and Chardin, and the popular success accorded to both Fragonard and Greuze dates from the 1760s. Jean-Baptiste Greuze (1725–1805), who had been a student at the Royal Academy in Paris, suddenly became famous in 1761 when he exhibited his *Village Bride* (the Louvre, Paris), a sentimental portrayal of middle-class rural life. Greuze's genre paintings were based on Dutch and also English prototypes (*e.g.,* Hogarth; see page 368), but they can easily be related to Chardin's works, and the artist's contemporaries did, in fact, consider him a follower of the older master. However, while a painting like Chardin's *Benediction* (fig. 326) was meant to be sentimentally engaging, Greuze's pictures, such as the *Punished Son* (1777–78; fig. 329), were intended to be morally edifying. The *Punished Son,* or *Return of the Prodigal Son,* as it is also known, showing the chastened son returning home to find his heartbroken father dead and noisily lamented, proclaims the inevitable outcome of filial irresponsibility. Such paintings obeyed Diderot's aesthetic imperative: "To render virtue lovable, vice hateful . . . , that is the task of every *honnête homme* who takes up the pen, the brush, or the chisel."[10] Understandably, Greuze became the darling of prerevolutionary moralists. The *Punished Son* was praised as a "history of the passions and of the human heart," drawn from the life of "honest citizens," and as great as any "Greek or Roman story."[11]

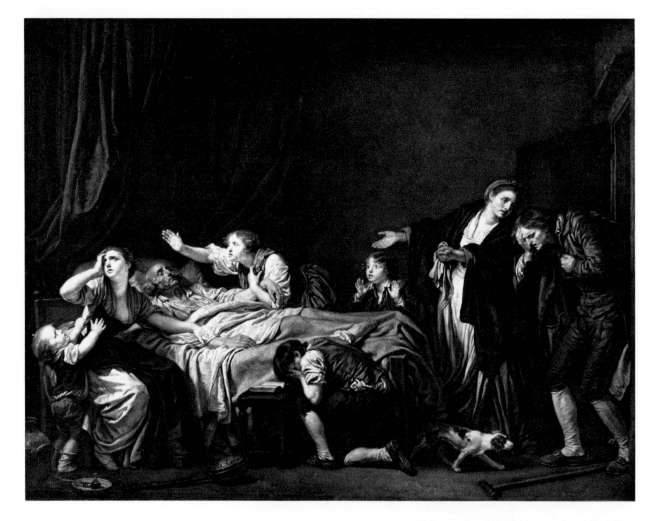

329. JEAN-BAPTISTE GREUZE. *Punished Son.* 1777–78. 51×65″. The Louvre, Paris

Greuze not only elevated genre subjects by investing them with didactic content, but frequently he adapted the noble forms and the dramatic rhetoric hitherto reserved for history painting to his depictions of the life of ordinary people. He borrowed poses and compositions from ancient sculptures and from the paintings of the great masters.[12] The composition of the *Punished Son* is based on Poussin's *Extreme Unction* (Duke of Sutherland Collection, National Gallery of Scotland, Edinburgh). Thus the art of Greuze points in the direction of Neoclassicism, which was to concentrate on moral values and revitalize the ideal forms of the great history painters. But, Greuze's moral posture was ultimately no more sincere than were Marie-Antoinette's rustic diversions. The artist created make-believe dramas of life in the country peopled by senti-

mentalized, "noble" peasants, and by pious maidens whose "natural" deshabille generally affords a titillating view of an ample bosom (fig. 330). By the 1780s Greuze was being overshadowed by a virile and truly serious art that heralded the Revolution. Greuze was gradually forgotten, and he died impoverished.

The Neoclassical style that captured France in the 1780s had been developing for several decades. As early as the 1740s attempts were being made to counter the seductive frivolities of modish painters like Boucher, and to reinstate the grave and grand manner of the great history painters of the last two centuries. Once again, the structural and expository values of drawing were asserted in opposition to the purely sensuous charms of color.[13] In France, these early efforts of stylistic reform are recorded in the not too

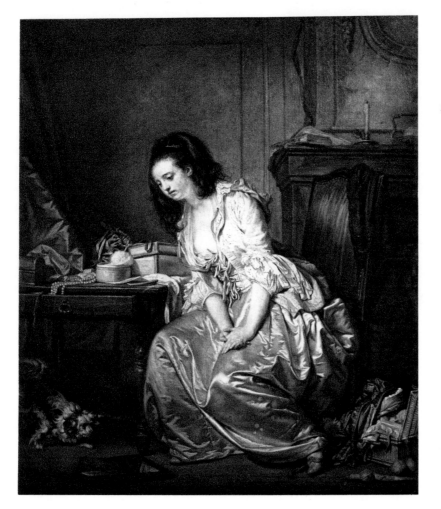

330. JEAN-BAPTISTE GREUZE. *Broken Mirror*. 1763. 21¾ × 17¾". Wallace Collection, London

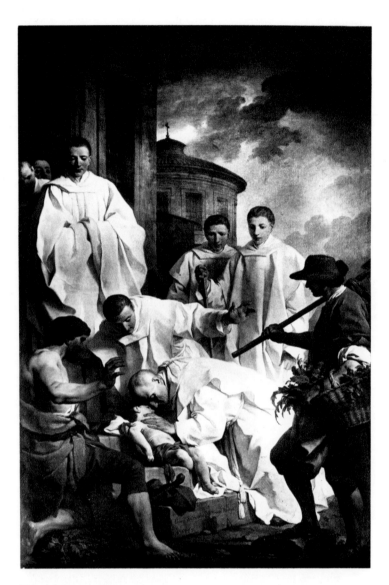

331. PIERRE-HUBERT SUBLEYRAS.
    St. Benedict Reviving a Child. 1744.
    S. Francesca Romana, Rome

successful works of artists like Joseph-Marie Vien (1716–1809) and Gabriel-François Doyen (1726–1806). The movement was international, however, and it drew its main inspiration from Italy, where it was supported by the artistic traditions of ancient and modern Rome as well as by the new archaeological discoveries of the time (in 1738 excavations began at Herculaneum and, in the next few years, at Paestum and Pompeii). One of the leading French artists representing this trend in Italy in the first half of the eighteenth century was Pierre-Hubert Subleyras (1699–1749). Subleyras went to Italy after winning a Prix de Rome in 1727, and he remained there for the rest of his life. His *St. Benedict Reviving a Child* (1744; fig. 331) has an almost fragile delicacy of form and color that belongs unmistakably to the eighteenth century. Nevertheless, this seriously composed, carefully constructed picture, with its restrained harmony of whites and its linear clarity, remains solidly in the classical tradition of Roman painting. Indeed, it was partly inspired by Sacchi's *Vision of St. Romuald* (colorplate 12), painted a hundred years earlier.

The style of Subleyras and others, with its serious subjects and elevated diction, remained a subsidiary current for many decades in the eighteenth century. However, this was the current that culminated in the art of Jacques-Louis David (1748–1825) and provided a style that could express the ideals of the Revolution. David was a student of Vien, who was Director of the French Academy in Rome from 1775 to 1781. David painted *Belisarius Begging for Alms* (fig. 332) in 1781, just after he returned to Paris from a five-year stay in Italy. The picture's grave subject, measured composition, solidly constructed forms, and emphatic linearism indicate its strong ties to classical aspects of seventeenth-century art. Indeed, the soldier who recognizes Belisarius and raises his hands in surprise, and the architectural landscape behind him, are designed in the spirit of Poussin.

Instantly, the noble and dignified paintings of David captured the imagination of a public

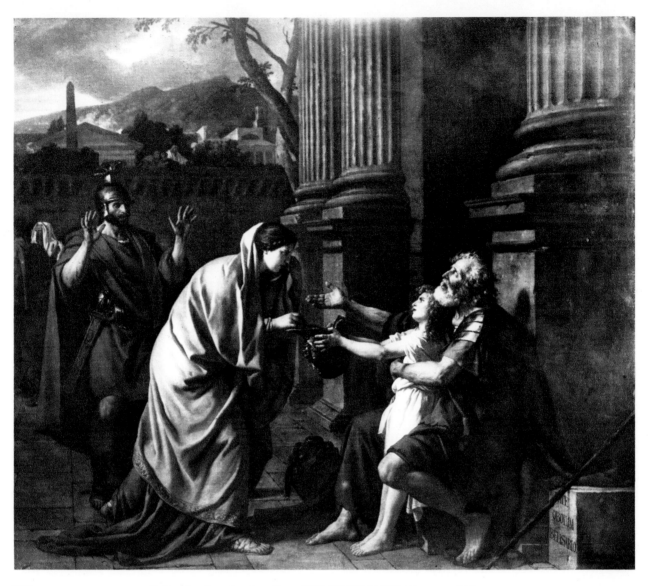

332. JACQUES-LOUIS DAVID. *Belisarius Begging for Alms*. 1781. 9'5½" × 10'3". Museum, Lille

333. JACQUES-LOUIS DAVID.
Oath of the Horatii.
1784. 10'10" × 14'.
The Louvre, Paris

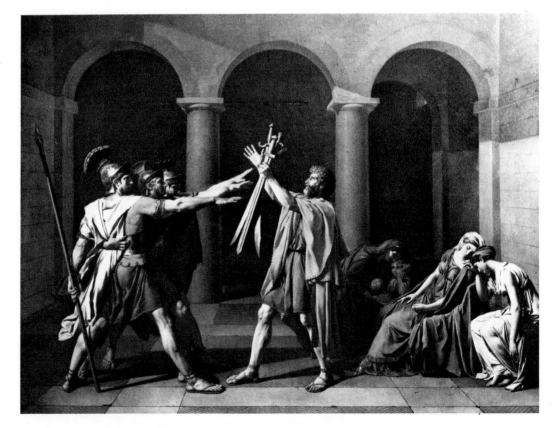

grown weary of the licentious charms of Fragonard and of the honeyed goodness of Greuze. *Belisarius* represents Justinian's great general: old, blind, and unjustly exiled by the state he so loyally served, he has been reduced to beggary. The point of the story was not lost at a moment when the nation was fast losing faith in its rulers. David's works of the next few years, like the *Oath of the Horatii* (1784; fig. 333) and the *Death of Socrates* (1787; Metropolitan Museum of Art, New York), are even more radical in content and more severe in style. The asymmetrical arrangement and the receding diagonal organization of the *Belisarius,* which lend it a Baroque character, were abandoned in favor of the strictly ordered planar compositions and movements that became typical of Neoclassical style.

With David Rococo art ended—his pupils later amused themselves by throwing bread pellets at Watteau's *Pilgrimage to Cythera.*[14]

SCULPTURE

In sculpture, as in painting, the aesthetic predilections of the eighteenth century led away from the heavy formality of the seventeenth century and encouraged the development of gay, lively subject matter and of a new freedom, immediacy, and lightness in forms and compositions. Despite its innovations, however, French sculpture of the eighteenth century is much less sharply separated from the main traditions of the previous century than is painting. Puget's relatively baroque style appealed to the current taste for movement and emotional display, and his works were an important source of inspiration for eighteenth-century sculptors. The other major sculptors of the *grand siècle,* Girardon and Coysevox, were both active through most of the second decade of the new century, and their work and instruction may be said to stand at the beginning of the history of the sculpture of the period. Through their students, especially Robert Le Lorrain, the Coustou brothers, and the elder Lemoyne, the influence of these artists was transmitted to Bouchardon, Falconet, Pigalle, and ultimately to Houdon.

With characteristic national restraint, French sculptors avoided the extremes of formal exuberance that are found, for example, in German sculpture of the period. As in contemporary French painting though, lighthearted, licentious subjects were enormously popular. Edmé Bouchardon (1698–1762) had a remarkable success with his *Cupid Making a Bow from the Club of Hercules* (1739–50; the Louvre, Paris). Etienne-Maurice Falconet (1716–1791) produced lovely images of lithesome nudity such as his *Nymph Leaving the Bath* (1757; the Louvre, Paris), destined to decorate Madame de Pompadour's Paris house. Falconet had earned a reputation for erotica with his *Menacing Cupid,* which he completed in a lifesize marble version in 1757 (fig. 334) for Madame de Pompadour. The graceful, gently spiraling pose of the figure is as typical of Rococo art as is the subject. Cupid smiles mischievously at the spectator and puts a warning finger to his lips, demanding silent complicity as he reaches into his quiver for a fatal arrow. (This figure was to make a felicitous appearance in Fragonard's painting *The Swing;* fig. 319). Related subjects remained popular until the end of the century. Jean-Baptiste Pigalle (1714–1785) excelled in the depiction of pairs of naked infants whose innocent games prove slyly suggestive. There is,

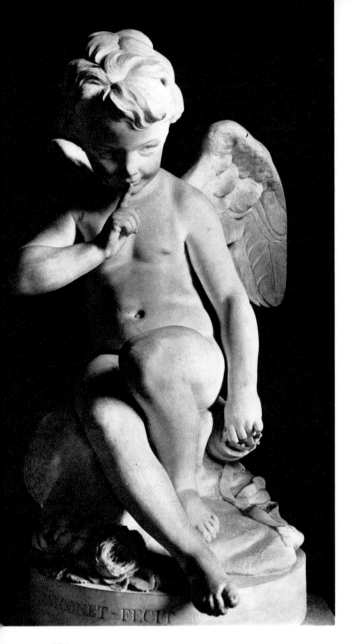

334. ETIENNE-MAURICE FALCONET.
Menacing Cupid. 1757.
Marble, height 35½".
The Louvre, Paris

for instance, Pigalle's chubby male baby holding an empty birdcage (fig. 335); the pendant figure, a female infant who has captured the bird, smiles a little maliciously as she offers her companion an apple in exchange. In the sculpture of Claude Michel, known as Clodion (1738–1814), a student of Pigalle's, the eroticism of eighteenth-century sculpture came to a florid and joyous conclusion. For the spontaneity of Clodion's designs, and the freedom and suppleness of his modeling, best appreciated in his small terracotta statues like the *Faun and Infant Fauns* (fig. 336), make

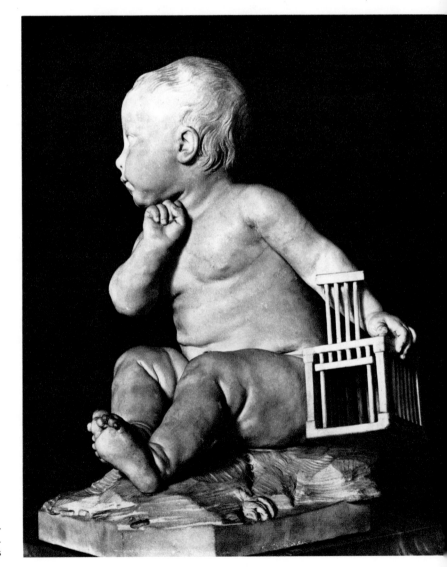

335. JEAN-BAPTISTE PIGALLE.
Child with Birdcage. 1749.
Marble, height 19". The Louvre, Paris

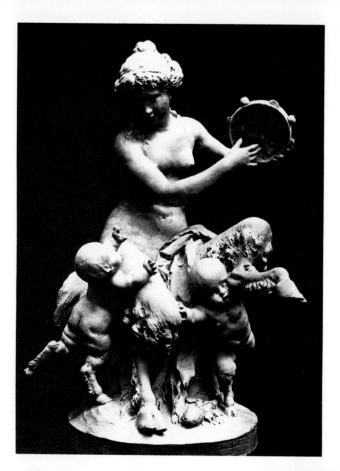

his sculpture an almost exact parallel of the painting of his contemporary Fragonard (see pages 310–11).

Such attractive and amusing works do not, however, represent the major sculptural accomplishments of the age, which were made in the fields of monumental and portrait sculpture. Bouchardon's equestrian statue of Louis XV (fig. 337)[15] in the Place de la Concorde in Paris, destroyed during the French Revolution, was an outstanding achievement. It harked back to Girardon's equestrian Louis XIV (fig. 176) and to its antique model, the statue of Marcus Aurelius in Rome. In Bouchardon's statue, however, a lightness of step and a general elegance of design are in striking contrast to Girardon's more ponderous and solemn composition. Another equestrian statue of the age, Falconet's monument to *Peter the Great* in Leningrad, illustrated here by a drawing (fig. 338),[16] is a landmark in the his-

336. CLAUDE MICHEL (CLODION).
Faun and Infant Fauns.
Late 18th century. Terracotta.
Cluny Museum, Paris

337. EDME BOUCHARDON.
Etching by L. Prevost
after *Equestrian Statue of Louis XV*
(finished 1763; destroyed
during the French Revolution)

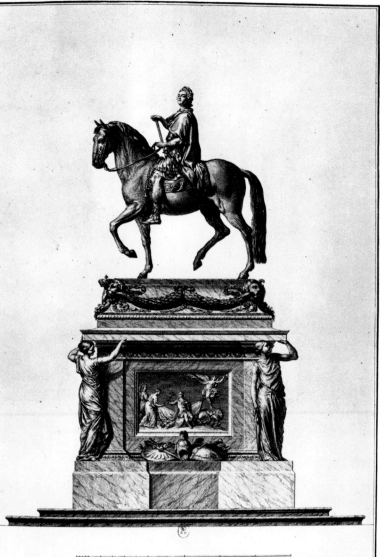

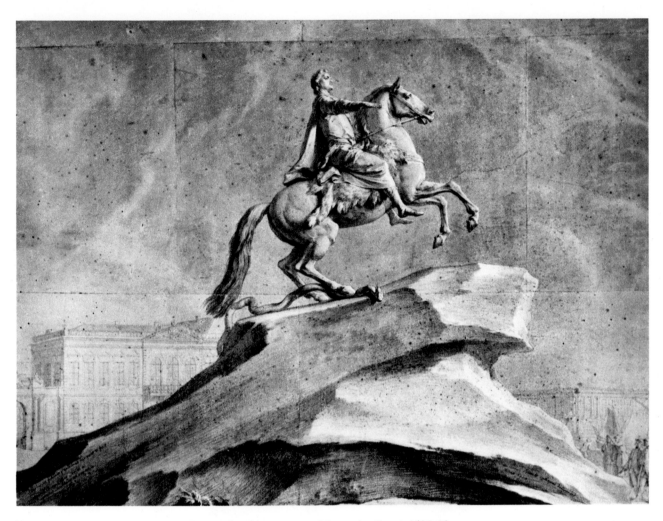

338. ETIENNE-MAURICE FALCONET. *Equestrian Monument of Peter the Great.* 1766–82.
Bronze statue on granite base, over lifesize. Leningrad (drawing by A. P. Losenko in Museum, Nancy)

tory of Western sculpture. Diderot suggested that Falconet should execute the statue, which Catherine II envisaged as a monument to her father. None of the artist's earlier works approached the ambitious scope of this project, but Falconet, with his passionate admiration for Puget (his reception piece for the Academy was a *Milo of Crotona*), was temperamentally as well as intellectually equipped to do justice to the task.[17] He went to Russia in 1766, and by 1770 he had completed a full-scale plaster model. The finished bronze statue was not unveiled in St. Petersburg until 1782, four years after the artist had returned to France.

Falconet's design makes a radical departure from the tradition of Girardon and Bouchardon. Rejecting the stately parade gait of the canonical *Marcus Aurelius,* Falconet turned instead to the more dynamic baroque type with a rearing horse, as in Bernini's equestrian statue of *Louis XIV-Marcus Curtius* at Versailles. Furthermore, the iconography of Falconet's monument belongs to a new age and differs notably from seventeenth- and early eighteenth-century equestrian statues. Peter the Great is presented neither as a conqueror nor as a ruler. He extends his arm in the gesture of the legislator, the civil reformer. Instead of being raised on the traditional classical pedestal, the Emperor of all the Russians is shown as he reaches the top of a long, clifflike granite boulder,[18] symbolizing the difficulties he surmounted in his effort of reform. His horse tramples the serpent of Envy underfoot.

Falconet's main rival in France was Pigalle,

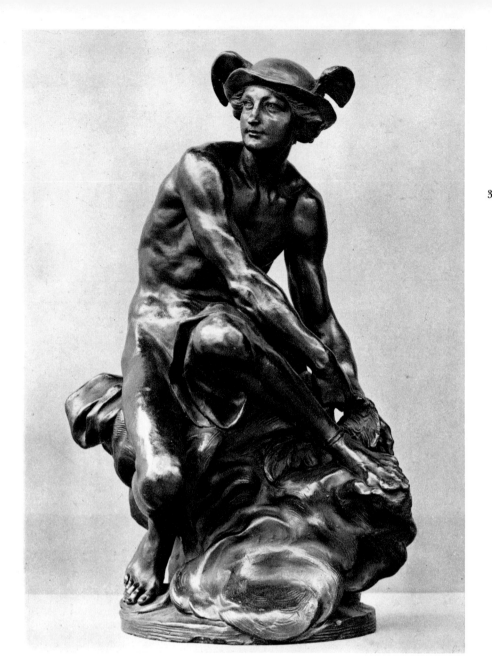

339. JEAN-BAPTISTE PIGALLE.
Mercury. 1736–39.
Terracotta (tinted bronze color),
height 22″.
The Metropolitan Museum of Art,
New York (Bequest of
Benjamin Altman, 1913)

whose reputation was established by his splendid *Mercury,* a work endowed with both grace and vigor by the complicated torsion of the pose. The first version of the statue, in terracotta (fig. 339; see also fig. 324), may have been made between 1736 and 1739 when Pigalle was in Rome, where he certainly studied the works of Bernini and his followers. Pigalle's style, which is remarkable for its gracefulness and its bold, naturalistic modeling, was admirably suited to portraiture as well as to the seductive and playful subjects that were so dear to the Rococo. However, Pigalle's most impressive work is the tomb of the Maréchal de

Saxe in the Church of St. Thomas, Strasbourg (fig. 340), commissioned in 1753 and completed in 1776. Here the artist displays his ability to compose on a large scale. The design seems free and animated, although the movements and the placement of the forms are controlled and carefully related. To the left of Louis XV's great general, who died in 1750, three terrified creatures—a lion, a leopard, and an eagle—represent Holland, England, and the Holy Roman Empire, vanquished by his military prowess. At the right, an infant symbolizes the Genius of War; weeping, he extinguishes his torch. The general stands be-

OPPOSITE: 340. JEAN-BAPTISTE PIGALLE.
Tomb of the Maréchal de Saxe. 1753–76. Marble.
St. Thomas, Strasbourg

fore a pyramid, symbol of the immortality that his deeds have assured to him, and that allows him to descend fearlessly to the tomb held open by Death. A lamenting figure of France tries vainly to intercede. At the lower left a despairing Hercules symbolizes the French armies. This is a rather cumbersome allegory, and the success of the group is essentially the result of Pigalle's ability to invest it with a ceremonial majesty and discreet vivacity.

Because the leading sculptors of the age continued to produce "ennobling," serious works in a grand style, the Neoclassical reaction was less urgent and less severe in sculpture than in painting. Nevertheless, the gradual development of a taste for quieter, more austere, and linear forms is easy to trace, and it is strongly reflected in the early works of Jean-Antoine Houdon (1741–1828). Houdon studied at the Royal Academy before going to Rome, where he stayed from

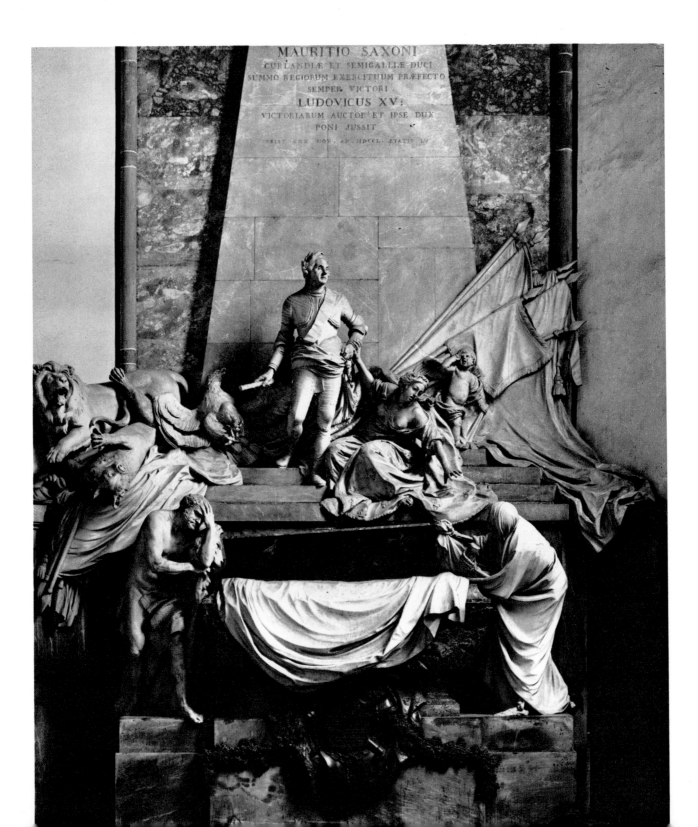

1764 to 1768. The masterpiece of his Roman period is the large *St. Bruno* (1766) in Santa Maria degli Angeli (fig. 341). The artist has abandoned the rhetorical conventions, the open, turning postures, and the animated drapery style of the Rococo. The figure is carved in broad, simple planes, and the silhouette is closed and almost symmetrical. Remaining within the confines of the niche, St. Bruno stands straight, with his head bowed and his arms folded over his chest in fervent, inward devotion. It is instructive to compare this statue with the figures in Subleyras' *St. Benedict Reviving a Child* of 1744 (fig. 331). Houdon's *St. Bruno* represents a further step in the direction of Neoclassicism initiated by the style of Subleyras and other members of his generation (see page 322).

Houdon is best known as a portraitist. Accomplishments in this field during the eighteenth century were no less brilliant in sculpture than in painting. The portrait tradition established in France by Coysevox was passed on through

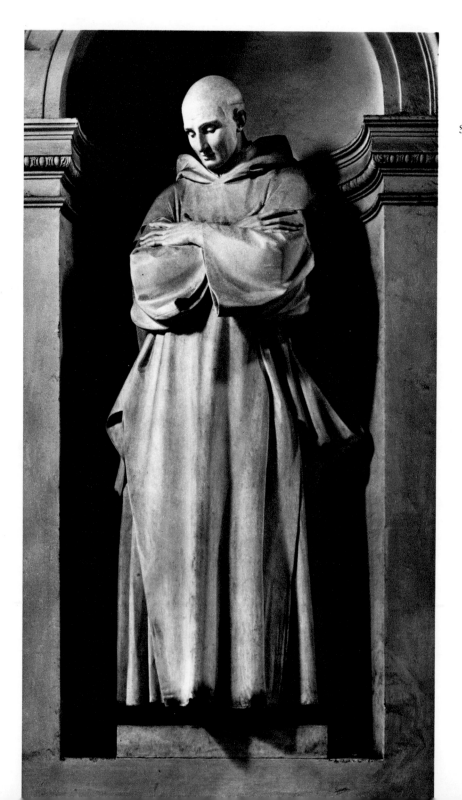

341. JEAN-ANTOINE HOUDON.
St. Bruno. 1766.
Marble, over lifesize.
S. Maria degli Angeli, Rome

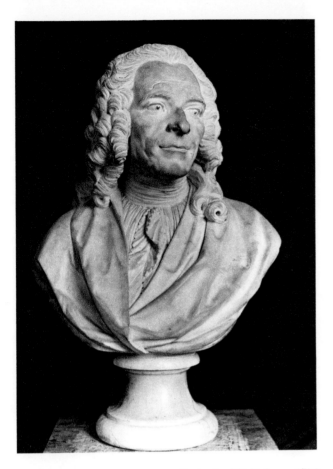

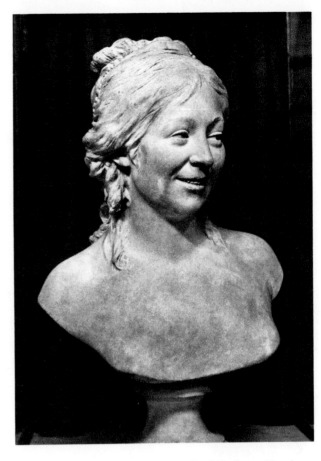

342. JEAN-BAPTISTE LEMOYNE II. *Portrait of Voltaire.* c. 1750. Marble, height 19¼″. Château de Challis (Oise)

343. JEAN-ANTOINE HOUDON. *Portrait of Madame Houdon.* c. 1787. Plaster, lifesize. The Louvre, Paris

the Costou and the Lemoyne (fig. 342), to Pigalle and Houdon.[19] Houdon was the favorite portrait sculptor of the progressive thinkers and politicians of the age. He portrayed Voltaire many times, as well as Rousseau, Diderot, Mirabeau, and finally Napoleon; in 1785 he came to America to portray Washington. Many of these statues are best understood in the context of Neoclassical style, which goes beyond the limits of this book. However, Houdon is a transitional figure. He is unsurpassed in rendering the vibrant delicacy of living flesh and the mobility of expression, and a portrait as late as about 1787, the bust of his wife (fig. 343), radiates a generous warmth, a lovely freshness, and a vivid spontaneity of expression that reflect the dominant aesthetic ideals of the eighteenth century. The portrait goes back to the informal portrait style of Coysevox (fig. 180); and, further back, to the most intimate of Bernini's portraits, *Costanza Buonarelli* (fig. 68). At the same time, it points ahead to the portrait sculpture of Rodin.

ARCHITECTURE

Like sculpture, eighteenth-century architecture in France was able to retain close ties to traditions of the previous century while responding to the new tastes of the age. From the beginning of the century French buildings were characterized by new elegance and charm, by lively inventiveness, and also by a fine awareness of the requirements of intimacy and convenience in architecture. Typically, achievements in domestic architecture dominated the age, and, because elegant

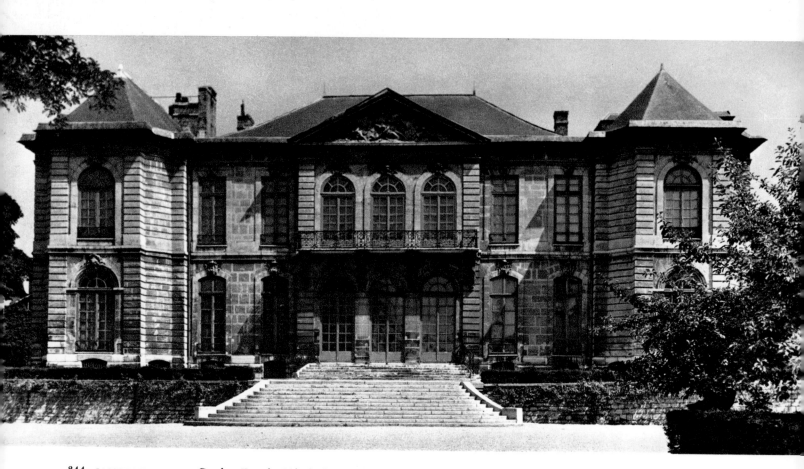

344. JACQUES V. GABRIEL. Garden Façade, Hôtel Biron (Musée Rodin). 1728–30. Paris

society in the eighteenth century was predominantly citified, there was less emphasis on great country châteaux than on *hôtels,* or town houses.

One of the finest Parisian houses of the first half of the century is the Hôtel Biron (now the Musée Rodin), built between 1728 and 1730 by Jacques V. Gabriel (1667–1742), who came from a family of architects related to the Mansarts. The garden façade of the Hôtel Biron (fig. 344) combines a classical feeling for restraint and harmonious proportions with an elegant liveliness of effect. The clarity of the arrangement of the masses of the building is emphasized by the plain wall surface, usual for eighteenth-century *hôtels,* which is tastefully relieved by the discreet rustication of the end pavilions and the frontispiece. The window enframements are sim-

ple and almost unornamented, but the tall windows themselves are varied in width and shape. The surface and outline of the house are beautifully enlivened by the rhythmic pattern of the windows, the contrasting forms of the pediment and the roofs, and by the relief of the wall, with its projections and rounded pavilions.

While ornament was generally used sparingly and with classical correctness on house exteriors, thus maintaining the dignity of the public façade, eighteenth-century interiors make a decorative display that is extraordinarily free and abundant, although compared to most German or Spanish decoration of the time (fig. 399), French designs generally seem restrained. The ornamental vocabulary of the century, which can be traced back to the last decades of the seventeenth century,[20] was rapidly elaborated around 1710 in works such as the Galerie Dorée in the Hôtel de Toulouse (fig. 345; 1713–19, now the Banque de France) by Robert de Cotte (1656–1735; see fig. 180), a pupil and assistant of J.-H. Mansart's. The Galerie Dorée seems an intimate, graceful, and glittering version of the Galerie des Glaces at Versailles (fig. 143). However, the style of interior decoration reached a peak of licentious gaiety around 1735 in works like the Salon Ovale in the Hôtel de Soubise (now the Archives Nationales; fig. 346) by another of J.-H. Mansart's students, Germain Boffrand (1667–1754). In such Rococo[21] interiors the last echoes of the geometric formality of the decorative style of the age of Louis XIV (figs. 145, 146) have been stilled. Now irregular, active curvilinear forms create intricate ornamental traceries over wall surfaces. The membering is typically thin and delicate, emphasizing the lightness and the height of the rooms. Paintings are part of the decorative furnishings, and mirrors collaborate with tall windows to fill interiors with

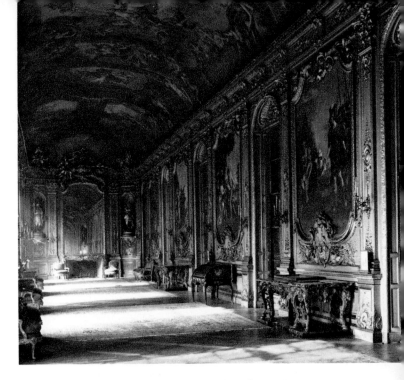

345. ROBERT DE COTTE. Galerie Dorée, Hôtel de Toulouse (Banque de France). 1713–19. Paris

346. GERMAIN BOFFRAND. Salon Ovale, Hôtel de Soubise (Archives Nationales). Begun 1732. Paris

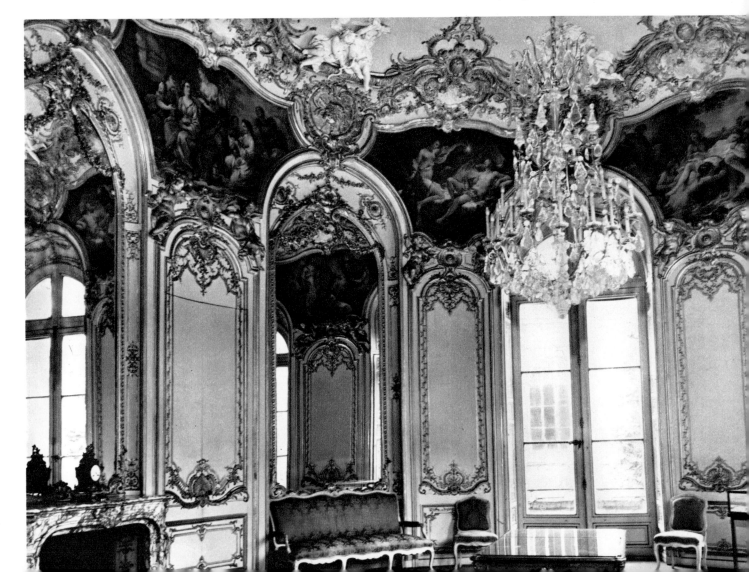

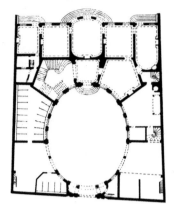

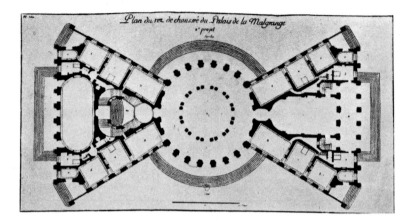

347. GERMAIN BOFFRAND. Plan, Hôtel Amelot. Begun 1710. Paris

348. GERMAIN BOFFRAND. Second Plan, La Malgrange. After 1711. Nancy

light and air and to catch the sparkle of gilding and the brightness of white and pastel surfaces.

In planning town houses, eighteenth-century architects showed remarkable ingenuity in satisfying their patrons' demands for convenience and comfort. They were no longer bound by those architectural ideals that led Madame de Maintenon to complain of Louis XIV: "With him only grandeur, magnificence, symmetry matter; it is infinitely worthwhile enduring all the draughts which sweep under the doors if only these can be arranged facing each other."[22] In Boffrand's plan for the Hôtel Amelot (begun 1710; fig. 347) one sees how irregular shapes and arrangements were designed to provide a maximum of usable well-lit space, to facilitate movement between rooms and floors, to make functional combinations (such as connecting the kitchen and dining room), and to assure privacy where needed.[23] The freedom with which rooms were shaped and placed added charm as well as convenience to interiors. The contemporary taste for animated, unusual forms encouraged the development of Rococo ornament, and, naturally, it also appreciated variety in plans, novel arrangements, irregular shapes, and curved corners. The forms of the Italian Baroque were, of course, an important source of inspiration for such designs, but these forms were treated with a new and characteristically French feeling for grace and refinement.[24]

Novelty and ingenuity, so highly prized in the eighteenth century, also characterize the more ambitious architectural projects of the age. Boffrand's second design for the château La Malgrange (after 1711; fig. 348) makes a radical departure from the traditional château plan, where there is a massing of closely related units. Here, four long wings (each an apartment) radiate, like the spokes of a wheel, from a circular center, the grand salon. Between the wings of the long axis the architect has inserted on one side the gallery and the grand staircase, and on the other side the dining room and a peristyle. The design was not executed, but the intended visual effect of the interplay of shapes and of the irregular spatial movement of the plan may be partly judged from Juvarra's closely related building at Stupinigi (fig. 374).[25]

La Malgrange was commissioned by Duke Leopold, who ruled the duchy of Lorraine (independent until 1766). Boffrand continued to work for Lorraine after 1730, when Leopold was succeeded by Louis XV's father-in-law, Stanislas Leczinski, the deposed king of Poland. However, Emmanuel Héré de Corny (1705–1763) was mainly responsible for the architectural distinction of Lorraine's capital, Nancy. Héré, who apparently never went to Paris, was greatly influenced by

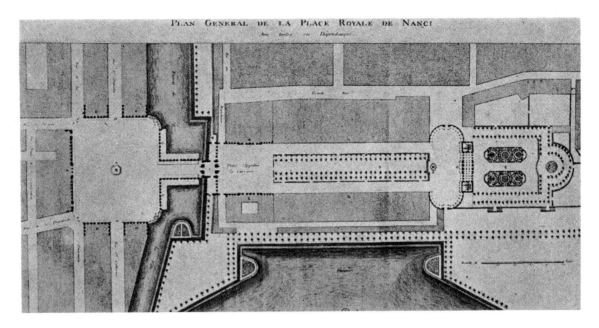

PLAN GENERAL DE LA PLACE ROYALE DE NANCI

349. EMMANUEL HERE DE CORNY.
Plan, Place Stanislas.
1752–55. Nancy

Boffrand, and his major achievement, the Place Stanislas in Nancy (1752–55), is a development of work already begun under Boffrand. The Place Stanislas is really a group of three connected squares (fig. 349). The oval Place du Gouvernement is defined by a graceful, undulating colonnaded screen (fig. 350). In front of the palace, across the short axis of this hemicycle, is the entrance to the Place de la Carrière. The long, nar-

350. EMMANUEL HERE DE CORNY.
Place du Gouvernement (The Hemicycle).
1752–55. Nancy

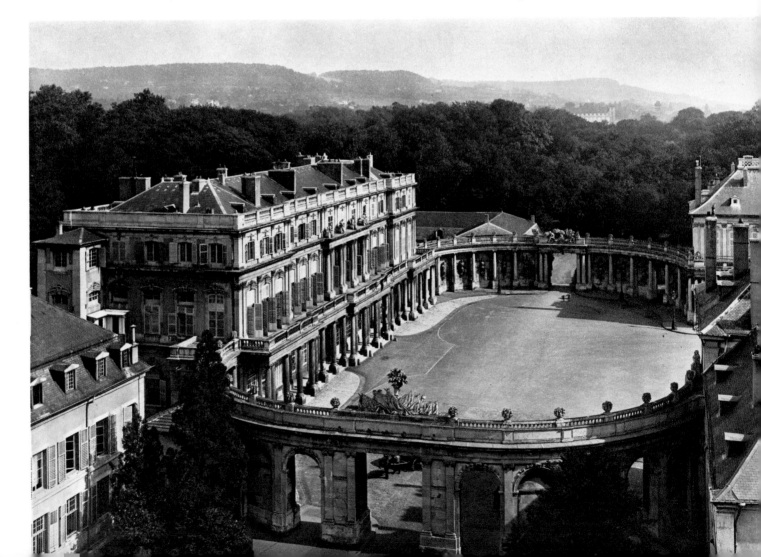

row old tournament ground is lined with trees and closed by symmetrical rows of houses. At the end of the *carrière* the space is cleared before a triumphal arch that leads to a bridge across the moat, beyond which opens the rectangular Place Louis XV. With its accented sequence of varied spaces and the refinement of its surrounding buildings, the Place Stanislas is one of the most enchanting ensembles in France.[26]

In Paris and at Versailles major architectural work was carried out during the last two decades of Louis XV's reign by Jacques-Ange Gabriel (1698–1782), the son of Jacques V. Gabriel. The younger Gabriel was responsible for the École Militaire and the Place de la Concorde (fig. 351) in Paris, and for important additions to Versailles, including the Royal Opera. However, his most attractive work is surely the Petit Trianon, an intimate residence secluded in the park of Versailles. The small house (seventy-nine by seventy-three feet in plan) was built between 1762 and 1768 for the king, who presented it to Madame du Barry. The west façade (colorplate 49) is splendid in the perfection of its proportions and in its poise and sophistication. The façade reads as a single rectangular unit, and the two stories— the division is suggested with the utmost discretion by the cornices of the lower windows—are drawn together by the giant Corinthian columns. However, the spacing of the bays and the slight projection of the columniated central section create a quiet rhythm across the façade, while the whole building is caught up by the rhythm and direction of the surrounding terrace which makes an easy descent into the gardens. The building is best seen when sunlight animates the central screen of windows and finely fluted columns and brings out the color of the white limestone.

Despite its lightness and elegance the Petit Trianon clearly signals the end of our period in architecture. The reaction to Rococo style was developing in architecture as well as in the other arts in the second half of the eighteenth century, and the regularity of Gabriel's design and his sharp, geometric definition of forms do, in fact, already assert the ideals of a new age. Indeed, the first great monument of Neoclassicism in French architecture, Soufflot's Panthéon in Paris, was begun in 1755, almost a decade before Gabriel began the Petit Trianon.

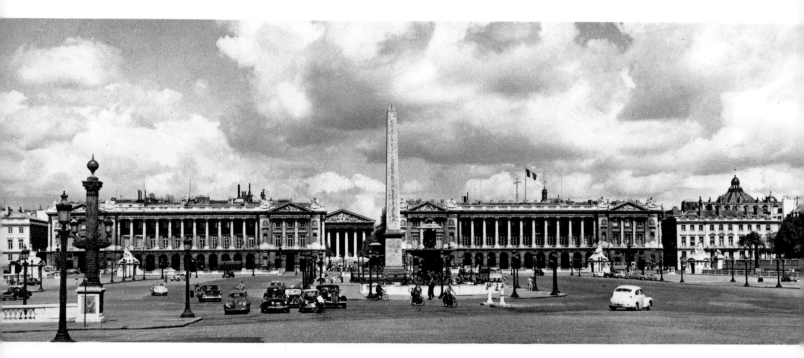

351. JACQUES-ANGE GABRIEL. Place de la Concorde. 1763. Paris

Colorplate 49. JACQUES-ANGE GABRIEL. West Façade, Petit Trianon. 1762–68. Versailles

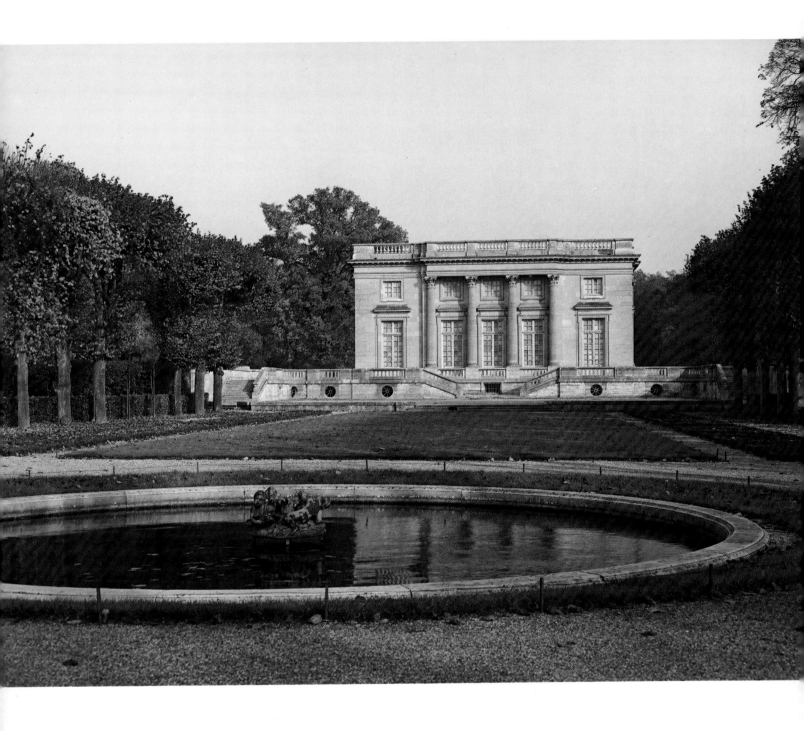

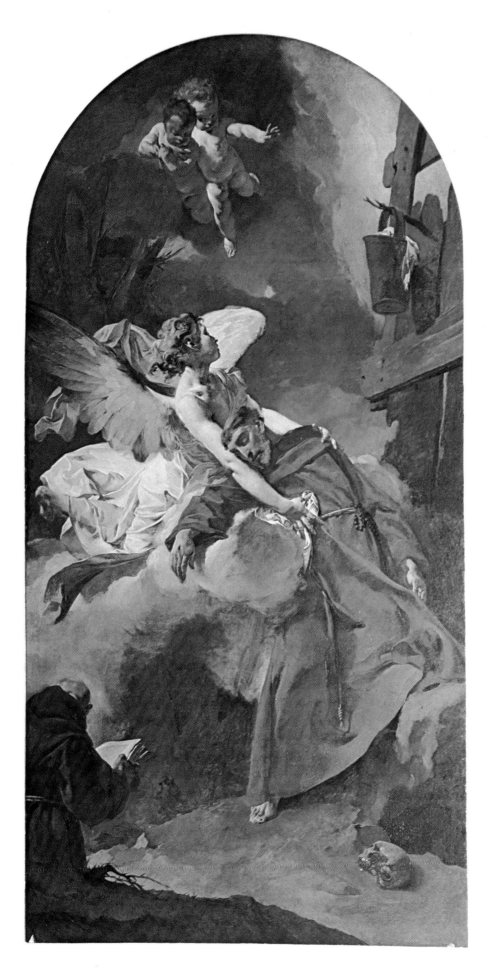

Colorplate 50.
GIAMBATTISTA PIAZZETTA.
Ecstasy of St. Francis. c. 1732.
12′4½″ × 6′1⅛″.
Museo Civico, Vicenza

8

Italy in the Eighteenth Century

PAINTING

In Italian painting the transition from the seventeenth to the eighteenth century was made almost imperceptibly. In the field of monumental decoration, for instance, the art of Luca Giordano, deriving largely from Pietro da Cortona, led directly to the works of Francesco Solimena (1657–1747) in Naples, Corrado Giaquinto (1703–1765) in Naples and Rome, Sebastiano Ricci (1659–1734) and Giambattista Tiepolo (1696–1770) in Venice. However, a survey of eighteenth-century painting in Italy reveals its distinctive characteristics, and also affirms the new importance of Venice, which now came to supplant Rome in supporting the most vigorous school of painting in the country.

In the eighteenth century Venice experienced a renascence; indeed, not since the sixteenth century had the city been endowed with so much native talent. One great Venetian painter of the beginning of the century, Giambattista Piazzetta (1683–1752), is best understood as a transitional figure. In paintings like the *Ecstasy of St. Francis* (c. 1732; colorplate 50), the tall format and the terse zigzag compositional pattern are characteristic of eighteenth-century design. However,

Piazzetta's style was still rooted in the previous century. Instead of the bright colors and spirited handling that were already coming to dominate the period, Piazzetta based his palette on dark, opalescent colors—deep browns, oranges, russets, blacks, blues, and grays—and he insisted on forceful contrasts of light and shade and on the plastic solidity of forms. The picture illustrates the moment after the Stigmatization, when St. Francis faints in the arms of an angel who has flown down swiftly to support him and to staunch the wound in his side. The figures are caught up in a feverish pattern of movement, and they glow in the hot light that, according to old accounts, "flamed forth" as St. Francis was miraculously marked with the wounds of the crucified Christ.

Piazzetta's work was a source of inspiration for the greatest Italian painter of the eighteenth century, another Venetian, Giambattista Tiepolo. Tiepolo had studied with the rather *retardataire* artist Gregorio Lazzarini, but Piazzetta's dark and relatively heavy manner was the main influence on his early work. However, by about 1730 Tiepolo developed a new luminous style. The sunlit brilliance of his coloring really represents a kind

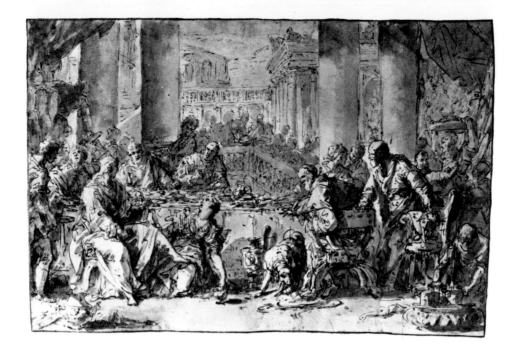

352. SEBASTIANO RICCI.
*St. Mary Magdalen
Anointing Christ's Feet.* c. 1725.
Drawing, 9⅝×13⅞".
Windsor Castle

of revival of sixteenth-century Venetian painting. Sebastiano Ricci had already developed a fine manner based largely on Veronese's work. Ricci's paintings and drawings are wonderful in their sprightly bravura, their glitter, and their breathless activity (fig. 352). But Ricci lacked the poetic genius of Tiepolo, who used a singing color and dazzling light, recalling Veronese, with an airy translucency and a freedom of touch that carry the spectator into a new world of imagination.

In sheer quantity Tiepolo's output is astonishing—whether one totals his paintings, drawings, and etchings, or measures the square feet of canvas, walls, and ceilings that he decorated. The artist was equipped by nature for great tasks, and his contemporaries knew it. Count Tessin, the Swedish Minister, recommended Tiepolo to his king in 1736: "Tiepolo is just the man for us," he wrote, ". . . a man of great wit, accommodating. . . ; his imagination is inexhaustible, his color is brilliant, and his speed amazing. He can complete a picture in less time than others take to grind their colors."[1] His technical virtuosity and prodigious inventiveness made Tiepolo the commanding figure of his time in the field of monumental decoration. He painted many great easel pictures, such as the passionate and deeply felt *St. Thecla*

Praying for the Plague-stricken (fig. 353), but his frescoes in churches and palaces more readily reveal the full range and fertility of his genius.

In 1744 Tiepolo completed the now destroyed ceiling fresco of the Church of the Scalzi in Venice (fig. 354), for which there is a beautiful and very freely painted sketch in Venice (colorplate 51). It represents the miraculous transportation of the Virgin's house from Nazareth to Loreto (with several intermediate stops), an event said to have occurred between 1291 and 1294. The ceiling seems painted away, dissolved by the luminosity of Tiepolo's color. The little house speeds across the sky, carried on a cloud and propelled by angels. The Madonna stands imperiously on the roof of her house, like a captain on the bridge of his ship. The sight of the Marian miracle overthrows the Heresies, who fall precipitously from the heavens. The view, seen not directly from below but tilted on an angle above the spectator, follows a pattern that Veronese had used consistently in ceiling designs. However, the dense cloud populated by boldly foreshortened angels serves to remind one of Correggio, whose works were the ultimate source of this tradition of illusionistic ceiling decoration.

It is instructive to compare Tiepolo's fresco

with Baciccio's treatment of a similar subject, painted some seventy years earlier in Il Gesù in Rome (fig. 122). Characteristically for the seventeenth century, Baciccio's painting emphasizes the central vertical axis, and is packed with figures. By contrast, Tiepolo's design is light and free. His forms seem small and scattered in the immense space of his painted heaven, but they are linked by an underlying pattern of movement that zigzags across the ceiling to create tension and excitement and to suggest the swiftness of the flight of the Holy House.

In Italy Tiepolo's activity was confined to the north—Venice, Vicenza, Udine, Bergamo, Milan. Outside Italy he was most appreciated in Germany and Spain (where he worked from 1762

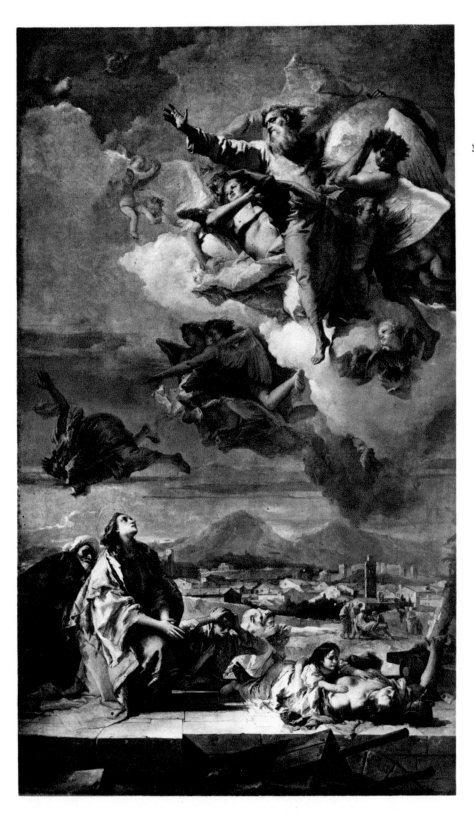

353. GIAMBATTISTA TIEPOLO.
*St. Thecla Praying
for the Plague-stricken.*
1759. 26½ × 15⅜".
Chiesa delle Grazie, Este

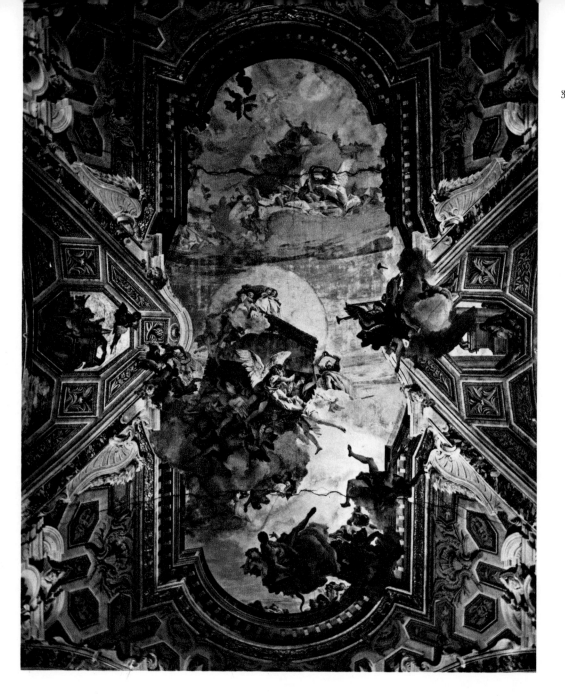

until his death), countries that had developed
flamboyant versions of the Baroque and Rococo
styles. In 1750 Tiepolo went to Würzburg, where
he stayed three years to fresco the new Residenz,
built by Balthasar Neumann (see pages 389, 391).
The extensive decoration is Tiepolo's supreme
masterpiece, and the ensemble of architecture
and painting (colorplate 58) is one of the greatest
artistic accomplishments of the eighteenth century. In the Kaisersaal of the Residenz, Tiepolo
illustrated scenes glorifying the twelfth-century
emperor Frederick Barbarossa. Oblivious to
questions of historical accuracy, Tiepolo created,
in such a painting as the *Marriage of Barbarossa*
(fig. 355), a wonderful fantasy in which the Middle Ages come to life in the costumes and surroundings of Veronese's Venice. The Neoclassical
period, and the critics and artists of Tiepolo's
time who anticipated Neoclassicism, condemned
him for such breaches of decorum and for his
indifference to the ideal of "the learned painter."
However, Tiepolo's picture provides the spec-

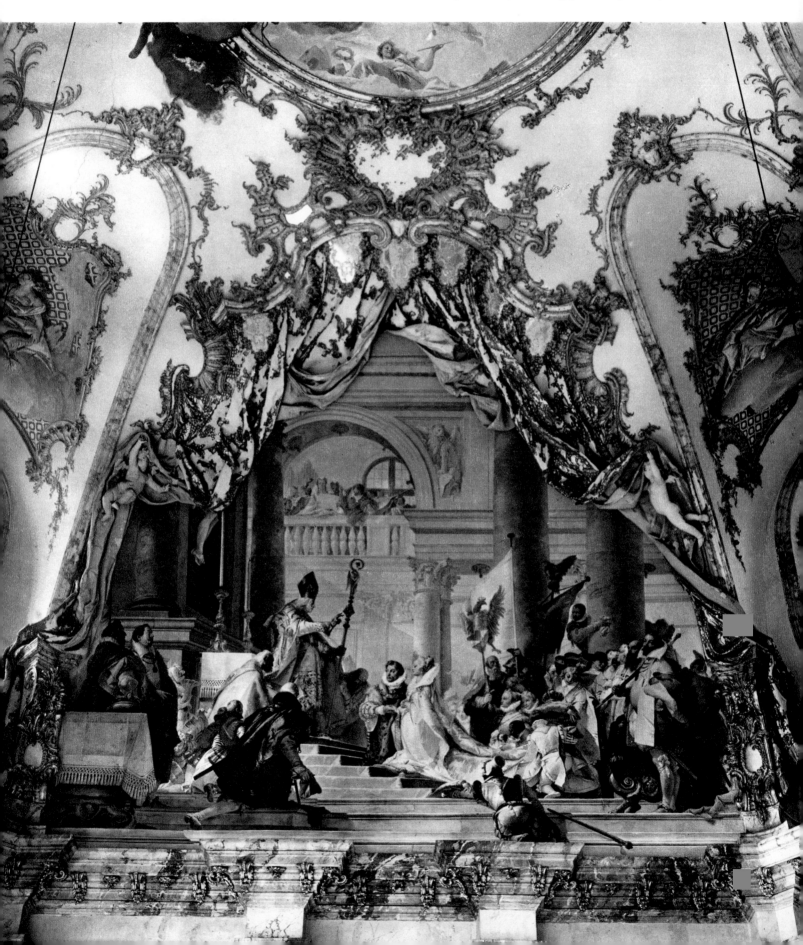

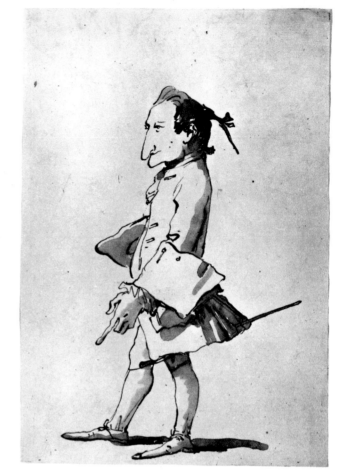

tator with an experience that might be compared
to watching a modern performance of *Richard III*
played in Elizabethan dress. The twelfth and sixteenth centuries are poetically merged by Tiepolo
in theatrical fantasy and pageantry; the time is
the fabulous age of "long ago." Tiepolo's works
suggest the analogy of the theater or the opera; in
the Kaisersaal the spectator sees a curtain (of
painted stucco) rise to reveal an elaborate set. Behind is a splendid architectural backdrop. Barbarossa's marriage is an enchanting spectacle, and
the brilliant colors—blues and golds, pinks and
lemon yellows—of the costumes and banners are
radiant in the cool, silvery light that floods the
stage.

Tiepolo's paintings, whether secular or religious, are certainly sincere. He was convinced of
the virtues of monarchy and of the truth of his religion. However, he avoided the weighty seriousness and even pomposity that so frequently characterize seventeenth-century art. Tiepolo's works
often sparkle with wit and playful levity. The solemnity of Barbarossa's marriage is lightened by
such conceits as the fantastically dressed dwarf
who kneels on the steps at the right, and by the
charming brown-and-white lap dog, just behind
the empress, watching the ceremony.

In a more private vein Tiepolo's incisive wit is
brilliantly revealed in his caricature drawings.
Caricature was established in Italy by the Carracci and their circle at the end of the sixteenth century, and it was practiced as a humorous diversion
by Bernini, among others, in the next century.
Tiepolo's age, with its sophisticated propensity
for skeptical self-criticism, with its taste for irony
and for witty conceits, delighted in caricature. Indeed, the professional caricaturist was a creation
of the eighteenth century.[2] For Tiepolo caricature
was only an amusing pastime, but his drawings
in this field are unsurpassed in quality. A splendid
example is in the Art Institute of Chicago (fig.

356). Here some long-nosed gentleman with pretensions to style is made marvelously ridiculous
by the proliferation of noses and tails that point
absurdly in all directions. The caricature shows
the artist's brilliant draftsmanship as well as his
humor. The luminosity of Tiepolo's washes creates space and air around the figure, and the accuracy and controlled speed of his brush and pen
render essentials with precision, economy, and
instantaneousness.

Eighteenth-century man's fondness for contem-
plating himself and his own world naturally encouraged the development of such fields as genre,
landscape, and view painting, all of which now
became important and popular enough to begin
to compete seriously with history painting for artistic primacy.[3] In Venice, Pietro Longhi (1702–
1785) had a great success with little scenes of contemporary life. Longhi's talents were limited, and
his paintings sometimes seem rather clumsy, but

they invariably achieve their modest aim of conveying the charms of the domestic life of the well-to-do, or of recording the attractive diversions of the everyday scene in Venice. In a delightful painting in the Ca' Rezzonico in Venice (fig. 357) he offers, as the sign on the wall at the right says, "A true portrait of a rhinoceros, brought to Venice in 1751. . . ."

Longhi established the conversation piece, the genre of polite society, in Italy. However, the Italian tradition of low-life scenes, which was rooted in the art of the Carracci as well as of Caravaggio's followers (see pages 73, 79), continued to enjoy great popularity. Among the eighteenth-century practitioners of this tradition was the Bolognese artist Giuseppe Maria Crespi, called Lo Spagnuolo (1665–1747), who was, in fact, the teacher of

Longhi (and also of Piazzetta). Crespi, whose style owes much to the work of Ludovico Carracci and Guercino, did not favor the high-keyed palette of the eighteenth century, and his paintings are characterized by strong, dramatic chiaroscuro effects. Genre painting represents only one aspect of Crespi's activity (see fig. 13), but even his history and portrait paintings are informed by a genre-like directness and intimacy of treatment. One of Crespi's most popular works, the *Flea Hunt* (fig. 358), supposedly belonged to a series of small pictures illustrating the gradual rise of a poor girl to fame and fortune as a singer. The *Flea Hunt* depicts an early stage in this typically eighteenth-century tale. The small room, its shabby furnishings in disorder, is lit by a ray of sunlight falling from a window above. The scene of the girl at her

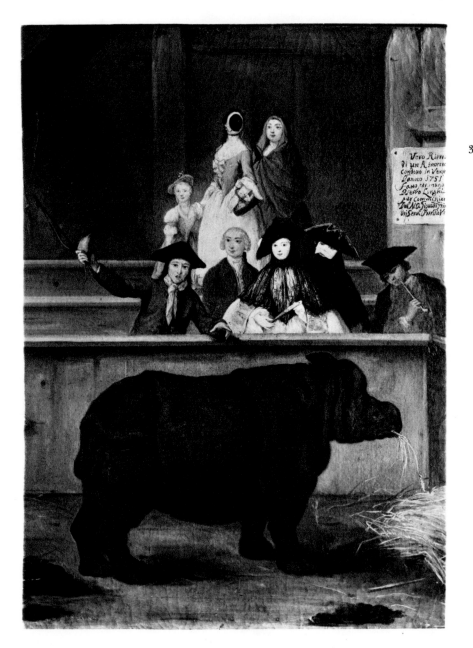

357. PIETRO LONGHI.
Rhinoceros. c. 1751.
23¾ × 18½".
Ca' Rezzonico, Venice

345

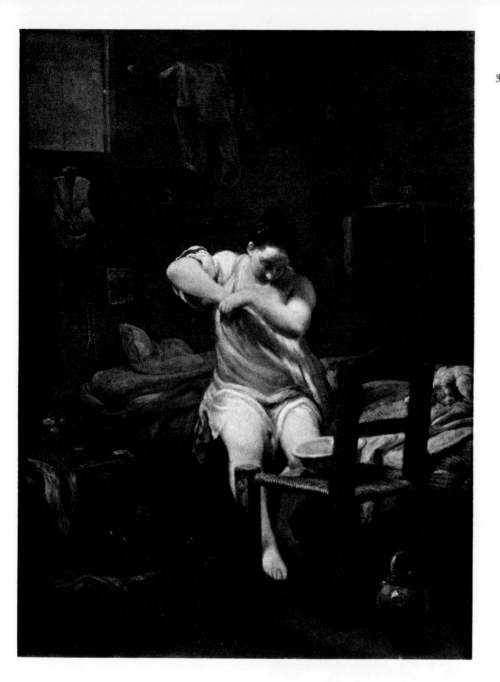

358. GIUSEPPE MARIA CRESPI.
Flea Hunt. c. 1707.
Copper, 18¼ × 13⅜".
Uffizi Gallery, Florence

toilet, searching herself for a flea, is at once amusing and poignant. While such a subject has precedents in the early seventeenth century, a comparison with La Tour's *Woman with a Flea* (fig. 150) underlines the new intimacy and sympathy of Crespi's approach.

Eighteenth-century taste encouraged not only paintings of familiar, everyday life but also scenes of fantasy and depictions of strange places and mysterious activities. Undoubtedly the most bizarre and also the most fascinating representative

of the latter trend was Alessandro Magnasco, called Lissandrino (1667–1749). Magnasco was a Genoese but spent a good part of his life in Milan. Among the most enigmatic of his works are scenes of religious practice; for instance, monks in a passion of penitential devotion, nuns working intently at their spinning wheels, or a crowded synagogue. The mode of presentation as well as the specific subjects give Magnasco's pictures their mysterious, hallucinatory quality. Such a painting as the *Monks in a Refectory* (fig. 359) might be

Colorplate 51.
GIAMBATTISTA TIEPOLO.
Translation of the Holy House to Loreto. c. 1743.
Oil sketch, 49½×33½".
Accademia, Venice

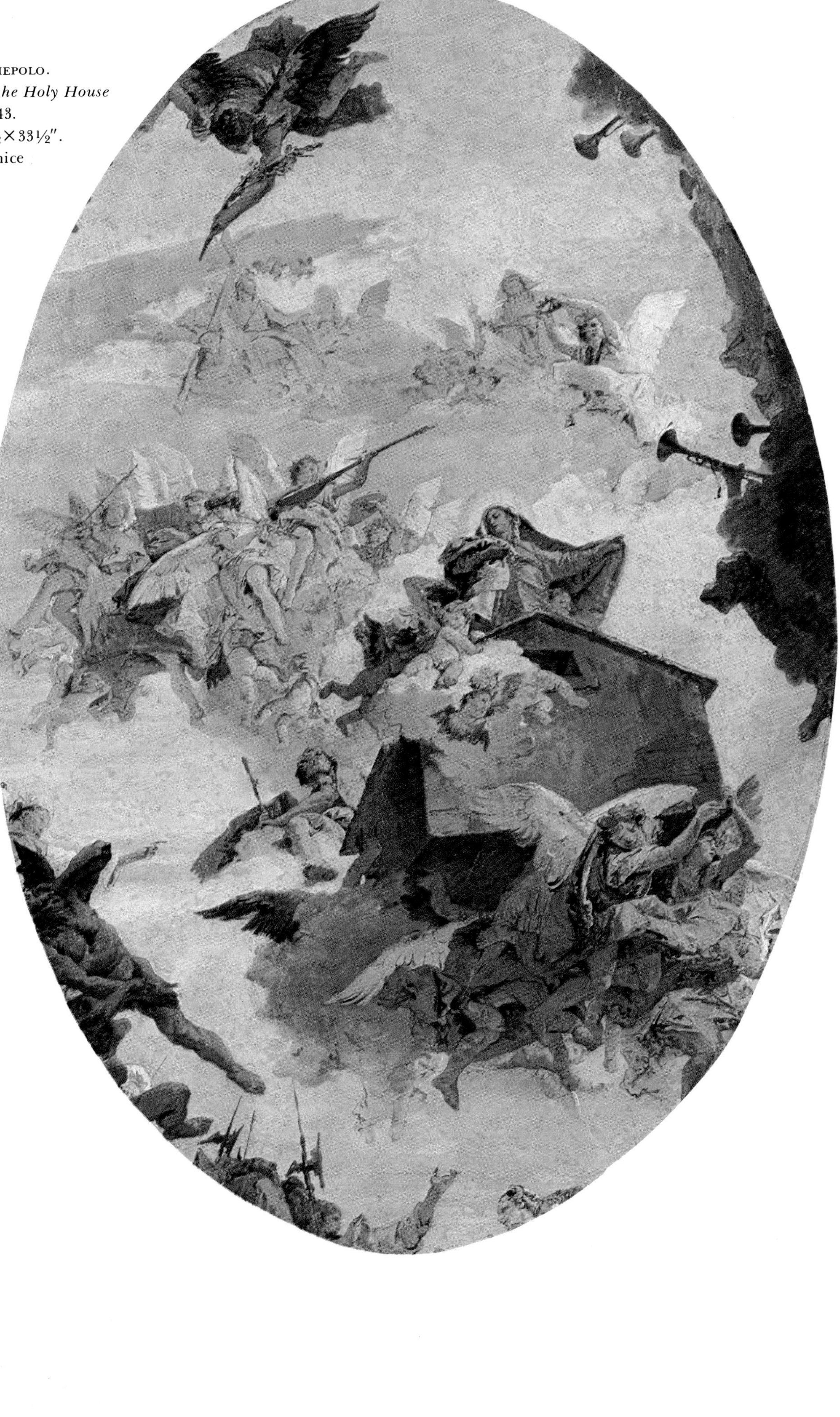

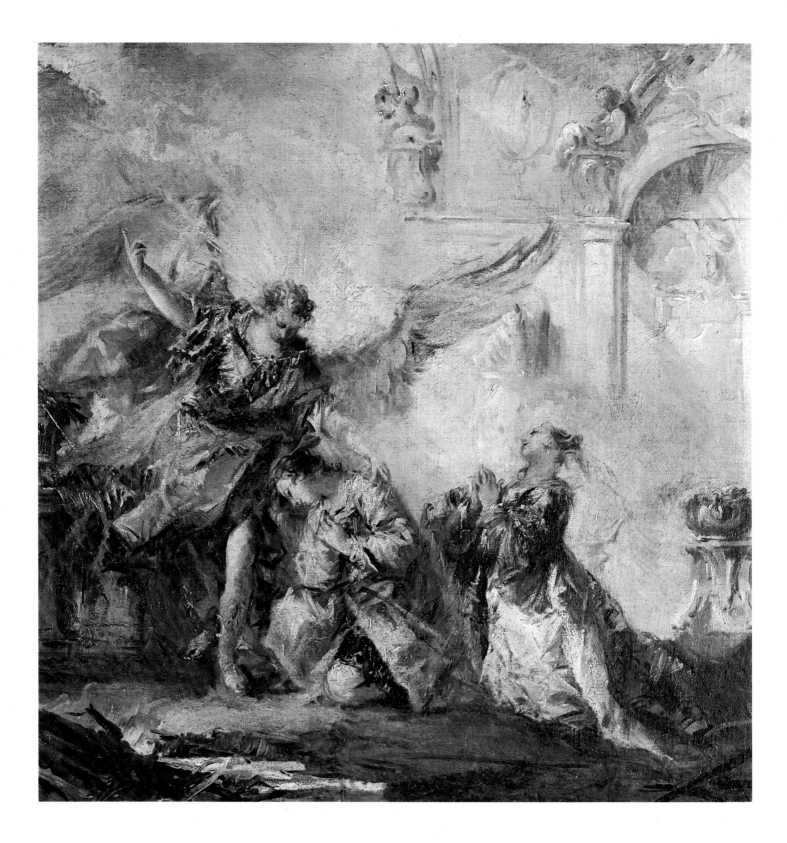

Colorplate 52. GIAN ANTONIO GUARDI. *Raphael Blessing Tobias and Sarah* (detail of Organ Panel). c. 1750.
Church of the Angelo Raffaele, Venice

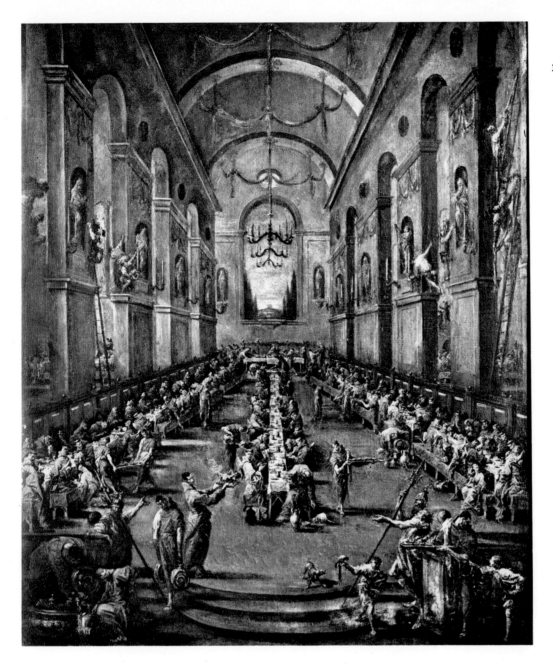

359. ALESSANDRO MAGNASCO.
Monks in a Refectory.
Early 18th century.
68½ × 55¾".
Museo Civico, Bassano

understood as an everyday scene of monastic life, but it is transformed by the high viewpoint and by the fantastically vast hall, which make the monks appear strangely diminutive. The sense of agitation in the elongated, gesturing figures, and such jarring details as the men on ladders scaling the walls, suggest a hidden level of meaning, but whether it lies in the direction of religious mysticism or religious satire is far from clear.[4]

Magnasco was undoubtedly influenced by the prints of Jacques Callot (fig. 149) and by the paintings of Salvator Rosa (fig. 114). Indeed, Rosa's style was one of the main sources of Magnasco's landscape paintings (usually macabre scenes of dense forests or stormy seashores inhabited by bandits, sorcerers, or friars) and of the nervous, rapid brush technique that contributes so much to the spectral quality of Magnasco's pictures. Magnasco's art was highly personal and he had no real following, but his style influenced the Venetian landscape painter Marco Ricci (1676–1729; the nephew of Sebastiano) and ultimately, through Ricci, Francesco Guardi.

In the eighteenth century the major accomplishments in Italian landscape painting were made by the *vedutisti,* the painters of views *(vedute).* View painting, which is really a subdivision of landscape painting, might be traced back to the topographical views that appear occasionally, for instance, in the backgrounds of early Renaissance pictures. However, in Italy it was only in the sixteenth and seventeenth centuries that artists began to take a serious interest in recording views for their own sake; and in the eighteenth century the great increase in tourism was a powerful stimulus for the further development of the field. Visitors to Italy (the ultimate goal of travelers from all parts of Europe) wanted souvenirs of their trip, and they created a vast market for views of famous and beautiful sites. Views of Rome's ancient and modern monuments were, of course, in great demand, and in that city Pannini (1691/2–1765) and Piranesi (see page 352) produced some of the finest *vedute* of the time. For enchanting and, in-

deed, almost magical vistas, however, the Venetian topography is unequaled in Italy, and it seems inevitable that Venice should have produced the two greatest view painters of the century, Canaletto and Guardi.

Giovanni Antonio Canal, called Canaletto (1697–1768), took up view painting around 1720. He had begun his career as a stage designer, which, in the eighteenth century, usually involved the creation of elaborate architectural perspectives.[5] This early training certainly underlies the artist's extraordinary mastery of perspective, and it undoubtedly contributed to his feeling for the poetic effects of the city scene. Paintings like the *Basin of San Marco* (fig. 360) have always been admired for their fidelity to topographical details and for their almost photographic accuracy in rendition. However, Canaletto was far from being an unselective or uncritical observer. His pictures are marvelously calculated; the details of the scene,

360. CANALETTO. *Basin of San Marco.* Early 1730s. 49¼ × 80¼". Museum of Fine Arts, Boston

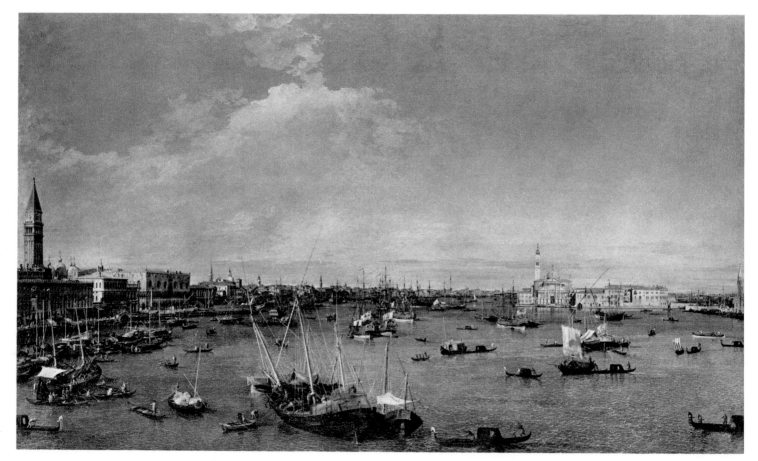

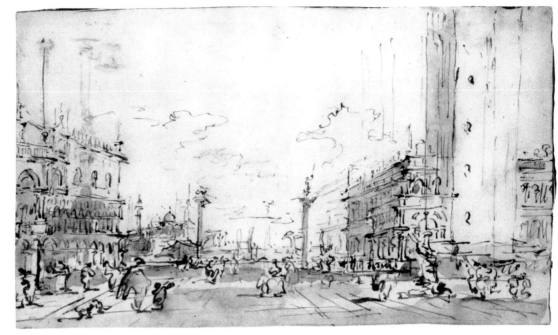

361. FRANCESCO GUARDI.
Piazzetta San Marco. c. 1765.
Pen and wash, 6 × 10¼″.
The Metropolitan Museum of Art,
New York (Rogers Fund, 1937)

the quality of the light, the luminosity of the air and water, the activity on the waterways and in the squares—all are made to combine with the vista to fix and to convey the real physiognomy of Venice.

Canaletto's art attracted numerous followers and imitators in Venice. Foremost among them was the artist's nephew, Bernardo Bellotto (1720–1780; fig. 397), who was also called Canaletto. In 1747 (a year after Canaletto went to England)[6] Bellotto left Venice for Dresden, and he stayed in eastern Europe until his death in Warsaw. However, in Venice another view painter, Francesco Guardi (1712–1793), who may have begun his work in the field by imitating Canaletto, eventually created one of the most original styles of the century, and one that contrasts strongly with Canaletto's smooth surfaces, deliberate brushwork, and sharply defined forms.

Francesco Guardi worked for a long period in the studio of his older brother Gian Antonio (1698–1760), a figure painter who has been rediscovered relatively recently; G. A. Guardi now appears almost certainly to be the author of a truly stupendous example of eighteenth-century colorism and spontaneous brushwork, the organ panels in the Church of the Angelo Raffaele in Venice (colorplate 52).[7] Francesco was first mentioned as a view painter in 1764 by a writer who considered him a pupil of Canaletto's. Whether or not Guardi actually studied with Canaletto, paintings like the *View of the Church of Santa Maria della Salute and the Old Customs House* (colorplate 53), although influenced by the older master, are informed by a spirit altogether different. Guardi works freely, with a loaded brush that seems to seize and momentarily hold the sparkle of Venice's light. His surfaces, rich and dense in color, evoke the vibrant ambience of the city. Figures and architecture are defined with spots of color and with a rapid, broken line; the brush merely sketches, suggests. Canaletto's Venice is the fabulous setting for a daily spectacle; Guardi, in his paintings and drawings (fig. 361), brings the city itself to life. He knows its pulse beat, and his touch animates arcades and windows, statues and church façades, sails of boats and the long poles of the gondoliers, the habitation as well as the inhabitants of Venice.

Besides views of the city the *vedutisti* also created topographical fantasies—views of imagined and poetically idealized cities and suburbs. Sometimes in these caprice views, several existing but geographically unrelated monuments were combined in a picturesque composition that charms or startles us by the unexpectedness of the juxtaposition; sometimes a view was created, like a

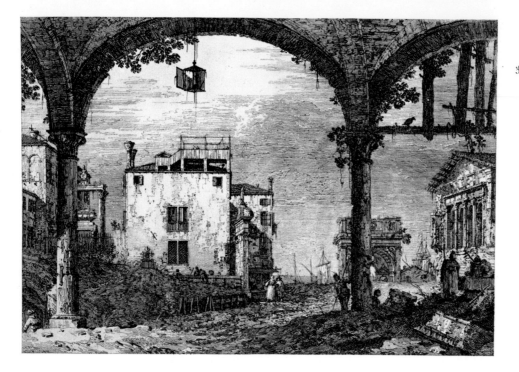

stage set, that is pure invention (fig. 362). Actually, stage design was an important source for the topographical, as well as the closely related architectural, caprice.

Probably the most famous group of eighteenth-century caprices is Giovanni Battista Piranesi's *Imaginary Prisons*. Piranesi (1720–1778), who went to Rome from Venice about 1740, had studied architecture, engineering, and stage design. In Rome, where there were few opportunities for commissions for grand architectural projects, he took up etching, having decided, he wrote, to "make my ideas known through pictures."[8] His designs are always daring and dramatic, but it is in the series of *Prison* etchings (the first states date from the mid-1740s, the second states from 1760–61) that the power of his romantic fantasy is most completely expressed. These prints, which were partly derived from an earlier project for opera scenery, are gripping in their overpowering sense of nightmare reality (fig. 363). Their expanded space and the rapid, flickering movements that animate it are stylistic characteristics that Piranesi shares with many eighteenth-century artists.

However, rather like Magnasco (fig. 359), he seized upon their bizarre, even hallucinatory possibilities. Man seems forever trapped in the vast gloom of Piranesi's dungeons, with their colossal towers, fearsome machinery, and maddening labyrinth of stairs and bridges.

Piranesi's etchings of Rome have much the same bizarre character as the *Prisons*. The artist contrasts diminutive figures with the colossal ruins of antiquity, seen, frequently, from a compelling, unexpected perspective and dramatized by brilliant atmospheric and chiaroscuro effects (fig. 364). However, Piranesi's views are always archaeologically correct in detail; it was, indeed, characteristic for the eighteenth-century to fuse a romantic nostalgia for the grandeur of the classical world with a serious, scholarly antiquarianism.

Actually, the archaeological enthusiasm of the time was one of the factors leading to an increasing demand for "classical" correctness in contemporary art and encouraging the development of an anti-Rococo trend. Rococo styles derived from the painterly, coloristic art of the baroque masters of the seventeenth century. They harked back to

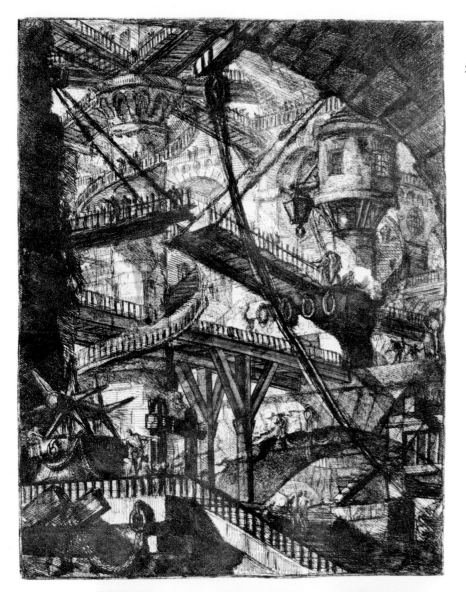

363. GIOVANNI BATTISTA PIRANESI.
Tower with Bridges,
from *Prison Caprices.* 1760–61.
Etching, second state.
The Metropolitan Museum of Art,
New York (Rogers Fund)

364.
GIOVANNI BATTISTA PIRANESI.
Interior of the Frigidarium,
Baths of Diocletian.
Etching.
The Metropolitan Museum of Art,
New York (Rogers Fund)

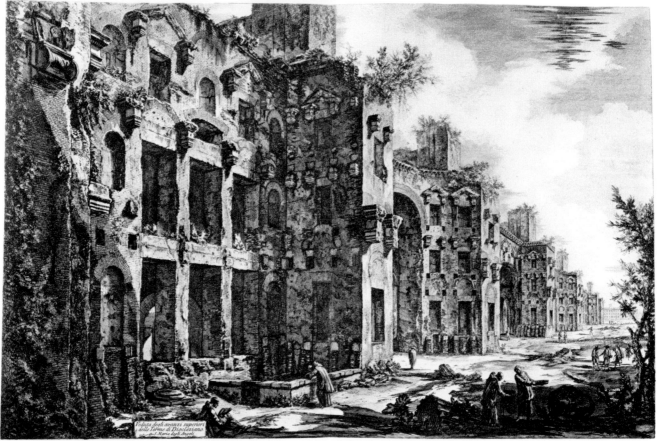

365. POMPEO BATONI. *Portrait of Count Razoumowsky.*
1766. 9'9½" × 6'5".
Collection Count Razoumowsky, Vienna

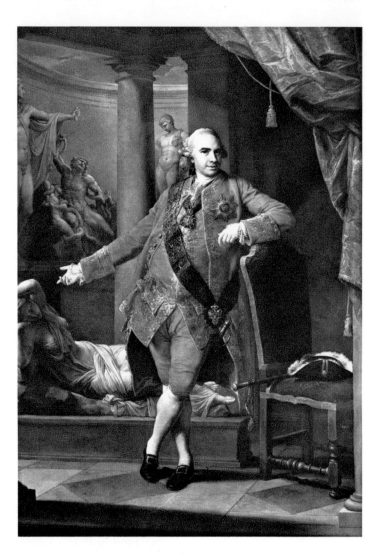

Guercino and Cortona rather than to Reni and
Sacchi, to Baciccio rather than Maratta. The baroque current itself was largely dependent on
north Italian art, and in the eighteenth century
Venice and other north Italian centers were naturally inclined to follow and develop it. However,
in Rome especially, and to some extent in Bologna, it was to be expected that the art of the ancients, of Raphael, and of Annibale Carracci and
other seventeenth-century "classicists" would continue to be emulated. Artists like Sebastiano Con-
ca (1680–1764), Marco Benefial (1684–1764),
Agostino Masucci (1691–1758), and Pompeo
Batoni (1708–1787), although not unaffected by
general eighteenth-century ideals of grace and
elegance, were the guardians of a tradition from
which a new wave of classicism was to rise and
eventually sweep over all Europe (see pages 321–
22). Batoni was one of the finest of these artists.
In his time he was famous both for his history

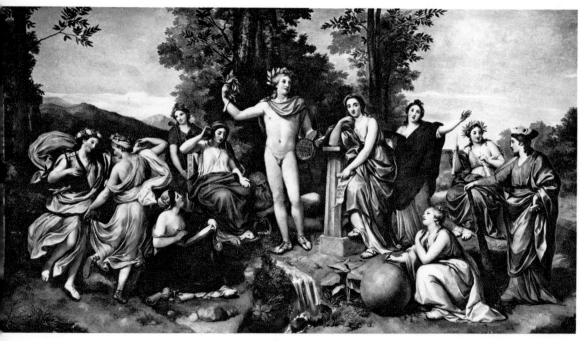

366. ANTON RAPHAEL MENGS. *Parnassus.* 1761.
Ceiling Fresco. Villa Albani, Rome

paintings and his portraits, but today the latter seem his best productions. Batoni's painting of the president of the St. Petersburg Academy of Science, Count Razoumowsky (fig. 365), who was in Rome in 1766, is treated with a new sobriety in drawing and composition. The count points to a collection of famous antique statues—the *Sleeping Ariadne,* the *Apollo Belvedere,* the *Laocoön,* and the so-called *Antinoüs*[9]—that embody his ideals and the ideals of the artist. Despite the informality of the pose and of the general arrangement, an archaeological chill seems to invade the scene. Such works mark the end of our period; indeed, in 1761 Anton Raphael Mengs (1728–1779), a close friend of the enormously influential historian and antiquarian Johann Joachim Winckelmann, had painted his celebrated *Parnassus* on a ceiling in the Villa Albani in Rome (fig. 366). By its reasoned application of linear and planar design principles, and by its evident derivations from ancient sculptures, Raphael, and Poussin, the *Parnassus* is nothing less than the first manifesto of the Neoclassical movement in painting.

SCULPTURE

Gianlorenzo Bernini had dominated seventeenth-century sculpture in Italy, and his work remained the main influence on Italian sculpture far into the next century. Even foreigners, like the French sculptors who began to play an important role in Rome soon after the foundation of the French Academy there in 1666, assimilated major aspects of Bernini's style. However, no sculptor in Italy after the death of Bernini approached the artistic range or quality of the master.

Of course, the ideals of the eighteenth century brought about significant changes in Italian sculpture. The baroque style was gradually transformed into a version of the Rococo as sculptors tended to stress elegance, lightness, and wit in their work. In their "serious" monuments, eighteenth-century sculptors often inclined toward sentimentality. However, the art of Bernini remained an inescapable precedent. When the talented Filippo della Valle (1697–1770) created his tomb of Innocent XII in St. Peter's (1746; fig. 367), he managed little more than a paraphrase of Bernini's famous tomb monuments in the same church (colorplate 2; fig. 61). Technical virtuosity in the

367. FILIPPO DELLA VALLE.
Tomb of Innocent XII.
1746. Colored marbles.
St. Peter's, Rome

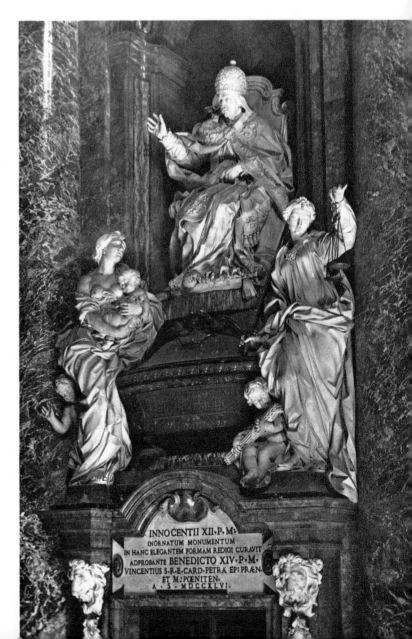

sculpture of the period is frequently dazzling; it is the primary attraction of the *Disinganno* by Francesco Queirolo (1704–1762) in the Cappella Sansevero dei Sangro in Naples (fig. 368). In this allegory the winged figure representing Intellect rescues Humanity from the Net of Deception. Queirolo's display of skill in execution is breathtaking, but the group shows nothing of the impassioned conviction with which Bernini treated a similar problem in his *Truth* in the Borghese Gallery, Rome.

Of the sculptors of the period, Pietro Bracci

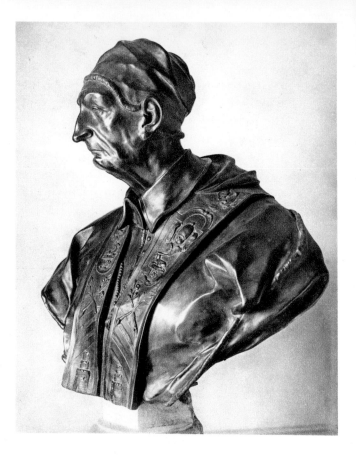

368. FRANCESCO QUEIROLO. *Allegory of Deception.*
Mid-18th century. Marble. Cappella Sansevero dei Sangro, Naples

369. PIETRO BRACCI.
Portrait of Pope Benedict XIII.
1724–30. Bronze, lifesize.
Signora Giusta Novelli
Collection, Rome

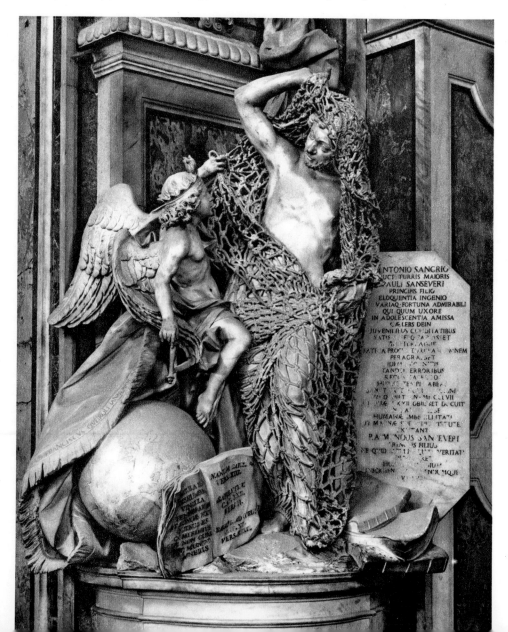

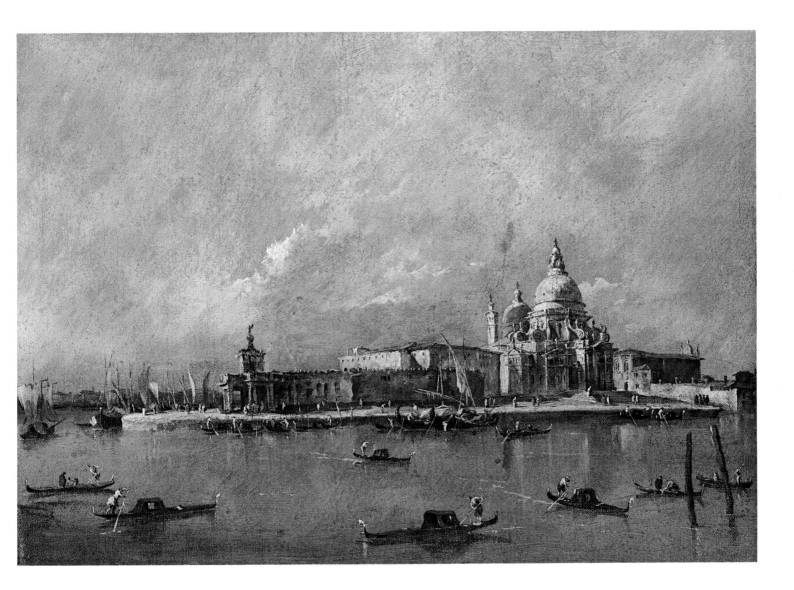

Colorplate 53. FRANCESCO GUARDI. *View of the Church of Santa Maria della Salute and the Old Customs House.*
c. 1785. 19×26¼″. Palace of the Legion of Honor, San Francisco

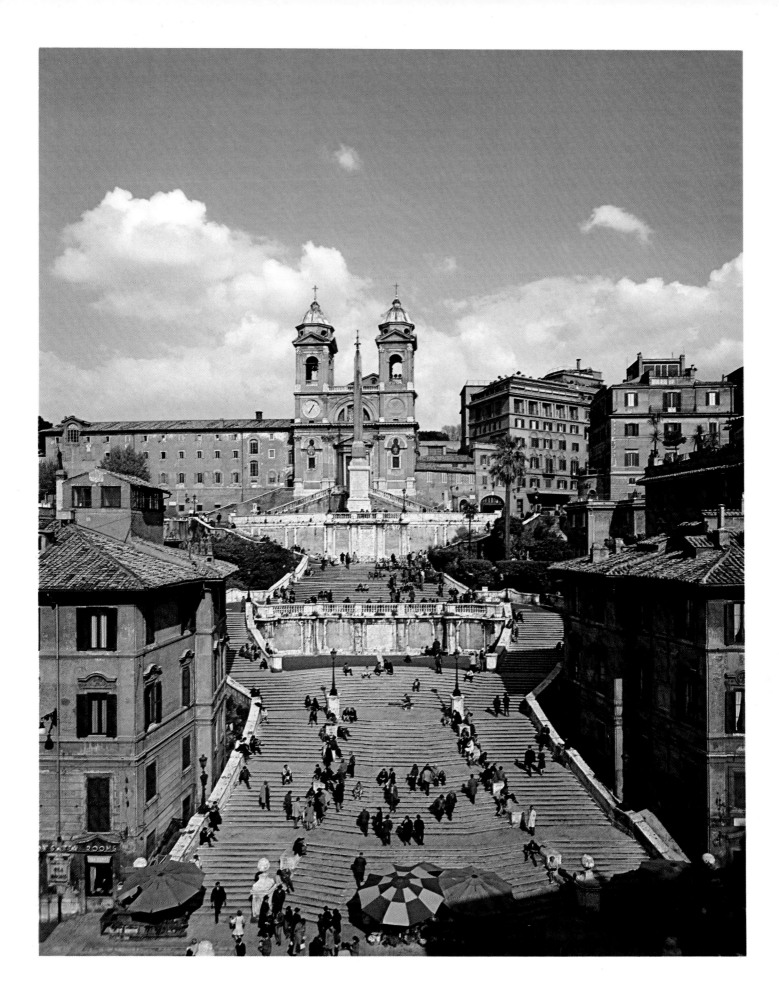

Colorplate 54. FRANCESCO DE SANCTIS. Spanish Steps. 1723–25. Rome

(1700–1773) stands out from among his contemporaries as a remarkably sensitive portraitist (fig. 369). It was Bracci too, who was responsible for much of the sculpture of the Trevi Fountain in Rome (fig. 370).[10] His elegant Neptune there makes a delightful Rococo interpretation of Bernini's baroque figure style. However, in sculpture Italy was overshadowed by France in the eighteenth century. Not until Antonio Canova (1757–1822) did a sculptor of truly international importance appear again in Italy. But Canova's Neoclassical style put an end to the Baroque and Rococo trends that had dominated Italian sculpture for about one hundred and fifty years.

370. NICOLA SALVI, GIUSEPPE PANNINI, PIETRO BRACCI, and FILIPPO DELLA VALLE. Trevi Fountain. 1732–62. Rome

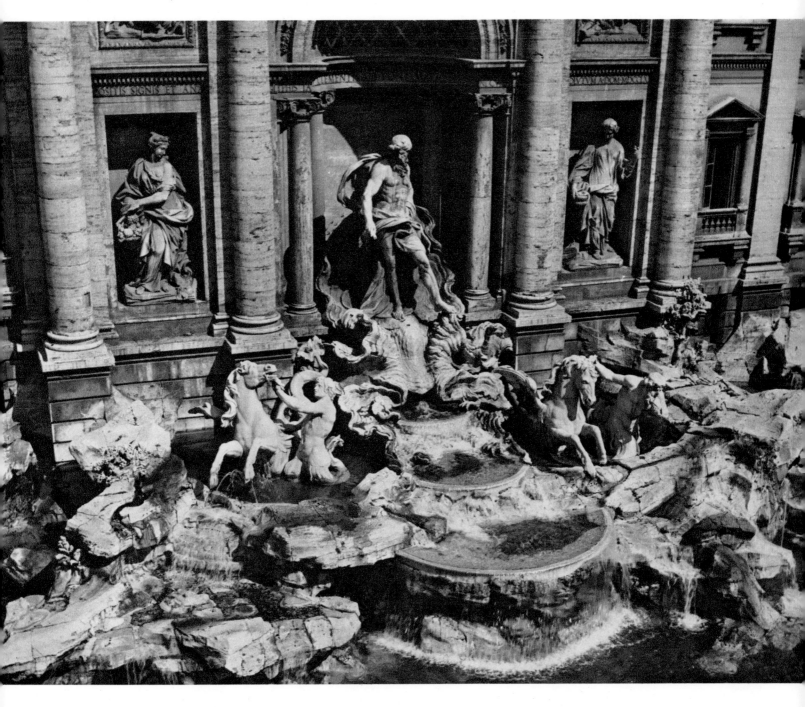

ARCHITECTURE

Italian architects in the eighteenth century rarely allowed themselves the kind of decorative license that characterizes so much of the architecture of the period in France and Germany; in fact, there are not very many architectural monuments in Italy from the eighteenth century that can properly be described as Rococo, if by that term we have in mind interiors like Boffrand's Salon Ovale (fig. 346) and façades like the Asam brothers' Church of St. Johann Nepomuk (fig. 413). Yet if Italian architects of the time generally showed more decorative restraint than their Northern colleagues, they nonetheless shared some characteristic approaches to planning, composition, and the use of light and shadow.

A comparison of the façade of San Giovanni in Laterano in Rome (1732–36; fig. 371) by Alessandro Galilei (1691–1737) with Carlo Maderno's façade of St. Peter's (fig. 20), built more than a century earlier, provides a striking example of how traditional forms were modified in Italy according to new, eighteenth-century architectural ideals. Galilei, whose design was chosen over twenty-two other entries in competition for the commission, based his façade on Maderno's scheme. However, his design is in every way lighter, more elegant, and more pictorial than Maderno's. At St. Peter's the columns that rest heavily on the ground express the great weight of the building; at San Giovanni the structure seems light and easily borne by the columns and pilasters, which rise from high pedestals. Galilei used an elegant Palladian motif and a delicate balcony on the second story of the central bay, and, compared to Maderno, he reduced the weight and expanse of the crowning pediment. Most important, he carved out great rectangular and arched openings in the façade that produce a lively, pictorial play of light and shade and create the effect of a kind of skeletal screen allowing a free flow between interior and exterior space. His intention, it seems, was to revise Maderno's scheme in order to suggest something of the character and open, graceful effect of a Roman temple front.[11]

In terms of planning, the most famous eighteenth-century monument in Rome is undoubtedly the Spanish Steps (colorplate 54; fig. 372), executed between 1723 and 1725 by Francesco de Sanctis (1693–1740).[12] The steps connect main traffic arteries in the city, and provide a dynamic, irregularly shaped link between the Church of Trinità dei Monti and the Piazza di Spagna. They expand

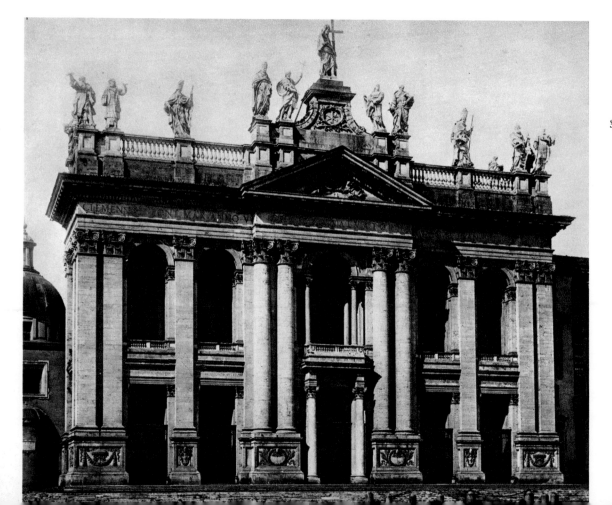

371. ALESSANDRO GALILEI. Façade, S. Giovanni in Laterano. 1732–36. Rome

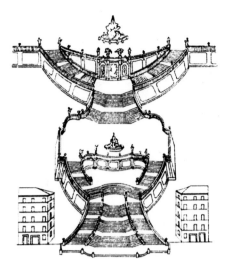

372. FRANCESCO DE SANCTIS.
Plan, Spanish Steps. 1723–25. Rome (see colorplate 54)

and contract horizontally, and in their vertical course their plan changes from concave to convex, while they are interrupted by broad terraces and divide at the top into two curving flights. This produces constantly shifting visual and spatial relationships for those using the stairs, and, from the piazza, the animation and perspective of the vista create one of Italy's most captivating passages of urban scenography. This feeling for the scenic possibilities of architecture has its source in works of the seventeenth century, but now its

importance increased greatly, affecting, as has been mentioned (pages 350–352), the history of painting as well as of architecture.

Among the distinguished architects active in Rome in the eighteenth century one must mention Filippo Raguzzini (c. 1680–1771) and Ferdinando Fuga (1699–1782). The former was responsible for the Piazza Sant'Ignazio (1727–28) and the latter for the Palazzo della Consulta (1732–37) and the façade of Santa Maria Maggiore (1741–43). However, the commanding Italian architect of the eighteenth century, Filippo Juvarra (1678–1736), worked outside of Rome. Juvarra was born in Messina, but about 1704 he went to Rome and joined the studio of Carlo Fontana. In 1714 he became architect to King Vittorio Amadeo II of Savoy, and thereafter, although he visited Portugal, London, Paris, and Madrid, his major work was done in and around Turin. Between 1717 and 1731 he built the Superga (fig. 373), a church high

373. FILIPPO JUVARRA.
Exterior, Superga,
Monastery Church.
1717–31. Near Turin

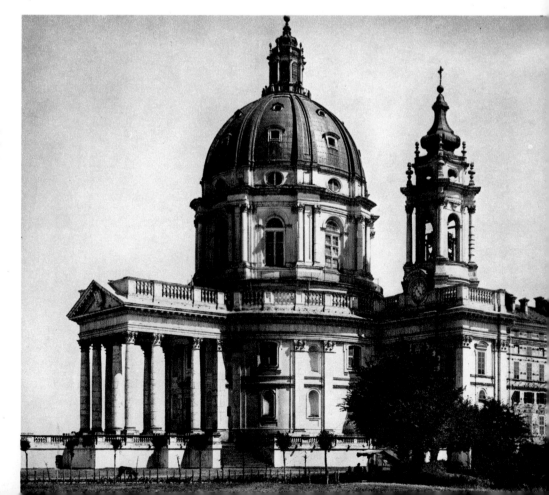

in the hills outside Turin. The central plan of the church and its high drum and dome suggest a relationship to the slightly earlier Church of the Invalides in Paris (fig. 147), which Juvarra would have known from engravings. Like Mansart's building it is a kind of crowning ornament for a larger structure, this time a monastery. However, although Mansart's design is remarkably open in its insistent use of large shadowed recesses, it seems to compose on a plane, and the façade clearly marks the boundary between interior and exterior space. Juvarra related his church to the monastery and to the space in front of it by a dynamic sequence of changing shapes that achieves an extraordinary pictorial effect. One third of the circular church is embedded in the old monastery, whose near, short side was refaced so that it corresponds to the exterior elevation of the new building. The bulk of the round church surges outward from the straight wall of the monastery; against the great cylinder is a cubical, airy portico, a variation of the classical scheme of the Pantheon in Rome. Vertically, the architect created a progression of three units of equal height—the body of the church, the drum, the dome—that merge easily as pilasters flanking niches give way to paired columns, which, in turn, yield to the tapering ribs of the dome. The drum and dome are majestically posed between the lighter, rather fanciful flanking towers.

The same inventive and sophisticated treatment of architectural forms is found in the royal hunting palace that Juvarra built at Stupinigi (1729–33; fig. 374), also outside Turin. The buildings are dominated by the great oval salon, from which four arms extend to create an X-shaped plan. Two of the arms continue out until they link up with other buildings and begin the vast hexagon enclosing a court that opens, on the farther side into a second, squarish court. Beyond this are the broad lawns of a large hemicycle (not Juvarra's responsibility). It is evident that the design, with its great spaces, its play of irregular shapes, and the elegance of the wall articulation, parallels contemporary

374. FILIPPO JUVARRA. Air View, Royal Hunting Palace. 1729–33. Stupinigi

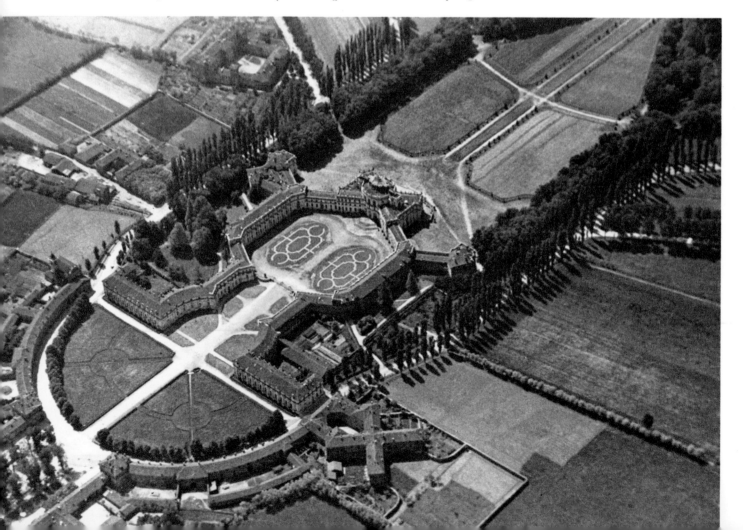

French architecture. One thinks of the spatial sequence and the graceful articulation of Héré's Place Stanislas (fig. 349) and, of course, of Boffrand's second plan for La Malgrange (fig. 348).[13] There were, in fact, important connections and an exchange of ideas in the eighteenth century between Italian and French architects, and between both these and German architects.[14]

The outstanding architectural monument of the eighteenth century in southern Italy is the twelve-hundred-room Royal Palace constructed at Caserta (fig. 375), some twenty miles north of Naples. The palace was begun in 1752 and finished in 1774, after the death of its architect, Luigi Vanvitelli (1700–1773). Vanvitelli, the son of a Dutch painter, Gaspard van Wittel, was born in Naples, but until he was called by Charles III to build the palace at Caserta he was active in Ancona, Siena, and Rome, where he was trained. The huge palace, surrounded by vast stretches of geometrically patterned gardens, was clearly designed to emulate and rival Versailles. Some details, like the chapel at Caserta, are, in fact, modeled on corresponding structures at Versailles. Nonetheless, Vanvitelli's palace is remarkably original in its

brilliant application of scenographic architectural principles. An analysis of the plan[15] reveals a multitude of changing, unexpected vistas and spatial combinations. From the entrance the spectator is treated to a view that extends through the whole width of the palace and along the main axis of the gardens beyond. The octagonal vestibules open on all sides and provide entrances onto the diagonal axes of the courtyards. The grand staircase (fig. 376), with its multiplicity of directions and plurality of visual effects, is the scenographic mas-

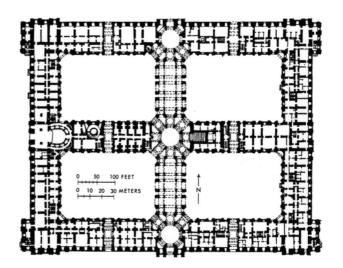

375, 376. LUIGI VANVITELLI.
Plan and Grand Staircase,
Royal Palace.
1752–74. Caserta

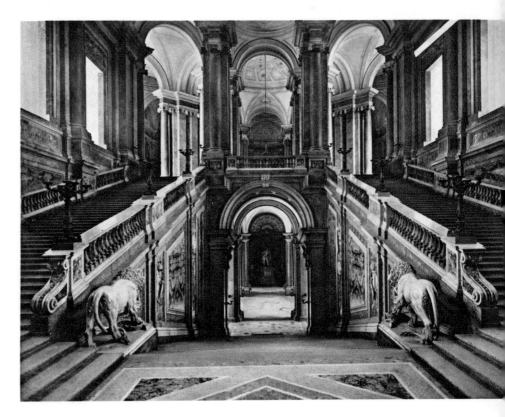

terstroke at Caserta. A broad first flight leads to a landing from which two lateral flights turn and rise to the light-filled vaulted octagonal space above, where a screen of arches interrupts, deflects, and redirects the view.

Despite the animated play of light and space at Caserta, the palace—in plan a rigidly organized and self-contained rectangular block enclosing four separated rectangular courtyards—points to the ideals of the coming Neoclassical age. However, it should be recognized that Vanvitelli, along with Juvarra and Galilei, belonged to a tradition, represented at the turn of the previous century by Carlo Fontana, that had always stressed formal discipline and rejected the inventive architectural irregularities that Borromini and others had introduced.

Of course, the Borrominesque trend had its followers in the eighteenth century. In Rome there were such architects as Specchi and Raguzzini, and in Piedmont this current had its most brilliant representative, Bernardo Antonio Vittone (1702–1770). Vittone, who studied with Juvarra in Turin, managed to reconcile aspects of his master's work with Guarini's architectural forms. The small Church of Santa Chiara (begun 1742) at Brà, not far from Turin, is one of the architect's masterpieces. The complicated flow of the interrelated spaces designed by Vittone is evident in the plan (fig. 377), where four slender piers define a main circular space surrounded by oval chapels. However, Vittone's tour de force is his design of the upper zone (fig. 378). Above the elegant high arches of the chapels and below the vault, the view opens out to a brilliantly lit wide gallery. The gallery greatly reduces the area of the vault, which seems stretched above the spectator like an inflated canopy with its four corners fixed to the piers. It is flooded by light from the lantern and from the unorthodox openings in each section of the vault. Through these "windows" one looks into the outer shell, where there is a painted heaven with saints and angels.

The luminous vaulting of Santa Chiara, almost fragile in its diaphanous delicacy, elegantly ornamented with thin, curvilinear decoration, and painted in lovely pale blue and gold, seems really to parallel French and German Rococo architecture. However, perhaps the term "barocchetto" ("little baroque"), favored by some scholars, most aptly describes this Italian eighteenth-century style. Indeed, it is evident that it was a child of the baroque tradition that goes back, through Guarini (fig. 47), to Borromini (fig. 42). It was the last child, too, for by the time Vittone died the Neoclassical reaction was conquering Europe.

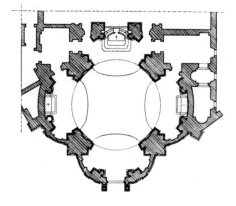

377. 378.
BERNARDO ANTONIO VITTONE.
Plan and Interior of Vault,
S. Chiara.
Begun 1742. Brà

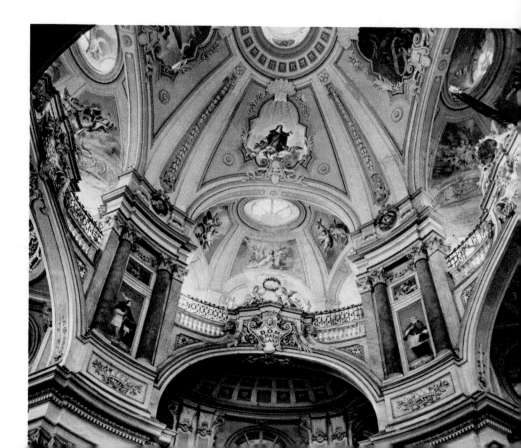

9

English Painting in the Eighteenth Century

The vigor and originality of British seventeenth-century architecture—not to mention British poetry and music—was not matched by British painting or sculpture. Up to the very end of the century not one of the native painters was of more than local significance; in sculpture this state of affairs continued throughout the eighteenth century. The classicizing John Michael Rysbrack of Antwerp (1694–1770) and the Berninesque Louis François Roubiliac of Lyons (1702/5–1762) were the most accomplished sculptors working in England. Large-scale commissions such as the ceiling of the Banqueting House in Whitehall and the vestibule at Hampton Court went to foreign artists (Rubens and Honthorst respectively). In portraiture—a field that provided the bulk of all commissions—no English artist was as successful with the wealthy patrons in the first half of the century as the Flemish Van Dyck (see pages 213–14) or, in the second half, the Dutch Pieter Van der Faes (better known as Sir Peter Lely; 1618–1680) and the German Gottfried (alias Godfrey) Kneller (1646–1723).[1] It may well be that the Stuarts, because of their close dynastic ties with Continental families and the persistent cultural

links maintained by them abroad, as well as the Hanoverians and their courts fostered a snobbish attitude comparable to that which prompted cultured Americans around 1900 to collect Barbizon School landscapes and English portraits rather than works by Mount and Homer, and to prefer Boldini to Eakins.

Whatever the reasons, it is clear that the English artists of talent and originality who finally appeared at the turn of the century felt they had to overcome a prejudice against native talent as well as the tyranny of the old masters. No one was more conscious of this situation, or fought the battle for recognition with more gusto, than William Hogarth (1697–1764), although James Thornhill (1675/77–1734), his father-in-law, had preceded him in this effort. There is a certain irony in the fact that these painters who protested so vigorously against the preference shown to foreigners were themselves deeply indebted to foreign art. Thornhill, surely the most forceful English painter of his generation, followed the grand decorative style of Baciccio and Pozzo (perhaps with some influence from Rubens) when he covered walls and ceiling of the vast "Painted Hall" at Green-

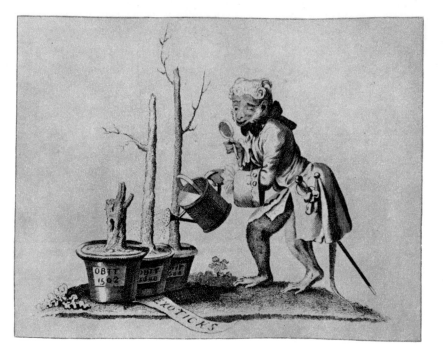

379. WILLIAM HOGARTH. *Exotics*
(engraved tailpiece to the
artist's catalogue). 1761.
Avery Architectural Library,
Columbia University, New York

wich (fig. 305) with illusionistic paintings. Only an Englishman, though, would have painted two ponderous warships into a ceiling decoration.[2]

Hogarth, too, was familiar with and influenced by foreign art both past and present, but he did his best to saw off the branch on which he sat. Moreover, he used his art to make fun of the "connoisseurs," represented by men like Lord Shaftesbury and Samuel Richardson, who admired the dark old masters that time had "smoked into worth." Inspired perhaps by Chardin's monkey-antiquarian (1740), Hogarth ridiculed, in the tailpiece of the exhibition catalogue of 1761, the connoisseur shown as a monkey watering a dead tree (fig. 379).[3]

Fortunately, Hogarth was more than a man with an ax to grind. He was a painter of remarkable flexibility and force. Even though not all Lely's women were "female insipidities," nor all of Kneller's men "unprepossessing males . . . in red coats" (like those decorating Thorne's Hall in Trollope's *Barchester Towers*), it is clear that Hogarth's pert Mary Edwards represents a new breed in English portraiture (colorplate 55). In his portrait of kindly Captain Coram (1740), middle-class respectability is rendered in the traditional terms of the state portrait, without demeaning the latter or making the former ludicrous.

Pictures as lively as these could never have come from the assembly line of the Lely or Kneller studios. In his desire to animate his models, however, Hogarth occasionally forced contrived narrative elements into his portraiture. This is particularly true of his portrait groups. In the picture of the Cholmondeley family (fig. 380), a good example of the so-called conversation piece, the younger boys unceremoniously romp across the furniture while little departed Cholmondeleys, in keeping with an old iconographic idea, fly overhead in the form of equally playful *putti*. The more ceremonious Graham children (1742; fig. 381) are engaged in a minor drama involving a music box, a caged canary, and a cat that is up to no good. In his portrait of David Garrick, the celebrated Shakespearean actor and playwright, Hogarth deflated the rhetoric of a declamatory pose by introducing Mrs. Garrick behind her husband's chair; unseen by him, she appears to be ready to snatch the pen from his hand. When he finally placed a stolid bulldog into a canvas containing also—as a picture within a picture—a portrait of himself, his audience surely recognized that the dog was taking the place traditionally reserved, in this context, for a muse or personification of fame.

As a humorist Hogarth followed the advice in

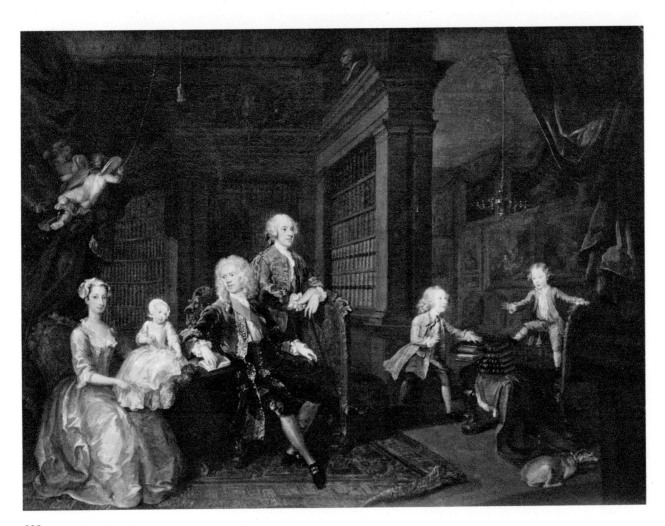

380. WILLIAM HOGARTH.
*Portrait of the
Cholmondeley Family.*
1732. 29½ × 38″.
Collection Marquis of
Cholmondeley, London

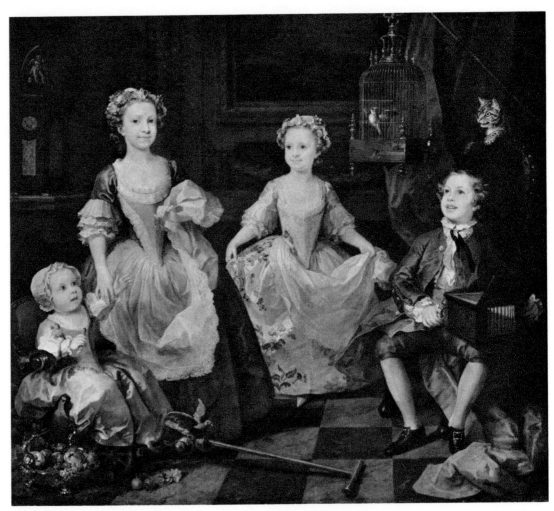

381. WILLIAM HOGARTH.
*Portrait of
the Graham Children.*
1742. 61¼ × 63¾″.
Tate Gallery, London

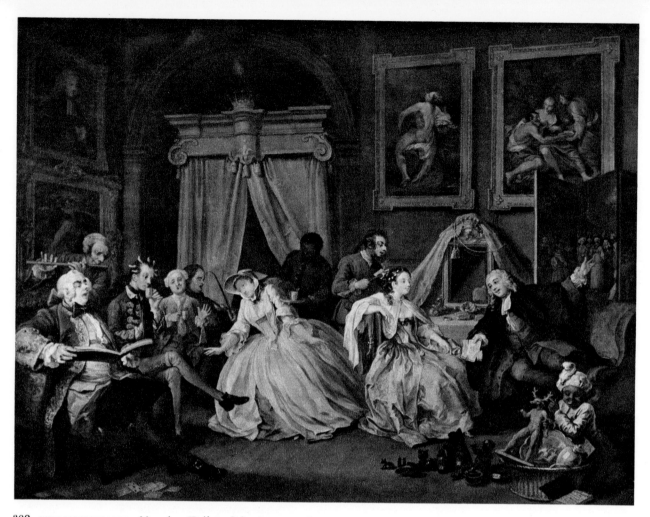

382. WILLIAM HOGARTH. *Morning Toilet of the Countess*. Scene IV, *Marriage à la Mode.*
1743–45. 27 × 35″. National Gallery, London

Horace's *Satires* (I, 1, 24) to use humor for moral ends. Illustrating in serial form the careers of "Mary Hackabout" *(Harlot's Progress)* or "Tom Rakewell" *(Rake's Progress),* he used the hallowed method of the narrative cycle to preach on the evils that befall the unchaste and the wastrel. His masterpiece in this genre, and like the others distributed with considerable financial success in engraved form, is *Marriage à la Mode* (1743–45). The ill-fated union between the flighty daughter of a *nouveau riche* and the unprincipled heir to the noble title of "Count Squanderfield" runs its pathetic if somewhat lurid course of dissipation, adultery, murder, and squalid death. Each tableau tells its part of the story in innumerable meaningful details. The old Dutch method of using paintings within pictures for special narrative effects

was used with unrelenting explicitness, especially in the scenes of the wedding contract, the levée of the countess, and her pitiful end. The connection with the theater and its conventions is particularly striking in *Marriage à la Mode.* The story itself, the behavior of the actors, and even the arrangement of the settings are clearly connected with the stage. It is no more than historic justice that one of the incidents, the *Morning Toilet of the Countess* (fig. 382), provided the model for one of the most effective operatic scenes of the modern stage, in the first act of Richard Strauss's *Der Rosenkavalier;* even Hogarth's little turbaned Negro boy reappears in the opera in a silent, though significant, role.

Marriage à la Mode is one of the clearest examples of the French influence on Hogarth's art.

368

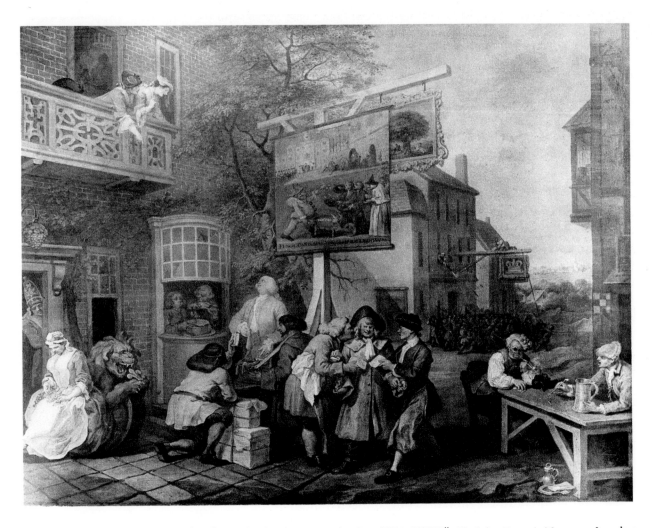

383. WILLIAM HOGARTH. *Canvassing for Votes*. Scene II, *An Election*. 1754. 40×50″. Sir John Soane's Museum, London

Just before painting this cycle he had been in France (1743). Whether or not he had actually seen Chardin's work, it is hardly accidental that *Marriage à la Mode* was painted with a pictorial delicacy and compositional deliberateness that far surpass all of Hogarth's earlier efforts in this vein. The best pictures of the set foreshadow the master's last works, which, in purely pictorial terms, are his freest. The four pictures known together as *An Election* (fig. 383), though more crowded and more grotesque than *Marriage à la Mode,* are painted with a truly stunning virtuosity, and the celebrated *Shrimp Girl* (fig. 384) pays homage to Frans Hals while anticipating the debonair bravura of Fragonard.

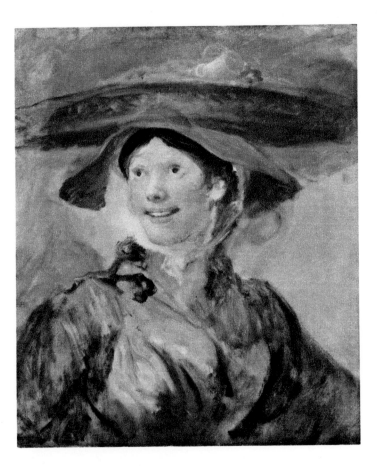

384. WILLIAM HOGARTH. *Shrimp Girl.*
Oil sketch, 25×20¾″.
National Gallery, London

With all the shortcomings of his art and character, his commercialism, his pugnaciousness, and his lapses into bad taste, Hogarth is the first English artist of international stature. His moralizing subjects, echoed in England in the works of Northcote, were adopted in France, though with less wit and inventiveness, by Greuze, under the influence of Diderot's enthusiasm for *"la peinture morale."* Moreover, the subsequent development of English and Continental caricature (Rowlandson, Gilray, Daumier) is profoundly in his debt.

Technically accomplished and psychologically incisive though they were, Hogarth's portraits apparently lacked that extra element of flattery that is an essential ingredient in social portraiture; he certainly never achieved the popularity as a painter of portraits that was enjoyed by two of his younger countrymen, Sir Joshua Reynolds (1723–1792) and Thomas Gainsborough (1727–1788). Both painters had a manner that must have been pleasing to their models, but they differed greatly in their approach. In a memorable analysis of their portraits, Edgar Wind not only pinpointed these differences but connected them with two basic attitudes of human behavior formulated by David Hume on the one hand and by Samuel Johnson, James Beattie, and Edmund Burke on the other.[4]

The basic conflict was alluded to in Reynolds' eulogy of Gainsborough after his rival's death. Ending years of mutual coldness, if not hostility, they had recently made peace, since each could not help recognizing the other's genius; Reynolds, conscious of his responsibilities as president of the Royal Academy, felt obliged to temper his praise of Gainsborough with a warning to his students. Gainsborough, he said, had seen the world "with the eye of the painter, not the poet."[5] This was a clear allusion to Horace's dictum that painting should follow poetry. Reynolds was deeply convinced that art was only worthy of the name if it poetically transfigured reality. In his own portraits he followed the "grand manner" of the French academicians, heightening the effect

through the addition of fitting formal or iconographic elements. Military heroes were rendered in dramatic light and heroic poses; actors were shown in favorite roles; and ladies were disguised as goddesses, saints, or vestal virgins if their social activity did not make a Thaïs or a Danaë appropriate. He also paid his respects to tradition by "quoting," more or less literally, from the ancients or the masters of the Renaissance.[6] Thus one lady holding a child might strike the pose of a Raphael *Madonna,* while another might evoke Salviati's *Allegory of Chastity.* Mrs. Siddons, famous as a dramatic actress, was modeled after Michelangelo's prophets on the Sistine Ceiling when Reynolds painted her as the Tragic Muse, enthroned between Pity and Terror (fig. 385).

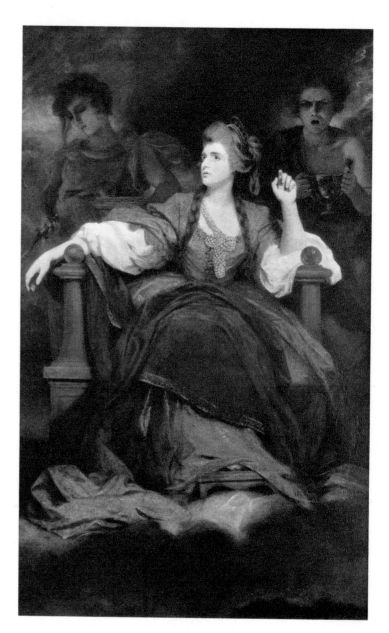

385. JOSHUA REYNOLDS. *Portrait of Mrs. Siddons as the Tragic Muse.* 1784. 93 × 57½"
Henry E. Huntington Library and Art Gallery, San Marino, California

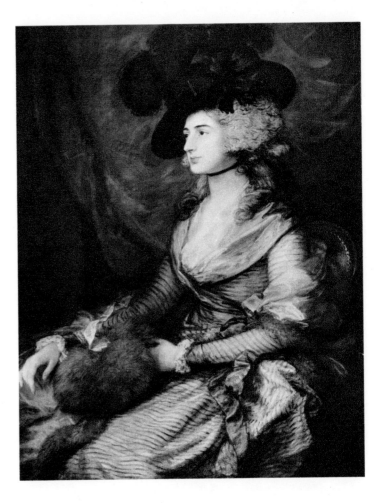

386. THOMAS GAINSBOROUGH.
Portrait of Mrs. Siddons. 1785.
49½×39".
National Gallery, London

All this was alien to Gainsborough's temperament and conception of art. Living in London only reluctantly, averse to all intellectual ambitions and pretensions, happiest when outdoors in nature or making music with friends, Gainsborough aimed at an art that could be described as "natural" in the sense in which Hume used the word. Just as to Hume the "natural" attitude of man was that which avoids both excessive pride and humility, so Gainsborough's models never posture or strut, and never pose as anything other than what they are—or what he felt they should be. For just as the Caroline society was probably quite unlike what Van Dyck made of it, so the ladies and gentlemen posing for Gainsborough were hardly the uniformly well-mannered, impassive, and slightly withdrawn beings in Gainsborough's canvases. Like Van Dyck, whom he worshiped, Gainsborough stressed slender proportions, elegant costumes, and a charming negligence of pose. Despite these similarities,

Gainsborough's figures can never be mistaken for anything but members of the fashionable society of eighteenth-century England. It is probably fair to say that Gainsborough's interpretation contributed more to shaping the historic image of that society than Reynolds' flashier portraits. And just as Watteau may have influenced the social behavior of eighteenth-century Frenchmen, Gainsborough's figures may have made an important contribution to the overt manners of English aristocracy; if nothing else, they shaped its popular image.

Thus, when Gainsborough painted Mrs. Siddons (fig. 386), he made no reference to her profession. Immaculately groomed and dressed with dazzling chic, she sits quietly on a chair, patiently posing for a painter who seems to have been enamored of the play of light on her striped dress, the soft undulations of her powdered hair, the extravagant silhouette of her plumed hat, but who did not give a farthing that his model was a

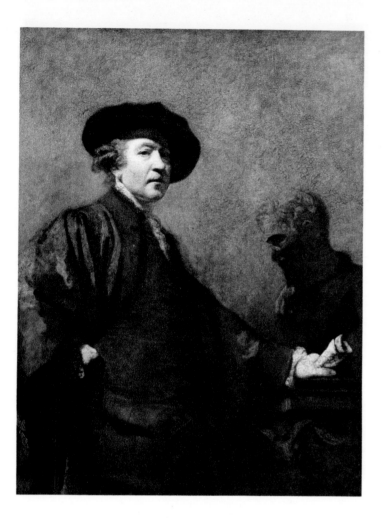

celebrated actress. Gainsborough's portrait of his
friend Dr. Schomberg nowhere hints that this
gentleman briefly stopping on a stroll in the country is a physician; and whereas Reynolds appears
in his self-portraits (fig. 387) either as the professional painter—once even borrowing an outfit
like Rembrandt's—or as the president of the
Royal Academy, Gainsborough's self-portraits are
in no way different from his other works.

Gainsborough's increasing success as a fashionable portraitist was bought at a price, as may be
seen in the contrast between his portrait of Mr.
and Mrs. Andrews (fig. 388) of about 1749 and
the picture known as the *Morning Walk* (fig. 389)
of 1785. Obviously the late work is the result of
skillful planning; the young couple walks in

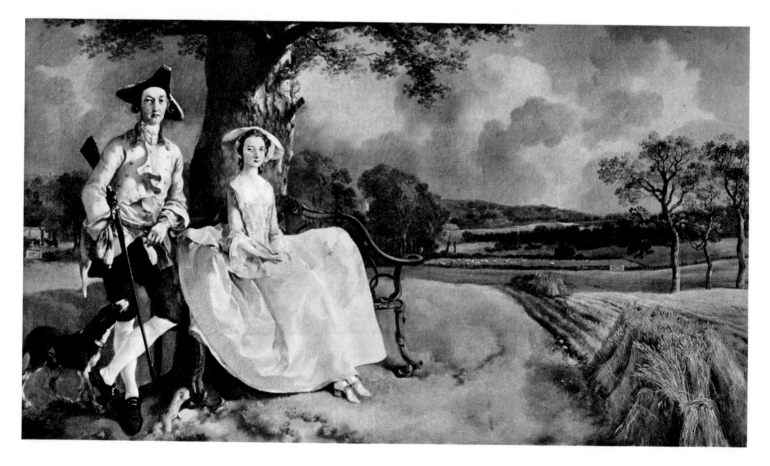

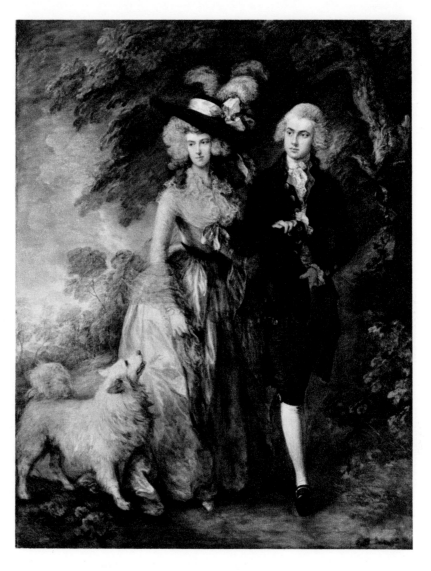

389. THOMAS GAINSBOROUGH.
Morning Walk. 1785. 93 × 70".
National Gallery, London

unison, and even the dog is in step. The execution has the shimmering lightness, the mercurial touch characteristic of Gainsborough's last years. The early work, by comparison, looks somewhat disjointed and unbalanced. And yet the young Andrews couple is real, and the scenery is part of a real English landscape. Gainsborough had begun his career by studying Dutch masters, and something of Dutch plainness still reverberates in the picture. Confronted with the unassuming solidity of the Andrews couple, the pair in the *Morning Walk* look as insubstantial as the landscape behind them. Toward the end of his life Gainsborough worked in this ethereal vein even when painting landscapes and rustic genre scenes, the so-called "fancy pictures" to which he devoted much time and thought.

Of the two great painters, Reynolds undoubtedly was the more versatile and the more vigorous. His range as portraitist includes not only the theatrical Mrs. Siddons (fig. 385) but also the frankly intimate Nelly O'Brien of 1762 (fig. 390). He had, above all, a sense of humor. Gainsborough's *Blue Boy* is nothing but a nostalgic evocation of Van Dyck. Reynolds' *Master Crewe as Henry VIII* is a witty paraphrase of Holbein. His masterpiece in this vein, however, is the portrait of *Garrick Between Tragedy and Comedy* (fig. 391; see page 366). Alluding to the famous type of the Choice of Hercules, best known from Annibale Carracci's example, Reynolds delightfully reverses the nature of the decision.[7] Instead of following Tragedy, who takes the place of Virtue in the Hercules pictures, Garrick follows Comedy

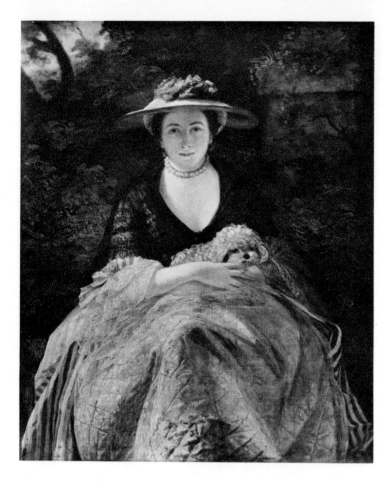

—Vice—not without an apologetic gesture, blaming it all on Comedy's irresistible pull.

The picture of Garrick's choice is not only of importance for a just appraisal of Reynolds; it is also revealing for the general artistic situation. No matter how serious Reynolds was as a representative and propagandist of the grand tradition, he could not resist poking fun at it when the situation permitted. Irony, wit, and a willingness not to take oneself too seriously are intellectual commodities more readily found in the eighteenth century than in the seventeenth. With the age of reason came also a gift for ironical self-examination. "Permit me to wear the beard of a philosopher till I pull it off and make a jest of it myself," Pope wrote to Swift (September 15, 1734). More subtly than Hogarth before him, Reynolds was capable of deflating the grand style of the Baroque, a clear sign that it had run its course.

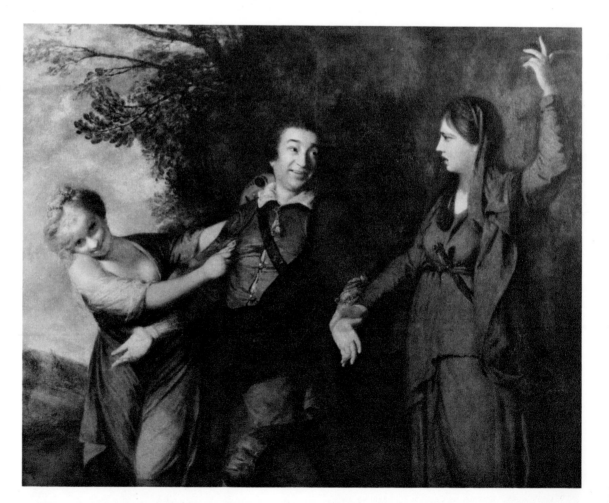

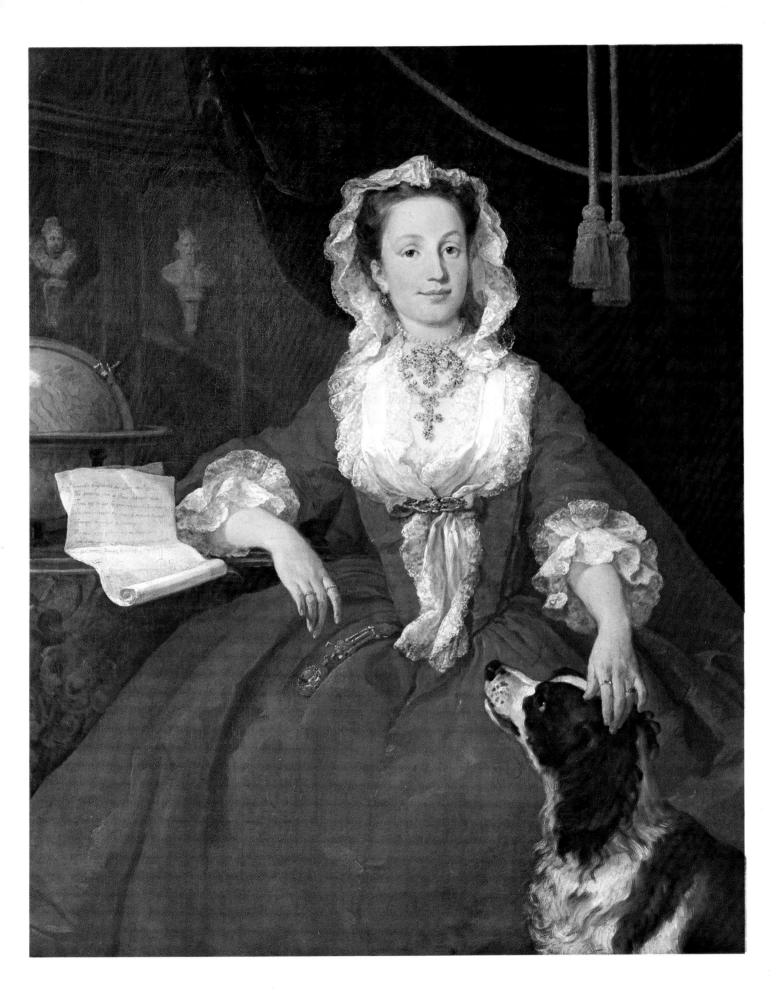

Colorplate 55. WILLIAM HOGARTH. *Portrait of Mary Edwards*. 1742. 49¾ × 40″. Copyright The Frick Collection, New York

Colorplate 56.   JOHANN BERNHARD and JOSEPH EMANUEL FISCHER VON ERLACH.
Interior of Prunksaal, Hofburg Library. Begun 1723. Vienna

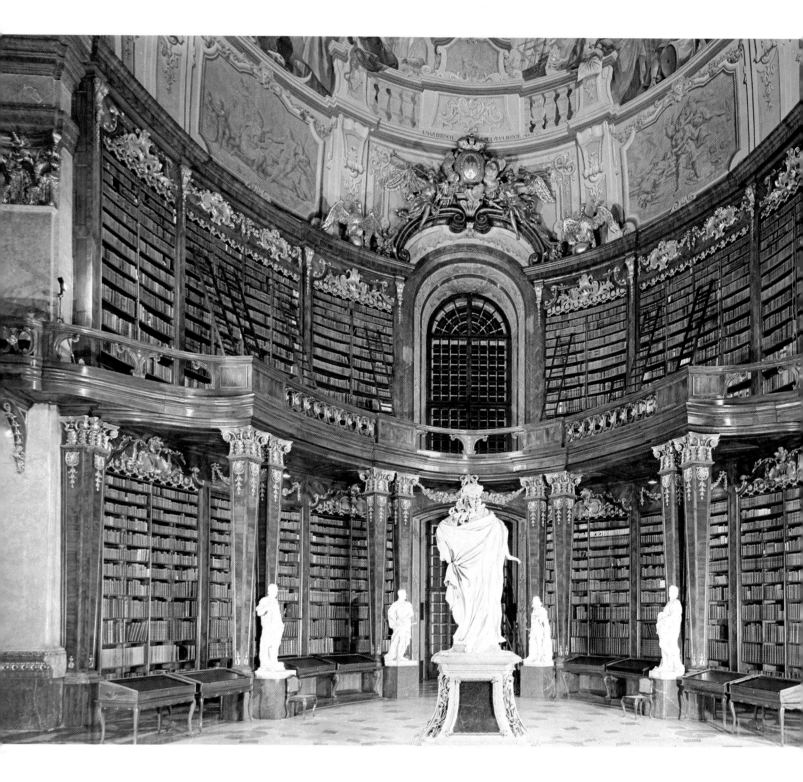

10

Germany and Austria in the Seventeenth and Eighteenth Centuries

ARCHITECTURE

No area of Europe had suffered more from the ravages of the Thirty Years' War (1618–48) than Germany. The speed of recovery varied from region to region, but so great had been the loss of life and goods, so impoverished were the leading social groups, and so low had fallen the literary and artistic standards that for a long time the level of German culture remained provincial. The only bright spot in a bleak picture was the preservation of craftsmen's skills. The miracle of German eighteenth-century art would have been impossible without a highly trained labor force capable of translating even the boldest ideas into concrete form.

Most major projects of the later seventeenth century were indeed entrusted to foreigners, chiefly Italian and French. Even in the eighteenth century foreign names, especially French, still abound, and some of the finest eighteenth-century works on German soil were produced by foreigners with special skills (Bustelli, the Galli Bibiena, and Tiepolo). Nevertheless, the majority of artists now active in Germany were indeed Germans. Contemporaries of the great German composers, from Bach and Händel to Gluck, Haydn, and

Mozart, they were their equals in their own field of activity.

The very word "German," however, ought to be used with some reservations. A German empire did in fact exist; the princes of the house of Hapsburg, residing in Vienna, were the duly elected emperors. In regard to effective political or economic control, however, the empire was hardly more than a fiction, and the "emperors" in Vienna never ruled more than their own Austria. "Germany" was a vast conglomeration of independent principalities governed by absolute rulers who could—and often did—dictate the religion of their subjects or sell them into military bondage.

Besides being split into a multitude of small states, Germany was deeply divided by religion. The largest Catholic countries—Bavaria and Austria—lay to the south; northern Germany was mostly Lutheran. For religious as well as geographic reasons the South gravitated to Italy, the North toward the Netherlands and Scandinavia. Yet, as the eighteenth century progressed, both regions fell increasingly under the spell of France, especially as the forces of the Enlightenment began to spread. Voltaire's occasionally stormy relationship with King Frederick the Great of Prussia was symptomatic of the process of cultural and intellectual reorientation.

The prince-bishops and abbots who ruled large areas of the Catholic regions almost invariably came from noble families. Perhaps the greatest of these was the Von Schönborn family, which at various times ruled many of the bishoprics. All were munificent builders of residences and churches.

Although the building mania, as it has been called, could be rationalized on the grounds that it kept money in domestic circulation, the basic motivation of many of these princelings appears to have been a "Versailles complex"—a desire to outdo others, no matter what the expense. More than one building reached posterity "in serf's shape" (*Knechtsgestalt*), to use Dehio's famous expression about Neresheim. There have also been losses, not the least through the bombing of World War II. Yet enough remains to permit us to study the last chapter in the history of the Baroque, and one of its finest.

The leading figures were architects. Their activity often extended far beyond the strictly artistic scope. Neumann, for instance, designed not only castles, churches, monasteries, and town houses but also bridges, pump works, fortifications, armories, spas, and even a glass factory. He also laid out streets and water conduits. During his heyday, no house could be built in Würzburg without his approval. In all large projects the architect was commander in chief of an army of sculptors, painters, carpenters, masons, glaziers, stuccoworkers, wallpaperers, and blacksmiths. Even international celebrities like Tiepolo worked within the framework staked out for them by the German architect.

Seen as a whole, German eighteenth-century art adopted those tendencies of the Baroque that tried to create an air of festivity and formal exuberance. In Protestant churches, which had to be much plainer in shape and decor than Catholic ones, it was the music that created the festive climate. For his orchestration of the music describing the Resurrection of Christ, Bach significantly relied on horns and trumpets, the traditional instruments to herald the entry or departure of a prince.

Appropriately, the German revival first manifested itself in Vienna. Being traditionally the eastern outpost of the Empire, Vienna was also the first to taste the fruits of the victories over the Turks, beginning in 1683 when Jan Sobieski broke the siege of Vienna, and continuing with the brilliant campaigns of Prince Eugene of Savoy. Almost immediately, the city on the Danube underwent a face-lifting that still determines her appearance.

In Johann Bernhard Fischer von Erlach (1656–1723)[1] and Johann Lukas von Hildebrandt (1668–1745)[2] Vienna had two of the most original architects of the age. Fischer had started as a sculptor, doing fountains and altars; during a prolonged stay in Italy (1685–86) he studied architecture, and he began his first buildings (for Salzburg) in the 1690s. Adopting ideas from both Borromini and Guarini, he filtered them through an essentially cool temperament, always aiming at lucidity and order. In his churches he preferred an oval plan for the main unit of space, placing it into the longitudinal axis; it so appears in his last and greatest church, the Karlskirche (Church of St. Carlo Borromeo) in Vienna (fig. 392), begun in 1715. Finished only after Fischer's death and less than faithful to his designs, the church still delights us with its uncluttered spaciousness, the warm beauty of its colors, and the pleasant rhythm of tall pilasters accentuating an alternating sequence of large arches and superimposed small ones. The famous façade (fig. 393), originally rising above the banks of the Wien River, is something of a grandiose freak. Putting into practice some of the ideas expounded in his book on a "historical architecture" (1721), Fischer combined in it elements of very different origin. A tall dome, rising on an unusually high tambour, dominates the center. Like Pietro da Cortona's dome of San Carlo al Corso (fig. 30), its cupola is

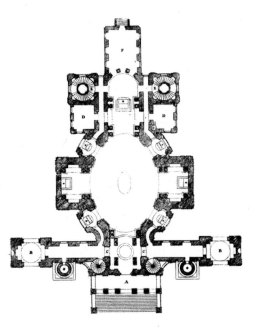

pierced by oval windows, but being turned by ninety degrees, they greatly contribute to the impression of soaring height. The dome surmounts a Pantheon-type porch of six Corinthian columns carrying a standard entablature and broad, unbroken pediment. To either side of the portico and in front of receding wings Fischer placed two high columns, covered with spiraling reliefs like their model, the Column of Trajan. The façade ends like that of St. Peter's, with bays containing arched passageways; these are crowned with stepped gables and picturesque, pagodalike roofs, piquantly reasserting the Baroque character of the whole composition.

Columns and archways are symbols of imperial triumph and were surely welcomed by Emperor

392, 393. JOHANN BERNHARD FISCHER VON ERLACH.
Plan and Façade, Karlskirche. Begun 1715. Vienna

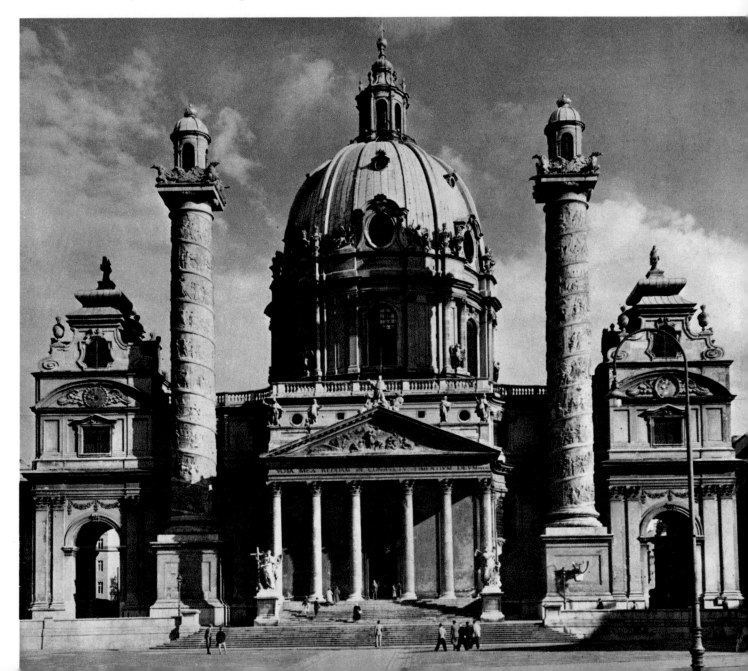

Charles VI, who had vowed the erection of the church during the plague of 1713; yet they also proclaim the freedom of the architect to avail himself readily of ideas from past ages and to combine them in any manner serving his purpose.

It is doubtful that Fischer aimed at a complete stylistic integration of all the parts of his façade. Nor is it surprising that the building remained an isolated case. Yet no matter how odd, it does have a strange, exotic beauty, foreshadowing, in some manner, the syncretistic idealism of Mozart's *Magic Flute*. The Baroque framework for the severely classical details of the design reminds us also of the eighteenth-century theatrical practice of dressing Roman heroes in wigs, and ancient goddesses in crinoline frocks.

Toward the end of his life Fischer made plans for the Hofburg. For its library he designed the famous Prunksaal (Hall of Splendor; colorplate 56), the largest and perhaps finest of all the splendid library rooms in Austrian and German palaces and monasteries, where the books themselves, bound in parchment or tooled leather, fulfill an eminently tectonic function among the free

rhythms of balconies and painted ceilings. The execution of the library lay in the hands of Fischer's gifted son Joseph Emanuel, who was also responsible for the finest single façade of the Hofburg complex, the Chancellery (Reichskanzlei; fig. 394), a model of elegant proportioning and delicate modulation on a monumental scale.

It was Fischer's great competitor, Lukas von Hildebrandt, however, who enriched Vienna with its most distinguished secular structure, the Palace of the Belvedere. Built as a summer residence for Prince Eugene of Savoy, it has retained much of its original enchantment even though all its parts have lost their furnishings and been turned into museums. The name "Belvedere" is taken from the garden pavilions that serve for casual entertainment or as goals for brief strolls.[3] Hildebrandt's Belvedere, however, is a full-fledged palace with separate buildings for servants. A spacious casino, known as the Lower Belvedere, lies across the lower end of a very long and relatively narrow property on a gentle hill outside the old city limits. The main building faces it at the other end, as the crowning feature

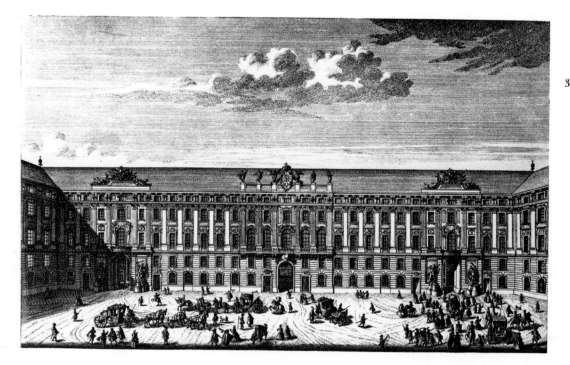

394. JOSEPH EMANUEL
FISCHER VON ERLACH.
Façade, Hofburg Chancellery.
1719. Vienna
(engraving by J. A. Corvinus)

OPPOSITE: 396. JOHANN LUKAS VON HILDEBRANDT.
Entrance Façade, Upper Palace, Belvedere.
1721–24. Vienna

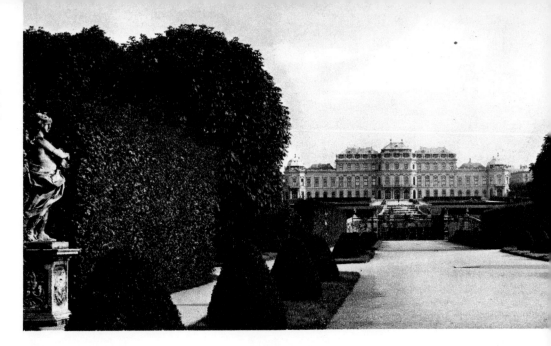

395. JOHANN LUKAS VON HILDEBRANDT.
View of Gardens and Upper Palace,
Belvedere. 1721–24. Vienna

of the composition (fig. 395). A garden with many terraces and fountains lies between them. Because of the drop of the ground, the garden façade of the upper Belvedere has one more story than the façade on the other side which contains the main entrance (fig. 396). The approaching visitor sees at first only a long one-story structure (though there are two higher units on either side of the central portico). A large basin in front adds a degree of informality by preventing an approach along a central axis. Once inside the arcaded portico, the visitor finds himself in an airy staircase from which he may either ascend to the main floor or descend toward the lower level and the gardens. (The magnificent panorama of Vienna visible from here in the eighteenth cen-

tury has been preserved in one of Bellotto's painstaking *vedute;* fig. 397.) The full poetry of the Upper Belvedere is seen only as one descends into the gardens and looks back; seen from a distance, the large building seems to float on top of the hill, its silhouette picturesquely accented by the corner pavilions and the high central body with its elegant French roof.

When Carlantonio Carlone, the last of the major Italian masters active in Austria, died in 1708, his place was taken by another native master, Jakob Prandtauer (1660–1726), the architect of Melk. Less intellectual than Fischer, and less sophisticated than Hildebrandt, Prandtauer possessed an elemental vigor and a unique sense of the spectacular. Both qualities make Melk an

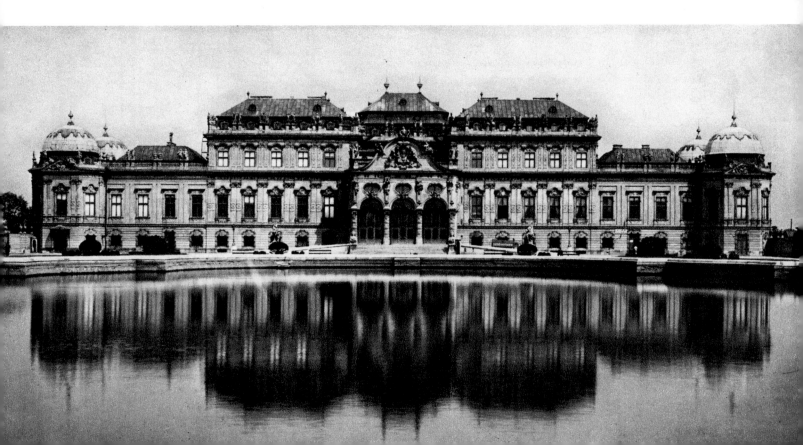

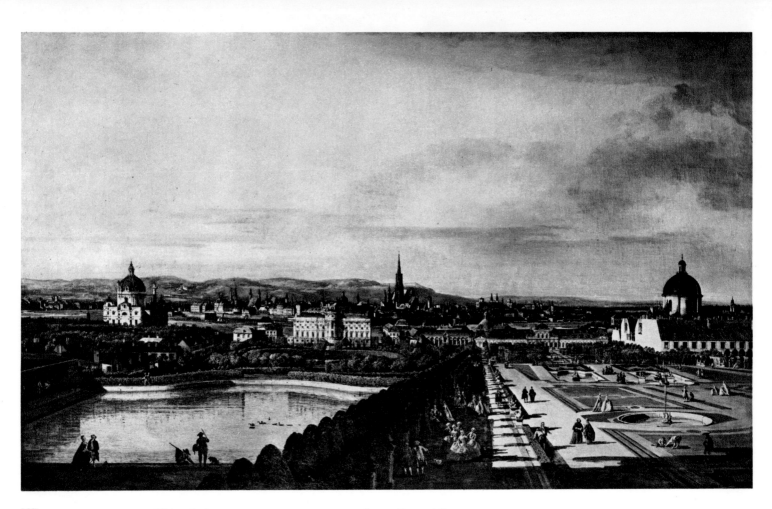

397. BERNARDO BELLOTTO. *View of Vienna from the Belvedere*. 1759/60. 53½ × 84¼"
Kunsthistorisches Museum, Vienna

exemplary representative of the late Baroque.
(They also may have been the reason Prandtauer
was never charged with a major job in the more
aristocratically refined world of Vienna.)

Melk's monastery and church rise on a steep
rock (colorplate 57; fig. 398); a branch of the
Danube that today passes only in front originally
flowed along one of its sides as well. Extending
from east to west for about eleven hundred feet,
the vast monastery buildings converge in two
arms toward the tip of the rock, containing on
their main level a large banquet hall at one end
and a delightful library at the other. From these
arms, which remain somewhat apart, an open
platform curves forward toward the river, linking
the two buildings and permitting a sweeping
view of the valley. The space between the converging ends of the monastery wings is filled by the
church. Partly screened below by the arcaded

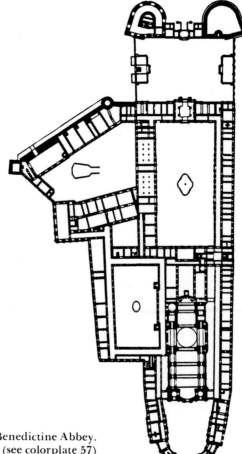

398. JAKOB PRANDTAUER. Plan, Benedictine Abbey.
Begun 1702. Melk (see colorplate 57)

platform, it rises to a dominant position by virtue of its dome and tall towers. Seen from afar, it emerges from the surrounding structures like a jewel from the prongs of a well-made setting. Nor was Prandtauer's role confined to devising a dramatic external effect. The interior of the church, in principle still following the pattern of Il Gesù, is distinguished by broad undulating moldings flowing around the church with the rhythmical majesty of a concerto grosso by Händel.

The complete integration of architectural structure and sculptural decor—essential in all Baroque buildings—was rarely more happily achieved than in the Dresden Zwinger, erected for August the Strong between 1710 and 1732.[4] The Zwinger is an open area—intended for performances of dances, operas, mock tournaments, the showing of fireworks, and similar diversions—enclosed by a succession of gate towers, corridors, and pavilions (fig. 399). These buildings were erected by two masters of equal genius, apparently working together in perfect harmony. Matthäus Daniel Pöppelmann (1662–1736), the architect, and Balthasar Permoser (1651–1732), the sculptor, had both studied in Italy. Indeed, Permoser was the foremost exponent in the North of Berninesque sculpture. Their collaboration can well be seen in one of the enclosure's key pieces, the "Wallpavillon" of 1716 (so called because it was built against the ramparts; fig. 400). The profusion of Permoser's sculpture is held in check by Pöppelmann's unfailing sense of proportion. The high open arcades below, and the equally high rounded windows above, create the necessary breathing spaces between Permoser's garlands, volutes, masks, escutcheons, flower urns, and exuberantly smiling bacchic caryatids. The sculpture, in fact, contributes substantially to the tectonic organization of the whole, by increasing the number of the caryatids—one, two, three—

400. MATTHÄUS DANIEL PÖPPELMANN and BALTHASAR PERMOSER. "Wallpavillon," Zwinger. 1716. Dresden

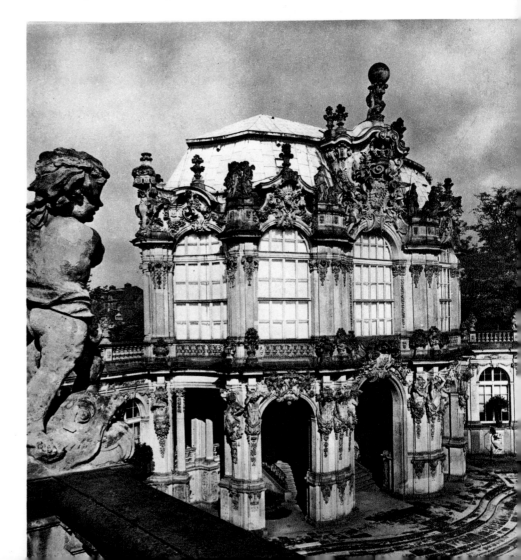

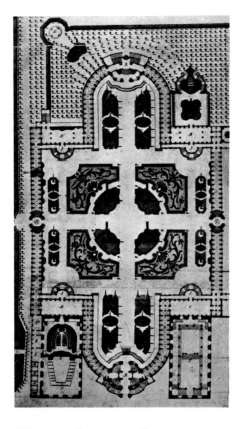

399. MATTHÄUS DANIEL PÖPPELMANN. Plan, Zwinger. 1710–32. Dresden

toward the middle, and by similarly enlarging the decorations of keystones and gables up to the triumphant explosion above the central window, Permoser helped realize Pöppelmann's intentions, stated clearly in the shape of the open arches and the gentle but unmistakable forward motion of the polygonally designed pavilion.

The particularly subtle balance of this edifice may be connected with new French influences.

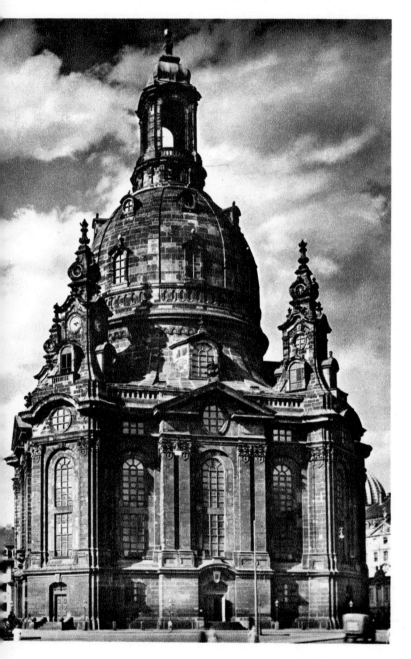

Pöppelmann had made a trip to Paris in 1715. The whole idea of the Zwinger is derived in some measure from the French *maison de plaisance,* and parts of the enclosure were devoted to the equally French idea of an *orangerie.* Pöppelmann, however, also knew Austrian models, some from personal acquaintance, others from the engravings of Decker's influential work published with the characteristic title *Der fürstliche Baumeister (The Princely Architect).* Yet when all is said and done, the Zwinger remains a work *sui generis,* unmatched in its buoyancy and cheer.

As a work of art, the Zwinger is a perfect foil for the prince for whom it was built, the ambitious, fun-loving, clever, and unprincipled King August (1670–1733), glorified as *Hercules Saxonicus* on top of the Wallpavillon. Although Saxony had been traditionally Lutheran, August had no compunction against becoming a Catholic when his newly won dignity as king of Poland made it expedient. The city of Dresden, however, remained a Lutheran stronghold: the Lutheran church, built on orders of its magistrate, turned out to be the largest Protestant church built during the entire age. Designed by the municipal "chief carpenter" Georg Bähr (1666–1738) and incorporating ideas of Johann Christoph Knöffel (1686–1752), the Frauenkirche (fig. 401) was begun in 1726 and after many difficulties, some of them financial, was finished in 1743, five years after Bähr's death. Like earlier Protestant churches it followed a central plan suited to sermons and community singing; yet it was as bold and unconventional for its time as—and probably more functional than—Wright's Guggenheim Museum is for ours. The interior is a high cylindrical shaft surrounded by five (later four) circles of "loges," seating thirty-six hundred people. Eight huge piers hold these galleries and support the bell-shaped dome, the full height of which is visible only from the outside. Only the flaring base of the

401. GEORG BÄHR. Frauenkirche.
1726–43. Dresden

384

Colorplate 57. JAKOB PRANDTAUER. Benedictine Abbey. Begun 1702. Melk

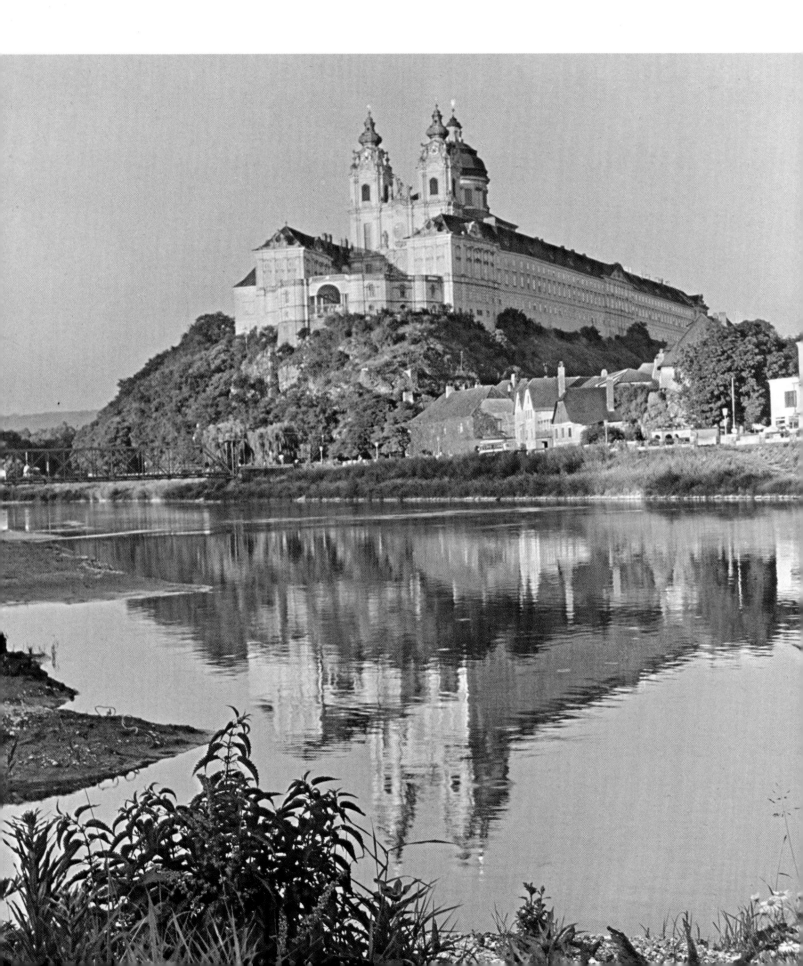

Colorplate 58. JOHANN BALTHASAR NEUMANN. Interior of Kaisersaal. Begun 1720
(frescoes by GIAMBATTISTA TIEPOLO, 1751–52). Residenz, Würzburg

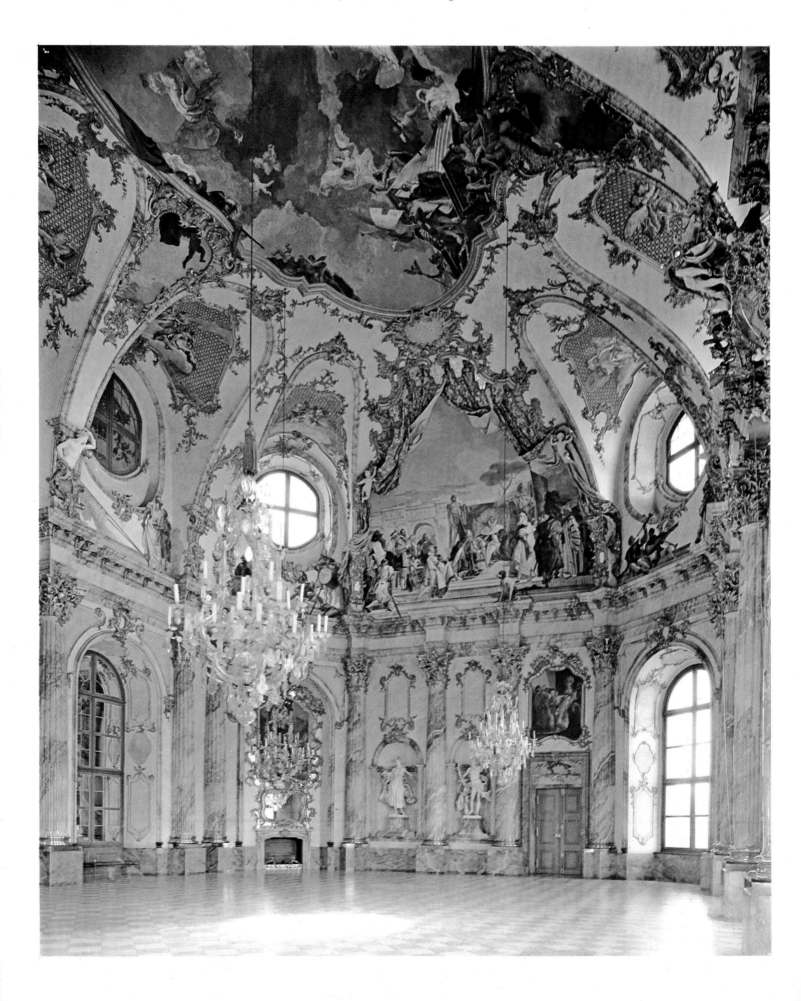

inner, shallower dome appears on the exterior, where it makes for a transition between the cylindrical core and the main shell of the building, which is square with blunted corners. Though the silhouette of the building is enriched by four graceful towers above these corners, its main feature is the dome, springing from the line at which the lower cupola turns from its concave beginning to its convex top, and ending with a high and airy lantern. Looking marvelously solid with its massive stone construction, the Frauenkirche seems indeed the very embodiment of Luther's sturdy faith. Yet following the fire-bombing of 1945 it collapsed, and unlike the Zwinger, has not been rebuilt.

In the years around 1700, developments in Vienna and Dresden were matched by the activities in Berlin, the young capital of the vigorous state of Prussia. Andreas Schlüter (1664–1714)[5] was the master capable of giving a distinct, and distinguished, physiognomy to the royal residence on the Spree River. Schlüter was trained as a sculptor, and like Bernini suffered the ignominy that a tower built from his designs had to be taken down because of faulty foundations. But whereas Bernini's career did not suffer seriously from this mishap, Schlüter's was practically ended by it. Dismissed from the court in 1706, he built little else, though the delightful Von Kamecke villa (fig. 402) dates from this period. When in 1713 he lost even his job as sculptor of the court, he left

Berlin and died a little later in St. Petersburg.

The misfortunes that had dogged him in life did not end with his death. Many of his buildings, including the Von Kamecke villa, were destroyed in World War II; the Royal Castle, which owed its most noble features to the period of Schlüter's activity (1698–1706), was severely damaged by bombs and finally razed by the East German government.

With it disappeared some of the most striking façades of the age (fig. 403). It is easy to trace individual motives of Schlüter's structures to Italian, French, and even classical models. Yet Schlüter achieved a synthesis having a severe grandeur all its own, notably in the entrance façades. These have either three or five bays, and, although the castle was designed by a sculptor, sculptural decor is used most sparingly. If Schlüter's architecture lacks the melodious grace of its Viennese contemporaries, it makes up for it by a certain sinewy virility befitting the hard and ambitious climate of the Prussian court

During the reign of the parsimonious King Frederick William I, Berlin suffered cultural stagnation. The arts were revived only when his son Frederick II the Great ascended the throne in 1740. By then tastes had changed; even a king preferred a secluded residence to a vast palace. Frederick II, an enthusiastic admirer of everything French and speaking that language more fluently than his own (though never correctly), built a country retreat near Potsdam that he

402. ANDREAS SCHLÜTER. Exterior, Von Kamecke House (destroyed). c. 1706. Berlin

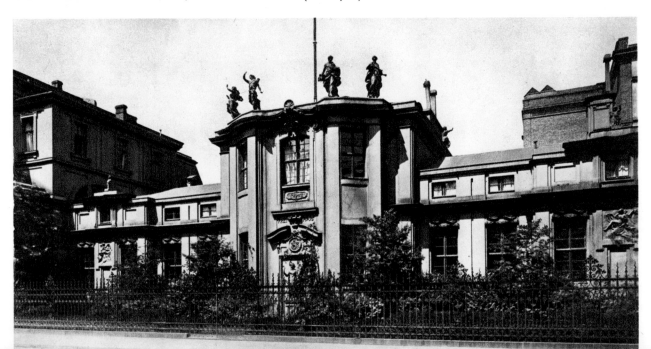

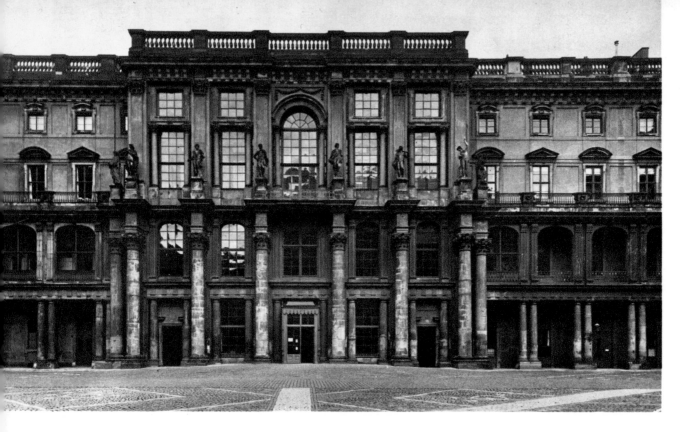

403. ANDREAS SCHLÜTER. Courtyard Façade, Royal Castle (destroyed). 1698–1706. Berlin

named Sanssouci (1745–47). Designed by a friend and born nobleman, Georg Wenzeslaus von Knobelsdorff (1699–1753), perhaps working from the king's own sketches, it is a long, low building, hugging the ground like a modern ranch house (fig. 404). Placed on a steep little hill, it is approached through a succession of garden terraces. The chief delight of Sanssouci is undoubtedly its sequence of lovely rooms embellished with Rococo ornaments of the airiest lightness (fig. 405). Its exterior, too, is most felicitous. The main feature of its decoration, the paired herms between high bay windows, was probably derived from Pöppelmann's Zwinger pavilions. But Per-

moser's figures there were part of a lavish decoration with little functional purpose; at Potsdam, the herms form an orderly phalanx beneath the clean lines of an unbroken entablature which they support with visible, if good-natured, strain.

Sanssouci clearly represents a new stylistic phase of eighteenth-century German art. This phase had begun around 1720 when a new generation of artists superseded the generation of Fischer von Erlach, Pöppelmann, and Schlüter. It was characterized by an increasing receptivity to the ideas and forms of the French Rococo, but its major contribution was the imaginative development

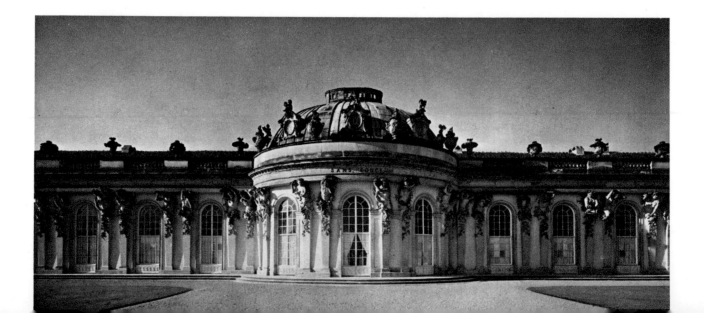

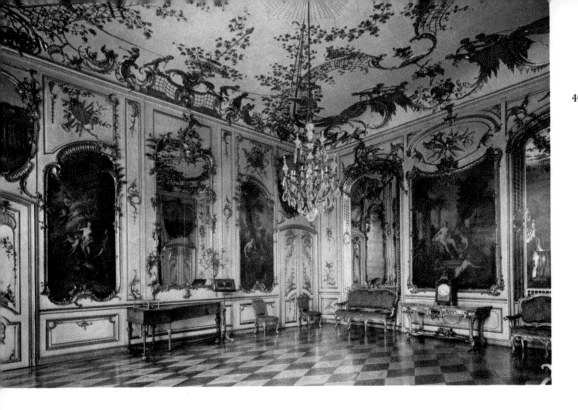

405. GEORG WENZESLAUS
VON KNOBELSDORFF.
Interior of Music Room,
Sanssouci.
1745–47. Potsdam

of the possibilities inherent in the Italian Baroque.

The most powerful figure of this period was Johann Balthasar Neumann (1687–1753).[6] His activity after his arrival in Würzburg in 1719 until his death fairly accurately spans the years most productive for German late Baroque architecture.

Like Lukas von Hildebrandt, Neumann had been a military engineer before he turned to architecture. The boldness of some of his structures can be credited to his technical expertise. More important, however, was his inventiveness and flexibility. Faced more than once with difficult situations, he thought up novel solutions with seemingly effortless speed.

The major project of his early years in Würzburg was the construction of the residence of the prince-bishops of Franconia, begun in 1720 and finished, except for some parts of the interior decoration, in 1744. Located at the far end of a gently rising and very large square, the red sandstone building (fig. 406) opens in the center with an unusually deep *cour d'honneur,* originally protected by an elaborate wrought-iron fence.

The projecting wings themselves are very wide, each one enclosing two courtyards, one behind the other.[7]

Neumann reserved the most striking effects for the interior (fig. 407). The famed staircase (1737–44) is not only one of the largest ever built,[8] but Neumann also introduced the novel idea of making the spatial shell considerably wider than the combined width of the three flights of stairs.[9] The visitor ascends the first flight in the center; after the halfway landing he proceeds on one of the flights doubling back, and he not only experiences the traditional progress from dimly lit spaces to luminous ones but also feels that the very boundaries of the room expand as he continues. When Tiepolo added his celebrated ceiling fresco he further developed this idea by massing along the rim of the painted zone a colorful crowd of people set before a rapid recession of trees and buildings. Thus the space of the staircase seems to extend sideways as well as upward.

A special effort was needed to prevent an anticlimax after such an introduction. Neumann succeeded in making the main reception room worthy of the staircase. In the grand Kaisersaal

389

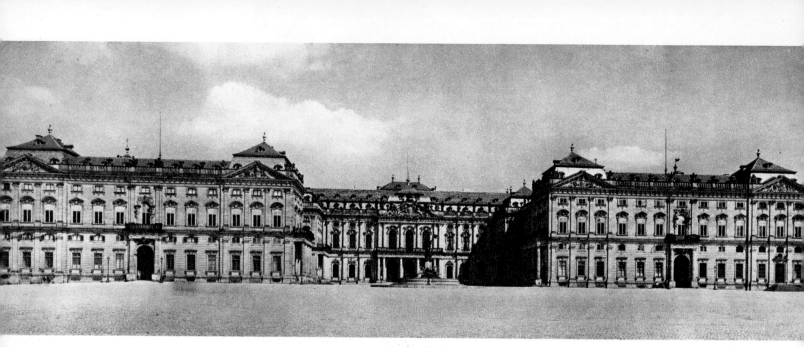

406. JOHANN BALTHASAR NEUMANN. Exterior, Residenz. 1720–44. Würzburg

407.
JOHANN BALTHASAR NEUMANN.
Interior Staircase, Residenz.
1737–44.
Würzburg (see colorplate 58)

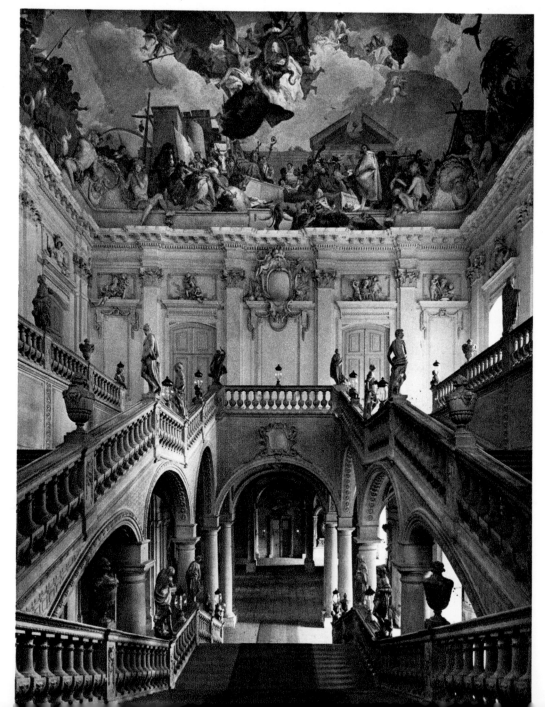

390

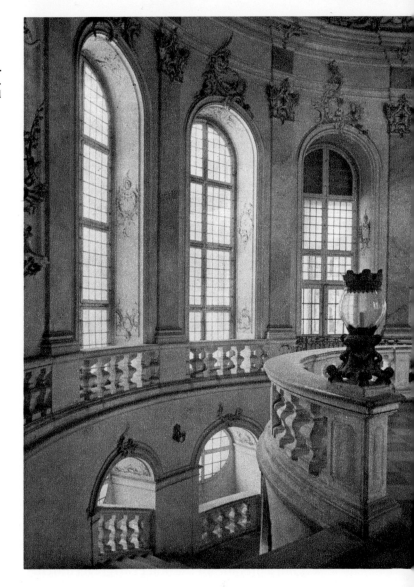

408. JOHANN BALTHASAR NEUMANN. Interior Staircase, Bishop's Palace. Begun 1731. Bruchsal

(Imperial Hall) the Tiepolo frescoes are only one voice—admittedly a soaring one—in the polyphony of colored marble, gilded ornaments, and crystal chandeliers spread over a room of majestic dimensions (colorplate 58; see also pages 342–44).

About ten years before, Neumann had been confronted with a similar problem, though without the freedom he enjoyed at Würzburg. His staircase at Bruchsal (fig. 408) is all the more remarkable as it had to be fitted into a cylindrical shaft not of his planning.[10] Ascending past dark, quasi-subterranean spaces, the visitor arrives on a circular platform floating like an island within the stately circumference of the walls and beneath the wide spread of a frescoed dome. After bridging the gap between platform and wall, he reaches again an Imperial Room, where the exuberant Rococo ornament of the walls crested over into the ceiling.

Impressive as Neumann's work was in the field of secular architecture, it was topped by his contribution to the design of churches. Three of these churches were of prime importance: the palace chapel in Würzburg and the churches of Vierzehnheiligen and Neresheim.

Two interrelated principles determine the character of these buildings. One is the complete unification of the interior in terms of overlapping circular or oval units; the other is the total emancipation of this interior from the outer shell of the building. Neither principle was novel. Both were inherent in the development that began with Borromini and was carried on in Italy by Guarini and Vittone. The idea of interpenetrating ovals applied by Guarini in the Church of Santa Maria della Providenza in Lisbon (a casualty of the earthquake of 1775) had been picked up by Lukas von Hildebrandt in his church at Gabel (1699) and above all by architects of the remarkable Dientzenhofer family. Hailing from Bavaria, this family, four of whose members were major ar-

chitects, was primarily active in Bohemia and Moravia, where they built several important churches during the critical years around 1700 (Guarini himself may have been in Prague in 1679). One of them, Johann Dientzenhofer (d. 1726), is generally credited with the monastery church of Banz, near Bamberg (1710–18), where, apparently for the first time, the curvatures of the walls were projected upward into the zone of the vaults (fig. 409).

Guarini was also the spiritual father of the differentiation between the stable outer shell and the free development of spatial units within. Yet in Neumann's churches, in contrast to Guarini's, the spatial "cushions" between the shells assume a major share in the effect of the interior. In a

Germany and Austria in the Seventeenth and Eighteenth Centuries / 391

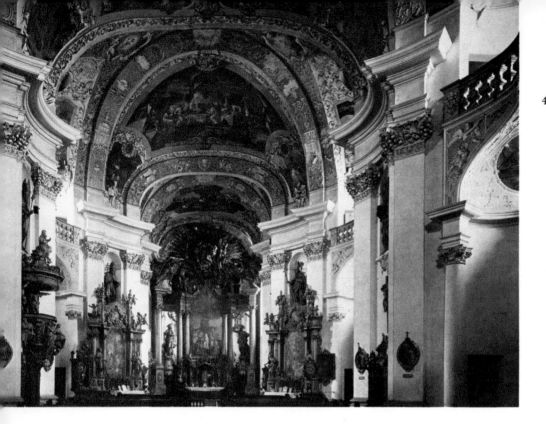

409. JOHANN DIENTZENHOFER.
Interior,
Benedictine Monastery Church.
1710–18. Banz

most revealing statement Neumann himself spoke of the *Durchsichtigkeit* (transparency) of his church interiors.

The principle of the interpenetration of curved spaces appears with Neumann first in the Würzburg chapel (1732—possibly in collaboration with Von Hildebrandt). This chapel, however, was but a prelude for the other two great churches. The first to be begun was Vierzehnheiligen, so called because it was dedicated to the fourteen saints known as "aids in need" *(Nothelfer)*. As it stands, the church was built from a second plan (fig. 410) that Neumann was forced to make in 1744, when the abbot decided to move the building farther east without changing the site marked for the main altar. Faced with this emergency, Neumann found a brilliant solution; he indeed delivered what he had promised: "ein meisterhaftes Werck."

No one can predict from the outside what the interior of the church might be like. Seen from without, the church looks like a traditional basilica with side aisles, transept, and apse.[11] Nothing in the interior (fig. 411) corresponds to these expectations.

There is indeed a transept of sorts. But whereas in traditional churches the crossing is emphasized, most often with the construction of a dome over it, this space in Vierzehnheiligen is sharply downgraded. All the adjoining spatial units encroach on its integrity. To the west and east lie truncated ovals (the western one indeed forming the largest spatial unit of the church) whose vaults extend into the "crossing" until their supporting arches touch. Spandrels of complex spherical form tie the circular arms of the transept into this decentralized configuration.

At the western end of the main oval the galleries flanking it give way, for the space of one bay, to a wide and high arch, suggesting a second transept —but again the vaults of the neighboring areas continue across it as they had done at the other end. The ambiguity of this pseudotransept is increased by the insertion of large altars at its lateral ends, a feature that tends to vitiate any sense of continuity in the "side aisles." Indeed, these subordinate spaces have completely irregular shapes, owing to the constantly changing width and curvature of the rooms arranged along the central axis. It is as if their shape resulted from

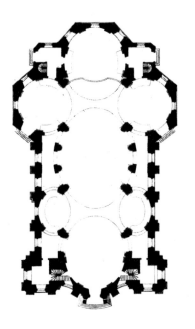

410. JOHANN BALTHASAR NEUMANN.
Plan, Vierzehnheiligen.
1743. Near Staffelstein

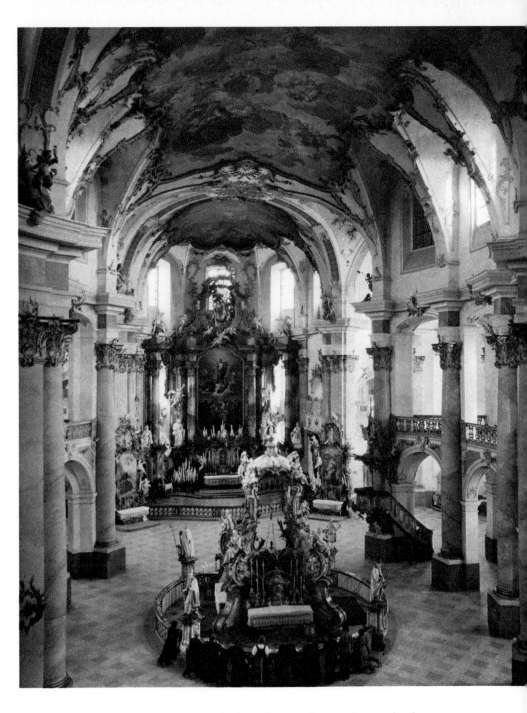

411. JOHANN BALTHASAR NEUMANN.
Interior, Vierzehnheiligen. 1743–72

their absorbing the pressures exerted by the main rooms.

As could be expected, the effect is irrational, but not bewildering. Rather, the visitor is transported by a curious sense of exhilaration as walls seem to move to and fro, vaults rise above deeply recessed spandrels; and the whole building seems to partake in a motion of joyous abandon. What Bernini had accomplished for the human figure Neumann finally achieved for a whole building:

to transform it into a worthy, and convincing, carrier of spiritual excitement.[12]

Neumann never saw the finished building. He died before the vaults were completed. He saw even less of his last great church, at the Benedictine Abbey of Neresheim (fig. 412). Begun in 1749, it was finished only in 1792, with columns of oak rather than marble, vaults of wood rather than reinforced stone, and decorated "with false colors and false altars."[13] With its length of 280

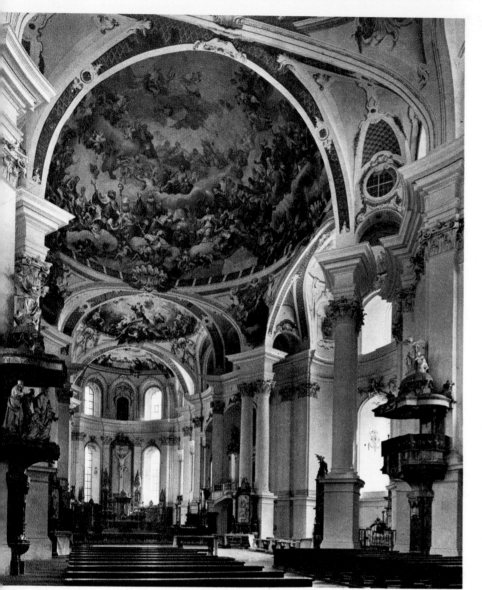

412. JOHANN BALTHASAR NEUMANN.
Interior, Benedictine Abbey Church.
1749–92. Neresheim

feet, Neresheim is bigger than Vierzehnheiligen, but it is more symmetrical and less intricate. While the principle of two shells is implicit in all parts of the building, it is given special emphasis in the "crossing." Here the inner shell is formed by four pairs of slender columns that carry the vault. The high spaces behind them provide Neumann's cherished transparency; they also help cushion the expansive thrust of the central room, permitting it to ebb out in the gentle curves of the crossarms.

Constructively as bold as Vierzehnheiligen, Neresheim is distinguished by a particularly graceful and lucid interaction of its spatial units. Its

cool and unimaginative decoration, however, robs it of much of its architectural rhythm.

Among Neumann's contemporaries, an unusually fascinating group of artists was working in Bavaria. Painters and sculptors as well as architects, the Asam brothers (Cosmas Damian, 1686–1739, and Egid Quirin, 1692–1750) created striking if somewhat theatrical effects in the churches of Rohr (1718) and Weltenburg (1717). The latter (colorplate 59) is famous for its silver statue of St. George above the high altar, perhaps the most successful visualization of a miraculous apparition (*pace* Bernini's *St. Theresa*) ever achieved. Best

Colorplate 59. EGID QUIRIN ASAM. *St. George*. 1735–36. Silver. Cloister Church, Weltenburg

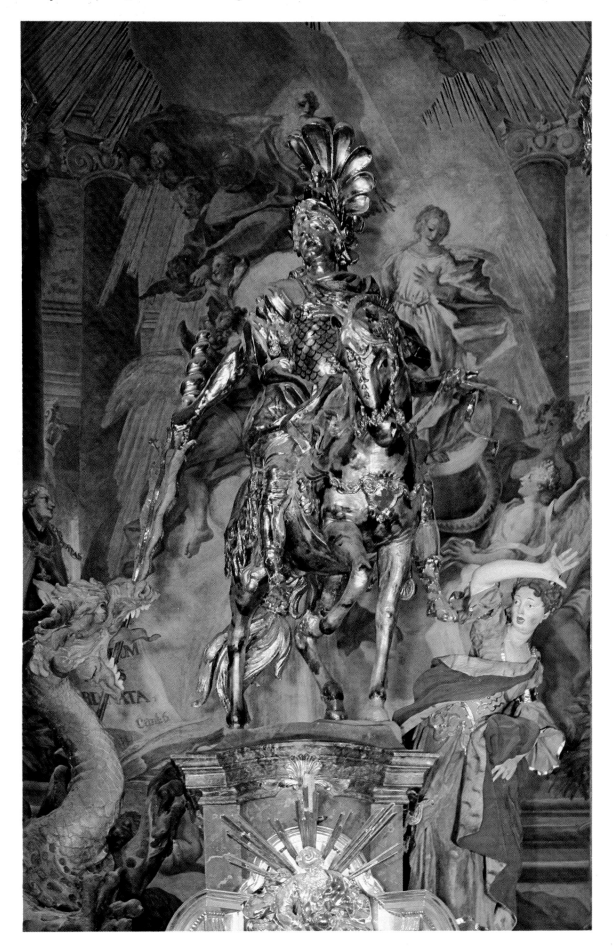

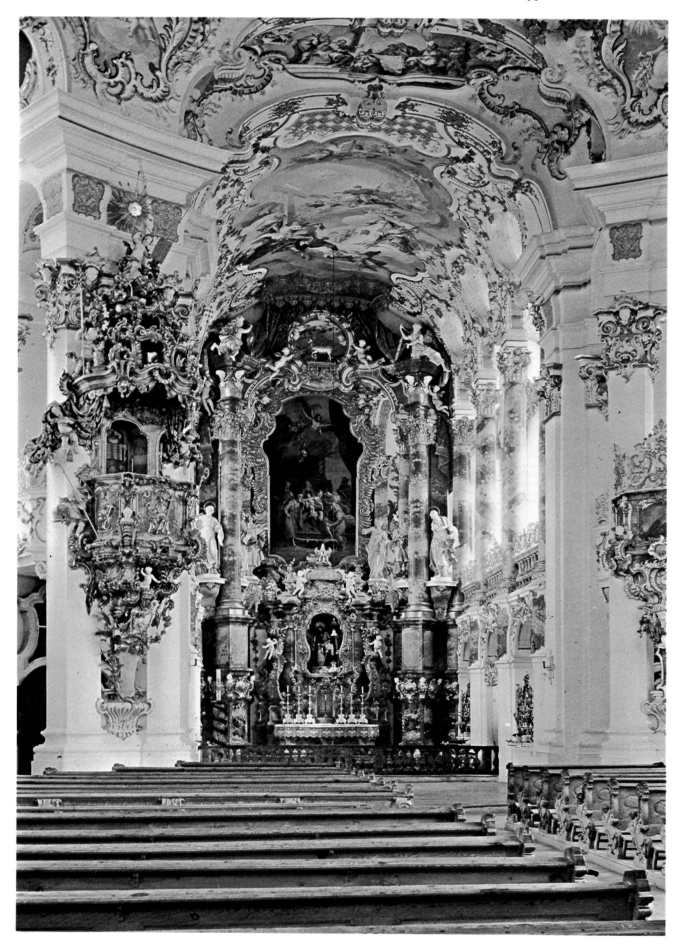

Colorplate 61.   FRANCESCO ANTONIO BUSTELLI. *Pantalone and Isabella*. c. 1760.
Porcelain, height c. 8″. Bayerisches Nationalmuseum, Munich

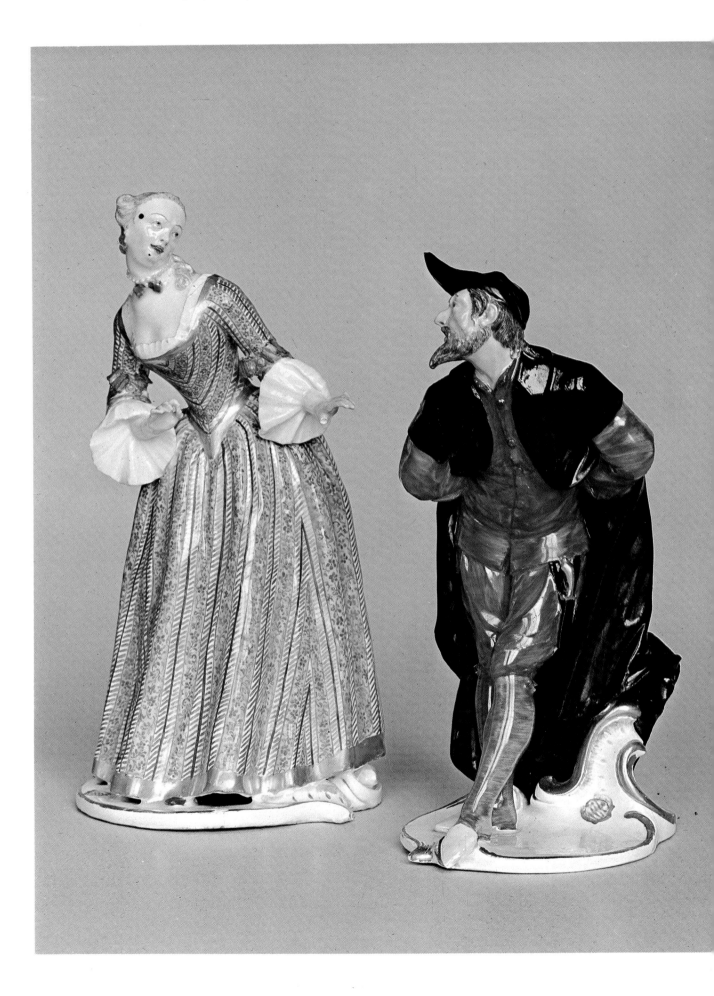

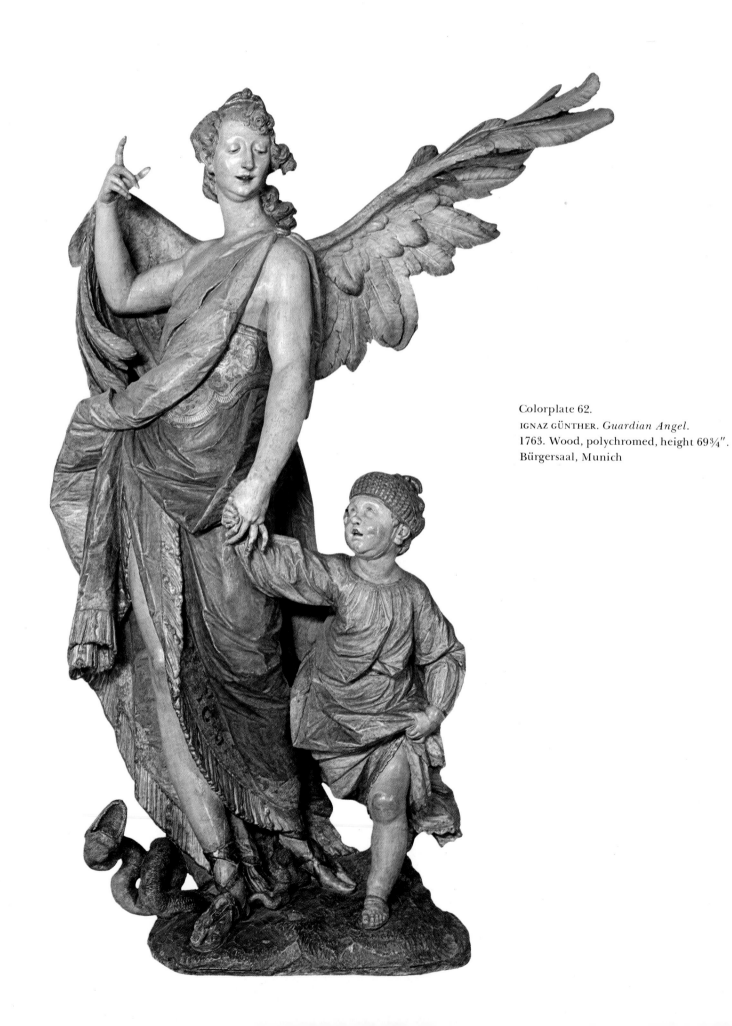

Colorplate 62.
IGNAZ GÜNTHER. *Guardian Angel*.
1763. Wood, polychromed, height 69¾″.
Bürgersaal, Munich

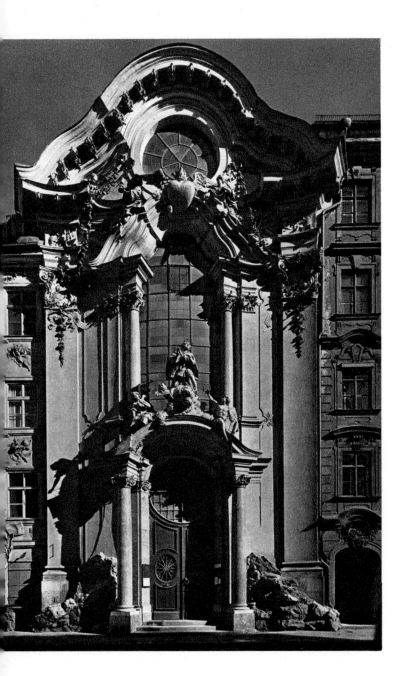

known among their works is the little church of St. Johann Nepomuk in Munich (1733). Its whimsical Borrominesque façade (fig. 413) rises from rough boulders like a Bernini fountain and is garnished with flower garlands and ribbons. The interior (fig. 414) repeats an effect first introduced in Weltenburg: through a perforation of the ceiling one sees a space of uncertain nature and dimensions, illuminated from hidden sources and all the more suggestive of a supernatural world as, silhouetted against it, there appears the Trinity, adored by angels, with a large crucifix as its principal feature.[14]

The slightly older Dominikus Zimmermann (1685–1766) was much less in demand than the Asam brothers, but was the architect of some of the most successful creations of the age. His masterpiece is the little pilgrimage church affectionately known as "Die Wies" (1746–54). Called by Pevsner "the perfect church of the German Baroque," it deserves this praise primarily because of the harmonious blending of structure and decoration. Whitewashed on the outside like any *Dorfkirche,* it is a jubilantly radiant house of God

413, 414. COSMAS DAMIAN ASAM and EGID QUIRIN ASAM. Façade and Interior, Church of St. Johann Nepomuk. 1733. Munich.

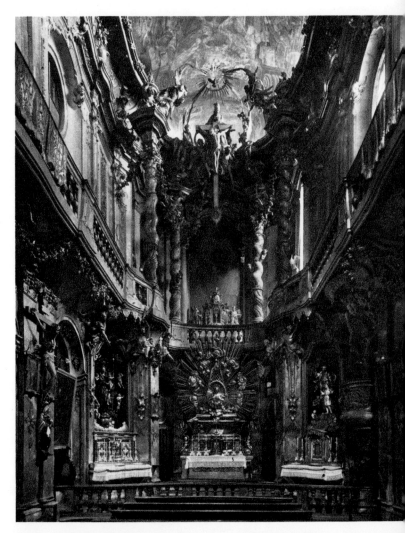

within (colorplate 60). The highest craftsmanship is lavished on every object from the blinding fireworks of the pulpit to the solid strength of the benches. Color is bright, almost garish; the paintings of the vault, by Dominikus' brother Johann Baptist Zimmermann (1680–1758), are among the finest of their kind.

Stucco played a prominent role in the decoration of these churches. The best of the German stucco sculptors, Josef Anton Feichtmayr (1696–1770), made of the simple pilgrimage church of Birnau above Lake Constance a veritable jewel of late Baroque decoration. The light interior of the single large room (fig. 415) is overlaid with stucco as a wedding cake is with frosting. Feichtmayr's work is saved from redundancy by the unbelievable variety of its forms and the sustained character of improvisation (fig. 416).

In the hands of these masters, the graceful French rocaille ornament of J.-A. Meissonier and G.-M. Oppenord was pressed into the service of one of the most riotous systems of decoration ever

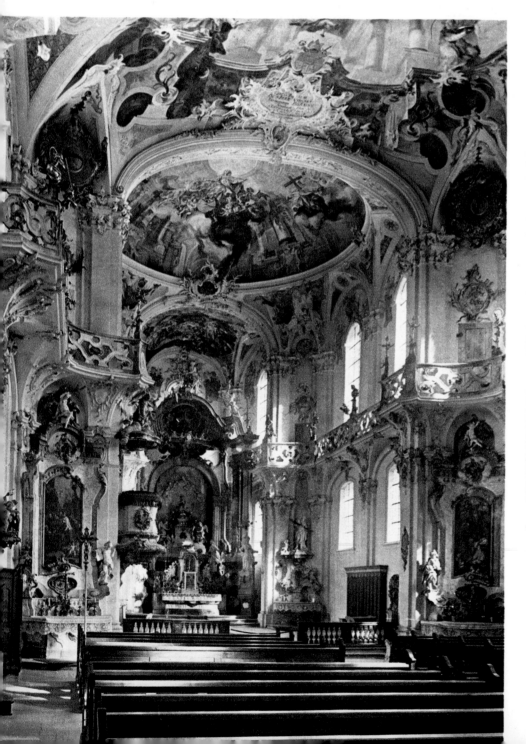

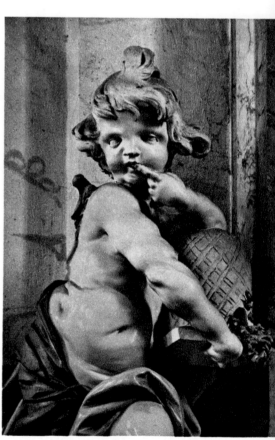

415, 416. JOSEF ANTON FEICHTMAYR.
Interior and Detail
of Sculptural Decoration,
Pilgrimage Church.
c. 1754. Birnau

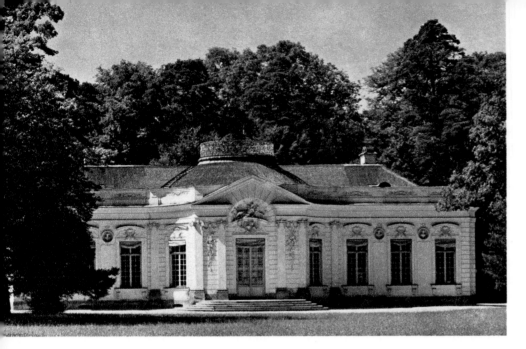

417, 418.
FRANÇOIS CUVILLIES THE ELDER.
Exterior and Interior of
Mirror Room, Amalienburg.
1734–39. Nymphenburg Park
(near Munich)

devised. The man who more than any other had been instrumental in the importation of these motifs into Germany was François Cuvilliés the Elder (1695–1768).

During a period spent in banishment, Max Emanuel, the Elector of Bavaria, had hired Cuvilliés as a court dwarf. When the Elector returned to Munich in 1714, the youth, a native of Soignies in the Hainaut, accompanied him and was educated at the court. His teacher in architecture was Joseph Effner, and like Effner before him he went to Paris to complete his studies.

Cuvilliés arrived in Paris precisely when the Rococo had become the fashionable style of society. When he returned in 1725, after an absence of five years, his familiarity with the latest French

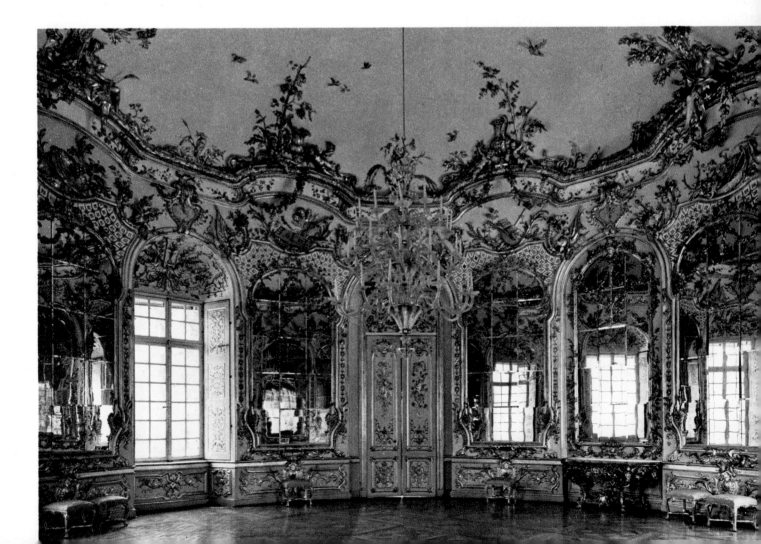

fashion aided him to supersede Effner as the favorite architect of the Bavarian court.

The masterpiece of his early career is the little *maison de plaisance* known as the Amalienburg (1734–39), one of several houses of pleasure distributed in the gardens of Nymphenburg. The exterior (fig. 417) of the low-set rectangle has an unpretentious look but is full of charming ideas.

The refined modesty of the exterior sharply contrasts with the profusely decorated interior. The walls of the central hall (fig. 418) are pierced by a free sequence of doors, windows, and mirrors. All available spaces between them contain crawling, sprouting, intertwining forms full of vital energy. Above them, gliding around the room in a leisurely sequence of rising and sinking curves, the parallel moldings of a rudimentary cornice hide rather than mark the transition between walls and ceiling; in fact, they themselves serve as platforms for little evanescent landscape idyls dissolved against the "sky." The tastefully limited colors (silver against yellow and light blue) add the last touch of sophistication.[15]

In the celebrated theater of the Munich Residenz (fig. 419), Cuvilliés achieved a maximum of opulence without neglecting the technical requirements of the stage, or the social stratification of the audience[16] (the decoration of the loges differs significantly from level to level). Of the few eighteenth-century theaters preserved (for instance at Schönbrunn in Vienna, and at Castle Drottningholm in Sweden), Cuvilliés' theater is surely the most festive. It offers a highly congenial setting for the eighteenth-century plays and operas that today are again performed on its stage.

Cuvilliés' buildings in Munich and Nymphenburg are the south German, and hence more voluble, parallel to the Rococo of Frederick the Great in Potsdam (see pages 387–88). Both represent the utmost extent of playfulness and grace achieved in the eighteenth century. Soon after they were built, official taste adopted the new preference for straight lines and right angles, for white surfaces and classical detail, that herald the dawn of a different world. For what had begun as a mere change in taste eventually grew into the aesthetic credo of a thorough social and political revolution. Whereas Cuvilliés' theater was obviously destined to serve an aristocratic society attached to a court, the theater built by K. G. Langhans in Potsdam (1795) was inscribed, on its plain and austerely rectilinear façade: *"Dem Vergnügen der Einwohner"*—"for the pleasure of the citizens."

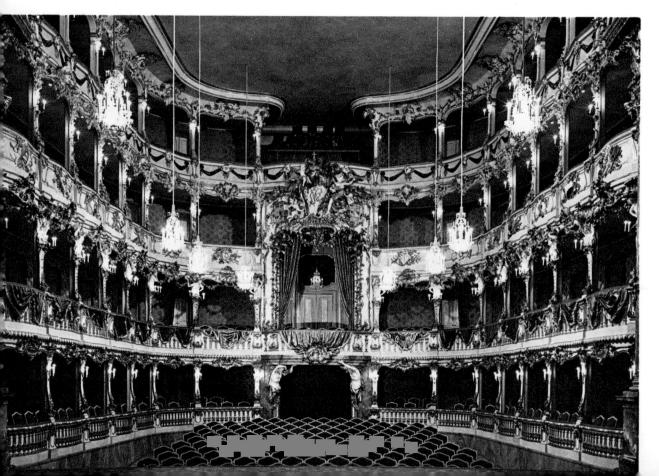

419.
FRANÇOIS CUVILLIES
THE ELDER.
Interior of Residenz
Theater. 1751–52.
Munich

SCULPTURE AND PAINTING

Few of the painters and sculptors active in Germany in the seventeenth century reached artistic levels comparable to those of artists of Italy, France, or the Netherlands. Of those who did, some left Germany to finish their careers abroad, such as Elsheimer (p. 208) or Liss (p. 103). Others returned to their homeland only after long periods spent elsewhere. Foremost among these were the sculptor Georg Petel (1601/2–1634) who worked in Rome, Genoa, and Antwerp (where he struck up a friendship with Rubens), and the painter Johann Heinrich Schönfeld (1609–1682/3) who spent eighteen years in Italy (chiefly Naples) before settling in Augsburg, then the leading art center in southern Germany. His works, suggesting contacts with Poussin, Mola, and Salvator Rosa, are characterized by a highly personal stress on ecstatic gestures, romantic settings, and a flickering light. His better known, and even more widely traveled contemporary, Joachim von Sandrart (1606–1688) was a much more academic painter. More than for his paintings he deserves to be remembered for his book on artists' biographies, the *Teutsche Academie* (Nuremberg, 1675–79), an invaluable source not only for German art but for Flemish and Dutch painting as well.

While the number of German sculptors and painters increased dramatically with the building boom of the eighteenth century, there were only a few men of superior genius. Around 1700, Andreas Schlüter—prominent as an architect as well—was without peer as a sculptor and not only in Germany (see page 387). Each of his works—the pulpit of the Marienkirche, the keystones of the Zeughaus (Arsenal; fig. 420), the allegories of the continents in the Rittersaal of the castle (now destroyed)—translates Berninesque formulations into a personal idiom capable of expressing a wide range of emotions and depicting forms in motion with a great deal of conviction. His masterwork, however, is the freestanding equestrian monument in bronze (1698–1709) erected in commemoration of Frederick William, the Great Elector of Prussia.[17]

Since Bernini's plans for an equestrian statue of Louis XIV pathetically came to naught,[18] Schlüter's *Great Elector* (fig. 421) is the grandest formulation of princely majesty produced in sculpture during the Baroque period. The idea of the absolute ruler, invested with his power by the grace of God, and not accountable to any human institution, has here been visualized with symbolic force. In one strikingly unified composition, two separate worlds have been depicted. One belongs to the prince riding high on his fiery charger, his leonine hair blown back by the wind, his dilated eyes looking toward distant goals. The other (fig. 422) is represented by four chained prisoners sitting far below him, some abjectly pondering their fate, others looking upward in his direction with expressions and gestures of awe. They are fixed to one spot: he moves out into space. They are helpless: he is all-powerful. They acknowledge his greatness: but he does not even realize they are there.

The German sculptors of the generation following Schlüter—Paul Egell (1691–1752), Egid Quirin Asam (1692–1750), and Raphael Donner (1693–1741), to mention three of the best—tended toward a lighter and more ingratiating art, in keeping with the general trends of their time.

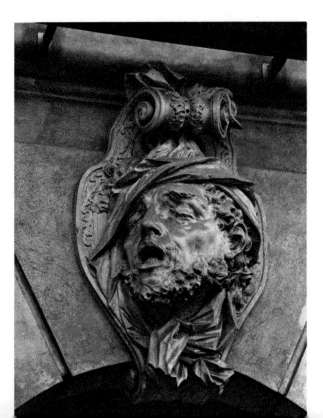

420. ANDREAS SCHLÜTER. *Dying Soldier.* 1696.
Keystone of Zeughaus (Arsenal), Berlin

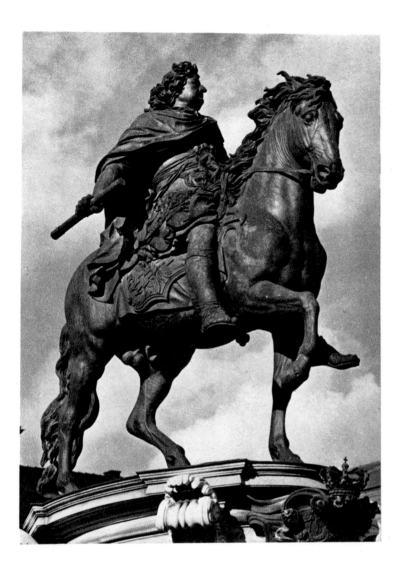

421. ANDREAS SCHLÜTER.
Equestrian Portrait of the Great Elector.
1698–1703. Bronze, over lifesize. Berlin

Asam, as we have seen, was fond of theatrical effects; Egell, active in Mannheim, produced works of strong emotional realism; Donner, in Vienna, aimed at a melodious flow of line and a controlled expression of feeling.

Donner was perhaps the most interesting sculptor of his generation. Some of his best pieces, all on a large scale, were cast in lead, a material that offers certain difficulties but that also rewards with an epidermis of low-keyed beauty differing greatly from the coldly glistening surfaces of bronze. Avoiding Berninesque freedom, Donner preferred a gentle classicism, modified occasionally by curious echoes of Mannerist preciousness, as if he had studied works of Giovanni Bologna or his Northern followers, Hubert Gerhardt and Adriaen de Vries.

Two of his major works were fountains commissioned—a fairly unusual practice—by the Vienna Magistrate. His works for churches consist of single large groups such as his *St. Martin,* in Hungarian uniform, for Bratislava (fig. 423), a huge lead casting over eight and a half feet high, and a late *Pietà* of lead in the Cathedral at Gurk, rising above the ciborium of the altar with its plaintive but restrained message of grief.

The tendency of the Rococo to appeal to a refined taste and to make even the smallest objects (snuffboxes, watches, fans) into delicate works of art is nowhere seen more delightfully than in objects made of porcelain. Originally known only to the Chinese, porcelain manufacture spread rapidly all over Europe after a domestic supply of kaolin—essential for the manufacture of hard-paste pottery (porcelain)—had been discovered by a Dresden potter early in the eighteenth century. Among the many gifted sculptors and paint-

422. ANDREAS SCHLÜTER.
Equestrian Portrait of the Great Elector (base).
Completed 1709. Bronze

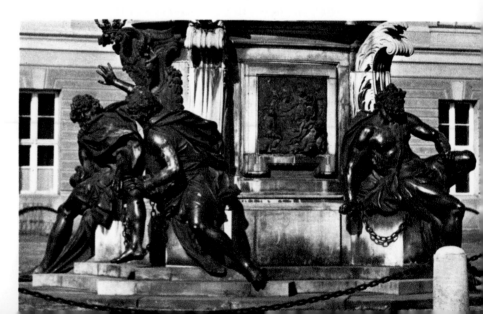

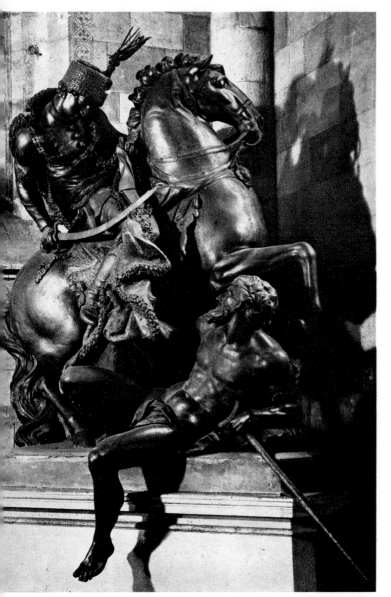

Foreign painters retained a strong position. Andrea Pozzo himself left Rome for Vienna in 1702, and in his wake came Francesco Solimena (from Naples), Carlo Carlone and Giovanni Antonio Pellegrini (from Venice), and Martino Altomonte (from Rome). Jacopo Amigoni (a Venetian) was active in Bavaria;[19] of Tiepolo's frescoes in Würzburg we have spoken before. The first Northerner to compete with them was Johann Michael Rottmayr (1654–1730), who had long worked in Venice before becoming the collaborator of Fischer von Erlach and Jakob Prandtauer. He was followed in Austria by Daniel Gran (1694–1757) and Paul Troger (1698–1762), in Germany by Cosmas Damian Asam (1686–1739), Johann Baptist Zimmermann (1680–1758), Johann Zick (1702–1762), and Matthäus Günther (1705–1788). All of them, in various degrees of perfection, continued the tradition of *quadratura* painting, which had become widely accessible through Pozzo's *Tractatus perspectivae pictorum et architectorum,* of which a German translation was published in Augsburg in 1719.

Baroque sculpture and painting in Germany ends with two figures of special stature. The sculptor, Ignaz Günther (1725–1775) of Munich, enriched Upper Bavaria with his spirited carvings; the painter, Anton Franz Maulpertsch (1724–1796; south German by birth), from Vienna furnished frescoes and altarpieces to places as far away as Dresden, Innsbruck, Kremsier, and Brünn.

Stylistically they had little in common, but they shared a certain extremism, a determination, each in his own way, to develop his style to its utmost potentialities. With Günther this meant the combination of an almost supercilious elegance with a good deal of earthy sensualism. Like Donner, Günther seems to have studied works of Mannerist artists, and his figures are as elongated as their sixteenth-century forerunners. Yet unlike Don-

ers working in this new medium one man stands out as an artist of the first rank: Francesco Antonio Bustelli (1723–1763). Born in Locarno, he appeared in Munich around 1760 as *modelleur* at the factory of Neudeck-Nymphenburg. Here he created the most original, witty, and superbly elegant porcelain figures ever designed. His finest pieces are a set of figures representing actors of the *commedia dell'arte* (colorplate 61). Like Watteau before him, Bustelli caught well the formalized freedom of this theatrical tradition, its humor, its playfulness, its choreographed gracefulness. Like Watteau's, Bustelli's career was ended abruptly by his early death, at the age of forty.

ner's cool and impersonally beautiful figures, Günther's are characterized by a voluptuous softness of forms, sensuously parted lips, sleepy eyes, fleshy but secretly agitated hands, and a suggestive swiveling of hips (colorplate 62).

Günther's eroticism, however, was only one facet of his artistic temperament. He was equally capable of rendering contemplation, transport, and deep-felt pathos. Whatever they do, his figures are the prey of an ever ready excitability. Only at the end of his life, in his *Pietà* for the Swabian town of Nenningen (fig. 424), do we meet a marked reduction of rhetoric and nervous tension. Even for the most sophisticated sculptor of the German Rococo, the time had come to adopt a style of greater calm and simplicity.

Resistance to the Neoclassical trends was complete in the paintings of Maulpertsch. From 1750 to his death Maulpertsch painted frescoes in nearly sixty different localities, not to mention his many altarpieces and oil sketches.[20] Indebted to many sources, Maulpertsch's style is a highly personal version of Baroque hyperbole. Confronted with the time-honored themes of martyrdom, ecstasy, and princely apotheosis, Maulpertsch unhesitatingly rendered his figures with outflinging gestures and extreme facial distortion (colorplate 63). They are set against mysterious, shadowy backgrounds, and are illuminated, but not clarified, by sudden flashes of light. With brushwork as bold and sure as that of Fragonard (his junior by only a few years), he put down his color in irregular patches that more often than not seem to pay no attention to the actual boundaries of his bodies. His oil sketches, particularly, are miracles of pictorial economy and of witty, if not irreverent, abbreviation.

Compared with Goya—his junior by twenty-two years—Maulpertsch remains very much the man of the late Baroque. But if Goya's historic role is defined as a link between the decorative colorism of the late Venetian school and the emotional colorism of the Romantics, then it is of some interest to realize that with Maulpertsch the old tradition had been kept alive to the very end of the eighteenth century.

424. IGNAZ GÜNTHER.
Pietà. 1774. Wood, 64⅛".
Friedhof Kapelle, Nenningen

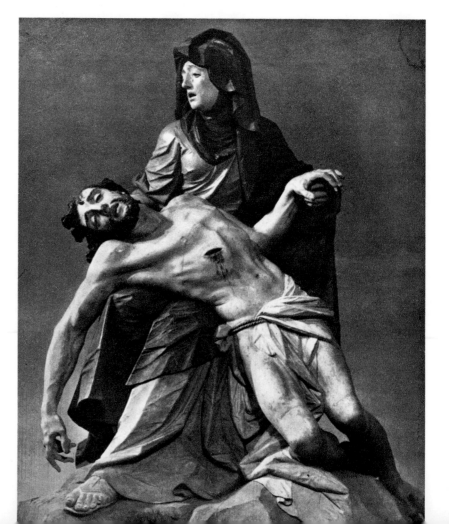

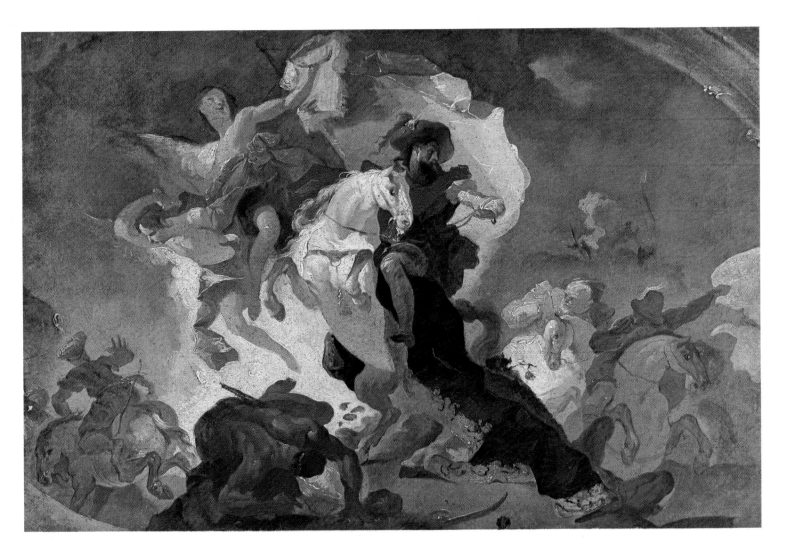

Colorplate 63. ANTON FRANZ MAULPERTSCH. *Victory of St. James of Compostela over the Saracens*. c. 1764.
Oil sketch on paper, 12½ × 18¾″. Oesterreichische Galerie, Belvedere, Vienna

Notes

The manuscript of this book was completed early in 1965, and only minor additions and revisions have been made since then. Thanks are owed to Patricia Egan for overall editorial assistance; also to Howard Hibbard who read Julius Held's chapter on Italian art and Rosalie L. Colie who gave editorial assistance with the Dutch chapter; also to José López-Rey, Richard Pommer, Charles Sterling, and Guy Walton, who read portions of Donald Posner's manuscript and gave him the benefit of their specialized knowledge.

INTRODUCTION TO BAROQUE ART

1. See O. Kurz, "Barocco: storia di una parola," *Lettere Italiane,* XII (1960), 414 ff. *Idem,* "Barocco, storia di un concetto," *Barocco europeo e barocco veneziano,* a cura di Vittore Branca (Venice, 1963), pp. 15 ff. See also B. Migliorini, "Etimologia e storia del termine 'barocco,'" *Accademia Nazionale dei Lincei,* Quaderno No. 52, CCCLIX (1962), 39 ff.
2. A. von Zahn, "Barock, Rococo, Zopf," *Zeitschrift für bildende Kunst,* VIII (1873), I ff.
3. Wölfflin's book had been preceded by C. Gurlitt, *Geschichte des Barockstiles in Italien* (Stuttgart, 1887).
4. E. Nencioni, *La Vita italiana nel seicento,* III (1895), 383; C. Ricci, *Vita Barocca* (Rome, 1904).
5. A. Riegl, *Die Entstehung der Barockkunst in Rom* (Vienna, 1908).
6. F. Nietzsche, *Menschliches, Allzumenschliches, Aphorismus 144,* in *Werke,* III, 1900, p. 78.
7. The most sweeping connection between Baroque and Counter Reformation was made by W. Weisbach, *Barock als Kunst der Gegenreformation* (Berlin, 1921). See also E. Mâle, *L'Art religieux après le Concile de Trente,* 2nd ed. (Paris, 1951).
8. R. Wittkower, *Art and Architecture in Italy: 1600 to 1750,* Pelican History of Art (Baltimore, 1958).
9. L. Venturi and L. Salerno, Introduction, *Il Seicento Europeo,* Exhibition (Rome, 1956).
10. O. Kurz, *art. cit.,* in *Lettere Italiane,* XII (1960), 423, 440–41.
11. F. Kimball, *The Creation of the Rococo* (Philadelphia, 1943), p. 4.
12. O. Kurz, *art. cit.,* in *Lettere Italiane,* XII (1960), 429.
13. For example, the Council of Europe exhibition held in Munich in 1958 titled "The Age of Rococo; Art and Culture of the Eighteenth Century."
14. H. Sedlmayr, "Zur Charakteristik des Rokoko," *Accademia Nazionale dei Lincei,* Quaderno No. 52, CCCLIX (1962), 347–48.
15. G. Briganti, "Baroque Art" in *Encyclopedia of World Art* (New York, 1960), cols. 255–67; *idem, Pietro da Cortona, o della pittura barocca* (Florence, 1962).
16. D. Posner, *Art Bulletin,* XLVI (1964), 413–14.
17. C. Le Brun, *Méthode pour apprendre à dessiner les passions* (Paris, 1698).
18. L. L. Martz, *The Poetry of Meditation* (New Haven and London, 1954; rev. ed. 1962).
19. M. H. Nicolson, *The Breaking of the Circle* (New York, 1960).
20. For a survey and critical discussion of the many different and often contradictory opinions about Baroque expressed in the recent literature the student is referred to Jan Bialostocki, "Barock: Stil, Epoche, Haltung," in his collection of essays *Stil und Ikonographie, Studien zur Kunstwissenschaft,* (Dresden, 1965), pp. 77–108; see also "A Symposium on Periods," *New Literary History, A Journal of Theory and Interpretation,* I (1970), 113 ff., especially H. W. Janson's passage on the Baroque, pp. 120–22.

1 ITALY IN THE SEVENTEENTH CENTURY

1. G. B. Armenini, *De' veri precetti della pittura* (Ravenna, 1587).
2. St. Philip Neri had wanted the Church of Il Gesù to remain unadorned; it was eventually turned into one of the most colorful churches of the period.
3. F. Haskell, *Patrons and Painters: a Study in the Relations Between Italian Art and Society in the Age of the Baroque* (New York, 1963).
4. See E. Mâle, *L'Art religieux après le Concile de Trente,* 2nd ed. (Paris, 1951).
5. R. Borghini, *Il Riposo* (Florence, 1584).

6. G. A. Gilio, *Due dialoghi ... degli errori ed abusi de' pittori ...* (Camerino, 1564), insisted that Christ be shown "bleeding, spat upon, with his skin torn, wounded, deformed, pale and unsightly" (p. 86). A. Possevino, *Tractatio de poësi et pictura ethica ...* (Rome, 1593), wants artists to paint "the pains of the martyrs, the tears of the crying, the suffering of the tortured, and the glory of the rising." See A. Blunt, *Artistic Theory in Italy: 1450–1600* (Oxford, 1940); see also R. Wittkower, *Art and Architecture in Italy: 1600 to 1750,* Pelican History of Art (Baltimore, 1958).

7. Pictures of the Immaculate Conception were particularly popular in Spain, where the doctrine was officially sanctioned in 1615, though it was accepted as dogma only in 1854.

8. As new names were added to the established roster of saints, artists often had to illustrate incidents never treated before. Following a lapse of sixty-five years the first new canonization was held in 1588, and in one memorable year (1622) no less than four saints were created (Ignatius, Francis Xavier, Philip Neri, and Theresa).

9. The importance of the location of St. Peter's tomb was again stressed when a modern scientific excavation was launched in 1940 to find the precise spot.

10. J. Molanus, *De historia SS. imaginum et picturarum pro vero earum usu contra abusus* (Louvain, 1594), Ch. XL, pp. 62–63: *"Cogitat ergo Christianus quando in templum ingreditur, se in coelum quoddam terrestre ingredi, ubi Deus impleat totam domum."* ("As the Christian enters the church he thinks to enter into a kind of terrestrial heaven where God fills the whole building.") Defending the luxury of interior decoration, he also says that it is unthinkable that Christian churches be inferior to Solomon's temple in expressing the splendor of the heavens.

11. N. Pevsner, *An Outline of European Architecture,* Jubilee edition (Baltimore, 1960), p. 374; see also P. Pecchiai, *Il Gesù di Roma* (Rome, 1952).

12. The Egyptian monument was "converted" to Christianity by an inscription and the erection of a cross on its top. Other relics of antiquity were drafted into the service of the Church, among them the Column of Marcus Aurelius and the Column of Trajan, which were crowned with the figures of St. Paul and St. Peter respectively.

13. Contrary to the conventional orientation of churches, St. Peter's has its entrance in the east end, its apse and altar in the west.

14. R. Wittkower, "S. Maria Salute: Scenographic Architecture and the Venetian Baroque," *Journal of the Society of Architectural Historians,* XVI (1957), 3 ff.

15. At a late stage of the development of ancient architecture some architects had also savored the picturesque interplay of concave and convex forms; for instance, the little round temple at Baalbek from the second century A. D. (see below, Ch. 6).

16. Pevsner, *op. cit.,* p. 395.

17. Wittkower, *Art and Architecture in Italy,* p. 133

18. As remarkable as his buildings are some of Guarino's views on architecture expressed in his *Architettura civile,* published posthumously in 1737 and reprinted in 1964. While an interest in Gothic architecture was not uncommon in the Baroque period, Guarino may have been the first to analyze the structural principles of Gothic designs. See E. Panofsky, "The First Page of Giorgio Vasari's 'Libro'," *Meaning in the Visual Arts* (New York, 1955), p. 169, and E. S. de Beer, "Gothic; Origin and Diffusion of the Term," *Journal of the Warburg and Courtauld Institutes,* XI (1948), 143. According to Wittkower (*op. cit.,* p. 274), "it does not appear far-fetched to conclude that the idea of his daring diaphanous domes ... was suggested to Guarini by his study and analysis of Gothic architecture."

19. See R. Wittkower, *Art and Architecture in Italy;* see also J. Pope-Hennessy, *Italian High Renaissance and Baroque Sculpture* (London, 1963).

20. See R. Wittkower, *The Sculpture of Bernini,* 2nd ed. (London, 1966). Bernini's drawings were published by H. Brauer and R. Wittkower, *Die Zeichnungen des Gianlorenzo Bernini* (Berlin, 1931). For Bernini's sculpture, see also H. Hibbard, *Bernini* (Baltimore, 1966).

21. The Order of the Teresians (the reformed branch of the Carmelites) was known as the discalced (barefoot) Carmelites because they wore sandals rather than shoes and stockings.

22. For Bernini's earliest portrait sculpture see I. Lavin, "Five New Youthful Sculptures by Gianlorenzo Bernini and a Revised Chronology of His Early Works," *Art Bulletin,* L (1968), 223–48.

23. See E. Panofsky, *Tomb Sculpture* (New York, 1964).

24. It was said that one of the Four Rivers extended his hand in horror at the sight of Borromini's façade. The gesture is indeed there, but the meaning associated with it is pure fantasy: Borromini had not even begun building his façade when the figure was put into place.

25. By placing a dove—emblem of the Pamphili family—on top of the obelisk, Bernini added a bit of flattery for the then reigning pope, Innocent X, a member of that family.

26. For the controversy between the artist and the Jesuit Fathers see F. Haskell, "P. Legros and a Statue of the Blessed Stanislas Kostka," *Burlington Magazine,* XCVII (1955), 287 ff.

27. G. A. Gilio, *Due dialoghi . . .* (Camerino, 1564), p. 121; A. Blunt, *Artistic Theory in Italy: 1450–1600,* Ch. VIII, especially pp. 107 ff.

28. The classic study concerning this period is W. Friedlaender, "The Anti-Mannerist Style," in *Mannerism and Anti-Mannerism in Italian Painting* (New York, 1965), pp. 47–83. See also F. Zeri, *Pittura e controriforma; l'arte senza tempo di Scipione da Gaeta* (Turin, 1957).

29. C. C. Malvasia, *Felsina pittrice* (Bologna, 1678), I, p. 377.

30. On the history of caricature see W. Hofmann, *Caricature from Leonardo to Picasso* (London, 1957), and E. H. Gombrich and E. Kris, *Caricature* (London, 1940). On the Carracci and caricature see especially D. Posner, *Annibale Carracci* (London, 1971), pp. 65 ff.

31. G. Paleotti, *Discorso intorno alle imagini sacre e profane* (Bologna, 1582), in P. Barocchi, *Trattati d'arte del cinquecento,* II (Bari, 1961), p. 408.

32. Malvasia, *op. cit.,* I, p. 392.

33. For Caravaggio's paintings of youths see D. Posner, "Caravaggio's Homoerotic Early Works," *Art Quarterly,* XXXIV (1971), no. 3.

34. See Ch. VI in W. Friedlaender's *Caravaggio Studies* (Princeton, 1955), the best modern interpretation of Caravaggio and his art.

35. Documentary discoveries of great importance concerning Caravaggio's work in San Luigi have been made and published by H. Röttgen, "Die Stellung der Contarelli-Kapelle in Caravaggios Werk," *Zeitschrift für Kunstgeschichte,* XXVIII (1965)), 47–68.

36. J. Hess has compared the figure of the Virgin to the ancient statue of a "barbarian woman" in the Loggia dei Lanzi in Florence: "Modelle e modelli del Caravaggio," *Commentari,* V (1954), 272–73; pl. LXXIV.

37. For Ribera's presence in Rome in 1615 see J. Chenault, "Ribera in Rome," *Burlington Magazine,* CXI (1969), 561. Arguments in favor of the view that Ribera studied with Ribalta are presented by D. Fitz-Darby in *Art Bulletin,* XXXV (1953), 71–72.

38. For the history of this group see G. J. Hoogewerff, *Die Bentveughels* (The Hague, 1952).

39. For the iconography of the Gallery see J. R. Martin, *The Farnese Gallery* (Princeton, 1965), pp. 83–145; also the important study by C. Dempsey, "*Et nos cedamus Amor:* Observations on the Farnese Gallery," *Art Bulletin,* L (1968), 363–74, where fundamental revisions of Martin's reading of the vault are made.

40. The major monument of this period, the *Crucifixion of St. Peter* in the Vatican Gallery, is dated 1604/5.

41. In the Sutherland collection. See *Mostra dei Carracci: Disegni,* 2nd ed. (Bologna, 1963), pp. 96–97.

42. G. P. Bellori, *Le Vite de' pittori, scultori et architetti moderni* (Rome, 1672), p. 372.

43. G. Bottari and S. Ticozzi, *Raccolta di lettere sulla pittura, scultura, ed architettura,* I (Milan, 1822), pp. 288–89.

44. For the history of these paintings see J. Walker, *Bellini and Titian at Ferrara* (London, 1956).

45. For an excellent discussion of the iconography of the ceiling see W. Vitzthum, "A Comment on the Iconography of Pietro da Cortona's Barberini Ceiling," *Burlington Magazine,* CIII (1961), 427–33.

46. Only five of the seven ceilings originally planned were executed; Cortona completed three and began a fourth, the *Sala d'Apollo,* which was finished in the 1660s by his student Ciro Ferri, who was entirely responsible for the fifth room, the *Sala di Saturno.*

47. See M. Missirini, *Memorie per servire alla storia della romana Accademia di S. Luca* (Rome, 1823), p.111.

48. C. Jouanny, *Correspondance de Nicolas Poussin* (Paris, 1911), pp. 134–35.

49. R. Enggass, "Bernini, Gaulli, and the Frescoes of the Gesù," *Art Bulletin,* XXXIX (1957), 303–5. But see F. Dowley in *Art Bulletin,* XLVII (1965), 294–300.

2 FRANCE IN THE SEVENTEENTH CENTURY

1. The rustication was inspired by Maria de' Medici's desire that the Palazzo Pitti in Florence be used as a model for the building. De Brosse had used rustication in his earlier château of Coulommiers, but there it is closer in character to the varied, decorative pattern of rustication used by Du Cerceau than to the Italian model.

2. By A. Blunt, who suggests that Rosato Rosati, the designer of San Carlo ai Catinari, may have been Lemercier's teacher in Rome: see *Art and Architecture in France: 1500 to 1700,* Pelican History of Art (Baltimore, 1957), p. 115.

3. The surviving material has been studied by A. Braham, "Mansart Studies I: The Val-de-Grâce," *Burlington Magazine,* CV (1963), 351–63, and P. Smith, "Mansart Studies II: The Val-de-Grâce," *ibid.,* CVI (1964), 106–15.

4. The church has been thoroughly studied by P. Smith in "Mansart Studies III: The Church of the Visitation in the Rue St. Antoine," *Burlington Magazine,* CVI (1964), 202–15.

5. To some extent irregularities are due to the nature of the site.

6. The high cut-off "Mansard" roof was used in the sixteenth century. Because Mansart popularized it his name is associated with it.

7. A. Laprade, who takes an extreme position and gives D'Orbay a major share of the responsibility for all Le Vau's late work, would exclude Le Vau from this project entirely: in *François d'Orbay* (Paris, 1960), pp. 179–82.

8. While in France, Bernini was anything but tactful in expressing his rather low opinion of French art. The contemporary account of his stay in Paris is P. Fréart de Chantelou, *Journal du voyage du Cavalier Bernin en France,* ed. L. Lalanne (Paris, 1885).

9. As Le Vau's assistant, D'Orbay was also involved, but Laprade's attempt to give him full responsibility for its design and execution is not convincing (*op. cit.,* pp. 132–56). For a discussion of Le Vau's claims see A. Braham and M. Whiteley, "Louis Le Vau's Project for the Louvre and the Colonnade," *Gazette des Beaux-Arts,* LXIV (1964), 347–62. The most recent discussions of the problem are M. Petzet, "Entwürfe zur Louvre-Kolonnade," in *Stil und Überlieferung in der Kunst des Abendlandes* (Berlin, 1967), III, 159–63, and R. Berger, "Charles Le Brun and the Louvre Colonnade," *Art Bulletin,* LII (1970), 394–403.

10. Published as *Cours d'architecture enseigné dans l'Académie,* 2 vols. (Paris, 1675–83).

11. A. Braham has suggested that Louis XIV actually planned to build the Bourbon funerary chapel at the Invalides instead of at St. Denis, and that Mansart's church there was commissioned as such: in "L'Église du Dome," *Journal of the Warburg and Courtauld Institutes,* XXIII (1960), 216–24. But see also P. Reuterswärd, "L'Église des Invalides," *L'Information d'histoire de l'art,* IX (1964), 7–18, and, for a full discussion of the monument, *idem, The Two Churches of the Hôtel des Invalides: a History of their Design* (Stockholm, 1966).

12. See F. G. Pariset, *Georges de La Tour* (Paris, 1948), pp. 122–24.

13. One notable "Caravaggesque" artist active in Paris was Claude Vignon (1593–1670). He was in Italy from about 1616 to about 1624 and was influenced by Fetti and Elsheimer as well as by Caravaggio.

14. La Tour's art seems related to the contemporary religious movement led by the Franciscans in Lorraine. See Pariset, *op. cit.,* especially pp. 320 ff.

15. B. Nicolson suggested that, like Dutch examples, La Tour's painting may be an allegory of the sense of touch; in *Burlington Magazine,* C (1958), 101, n. 14.

16. M. Faré, *La nature morte en France,* 2 vols. (Paris, 1962).

17. A. Félibien, *Entretiens sur les vies et les ouvrages des plus excellens peintres, anciens et modernes* (Trévoux, 1725), III, p. 398.

18. On the Long Gallery see A. Blunt, *Burlington Magazine,* XCIII (1951), 369–76, and *ibid.,* XCIV (1952), 31; also A. Blunt and R. Hughes-Hallett, *The Drawings of Nicolas Poussin,* IV (London, 1963), 11–24; and D. Wild, "Nicolas Poussin et la décoration de la Grande Galerie du Louvre," *La Revue du Louvre,* XVI (1966), 77–84.

19. On Poussin's relation to neo-Stoical trends in France see especially M. Alpatov, "Poussin Problems," *Art Bulletin,* XVIII (1936), 264–65 and *passim,* and A. Blunt, *Nicolas Poussin* (New York, 1967), I, pp. 157–76.

20. See the interesting study by P. Desjardins, *La Méthode des classiques français: Corneille, Poussin, Pascal* (Paris, 1904).
21. See A. Blunt, *Nicolas Poussin* (New York, 1967), I, *passim.*
22. See especially A. Blunt, "The Heroic and Ideal Landscape in the Work of Nicolas Poussin," *Journal of the Warburg and Courtauld Institutes,* VII (1944), 154–68; and E. H. Gombrich, "The Subject of Poussin's *Orion," Burlington Magazine,* LXXXIV (1944), 37–38.
23. The date is disputed; see D. Mahon, "Réflexions sur les paysages de Poussin," *Art de France,* I (1961), 126–29. For the interpretation I am following Blunt, *Nicolas Poussin* (New York, 1967), I, p. 299.
24. See B. Dorival, "Poussin et Philippe de Champaigne," in *Nicolas Poussin (Actes du Colloque Poussin)* (Paris, 1960), pp. 57–70.
25. A. Blunt, *Art and Architecture in France: 1500 to 1700,* p. 244.
26. See A. Fontaine, *Les Doctrines d'art en France* (Paris, 1909).
27. The series is studied in D. Posner, "Charles Le Brun's *Triumphs of Alexander," Art Bulletin,* XLI (1959), 237–48.
28. Sarrazin directed the work, but the execution is mainly by his assistants and students.
29. Puget's certain paintings are not especially distinguished, and there is still considerable confusion between his work in this field and the work of Jean-Baptiste de la Rose and other Provençal painters.
30. For Puget's work for the church see G. Walton, "Pierre Puget's Projects for the Church of Santa Maria Assunta di Carignano," *Art Bulletin,* XLVI (1964), 89–94, and *idem,* "A Terra-Cotta Sketch by Pierre Puget," *Museum Monograph II. The City Art Museum of St. Louis* (1970).
31. Three of the nymphs were the responsibility of the sculptor Thomas Regnaudin. The present "rustic" setting was designed by Hubert Robert (see page 313).

3 SPAIN IN THE SEVENTEENTH CENTURY

1. See especially J. Ainaud de Lasarte, "Ribalta y Caravaggio," *Anales y Boletín de los Museos de Barcelona,* V (1947), 346–63. It is also possible that Ribalta's late work was influenced by paintings of the young Ribera then arriving in Spain.
2. It is after the *Crucifixion of St. Peter* in Santa Maria del Popolo in Rome, and is apparently a copy of a copy. See J. Ainaud de Lasarte, "Francisco Ribalta: Notas y comentarios," *Revista Goya,* No. 20 (1957), 86–89.
3. I cannot agree with such writers as Soria who consider Zurbarán's art more indebted to the style of the mediocre Roelas or to Flemish late Mannerism than to Caravaggio. See G. Kubler and M. Soria, *Art and Architecture in Spain and Portugal and Their American Dominions: 1500 to 1800,* Pelican History of Art (Baltimore, 1959), pp. 243–44.
4. It has been suggested that Zurbarán's paintings can be related to the teachings of the heretical "Quietists," who were especially active in Seville and Llerena, the cities where the artist spent most of his life; see M. Soria, *Francisco Zurbarán* (New York, 1953), p. 23.
5. For the development of Spanish and European still-life painting, see respectively J. Cavestany, *Floreros y bodegones en la pintura española* (Madrid, 1940), and C. Sterling, *Still Life Painting from Antiquity to the Present Time,* trans. J. Emmons (New York, 1959).
6. The history of the *bodegón* is closely related to the history of still-life painting. See the books mentioned in note 5 above.
7. On the relationship of artistic methods and visual perception see the brilliant book by E. H. Gombrich, *Art and Illusion,* 2nd ed. (New York, 1961).
8. See J. López-Rey, *Velázquez* (London, 1963), especially pp. 37–40.
9. The sources that have been suggested for the picture are listed by López-Rey, who however, finds all of them unconvincing. His discussion of the history and significance of the painting is admirable (*op. cit.,* pp. 64–69, and *idem, Velázquez' Work and World* [London, 1968], pp. 75–79).
10. E. du Gué Trapier has called attention to its similarity to paintings of domestic interiors by Dutch masters; see her *Velázquez* (New York, 1948), p. 347. However, when the relationship is most striking the Dutch pictures appear to have been painted too late to have influenced Velázquez. Possibly, similar

paintings by the Bambocccianti that Velázquez could have seen during his second Italian trip influenced his *Maids of Honor*. In any event, in his monumental treatment of the subject Velázquez has no parallel anywhere. In presentation and partly in subject the painting suggests comparison with Vermeer's *Artist in His Studio* (colorplate 43; p. 278).

11. See E. Harris, *Spanish Painting* (New York, 1937), p. 20.

12. The *Immaculate Conception* by Reni now in the Metropolitan Museum in New York was originally in the Cathedral of Seville.

13. On Leal and themes of death see J. Brown, "Hieroglyphs of Death and Salvation: The Decoration of the Church of Hermandad de la Caridad, Seville," *Art Bulletin*, LII (1970), 265–77.

14. A photograph of Pedro de Mena's *Madonna* somewhat differently draped can be seen in R. de Orueta, *La Vida e la obra de Pedro de Mena y Medrano* (Madrid, 1914), fig. 148.

4 FLEMISH PAINTING IN THE SEVENTEENTH CENTURY

1. The basic work on Rubens remains M. Rooses, *L'Oeuvre de P. P. Rubens* (Antwerp, 1886–92). The documents, including the master's letters, were published by C. Ruelens and M. Rooses, *Correspondance de Rubens et documents epistolaires* (Antwerp, 1887–1909). English translation of Rubens' letters (with additions): R. S. Magurn, ed., *The Letters of Peter Paul Rubens* (Cambridge, Mass., 1955).

2. Of the original building only minor parts have survived including a tripartite portico dividing the courtyard from the garden. Beginning in 1931, the city of Antwerp has reconstructed the original building, chiefly from the evidence of old engravings. It is now a museum.

3. D. Dubon, *Tapestries from the Samuel H. Kress Collection at the Philadelphia Museum of Art: The history of Constantine the Great designed by Peter Paul Rubens and Pietro da Cortona* (London, 1964).

4. O. von Simson, *Zur Genealogie der weltlichen Apotheose im Barock* (Strassburg, 1936); Jacques Thuillier and Jacques Foucart, *Rubens' Life of Marie de'Medici* (New York, 1970).

5. See Oliver Millar, "The Whitehall Ceiling," *Burlington Magazine*, XCVIII (1956), 258 ff.

6. See Juergen Schulz, *Venetian Painted Ceilings of the Renaissance* (Berkeley and Los Angeles, 1968); and J. S. Held, "Rubens's Glynde Sketch and the Installation of the Whitehall Ceiling," *Burlington Magazine*, CXII (1970), 274 ff.

7. All the arches were reproduced in print, and the meaning of every detail learnedly explained, in C. Gevartius, *Pompa introitus . . . Fernandi* (Antwerp, 1642).

8. See H. Weizsäcker, *Adam Elsheimer, der Maler von Frankfurt* (Berlin, 1936 and 1953).

9. For Rubens' drawings see G. Glück and F. M. Haberditzl, *Die Handzeichnungen von Peter Paul Rubens* (Berlin, 1928); J. S. Held, *Rubens, Selected Drawings* (London, 1959); L. Burchard and R.-A. d'Hulst, *Rubens Drawings* (Brussels, 1963).

10. G. Glück, *Van Dyck; Des Meisters Gemälde* (London, 1931); for Van Dyck's drawings see H. Vey, *Die Zeichnungen Anton van Dycks* (Brussels, 1962).

11. The model was Susanne Fourment, elder sister of Rubens' wife; the painting may have been done about 1622, when she married Arnold Lunden, and eight years before Rubens married Hélène.

12. Thomas Howard, the second earl of Arundel (1585–1646), formed the first great collection of ancient sculptures in England. Rubens painted his portrait in 1629–30 during his visit to London. A preparatory drawing is at the Sterling and Francine Clark Art Institute, Williamstown, Massachusetts.

13. M. Rooses, *Jacob Jordaens*, trans. E. C. Broers (New York, 1908). For Jordaens' drawings see R.-A. d'Hulst, *De Tekeningen van Jakob Jordaens* (Brussels, 1956).

14. Jordaens also contributed two canvases to the cycle on Claudius Civilis in the Amsterdam town hall; (see page 247).

5 DUTCH PAINTING IN THE SEVENTEENTH CENTURY

1. The most recent treatment of seventeenth-century Dutch art is J. Rosenberg, S. Slive, and E. H. ter Kuile, *Dutch Art and Architecture: 1600 to 1800*, Pelican History of Art (Baltimore, 1966).

2. Rembrandt's insolvency, which resulted in the forced sale of his house and collections (1656–58), was largely caused by the unsound conduct of his business, aggravated by his ardent desire to collect precious objects.

3. See W. Stechow, *Dutch Landscape Painting of the Seventeenth Century* (London, 1966).

4. See H. van de Waal, *Drie Eeuwen vaterlandsche Geschieds-Uitbeelding, 1500–1600* (The Hague, 1952).

5. The connection between genre scenes and didactic meditation is particularly close in the works of the popular poet Jacob Cats (1557–1660); see also E. de Jongh, *Zinne-en minnebeelden in de Schilderkunst van de zeventiende eeuw* (n. p., 1967).

6. This device was later developed by William Hogarth into a veritable game of hide-and-seek.

7. See I. Bergström, *Dutch Still-life Painting in the Seventeenth Century*, trans. C. Hedström and G. Taylor (New York, 1956). Still lifes of flowers also often have *vanitas* associations.

8. The language of Dutch poets underwent a similar development, as has been pointed out by J. G. van Gelder, *Jan van de Velde* (The Hague, 1934).

9. B. Nicolson, *Hendrick Terbrugghen* (London, 1958).

10. For Hals, see now the excellent monograph by Seymour Slive, *Frans Hals*, 2 vols. (London, 1970).

11. A. Riegl, *Das holländische Gruppenporträt*, 2 vols. (Vienna, 1931).

12. With one exception, a painting only partly done by Hals, all his group portraits are preserved in the Frans Hals Museum in Haarlem.

13. The last complete publications of Rembrandt's paintings are K. Bauch, *Rembrandt: Gemälde* (Berlin, 1966) and H. Gerson, *Rembrandt Paintings* (Amsterdam, 1968). For Rembrandt's etchings see L. Münz, *Rembrandt's Etchings,* 2 vols. (London, 1952) and Christopher White, *Rembrandt as an Etcher* (London, 1969). The standard work on Rembrandt's drawings is O. Benesch, *The Drawings of Rembrandt* (London, 1954–57).

14. Sir Kenneth Clark, *Rembrandt and the Italian Renaissance* (New York, 1966).

15. Huygens described this picture in his autobiography, written about 1629/30, in which he also makes very acute observations about Rembrandt, who was then only twenty-four years old. See C. Hofstede de Groot, *Die Urkunden über Rembrandt, 1575–1721* (The Hague, 1906).

16. See W. S. Heckscher, *Rembrandt's Anatomy of Dr. Nicolaas Tulp* (New York, 1958).

17. The original source for the life of Claudius Civilis is Tacitus' *Histories;* the Batavian revolt took place in A.D. 69. How it ended is not known, since that part of the story was in one of the lost books of Tacitus.

18. From the evidence of X-rays it can be seen that Rembrandt tried out different compositional arrangements before deciding on the one now visible. He was particularly hesitant about the placing of the guild servant.

19. Julius S. Held, *Rembrandt's "Aristotle" and other Rembrandt Studies* (Princeton, 1969).

20. See J. A. Emmens, "Ay Rembrandt maal *Cornelis* stem," *Nederlands Kunsthistorisch Jaarboek,* VII (1956), 133.

21. Originally the picture contained the figure of a scribe, which has been cut away.

22. Contrary to the proposed identification of the story as the dismissal of Uriah, the traditional title appears to be the correct one; see M. Kahr, "A Rembrandt Problem: Haman or Uriah?," *Journal of the Warburg and Courtauld Institutes,* XXVIII (1965), 258.

23. Isaac van Ostade, whose landscapes and farm interiors were more original than the pictures of his more famous brother Adriaen, and Paulus Potter, who gave dignity and power to landscapes with animals, both died at twenty-eight. The witty Willem Buytewech, influential as etcher as well as painter, lived to the age of thirty-three; Jan Both, the leader of the Italianate landscape school, to thirty-four; Adriaen van de Velde, creator of quiet rustic idyls, to thirty-five; Willem Duyster, painter of spirited soldiers' scenes, to thirty-six; and Gabriel Metsu, who excelled in domestic genre, to thirty-eight. Jan Baptist Weenix, one of the most versatile artists of his time, was about forty when he died, Terbrugghen forty-one, and Vermeer forty-three.

24. See L. Gowing, *Vermeer* (London, 1952).

25. See H. Sedlmayr, "Der Ruhm der Malkunst," *Festschrift für Hans Jantzen* (Berlin, 1951), p. 169; also J. G. van Gelder, *De Schilderkunst van Jan Vermeer,* with commentary by J. A. Emmens (Utrecht, 1958).

6 NORTHERN EUROPEAN ARCHITECTURE IN THE SEVENTEENTH AND EIGHTEENTH CENTURIES

1. J. Summerson, *Architecture in Britain: 1530 to 1830,* Pelican History of Art (Baltimore, 1958), pp. 174 ff.
2. Leyden (1657) and Gouda (1668) built by Pieter Post. Another one, in Groningen, now destroyed.
3. Jones's copy of Palladio's work, with his own annotations, still survives at Worcester College, Oxford (Summerson, *op. cit.,* p. 66).
4. With the addition in the 1660s of two more bridges carrying superstructures in harmony with the main lines of the original buildings, Queen's House assumed the semblance of a solid square block. Recent excavations have laid bare parts of the old cobblestone roadbed that passed underneath.
5. See P. Palme, *Triumph of Peace, a Study of the Whitehall Banqueting House* (London, 1957).
6. This podium contains the vaulted wine cellar made famous by Ben Jonson's poem in commemoration of its dedication (*Works,* VIII, 220 ff).
7. It has been attributed to Jones by N. Pevsner, *An Outline of European Architecture,* Jubilee edition (Baltimore, 1960), pp. 218–19.
8. See K. Fremantle, *The Baroque Town Hall of Amsterdam* (Utrecht, 1959).
9. See T. Paulsson, *Scandinavian Architecture* (London, 1958).
10. The apex of the inner dome reaches no higher than the level at which the semicircle of the outer one begins. Since the wood construction of the latter would have been incapable of supporting the slender but very high lantern, Wren surmounted the inner dome with a conical masonry dome and permitted a glimpse of this curious auxiliary structure through a circular opening (shades of the Roman Pantheon!) in the center of the lower dome.
11. St. Stephen's was built for the company of grocers.
12. M. Whinney and O. Millar, *English Art, 1625–1714* (Oxford, 1957), p. 160.

7 FRANCE IN THE EIGHTEENTH CENTURY

1. The fundamental study is P. Marcel, *La Peinture française, 1690–1721* (Paris, 1906).
2. On the subject of the painting see M. Levey, "The Real Theme of Watteau's *Embarkation for Cythera,*" *Burlington Magazine,* CIII (1961), 180–85. H. Bauer's arguments ("Wo liegt Kythera," in *Wandlung des Paradiesischen und Utopischen* [Berlin, 1966], pp. 251–78) for rejecting Levey's conclusions do not seem convincing to me.
3. Cited in G. Wildenstein, *The Paintings of Fragonard* (London, 1960), p. 13, n. 2.
4. E. and J. de Goncourt, *French XVIII Century Painters,* trans. R. Ironside (New York, 1948), p. 309.
5. For the complete account of the circumstances of the commission see *ibid.,* p. 282, n. 39.
6. Fragonard was in Italy a second time in 1773–74. It is an indication of the new importance of the "minor" categories in the eighteenth century that Natoire, while director of the French Academy in Rome, especially encouraged the students to make landscape studies in the countryside.
7. In collaboration with the architect Mique, Robert transformed Le Nôtre's work at the Petit Trianon at Versailles into an English garden. Robert was also responsible for the present "picturesque" setting of Girardon's *Apollo and the Nymphs* group (see fig. 177).
8. It is interesting that one version of the *Benediction* (see fig. 326) was commissioned as a pendant for a genre piece by D. Teniers.
9. The medium was first made fashionable by the Venetian portraitist Rosalba Carriera, who visited Paris in 1720–21.
10. Cited by M. Florisoone, *Le Dix-huitième siècle* (Paris, 1948), p. 67.
11. Sautreau de Marsy in a letter to the *Journal de Paris* in 1778. See L. Hourticq, *Greuze* (Paris, 1913), pp. 76–77.
12. See W. Sauerländer, "Pathosfiguren im Oeuvre des Jean-Baptiste Greuze," *Festschrift Walter Friedlaender* (Berlin, 1965), pp. 146–150.
13. An important study is J. Locquin, *Le Peintre d'histoire en France, de 1747 à 1785* (Paris, 1912).
14. See E. and J. de Goncourt, *op. cit.,* p. 108.

15. The statue, not quite finished at Bouchardon's death, was completed by Pigalle in 1763. Pigalle's contribution does not seem to have been significant.

16. The drawing, made by Losenko after Falconet's model, is in the Museum of Nancy. It was commissioned in 1770 by Falconet himself as a preparation for an engraving. Unfortunately, available photographs of the monument do not include the whole of the base, which is essential for the intended effect.

17. On the choice of Falconet, it must also be recorded that while Pajou asked 600,000 *livres* to execute the statue, and Coustou 450,000, Falconet asked 300,000 and settled for 200,000.

18. The idea of using a great rock for a base goes back to Bernini. See R. Wittkower, "The Vicissitudes of a Dynastic Monument," *Essays in Honor of Erwin Panofsky* (New York, 1961), I, especially pp. 515–16.

19. Houdon studied under J.-B. Lemoyne and Pigalle at the Royal Academy.

20. See especially F. Kimball, *The Creation of the Rococo* (Philadelphia, 1943).

21. When used in its narrowest sense, the term "rococo" refers to the decorative style of the reign of Louis XV.

22. Quoted in P. Lavedan, *French Architecture* (Baltimore, 1956), p. 198.

23. Actually, these designs represent the perfection of a tradition of town-house planning that had been established in the seventeenth century, when important innovations were made by such architects as François Mansart, Louis Le Vau, Antoine Le Pautre (1621–81), and Pierre Bullet (1639–1716).

24. It is interesting that Boffrand condemned Borromini and Guarini for "theatricality": see G. Boffrand, *Livre d'architecture* (Paris, 1745), pp. 8–9.

25. On the relationship of the two designs see below, ch. 8, n. 13.

26. See, especially on the political significance of the ensemble, P. Marot, *La place royale de Nancy. Image de la réunion de la Lorraine à la France* (Nancy, 1966).

8 ITALY IN THE EIGHTEENTH CENTURY

1. Quoted in A. Morassi, *G. B. Tiepolo* (London, 1955), p. 1. The plan was to have Tiepolo decorate the new Royal Palace in Stockholm, but the artist's price was found prohibitive.

2. For literature on the history of caricature see above, ch. 1, n. 30.

3. The ultimate result of this, of course, was the complete breakdown of the hierarchy of the categories in the nineteenth century. It is interesting that in 1784 a speaker at the Venetian Academy argued the superiority of view painting over painting of the nude. See F. Haskell, "Francesco Guardi as Vedutista and Some of his Patrons," *Journal of the Warburg and Courtauld Institutes,* XXIII (1960), 264.

4. Cf. G. Syamken, *Die Bildinhalte des Alessandro Magnasco* (Hamburg, 1965).

5. A useful introduction to this subject is J. Scholz and A. H. Mayor, *Baroque and Romantic Stage Design* (New York, 1950).

6. Canaletto spent most of the period from 1746 to 1755 in England.

7. On the Guardi brothers see especially *Mostra dei Guardi* (Venice, 1965).

8. Quoted in A. H. Mayor, *Giovanni Battista Piranesi* (New York, 1952), p. 5. On Piranesi as an architect see W. Körte, "G. B. Piranesi als praktischer Architekt," *Zeitschrift für Kunstgeschichte,* n.f., II (1933), 16–33; and R. Wittkower, "Piranesi as Architect," in the catalogue *Piranesi,* Smith College Museum of Art (Northampton, Massachusetts, 1961), pp. 99–109.

9. All these statues are in the Vatican Museum.

10. Bracci, Filippo della Valle, and Queirolo were among the artists responsible for the sculptural decoration of the Fontana di Trevi in Rome. For that monument, see A. Schiavo, *La Fontana di Trevi e le altre opere de Nicola Salvi* (Rome, 1956).

11. See V. Golzio, "La Facciata de S. Giovanni in Laterano e l'architettura del Settecento," *Miscellanea Bibliothecae Hertzianae* (Munich, 1961), p. 455 and especially pp. 462–63.

12. Cf. W. Lotz, "Die Spanische Treppe," *Römisches Jahrbuch für Kunstgeschichte,* XII (1969), 41–94.

13. In his *Livre d'architecture* (Paris, 1745), Boffrand actually claimed responsibility for the plan of Stupinigi. The claim is at best exaggerated, though Juvarra may have been familiar with Boffrand's design. The relationship and the sources of the two schemes are discussed by R. Pommer, *Eighteenth-Century Architecture in Piedmont* (New York, 1967), pp. 69–71.

14. The importance of these connections, especially as they affected architecture in Piedmont, is discussed by Pommer, *op. cit.*

15. For a concise, penetrating analysis of the building see R. Wittkower, *Art and Architecture in Italy: 1600 to 1750,* Pelican History of Art (Baltimore, 1958), pp. 261–63.

9 ENGLISH PAINTING IN THE EIGHTEENTH CENTURY

1. The situation had been very much the same in the sixteenth century, when Holbein and his school dominated British portraiture in the first half, Marcus Gheeraerdts and various other Continental painters in the second.

2. The best general account of British painting of this period is E. Waterhouse, *Painting in Britain: 1530 to 1790,* Pelican History of Art (2nd ed.; Baltimore, 1962).

3. In a famous passage he also paraphrased wittily the gibberish of the "experts." A similar satire on art experts is found in the tale of the returned son in Oliver Goldsmith's *The Vicar of Wakefield* (London, 1766).

4. E. Wind, "Humanitätsidee und heroisiertes Porträt in der englischen Kultur des 18. Jahrhunderts," *Vorträge der Bibliothek Warburg* (Leipzig–Berlin, 1930/31), pp. 156 ff.

5. Sir Joshua Reynolds, *Discourses on Art,* ed. R. Lavine (New York, 1961), Discourse No. XIV.

6. For the problem of quotation in art see H. Walpole, *Anecdotes* (ed. 1849), I, XVII.

7. See E. Panofsky, *Hercules am Scheidewege, und andere antike Bildstoffe in der neueren Kunst* (Leipzig–Berlin, 1930).

10 GERMANY AND AUSTRIA IN THE SEVENTEENTH AND EIGHTEENTH CENTURIES

1. H. Sedlmayr, *Johann Bernhard Fischer von Erlach* (Vienna, 1956).

2. B. Grimschitz, *Johann Lukas von Hildebrandt* (Vienna, 1959).

3. Fischer von Erlach had erected a Belvedere for the Palais Liechtenstein in 1687.

4. The name "Zwinger" was given to the open spaces behind fortified walls. The Dresden Zwinger, never completely finished as Pöppelmann had planned it, was restored between 1924 and 1936, after having suffered many indignities and losses. Yet in February, 1945, it was virtually all destroyed, along with most of Old Dresden, by aerial bombardment (that left the outlying war-industries intact!). A modern reconstruction, finished 1964, preserves its outward appearance. See F. Löffler, *Das alte Dresden,* 5th ed. (Leipzig, 1965).

5. H. Ladendorf, *Der Bildhauer und Baumeister Andreas Schlüter* (Berlin, 1935).

6. M. H. von Freeden, *Balthasar Neumann* (Munich–Berlin, 1953).

7. The plan of the whole, with its felicitous rhythm of salients, is Neumann's work even though certain parts (none belonging to the façade) may have been modified at the suggestion of the foreign artists consulted, among them Johann Lukas von Hildebrandt.

8. Hildebrandt had doubted that it could be vaulted.

9. Neumann had planned to duplicate these stairs with others like them in the opposite wing!

10. See the description of this staircase by Pevsner in *An Outline of European Architecture,* Jubilee edition (Baltimore, 1960), pp. 486–87.

11. The only curved form on the outside is the convex part in the center of the two-tower façade. Two-tower façades had always been popular in the North, and the narrow, high proportions of Vierzehnheiligen are indeed reminiscent of Gothic prototypes.

12. In the relatively sparing decor the great central tabernacle plays a vital role. Designed by J. J. M. Küchel and (in his words) "pierced in a specially novel fashion," this tabernacle, containing the altar of the patron saints, is a worthy eighteenth-century successor to Bernini's baldachin of St. Peter's.

13. W. Pinder, *Deutscher Barock,* 2nd ed. (Königstein and Leipzig, 1924), p. 125.

14. The idea as such was not entirely new; it had been introduced by Jules Hardouin-Mansart in the dome

of the Church of the Invalides in Paris (see pages 142–145), which in turn was developed from a design by François Mansart for the Bourbon Chapel at St. Denis: see A. Blunt, *Art and Architecture in France: 1500–1700,* Pelican History of Art (Baltimore, 1953), p. 212.

15. J. B. Zimmermann assisted Cuvilliés in the execution of this decoration.

16. The theater has been rebuilt after its destruction in World War II; most of the original decor had been saved in a shelter, and the old color scheme has been freed from later coats of paint.

17. Placed originally on a bridge over the River Spree, near the Royal Castle, the Monument has been moved to the courtyard of Charlottenburg.

18. Bernini had planned an equestrian portrait of the king placed on top of steep cliffs—a new Hercules on the mountain of Virtue. Appreciated as little as Bernini's façade design for the Louvre, his sculpture ended up, considerably transformed, as a piece of garden decoration in Versailles. See R. Wittkower, "The Vicissitudes of a Dynastic Monument," *Essays in Honor of Erwin Panofsky* (New York, 1961), I, p. 497.

19. Some of these painters were active elsewhere as well. Pellegrini, for instance, worked in England, Flanders, Holland, and France. Amigoni, too, spent long periods in England any Spain, as well as in Bavaria.

20. With few exceptions all his sketches are in Austrian collections.

Chronological Chart

Before 1550

St. Ignatius of Loyola (1491–1556; canonized 1622)
St. Francis Xavier (1506–52; canonized 1622)
Vignola (Giacomo Barozzi; 1507–73)
St. Theresa of Avila (1515–82; canonized 1622)
St. Philip Neri (1515–95; canonized 1622)
Martin Luther posts 95 theses at Wittenberg, 1517
Felice Peretti (1521–90); Pope Sixtus V
Federico Barocci (1535–1612)
St. Charles Borromeo (1538–84; canonized 1610)
Society of Jesus founded 1540
Council of Trent (1545–63)

1550–59

Camillo Borghese (1552–1621); Pope Paul V
Paul Bril (1554–1626)
Ludovico Carracci (1555–1619)
Carlo Maderno (1556–1629)
Agostino Carracci (1557–1602)

1560–69

Annibale Carracci (1560–1609)
Cavaliere Cesare d'Arpino (1568–1640)
Joos de Momper (1564–1636)
Francisco Ribalta (1565–1628)
Il Gesù, Rome (Vignola), begun 1568
Netherlands begins revolt against Spain, 1568
Jan Brueghel (1568–1625)
Maffeo Barberini (1568–1644); Pope Urban VIII
Juan Martinez Montanes (1568–1649)

1570–79

Giovanni Battista Caracciolo (Battistello; c. 1570–1637)
Salomon de Brosse (1571–1626)
Caravaggio, Michelangelo Merisi da (1573–1610)
Inigo Jones (1573–1652)
Giambattista Pamphili (1574–1655); Pope Innocent X
Guido Reni (1575–1642)
Gregorio Fernandez (1576–1636)
Stefano Maderno (1576–1636)
Peter Paul Rubens (1577–1640)
Adam Elsheimer (1578–1610)
Francesco Albani (1578–1660)

1580–89

Francesco Mocchi (1580–1654)
Frans Hals (c. 1580–1666)
Northern provinces of the Netherlands absolve themselves from allegiance to Spain, 1581
Bernardo Strozzi (1581–1644)
Domenichino (Domenico Zampieri; 1581–1641)
Giovanni Lanfranco (1582–1647)
Pieter Lastman (1583–1633)
Francesco Maria Ricchino (1583–1658)
Papacy of Sixtus V, 1585–90
Jacques Lemercier (c. 1585–1654)
Hendrick Terbrugghen (1588–1629)
Antoine Le Nain (1588–1648)
Jacques Sarrazin (1588–1660)
Reign of Henry IV of France, 1589–1610
Domenico Fetti (1589–1623)
Hercules Seghers (1589/90–after 1632)

1590–99

Simon Vouet (1590–1649)
Gerard Honthorst (1590–1656)
Esaias van de Velde (c. 1591–1630)
Jusepe de Ribera (Lo Spagnoletto; 1591–1652)
Guercino (Giovanni Francesco Barbieri; 1591–1666)
Jacques Callot (1592/93–1635)
Il Bamboccio (Pieter van Laer; 1592/95–1642)
France becomes Catholic power with the conversion of Henry IV, 1593
Louis Le Nain (1593–1648)
Georges de La Tour (1593–1652)
Jacob Jordaens (1593–1678)
Valentin de Boulogne (1594–1632)
François Duquesnoy (1594–1643)
Nicolas Poussin (1594–1665)
Alessandro Algardi (1596–1654)
Constantijn Huygens (1596–1687)
Farnese Gallery ceiling, Rome (Annibale Carracci), 1597–1600
Jan Liss (1595/97–1629/30)
Jan van Goyen (1596–1656)
Pietro da Cortona (1596–1669)
Façade of Santa Susanna, Rome (Maderno), 1597–1603
Sebastien Stoskopff (1597–1657)
Pieter Jansz. Saenredam (1597–1665)
Edict of Nantes establishes religious toleration in France, 1598
Jacob van Campen (1598–1657)
Francisco de Zurbaran (1598–1664)
François Mansart (1598–1666)
Gianlorenzo Bernini (1598–1680)
Baldassare Longhena (1598–1682)

Contarelli Chapel, S. Luigi dei Francesi, Rome (Caravaggio), 1599–1600
ANTHONY VAN DYCK (1599–1641)
DIEGO RODRIGUEZ DE SILVA Y VELAZQUEZ (1599–1660)
ANDREA SACCHI (1599–1661)
FABIO CHIGI (1599–1667); Pope Alexander VII
FRANCESCO BORROMINI (1599–1667)

1600–1609

JACQUES BLANCHARD (1600–38)
GIOVANNI BENEDETTO CASTIGLIONE (c. 1600/10–65)
SALOMON VAN RUYSDAEL (c. 1600–1670)
CLAUDE LORRAIN (Claude Gellée; 1600–82)
ALONSO CANO (1601–67)
PHILIPPE DE CHAMPAIGNE (1602–74)
Queen Elizabeth I of England dies, 1603
Carlo Maderno appointed architect of St. Peter's, 1603
Annunciation, St. Peter's (Francesco Mocchi), 1603–8
AERT VAN DER NEER (1603–77)
Papacy of Paul V, 1605–21
ADRIAEN BROUWER (1606–38)
LAURENT DE LA HIRE (1606–56)
ARTUS QUELLINUS I (1606–68)
REMBRANDT VAN RIJN (1606–69)
MATHIEU LE NAIN (1607–77)
Holland's independence recognized by Spain, 1609

1610–19

Maria de' Medici regent of France 1610–24, during minority of Louis XIII
Reign of Louis XIII of France, 1610–43
ADRIAEN VAN OSTADE (1610–85)
DAVID TENIERS (1610–90)
CARLO RAINALDI (1611–91)
LOUIS LE VAU (1612–70)
FRANS POST (c. 1612–80)
Aurora, Casino Rospigliosi (Reni), 1613–14
BARTHOLOMEUS VAN DER HELST (1613–70)
CLAUDE PERRAULT (1613–88)
ANDRE LE NOTRE (1613–1700)
Last Communion of St. Jerome (Domenichino), 1614
Luxembourg Palace, Paris (De Brosse), begun 1615
SALVATOR ROSA (1615–73)
GASPARD DUGHET (1615–75)
EUSTACHE LE SUEUR (1616–55)
GERARD TERBORCH (c. 1617–81)
BARTOLOME ESTEBAN MURILLO (1617–82)
Thirty Years' War begins 1618
Banqueting House, Whitehall Palace, London (Inigo

Jones), 1619–22
PHILIPS KONINCK (1619–88)
CHARLES LE BRUN (1619–90)

1620–29

AELBERT CUYP (c. 1620–91)
PIERRE PUGET (1620–94)
Aurora, Casino Ludovisi, Rome (Guercino), 1621
ALLAERT VAN EVERDINGEN (1621–75)
Medici Cycle, Palace of Luxembourg, Paris (Rubens), 1622–25
CAREL FABRITIUS (1622–54)
JUAN DE VALDES LEAL (1622–90)
Papacy of Urban VIII, 1623–44
ANTONIO RAGGI (1624–86)
Baldachin, St. Peter's (Bernini), 1624–33
Cardinal Richelieu, chief minister and adviser to Louis XIII, 1624–42
GUARINO GUARINI (1624–83)
Assumption of the Virgin, S. Andrea della Valle (Lanfranco), 1625–27
Reign of Charles I of England, 1625–49
CARLO MARATTA (1625–1713)
Tomb of Urban VIII, St. Peter's, Rome (Bernini), 1628–47
JACOB VAN RUISDAEL (1628/29–82)
PEDRO DE MENA (1628–88)
FRANÇOIS GIRARDON (1628–1715)
Divine Wisdom, Palazzo Barberini (Sacchi), 1629–31
PIETER DE HOOGH (1629–after 1684)

1630–39

JOB BERCKHEYDE (1630–1693)
FRANÇOIS D'ORBAY (1631–97)
JAN VERMEER (1632–75)
CHRISTOPHER WREN (1632–1723)
Mauritshuis, Rotterdam (Van Campen and C. Huygens), 1633–35
Triumph of the Barberini, Barberini Palace (Cortona), 1633–39
LUCA GIORDANO (1634–1705)
Charles I at the Hunt (Anthony van Dyck), 1635
MELCHIORRE CAFFA (1635–67/68)
The Smokers (Brouwer), c. 1636
CHARLES DE LA FOSSE (1636–1716)
Rape of the Sabine Women (Poussin), c. 1636
JAN VAN DER HEYDEN (1637–1712)
GERRIT BERCKHEYDE (1638–1698)
San Carlo alle Quattro Fontane, Rome (Borromini), 1638–41; façade c. 1665

MEINDERT HOBBEMA (1638–1709)
GIOVANNI BATTISTA GAULLI (Baciccio; 1639–1709)

1640–49

Poussin in Paris, 1640–42
Reign of Frederick William, the Great Elector of Brandenburg, 1640–88
ANTOINE COYSEVOX (1640–1720)
Night Watch (Rembrandt), 1642
Château of Maisons (Mansart), 1642–46
Cardinal Mazarin governs France (1643–61) during minority of Louis XIV
Reign of Louis XIV of France, 1643–1715
Fraga Portrait of Philip IV (Velázquez), 1644
Papacy of Innocent X, 1644–55
St. Theresa in Ecstasy, Sta. Maria della Vittoria (Bernini), 1645–52
JULES HARDOUIN-MANSART (1646–1708)
Peace of Westphalia, 1648
Royal Academy of Painting and Sculpture founded in Paris, 1648
Charles I of England beheaded, 1649; Commonwealth under Cromwell, 1649–53; Protectorate, 1653–59

1650–59

BALTHASAR PERMOSER (1651–1732)
Aristotle with the Bust of Homer (Rembrandt), 1653
Guardsman (Fabritius), 1654
NICODEMUS TESSIN THE YOUNGER (1654–1728)
Jewish Cemetery (J. van Ruisdael), c. 1655
Papacy of Alexander VII, 1655–67
The Maids of Honor (Velázquez), 1656
Colonnade of St. Peter's, Rome (Bernini), begun 1656
JOHANN BERNHARD FISCHER VON ERLACH (1656–1723)
ROBERT DE COTTE (1656–1735)
NICOLAS DE LARGILLIERE (1656–1746)
Château of Vaux-le-Vicomte (Le Vau), 1657–61
FRANCESCO SOLIMENA (1657–1747)
View of Delft (Vermeer), c. 1658
SEBASTIANO RICCI (1659–1734)
HYACINTHE RIGAUD (1659–1743)

1660–69

Reign of Charles II of England, 1660–85
JACOB PRANDTAUER (1660–1726)
Louis XIV, assisted by Colbert, assumes absolute rule of France, 1661
Oath of Claudius Civilis (Rembrandt), 1661/62
ANTOINE COYPEL (1661–1708)
MATTHÄUS DANIEL PÖPPELMANN (1662–1736)

Women Regents of the Old Men's Home at Haarlem (Hals), 1664
ANDREAS SCHLÜTER (1664–1714)
JOHN VANBRUGH (1664–1726)
Triumphs of Alexander, Louvre (Le Brun), 1661–68
GIUSEPPE MARIA CRESPI (Lo Spagnuolo; 1665–1747)
Great Fire of London, 1666
French Academy in Rome founded, 1666
GEORG BÄHR (1666–1738)
Colbert creates Buildings Council—Le Vau, Le Brun, Perrault—to complete Louvre, 1667
JACQUES V. GABRIEL (1667–1742)
ALESSANDRO MAGNASCO (Lissandrino; 1667–1749)
GERMAIN BOFFRAND (1667–1754)
JOHANN LUKAS VAN HILDEBRANDT (1668–1745)
Construction of Versailles begun 1669

1670–79

Colbert establishes Royal Academy of Architecture in 1671
Milo of Crotona (Puget), 1671–82
CLAUDE GILLOT (1673–1722)
Tomb of Cardinal Richelieu (Girardon), 1675–94
St. Paul's Cathedral, London (Wren), 1675–1710
Ceiling Fresco, Il Gesù, Rome (Baciccio), 1676–79
Church of the Invalides, Paris (J. Hardouin-Mansart), 1676–1706
FILIPPO JUVARRA (1678–1736)

1680–89

FILIPPO RAGUZZINI (c. 1680–1771)
Peter the Great (r. 1682–1725) westernizes Russia
JAMES GIBBS (1682–1754)
PEDRO DE RIBERA (c. 1683–1742)
GIAMBATTISTA PIAZZETTA (1683–1752)
ANTOINE WATTEAU (1684–1721)
Louis XIV revokes Edict of Nantes, 1685
DOMINIKUS ZIMMERMANN (1685–1766)
COSMAS DAMIAN ASAM (1686–1739)
JOHANN BALTHASAR NEUMANN (1687–1753)

1690–99

ALESSANDRO GALILEI (1691–1737)
PAUL EGELL (1691–1752)
EGID QUIRIN ASAM (1692–1750)
FRANCESCO DE SANCTIS (1693–1740)
RAPHAEL DONNER (1693–1741)
RICHARD BOYLE (1694–1753)
FRANÇOIS CUVILLIES THE ELDER (1695–1768)
JOSEF ANTON FEICHTMAYR (1696–1770)
GIAMBATTISTA TIEPOLO (1696–1770)

WILLIAM HOGARTH (1697–1764)
CANALETTO (Giovanni Antonio Canal; 1697–1768)
FILIPPO DELLA VALLE (1697–1770)
Equestrian Portrait of Frederick William, the Great Elector (Schlüter), 1698–1709
EDME BOUCHARDON (1698–1762)
PIERRE-HUBERT SUBLEYRAS (1699–1749)
GEORG WENZESLAUS VON KNOBELSDORFF (1699–1753)
JEAN-BAPTISTE SIMEON CHARDIN (1699–1779)
FERDINANDO FUGA (1699–1782)
JACQUES-ANGE GABRIEL (1698–1782)

1700–1709

Royal Palace, Stockholm (N. Tessin the Younger), c. 1700
PIETRO BRACCI (1700–73)
LUIGI VANVITELLI (1700–73)
NICOLAI EIGTVED (1701–54)
BERNARDO ANTONIO VITTONE (1702–70)
PIETRO LONGHI (1702–85)
FRANÇOIS BOUCHER (1703–70)
FRANCESCO QUEIROLO (1704–62)
MAURICE QUENTIN DE LA TOUR (1704–88)
Blenheim Palace, Woodstock (Vanbrugh), 1705–22
MARCUS TUSCHER (1705–51)
EMMANUEL HERE DE CORNY (1705–63)
FRANCISCO SALZILLO (1707–83)
POMPEO BATONI (1708–87)
Zwinger, Dresden (M. D. Pöppelmann), 1709–19

1710–19

Act passed in England to build 50 new churches, 1711
FRANCESCO GUARDI (1712–93)
Reign of Frederick William, the Great Elector, 1713–40
JEAN-BAPTISTE PIGALLE (1714–85)
Karlskirche, Vienna (J. B. Fischer von Erlach), begun 1715
Reign of Louis XV of France, 1715–74
ETIENNE-MAURICE FALCONET (1716–91)
JOSEPH-MARIE VIEN (1716–1809)
Superga, Turin (Juvarra), 1717–31
Pilgrimage to Cythera (Watteau), c. 1718

1720–29

Residenz, Würzburg (J. B. Neumann), begun 1720
GIOVANNI BATTISTA PIRANESI (1720–78)
Gersaint's Signboard (Watteau), 1721
Palace of the Belvedere, Vienna (J. L. von Hildebrandt), 1721–24
Spanish Steps, Rome (De Sanctis), 1723–25

JOSHUA REYNOLDS (1723–92)
FRANCESCO ANTONIO BUSTELLI (1723–63)
ANTON FRANZ MAULPERTSCH (1724–96)
JEAN-BAPTISTE GREUZE (1725–1805)
IGNAZ GÜNTHER (1725–75)
THOMAS GAINSBOROUGH (1727–88)
ANTON RAPHAEL MENGS (1728–79)
Royal Hunting Palace, Stupinigi (Juvarra), 1729–33

1730–39

Hôtel de Soubise, Paris (Boffrand), begun 1732
Soap Bubbles (Chardin), c. 1732
Trasparente, Cathedral of Toledo (Tomé), 1732
JEAN-HONORE FRAGONARD (1732–1806)
HUBERT ROBERT (1733–1808)
Amalienburg, near Munich (Cuvilliés), 1734–39
Mercury (Pigalle), 1736–39
Excavations begin at Herculaneum, 1738; later at Paestum and Pompeii
CLODION (Claude Michel; 1738–1814)

1740–49

Reign of Frederick II the Great, King of Prussia, 1740–86
LOUIS-GABRIEL MOREAU THE ELDER (1740–1806)
JEAN-ANTOINE HOUDON (1741–1828)
Marriage à la Mode (William Hogarth), 1743–45
Sanssouci, Potsdam (Knobelsdorff), 1745–47
JACQUES-LOUIS DAVID (1748–1825)
Amalienborg, Copenhagen (M. Tuscher and N. Eigtved), begun 1749

After 1750

Frescoes in Residenz, Würzburg (G. B. Tiepolo), 1751–52
Place Stanislas, Nancy (Héré de Corny), 1752–55
Royal Palace, Caserta (Vanvitelli), 1752–74
Parnassus, Villa Albani (Mengs), 1761
Petit Trianon, Versailles (J.-A. Gabriel), 1762–68
Happy Accidents of the Swing (Fragonard), 1767
Royal Crescent, Bath (J. Wood the Younger), 1767–75
Equestrian Monument of Peter the Great (Falconet), 1770–82
Reign of Louis XVI of France, 1774–93
Punished Son (Greuze), 1777–78
Oath of the Horatii (J.-L. David), 1784
Portrait of Mrs. Siddons as the Tragic Muse (Reynolds), 1784
Portrait of Mrs. Siddons (Gainsborough), 1785

Selected Bibliography

Asterisks (*) indicate that titles are available in paperback.

GENERAL

Adhémar, J. *Graphic Art of the 18th Century.* London: Thames & Hudson, 1964.

Bazin, G. *The Baroque.* Greenwich, Conn.: New York Graphic Society, 1968.

————. *Baroque and Rococo Art.* New York: Praeger, 1964.*

Holt, E. *A Documentary History of Art.* Vol. 2. New York: Anchor, 1958.*

Kaufmann, E. *Architecture in the Age of Reason.* Cambridge: Harvard University Press, 1955.

Kitson, M. *The Age of Baroque.* New York: McGraw-Hill, 1966.

Lee, R. *Ut Pictura Poesis: The Humanistic Theory of Painting.* New York: Norton, 1967.*

Levey, M. *Rococo to Revolution.* New York: Praeger, 1966.*

Millon, H. *Baroque and Rococo Architecture.* New York: Braziller, 1961.*

Panofsky, E. *Idea: A Concept in Art Theory.* Columbia: University of South Carolina Press, 1968.

Pevsner, N. *An Outline of European Architecture.* 6th Jubilee ed. Baltimore: Penguin Books, 1960.*

Rosenblum, R. *Transformations in Late Eighteenth Century Art.* Princeton: Princeton University Press, 1967.*

Scholz, J., and Mayor, A. H. *Baroque and Romantic Stage Design.* New York: H. Bittner, 1950.

Schönberger, A., and Soehner, H. *The Rococo Age.* New York: McGraw-Hill, 1960.

Sterling, C. *Still Life Painting from Antiquity to the Present Time.* New York: Universe Books, 1959.

Tapié, V.-L. *The Age of Grandeur. Baroque Art and Architecture.* 2nd ed. New York: Praeger, 1966.*

Wölfflin, H. *Principles of Art History.* New York: Dover, c. 1950.*

ITALY

d'Ancona, P. *Tiepolo in Milan: The Palazzo Clerici Frescoes.* Milan: Edizione del Milione, 1956.

Bellori, G. P. *The Lives of Annibale and Agostino Carracci.* Translated by C. Enggass. University Park: Pennsylvania State University Press, 1968.

Blunt, A. *Artistic Theory in Italy: 1450–1600.* Oxford: Oxford University Press, 1940.*

————. *The Drawings of G. B. Castiglione and Stefano della Bella at Windsor Castle.* London: Phaidon, 1954.

Blunt, A., and Cooke, H. L. *Roman Drawings of the XVII & XVIII Centuries . . . at Windsor Castle.* London: Phaidon, 1960.

Blunt, A., and Croft-Murray, E. *Venetian Drawings of the XVII & XVIII Centuries . . . at Windsor Castle.* London: Phaidon, 1957.

Constable, W. G. *Canaletto.* 2 vols. Oxford: Oxford University Press, 1962.

Enggass, R. *The Painting of Baciccio.* University Park: Pennsylvania State University Press, 1964.

Fiocco, G. *Venetian Painting of the Seicento and Settecento.* New York: Harcourt, Brace, 1929.

Friedlaender, W. *Caravaggio Studies.* Princeton: Princeton University Press, 1955.*

————. *Mannerism and Anti-Mannerism in Italian Painting.* New York: Schocken Books, 1965.*

Haskell, F. *Patrons and Painters: A Study in the Relations Between Italian Art and Society in the Age of the Baroque.* New York: Knopf, 1963.

Hind, A. M. *Giovanni Battista Piranesi.* London: The Cotswold Gallery, 1922.

Kitson, M., intro. *The Complete Paintings of Caravaggio.* New York: Abrams, 1969.

Knox, G. *Tiepolo Drawings in the Victoria and Albert Museum.* London: H. M. Stationery Office, 1960.

Kurz, O. *Bolognese Drawings of the XVII & XVIII Centuries . . . at Windsor Castle.* London: Phaidon, 1955.

Levey, M. *Painting in XVIII Century Venice.* London: Phaidon, 1959.

Mahon, D. *Studies in Seicento Art and Theory.* London: Warburg Institute, 1947.

Manning, R., and B. S. *Genoese Masters: Cambiaso to Magnasco, 1550–1750.* Dayton Art Institute, 1962.

Martin, J. R. *The Farnese Gallery.* Princeton: Princeton University Press, 1965.

Maxon, J., ed. *Painting in Italy in the Eighteenth Century: Rococo to Romanticism.* Chicago: Art Institute of Chicago, 1970.

Mayor, A. H. *Giovanni Battista Piranesi.* New York: H. Bittner, 1952.

Milkovich, M. *Bernardo Strozzi: Paintings and Drawings.* Binghamton, N. Y.: State University, Art Gallery, 1967.

———. *Sebastiano and Marco Ricci in America*. Lexington: University of Kentucky, 1966.

Moir, A. *The Italian Followers of Caravaggio*. 2 vols. Cambridge: Harvard University Press, 1967.

Morassi, A. *G. B. Tiepolo*. London: Phaidon, 1955.

———. *A Complete Catalogue of the Paintings of G. B. Tiepolo*. London: Phaidon, 1962.

Nissman, J., and Hibbard, H. *Florentine Baroque Art*. New York: The Metropolitan Museum of Art, 1969.

Olsen, H. *Federico Barocci*. 2nd rev. ed. Copenhagen: Munksgaard, 1962.

Parker, K. T. *The Drawings of Antonio Canaletto . . . at Windsor Castle*. London: Phaidon, 1948.

Pignatti, T. *Pietro Longhi*. London: Phaidon, 1969.

Pommer, R. *Eighteenth-Century Architecture in Piedmont*. New York: New York University Press, 1967.

Pope-Hennessy, J. *The Drawings of Domenichino . . . at Windsor Castle*. London: Phaidon, 1948.

———. *Italian High Renaissance and Baroque Sculpture*. 3 vols. London: Phaidon, 1963.

Posner, D. *Annibale Carracci*. 2 vols. London: Phaidon, 1971.

de Rinaldis, A. *Neapolitan Painting of the Seicento*. New York: Harcourt, Brace, 1929.

Röthlisberger, M. *Claude Lorrain: The Drawings*. Berkeley and Los Angeles: University of California Press, 1969.

———. *Claude Lorrain: The Paintings*. New Haven: Yale University Press, 1961.

Shaw, J. Byam. *The Drawings of Domenico Tiepolo*. London: Faber & Faber, 1962.

———. *The Drawings of Francesco Guardi*. London: Faber & Faber, 1951.

Sutton, D., and Mahon, D. *Artists in 17th Century Rome*. London: Wildenstein, 1955.

Thomas, H. *The Drawings of Giovanni Battista Piranesi*. New York: Beechhurst, 1954.

Trapier, E. du G. *Ribera*. New York: Hispanic Society of America, 1952.

Wallis, M. *Canaletto [Bellotto, The Painter of Warsaw]*. Warsaw: Panstwowy Instytut Wydawniczy, 1954.

Waterhouse, E. *Baroque Painting in Rome: The Seventeenth Century*. London: Macmillan, 1937.

———. *Italian Baroque Painting*. Rev. ed. London: Phaidon, 1969.*

Wittkower, R. *Art and Architecture in Italy: 1600 to 1750*. Pelican History of Art. 2nd rev. ed. Baltimore: Penguin Books, 1965.

———. *The Drawings of the Carracci . . . at Windsor Castle*. London: Phaidon, 1952.

———. *The Sculpture of Bernini*. 2nd ed. London: Phaidon, 1966.

Wittkower, R., et al. *Art in Italy, 1600–1700*. Detroit Institute of Arts, 1965.

FRANCE

Bechtel, E. de T. *Jacques Callot*. New York: Braziller, 1955.

Berger, R. *Antoine Le Pautre*. New York: College Art Association of America, 1969.

Blomfield, R. *A History of French Architecture, 1494–1661*. London: G. Bell & Sons, 1911.

———. *A History of French Architecture, 1661–1774*. 2 vols. London: G. Bell & Sons, 1921.

Blunt, A. *Art and Architecture in France: 1500 to 1700*. Pelican History of Art. Baltimore: Penguin Books, 1957.

———. *François Mansart*. London: Warburg Institute, 1941.

———. *The French Drawings at Windsor Castle*. London: Phaidon, 1945.

———. *Nicolas Poussin*. 2 vols. New York: Pantheon Books, 1967.

Crelly, W. *The Painting of Simon Vouet*. New Haven: Yale University Press, 1962.

Dilke, Lady. *French Architects and Sculptors of the XVIIIth Century*. London: G. Bell & Sons, 1900.

Fox, H. *André Le Nôtre*. London: B. T. Batsford, 1962.

Friedlaender, W. *Nicolas Poussin*. New York: Abrams, 1965.

Friedlaender, W.; Blunt, A.; et al. *The Drawings of Nicolas Poussin*. 4 vols. London: Warburg Institute, 1939–63.

de Goncourt, E. and J. *French XVIII Century Painters*. New York: Phaidon, 1948.

Kimball, F. *The Creation of the Rococo*. Philadelphia Museum of Art, 1943.*

Lavedan, P. *French Architecture*. Baltimore: Penguin Books, 1956.*

Montagni, E. C. *The Complete Paintings of Watteau*. New York: Abrams, 1971.

de Nolhac, P. *Versailles and the Trianons*. New York: Dodd, Mead, 1906.

Parker, K. T. *The Drawings of Antoine Watteau*. London: B. T. Batsford, 1931.

Rosenberg, P. *Chardin*. Geneva: Skira, 1963.

Savage, G. *French Decorative Art, 1638–1793*. New York: Praeger, 1969.

The Splendid Century; French Art: 1600–1715. New York: The Metropolitan Museum of Art, 1960–61.

Sutton, D. *France in the Eighteenth Century*. London: Royal Academy, 1968.

———. *French Drawings of the Eighteenth Century*. London: Pleiades Books, 1949.

Thuillier, J. *Fragonard*. Geneva: Skira, 1967.

Thuillier, J., and Châtelet, A. *French Painting from Le Nain to Fragonard*. Geneva: Skira, 1964.

Ward, W. *The Architecture of the Renaissance in France, 1495–1830*. 2 vols. 2nd rev. ed. London: B. T. Batsford, 1926.

Wildenstein, G. *Chardin*. Greenwich, Conn.: New York Graphic Society, 1969.

———. *The Paintings of Fragonard*. London: Phaidon, 1960.

SPAIN AND LATIN AMERICA

Baird, J. A. *The Churches of Mexico, 1530–1810*. Berkeley: University of California Press, 1962.

Bevan, B. *History of Spanish Architecture*. New York: Scribner, 1939.

Darby, D. F. *Francisco Ribalta and His School*. Cambridge: Harvard University Press, 1938.

Harris, E. *Spanish Painting*. New York: Hyperion Press, 1937.

Justi, K. *Diego Velázquez and His Times*. London: H. Grevel, 1889.

Kelemen, P. *Baroque and Rococo in Latin America*. New York: Macmillan, 1951.*

Kubler, G., and Soria, M. *Art and Architecture in Spain and Portugal and their American Dominions: 1500 to 1800*. Pelican History of Art. Baltimore: Penguin Books, 1959.

López-Rey, J. *Velázquez*. London: Faber & Faber, 1963.

———. *Velázquez' Work and World*. London: Faber & Faber, 1968.

Proske, B. *Juan Martínez Montañés*. New York: Hispanic Society of America, 1967.

Soria, M. *The Paintings of Zurbarán*. 2nd ed. New York: Phaidon, 1955.

Trapier, E. du G. *Valdés Leal*. New York: Hispanic Society of America, 1960.

———. *Velázquez*. New York: Hispanic Society of America, 1948.

Weisbach, W. *Spanish Baroque Art*. Cambridge, Eng.: The University Press, 1941.

Wethey, H. *Alonso Cano*. Princeton: Princeton University Press, 1955.

———. *Colonial Architecture and Sculpture in Peru*. Cambridge: Harvard University Press, 1949.

NORTHERN EUROPE

Paulsson, T. *Scandinavian Architecture*. London: L. Hill, 1958.

FLANDERS

Burchard, L., and d' Hulst, R. A. *Rubens Drawings*. 2 vols. Brussels: Arcade, 1963.

Evers, H. G. *Peter Paul Rubens*. Munich: Bruckmann, 1942.

Gerson, H., and ter Kuile, E. H. *Art and Architecture in Belgium: 1600 to 1800*. Pelican History of Art. Baltimore: Penguin Books, 1960.

Glück, G. *Van Dyck; Des Meisters Gemälde*. Klassiker der Kunst. Stuttgart: Deutsche Verlags-Anstalt, 1931.

Held, J. S. *Rubens, Selected Drawings*. 2 vols. London: Phaidon, 1959.

d'Hulst, R.-A. *De Tekeningen van Jakob Jordaens*. Brussels: Paleis der Academiën, 1956.

Magurn, R. S., ed. *The Letters of Peter Paul Rubens*. Cambridge: Harvard University Press, 1955.

van Puyvelde, L. *The Sketches of Rubens*. London: K. Paul, Trench, Trubner, 1947.

Rooses, M. *Jacob Jordaens, His Life and Work*. New York: Dutton, 1908.

———. *L'Oeuvre de P. P. Rubens*. 5 vols. Antwerp: Joseph Maes, 1886–92.

Vey, H. *Die Zeichnungen Anton van Dycks*. 2 vols. Brussels: Arcade, 1962.

Wedgwood, C. V. *The World of Rubens*. New York: Time-Life Books, 1967.

HOLLAND

Benesch, O. *The Drawings of Rembrandt*. 6 vols. London: Phaidon, 1954–57.

Bergström, I. *Dutch Still-Life Painting in the Seventeenth Century*. New York: T. Yoseloff, 1956.

Gerson, H. *Rembrandt Paintings*. New York: Reynal, 1968.

Gowing, L. *Vermeer*. London: Faber & Faber, 1952.

Haak, Bob. *Rembrandt: His Life, His Work, His Time*. New York: Abrams, 1969.

Held, Julius S. *Rembrandt's "Aristotle" and other Rembrandt Studies*. Princeton: Princeton University Press, 1969.

Münz, L. *Rembrandt's Etchings*. 2 vols. London: Phaidon, 1952.

Rosenberg, J. *Rembrandt: Life and Work*. London: Phaidon, 1964.*

Rosenberg, J.; Slive, S.; and ter Kuile, E. H. *Dutch Art and Architecture: 1600 to 1800*. Pelican History of Art. Baltimore: Penguin Books, 1966.

Slive, S. *Frans Hals*. 2 vols. London: Phaidon, 1970.

Stechow, W. *Dutch Landscape Painting of the Seventeenth Century*. London: Phaidon, 1966.

White, C. *Rembrandt as an Etcher*, 2 vols. University Park: Pennsylvania State University Press, 1969.

ENGLAND

Summerson, J. *Architecture in Britain: 1530 to 1830*. Pelican History of Art. 3rd rev. ed. Baltimore: Penguin Books, 1958.

Waterhouse, E. *Gainsborough*. London: Edward Hulton, Ltd., 1958.

———. *Painting in Britain: 1530 to 1790*. Pelican History of Art. 2nd ed. Baltimore: Penguin Books, 1962.

Whinney, M., and Millar, O. *English Art, 1625–1714*. Oxford History of English Art. Oxford: Clarendon Press, 1957.

GERMANY AND AUSTRIA

von Freeden, M. H. *Balthasar Neumann*. 2nd ed. Munich: Deutscher Kunstverlag, 1963.

Grimschitz, B. *Johann Lukas von Hildebrandt*. 2nd ed. Vienna: Herold, 1959.

Hempel, E. *Baroque Art and Architecture in Central Europe*. Pelican History of Art. Baltimore: Penguin Books, 1965.

———. *Geschichte der deutschen Baukunst*. 2nd ed. Munich: Bruckmann, 1956.

Hitchcock, H.-R. *Rococo Architecture in Southern Germany*. London: Phaidon, 1969.

Rococo Art from Bavaria. London: Lund Humphries, 1956.

Sedlmayr, H. *Johann Bernhard Fischer von Erlach*. 2nd ed. Vienna: Herold, 1956.

Index

Page numbers are in roman type. Figure numbers of black-and-white illustrations and colorplates are specifically so designated. Names of artists and architects are in SMALL CAPS. Titles of works are in *italics*.

428

List of Credits

The authors and publisher wish to thank the libraries, museums, and private collectors for permitting the reproduction in black-and-white of paintings, prints, and drawings in their collections. Photographs have been supplied by the owners or custodians of the works of art except for the following, whose courtesy is gratefully acknowledged:

Thomas Agnew & Sons, London (212); Alinari (including Anderson and Brogi), Florence (7, 11, 13, 15–17, 19, 20, 24, 27, 28, 32, 33, 35, 38, 39, 45, 50–60, 62–67, 69, 72, 73, 75, 77, 78, 82, 83, 85, 99, 102, 103, 105–7, 109, 120, 122–24, 218, 219, 341, 343, 354, 358, 359, 366, 368, 371, 373, 376); Wayne Andrews, Grosse Pointe, Mich. (44, 346, 351, 393); T. and R. Annan & Sons, Glasgow (184); Archives Photographiques, Paris (128, 130, 133, 136, 137, 320, 328, 342, 344, 345, 350); Archives Centrales Iconographiques, Brussels (207, 208, 242); Archivio Fotografico, Musei Vaticani, Rome (30); Atelier Gerlach, Vienna (395); Max Baur, Dresden (401); Bayerische Verwaltung der staatlichen Schlösser, Gärten und Seen, Munich (418, 419); Biblioteca Ambrosiana, Milan (203); Bibliothèque Nationale, Paris (126, 135, 138, 139, 141, 337); Bildarchiv Oesterr. Nationalbibliothek, Vienna (394); Osvaldo Böhm, Venice (353); Bruckmann, Munich (402); J.-E. Bulloz, Paris (140, 321, 332, 340); Gabriele Busch-Hauck, Frankfort (118, 226, 256, 285); Campbell, *Vitruvius Britannicus,* Vol. I, pl. 62 (307); Compagnie Aérienne Française, Suresnes (144); A. C. Cooper, London (380); Copyright Country Life, London (134); Courtauld Institute of Art, University of London, London (117); De' Rossi, *Insignium Roma Temporium* (49); Deutsche Fotothek, Dresden (86, 399, 420); A. Dingjan, The Hague (228, 250–52, 260, 274, 281, 286); R. B. Fleming, London (308); Carlo Fontana, *Templum Vaticanum,* Rome, 1694 (36); Fotocielo, Rome (34); Fototeca Unione, Rome (18, 70, 71); John R. Freeman, London (253, 264); Gabinetto Fotografico Nazionale, Florence (84, 367); Gabinetto Fotografico Nazionale, Rome (22, 26, 61, 68, 74, 76, 87, 89, 95, 104, 108, 110, 111, 119, 121, 125, 331, 365, 369); Giraudon, Paris (91, 93, 112, 129, 248, 267, 315–17, 323, 326, 329, 334–36); Helga Schmidt Glassner, Stuttgart (414); L. Hautecoeur, *Histoire de l'Architecture Classique en France,* Paris, Vol. III, p. 61 (348), p. 482 (349); Istituto Centrale del Restauro, Rome (88, 90); Peter Keetman, Am Chiemsee (417); A. F. Kersting, London (289, 300); G. E. Kidder-Smith, New York (25, 46); Jeannine Le Brun, Kostanz (415, 416); Lennart af Petersens, Stockholm (293); Lott, Nancy (338); Foto Marburg, Marburg / Lahn (21, 31, 41–43, 143, 313, 355, 396, 400, 403, 404, 406, 409); A. and R. Mas, Barcelona (92, 181–83, 186, 188–90, 193, 196–98, 200–202); Ministry of Works, London, Crown Copyright (304, 305); Moncalvo, Turin (374); Eric Müller, Kassel (407, 412); A. Muñoz, *Roma Barocca,* Milan, 1919, p. 98 (14); Ernest Nash, Rome (377); Copyright National Buildings Record, London (306, 310); Nationalmuseet, Copenhagen (296, 297); Nordiska Museet, Stockholm (294, 295); Augusto Pedrini, Turin (378); Penguin Books, Baltimore (127, from A. Blunt, *Art and Architecture in France: 1500 to 1700,* fig. 12; 199, from G. Kubler and M. Soria, *Art and Architecture in Spain and Portugal and Their Dominions: 1500 to 1800,* fig. 10; 40, from R. Wittkower, *Art and Architecture in Italy: 1600 to 1750,* fig. 12); A. Renger-Patzsch, Wamel-Dorf über Soest (408); Eduard Renner, Frankfort (411); Toni Schneiders, Lindau-Schachen (421); Service Photographique, Versailles (142, 204, 211, 221, 312, 314, 333); Slovak Institute for the Care of Monuments, Bratislava (423); Edwin Smith, London (299, 303, 309); Soprintendenza ai Monumenti del Piemonte, Turin (47, 48); George Spearman, Windsor (352); Staatliche Schlösser und Garten, Potsdam-Sanssouci (405); Walter Steinkopf, Berlin (239, 261, 422); A. Stratton, *Life... Wren,* p. 33 (298); Thomas Photos, Oxford (310); Fritz Thudichum, Munich (413); Vaghi, Parma (81); A. Villani & Figli, Bologna (79, 80, 96, 98, 101); H. Roger Viollet, Paris (147); Vizzavona, Paris (388).